S0-BCS-892

THE POE CLAN VOL. 2

MOTO HAGIO

TRANSLATED BY RACHEL THORN

THE POE CLAN VOL. 2

MOTO HAGIO

FANTAGRAPHICS BOOKS

CONTENTS

THE POE CLAN · VOL. 2

Translation: Rachel Thorn
Editor: Kristy Valenti
Designer: Justin Allan-Spencer
Production: Christina Hwang & Paul Baresh
Production Assistance: Aidan Lee
Associate Publisher: Eric Reynolds
Publisher: Gary Groth
Publicity: Jacq Cohen

This edition is copyright © 2022 Fantagraphics Books, Inc.

POE NO ICHIZOKU Vol,2 by Moto HAGIO © 2007 Moto HAGIO. All rights reserved. Original Japanese edition published by SHOGAKUKAN. English translation rights in U.S.A., Canada, England, Ireland, Australia, and New Zealand arranged with SHOGAKUKAN through Tuttle-Mori Agency, Inc, Tokyo.

Permission to quote or reproduce material must be obtained from the publisher.

Fantagraphics Books, Inc.
7563 Lake City Way NE
Seattle, WA 98115

(800) 657-1100 • www.fantagraphics.com.
Follow us on Twitter and Instagram @fantagraphics and on Facebook at Facebook.com/Fantagraphics.

ISBN: 978-1-68396-572-5
Library of Congress Control Number: 2018963702

First Printing: 2022
Printed in China

LAST TIME

IN THE 1740S, Edgar and Marybelle, a noble's natural children, are abandoned in a forest and found by Old Hannah. She takes them to the Poe Clan — a race of unageing, supernaturally healing "vampirnellas" who feed on the blood-energy of the living — who adopts them. The Poes while away the centuries in a village where time and geography have no meaning, growing roses that serve as a substitute for blood-energy. Using his little sister, Marybelle, as leverage, the clan intends to make Edgar one of their own when he reaches adulthood. But, when he is fourteen, humans attack the village. The Poes' powerful king turns him.

Tragic events lead Edgar to then turn Marybelle into a vampirnella when she is thirteen. Their half-brother, Oswald, goes on to become Earl Evans. He marries Madonna. Their descendants are destined to cross paths with the lost siblings. Edgar and Marybelle become the wards of two vampirnellas, Frank and Sheila, a.k.a. Baron and Baroness Portnell. In 1865, while hunting, Glensmith, Lord Longbird, meets the immortal Marybelle and Edgar. He writes about them in his diary, thereby passing down their legend through his bloodline, who are also destined to intertwine again with the immortal children.

In 1879, the siblings befriend Alan Twilight, a spoiled child of wealth, and the Portnells' secret is discovered. A panic-stricken Dr. John Clifford murders Sheila and Marybelle, the latter with a silver bullet. Grief-stricken, Frank perishes as well. And so, now alone, Edgar invites Alan to share eternal life with him. Frozen in adolescence for eternity, Edgar's and Alan's adventures continue into the next century. In 1959, they enroll in a German boarding school to unravel the mystery of the death of a certain pupil. Their classmates, Killian, Matthias, and Theo, come to learn that there's something not quite human about Edgar and Alan...

PUBLICATION HISTORY

These stories were originally published in 1975 and 1976 in monthly and weekly comics magazines aimed at girls. The chapters, arranged in publishing order, are not chronological in terms of the narrative, and therefore jump back and forth in time.

THE DOCTOR
CHARLES
ELIZABETH
JANE
GLENSMITH
EUSTACE
OSWALD
MADONNA
OLD HANNAH
LADY EVANS, OSWALD'S STEPMOTHER
MARYBELLE
THE KING OF THE POE CLAN
LORD EVANS, OSWALD'S FATHER

MARGOT
LADY SHEILA PORTNELL
KILLIAN
JOHN CLIFFORD
LORD
FRANK
PRTNELL
MATTHIAS
ALAN TWILIGHT
ROBIN CARR
EDGAR
THEO
HERR GRAF
ISAIAS (ISSAI)

CHAPTER 1

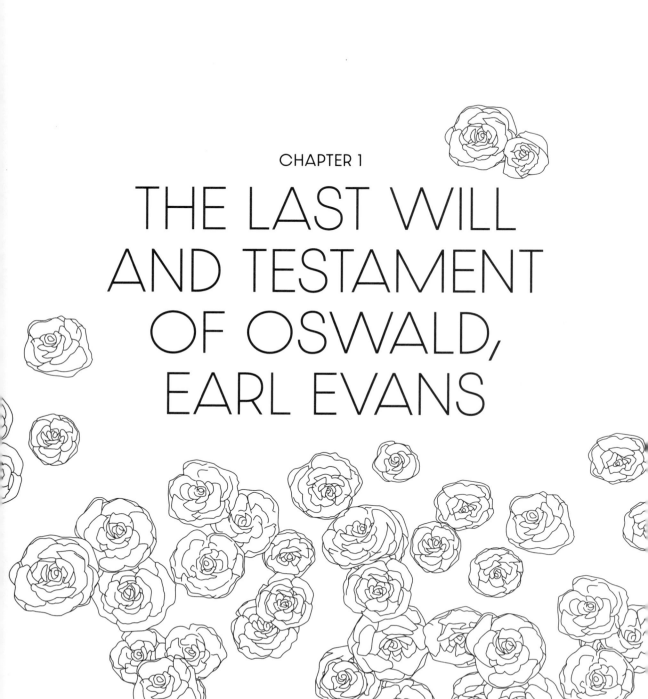

THE LAST WILL AND TESTAMENT OF OSWALD, EARL EVANS

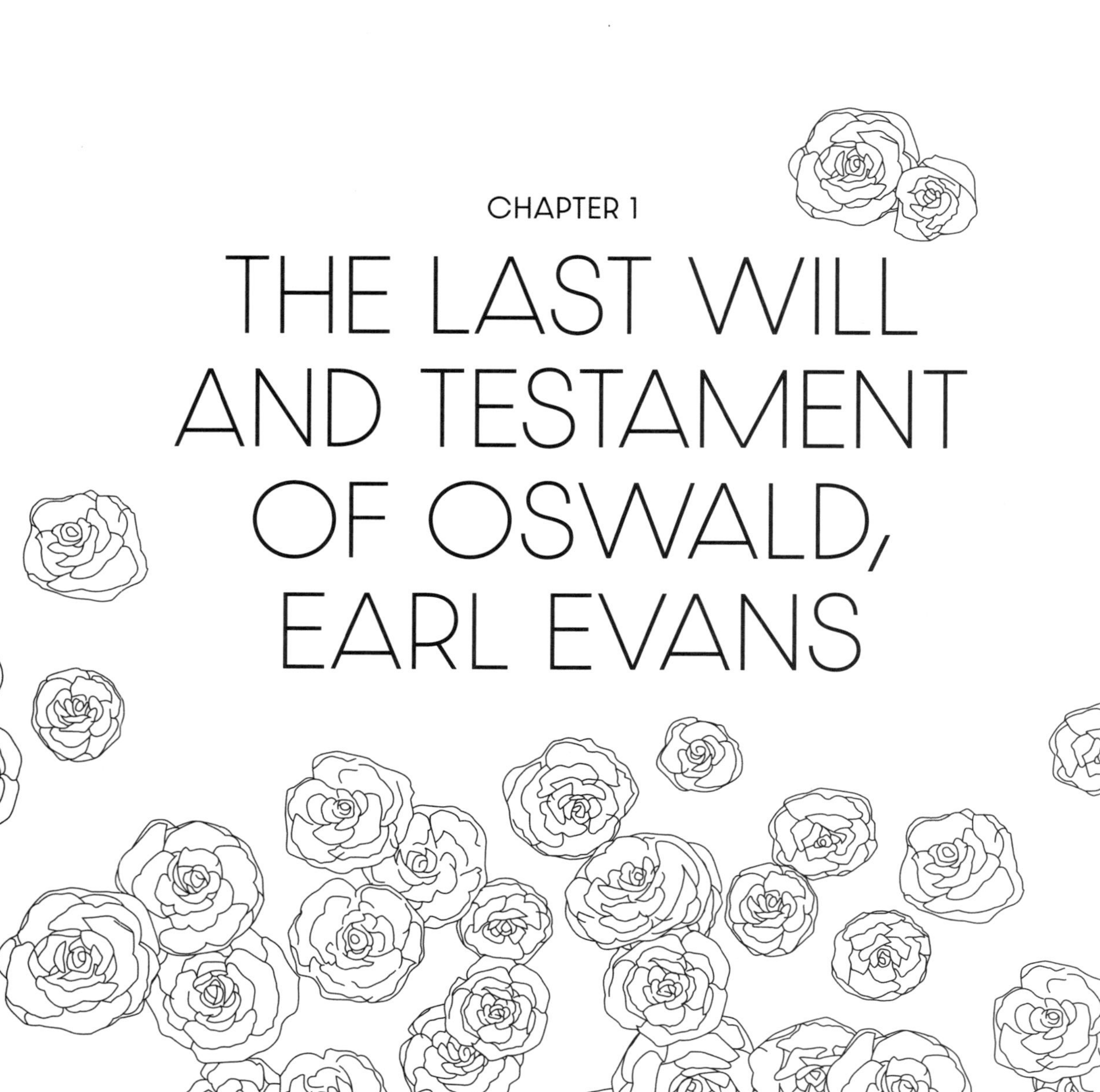

IN THE NAME OF GOD, AMEN.
BUILT UPON THE LIVES OF SO MANY
OTHERS ARE OUR LIFETIMES.
I SHALL NEVER FORGET TWO WHO BY
RIGHTS SHOULD BE LONG DEAD TO
THIS WORLD--MY SIBLINGS.
KNOWING FULL WELL IT IS BUT FOLLY:
I NONETHELESS SET DOWN HERE THIS
LAST WILL AND TESTAMENT.
I DO IT MERELY TO EASE MY OWN MIND.
AND YET....

CRACK
HAH! HAH!
I'D SAY IT'S TREE OR FOUR HOURS TO LITTLE HEAVEN, GUVNOR!
RIGHT. DON'T SPARE THE HORSES!
SMACK
FINE WEATHER FOR A DRIVE NOW, INNIT!

IF I FAIL TO CATCH UP WITH THEM AT LITTLE HEAVEN...
AND MARYBELLE IS WAITING FOR ME...
THREE OR FOUR HOURS...

AH-H-H
KLUNK
!
WHAM!

A CAR FELL OFF THE CLIFF AT THE SEVEN TURNS!
SWALLOWED UP IN THE TORRENT, IT WAS! IT'S HEADING TOWARDS THE MANOR!
WHAT'S ALL THAT COMMOTION?
A CARRIAGE IN THE RIVER, M'LORD.
A CARRIAGE?
WHACK
GIMME A HAND! SOMEONE'S INSIDE!
GOOD! IT'S CAUGHT ON THE ROCKS!
HEAVE TO, MEN!

TMP
FATHER! WAIT! PLEASE WAIT!
COME! WE CAN'T WAIT ANY LONGER.
EDGAR WILL COME! I'M SURE! THERE MUST BE SOMETHING HOLDING HIM UP!
IT'S MORE IMPORTANT THAT WE BE AT THE GATHERING ON TIME.
DON'T WORRY, MARYBELLE. IT'S EDGAR, AFTER ALL. HE'LL BE FINE.
YOU'RE FORTUNATE, M'LORD. IT'S JUST NOW STOPPED RAINING.

A VAMPIRNELLA CAN BE KILLED WITH A SILVER BULLET THROUGH THE HEART, OR A WOODEN STAKE. I SUPPOSE THE HEART IS ITS WEAK POINT.
A VAMPIRNELLA WHO'S LIVED FOR HUNDREDS OF YEARS WILL PROMPTLY DRY UP, CRUMBLE INTO DUST, AND BE BLOWN AWAY. IT SEEMS THAT NOT ONLY THE BODY, BUT THE CLOTHES, TOO, BEING VERY OLD, TURN TO DUST.
BUT WHAT IF A VAMPIRNELLA, HAVING AN AVERSION TO SILVER, WERE TO BE WEARING A GOLD RING, OR A COPPER BUCKLE? WOULDN'T PRECIOUS METALS BE LEFT BEHIND?

WHAT IF A VAMPIRNELLA WAS WEARING NEW UNDERPANTS? WOULD THE UNDERPANTS REMAIN? CLOTHING OR BUTTONS MIGHT END UP DISPLAYED IN THE BRITISH MUSEUM WITH SIGNS SAYING, "UNDERPANTS WORN BY A VAMPIRNELLA." THAT WOULDN'T BE TERRIBLY ROMANTIC.
WHAT I THINK IS THAT PERHAPS WHEN A VAMPIRNELLA TAKES A STAKE TO HEART OR WHAT HAVE YOU, AT THE MOMENT THE BALANCE MAINTAINING ITS EXISTENCE IN THIS WORLD IS LOST, IT FALLS STRAIGHT INTO A SORT OF HOLE LEADING TO ANOTHER DIMENSION. AT LEAST THAT WAY, YOU WOULDN'T HAVE LEFT-BEHIND UNDERPANTS.

--MOTO HAGIO

LORD EVANS!
WHERE'S THE CARRIAGE?
M'LORD!
M'LORD!
NO, HE'S NOT FAMILIAR TO ME. IS HE DEAD?
YES, M'LORD, HE WAS ALREADY DEAD WHEN WE PULLED HIM OUT.
STRANGLED BY THE STRING OF HIS CAPE, I SHOULD SAY.
CRUSHED TO PIECES, IT WAS! FLOATED FARTHER DOWNSTREAM!
WAS HE A GUEST OF THE MANOR, M'LORD?
HE'S JUST A CHILD.
AND SO LOVELY.
THE LORD IS MY SHEPHERD.
I SHALL NOT WANT.
HE MAKETH ME TO LIE DOWN.
IN GREEN PASTURES.

SHALL WE PUT THE CHILD'S REMAINS IN THE CELLAR, M'LORD?
YES.
WHEN THE STORM'S PASSED WE'LL GIVE HIM A PROPER FUNERAL.
HE WAS FOUND ON MY LAND. IT'S THE LEAST I CAN DO.
I WONDER WHAT FAMILY THE POOR BOY HAILED FROM.
HE WAS WEARING FINE CLOTHES, HE WAS.
I WONDER IF THERE WAS ANYONE ELSE WITH HIM.
PARENTS OR SIBLINGS.
NO ONE COULD HAVE SURVIVED THAT.
IT SEEMS YOU CAME TO US AT A BAD TIME, DOCTOR.
GOOD NIGHT, M'LORD.
NO ONE COULD HAVE SURVIVED THAT.

PIT
PIT
TWITCH
PIT
PIT
PIT
PIT
PIT
RATTLE
RATTLE
RATTLE
RATTLE
RATTLE
PIT
PIT
PIT

TMP
RATTLE RATTLE
RATTLE RATTLE
RATTLE RATTLE
TMP
RATTLE RATTLE
WHOOO RATTLE
TMP
RATTLE RATTLE RATTLE
DOC-TOR !!
THOSE EYES... THOSE BLUE EYES... BLOOD... VIOLETTA...
S- SOME-ONE!

A BLOW TO THE HEAD MUST HAVE THROWN HIM INTO A COMA.
A COMA FROM WHICH HE HAS MIRACULOUSLY AWOKEN.
IT'S THE DAMNEDEST THING. AND YET HE LIVES.
HIS RESPIRATION AND PULSE ARE LESS THAN HALF THE NORMAL RATE. HIS TEMPERATURE IS ALSO EXTREMELY LOW.
BUT WILL HE SURVIVE?
I DON'T WANT A DEATH IN MY HOME. NOT ANOTHER.
HE HASN'T OPENED HIS EYES ONCE, DOCTOR. HE JUST SLEEPS.
HASN'T EATEN A BITE OR HAD A SIP OF WATER.
IT'S BEEN MORE THAN TEN DAYS!
YES, IT'S ALMOST AS IF HE'S HIBERNATING.

POOR LORD HENRY, SADDLED WITH A BURDEN LIKE THAT.
OH, YOU MUSTN'T SAY SUCH THINGS! HE COULD BE THE SCION OF SOME LORD, YOU KNOW!

WHAT IF HE NEVER WAKES?
THEN HE'LL DIE, EVENTUALLY.

HIS EYES WERE SO BLUE.

LIKE MY VIOLETTA'S. LIKE THE BLUE, BLUE EYES OF MY DARLING WIFE WHO FELL ILL, SPIT UP BRIGHT RED BLOOD, AND PASSED ON, LEAVING ME ALONE.

PLEASE. OPEN YOUR EYES.

ROGER!
DEAREST BROTHER!!
THE FIRST CAMELLIAS ARE BLOOMING, AND I HAVE RETURNED!
MY LITTLE BROTHER, ROGER.
ROGER, MEET DR. DODD.
HELLO
WONDERFUL TO MEET YOU, ROGER.
THIS IS YOUR FIRST VISIT TO OUR HOME, DOCTOR. TELL ME, DO YOU SKATE?
THE POND FREEZES OVER THIS TIME OF YEAR AND VISITORS COME TO SKATE.
WHY, I USED TO SKATE EVERY WINTER IN FRANCE.
THE FIRST CAMELLIAS HAVE BLOOMED, M'LORD.
AND AREN'T THEY LOVELY!
PUT THEM IN THE ROOM OF OUR SLEEPING BEAUTY. PERHAPS THE FRAGRANCE WILL OPEN HIS EYES.
SLEEPING BEAUTY?

AH-H-H-H-H-H-H-H-H
AHHHHH
BAM!
BAM
BAM!
WHERE'S IT COMING FROM!?
WHO'S SCREAMING!?
IT'S A CHILD!
SO THE CAMELLIAS DID WAKE YOU UP.
THERE, THERE.
YOU'RE SAFE. YOU'RE SAFE.
THANK GOD!

WHAT'S YOUR NAME, SON? HM? YOUR NAME?
YOUR NAME?
YOUR NAME?
YOUR NAME?
YOUR NAME?
EDGAR...
ED-GAR...
IT'S HIM!
WHERE AM I?

WITH REST AND CARE, HE MAY REGAIN HIS MEMORIES.
HE'S NO NEWBORN.
HE COULD RETURN TO NORMAL. ISN'T THAT RIGHT, DOCTOR?
IT'S HARD TO SAY.
WELL, THAT'S SOME FINE BAGGAGE YOU'VE PICKED UP, EH BROTHER?
A KID WHO MAY AS WELL BE A NEWBORN!
IT'S CURIOUS THAT HIS NAME IS EDGAR.
A SINGLE NAME, "EDGAR," ISN'T MUCH TO WORK WITH.
WHAT'S THAT YOU'VE GOT THERE?
KLAK
QUITE AN OSTEN-TATIOUS LITTLE BOX, ISN'T IT?
THIS IS THE LAST WILL AND TESTAMENT OF OSWALD, LORD EVANS.
OUR GRAND-FATHER.

GRAND-FATHER? NEVER KNEW HIM.

OUR GRANDFATHER DIED BEFORE WE WERE BORN.
HE WROTE THIS WILL AND EN-TRUSTED IT TO OUR FATHER.
TEN YEARS AGO, ON HIS DEATH-BED...
FATHER ENTRUSTED IT TO ME, HIS OLDEST SON.
IT WAS SUCH A PECULIAR WILL...
...I REMEMBER ITS CONTENTS QUITE WELL.

OH?
PECULIAR, YOU SAY?

TO MY DESCEN-DANTS.
SHOULD PERSONS NAMED EDGAR AND MARYBELLE APPEAR BEFORE THE DESCENDANTS OF THE EVANS ESTATE...
...SAID DESCENDANTS ARE TO DONATE THE ENTIRE EVANS FORTUNE TO THEM, REGARDLESS OF THEIR STATION, NATIONALITY, OR AGE...
HUH?
...FOR ALL MEMBERS OF THE EVANS FAMILY UNTIL THE END OF TIME OWE THOSE WHO BEAR THOSE NAMES A DEBT SO GREAT THAT IT CAN NEVER BE REPAID.

YOU CAN'T BE SERIOUS! OLD OSWALD MUST HAVE BEEN **MAD!**
ROG-ER!
B-DUMP

GIVE ME THAT! I CAN'T BELIEVE YOU'VE EVEN KEPT IT! I'LL TEAR IT TO PIECES AND THAT'LL BE THE END OF THAT NONSENSE!
ROGER! CALM YOURSELF!

IT HAS NO LEGAL VALIDITY. "1780. OSWALD O., EARL EVANS."

FLUMP
WELL, OF COURSE IT DOES-N'T!

THEN ALL WE NEED IS A MARYBELLE.

AN INTERESTING WILL, AND AN INTERESTING COINCIDENCE.
WHAT COINCIDENCE!? EDGAR IS A PERFECTLY COMMON NAME!

REALLY! "SHOULD EDGAR AND MARYBELLE APPEAR." HAH!
1780!? THAT WILL IS FORTY YEARS OLD!

SO ARE YOU SAYING YOU'D HAND OVER YOUR ENTIRE FORTUNE TO THE EDGAR SLEEPING UPSTAIRS?
IF THIS FAMILY HAS GOLD TO GIVE AWAY TO STRANGERS, I WISH THEY WOULD GIVE SOME OF IT TO ME!
SNIP

I BELIEVE OUR GRANDFATHER FELT HE OWED TWO PEOPLE BY THESE NAMES A DEBT THAT COULDN'T BE ERASED WITH GOLD.

NOT ALL OF OUR FORTUNE, PERHAPS...

ARE YOU HARD UP FOR MONEY, THEN, ROGER?

...UNTIL EDGAR'S MEMORY RETURNS.
OR PERHAPS FOR LONGER THAN THAT.
...BUT WE COULD HONOR GRANDFATHER'S WISHES IN SOME SMALL WAY...
I HAVE NO SON OF MY OWN.
WHY NOT ADOPT ONE?
BLUE, BLUE EYES.
MY WIFE WAS HEAVY WITH CHILD...
...WHEN SHE FELL ILL.
LORD EVANS...
HAD THE BABY BEEN BORN...
...HE MIGHT HAVE HAD EYES OF BLUE.
HMPH! A FINE HOBBY!
DO YOU LIVE IN LONDON, ROGER?
I'VE BEEN TO PARIS, TOO!
NOW THERE'S A DAZZLING CITY FOR YOU! QUITE TO MY LIKING.
LONDON IS DREARY, BUT NOT ENTIRELY LACKING IN ENTERTAINMENT.

EACH YEAR AROUND THIS TIME HE RUNS LOW ON FUNDS.
YOU DON'T SAY! WHAT KIND OF BUSINESS?

SO WHY DOES YOUR BROTHER, WITH HIS FLASHY TASTES, COME TO THE COUNTRYSIDE?
AH. HE MAKES BUSINESS INVEST-MENTS, DON'T YOU KNOW.

I'M SURE I DON'T KNOW. BUT WHATEVER THE REASON, I'M JUST GLAD HE COMES TO SEE ME.
EDGAR! DON'T BREAK THE STEMS. YOU'LL CUT YOURSELF ON THE THORNS.

JUST LIKE FATHER AND SON, AREN'T THEY NOW? THEY DO GET ALONG.
M'LORD IS ABSOLUTELY SMITTEN.
EVERY DAY HE SHOWS HIM NEW THINGS...
...HOPING TO JOG SOME MEMORY.

SNOW

WHITE CAMEL-LIAS
RED CAMEL-LIAS
TREES
TREE-TOPS
BIRDS

I DARE SAY WE'VE BEEN ABANDONED, ELLEN!

PULL THE REINS!
PULL NOW!

EXCELLENT! YOUR BODY REMEMBERS, EVEN IF YOUR MIND DOESN'T.

AH

ED-GAR!

WHAT I'M SAYING IS...
...FOR SOME REASON THIS LAD'S HEART BEATS JUST FORTY-FIVE TIMES PER MINUTE!
NOW JUST IMAGINE WHAT HAPPENS WHEN HE'S PRESSED TO STRAIN HIMSELF!
UNDER-STOOD, DOCTOR! UNDER-STOOD!

HMPH! WHAT A BOTHER THAT BRAT IS!
MASTER ROGER, A LETTER FOR YOU.

DAMNED DEBT-COLLECTORS HOUNDING ME TO THE ENDS OF THE EARTH!

OH, UNCLE!

UNCLE!

WELL, WELL.
FROM HIS LATE WIFE'S SIDE OF THE FAMILY.
THEY'RE HENRY'S NIECE AND NEPHEW.
WELL!
MASTER ROGER! MISS LINDA OF GREENAWAY AND MASTER ERNEST ARE HERE!

MARY-BELLE!
OH, WAIT! THIS TIME WE BROUGHT A FRIEND.

HAHA! WELCOME, LADY AND GENTLE-MAN.
OH, UNCLE ROGER'S HERE! IT'S BEEN A WHOLE YEAR!
IS OUR HANDSOME UNCLE ROGER STILL UNMARRIED?

MARY-
BELLE
!?
WELL,
WELL.
ALLOW ME TO INTRODUCE MARYBELLE, DAUGHTER OF THE BARON PORTNELL.
SHE JUST MOVED IN NEXT DOOR TO OUR HOME IN LONDON A MONTH AGO.
WE'VE BECOME BOSOM FRIENDS, HAVEN'T WE, MARYBELLE? ERNEST?

IS THE POND FROZEN? ALL THE WAY TO THE SUMMER HOUSE?
OH, WHERE'S UNCLE HENRY?
...SO WE INVITED HER TO COME SKATING!
MARYBELLE'S FATHER AND MOTHER ARE TRAVELING, YOU SEE...
IT SEEMS ELLEN HAS FOUND UNCLE H--
!
THE MAN'S INCORRIGIBLE!!
DR. DODD!
EDGAR'S FAINTED AGAIN!
GOOD GRACIOUS!
EDGAR?
THERE'S A BOY WITH HIM. WHO'S THAT?

POSTSCRIPT:
A READER SENT ME A LETTER ASKING WHY EDGAR, A VAMPIRNELLA, WOULD HAVE A PULSE. BY NATURE, A VAMPIRNELLA HAS NO PULSE. NOR WOULD THEY HAVE A NORMAL BODY TEMPERATURE OR HAVE A NEED TO BREATHE. THEY DON'T SWEAT, AND THEY DON'T NEED TO USE THE RESTROOM, OR EAT MEAT OR BREAD. THEY'RE NOT SUPPOSED TO HAVE A SHADOW, EITHER, BUT OF COURSE THAT WOULD BE A DEAD GIVEAWAY THAT THEY'RE NOT HUMAN.

PERHAPS IT WAS THE PRODUCT OF LORD PORTNELL'S CONSTANT INSISTENCE THAT EDGAR BEHAVE LIKE A HUMAN. PERHAPS WHEN HE LOST HIS MEMORY, HIS PSYCHOLOGICAL AGE REGRESSED TO THE POINT WHERE HE BELIEVED HIMSELF TO BE HUMAN. OR PERHAPS THE SHOCK OF THE ACCIDENT CAUSED HIS MIND TO BE TAKEN OVER BY A DESIRE TO RETURN TO HUMANITY, AND HE LOST HIS MEMORY OF BEING A VAMPIRNELLA.

--MOTO HAGIO

I HOPE YOU'LL BEFRIEND HIM AS YOU WOULD A SON OF MY OWN.
OF COURSE.

WE'RE ABOUT THE SAME AGE, AFTER ALL.
I'M SURE WE'LL BE FAST FRIENDS, UNCLE HENRY.

IT'S SO TERRIBLY ROMANTIC!
GOOD GRACIOUS, WHAT A TALE!
AND YOU SAY THIS POOR CHILD DOESN'T REMEMBER A THING?

MARYBELLE AND EDGAR. THE ACTORS ARE GATHERED, EH?
DON'T BE RIDICULOUS. IT'S... MERE COINCIDENCE.

I'M LINDA. MY, SUCH PRETTY BLUE EYES!
GOOD TO MEET YOU, EDGAR. I'M ERNEST.

I DIDN'T EXPECT TO FIND SUCH A PRETTY BOY OUT HERE IN THE COUNTRY. BE STILL, MY BEATING HEART! HA HA.
MARY-BELLE
WHAT IS IT, DEAR? ARE YOU HOMESICK?
OUT WITH IT, NOW. THIS IS THE SECOND TIME TODAY YOU'VE CRIED.
!
IS IT ON ACCOUNT OF THAT BOY! OH, MY!
YOU POOR DEAR! LOVE AT FIRST SIGHT! AND YOUR FIRST LOVE, NO DOUBT! THERE, THERE, DON'T CRY.
I'LL JUST HAVE TO MAKE DO WITH ERNEST OR UNCLE ROGER. I SHALL BE YOUR CO-CONSPIRATOR IN THIS ROMANCE, MARYBELLE!

WELCOME BACK, LORD PORTNELL! NO, I'M TERRIBLY SORRY, BUT YOUR SON NEVER CAME.
LET'S SEE. I RECKON T'WAS A MONTH AGO. CAR FELL OFF THE CLIFF, YOU SEE.
LORD EVANS RESCUED THE LAD AN' THEY SAY E'S BEEN CARING FOR 'IM EVER SINCE.
EVANS? THAT'S THE HOUSE EDGAR HAILS FROM. PROBABLY FEELING NOSTALGIC AND DECIDED TO STAY ON.
HE MIGHT BE INJURED, FATHER. I'M WORRIED.
THEN I'LL STAY NEARBY.
UNTIL YOU AND MOTHER PASS THIS WAY AGAIN.
HOW DO YOU PLAN TO APPROACH HIM?
I'VE HEARD THEY HAVE RELATIVES IN LONDON WHO VISIT EVERY WINTER TO SKATE.
YOU COULD APPROACH THEM AND GET YOURSELF INVITED ALONG.
WELL, HERE I AM...
...ONLY TO FIND EDGAR HAS FORGOTTEN EVERYTHING.
HAVE YOU REALLY FORGOTTEN ME, TOO, EDGAR?
HAVE YOU FORGOTTEN US ALL?

UNCLE, THE ICE DOESN'T LOOK VERY FIRM.
GIVE IT ANOTHER WEEK. THEN IT'LL BE FROZEN SOLID.
YOU'LL BE ABLE TO WALK OUT TO THE SUMMER HOUSE ON THE ISLAND, THEN.
HAVE YOU EVER SKATED BEFORE, MARYBELLE?
NO, I HAVEN'T.
WE'LL TEACH YOU! YOU'LL LEARN IN NO TIME.
THE VERY PICTURE OF A HAPPY FAMILY.
IF ONLY THE LADY WERE ALIVE TO SEE IT, EH, ELLEN?
EDGAR!

YOU MUSTN'T BREAK THE FLOWER STEMS. I SEE YOU HAVEN'T BROKEN THAT HABIT.
MARY--
HM?
OH...!
YOU KNOW HIS HABITS WELL, DON'T YOU?
OH! IF IT ISN'T MY HANDSOME UNCLE ROGER!
WHAT'S THAT? MARYBELLE AND EDGAR, YOU SAY?
MARYBELLE...
LINDA!
OH, ERNEST, YOU MUSTN'T STAND IN THE WAY ROMANCE!
DON'T BE SILLY!
YOU REALLY ARE DENSE, AREN'T YOU? JUST LOOK AT HER.
SHE ONLY HAS EYES FOR EDGAR.

YOU ONLY EVER CUT THE WHITE CAMELLIAS, ELLEN.
YES. THE EARL IS FOND OF THEM.
ELLEN, DO YOU LOVE LORD HENRY?
WHA--
I WOULDN'T DARE, MISS. IT'S JUST... IT'S JUST THAT...
AND BESIDES, MY EYES AREN'T BLUE.
THEY SAY THE LADY HAD THE MOST BEAUTIFUL BLUE EYES.
MAY SHE REST IN PEACE.
THE EARL LOVES HER STILL.
EYES LIKE EDGAR'S?
OH, YES, LOVELY EYES.
SO I'M AFRAID ALL I CAN OFFER M'LORD...
...IS THESE FLOWERS.

I HAVE SOMETHING FOR YOU, ELLEN.
WELL! AND WHAT WOULD THAT BE, MISS MARY-BELLE?
IT'S JUST ES-SENCE OF ROSE.
ADD SOME TO TEA AND IT WILL TAKE ON A WONDERFUL FRAGRANCE.
ROSE?
BUT IT HAS ANOTHER, SECRET EFFECT. IT'S A LOVE POTION!
THEY SAY THE ROSE IS THE FLOWER OF LOVE. I'M SURE IT WILL GET THROUGH TO HIM.
THAT'S JUST AN OLD WIVES' TALE.
I DON'T CARE IF IT IS. PLEASE. GIVE SOME TO EDGAR. FOR ME.
HM. A PECULIAR FRAGRANCE. WHAT BRANDY IS THIS?
I ADDED ESSENCE OF ROSE, M'LORD.
I HEARD THE ROYALTY IN PARIS DRINK IT THIS WAY.
FIRST I'VE HEARD OF IT.

EITHER WAY, I QUITE LIKE IT!

THE WAY MARYBELLE LOOKS AT EDGAR IS...

AND YOU'LL REMEMBER ME.

PLEASE, EDGAR. PLEASE.

PLEASE GET WELL. ONCE YOU'RE IN BETTER HEALTH, YOUR FEELINGS SHOULD BECOME CLEARER.

YOU'LL ALWAYS HAVE ME, ERNEST.

REALLY, ERNEST. YOUR EYES ARE POSITIVELY WILD WITH JEALOUSY.

...IS MARYBELLE.
THE GIRL WHO CHASED A WHITE BALL THROUGH THE BROKEN WALL.
SURELY YOU HAVEN'T FORGOTTEN THE DAY WE FIRST MET?
LINDA STARTED TALKING TO YOU RIGHT AWAY...
...BUT SINCE THAT DAY, I SEE NOTHING BUT YOU.
BUT NOW LOOK AT YOU.
I WON'T LET A PERFECT STRANGER TAKE YOU FROM ME!
SHISH

IT SEEMS MARYBELLE'S IN LOVE WITH YOU.
SICKLY, AMNESIAC YOU.

IT WAS THOSE BLUE EYES OF YOURS, APPARENTLY. DO YOU UNDERSTAND?

HEY.
....

EDGAR! I HAVE SOMETHING TO TELL YOU.
THEY...
...LOOK ALIKE!?

HAH! HE'S NOTHING BUT A HALFWIT.
CAN'T TALK.
DOESN'T UNDERSTAND A WORD HE HEARS!

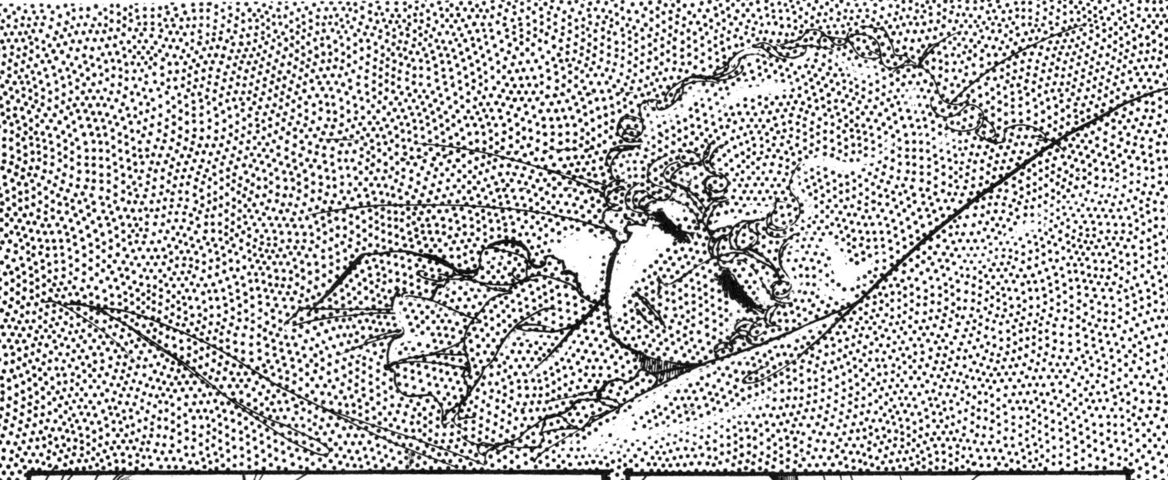

OUR RESIDENT GOSSIP, LINDA, TELLS ME MISS MARYBELLE PORTNELL IS IN LOVE WITH EDGAR.
I... I'M SURE I WOULDN'T KNOW, M'LORD.

MARYBELLE AND EDGAR...

ARE THE CHILDREN GETTING ON?
YES, M'LORD.
EXCELLENT. EDGAR'S COLOR IS MUCH IMPROVED.

TELL ME, ELLEN.
IMAGINE I ADOPT EDGAR FORMALLY.
FURTHER IMAGINE THAT MARYBELLE JOINS THE EVANS FAMILY AS EDGAR'S BRIDE.
WOULD THAT BE THE MOST FANCIFUL OF DREAMS?
OH, M'LORD!

ROGER! I MERELY--
PERHAPS NOT AS FANCIFUL AS YOU THINK!
BAM!
I, FOR ONE, AM OPPOSED! REALLY, BROTHER, YOU ARE MUCH TOO SENTIMENTAL!
I BELIEVE OSWALD EARL EVANS FORESAW ALL OF THIS IN A DREAM!
THAT'S WHY HE WROTE THAT EXTRAORDINARY WILL!
STUFF AND NONSENSE! SAW IT IN A DREAM? A PROPHECY?
HA HA HA HA
ALL BECAUSE THAT BRAT SHOWED UP ON OUR DOORSTEP!
ALL FOR THE SAKE OF THAT ONE LITTLE BRAT.

ERNEST! ERNEST! I CAN'T STOP! I'M GOING TO-- AH!
WHUMP
SEE! YOU'VE GOT IT! NOTHING TO IT, EH?
HUFF HUFF
HUFF HUFF HUFF
YOU'RE CRUEL, ERNEST!
THIS ICE IS SO SLIPPERY!
MARY-BELLE. I LOVE YOU.

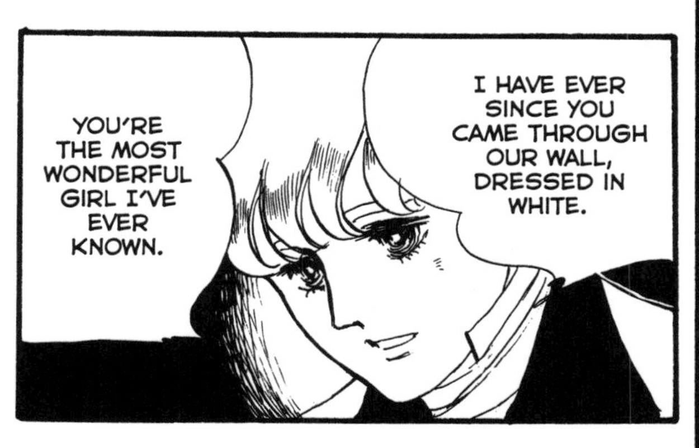

I HAVE EVER SINCE YOU CAME THROUGH OUR WALL, DRESSED IN WHITE.
YOU'RE THE MOST WONDERFUL GIRL I'VE EVER KNOWN.

I WANT TO CATCH YOU. HOLD YOU. FOR THE REST OF MY LIFE.
OH, DO ANSWER ME, MARYBELLE. DO YOU HATE ME?
MARY-
BELLE?

I DON'T HATE YOU.

I DON'T.

BUT...

BUT...

MARY-
BELLE!!

MARYBELLE! I LOVE YOU!
NO MATTER HOW MUCH YOU LIKE ME, I CANNOT REQUITE YOUR LOVE.
I CAN NEVER GROW BEYOND THAT.
I'M SORRY. I'M SO SORRY.
I WILL NEVER...
BUT YOU MUSTN'T! YOU MUSTN'T!
I WILL NEVER BE ANYTHING BUT A THIRTEEN-YEAR-OLD GIRL.
EDGAR IS THE ONLY OTHER INHABITANT OF MY WORLD.
EDGAR IS ALL I HAVE.
ROMANCE IS UNTHINKABLE.
I WILL NEVER BE ANYTHING BUT EDGAR'S LITTLE SISTER.

SHIK
EDGAR!
AH!
FLUMP
ED-
GAR.

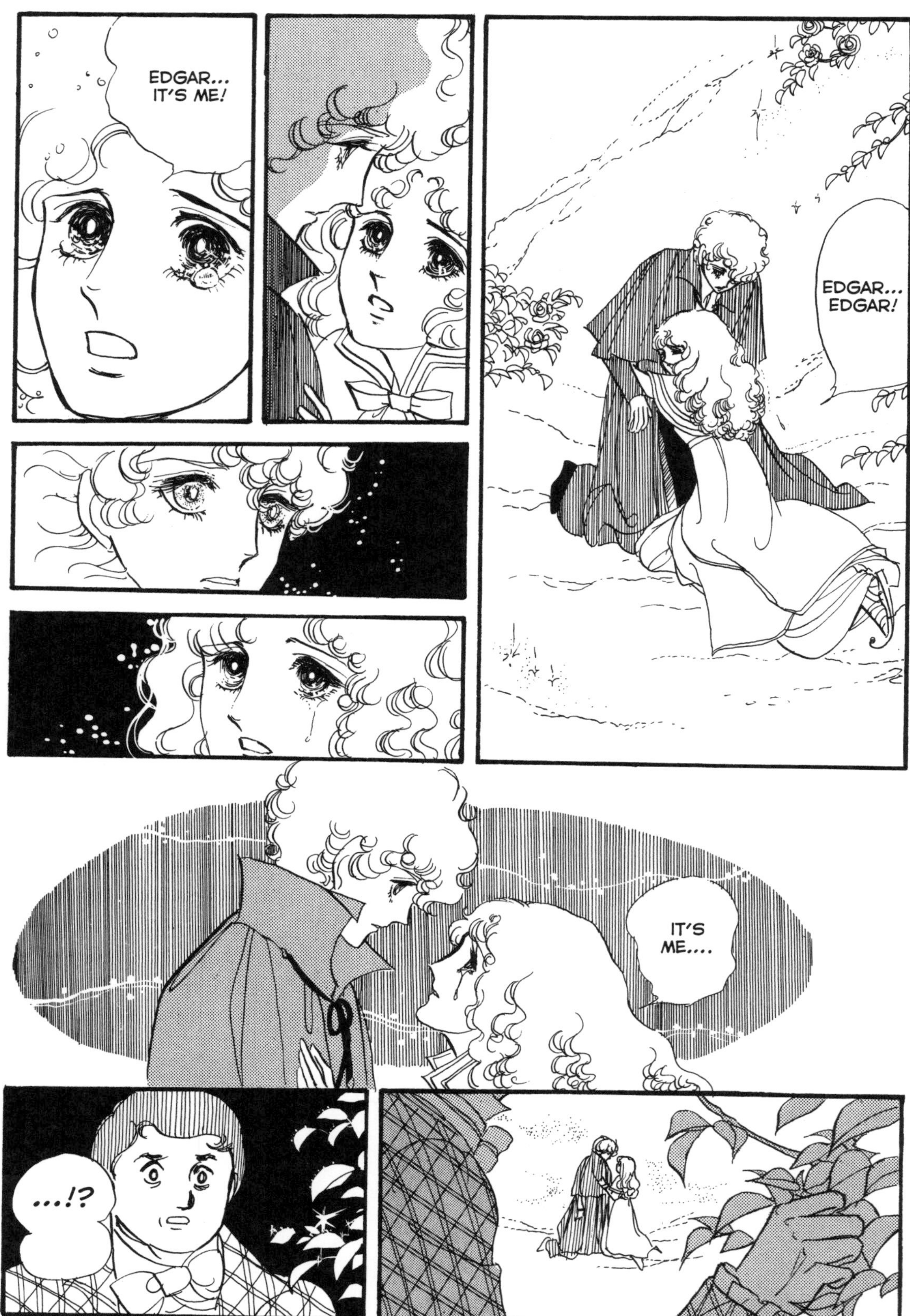
EDGAR... IT'S ME!
EDGAR... EDGAR!
IT'S ME....
...!?

MASTER EDGAR?
IT'S ME

EDGAR
EDGAR

IT'S ME

AND HOW FAR DID YOU WALK TODAY? YOU'VE GROWN SO STRONG OF LATE.
M'LORD IS QUITE PLEASED.

ALLOW ME TO WIPE YOUR FACE AND HANDS BEFORE YOU RETIRE.

IF YOU ARE SUFFERING, YOU MUST PRAY.
YOU NEEDN'T SAY THE PRAYER OUT LOUD.
!?
WHAT IS IT, CHILD?
WH--
NOW REST. I SHALL READ TO YOU FROM THE BIBLE.
THE LORD IS WATCHING OVER YOU. ALWAYS.
HERE.
THAT YOU MAY RECOVER ALL THE MORE QUICKLY...

I DON'T KNOW WHO EDGAR IS...
...NOR WHENCE HE CAME...
...BUT I BELIEVE HE STRUGGLES TO REMEMBER...

ELLEN IS A FINE GIRL. I'M DEEPLY GRATEFUL FOR HER.
AND A BEAUTY, TOO.

...THOUGH HE SAYS NARY A WORD.
WHAT IS IT, DR. DODD?

NOTH-ING.

HENRY'S MAD ABOUT THAT CHILD. HE CAN'T JUDGE THE SITUATION OBJECTIVELY.
WELL I CAN. WHAT IS IT?

ALL RIGHT. I'LL TELL YOU. I BELIEVE THOSE TWO KNOW EACH OTHER, ROGER.
WHICH TWO?

EDGAR AND MARY-BELLE.

DON'T TELL ME YOU'VE LET OSWALD'S WILL GET TO YOU, TOO!?

BOTH EDGAR AND MARYBELLE ARE UTTER NEWCOMERS TO US.
STRANGERS.

WHAT YOU MEAN IS...?
WHAT I MEAN IS...

ALL I KNOW IS, SOME BRAT WHO BY RIGHTS SHOULD BE DEAD...
...IS AFTER THE EVANS FORTUNE!!

IF THOSE TWO KNOW EACH OTHER, WHY DOESN'T MARYBELLE SAY SOMETHING!?

ROGER, YOU ARE MOST DEFINITELY NOT OBJECTIVE.
IF THE BRAT WON'T DIE, I'LL KILL HIM MY--

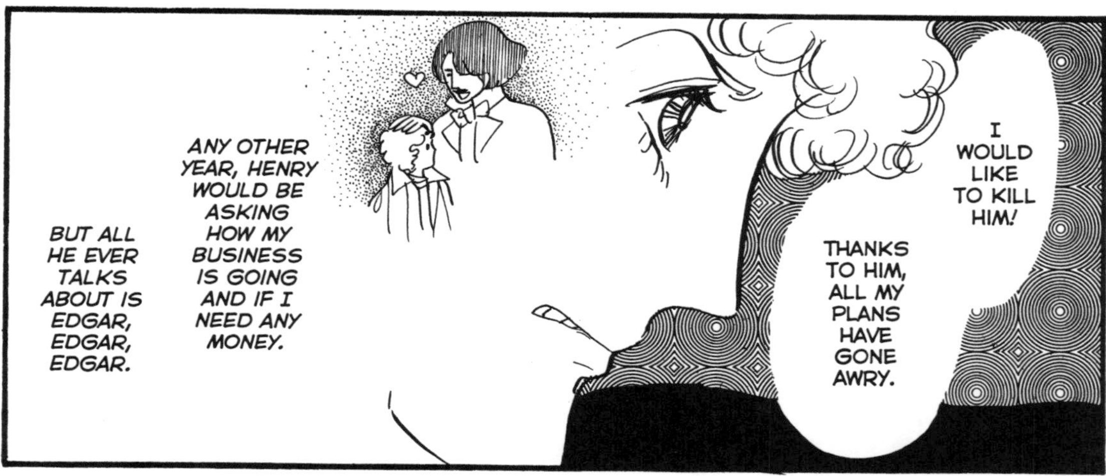
I WOULD LIKE TO KILL HIM!
THANKS TO HIM, ALL MY PLANS HAVE GONE AWRY.
ANY OTHER YEAR, HENRY WOULD BE ASKING HOW MY BUSINESS IS GOING AND IF I NEED ANY MONEY.
BUT ALL HE EVER TALKS ABOUT IS EDGAR, EDGAR, EDGAR.

IT'S POSITIVELY SICKENING.
"HIS EYES ARE LIKE MY LATE WIFE'S, THE POOR LAD." "HE'S SO SWEET."
BUT WHY WAIT FOR A MIRACLE...
...WHEN I CAN CAUSE ONE?
CRACKLE
IF ONLY HE AND EDGAR WERE TO FALL OFF A CLIFF TOGETHER AND DIE...!
IF IT WEREN'T FOR MY BROTHER, IT WOULD ALL BE MINE. YES.
BECAUSE I'M THE SECOND SON AND DIDN'T INHERIT THE FAMILY FORTUNE AND TITLE, THAT'S WHY!
WHY MUST I SUFFER LIKE THIS, YEAR AFTER YEAR?
AH, HENRY, LORD EVANS! I FEAR YOUR LUCK HAS RUN OUT.
I'M HARDLY INCAPABLE OF A MURDER OR TWO.
FAREWELL, CURSED DEBT!
FORGIVE ME, FATHER ...

HAHA HA
GOOD MORNING, MASTER EDGAR.
MY, SUCH A LOVELY CRUCIFIX.
HE SMILED!
HA HA!
WHY, YOU WRETCH-ED BOY!
COME BACK HERE, ERNEST!
HA HA HA
SHAKE
SPLASH
AHH!
A CRU-CIFIX ...!

WELL, WELL! GOOD MORNING, BLUE EYES! NOW THAT'S A SHABBY CRUCIFIX. BUT IT'S LOVELY! SILVER, ISN'T IT? IT SUITS YOU.
HA HA! MAY I HAVE SOME TEA, PLEASE! I'M PARCHED!

....

GOOD HEAVENS, UNCLE ROGER! YOUR EYES ARE SO BLOODSHOT!
YES. EHEM. AFRAID I WAS UP MOST THE NIGHT THINKING.

OH, A PHILOS-OPHER! THINKING ABOUT WHAT?
OH... UM...
I CAN'T TELL HER I WAS PLAN-NING MUR-DER.

WHAT SHOULD I DO?
A SILVER CROSS!

NO... NO!
SILVER... THE ONE ELEMENT OUR BODIES CAN NEVER ASSIMILATE.
AND THE CRUCIFIX, OR RATHER THE FAITH BEHIND IT, FILLS ME WITH FEAR.
FATHER AND EDGAR DON'T FEAR IT, BUT I LACK THEIR STRENGTH
WHAT SHOULD I
ER-NEST!
ISN'T IT PRETTY? LOOK! A PERFECT SNOWFLAKE.
WHY SO GLUM? IT'S SO MUCH NICER WHEN YOU SMILE.
....
THERE IS SOMETHING I DESIRE ABOVE A SNOWFLAKE, ERNEST.
JUST SAY THE WORD.

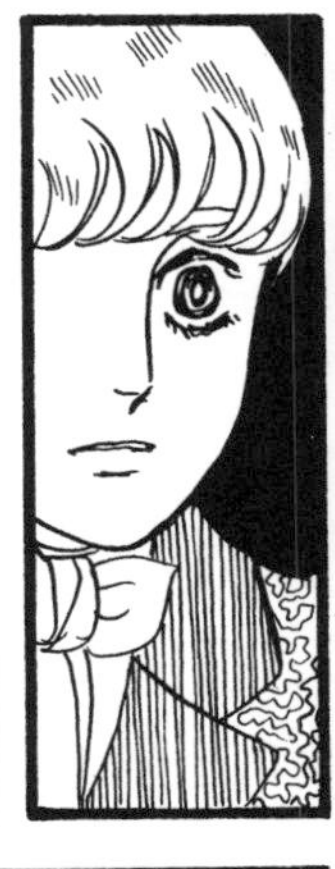

YES. I WANT IT. WON'T YOU GET IT FOR ME?

WERE YOU LYING WHEN YOU SAID YOU LOVE ME?

FOR YOU, MARYBELLE...

...SHOULD YOU DESIRE IT, THOUGH IT COST ME MY SANITY...

...I WOULD TAKE THE QUEEN'S HAIRPIN OR THE APPLE OF EDEN.

I MOST STRONGLY OBJECT! WE HAVE NO IDEA WHO HE IS!

BAM!

YOU OBJECT!? I'M NOT ASKING YOUR OPINION. I'M SAYING THAT IS WHAT I WISH.

BUT HENRY, THERE'S NO NEED TO LEGALLY ADOPT HIM! IF HE SHOULD PROVE TO--

AHHH

COME ON, NOW! I JUST WANT TO LOOK AT IT!

AH... AH!

I'LL GIVE IT RIGHT BACK!

UNCLE HENRY!

ER-NEST!

BAM!

UNCLE HENRY...
YOU DISAP-POINT ME, ERNEST. BULLYING THE WEAK.

BUT I JUST--
DIDN'T YOU TELL ME YOU WOULD BE FAST FRIENDS?
HE'S ILL. HE'S NO DIFFERENT FROM A CHILD OF FIVE OR SIX!

BAM!

...IT'S QUITE CLEAR THAT YOUR UNCLE DOESN'T LOVE YOU AS MUCH AS HE DOES THAT BLUE-EYED BOY.
YES, AND WHAT'S MORE...
HE'S BEEN GOING ON ABOUT MARRYING EDGAR TO MARYBELLE, DON'T YOU KNOW?
ROG-ER!
CHIN UP, ERNEST. HENRY IS JUST IN A FOUL MOOD, THAT'S ALL.
HE DIDN'T HAVE TO YELL LIKE THAT.
HE'S NEVER ONCE YELLED AT ME BEFORE.
WHY SHOULD I? HE WAS CONSULTING YOU ON THAT VERY MATTER, WASN'T HE?
LORD KNOWS WHAT HENRY SEES IN THAT BRAT!
DO HOLD YOUR TONGUE!
MAR-RY!?
BY RIGHTS HE SHOULD BE DEAD! TRYING TO CHEAT HENRY, HE IS! I'D LIKE TO WRING HIS NECK!

I KNOW I REPEAT MYSELF...
...BUT I AM QUITE FOND OF THIS ROSE ESSENCE!
I'D PROBABLY END UP POISONING MYSELF!
ES-SENCE, EH?
I COULD TRY POISONING THEIR CUPS.
ERNEST
I DO WISH YOU'D TAKE EDGAR'S CRUCIFIX.
MARRY EDGAR TO MARY-BELLE...
I HAD NO IDEA UNCLE HENRY HAD SUCH PLANS.
IT'S AS BALMY AS SPRING TODAY! WE MUST GO OUTDOORS!
TIME FOR OUR AFTERNOON SKATE! LET'S GO!

HENRY, IF I COULD HAVE A WORD.

A WORD?

a! apple pie!

I WAS HOPING A BRISK GALLOP WOULD SHAKE THIS MOOD OF MINE, BUT NOW--

!

I WAS GOING TO GO ON MY OWN...

ERNEST! BE A DEAR AND TAKE EDGAR WITH YOU.

...

JUST ONE TIME AROUND THE POND.

HOLD ON. THE SILVER CRUCIFIX.

THIS IS THE PERFECT CHANCE!

HENRY.
IDENTITY? BUT HE'S LOST HIS MEMORY. YOU KNOW THAT!

I THINK IT'S FINE OF YOU WANT TO TAKE EDGAR IN. HOWEVER...
...AS YOUR FRIEND, I AM ASKING YOU TO WAIT UNTIL YOU HAVE CONFIRMED HIS IDENTITY.

YOUR PLANS FOR EDGAR.
WHAT'S ON YOUR MIND?

I...
I'M NO FORTUNE TELLER. NO PROPHET. I'M A DOCTOR. BUT I BELIEVE IN LEGENDS. I BELIEVE IN THE EXISTENCE OF GOD AND THE DEVIL.

I CAN'T STOP THINKING ABOUT OSWALD, LORD EVAN'S LAST WILL AND TESTAMENT!

SHE SAID IT TWICE, WHEN NO ONE ELSE WAS AROUND. "EDGAR. IT'S ME."

LISTEN. MARYBELLE KNEW OF EDGAR'S HABIT OF BREAKING BRANCHES AS HE WALKS, EVEN THOUGH SHE'D JUST MET HIM. I THOUGHT NOTHING OF IT AT THE TIME.
BUT THEN
SHE SAID, "IT'S ME."

CALL IT INTUITION. THOSE TWO KNOW EACH OTHER.
PERHAPS SHE'S WAITING FOR EDGAR TO REGAIN HIS MEMORY.
PERHAPS SHE'S WAITING TO SEE WHAT HAP-PENS.
BUT IF THEY KNOW EACH OTHER, WHY DOESN'T MARYBELLE SAY SO?
YOU HAVE FINE INTU-ITION, DOCTOR.
MARYBELLE, AT LEAST, CAME HERE BY DESIGN!
WE KNOW NOTHING ABOUT THEIR PAST. THEY ARE THE STRANGEST OF STRANGERS.

CLOP
FOR A CONVAL-ESCENT
HE CERTAINLY IS A SEASONED RIDER.
THE CRUCIFIX!
WHAT AM I THINKING? I'VE GOT TO HURRY. IT'S LESS THAN FOUR MILES AROUND THE POND.
HEY! IT'S GETTING CLOUDY! TIME TO GO HOME! LADIES!
LINDA! LINDA! LET'S GO!

FOOSH
I THINK A STORM'S COMING.
REALLY! WHAT A TOMBOY THAT GIRL IS!

I'M GOING TO TAKE A SPIN AROUND THE SUMMER HOUSE! GO ON AHEAD!

YOUR FRAGRANCE GOLDEN BE

YOU TANGLE ME UP O, DAPHNE, I LOVE THEE

YOU TANGLE ME UP

AREN'T YOU COLD?
NO.
OH!

OS-WALD?
HA HA
NOW THERE'S AN OLD SONG! I'M SURPRISED I REMEMBER IT. MY LATE FATHER USED TO SING IT.

OSWALD? MY FATHER'S NAME WAS CLIFFORD.
OSWALD WAS MY GRANDFATHER'S NAME, BUT I NEVER KNEW HIM.
OH! I SEE ...

O, DAPHNE BUSH O, DAPHNE BUSH YOUR FRAGRANCE GOLDEN BE
YOU TANGLE ME UP YOU TANGLE ME UP O, DAPHNE, I LOVE THEE

?
?
?
?
?
OF COURSE. IT'S 1820. IT'S BEEN DECADES SINCE WE PLAYED AND SANG THAT SONG TOGETHER.
YOU KNOW, YOU REMIND ME OF OSWALD, ROGER. YOUR VOICE, TOO!
HE WAS SO KIND.
ZOOSH
HEE-E-E-E
AHHH
WHUMP
NOW'S MY CHANCE!

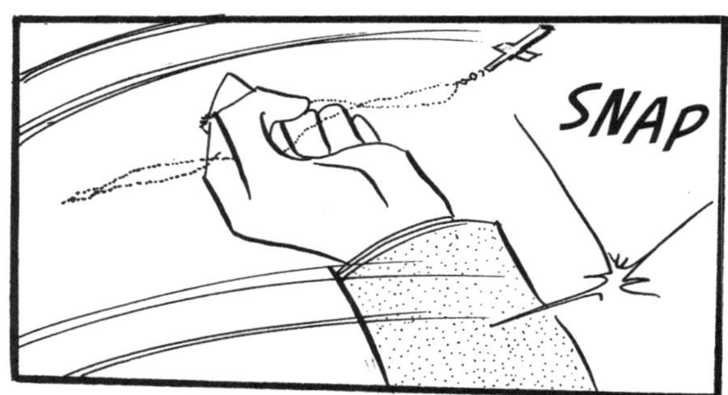
SNAP

LOOK AT YOU! JUST LYING THERE, LIKE--
I'VE GOT IT! HAH!

BY RIGHTS, YOU SHOULD BE DEAD! NOW GIVE ME THAT!
AH!
VOOM
CRACK
SNAP

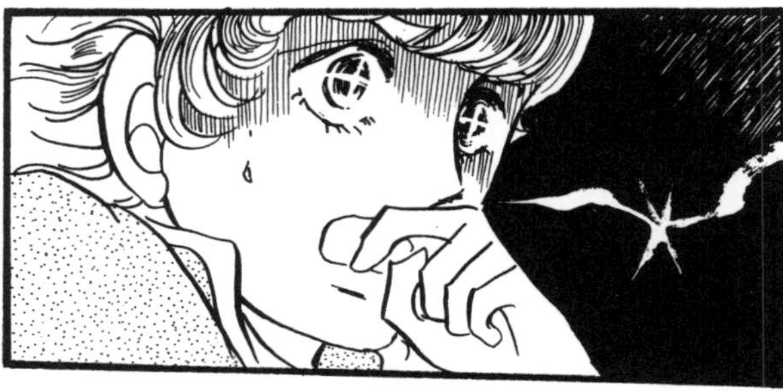

IS... IS HE... DEAD!?
AH... EDGAR...

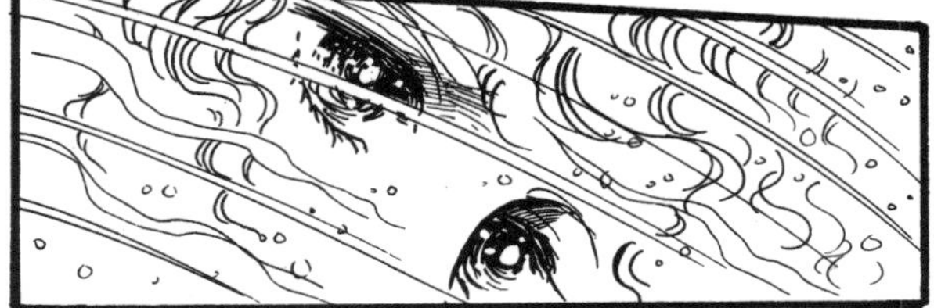

AH!

AH!
HE'S WATCH-ING ME
A WATER DEMON
HE'S UNDER WATER... YET LIVES?
UNDER WATER...!
SPLASH
FLOOMP

WHA--!?
WHA--!?
AHHHHHH!!!!!

AHH!
A-AH!
LINDA!
TMP!
WHUMP!
ERNEST! YOUR NECK IS BLEEDING!
WHAT...!? WHAT...!?
OH, ERNEST!
CLOP

BAM
UNCLE!!

IT'S ME.
EDGAR. IT'S ME.

WHAT ON EARTH ARE YOU DOING!?
OH, UNCLE! UNCLE!
ERNEST! YOU'RE SOAKED!
HELP LINDA!

LINDA? ER- NEST?
MARY- BELLE !

EDGAR! THE BOY YOU LOVE... HE'S NOT HUMAN! IT WAS SO FRIGHTENING! ERNEST'S NECK... HIS NECK!

HE'S A MONSTER! HIS EYES WERE GLOWING! I SWEAR IT! DO SOMETHING!
WERE YOU FIGHTING AGAIN!?

THE MOMENT I PULLED OFF HIS CRUCIFIX.

HE... HE BIT ME! ON THE NECK!
NECK? WHAT ABOUT YOUR NECK?

HE BIT YOU?

MARY-BELLE!?

MY LONG WAIT IS OVER. NOW I CAN TAKE HIM AWAY!

THEN HIS MEMORY HAS RETURNED.

WAIT! WHERE ARE--
RE-TURNED? TAKE HIM AWAY?
MARY-BELLE!

WHAT SORT OF GAME ARE YOU ALL AT!? WHERE'S EDGAR!?
HE'S NOT HUMAN!

THEN... MARY-BELLE, TOO...

DOC-TOR!

THE OLD TALES SAY THAT IT'S VAMPIRNELLA WHO BITE A PERSON ON THE NECK. WHAT IF...
YOU'RE THE ONE WHO'S GONE MAD! DID EDGAR RAVAGE ANY ROSES HERE? WELL?

I'M AFRAID THERE'S NOTHING BUT CAMELLIAS HERE. WAIT.
WHEN DID YOU START DRINK-ING ROSE ES-SENCE?

MARY-BELLE GAVE THAT TO ME, SIR.

THIS IS PERFECT. I DON'T BELIEVE IN DEMONS...
...BUT PLAYING ALONG IS A GOOD EXCUSE TO GO AFTER EDGAR!
HENRY, I'LL GO WITH YOU!
HEN-RY!
DOC-TOR!
I'M GOING AFTER THEM! LOCK ALL THE DOORS!

WHERE'S EDGAR!? FIND EDGAR!
THEN WE'LL GET SOME ANSWERS!

ERNEST, LET'S GET YOU INTO SOME DRY CLOTHES.

M' LORD ?
KLAK

UNCLE HENRY!?
UNCLE ROGER!?

KNOCK
KNOCK
KNOCK

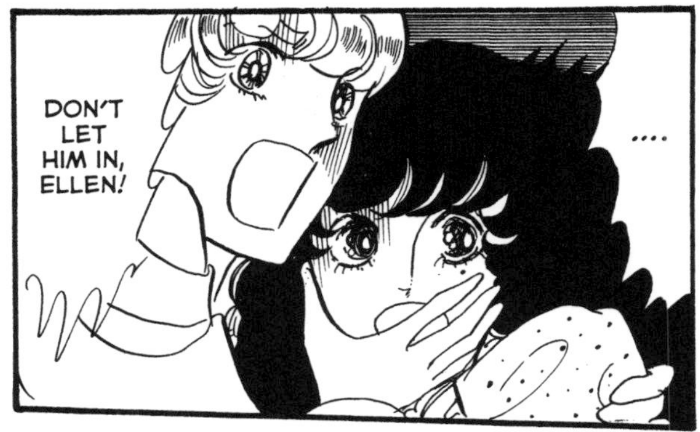
DON'T LET HIM IN, ELLEN!
....

... WHERE IS SHE?

MARY-BELLE ISN'T HERE.

RMBL RMBL

SHE'S OUTSIDE, MASTER EDGAR. OUTSIDE.
TMP

EDGAR!
EDGAR!
IN HIS WEAKENED STATE, HE'LL ...!
HE COULD BE ANYWHERE, BROTHER!
EDGAR!
NOW'S MY CHANCE. ONE SHOT.
I'LL SAY IT WAS AN ACCIDENT.
FORGIVE ME, FATHER, FOR WHAT I AM--
FLASH

RMBL
RMBL
RMBL
BROTH-
ER!
ED-
GAR!
ROGER, WHAT ARE YOU DOING!?
EDGAR! IT'S ME!
THAT'S NOT EDGAR! I GUARANTEE IT! YOU PULLED SOMETHING AWFUL FROM THE RIVER!
IT'S A DEVIL!
YOU... YOU...! BROTHER, I TELL YOU...
STOP! ROGER!
IF WE DON'T KILL HIM, HE'LL KILL US! LET GO, HENRY! WAHH!!
FLASH
IT'S ED-
GAR!

CRACK!

DAMN, I CAN'T REMEMBER A SINGLE HYMN!
YOU SNEAKY BASTARD. YOU AND MARYBELLE WERE IN CAHOOTS THE WHOLE TIME!
IS THIS HOW MY GREEDY LITTLE LIFE ENDS? THE LORD IS MY SHEPHERD...
AH!
WHERE IS SHE?
ED-GAR!

MARY-BELLE?
YES!
MARY-BELLE!
YES! YES!

WHERE HAS MY EDGAR GONE?
WHERE ARE THOSE BLUE EYES?
VIOLETTA?
GAZ-ING FOR SO VERY LONG ...
WHO? SOMEONE IS GAZING AT ME.
ELLEN?
YOU WERE STRUCK BY LIGHT-NING...
... M' LORD.

....

OH, DO GET WELL SOON, M'LORD.

WHAT A FINE GIRL. SUCH WARM, BROWN EYES.
WHEN I'M ABLE TO TALK AGAIN, I SHALL ASK HER HAND IN MARRIAGE, NO MATTER WHAT ANYONE SAYS ABOUT IT.

YOU WERE REALLY IN LOVE WITH MARYBELLE, WEREN'T YOU, ERNEST?
BUT THERE'S NO POINT IN FALLING IN LOVE WITH THE DUSK OR THE MOONLIGHT, IS THERE, LINDA?

YOU TANGLE ME UP YOU TANGLE ME UP
O, DAPHNE, I LOVE THEE

O, DAPHNE BUSH O, DAPHNE BUSH YOUR FRAGRANCE GOLDEN BE

WHAT A CLOD YOU ARE, ROGER EVANS. YOU TRY TO KILL YOUR BROTHER, END UP SAVING HIM, AND GET STRUCK BY LIGHTNING IN THE BARGAIN.

LONDON

YES, SIR! THIS HOUSE DID INDEED ONCE BELONG TO OSWALD LORD EVANS.
AFRAID I DON'T KNOW MUCH ABOUT HIM, OTHER THAN THAT HE WAS HANDSOME, HE LOVED HIS WIFE, AND HE WAS A PLAYBOY. OR SO THEY SAY.

THERE ON THE LANDING HANGS A PORTRAIT. PERHAPS ONE OF YOUR ANCESTORS, SIR?

ISN'T SHE LOVELY?

AND HOW MAY I ASSIST YOU?
ABOUT EDGAR AND MARY-BELLE...

MARYBELLE... AH. THE DAUGHTER OF DUKE ART WAS ADOPTED BY LORD EVANS. HER NAME WAS MARYBELLE. SHE WAS THIRTEEN YEARS OF AGE.
WELL, KEEP IN MIND THAT IN THOSE DAYS...
..."ADOPTION" OF A GIRL MIGHT BE A EUPHEMISM FOR TAKING IN A CONCUBINE.
AT ANY RATE...
...THE YOUNG LADY DIED IMMEDIATELY AFTERWARDS.

END OF CHAPTER 1. FIRST PUBLISHED IN **SPECIAL EDITION SHŌJO COMIC**, JAN-FEB 1975

CHAPTER 2

PENNY RAIN

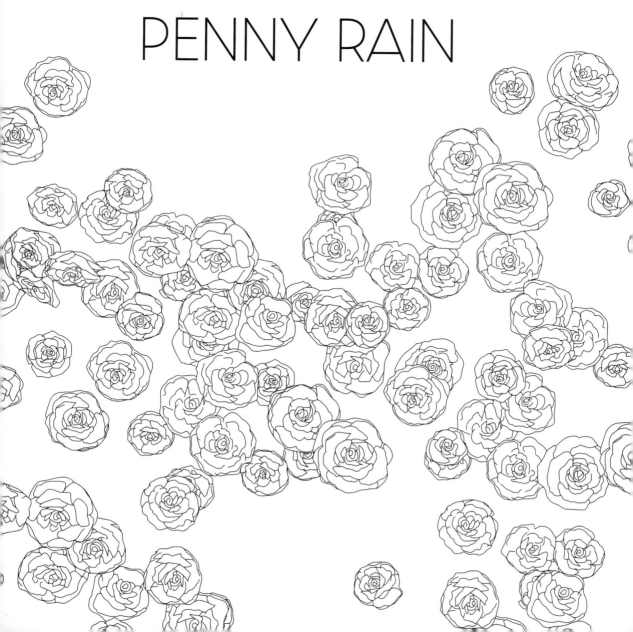

PIT PAT PIT PAT
PIT PAT PIT PAT
THAS ALWAYS THIS WAY THIS TOIME O' YEAR.
NO SUNSHOINE. NUTH'N BUT CLOWDS AN' FOG.
AN' NOW THAS RAIN'N!
SO, LITTLE MAASTER.
YOO SAY YOO'RE CUMM'N FR'M EWBOURNE?
SPLOSH SPLOSH
SPLOSH SPLOSH
OI CER-TAINLY DO, MAAS-TER.
MORE LIKE "PENNY RAIN."
ARE YOO SURE YOO WANNA TAKE THE HOIGHWAY TER WISH IN ALL THIS HERE RAIN?
YOU CALL THIS RAIN?
HM-MM
SHIVER
MAAS-TER?
THAT'S RIGHT.

!
TUMP
UMPH!?
CLOP CLOP CLOP
OI'D RAATHER BE UP THE PUB...
DAMNED RAIN.
THE HOSSES WILL BE THE WUSSER FOR UT.
SPLASH SPLASH
WOULDN'T BE SURPROISED IF HOIGHWAYMEN--
...HAVV'N A PINT AN' MAYK'N A STITCH WITH A PRETTY MAID.
SPLASH
SHIVER
SPLASH SPLASH
SPLASH!
THIS HERE RAIN IS COWD. PAARDON ME, SON.
HELLO.
SNAP

SPLASH
SPLASH

CLUNK
CLUNK
WE'RE HOIGH-WAYMEN, SEE?
THIS HERE HOIGH-WAY'S OURS.
HA HA. BAD SPOT OF LUCK FOR YOO, LAD.

TH-ERE'S A GOOD LAD.

YOUR MON-EY.

TUMP

ROIGHT
KLAK

YOO ALONE? OI RECK'N SO. WOS THIS.
KNOCK
KNOCK

PASSEN-
GER? A
WOMAN?
A KID WITH
MONEY.
HE'S A
GOOD LAD.

HARD
TER
FOIND
GAME
IN THIS
HERE
RAIN.
NO
GOOD,
DAD.
JEST
ONE
CAR-
RIAGE.
HOW'D
UT
GOO
?
KILLED THE
DROIVER.
BROUGHT THE
PASSENGER.

OI SEE. AN'
WOS THE
BIG BOX?
KLAK

HMMM

TAP

KLAK

WHAT?

A CORPSE.

WELL, OPEN UT UP.

HOW SHOULD OI KNOW? LOIKE OI SAY. THAS A CORPSE.

THAS JEST A CHILD.

WOS THIS ALL ABOWT?

STRANGE KID. NO CROY'N. NO WHING'N.
....
COME ALONG T'GETHER.
LOCK'M UP, GEE. HE'LL FETCH A RANSOM.
AN' THIS?
CLOP
CAN'T DO NUTHEN WITH A CORPSE. BURY'M SOMEWHERE WHEN THIS HERE RAIN LETS UP.
THAS A FAMILY BUSINESS. THU-TEEN BROTHERS AN' DAD'S THE BOSS.
DO AS YOO'RE TOWD AN' NO ONE WILL PICK ON YER.
WE'RE GOOD-NATURED AS HOIGHWAY-MEN GOO, YER KNOW.
CRASH

COOD-A-HELL -- WOS THAT NOISE!? GEE...?

WHAT IN THE NAME O'--!
BAM!

BLAM BLAM BLAM

WHAT!? WHAT ARE YOO!? WHAT IN--
BLAM

WOOSH
WOOSH
WOOSH
WOOSH
CLATTER
SNAP!
TMP TMP
HURRY

HURRY
HURRY
HURRY TO THE LITTLE MANOR IN WISH.
ALAN WILL WAKE.
YOUNG MAASTER PORTNELL!
THAS ME! DO YOO REMEMBER ME, M'LORD? OWD DON!
OI TOOK CARE O' YOUR HOSSES WHEN YOUR FAMILY PASSED THIS WAY LAAST YEAR!
YES.
I'M HEADED FOR THE MANOR.
FER THE MANOR?

THE BARON SAY HE'D STOP BOY IN SIX OR SEVEN MONTHS' TOIME.
OI'D BIN THINK'N THAS ABOWT TOIME YOO CAME.
THE MANOR'S QUOITE CLEAN, M'LORD. BUT THIS TOIME O' YEAR...
...THERE'S NOT MUCH TER SEE, OI'M AFRAID. THERE'S NUTHEN IN BLOOM.
TRAVEL'N ALONE, M'LORD? WHERE ARE THE BARON AND MISS MARYBELLE?
OH. FORGIVE ME FER SPEAK'N OWT O' TURN.

STAY AWAY FROM THE MANOR.
YOO KNOW WHERE THE WOOD AND THE PROVISIONS ARE, M'LORD? IF YOO NEED ANY HELP, OI'LL SEND MOY DAUGHTER AROWND.
PLE-ASE.
YES, JUST LEAVE IT THERE.
SHALL OI JEST LEAVE THIS HERE, M'LORD? NOT VERY HEAVY FER UTS SOIZE, IS UT?
WANT'N TER BE ALL ALONE IN A BIG HOWSE LOIKE THAT. NOT VERY FRIENDLY.
THAS NOT FER US COMMON FOLK TER MAKE SENSE O' THE WAYS O' NOBLES.
WELL, OI S'POSE HE'LL CALL IF HE NEEDS ANYTHING.
THEY'VE POPPED UP WITHOWT WARN'N AFORE.
OI'M SURE THE BARON AND THE OTHERS'LL BE ALONG SOON ENOUGH.

カチリ

TMP
NOTHING TO BUT WAIT FOR THE LONG NIGHT TO PASS.

...LATE TONIGHT, OR AROUND DAWN.

IT'S BEEN A BIT MORE THAN A FULL DAY NOW.
PER-HAPS HE'LL WAKE...

CRACK
POP POP

I WONDER WHO PUT THESE WILDFLOW-ERS HERE.

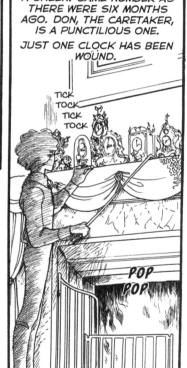

EVERY CLOCK, POLISHED TO A SHEEN. SAME NUMBER AS THERE WERE SIX MONTHS AGO. DON, THE CARETAKER, IS A PUNCTILIOUS ONE.
JUST ONE CLOCK HAS BEEN WOUND.
TICK
TOCK
TICK
TOCK
POP POP

AWAKE, YE MYTHS
AWAKE YE NOW
DREAMS DREAMT BY TIME
ART I AND THOU
FOR ANCIENT TALES,
AWE OF UNKNOWN
SUCH BE OUR SEEDBED
AND OUR SONG
O, ALAN, NOW
BID THEE FAREWELL
TO TRANSIENT WORLD
WHERE MORTALS
DWELL
FOR THOU DOST KNOW
WHO WE TWO BE
AND WHITHER THOU
AND I JOURNEY
AWAKE NOW, QUICK
AND BY MY SIDE
THE CHARIOT
ETERNAL RIDE

YOU!
YOU!
MY LITTLE SONGBIRD
MY LOVE
LOCKS OF SILVER
EDGAR!!
EDGAR!!
YOU!
YOU!
EDGAR
EDGAR

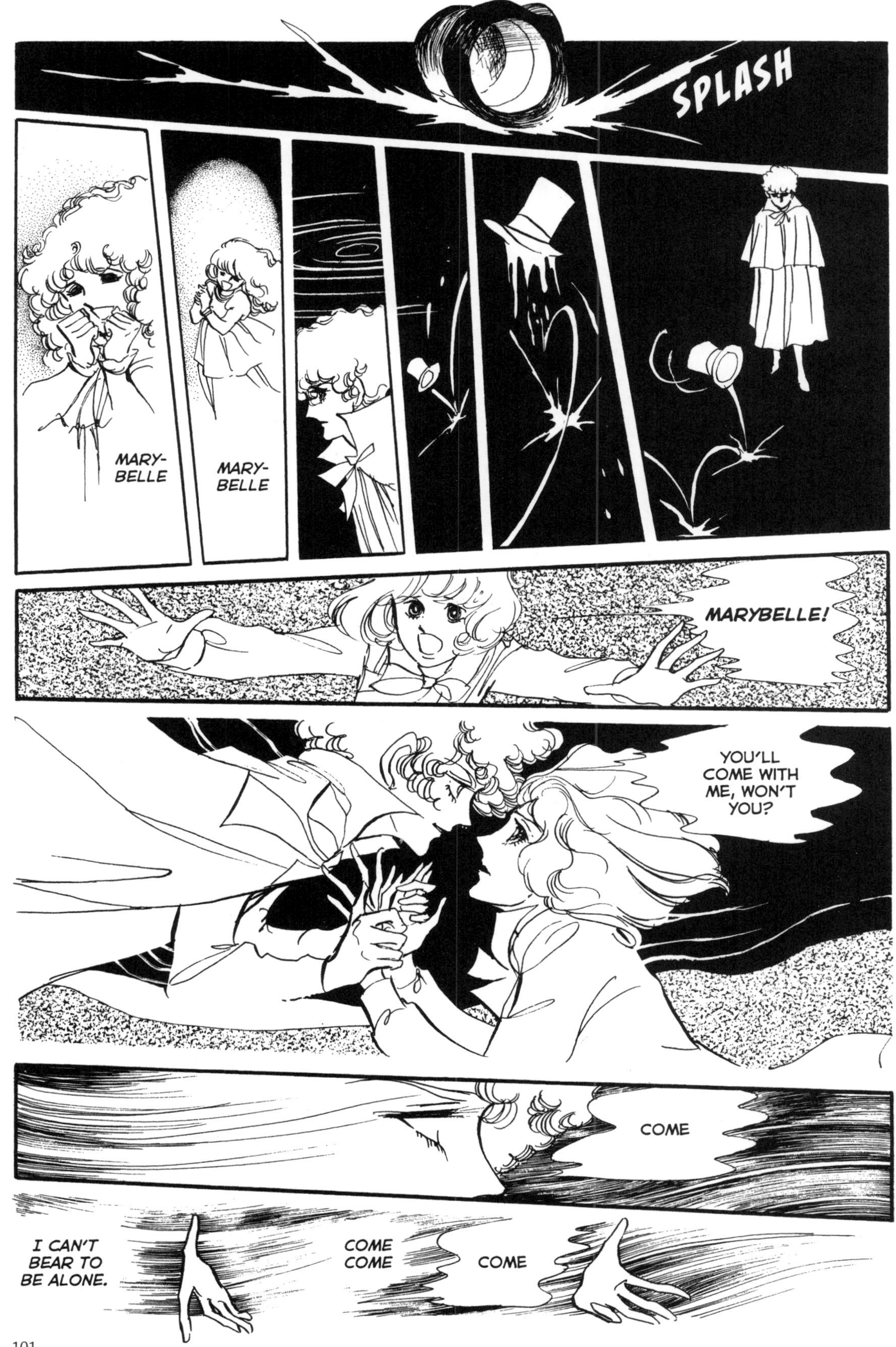
SPLASH
MARY-
BELLE
MARY-
BELLE
MARYBELLE!
YOU'LL COME WITH ME, WON'T YOU?
COME
I CAN'T BEAR TO BE ALONE.
COME
COME
COME

MORNING? WHAT WAS THAT SOUND?
TMP
KLAK
OH!

WHO ARE YOU!?
OI... OI...

...BROUGHT SOME VEGETABLES, M'LORD. FAATHER SAY NOT TER DISTURB YOO, SO OI...

....
I'VE NO NEED FOR VEGETA-BLES.

B--BUT FAATHER TOWD ME TER BRING 'EM, M'LORD.

ARE YOU THE ONE WHO WOUND JUST ONE CLOCK?
F--FAATHER TOWD ME TO, M'LORD.
AND YOUR FATHER TOLD YOU TO PUT FLOWERS IN A VASE, TOO?
SO THAT'S DON THE CARE-TAKER'S DAUGH-TER.
IT'S SO DARK YOU'D HARDLY KNOW IT WAS MORNING.
NOW HOW'S ALAN?
KLAK
WILL THIS RAIN NEVER LET UP?

THE TRANSFORMATION IS NOT YET COMPLETE.
HE SLEEPS STILL.
CRACK POP
POP CRACK
TICK TOCK TICK TOCK TICK TOCK TICK TOCK
KREE
HM!?
NO!
TMP
WHY...?

CRACK

POP
POP POP
CRACK

IT CAN'T BE. I INFUSED HIM WITH MORE THAN ENOUGH OF MY BLOOD. MY ENERGY. MY BLOOD SHOULD BE QUITE RICH. I RECEIVED IT DIRECTLY FROM THE KING OF THE POE CLAN HIMSELF.
POP CRACK
POP
THERE ARE RARE CASES...

...WHEN THE BLOOD WILL NOT COMMINGLE, AND THE BODY STIFFENS AND DIES.

IT CAN'T BE. I WON'T ALLOW IT!
POP
CRACK
COME TO THINK OF IT, SHEILA TOLD ME IT TOOK THREE WHOLE DAYS FOR ME TO TRANSFORM.

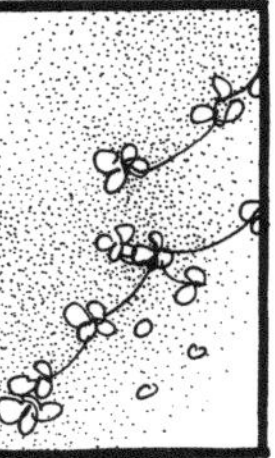
AND THIS IS ONLY DAY TWO. I'M SURE ALAN'S TRANSFORMATION IS SIMPLY PROGRESSING MORE SLOWLY THAN NORMAL.
I'M SURE HE'LL WAKE SOON.
WHY, EVEN MARYBELLE...

EVEN MARYBELLE...
MARYBELLE...
...AWOKE AFTER JUST ONE DAY WHEN I MADE HER ONE OF US.
MARYBELLE AMONG THE FLOWERS... HOW I LOVED THAT CHILD.
BUT SHE WAS ALWAYS SUSCEPTIBLE...
...TO DAMP AIR, AND COLD NIGHT WINDS, AND THE NOONDAY SUN.
I OFTEN EXCHANGED ENERGY WITH HER.
THE HOT BLOOD THAT RAN BETWEEN OUR FINGERTIPS AND COURSED THROUGH OUR VEINS... OLD BLOOD CONSUMED AND MADE NEW...
MARYBELLE AND I WERE INSEPARABLE.
SOMETIMES SHE WOULD SLEEP A FULL FORTNIGHT.
IT'S YOUR FAULT MARYBELLE IS SO WEAK, EDGAR.

YOUR BLOOD WAS A POOR MATCH FOR HER.
HOW THAT COULD BE WHEN YOU'RE BLOOD IS SO RICH...
...I'LL NEVER KNOW.
WELL, YOU ARE PECULIAR FOR ONE OF OUR CLAN. YOU'RE STRANGE. YOU'RE ABNORMAL. YOU'RE ECCENTRIC.
YOU STILL SOMETIMES DESIRE TO BECOME HUMAN AGAIN.
SCATTERING ROSES LIKE YOU DO...!
NOT SOME-TIMES!
I ALWAYS WANTED TO BE HUMAN AGAIN.
YET I TOOK MARYBELLE BY THE HAND...
EDGAR! EDGAR!
...AND KILLED HER! I KILLED HER.
MADE HER ONE OF US.

EDGAR! EDGAR!
ALAN, PLEASE WAKE UP!
ALONE I AM HOUNDED BY MEMO- RIES.
WHY WON'T YOU OPEN YOUR EYES?
EVEN IF IT WAS A MISTAKE TO BRING YOU TO THIS...
EVEN IF I'M A CREATURE THAT HAS NO RIGHT TO LIVE...
...I BEG YOU TO OPEN YOUR EYES.
ALAN RAIN... RAIN...
IT'S SO DARK ...
COULD THE RAIN BE THE CAUSE?

I CAN'T BEAR TO BE ALONE.
THIS DAMPNESS? THIS HEAVY, CLOYING DAMPNESS?
MARYBELLE, TOO, WAS ALWAYS WEAKENED BY WATER.
IS THIS WHAT KEEPS ALAN FROM WAKING?
IF THE RAIN WOULD STOP...
IF IT WOULD JUST STOP...
CRACK POP POP
POP CRACK
COME COME
COME
I CAN'T BEAR TO BE ALONE.

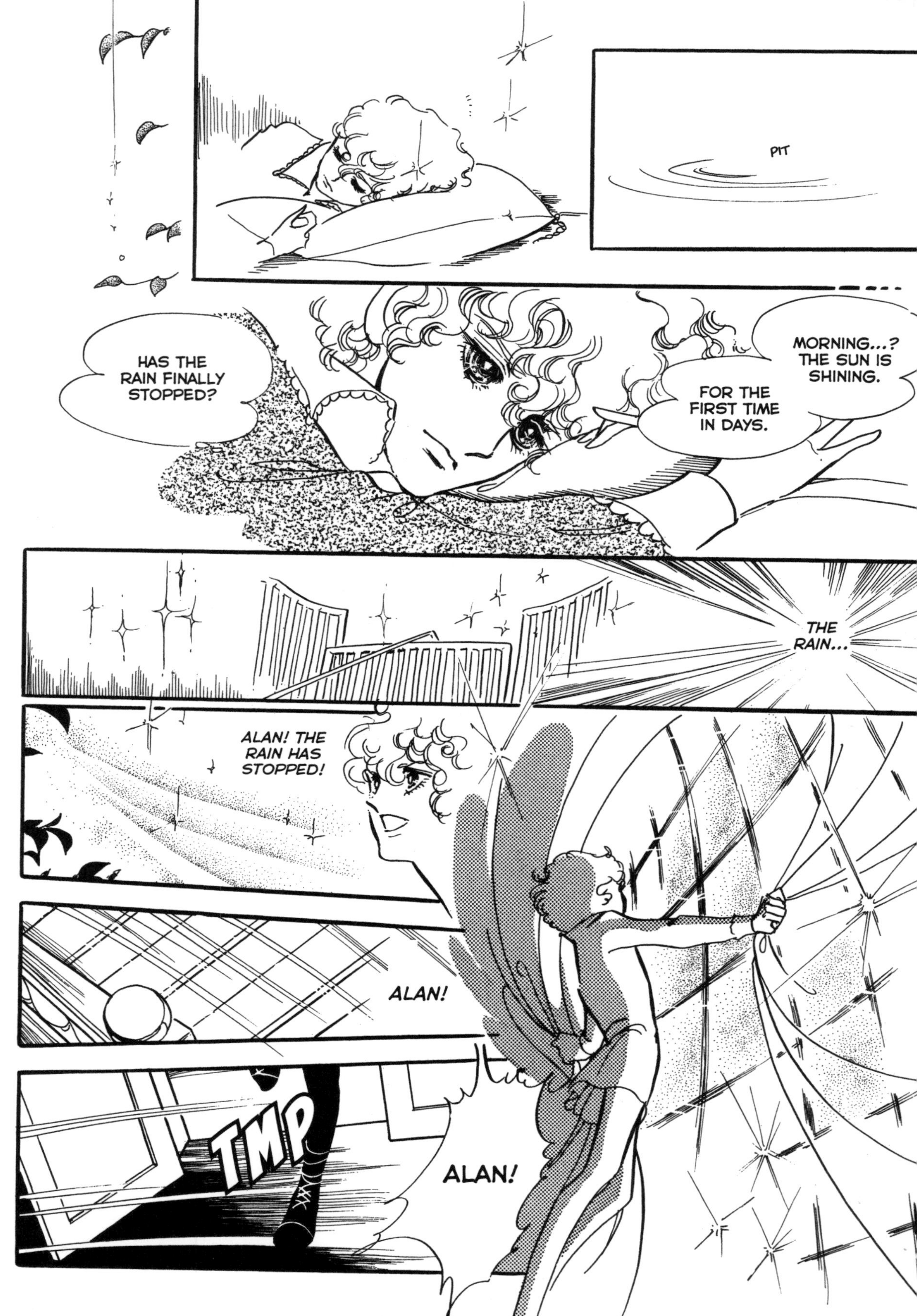
PIT
MORNING...? THE SUN IS SHINING.
FOR THE FIRST TIME IN DAYS.
HAS THE RAIN FINALLY STOPPED?
THE RAIN...
ALAN! THE RAIN HAS STOPPED!
ALAN!
TMP
ALAN!

ALAN!?
ALAN...

HE WENT OUT!? NO!
HE'S ONLY JUST AWOKE!
HE HASN'T SLAKED HIS THIRST!
BUT WHERE? WHERE!? WHERE!?
ALAN!
IF HE SHOULD ATTACK A HUMAN...
ALAN
...OR BE KILLED HIMSELF!
SPLASH
YOUNG MAASTER!
DON!
OI WAS JEST CUMM'N TER WARN YER, M'LORD! DON'T GOO OWTDOORS! MOY DAUGHTER... SHE WAS KILLED BOY THE HOIGHWAYMEN.

BUT FAATHER TOWD ME TO, M'LORD.

WHEN !?

TWO DAYS AGOO.

DO YOO KNOW HOW TER USE A GUN, YOUNG MAASTER?

THEY USUALLY KEEP TER THE HOIGHWAY, BUT OI S'POSE THE RAIN KEPT FOLKS FROM TRAVEL'N, AN' THE BANDITS TOOK TO ATTACK'N VILLAGERS.

THE VILLAGERS AN' CONSTABLE HAVE KILLED FOUR SO FAAR.

WHERE ARE YOU, ALAN?
THE REMNANTS OF THAT GANG THAT ATTACKED MY CARRIAGE, NO DOUBT.
RIGHT.
THEY WERE CHASED INTER THAT THERE FORREST, SO OI DON'T THINK THEY'LL COME THIS WAY, BUT JEST IN CASE...
THERE'S STILL TWO ON THE LOOSE!
....
IF YOO SEE 'EM, M'LORD, YOU SHOOT 'EM DEAD, YOO HEAR? SHOOT 'EM DEAD!
WITH THE WHOLE VILLAGE HUNTING THE WOODS TO THE WEST, THEY'RE SURE TO BE CAUGHT BY EVENING.
WHERE HAVE YOU WANDERED OFF TO?

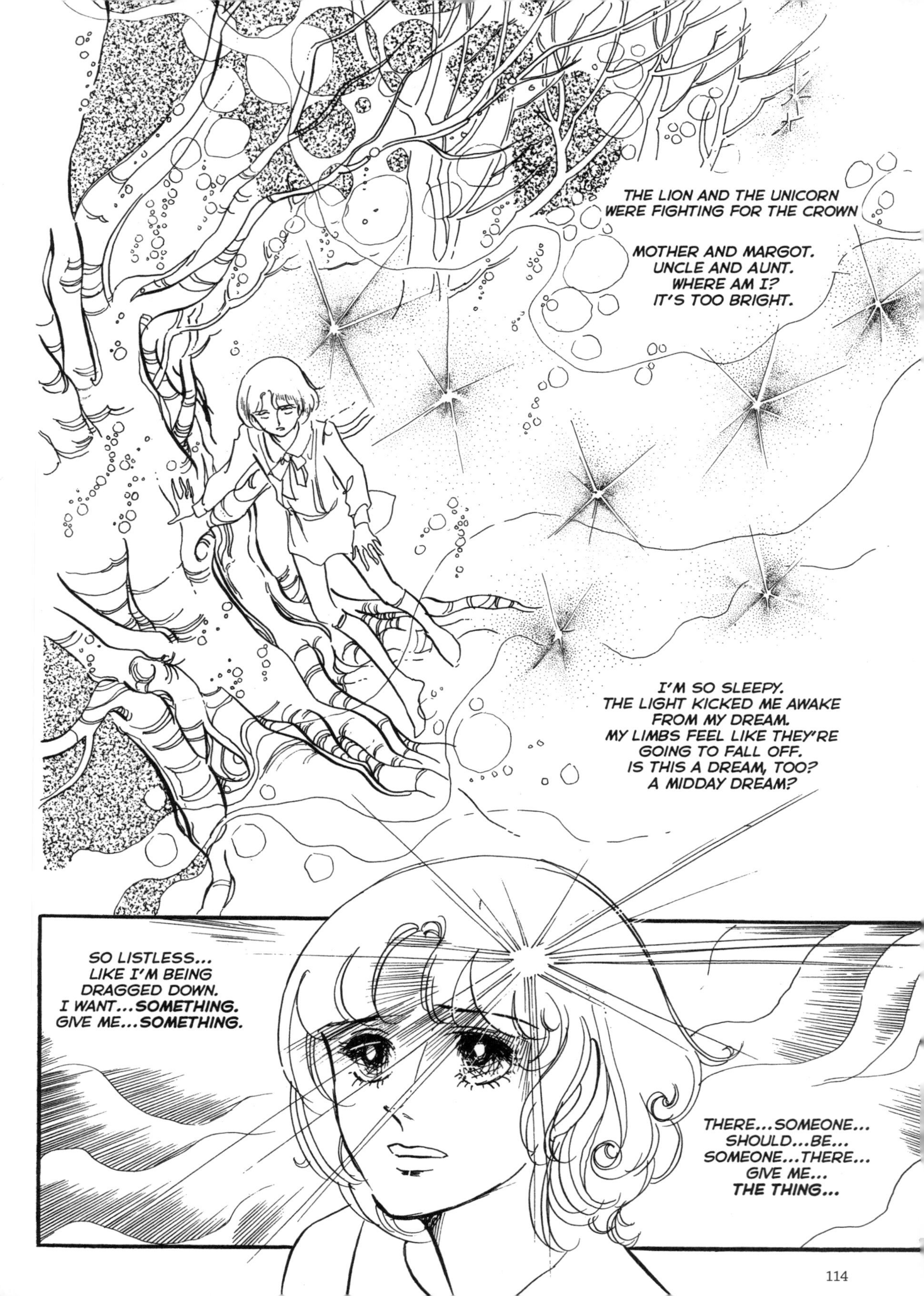
THE LION AND THE UNICORN
WERE FIGHTING FOR THE CROWN
MOTHER AND MARGOT.
UNCLE AND AUNT.
WHERE AM I?
IT'S TOO BRIGHT.
I'M SO SLEEPY.
THE LIGHT KICKED ME AWAKE
FROM MY DREAM.
MY LIMBS FEEL LIKE THEY'RE
GOING TO FALL OFF.
IS THIS A DREAM, TOO?
A MIDDAY DREAM?
SO LISTLESS...
LIKE I'M BEING
DRAGGED DOWN.
I WANT...SOMETHING.
GIVE ME...SOMETHING.
THERE...SOMEONE...
SHOULD...BE...
SOMEONE...THERE...
GIVE ME...
THE THING...

TAP
BUT HE MUST BE A BRAT FROM THE MANOR ON THE HILL, ROIGHT?
THE VILLAGERS ARE SEARCH'N THE WEST SOIDE O' THE FORREST.
WOS THIS?
HE'S NOT EVEN WEAR'N SHOES?
STAND UP OI SAY... STAND UP!
WE'LL HOIDE IN THE MANOR TILL NOIGHT.
SNEAK AWAY IN THE DAARK. THOSE VILLAGERS ARE BLOODTHIRSTY.
WALK! WALK, DAMN UT!
WOS WRONG WITH 'EM? OI THINK HE'S SICK.
THAS START'N TER RAIN AGAIN.
HOW'S YER WOUND?
YOO JEST KEEP AN OYE OWT FER THEM THERE DAMNED VILLAGERS.
OI SWEAR OI'LL KILL 'EM ALL SOME-DAY.
BLAM

WHUMP
BLAM
ISAAC !!
ZING!
WELL, WELL. AM OI GLAD TER SEE YOO AGAIN.
CLACK
YOO FIRED BOTH ROWNDS. TOO BAD, KID.
NOW LISSEN HERE.
YOO LITTLE DAVIL.

THE BOY YOU HAVE THERE...
KEEP YER HANDS UP, IF YOO DON'T WANT TER BE SHOT ALONG WITH THIS HERE KID.
OI SHOULD'VE SHOT YOO DEAD WHEN OI FOWND YOO ON THE HOIGH-WAY!
COME OVER HERE.
OI'M GONNA KILL YOO IN MOY OWN SWEET TOIME. AS PAYBACK FER MOY DAD AN' BROTHERS.
HANDS ...
AH!
OI SAY HANDS UP!
...IS THE CORPSE THAT WAS IN THAT BOX.
WAH!!
SSSSSS
BLAM

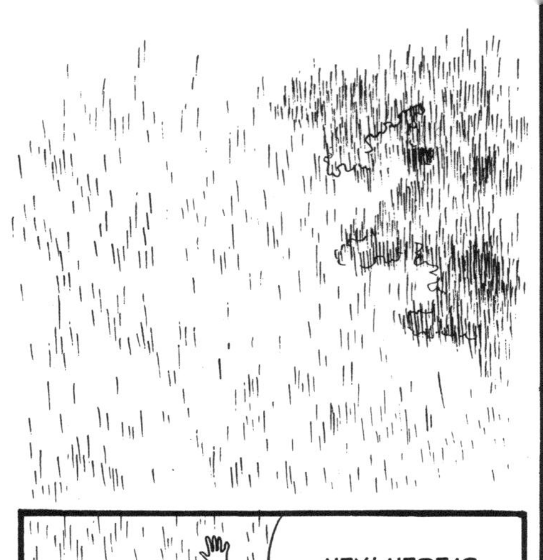

HEY! HERE'S ONE! NO, TWO! DEAD!

IS THIS THE LAAST O' THE GANG?
DO YOO S'POSE THEY KILLED EACH OTHER?

DEAD BEFORE HE EVEN KNEW WHO HE WAS DEALING WITH!

ALAN'S FIRST KILL...!
POOR MAN.

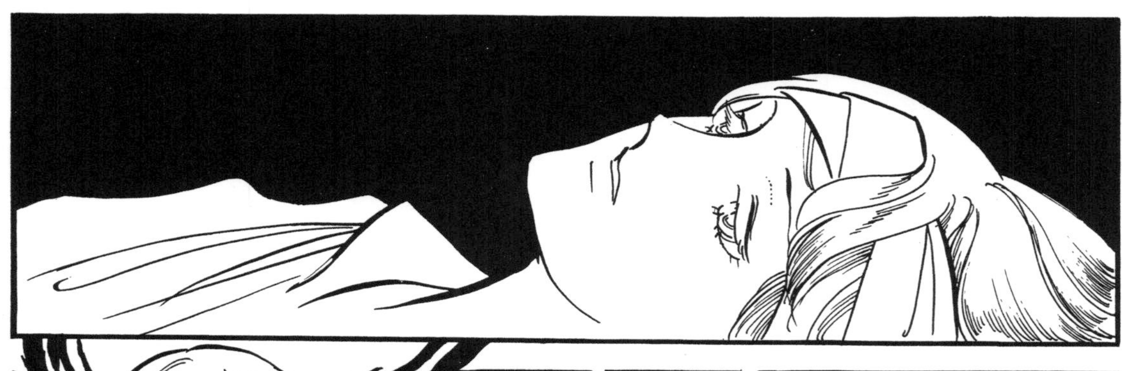

ALAN

I WON'T TAKE A VILLAGER. THE PEOPLE OF WISH LOOK AFTER THEIR OWN!!
SPLASH
SPLASH
SPLASH
SPLASH

A SUDDEN TRANSFORMATION AND SUDDEN AWAKENING. ALAN IS STILL HALF- ASLEEP. AND ON TOP OF IT ALL THIS WOUND...
IF THIS RAIN WOULD JUST STOP, THE WOUND WOULD HEAL QUICKLY. DAMN THIS ACCURSED DAMP!
HE'S LOSING TOO MUCH BLOOD. AT THIS RATE...

SPLASH

BUMP
BUMP

AH!

OHHH

CLATTER

WHAT THE DEVIL!?

AHHHH

AH!

KLAK!

NOT MUCH BLOOD IN HER. BUT IF I LEAVE HER HERE, SHE'LL EITHER STARVE OR FREEZE TO DEATH.

SNIFF
HIC
SHE LOOKS LIKE A PORCELAIN DOLL.

WHAT'S YOUR NAME?
LIDDY.

EVEN IF SOMEONE SHOULD FIND HER...

THERE'D BE NO HAPPY ENDING FOR AN ORPHANED NOBLE GIRL.

POP CRACK
POP POP

FIRE ...
I'LL GET THIS DAMP AIR DRY ENOUGH SOON.
HOW DO YOU FEEL ?

I DON'T KNOW. I FEEL SO GROGGY. I CAN'T TELL DREAM FROM REALITY. CAN'T EVEN REMEMBER WHEN I WOKE UP.

BUT YOU RECOGNIZE ME?
YES.

AND YOU KNOW WE'RE ABOUT TO BEGIN A VERY LONG JOURNEY.
...YES.
CRACK POP POP
AND YOU KNOW YOU DON'T NEED TO REMEMBER ANYTHING FROM THE PAST?
...YES.
THEN ONCE THIS RAIN STOPS...
...WE'LL SET OFF.
WHAT IS THAT DOLL I SEE THERE? OR IS THAT A DREAM?
THIS DOLL IS LIDDY.
WE'RE TAKING HER WITH US.
AND WE'RE GOING TO RAISE HER.

I SAW AN ELF HEELS OVER HEAD SPRING 'CROSS A FIELD WHERE FLOWERS SPREAD
THUS MYTH BEGINS
FOR GARDEN'S GLOOM SWEET FAIRIES DANCE TO PLEASE THE MOON AND TO THE CHILD WHO'S MET HIS END THE STEM AND ROOT OF ROSES SEND FOR NARCISSUS TRAPPED BY HIS SIGHT AN OFF'RING OF A BRIDE IN WHITE

AWAKE ALL MYTHS
FROM SLEEP RELENT
FOR THOU ART DREAMS
THAT TIME HAS DREAMT
O, DRAGON GRAND
O, PEGASUS
O FAWNS! O PRIDEFUL ICARUS!

END OF CHAPTER 2

FIRST PUBLISHED IN **SPECIAL EDITION SHÔJO COMIC**, MAY 1975

CHAPTER 3

LIDDY, IN THE FOREST

I STILL REMEMBER THEM. ONE WAS NAMED EDGAR. THE OTHER, ALAN.
THEY USED TO CALL ME "LIDDY DOLL."

...SOMETIMES A FIELD OF FLOWERS...

...SOMETIMES A VALLEY...
...OR A YEW FOR-EST...

OURS WAS A NOMADIC LIFE.
EACH SUMMER, WE MOVED FROM ONE FOREST TO ANOTHER.

SOMETIMES A BIRCH FOREST...

WE WERE ALWAYS IN A FOREST.

BUT THEY WOULD ALWAYS COAX ME
AND I'D BE READY FOR THE NEXT FOREST.

NOW LIDDY DOLL. THE PLACE WE'RE GOING TO HAS PEACH TREES.
PEA-CH?
THEY HAVE THE LOVELIEST BLOSSOMS.
YOU REALLY MUST SEE THEM.

SOME-TIMES I WOULD FUSS.
NO! NO! I LIKE IT HERE! I WANT TO STAY HERE!
NOW, LID-DY.

SUMMERS IN THE FOREST WOULD PASS IN THE BLINK OF AN EYE.
SPLASH
SPLASH
SPLASH
LIDDY!
AH-CHOO!

I WAS QUITE THE TOMBOY.
AND I LOVED TO BE BABIED.
WHY ARE THERE TINY BIRDS AND BIG BIRDS?

THE TWO OF THEM WERE MY ENTIRE WORLD.
THEY SEEMED TO KNOW EVERY-THING.
BABY BIRDS? WHAT'S A BABY?

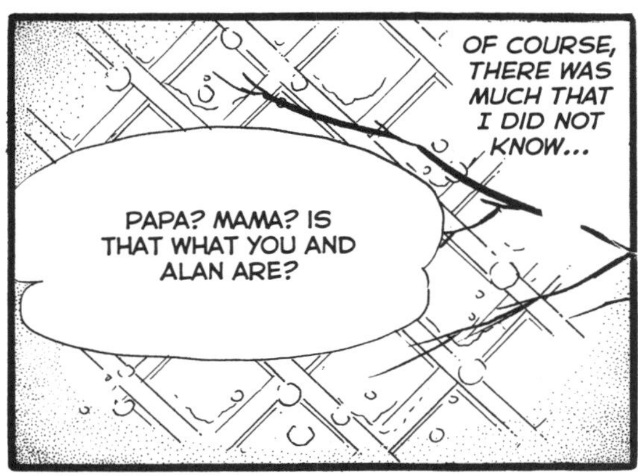

OF COURSE, THERE WAS MUCH THAT I DID NOT KNOW...
PAPA? MAMA? IS THAT WHAT YOU AND ALAN ARE?

AFTER ALL, AT THAT POINT I HAD NEVER EVEN SEEN ANOTHER HUMAN BEING EXCEPT FOR EDGAR AND ALAN.
...AND YET I LEARNED SO VERY MUCH FROM THEM.

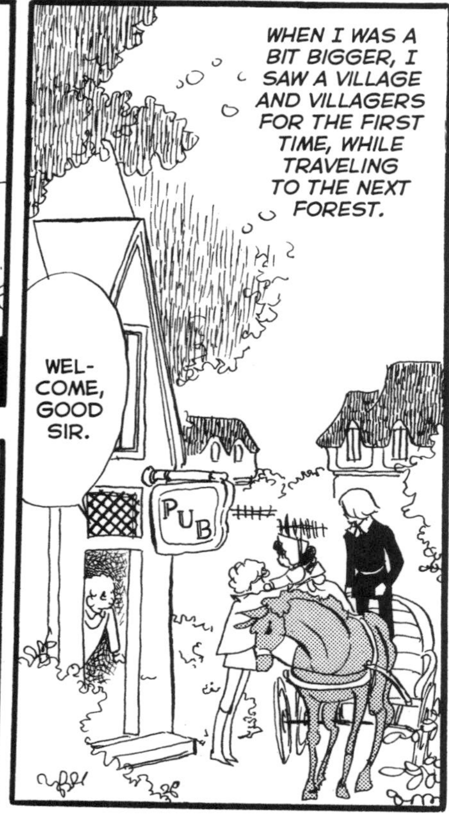
WHEN I WAS A BIT BIGGER, I SAW A VILLAGE AND VILLAGERS FOR THE FIRST TIME, WHILE TRAVELING TO THE NEXT FOREST.
WEL-COME, GOOD SIR.
PUB

LIDDY'S EYES ARE GOING TO POP RIGHT OUT OF HER HEAD.

I WASN'T AFRAID, SINCE EDGAR AND ALAN WERE WITH ME...
...AND YET...

CHILDREN SMALLER THAN ME.

ENORMOUS PEOPLE, LARGER THAN EDGAR AND ALAN.

WHY?
WHY?
WHY?
WHY?

WHY ARE THERE SO MANY PEOPLE? DO THEY LOOK FOR NEW FORESTS IN THE SUMMER, TOO? WHAT ARE THE BIG PEOPLE? WHAT ARE THE LITTLE PEOPLE?
I HATE COLD CHICKEN.
TINK TINK
EAT UP.
EACH YEAR, PEOPLE GET A LITTLE BIT BIGGER.
YOU'RE ABOUT SEVEN THIS YEAR.

AND YOU?
ABOUT FOUR-TEEN.

NO! I MEAN WHY DON'T YOU AND ALAN EAT CHICKEN!?
YOU ALWAYS MAKE ME EAT IT!

IT WAS TRUE.
I NEVER SAW THEM EAT MORE THAN A NIBBLE. THEY DRANK ONLY A FRAGRANT TEA.
WELL, YOU SEE...

I'M GOING TO GROW BIGGER THAN EDGAR?
BUT EDGAR IS TWICE MY SIZE.
BLINK
NOW EAT.
LIDDY WILL GROW BIGGER.
LIDDY WILL GROW BIGGER THAN US.
MUNCH MUNCH
WELL, THEN, I WON'T GROW ANY BIGGER EITHER!
TINK!
WE... WILL NOT GROW ANY BIGGER.
AND YOU?
AND ALAN?
AS RED AS THE MOST SINFUL BLOOD THEY WERE, AND SO BEAUTIFUL.
IN EVERY HOUSE WE MOVED TO, ROSES SPRAWLED IN THE GARDEN AND WINDOW BOXES.
SWAYING IN THE BREEZE AS IF THEY HAD SOMETHING THEY WANTED TO SAY.

THERE WAS HARMONY IN OUR SILVAN WORLD.
THE DAYS PASSED LIKE SONGS.
AND YET AT TIMES...
...I WOULD FEEL ANXIOUS.
BAM!
EDGAR! YOU MUSTN'T PICK ON ALAN!
HE'S CRYING, YOU KNOW!
AT TIMES THEY WOULD FIGHT.
I ALWAYS TOOK ALAN'S SIDE.
WHY ARE YOU FIGHTING?
BECAUSE HE WAS THE WEAKER ONE.
BECAUSE EDGAR HATES ME!
THAT'S NOT TRUE.
IT IS TRUE! AND HE HATES YOU, TOO!
...NO ...
IT'S TRUE. HE'S ALWAYS SAYING HE'S GOING TO CHASE YOU AWAY!
LID-DY!

WHERE COULD SHE BE? I CAN'T FIND HER ANYWHERE. ALAN, DO YOU KNOW WHERE SHE IS?

HM!?

CHASE HER AWAY!? YOU SAID THAT TO LIDDY!?
WELL, IT'S TRUE, ISN'T IT!?

BUT SHE--
BAW-W!

LIDDY! HAVE YOU BEEN IN THERE THIS WHOLE TIME?
WAH
WAH
WAH

YOU WON'T CHASE ME AWAY, WILL YOU?
OF COURSE NOT.
YOU DON'T HATE ME, DO YOU?
NOT EVEN A LITTLE!

AND ALAN?
OF COURSE NOT.
WE'RE ALL GOING TO GROW BIG TOGETHER, AREN'T WE?
THAT'S RIGHT.

BUT IN THE END...
...I HAD TO LEAVE THE FOREST.

I MUST SAY, YOU'RE QUITE THE ECCENTRIC.
WHY DO YOU WANT TO HEAR CHILDHOOD STORIES OF DUBIOUS VERACITY FROM AN OLD WOMAN LIKE ME, LORD ORBIN?

I AM INEXORABLY DRAWN TO TALES OF BOYS NAMED EDGAR, MADAM.
BUT WE CAN TALK ABOUT ME SOME OTHER TIME.
DO PLEASE CONTINUE, MADAM LYDIA THODOSA.

SO YOU EVENTUALLY CAME BACK FROM THE FOREST TO THE TOWN?
YES. TO MY GRANDMOTHER.

EVER SINCE I WENT MISSING AT AGE TWO, MY GRANDMOTHER HAD SEARCHED FOR ME TIRELESSLY.
MY PARENTS WERE MURDERED WHILE TRAVELING BY CARRIAGE, AND PRESUMABLY I WAS KIDNAPPED.

THERE ARE BLANKS IN MY MEMORY.

I DON'T KNOW HOW I FIRST MET EDGAR AND ALAN.

OR IF THEY KNEW ABOUT MY PARENTS' DEATHS.

I DON'T KNOW HOW EDGAR FOUND MY GRANDMOTHER.

ANYWAY, I LIVED WITH THEM.

IT WAS THE SPRING OF MY TENTH YEAR.

I REMEMBER THE LAST DAY.

IT WAS A COLD, EARLY SPRING NIGHT, AND THERE WAS A FIRE IN THE HEARTH.

EDGAR TOLD ME A VERY LONG STORY.

UNFORTUNATELY, HOWEVER, I COMPLETELY FORGOT THE CONTENT OF THE STORY.
IT WAS AN EXCITING STORY OF ADVENTURE, AND IT FEATURED GLISTENING, GOLDEN APPLES.

IT WAS AN OLD TALE FROM NORTHERN EUROPE.
MANY YEARS LATER (WHEN I WAS VERY MUCH AN ADULT), I CAME ACROSS THE SAME STORY IN A BOOK.

I READ IT OVER AND OVER, AND EACH TIME I DID...
IT WAS THE SAME STORY EDGAR HAD TOLD ME THAT NIGHT.

...I RECALLED THE WARMTH AND LIGHT OF THE FIRE, AND THE PALPITATIONS OF MY HEART AS I LISTENED.

CLOP
CLOP
CLOP

TO THE NEXT FOREST? ISN'T IT A BIT EARLY IN THE YEAR?
WHERE ARE WE GOING?
THE NEXT DAY, WE CLIMBED IN OUR CARRIAGE AND SET OUT.

ALTHOUGH I HAD ONCE SEEN A VILLAGE, TO SEE HOUSES AS PLENTIFUL AS TREES, TO SEE WINDOWS PLENTIFUL AS LEAVES, AND IN EACH A FACE, AND ANOTHER FACE, AND ANOTHER...

WHILE I WAS STILL REELING FROM THE SHOCK OF MY FIRST SIGHT OF A CITY...

...OUR CARRIAGE STOPPED IN FRONT A GREAT HOUSE.

KNOCK

KNOCK

I'M YOUR GRANDMOTHER! HOW I'VE SEARCHED FOR YOU, LYDIA! I FELT CERTAIN YOU WERE ALIVE!
EDGAR! ALAN!

LYDIA! LYDIA! I'M YOUR GRAND-MOTHER!
NO! ED-GAR!

BAM BAM BAM BAM
EDGAR!
EDGAR !!

CLOSE THE DOOR! DON'T LET HER OUT!

WHAT'S HAPPENING? WHAT'S HAPPENING? THEY'RE GONE.
WHY? WHY DID THEY CHASE ME AWAY?
LYD-IA...

UNH ...

BUT UNTIL I DID, I USED TO RUN FEVERS, AND HIDE MYSELF AWAY, REFUSING TO SAY A WORD.
BUT THE DOG THEY BOUGHT FOR ME FINALLY BROKE DOWN MY WALL.
BUT I WAS A GROWING GIRL OF TEN.
I BECAME VERY FOND OF THE COUNTRY HOUSE WHERE I WAS TAKEN TO CONVALESCE.
AND I LEARNED TO LOVE THE GRANDMOTHER, WHO NEVER STOPPED SMILING AT ME.
I ADJUSTED, OF COURSE.
AND SO I WAS BROUGHT BACK FROM THE WORLD OF THE FOREST AND AWOKE IN THE WORLD OF MAN.
AND I TOOK MY FIRST STEPS OUT INTO THAT WORLD.
I BEGAN TO LEARN ALL SORTS OF THINGS. ABOUT MANNERS AND PEOPLE AND TOWNS AND GOSSIP AND RELATIONSHIPS AND MURDER...
ABOUT NEWSPAPERS AND FLATTERY AND PARTIES.
I LEARNED THAT CHILDREN WHO WORE NICE CLOTHES HAD IMPORTANT FATHERS.
YOU WANT SOME TEA, GRANDMA?
LYDIA, A LADY ASKS, "WOULD YOU CARE FOR SOME TEA, GRANDMOTH-ER?"
AND THAT PEOPLE WHO WORE DIRTY CLOTHES WEREN'T RICH.
THE OBSCURE WAS STARTING TO BECOME CLEAR.

ALAN AND I...
WON'T YOU GROW BIGGER, EDGAR?
...I HAD A REALIZATION.
AND SUDDENLY...
IT WAS AS IF...
...THEY WERE IMAGES IN A PAINTING.
JUST WHAT WERE THE PARENTS WHO RAISED ME?
EACH SUMMER, IN PURSUIT OF NEW ROSES...
...HEADING TO A NEW FOREST...?
EAT YOUR COLD CHICKEN SO THAT YOU CAN GROW.
AND YOU?
FOURTEEN...
WE... WILL NOT GROW ANY BIGGER.
NOT GROW ANY BIGGER
THEY STAY THE SAME. ONLY I GROW OLDER WITH EACH YEAR.
THAT'S WHY THEY ABANDONED ME.
ONLY I GROW OLDER...

EVERY NIGHT I SLEPT WITH THE WINDOW OPEN.

THE ONLY WAY TO STOP GROW-ING OLDER IS TO DIE.
BUT I WASN'T ABOUT TO DIE.
AND YET...
...I THOUGHT THEY MIGHT COME TO SEE ME SOMETIME.

AND THEN...
...THE DAY CAME WHEN I CLOSED THE WINDOW.

I MARRIED.

I WAS CONTENT.
THE DAYS WERE FULL AND HAPPY.
I LOVED MY HUS-BAND. I CARED FOR MY CHILDREN. I TALKED ABOUT LIFE WITH MY FRIENDS.
I SEEMED FOR ALL THE WORLD LIKE A LADY WHO HAD BEEN RAISED BY GOOD PARENTS IN A GOOD HOME IN THE CITY SINCE THE DAY I WAS BORN.
THEN EVEN MORE YEARS PASSED.
...DE-SPITE IT ALL...
...I WOULD BE OVERCOME WITH GRIEF.
CRACK
POP
POP
BUT ONCE IN A WHILE...
GRIEF FOR THE ME THAT ONCE WAS.

END OF CHAPTER 3

FIRST PUBLISHED IN **SPECIAL EDITION SHŌJO COMIC**, JUNE 1975

JULY 1966
I ONLY RECENTLY ACQUIRED THIS OLD HOUSE.
I'M AFRAID IT ISN'T EVEN WIRED FOR ELECTRICITY YET.
THANK YOU ALL FOR COMING.
ALLOW ME TO DRAW YOUR ATTENTION TO THIS PAINTING.

BUT THIS IS A COPY.
SEE? THE FACE IS DIFFERENT.
IN-DEED.
OH! *THE RED BOY!* MASTER LAMBTON!
A SEVENTEENTH-CENTURY PORTRAITIST, THOMAS LAWRENCE REMAINS BELOVED THROUGHOUT THE WORLD FOR PAINTINGS OF SMILING LADIES AND DARLING BOYS.
THIS WAS PAINTED BY THE FORMER MASTER OF THIS MANOR, SIR ARTHUR QUENTIN.
HA! LET ME GUESS.
THIS QUENTIN FELLOW COPIED LAWRENCE'S PAINTING...
...THEN SUBSTI-TUTED HIS OWN SON'S FACE.
HE DIDN'T HAVE A SON.
WELL, THEN, A NEPHEW OR GRANDSON.

SIR ARTHUR QUENTIN PREFERRED LANDSCAPES AND STILL LIFES.
THIS: THE ONLY HUMAN HE EVER PAINTED, APART FROM HIMSELF.
THE DATE ON THE PAINTING IS THE THIRTIETH OF SEPTEMBER, 1888.
NOW LOOK AT THIS. SIR ARTHUR'S LAMBTON AGAIN, BUT IN A DIFFERENT POSE.
FIFTEENTH OF OCTOBER, 1888.
AND A THIRD LAMBTON. SAME YEAR, FIFTH OF NOVEMBER.
LOOK AT THIS CHAIR.
THE FOURTH.
LAMBTON SITTING ON THE ARM OF THE CHAIR.
THERE ARE ELEVEN PORTRAITS OF THIS BOY ALL TOGETHER.
LET'S LOOK AT THEM ALL, SHALL WE?
CHARLOTTE, IT IS THE VERY CHAIR YOU SIT ON NOW.
OH!

CHAPTER 4

THE TALE THAT LAMBTON TELLS

THE FIFTH. LAMBTON STANDING NEXT TO THE CHAIR.
OF COURSE, HIS NAME REALLY COULDN'T HAVE BEEN LAMBTON.
BUT SIR ARTHUR SEEMED TO THINK OF THIS BOY AS HIS OWN LAMBTON.
HE MAY HAVE EVEN CALLED HIM THAT.
YOU KNOW, ROGER, THAT BOY LOOKS A BIT LIKE *YOU*, DON'T YOU THINK?
CUT IT OUT!

THE PORTRAITS OF THE BOY ARE PAINTED AT A PACE OF ROUGHLY TWENTY DAYS PER PAINTING.
THE SIXTH. LAMBTON STANDING BY THE WALL.
THE SEVENTH. LAMBTON BY THE FIRE.
THE EIGHTH. LAMBTON STANDING AT THE FOOT OF THE STAIRS.
THE NINTH. LAMBTON BY THE WINDOW.
NOTICE WITH EACH PAINTING...
...THE BOY IS GRADUALLY MOVED FROM INDOORS TO OUTDOORS.
MY! SPRING!
THE TENTH. LAMBTON IN THE GARDEN.

THIS IS THE FIN WORK DATED T TWENTIE OF MA 1889

SIR ARTHUR NEVER PAINTED AGAIN...

...AND THREE MONTHS LATER, IN LATE AUGUST, HE PASSED, AGED THIRTY-THREE.

APPARENTLY, HE WAS ILL IN HIS LAST YEARS.

HE SPIT UP A GREAT DEAL OF BLOOD.

IT BEARS THE TITLE *ROOM WITHOUT LAMBTON.*

HE PAINTED HIS SELF-PORTRAIT WITH RIGHT PROFILE FACING THE MIRROR.

SI ARTH THOM QUEN

--LOST HIS LEFT EAR IN A CHILDHOOD ACCIDENT AND HAD A SCAR ALONG HIS JAW.

HE WORE HIS HAIR LONG TO HIDE IT.

HE WAS STUBBORN AND SULLEN, CURT TO HIS ART DEALERS, WAS NEVER VISITED BY FAMILY OR NEIGHBOR, AND NEVER MARRIED.

HE LIVED ALONE IN THIS HOUSE

WITH ONLY AN OLD MANSERVANT TO SEE TO HIS NEEDS.

MR. ORBIN.
AS TO THE IDENTITY OF THIS BOY...
...THERE IS NO RECORD.
DID YOU INVITE US HERE JUST TO PRESENT US WITH A RIDDLE?
WHO CARES WHO THE BOY WAS?
SO AN OBSTINATE MAN...
...TOOK A SHINE TO SOME KID AND PAINTED A BUNCH OF PORTRAITS OF HIM.
WHAT OF IT?
AH, BUT THERE IS MORE TO TELL ABOUT THIS BOY.
MORE?
MR. DONALD MARSHALL. IF YOU WOULD BE SO KIND.
I'M THE ONE WHO FOUND THE PAINTING OF LAMBTON.
IT ALL BEGAN...
...WITH A SERIES OF COINCI-DENCES.

AH

PLIP

I WAS A UNIVERSITY STUDENT ENJOYING SOME SUMMER TRAVEL.
IT WAS FIFTEEN YEARS AGO.
I WAS WALKING ALONG THE RIVER SOAR, IN THE DIRECTION OF LEICESTER.

IT STARTED TO POUR, AND I DASHED FOR A NEARBY MANOR.
OOP!

THE QUENTIN MANOR.
WHAT THE--!?

TERRIBLY SORRY! THE DOOR WAS OPEN, SO I...
THE RAIN, YOU SEE...

I SEE! NO HARM DONE.
I'M THE REALTOR.

LISTEN TO THAT THUNDER!
I WAS JUST HERE LOOKING THE PLACE OVER.
THE HOUSE IS FOR SALE, YOU KNOW.
I SEE.
PRETTY OLD, AS YOU CAN TELL!

IF YOU SAY SO. AN ART STUDENT, ARE YOU?
NO, IT'S A COPY. FACE IS WRONG. YOU KNOW. THOMAS LAWRENCE?

CARE TO BUY IT? IT'S QUITE A BAR-GAIN!
I'M JUST A POOR STUDENT, I'M AFRAID.

NO ONE'S TAKING THE HOUSE.
IF YOU LIKE IT, YOU MAY AS WELL TAKE IT.

FLASH
WELL, IT HAD BETTER SELL SOON. THE TAXES JUST GO UP AND UP!

MAS-TER LAMB-TON !?

CAUGHT THE TRAIN TO BIRMINGHAM JUST IN TIME.
HE GAVE ME A RIDE TO LEICESTER.

THE LAMBTON WITH A DIFFERENT FACE TOOK MY FANCY.
SO I TOOK IT AS A MEMENTO OF THIS TRIP.

IF I MAKE MY CONNECTION, I'LL BE BACK IN MY FLAT IN LONDON BY TONIGHT.
RIGHT.
KLAK

SOON ENOUGH, THE RAIN LET UP.

I HADN'T YET LOOKED AT THE PAINTING CAREFULLY. I TOOK A SEAT AND MINDED MY OWN BUSINESS.
NOW THAT'S A LOT OF ROSES! HEADED TO A PARTY, I FANCY.

T-TMP
T-TMP
T-TMP
THE ANNIVERSARY OF THE DEATH OF SIR ARTHUR QUENTIN.
MUCH LATER, I REALIZED THIS HAD BEEN THE TWENTY-FIRST OF AUGUST.
T-TMP
T-TMP

T-TMP
T-TMP
T-TMP
T-TMP

WHACK!

OUR STOP.
RIGHT.

D-DMP!

ED-
GAR!
EDGAR
EDGAR
IT'S ALL RIGHT. I'M FINE.

H-- HOLD UP!
WE'D BEST HURRY.
HOLD UP!
HOLD UP!

TMP
YOU THERE!

W--WAIT, I THOUGHT *YOU* WERE THE ONE WHO WAS HURT!?
HE FAINTED WHEN HE SAW THE BLOOD. HE'LL BE FINE.

I'M SO SORRY. YOU NEED TO SEE A DOCTOR!
YEAH. I'M ALL RIGHT.
ALAN, CAN YOU STAND?

HEY!
THIS IS MY RESPON-SIBILITY! I-- HEY!
FINE!? THAT WAS A LOT OF BLOOD!
OH!
HEY!
YOU TWO!
WE'VE GOT TO GET YOU TO A HOSPITAL!
I'M FINE.
HOLD UP!
TMP
KREE
MANOR PARK
NOR PA
ENTRANCE

WHA ...?
THE BLEEDING'S ALREADY STOPPED.
IT'S NOT SUCH A BAD CUT. SEE?
THANKS FOR WALKING US HOME. THAT'S OUR HOUSE OVER THERE.
OF ALL THE... YOU CAME TO A *PARK* IN YOUR CONDITION!?
AT LEAST ALLOW ME TO APOLOGIZE TO YOUR PARENTS.
NO PARENTS.
JUST THE TWO OF US.
GOOD DAY.
PERHAPS HE MEANT HIS PARENTS ARE OUT?
THEY DON'T LOOK LIKE RUNAWAYS.
???
ANYWAY, I SUPPOSE HE WASN'T TOO BADLY HURT...? HM...
MANOR PARK

SO I HEADED BACK TO THE BOYS' HOUSE...
...TO ASK IF THEY'D PUT ME UP FOR THE NIGHT.
WAS IT THIS WAY?
OR THAT WAY?
OF ALL THE... IS THERE A HOTEL?
IN THIS VILLIDGE? 'ARDLY ... 'APPEN YOU COULD BE UZEN A BENCH THORGH!
WELL I'LL BE...
STATION
THAT WERE LASST TRAIRN JOOST LEFT.
WHA--!?
PWEET
THE RED ROSES WERE BURNING IN THE FIREPLACE.
MANOR PARK
HERE WE ARE!
KNOCK KNOCK
HELLO! ANYONE HOME?
EDGAR, WAS IT? HELLO!
EDGAR! ARE YOU IN THERE?
KREE
SOME-ONE'S HERE.

AH HA HA
HA HA HA
WHERE ARE THEY?
YELLOW ROSES... MOONLIGHT...

BAM!

UM.
SO SORRY.

LOOKS LIKE SOMEONE MISSED HIS TRAIN.
SOMEONE DID, YES. I KNOW THIS TERRIBLY FORWARD OF ME, BUT...
...THINK YOU COULD HELP A CHAP OUT?
OH, LET ME SHOW YOU MY UNI ID.

PAT
PAT
PAT
STOP IT, ALAN.

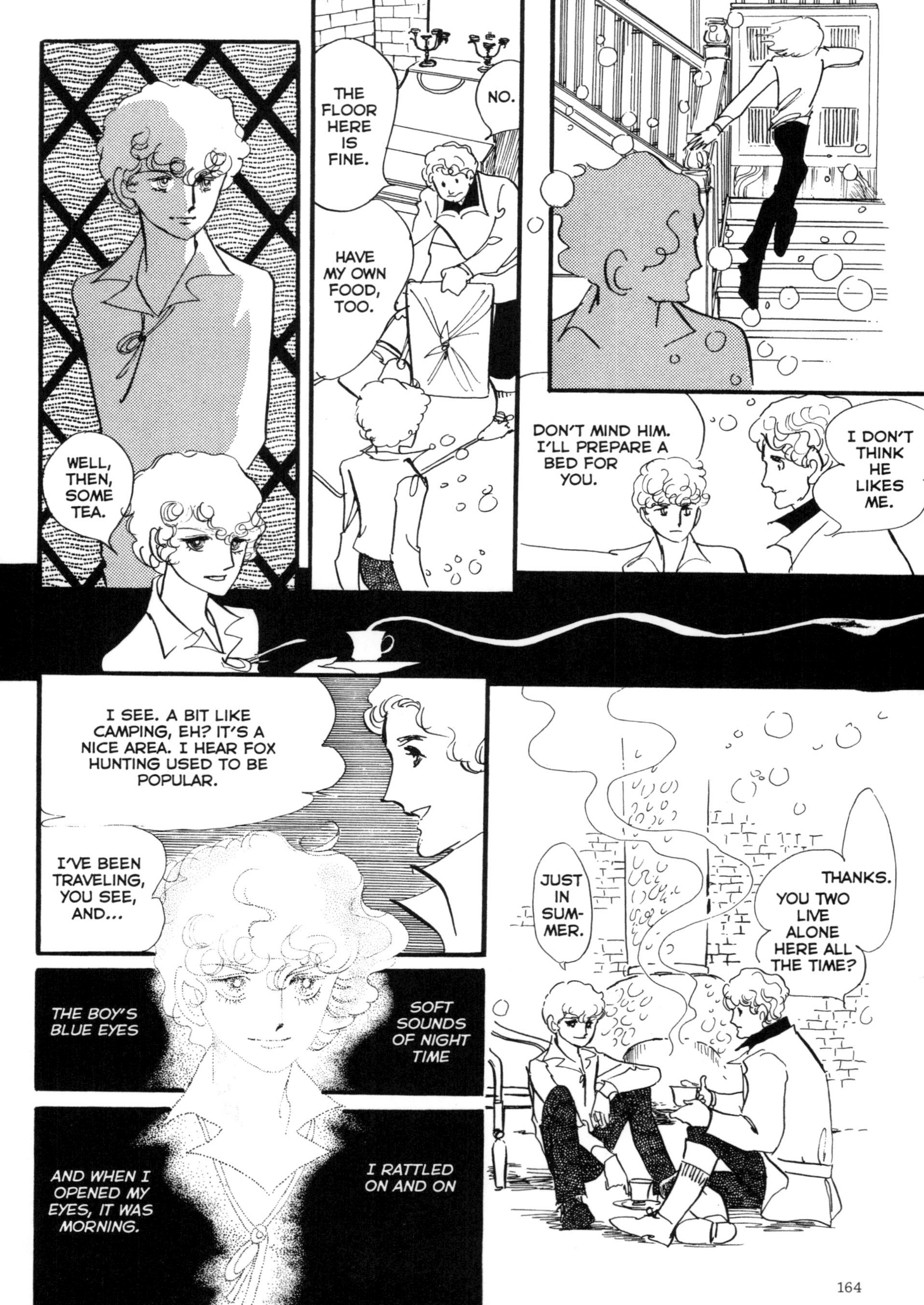
WELL, THEN, SOME TEA.
THE FLOOR HERE IS FINE.
NO.
HAVE MY OWN FOOD, TOO.
DON'T MIND HIM. I'LL PREPARE A BED FOR YOU.
I DON'T THINK HE LIKES ME.
I SEE. A BIT LIKE CAMPING, EH? IT'S A NICE AREA. I HEAR FOX HUNTING USED TO BE POPULAR.
I'VE BEEN TRAVELING, YOU SEE, AND...
THANKS.
YOU TWO LIVE ALONE HERE ALL THE TIME?
JUST IN SUM-MER.
SOFT SOUNDS OF NIGHT TIME
THE BOY'S BLUE EYES
I RATTLED ON AND ON
AND WHEN I OPENED MY EYES, IT WAS MORNING.

OH! IS THAT SO? THANKS FOR PUTTING ME UP.
YOUR TRAIN LEAVES AT NINE, YOU KNOW. NOT MUCH TIME.
THE ROSES HAD ALL BEEN BURNED.
WHY DON'T YOU JUST KILL HIM!?
AH. OUR GUEST IS AWAKE.
....
THERE'S SOMETHING OFF ABOUT THOSE TWO, BUT THEY DID GIVE ME A PLACE TO SLEEP, SO WHO AM I TO COMPLAIN?
LOOKS ALL RIGHT.
BLOOD! HOPE IT DIDN'T GET ON THE PAINTING.
DON'T WANT THIS FALLING AGAIN, SO I'LL HOLD ON TO IT.
JUST IN TIME.

YES.
THE FACE IS DIFFERENT, THOUGH.
THE RED BOY, EH?
SAY, NOW. THIS LAD LOOKS LIKE EDGAR. HE HAS THE SAME--
NO. IT'S IDENTICAL TO HIM.
IT IS HIM.
AND THE FAUN PLAYED HIS FLUTE BY THE LIGHT OF THE MOON
TMP!

*LISTED BUILDING: A BUILDING REGISTERED BY AND UNDER THE PROTECTION OF THE HISTORIC BUILDINGS AND MONUMENTS COMMISSION FOR ENGLAND.

THREE YEARS LATER, IN NINETEEN-FIFTY-THREE, I WROTE A SHORT STORY ABOUT THE LISTED BUILDING AND MY LAMBTON
AND PUBLISHED IT IN OUR UNIVERSITY'S LITERARY COTERIE JOURNAL.
I TITLE IT "LAMBTON."
THE CARETAKER UNLOCKED THE DOOR, AND INSIDE WE FOUND THE ASHES OF THE ROSES IN THE FIREPLACE.
THE CARETAKER WAS FURIOUS THAT SOME KIDS HAD USED IT AS THEIR PERSONAL COTTAGE.
THEY WERE GONE.
HAD THEY REALLY JUST BEEN A PAIR OF MISCHIEVOUS KIDS?
IT COULDN'T BE. THEY WERE TOO...
TOO...
IN THE MOONLIGHT, THEY HAD SEEMED TOO... TRANSLUCENT.

THEN, A FEW YEARS LATER...
...I RECEIVED A LETTER AND A BOOK OUT OF THE BLUE.
IT WAS JANUARY 1964. I HAD GRADUATED UNIVERSITY AND WAS WORKING AT A PUBLISHING HOUSE. THIRTY-FIVE AND SINGLE.
THE LETTER WAS FROM A READER OF A MAGAZINE WE PUBLISHED.
SHE SAID SHE HAD READ MY "LAMBTON" YEARS AGO...
...AND HAD RECENTLY READ A BOOK TRANSLATED FROM GERMAN THAT SEEMED QUITE SIMILAR TO MY STORY. THE BOOK WAS ENCLOSED.
THE BOOK WAS TITLED "GLENSMITH'S DIARY."
Glensmith's Diary
and Other Short Stories
Margaret Hesson
THE AUTHOR WAS A WEST GERMAN WOMAN NAMED MARGARET HESSEN.
GLENSMITH BECAME LOST IN THE FOG AND WAS LED TO THE VILLAGE OF POE, WHERE FIELDS OF ROSES BLOOM.
IT WAS THE SECRET HOME OF A CLAN OF IMMORTAL VAMPIRNELLA. (VAMPIRNELLA!)
THERE HE MET THE BOY EDGAR AND HIS SISTER MARYBELLE. AFTER TWO NIGHTS THERE, HE RETURNED HOME, BUT, TRY AS HE MAY, HE WAS NEVER ABLE TO FIND THE ENTRANCE TO THE VILLAGE AGAIN.
WELL, I'LL BE DAMNED.
EDGAR? A FOURTEEN-YEAR-OLD BOY WITH BLUE EYES AND CURLY HAIR...
THAT DESCRIBES MY LAMBTON TO A TEE!

SHE'S LOVELY! BUT IS IT FRÄULEIN OR FRAU?

I AM MARGARET HESSEN.

MR. DON MAR-SHALL?

I IMMEDIATELY BOOKED A FLIGHT FROM LONDON TO FRANKFURT.

NO RING! SO FRÄULEIN IT IS!

YOU CAN IMAGINE MY SHOCK WHEN I READ YOUR LETTER.

WAIT, THIS ISN'T WHY I CAME ALL THIS WAY.

HERE WE HAVE YOUR BOOK OF ELEVEN YEARS AGO, ***LAMBTON***.

AND HERE WE HAVE ***GLENSMITH'S DIARY***, MY GREAT GRANDFATHER'S TAKE WRITTEN A CENTURY AGO.

BY MARGARET HESSEN

GLENSMITH'S DIARY

COTERIE

THE COMMON THREAD THEY SHARE IS...

EDGAR
HOW COULD THESE BOYS HAVE SO MUCH IN COMMON?

SURELY YOU HAVE A DREAM?
AND THAT IS WHY I WRITE. WHEN I WRITE, I CAN BECOME A CHILD AGAIN, AND MAKE USE OF MIRACLES AND MAGIC.
YOU'RE QUITE THE ROMANTIC, MISS HESSEN.
BECAUSE THEY ARE ONE IN THE SAME, MR. MARSHALL. AFTER ALL, VAMPIRNELLA LIVE A VERY LONG TIME.
...A DREAM...?
BUT THE PRICE ONE PAYS TO BECOME AN ADULT...
...IS THE MAGIC AND DREAMS OF CHILD-HOOD.
WHEN I WAS LITTLE GIRL, I BELIEVED EVERY WORD OF IT.
MY GRANDMOTHER WOULD TAKE THIS OLD DIARY AND TELL ME GLENSMITH'S STRANGE TALE OF THE VILLAGE POE.
DAS IST ABER EIN SELTSAMER LAMBTON. DER IST EDGAR PORTNELL WIE AUS DEM GESICHT GESCHNITTEN.
NICE TO MEET YOU.
HALLO, LUIS. MY NEPHEW. HE'S JUST STARTED UNIVERSITY.
TANTE MARGA-RET!
BAM
KLASH
DON MARSHALL. CHARMED.

WHEN I WAS A FOURTH-YEAR STUDENT HERE AT GABRIEL SWISS GYMNASIUM...
...THEY TRANSFERRED HERE FROM ENGLAND.
ALAN TWILIGHT...
AND EDGAR PORTNELL.
EDGAR PORTNELL AND ALAN TWILIGHT.
SURE ENOUGH, THERE THEY WERE IN THE SCHOOL RECORDS.
BUT THEY WERE ONLY HERE FOR TWO MONTHS.
THEN THEY MOVED ON.
IT WAS UNNERV-ING.
IN HOW MANY LANDS, SPANNING HOW MANY AGES, ARE RECORDS TO BE FOUND THAT JUST HAPPEN TO CONTAIN THE NAME "EDGAR PORTNELL?"
LUIS TOLD ME AS MUCH ABOUT EDGAR AND ALAN AS HE COULD RECALL.
LAMBTON. THE HUNTING LODGE.
GLENSMITH'S DIARY. AND NOW GABRIEL SWISS GYMNASIUM.

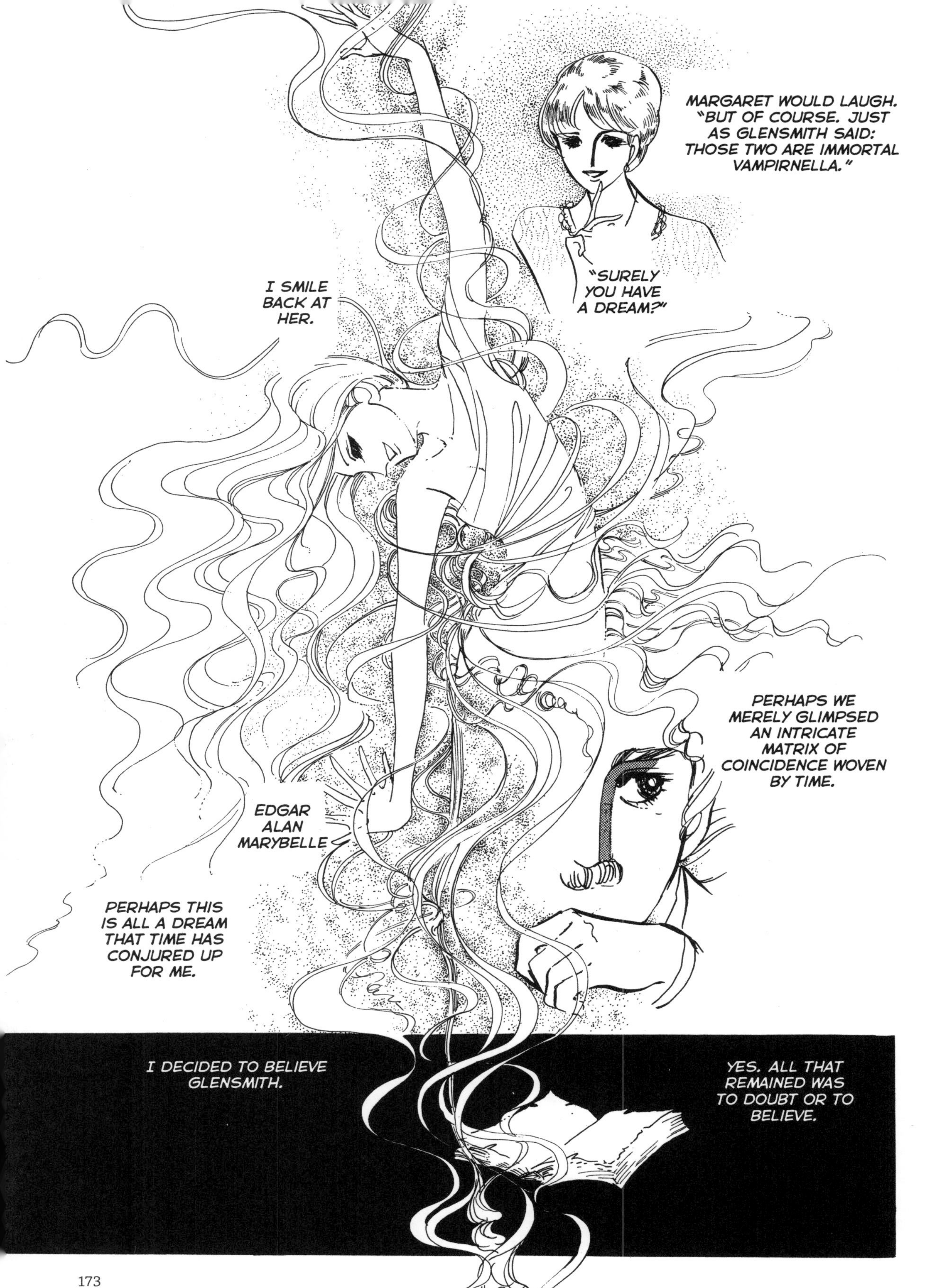
MARGARET WOULD LAUGH. "BUT OF COURSE. JUST AS GLENSMITH SAID: THOSE TWO ARE IMMORTAL VAMPIRNELLA."
"SURELY YOU HAVE A DREAM?"
I SMILE BACK AT HER.
PERHAPS WE MERELY GLIMPSED AN INTRICATE MATRIX OF COINCIDENCE WOVEN BY TIME.
EDGAR ALAN MARYBELLE
PERHAPS THIS IS ALL A DREAM THAT TIME HAS CONJURED UP FOR ME.
YES. ALL THAT REMAINED WAS TO DOUBT OR TO BELIEVE.
I DECIDED TO BELIEVE GLENSMITH.

THE FOLLOWING SUMMER, IN NINETEEN-SIXTY-FIVE, WE PUBLISHED A LITTLE BOOK TITLED THE VAMPIRNELLA HUNT.
THE VAMPIRNELLA HUNT
MARGARET CAME BACK TO ENGLAND WITH ME AND WE WERE MARRIED.
AND THAT IS OUR PART OF THE STORY.
WHAT A FAB STORY! SPANNING TWO COUNTRIES!
HA HA. VAMPIRNELLA INDEED.
THAT BOY PLAYED CUPID FOR THE TWO OF YOU.
"THE VAMPIRNELLA HUNT."
I CAME ACROSS IT AT A BOOKSTORE LAST YEAR AND IMMEDIATELY WENT TO SEE MR. MARSHALL.
THEN I CAME HER TO THE QUENTIN MANOR AND PURCHASED IT.
THEN I TRACKED DOWN THESE TEN PAINTINGS.
I ALSO INVESTIGATED SIR ARTHUR QUENTIN.
AND SO NOW YOU'VE GATHERED HERE TO PLOT OUT YOUR NEXT BOOK?

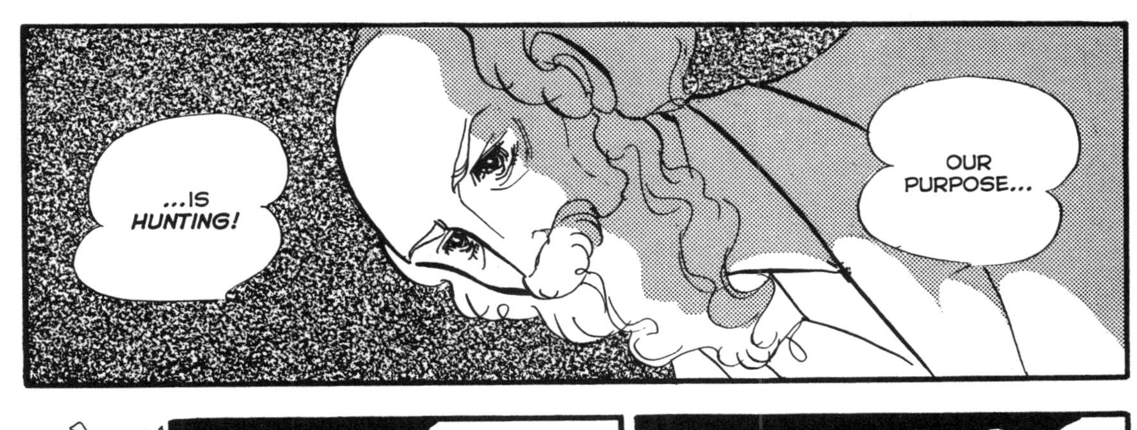

HUNT-ING?
A BOY WHO DOESN'T EXIST?
AH, BUT HE DOES. I MET HIM MYSELF, LONG AGO.
AND NOT JUST ME.
SHE KNEW HIM, TOO.
HER NAME WAS LYDIA. SHE HAS LONG SINCE PASSED.
SHE DISAPPEARED WHEN SHE WAS JUST A TODDLER. SHE CLAIMED THAT, FOR EIGHT YEARS, SHE LIVED WITH EDGAR AND ALAN.
SHE WAS RAISED BY THE TWO BOYS IN THE FOREST.
OH, YES. THEY EXIST. BEYOND TIME!
AND I HAVE BEEN CHASING THEM FOR THIRTY YEARS.
IF WE CAN FILL IN THE BLANKS, SET A TRAP, THEN LURE THEM INTO IT...
...THEY WILL SURELY REVEAL THEM-SELVES!
...!

YOU SEE...
...ARE CRUCIAL PIECES ON THIS CHESS BOARD.
AH, BUT YOU TWO...
I ACCEPTED YOUR INVITATION OUT OF CURIOSITY, BUT I CAN'T--
UNFORTUNATELY, I AM NO VAMPIRNELLA ENTHUSIAST.
ROGER!
WITH ALL DUE RESPECT, THIS IS TWADDLE!
THE EVANS FAMILY TREE
OSWALD MADONNA
(MARRIED 1757)
CLIFFORD
WIFE
(1778)
(BORN 1784) (BORN 1790)
HENRY
ELLEN
(1820)
(TWINS)
ROGER
WIFE
(1823)
MARY
ANNE
HENRY
ROGER
(COUSINS)
(DIED AT BIRTH)
MARRIED IN 1839 (WHEN BOTH WERE 16)
(BORN 1846)
ROGER
WIFE
(1876)
OSCAR
WIFE
(1897)
(BORN 1910)
BEN
WIFE
(1924)
OSCAR
WIFE
(BORN 1945)
(DIED AT BIRTH)
JAMES
WIFE
(1943)
HENRY
ROGER
CHARLOTTE
EDITH
...YOU TWO ARE DESCENDANTS OF OSWALD, EARL EVANS!
WHAT!?
OSWALD EVANS!?

THE BUILDING WAS A MANOR, GIFTED TO THE CITY BY CLIFFORD, EARL EVANS, IN SEVENTEEN-EIGHTY-THREE. I SUPPOSE THEY HAD FALLEN ON HARD TIMES.
YES, MR. EVANS.
ONE WINTER, TWENTY-ONE YEARS AGO, THERE WAS A FIRE AT THE EVANS LIBRARY IN LONDON, AND WHAT REMAINED OF THE BUILDING WAS TO BE TORN DOWN.
I STOPPED BY TO TAKE A LOOK.
ANYWAY, THERE, AMONG THE OLD BOOKS AND RECORDS, I FOUND THIS WILL AND THESE NOTES LEFT BY A CERTAIN DOCTOR DODD.
THEY SAY HE WAS A HANDSOME MAN.
WELL, THIS WILL WAS PASSED DOWN...
...AND WHEN HENRY'S TIME CAME--
YOU SAY THIS DOTTY WILL WAS WRITTEN BY...
...MY ANCESTOR!?
SHOULD PERSONS NAMED EDGAR AND MARYBELLE APPEAR BEFORE THE DESCENDANTS OF THE EVANS ESTATE...
...SAID DESCENDANTS ARE TO DONATE THE ENTIRE EVANS FORTUNE TO THEM, REGARDLESS OF THEIR STATION, NATIONALITY, OR AGE.
1780. OSWALD O., EARL EVANS.
YES, IT'S COMMON IN THE EVANS LINE FOR A FIRST SON TO BE NAMED HENRY WHILE THE SECOND IS NAMED ROGER.
HEN-RY!?

WHEN HENRY WAS EARL, EDGAR MADE AN APPEARANCE.
JANUARY, EIGH-TEEN-TWENTY.
THE EVENTS WERE RECORDED BY THIS DOCTOR DODD, WHO WAS STAYING AT THE MANOR.
A BLUE-EYED BOY HENRY HAPPENED TO FISH OUT OF THE RIVER SAID HIS NAME WAS EDGAR.
AND SO, REMEMBERING THE WILL, HENRY CARED FOR THE BOY.
LATER, A GIRL NAMED MARYBELLE APPEARED, AND THEY VANISHED TOGETHER.
BUT DODD RECORDS THAT DURING HIS STAY, EDGAR SUCKED THE BLOOD OF A BOY NAMED ERNEST.
SUCKED HIS BLOOD!?
IT'S JUST AN OLD FABLE, CHAR-LOTTE!
DODD WROTE THAT HE BELIEVED THE TWO TO BE VAMPIRNELLA.
THE DOCTOR LOOKED INTO EVANS' WILL
AND THE EVANS' FAMILY LINE.

THEIR NAMES WERE EDGAR AND MARYBELLE.
THEY WERE SAID TO HAVE DIED IN INFANCY.
OSWALD, WHO WROTE THE WILL, HAD HALF-SIBLINGS BY ANOTHER MOTHER.
VAMPIR-NELLA INDEED!
BUT IT'S JUST AN OLD FABLE!
HE HAD ANOTHER BROTHER, NAMED EUSTACE...
...BUT HE, TOO, DIED YOUNG.
LATER, THE FAMILY ADOPTED A GIRL OF THIRTEEN, NAMED MARYBELLE.
BUT SHE, TOO, SOON DIED.
GRA-CIOUS...
HOW-EVER...
PRECISELY. IT MADE NO SENSE.
SEE? IT'S JUST A FAIRY TALE. NOTHING MAKES SENSE.
HENRY, EARL EVANS, ACTUALLY MET EDGAR.
IN HIS WILL, OSWALD HAD PROPHESIED, THREE HUNDRED YEARS AGO...
THAT ONE DAY HIS DESCENDANTS WOULD MEET THIS "EDGAR" AND "MARYBELLE"...
...WHO WOULD...
...CROSS...
...THE SEA OF TIME...

...THE SEA OF TIME...
YES. AS YOU HEARD, EDGAR AND ALAN TRANSFERRED TO MY SCHOOL.
LUIS? THE ONE MR. MARSHALL SAID WENT TO SCHOOL WITH EDGAR?
AND NOW, IT IS TIME FOR *YOUR* TALE, LUIS BARD.
WELL
MR. MARSHALL AND HIS FRIENDS WERE QUITE FIXATED ON EDGAR.
I THOUGHT MAYBE ONE OF THEM COULD TELL ME MORE ABOUT EDGAR AND ALAN.
THIS SPRING, WHILE TRAVELING WEST GERMANY ON BICYCLE...
...I DECIDED TO VISIT SOME OLD FRIENDS.
BZZZZ

MY FIRST VISIT WAS TO THE HOME OF KILLIAN BRUNSCHWIG, BUT HE WAS NOT THERE.
I...
...DON'T KNOW...
...WHEN HE'LL COME HOME.
HIS ROOM WAS IN PERFECT ORDER.
HIS FOSTER FATHER SAID...
...THEY KEPT THE ROOM READY FOR HIS RETURN.
THIS IS A BOOK ON GERMAN HISTORY THAT KILLIAN WAS FOND OF.
THE DAY HE LEFT, IT WAS SITTING ON HIS BED. IF YOU'RE A FRIEND OF KILLIAN'S, PLEASE TAKE IT HOME WITH YOU.
HE...
HE MAY NEVER RETURN.
* Leb wohl, bis wir uns wiedersehen
*GOODBYE, UNTIL WE MEET AGAIN.
RETURN?
FROM WHERE?
EAST GERMANY?
WE ALL KNEW THAT KILLIAN HAD COME FROM EAST GERMANY WHEN HE WAS LITTLE.
AND THAT HIS FATHER WAS STILL SOMEWHERE IN EAST GERMANY.
I HAD BEEN CLOSE TO KILLIAN.
I THOUGHT OF OUR OLD CLASS PRESIDENT, THEO.

HE HAD GONE OFF TO BONN FOR UNIVERSITY.
OVER THERE
THEODOR
KNOCK KNOCK KNOCK
I'M NOT HERE!!
THEO
IT'S ME. LUIS BARD.
TMP!
WELL!
I HAVEN'T SEEN YOU SINCE GRADUATION!
I SEE YOU HAVEN'T CHANGED.
SIT DOWN! I'LL MAKE TEA!
CLATTER
YIKES!

UM... ARE YOU STUDYING HEMATOLOGY OR SOMETHING?
YOU MEAN THIS? HA HA. CARE TO CONTRIBUTE?
I'M COLLECTING FROM EVERYONE ON CAMPUS. AS YOU CAN IMAGINE, I'M NOT VERY POPULAR.

LIKE SOME KIND OF VAMPIRNELLA!
YOU ALWAYS WERE INTERESTED IN BLACK MAGIC.
THIS BOOK!
OH, THAT.
IT'S KILLIAN'S. HIS UNCLE GAVE IT TO ME.

Leb wohl, bis wir uns wiedersehen
THEO!
GIVE IT TO ME.
HUH?
COME ON! ALL HE LEFT ME WAS BLOOD! I DON'T HAVE ANYTHING ELSE TO REMEMBER HIM BY!
YOU MEAN KILLIAN CAME HERE?
HE DID.
TO GIVE ME A GENEROUS DONATION OF BLOOD. IN PARTING.
IT'S HIS FAULT I STARTED STUDYING BLOOD.
THIS IS WHERE BLACK MAGIC LED ME.
I... I HAVE TO FIND IT.
THAT WHOLE EPISODE...
...SEEMS LIKE A NIGHTMARE.
BUT, DAMMIT, THEY WERE REAL! THOSE TWO TRANSFER STUDENTS!
YOU MEAN EDGAR AND ALAN!?

AND THAT'S WHEN HE TOLD ME.

ABOUT EDGAR AND ALAN.

I DIDN'T COME HERE TO TRADE GHOST STORIES!
THEODOR BRONIS?
WELL, THEN, ENLIGHTEN US, THEO.
BUT LEGENDS ARE JUST LEGENDS! THEY AREN'T REAL!
YOU'VE BEEN GOING ON ABOUT VAMPIRNELLA OR DRACULA OR WHATEVER!
YOU WANT THE BOOK, DON'T YOU?
THOSE TWO... EDGAR AND ALAN... TRANSFERRED TO OUR SCHOOL AT THE END OF MARCH.

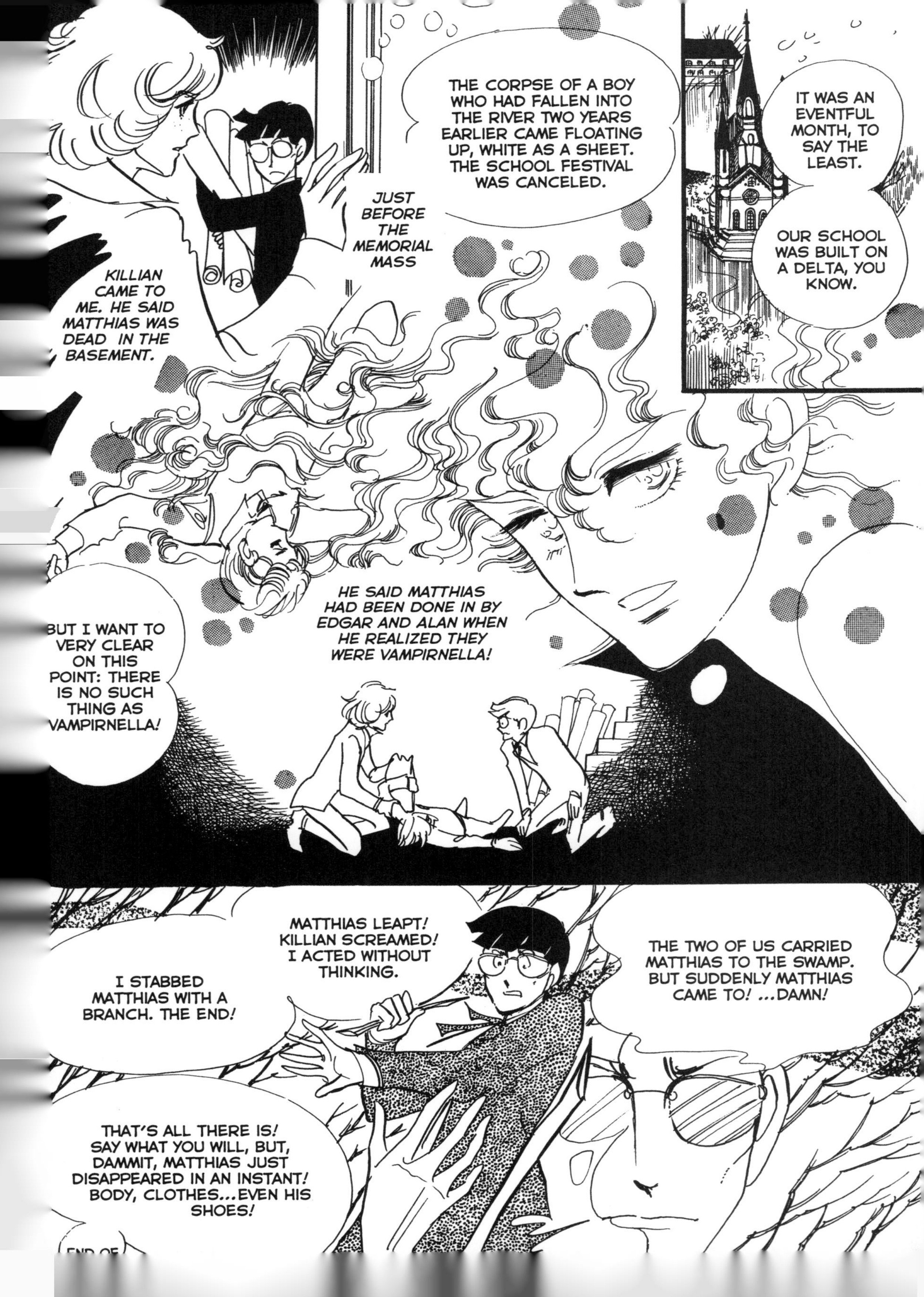
IT WAS AN EVENTFUL MONTH, TO SAY THE LEAST.
OUR SCHOOL WAS BUILT ON A DELTA, YOU KNOW.
THE CORPSE OF A BOY WHO HAD FALLEN INTO THE RIVER TWO YEARS EARLIER CAME FLOATING UP, WHITE AS A SHEET. THE SCHOOL FESTIVAL WAS CANCELED.
JUST BEFORE THE MEMORIAL MASS
KILLIAN CAME TO ME. HE SAID MATTHIAS WAS DEAD IN THE BASEMENT.
HE SAID MATTHIAS HAD BEEN DONE IN BY EDGAR AND ALAN WHEN HE REALIZED THEY WERE VAMPIRNELLA!
BUT I WANT TO VERY CLEAR ON THIS POINT: THERE IS NO SUCH THING AS VAMPIRNELLA!
THE TWO OF US CARRIED MATTHIAS TO THE SWAMP. BUT SUDDENLY MATTHIAS CAME TO! ...DAMN!
MATTHIAS LEAPT! KILLIAN SCREAMED! I ACTED WITHOUT THINKING.
I STABBED MATTHIAS WITH A BRANCH. THE END!
THAT'S ALL THERE IS! SAY WHAT YOU WILL, BUT, DAMMIT, MATTHIAS JUST DISAPPEARED IN AN INSTANT! BODY, CLOTHES...EVEN HIS SHOES!

HA HA
SHOES, TOO?
KILLIAN HAD BEEN BITTEN. HIS NECK WAS BLEEDING A BIT.
BEFORE THE DAY WAS OUT...
...EDGAR AND ALAN SAID THEY WERE MOVING AGAIN, AND THEY LEFT THE SCHOOL.
END OF STORY!
WAS KILLIAN WORRIED ABOUT THE BITE?
OF COURSE HE WAS! WHAT A RIDICULOUS QUESTION!
BUT IF THOSE TWO WERE VAMPIR-NELLA--
OH, YES! I KNOW! ACCORDING TO THE LEGEND...
EVERY NIGHT THEY SET OUT IN THE MOONLIGHT, SEARCHING FOR BLOOD, WANDERING SHADOWLESS. THEY CAUSE ROSES TO WITHER. THEY FEAR THE CRUCIFIX. THEY FEAR RUNNING WATER. THEY SLEEP IN OLD GRAVES.
...WHEN SOMEONE HAS THEIR BLOOD SUCKED BY A VAMPIRNELLA, THEY DIE AND ARE REBORN AS A VAMPIRNELLA.
NOTHING BUT FAIRY TALES! I'M TELLING YOU THERE'S NO SUCH THING!

ARE THEY *HUMAN?*
THEY'RE ...!
WHY DO YOU COL-LECT BLOOD?
TO STUDY IT!
I DON'T *KNOW!*
TIME TRAV-ELERS? ROSE ENTHUSI-ASTS?
WHAT ...
...ARE THEY?
WELL, THEN, WHAT *DOES* EXIST?
...SOME SORT OF... LIFE FORM... DIFFERENT TO US.
NO...
THEY ARE...
NO!
THEY AREN'T, ARE THEY?
I WONDER WHERE--OR IF--THEY ARE RIGHT NOW.

AT THIS SELF-SAME MOMENT, IS THAT BLUE-EYED BOY...

...STANDING ON A CORNER IN SOME TOWN, SOME CITY?

TIME PASSES THEM BY.

FROM THEIR POINT OF VIEW, TIME STANDS STILL.

IT IS THE WORLD AROUND THEM THAT CHANGES. IT IS WE WHO CHANGE.

EVEN IF ONLY IN DREAM...

...I WOULD SO VERY MUCH LIKE TO ENCOUNTER THAT MIRACLE ONCE MORE.

DOES ANYONE ELSE SMELL SOMETHING BURNING?

WHY, YES, I DO.

AHH!!
VWOOOSH
STAY CLOSE TO THE FLOOR! THE SMOKE--!
BAM
FIRE!
T-DMP!
THIS WAY IS BLOCKED! DON! THROUGH THAT DOOR! THE STAIRS!
QUICK! BEFORE THE STAIRS COLLAPSE! COVER YOUR MOUTHS!
BUT MR. ORBIN! THE PIC-TURES!
THE FLAMES ARE HERE, TOO!
THE GROUND FLOOR'S BURNING!

AH!
CHAR-LOTTE!
SHE WAS JUST HERE!
NEVER MIND THE PICTURES, DON! HURRY!
MAG-GIE!
THE EXIT'S TO THE LEFT!
HANG ON, EVERY-ONE!
ROGER! LOOK OUT!!
CHAR-LOTTE!
CRASH
THE PIC-TURES...

ROGER! HELP ME!
I...I JUST WANTED TO SAVE ONE PICTURE...
WHERE ARE THE STAIRS!?
ROG-ER
KOFF
KOFF
ROGER!
HENRY!
ROGER!
THIS WAY! COME ON!
AH...

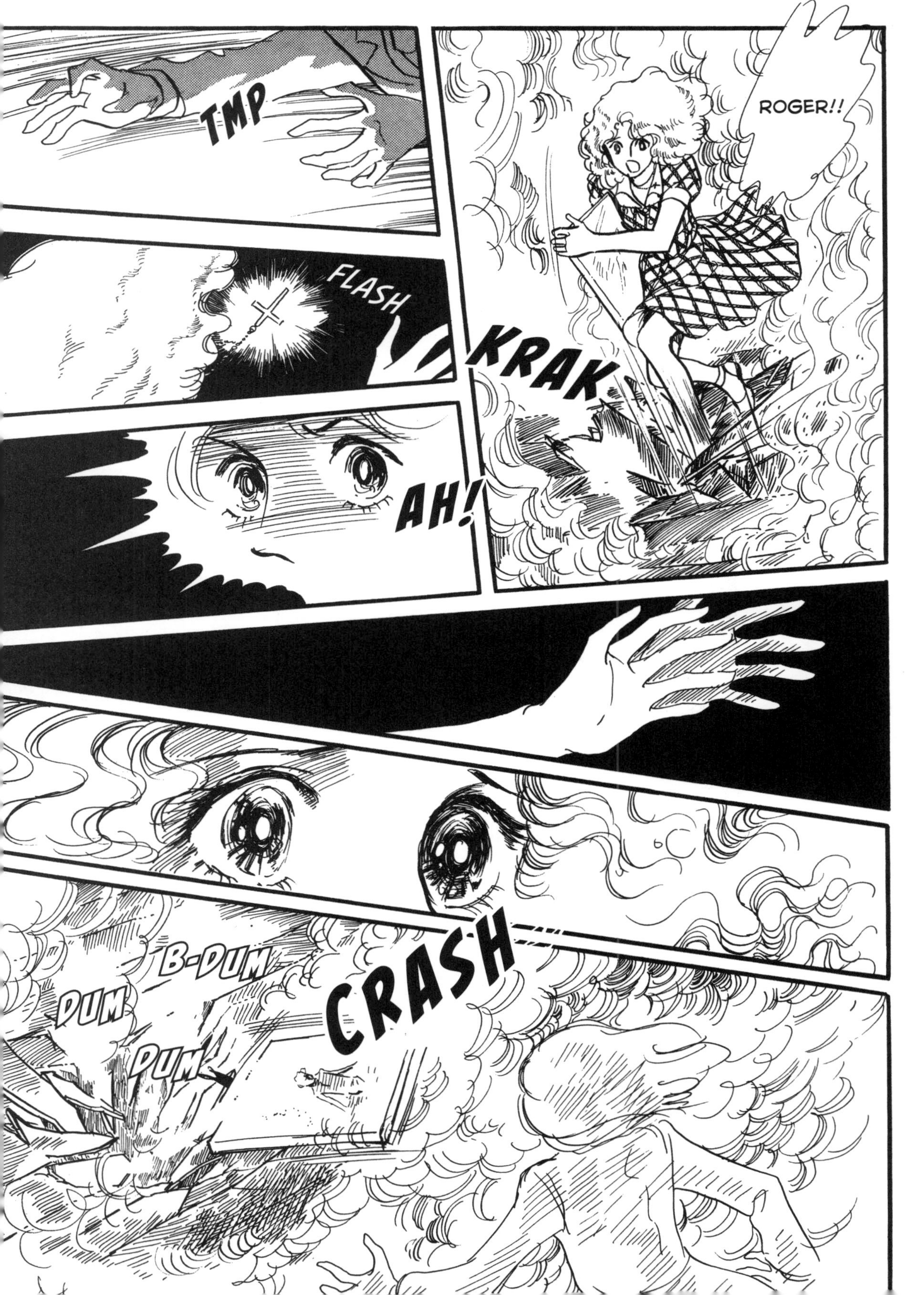
TMP
ROGER!!
FLASH
KRAK
AH!
CRASH
B-DUM
DUM
DUM

ROGER
ROGER
SAY
DO YOU SUPPOSE
THEY'RE OUT THERE SOMEWHERE... EVEN NOW?
WHERE'S CHARLOTTE!?
CHAR-LOTTE ...
ROG-ER
ROG-ER
AH ...
ROG-ER

NOTHING LIKE THIS HAS EVER.... TO THINK THEY WOULD GO TO SUCH TERRIBLE LENGTHS!
YOU MUST HAVE LEFT THE STOVE BURNING AT DINNER TIME.
CRACK
NO! I'M CERTAIN I TURNED IT OFF. BESIDES, WHO ELSE WOULD WANT TO MASSACRE A GROUP GATHERED TO DISCUSS FANTASY?
THIS ...
THIS IS ALL *YOUR* FAULT!
IF YOU HADN'T HELD THIS MEETING...
...HADN'T GATHERED US HERE...!
ROGER!
IF I HADN'T ACCEPTED...
CHARLOTTE...
CHAR...

1780 OSWALD O., EARL EVANS, WRITES HIS WILL
1783 CLIFFORD, EARL EVANS, DONATES A MANOR TO THE CITY TO BE USED AS A LIBRARY
1820 HENRY, EARL EVANS, MEETS EDGAR AND MARYBELLE
1879-1887 LYDIA LIVES IN THE FOREST WITH EDGAR AND ALAN
1888-1889 LORD QUENTIN PAINTS HIS LAMBTON
1934 ORBIN MEETS EDGAR
1940 ORBIN MEETS LYDIA
1945 ORBIN DISCOVERS EVANS' WILL IN THE LIBRARY
1950 DON MARSHALL FINDS THE LAMBTON PAINTING IN AN OLD MANOR; SPENDS A NIGHT WITH EDGAR AND ALAN IN THE HUNTING LODGE
1953 DON MARSHALL PUBLISHES "LAMBTON" IN A COTERIE JOURNAL
1959 EDGAR AND ALAN ATTEND THE GABRIEL SWISS GYMNASIUM IN WEST GERMANY
1960 MARGARET HESSEN PUBLISHES "THE LAST WILL AND TESTAMENT OF OSWALD, EARL EVANS"
1964 DON AND MARGARET MEET AND ARE MARRIED
1965 DON AND MARGARET PUBLISH "THE VAMPIRNELLA HUNT"
ORBIN READS IT AND THEY JOIN FORCES
THEY PURCHASE THE QUENTIN MANOR AND TRACK DOWN NUMEROUS PAINTINGS
1966 LUIS VISITS THEO
FIRE BREAKS OUT AT A GATHERING IN THE QUENTIN MANOR
CHARLOTTE EVANS PASSES (AGED 14)

END OF CHAPTER 4. FIRST PUBLISHED IN **SPECIAL EDITION SHÔJO COMIC**, JULY 1975

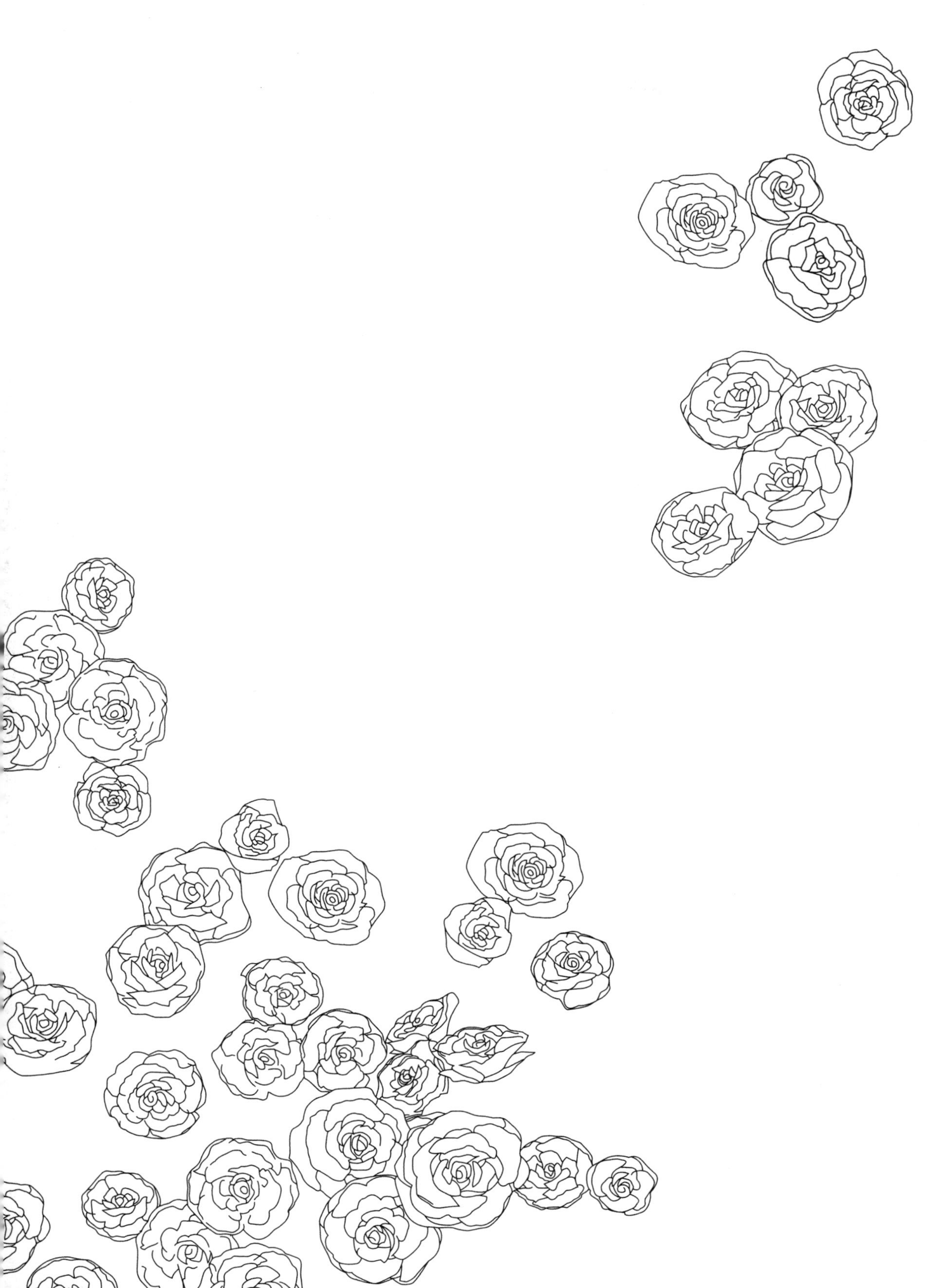

CHAPTER 5

PICCADILLY, SEVEN O'CLOCK

GONG
KREE
SLUMP
THUMP
GONG
ORANGES AND LEMONS

AHHH
AHHH
SAY THE BELLS OF ST. MARTIN'S
YOU OWE ME FIVE FAR-THINGS,
SAY THE BELLS OF ST. CLEMENT'S
AHHH
B-BEEP
TMP TMP
BLI-MEY!
WHAT IN THE--
BEEP
B-BEEP
A MURDER !?
THERE'S BEEN A MURDER!
TURN ON TO REGENT STREET.
COMING UP ON PICCADILLY CIRCUS, GUV.
TMP
TMP B-BEEP
TMP
GONG

SAY THE BELLS AT OLD BAILEY.
WHEN WILL YOU PAY ME? ♬
IN A FLAT UP THE STREET.
SOME HOOLIGAN WAS KILLED.
THE FLAT BELONGS TO LORD POLISTER, BUT HE'S GONE MISSING!
ED-GAR!
SORRY, GUV. WE'RE STUCK.
WE'LL GET OFF HERE.
DID YOU HEAR THAT?
I HEARD.
CHATTER CHATTER
MOVE ALONG, MOVE ALONG! CLEAR OFF, NOW!
YOU CAN'T STOP THAT CARRIAGE HERE!
OFF YOU GO!
YAP YAP
WHEN I GROW RICH, ♬
SAY THE BELLS AT SHOREDITCH.
I KNOW THAT HOOLIGAN!
NAME'S COOK! ALWAYS DRINKING IN PICCADILLY!
ONE CLEAN STAB, I HEERD.
HOPE THAT PRETTY DAUGHTER O' HIS IS ALL RIGHT!
YAP
YAP

GONG
GONG
WELL, WHAT ARE WE GOING TO DO, EDGAR? WE CAME TO SEE LORD POLISTER, DIDN'T WE?
IT SOUNDS LIKE A FUNERAL BELL, DOESN'T IT?
WHEN WILL THAT BE?
SAY THE BELLS OF STEPNEY.
WHAT!? EDGAR, WHAT ARE WE GOING TO DO?
I DO NOT KNOW,
SAYS THE GREAT BELL AT BOW.
GONG
HEY, LADD!
HOTEL ORIENT
PAUL!
DID YOU HEAR!? ABOUT THE MURDER ON REGENT STREET!?
YEAH, I'M WORRIED ABOUT LILIA.
BUT YOU SAW HER LAST NIGHT IN PICCADILLY, DIDN'T YOU?
NO.
SHE DIDN'T SHOW.

WELL, NOW.
WAS HIS LORDSHIP A SCHOLAR OF GEOGRAPHY AND HISTORY NOW?
AS I SEE IT...
...COOK SNUCK IN THROUGH THE SERVICE ENTRANCE AND LORD POLISTER TOOK HIM BY SURPRISE.
M... MY UNCLE ...?
THERE, THERE, YOUNG LADY.
SELF-DEFENSE, IT WAS. COOK WAS A BIG MAN. AND HE HAD A HUGE KNIFE, TO BOOT.
'E'S A GREAT MAN. ALWAYS TRAVELING FOR RESEARCH AN' SUCH.
WHOA!
JUS' YESTERDAY 'E WAS PACKING 'IS TRUNK.
BUT THEN A TELEGRAM CAME AN' HE CALLED OFF 'IS TRIP.
MAY I?
ARRIVE TOMORROW PORTNELL
AROUND THREE A.M. THIS MORNING...
...AN OFFICER SAW A MAN CARRYING A LARGE TRUNK.
YESTERDAY, UNCLE SAID HE WAS LEAVING ON A TRIP, SO I ARRANGED TO MEET MY LOVER, PAUL.
BUT THEN THAT TELEGRAM CAME, AND HE CANCELED, SO I COULDN'T LEAVE THE HOUSE. AND THIS MORNING, A MAN IS DEAD.
WHO'S THIS PORTNELL?
I COULDN'T SAY, SIR.
UNCLE...
WHERE HAVE YOU GONE WITH THAT BLACK TRUNK OF YOURS?

WHERE HAVE YOU DISAPPEARED TO...?
YET YOU FORBADE ME FROM SEEING PAUL
MORE A FATHER THAN AN UNCLE I WAS AN ORPHAN AND YOU RAISED ME AS YOUR OWN
OH, UNCLE DEAR UNCLE
SCOTLAND YARD SHALL NOT REST UNTIL YOUR UNCLE HAS BEEN FOUND.
YOU MUST SEND HIM A LETTER, MISS! I SHALL TAKE IT TO HIM MYSELF.
PAUL ...
IF ONLY PAUL WERE HERE!
EDGAR PORTNELL...
...AT YOUR SERVICE, M'LADY.
TMP
PAUL ...!?
KNOCK KNOCK KNOCK

HE WAS BOASTING
OF RAISING THE MOST WONDERFUL CHILD.
THESE BOYS...
...ARE UNCLE'S ASSOCI-ATES?
PORT-NELL !?
WE HAVE CAUGHT YOU AT A TERRIBLE TIME.
LORD POLISTER HAS SPOKEN OF YOU.
I'M FRIGHTFULLY SORRY. I WAS TOLD NOTHING OF YOUR VISIT.
THOUGH IT'S BEEN QUITE A WHILE SINCE I LAST SAW HIM.
I WAS SO LOOKING FORWARD TO SEEING HIM AGAIN.
DO TELL ME HOW HE HAS BEEN.
UNCLE HASN'T CHANGED A BIT SINCE I FIRST MET HIM.
DOES HE STILL HAVE A MOUS-TACHE?
AND DOES HE STILL WINK ALL THE TIME?
YES. HE'S TERRIBLY HANDSOME... ...AND KIND.
HE'S FOREVER SAYING
"COME, MY LILIA."

MY DEAR FATHER
ALWAYS THE SAME
WITH HIS BRIGHT BLONDE HAIR AND HIS BRIGHT EYES AND HIS FONDNESS FOR ABSINTHE
POURING HIS ABSINTHE WAS ALWAYS MY JOB
"COME, MY LILIA."
HE WAS A GOOD MAN.
RATHER CHARITABLE-- EVEN CREDULOUS. FOR A POE, THAT IS.
TALKING ABOUT 'IS LORDSHIP AS IF 'E'S DEAD!
STOP THAT THIS MINUTE!
FRIEDA!
WOULD YOU MIND SHOWING US LORD POLISTER'S ROOM?
BUT...
WHY?
WE MAY FIND SOME CLUE AS TO HIS WHEREABOUTS.
AND IF WE DO
WE CAN PASS IT ON TO THE POLICE
AND IT MIGHT HELP THEM IN THEIR SEARCH.
KREE

HE'S CUT OUT THE RUTLAND REGION!

DO YOU SUPPOSE THIS IS WHERE HE WENT?
HE PROBABLY PLANNED TO GO THERE, YES.
WITH HIS TRUNK? IN THE MIDDLE OF THE NIGHT?

WE'LL BE BACK. WE HAVE AN URGENT ERRAND.
WAIT!
FOR... MY SAKE?
ALAN!
YOU MEAN LORD POLISTER NEVER TOLD YOU ANYTHING?
FOR YOUR SAKE.
YOU MEAN LORD POLISTER NEVER TOLD YOU ANYTHING?
WHY DO YOU KNOW THINGS ABOUT UNCLE THAT EVEN I DON'T KNOW?
BAM
WAIT! WHY...
...DO YOU KNOW...
TWO BOYS, YOU SAY? NO MORE THAN FOURTEEN?
THEY SAID THEY'LL BE BACK.
HMM... RUTLAND, EH?
PORTNELL! THE ONE WHO SENT THE TELEGRAM!? WHY DIDN'T YOU CALL ME!?
DO THOSE BOYS KNOW SOME-THING!?

PUB
disci
PUB
EDGAR.
HOW MANY PUBS DO WE HAVE TO VISIT?
I'M LOOKING FOR SOMEONE.
LORD POLISTER? SURELY HE'S NOT IN LONDON. I'D WAGER HE'S GONE OFF TO RUTLAND?
HE...
...HAS NEVER ONCE FAILED TO KEEP A PROMISE.
HE WAS LOOKING FOR THE VILLAGE OF POE.
HOME OF THE ROSES, NESTLED IN THE VALLEY OF TIME.
HE SENT A LETTER SAYING HE'D FOUND THE ENTRANCE.
THAT HE'D TAKE US WITH HIM IF WE GOT HERE IN TIME FOR THE DEPARTURE DATE.
WE WERE DELAYED BY A CARGO TRAIN ACCIDENT.
HE WAS SURELY WAITING FOR US.
HE SAW THE TELEGRAM, SET DOWN HIS TRUNK, AND DELAYED HIS DEPARTURE.
HE ....
...?

SAY, D'YOU 'EAR THE NEWS THIS MORNING?

THAT CON GOOD LOUT, COOK! I KNEW 'E'D COME TO A BAD END!

KREE

I WISH 'E 'AD PAID OFF 'IS TAB BEFORE 'E UP AN' KICKED THE BUCKET, THOUGH!

THIS MUST BE THE PLACE.

ED-GAR?

YOU THE MASTER 'ERE?

AND WHAT IF I AM, LAD?

I WAS ASKED TO COME PAY OFF THAT TAB.

COOK'S TAB.

NOW 'OO ON EARTH WOULD PAY THAT OLD DRUNK'S TAB?

WHAT DIFFERENCE DOES IT MAKE AS LONG AS IT'S PAID?

WHY, THE LADD WHAT WORKS AT THE ORIENT 'OTEL!
WAIT...
WHICH LADD?
FIP!
MUCH OBLIGED! SAY, IS LADD COMING AROUND TO DRINK AGAIN TONIGHT?
HM!
EVENIN', INSPECTOR!
A PINT.
GONG
EDGAR!
YOU'LL SEE.
KREE
SIGH
THE ORIENT? JUST WHAT ARE YOU UP TO, EDGAR!?
COME ON! WE'RE STAYING AT THE ORIENT TONIGHT.

THEY PAID OFF COOK'S TAB.
B-BUT I DON'T KNOW A THING ABOUT THAT!

A PAIR O' LADS, MAYBE FOURTEEN, WERE JUST HERE. SAID YOU SENT 'EM.
SPLURT
ME!?

OI, LADD!
HEY
KREE

TWO LADS, YOU SAY!?
DID ONE HAVE CURLY BLONDE HAIR? FANCY CLOTHES?
GULP
WHOT!? DON'T TELL ME T'WAS YOU 'OO PAID THAT TAB!?
THAT WAS FIVE QUID!

GONG

YOU CALL ME IF THOSE LADS COME BACK, YOU HEAR?
ARE THEY IN SOME KIND OF TROUBLE?

I DON'T KNOW.
TING
I DON'T KNOW NUFFIN'!

THEY SEEMED TO KNOW SOME-THING.
COOK'S TAB? BUT WHY...?
TWO LADS...? ASSOCI-ATES OF LORD POLISTER ...?
JUST WHAT DO THEY KNOW?

HOTEL ORIENT
VERY GOOD, SIR. AND YOUR LUGGAGE?
WE LEFT IT AT THE STATION.

SO WHAT BUSINESS DO WE HAVE AT THIS HOTEL? WHY DID YOU PAY THAT TAB?
DING DING DING
I'M LOOKING FOR A BLACK TRUNK.

THE ONE LORD POLISTER TOOK WITH HIM ON HIS TRIP!?
HE DIDN'T GO ON ANY TRIP.

OH, AS IF YOU KNOW! WELL, THEN, WHERE *IS* LORD POLISTER!?

HUSH!

THAT'S LILIA'S MAID. WHAT'S SHE DOING HERE?
NOW THERE'S A HANDSOME LAD. ONE A YOUNG LASS COULD FALL FOR.
A LASS LIKE LILIA.

PAUL! SHOW OUR GUESTS TO THEIR ROOM!
RIGHT AWAY, SIR!
BUMP
OH, I'M TERRIBLY SORRY.
BAM
PAUL!?
TMP
ARE YOU ALL RIGHT?
FINE, THANK YOU.
AH! YOU FILCHED HIS LETTER! THAT'S LOW, EDGAR!
DRASTIC MEA-SURES, AND ALL THAT.
FORGIVE ME, PAUL
I COULD NOT KEEP OUR DATE LAST NIGHT.
UNCLE'S TRIP WAS CANCELED
AND I COULDN'T LEAVE THE HOUSE.
I'LL BE WAITING FOR YOU TOMORROW
HM? AH!
?
?

SNEAKING AROUND BEHIND LORD POLISTER'S BACK, EH?
HE WON'T LIKE THIS!
WH-- WHO ARE YOU TWO?

AT PICCADILLY CIRCUS, SEVEN O'CLOCK
FRIEDA AND I WILL BE AT THE MARKET.
OH! THAT LETTER!
HELLO, PAUL.

ASSOCIATES OF HIS.
WE MET WITH LILIA TODAY.

YOU DID!? IS SHE ALL RIGHT!?

TERRIBLE BUSINESS SHE GOT CAUGHT UP IN!
POOR GIRL...
IS SHE ALL RIGHT?
DO YOU LOVE HER?

I... I DO.

WELL, THAT'S TOO BAD. SHE HAS LORD POLISTER, AFTER ALL!

GONG
SAY THE BELLS OF ST. CLEMENT'S
ALAN!
YOU'RE MISSING THE POINT!
SO I SEE WHY HE WOULD BE OPPOSED...
♪ ORANGES AND LEMONS
I KNOW I'M JUST A HUMBLE BELLBOY.
SAY THE BELLS OF OLD BAILEY.
WHEN WILL YOU PAY ME?
...BUT I KNOW ONE DAY HE'LL UNDERSTAND.
YOU OWE ME FIVE FARTHINGS,
GONG
SAY THE BELLS OF ST. MARTIN'S.
I DO LOVE HER.
SO VERY MUCH.
IT WAS A YEAR AGO WE MET.
TRAFALGAR SQUARE IN THE SNOW. KENSINGTON GARDENS IN THE SPRING.... WHEREVER WE'RE TOGETHER, WE'RE HAPPY.
IN THE NAVE OF ST. PAUL'S AND WALKING IN ST. JAMES PARK...
WE'RE JUST SO HAPPY TOGETHER.
GONG
GONG
GONG
GONG
THE BELLS OF LONDON RING THE BELLS OF LONDON RING
ORANGES AND LEMONS. ROAST BEEF AND MARSHMALLOWS. JOY AND SORROW. FATE AND HAPPENSTANCE... ANGELS AND DEVILS.

IT SOUNDS LIKE A FUNERAL BELL.

WHAT ...?

I GAVE HIM THE LETTER, MISS. HE WAS HALF OUT HIS MIND WI' WORRY FOR YOU.

TOMORROW AT SEVEN!

THANK YOU, FRIEDA.

PAUL, PLEASE PRAY WITH ME THAT UNCLE IS FOUND SOON.

HE RAISED ME. HE'S PRECIOUS TO ME.

YOU'RE MEETING HER TOMORROW? WHY NOT TONIGHT?
I CAN'T. I WORK TILL TWO TONIGHT.
AND I JUST GOT LADD TO TRADE SHIFTS WITH ME LAST NIGHT.
LADD'S A BELLHOP HERE.

LADD!
TRADED SHIFTS!

THE TWO O' THEM WAS JUST DRINKING TOGETHER LAST NIGHT AT THE CORNER TABLE.

I BELIEVE... YOU COULD MAKE LILIA HAPPY.
EDGAR!

LADD? WHY?
BACK TO THAT PUB.
TO SEE LADD.
IT SEEMS LORD POLISTER HASN'T TOLD HER ANYTHING YET, BUT--
YOU KNOW PAUL AND LILIA CAN NEVER BE TOGETHER!
WHY WOULD YOU SAY SUCH A THING!
HEY, WHERE ARE YOU GOING?
SO LILIA PLANNED TO MEET HER LOVER WHILE HE WAS AWAY.
LORD POLISTER WAS SUPPOSED TO TRAVEL YESTERDAY.
SO HER LOVER PAUL...
...ARRANGED TO HAVE LADD TAKE HIS SHIFT.
I'VE GOT A DATE.
LADD HEARD THAT AND BROKE IN WITH COOK.
A CHANCE!
THEY THOUGHT THEY'D MAKE QUITE A HAUL.
BUT!
THE MASTER OF THE HOUSE WAS HOME.
WE NEED THAT TRUNK. THE MAP MAY BE IN IT.
AND YET, THE BLACK TRUNK WAS MISSING.
BECAUSE THE MASTER OF THE HOUSE WAS WAITING FOR *US*.

SO YOU'RE SAYING PAUL'S FRIEND LADD...
...HAS THE TRUNK? SO, WHAT ABOUT LORD POLISTER?
WHERE IS HE?
YOU STILL DON'T GET IT?

PUB PINGE

CLOSING TIME, LADD!
RIGHT.
OH!
TING

YOU CALL ME IF THOSE LADS COME BACK, YOU HEAR?
GULP
YOU'RE LADD?
HM? 'OO'RE YOU?
I HAVE A MESSAGE FOR YOU.
HUH?

A TALL HANDSOME MAN.

WH-WH-WHO GAVE YOU THIS!?

HE'S WAITING FOR YOUR ANSWER.

WHUH!?

I WILL PAY £100 FOR THE TRUNK

-POLISTER

100!!

YOU JUS' 'ANG ON, LAD, AN' YOU'LL 'AVE A TUPPENCE FER YER TROUBLE.

7AM PICADILLY

NEVER MIND. NOW IT'S JUST A MATTER OF TIMING.
IT LOOKS LIKE HE'S CALLING THE POLICE, EDGAR.

FANCY THAT. HE CHOSE THE SAME TIME AS LILIA'S DATE.

A HUNDRED POUNDS! THAT POLISTER BLOKE'S HIDIN' SOMFIN' FER SURE.

COOK 'N ME GOT IN ALL RIGHT
BUT THEN WE HEARD SOME-ONE
WHO?
I GRAB THE NEAREST THING AND SCARPERED OUTTA THERE.

NEXT DAY I 'EARD 'IS LORDSHIP WAS 'OME!
AND PAUL TOLD ME 'E'D BE OUT!

IT'S TOO BAD ABOUT COOK...
...BUT IT'S A STROKE O' LUCK FER ME!

COOK HAD A KNIFE.
A BIG ONE.
POLISTER MURDERED, STABBED STRAIGHT IN THE HEART
AND LIKE AN EXPLOSION WAS GONE IN THE BLINK OF AN EYE
HE'D BEEN RAISING HIS OWN BRIDE.
WITH HIS BRIGHT BLONDE HAIR AND HIS BRIGHT EYE AND HIS FONDNESS FOR ABSINTHE
WHEN SHE TURNED TWENTY...
...SHE'D BE WELCOMED TO THE CLAN.
BUT FIRST, HE'D HAVE TO FIND THE VILLAGE. TO FIND THE KING OF THE CLAN.
BUT NOW, HE'S GONE. GONE.

GONG
GONG
GONG

GONG
YOU YOUNG GENTS IN NEED OF A CAR?

AND YOU'RE CERTAIN UNCLE WILL APPEAR?
OH, YES!
IT'S JUST AS I SUSPECTED.
THOSE TWO LADS HAVE SOMETHING TO DO WITH THE EARL'S DISAPPEARANCE!

HM?
AH!

WE'LL KEEP OUR DISTANCE. SIGNAL US WHEN THE EARL SHOWS UP!

PAUL!
LILIA!
PAUL. PAUL.
IT'S BEEN SO LONG. YOU'RE SO THIN. NOT SLEEPING WELL?
HE... HE'S LOOKING FOR--
WHO'S THAT?
EH-HEM!
EH-HEM!!

PWEET!
'E'S SPOTTED US! CATCH 'IM!
TMP!
BLIMEY! IT'S POLISTER'S KID!!
OOPS!
THAT'S UNCLE'S TRUNK!!
LADD !?

PWEE-PWEE PWEE PWEE
IT'S A BLOODY TRAP!
WAH!

THE TRUNK!
M-MY 'UNDRED QUID!
HUFF HUFF
CRACK

HEY! LADD! OVER HERE!

AFTER THE CAR! THE CAR!!
WAH!!
GET YER MITTS OFF! IT'S MY 'UNDRED!

WHACK
TA-TA!

UNGH!
WHUMP

'UNDRED?
LOOK! A HUNDRED QUID!
GET THIS CAR OUTTA THE WAY! MOVE IT!
WHAT'S GOIN' ON?
THAT BLOKE'S DIVVY.

To my darling daughter
I shall be praying from
afar for your happiness
with your young man.
A. Polister

NO! LOOK! THERE'S A LETTER, TOO!

YOU NEED GLASSES, YOU TWIT! LOOK! THESE ARE BLANK PIECES OF PAPER!
WHAT!?

I shall be praying from afar
UNCLE...
ONE... ONE...ONE HUNDRED QUID...
WH...WH... WH...
ON YOUR FEET, LADD!
LET'S GO DOWN TO SCOTLAND YARD AND HEAR YOUR STORY, EH?
BUT...WHY, UNCLE?
WHY DID YOU HAVE TO GO?
...FOREVER SAYING...
"COME, MY LILIA."
WILL HE EVER COME BACK?
LILIA...
IT CAN'T BE TRUE...
I WONDER IF THOSE BOYS KNEW ANYTHING ABOUT IT.

END OF CHAPTER 5

FIRST PUBLISHED IN **SPECIAL EDITION SHÓJO COMIC**, AUGUST 1975

CHAPTER 6

THE FLOWERS AND BIRDS OF A FARAWAY LAND

SINCE THAT DAY I HAVE DREAMED OF NOTHING BUT YOU
THE FOREST BREEZE A CASTLE IN THE DISTANCE JOY AMONG THE FLOWERS
WITH YOU AND YOUR EYES OF GREEN

WHAT HAVE WE HERE?
FLOWER FILCHING WILL NEVER BE A CRIME. I'D BE HAPPY TO CUT SOME FOR YOU.
DO COME IN. THE GATE'S OPEN.
FORGIVE ME. THEY'RE SO LOVELY, I JUST--
YOU'RE NOT FROM AROUND HERE, ARE YOU?
NO, I JUST AR-RIVED.
FROM WHERE? OH! SUCH BLUE EYES.
I HAVE CAPTURED A UNICORN IN MY GARDEN.

DO YOU KNOW THIS ONE?
I THOUGHT YOU WERE GOING TO CUT ME A ROSE?

NOW COME AND SING A SONG, MY UNICORN PRISONER.

ONE ROSE FOR EACH VERSE.
FAIR ENOUGH.
Long Long Time ago

A long long Time ago

my little baby

WELCOME. LET ME INTRODUCE A NEW FRIEND. HE'S JUST ARRIVED IN OUR TOWN. ISN'T THAT RIGHT?
THIS IS THE TOWN CHOIR I'VE PUT TOGETHER. YOU SIMPLY MUST JOIN US. YOU HAVE A LOVELY VOICE.

JOE, BE A DEAR AND GET THINGS STARTED.
WELL, WAIT WHILE I CUT YOUR ROSES.
BUT I'M AFRAID I WON'T BE HERE FOR LONG.
AND I HAVE A FRIEND WAITING FOR ME AT THE MOMENT.
GOOD DAY, MISS BYRD.
GOOD DAY, DOCTOR HILLS.
HOW HAPPY SHE SEEMS. AND SHE DIDN'T ASK ME A THING ABOUT MYSELF.
I'LL SEE YOU TOMORROW, MY UNICORN. MY NAME'S ELSIE.
DO YOU LIKE TO SING?
I DON'T HATE IT.
NOW, THEN, BE CAREFUL NOT TO PRICK YOURSELF.
MY NAME... IS EDGAR.
WHO'S THAT KID?
AN OUT-SIDER.

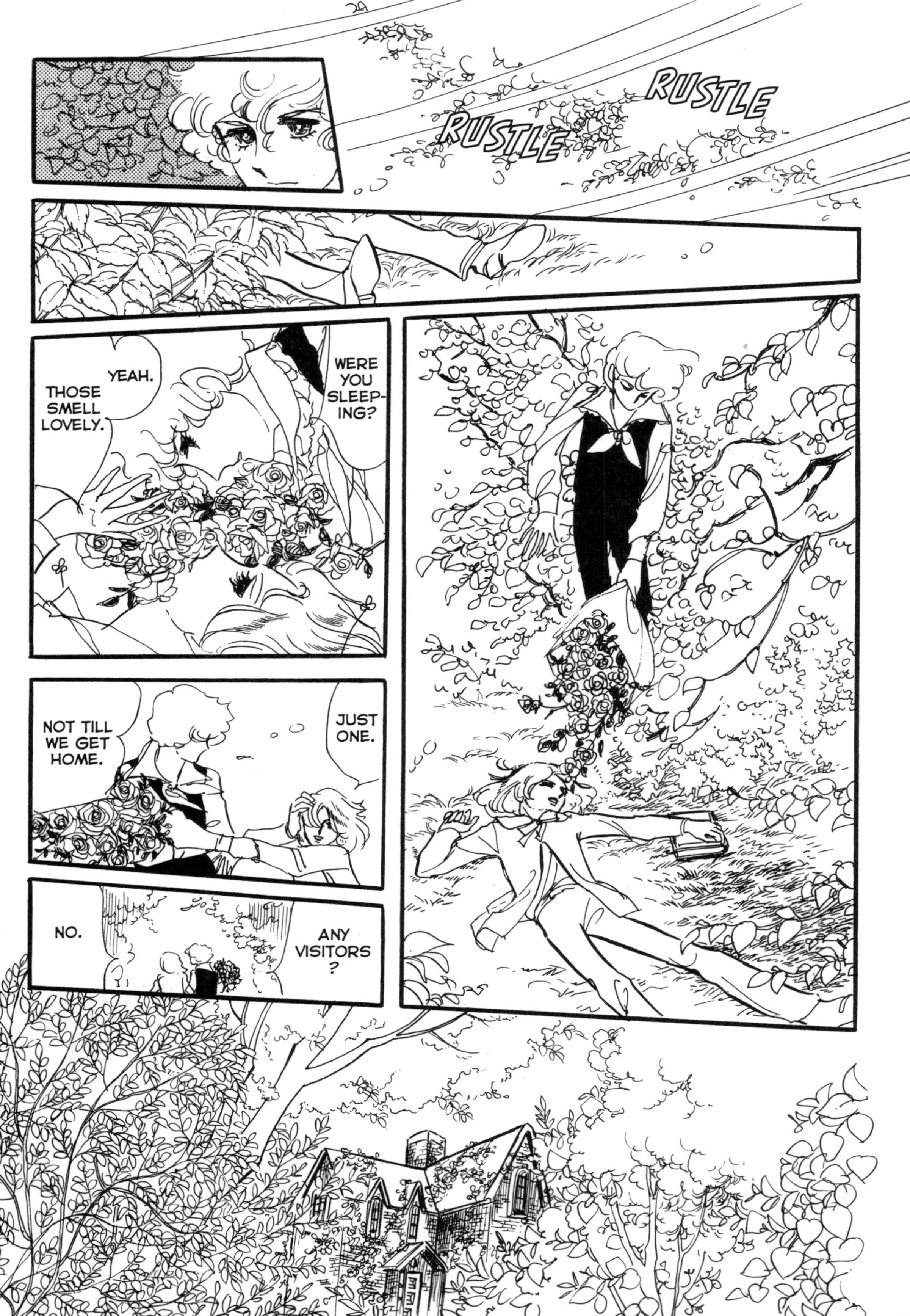
RUSTLE
RUSTLE
WERE YOU SLEEPING?
YEAH. THOSE SMELL LOVELY.
JUST ONE.
NOT TILL WE GET HOME.
ANY VISITORS?
NO.

WHERE DID YOU GET THEM?
FROM THE ROSE GARDEN OF A MISS ELSIE, WHO LIVES ON THE EDGE OF TOWN.
YOU DON'T SAY? WHAT'S SHE LIKE? IS SHE PRETTY?
VERY PRETTY.
SHE LEADS A CHOIR. I'VE BEEN HOOKED INTO SINGING. WANT TO JOIN?
WHY WOULD I?
IT'S QUIET HERE, BUT I WORRY LEAVING YOU ALONE. YOU DO TEND TO MAKE A MESS OF THINGS.
I DO *NOT!*
ANYWAY, WHO AM I TO TURN DOWN AN OFFER OF FRESH ROSES?
BUT DO TAKE CARE NOT TO END UP ON THE WRONG END OF A STAKE. IF OUR COVER IS BLOWN, WE'RE DONE FOR.
LIKE OUR POOR MARY-BELLE.

HELLO, ELSIE!
HELLO, BOYS!
OH! EDGAR!
COME IN, COME IN! THE GATE'S OPEN. I'M SO GLAD YOU CAME.
YOU ARE?
I AM.
LOOK! HE'S BACK!
WHAT, THAT OUTSIDER KID?
THE GATE IS OPEN, MY BLUE-EYED UNICORN
SO ENCHANTING WAS THE WOMAN'S SMILE
THAT THE UNICORN ALLOWED HIMSELF TO BECOME A CAPTIVE OF HER ROSE GARDEN

LOOK AT HIM MOONING OVER MISS ELSIE.
HMPH! I DON'T LIKE IT!

YOU ARE A TENOR. SUCH A LOVELY VOICE.
SOME LOVELY NEW SHEET MUSIC JUST ARRIVED BY POST.
I WANT YOU TO ALL LEARN IT BY NEXT WEEK.

YES, MY FAVORITE! APPLE PIE! WE USED THE APPLES JOE BROUGHT ON MONDAY.
PIE!

THE PIE TURNED OUT JUST FINE, MISS ELSIE.
WONDER-FUL! LET'S HAVE TEA!

A WAS AN APPLE PIE

B BIT IT

C CUT IT

D DEALT IT
E EAT IT
F...

MAY I HAVE SOME ROSES?
AS MANY AS YOU LIKE.

HMPH!

GOOD AFTER-NOON, MISS BYRD.
GOOD AFTER-NOON, DR. HILLS.

THIS ROSE GARDEN BELONGED TO THE AUNT WHO RAISED ME, AND WHO PASSED FIVE YEARS AGO.
I'M AFRAID I'M NOT AS GOOD AT TENDING IT SHE WAS.
BUT IT'S IN BLOOM FROM JUNE TILL CHRISTMAS EVERY YEAR AND I LOVE IT DEARLY.
YOU ARE SUR-ROUNDED BY THINGS YOU LOVE.
YOU SEEM SO HAPPY, DELIGHTING IN EVERY LITTLE THING.
STRAY HAIRS SILVER IN THE SUNLIGHT
STIR MEMORIES OF A LONG LOST GIRL

HEY!

BUT SHE'S LIKE A LITTLE GIRL.

SORRY. NOT INTERESTED IN OLDER WOMEN.

IS SHE REALLY SO WONDER-FUL?
SHE REALLY IS. WANT TO COME ALONG?

HOLD UP! WERE DO YOU LIVE, ANYWAY?
I HAVEN'T SEEN YOU AT CHURCH. DON'T GO GETTING ANY FUNNY IDEAS JUST BECAUSE ELSIE'S SO NICE!
OUTSIDER!

BOO HOO HOO

GOOD AFTER-NOON, MISS BYRD.
GOOD AFTER-NOON, DR. HILLS.
OH! DO THE BABIES NEED THEIR NAPPIES CHANGED!?
CLANG
AH!
BOO HOO

NOW YOU TWO MAKE UP. AS A FAVOR TO ME.
B-BUT HE...
YOU BOYS SHOULD PUT THAT ENERGY TO BETTER USE THAN FIGHTING.
YEOW!
BUT HE WHAT?
BOYS! BOYS!
FOND OF OLDER WOMEN, EH?
I'LL EVEN LEND YOU MY BIKE IF YOU LIKE. JUST DON'T GET FRESH WITH ELSIE, HEAR?
I CAN'T SAY NO TO ELSIE, SO WE'LL SIGN A PEACE TREATY.
SURE. THAT DOCTOR PASSES EVERY DAY. DON'T YOU THINK THEY'D MAKE A NICE COUPLE?
ELSIE'S STILL YOUNG!
ELSIE WILL NEVER MARRY ANYBODY!
YOU DON'T KNOW ANY-THING.

SHE WAS STOOD UP BY A LOVER.

WHY?

MY MUM TOLD IT HAPPENED ABOUT TEN YEARS AGO.
HE WAS HANDSOME AND PENNILESS AND THEY WERE IN LOVE, BUT HE ENDED UP MARRYING A MERCHANT'S DAUGHTER FOR HER MONEY.

SO MUM SAYS ELSIE REFUSES TO MARRY BECAUSE SHE'S STILL BITTER ABOUT IT.
"HELL HATH NO FURY," EH?
YOU SEEM SO HAPPY, DELIGHTING IN EVERY LITTLE THING.

THE SCENT OF MEMORIES LINGERS ABOUT HER.

STAY INDOORS. YOU KNOW THE DAMP DOESN'T AGREE WITH YOU.

EDGAR! DON'T TELL ME YOU'RE GOING OUT IN THIS WEATHER!?

I DIDN'T THINK ANYONE WOULD COME IN THIS WEATHER. DO YOU LIVE NEARBY?
OF COURSE I CAME. I'M YOUR CAPTIVE UNICORN.

GOOD-NESS! EDGAR!

IT SHOULD LET UP BY EVENING. THIS SHOULD BRING THE GREEN BACK TO THE LAWN!

IT'S DR. HILLS. MAKING A HOUSE CALL IN THE POURING RAIN.

AND, I'LL ADD, GOING OUT OF HIS WAY TO PASS *THIS HOUSE*.

BUT RUMOR HAS IT YOU REMAIN SINGLE OUT OF SPITE BECAUSE A LOVER STOOD YOU UP.

I HEAR THE DOCTOR HAS PROPOSED TO YOU, ELSIE. AND NOT JUST ONCE.

THERE'S THAT ENIGMATIC SMILE AGAIN.

TELL ME ABOUT IT.

HE'D JUST ARRIVED FROM HOLBEACH THAT SUMMER, AND I FELL IN LOVE WITH HIM.
I WAS SIXTEEN. HE WAS TWENTY.

I SAW...A CASTLE.

IT WAS A MARVELOUS SUMMER.
BUT THEN I LEARNED HE HAD A FIANCÉE.

"HAROLD LEE IS AN AMBITIOUS MAN," MY AUNT SAID. "HE'S POOR AND IN DEBT AND HIS FIANCÉE IS RICH. HE CAN'T BE TRUSTED."
BUT HE ASKED ME TO WAIT FOR HIM. HE SAID HE WOULD BREAK OFF THE ENGAGEMENT AND COME BACK TO ME.

I WAS CRUSHED. I BELIEVED IN HIM...

...BUT I ALSO BELIEVED IN FATE.

I THOUGHT IF I LET HIM GO, HE WOULD NEVER COME BACK.

THE NIGHT BEFORE HE WAS TO LEAVE, WE WENT FOR A WALK IN THE FOREST, LIKE A COUPLE OF LOST CHILDREN.
WE STEPPED OUT OF THE FOREST AT THE TOP OF A CLIFF. AND I SAW... I SAW A CASTLE.

AND I SAID, "LOOK! A CASTLE!"
AS THE WORDS CAME OUT OF MY MOUTH, I REALIZED IT WAS A TRICK OF THE MOONLIGHT. IT WAS JUST TREES.
THERE WAS NO CASTLE.

BUT HE SAID,
"YES, I SEE IT! IT'S A CASTLE."

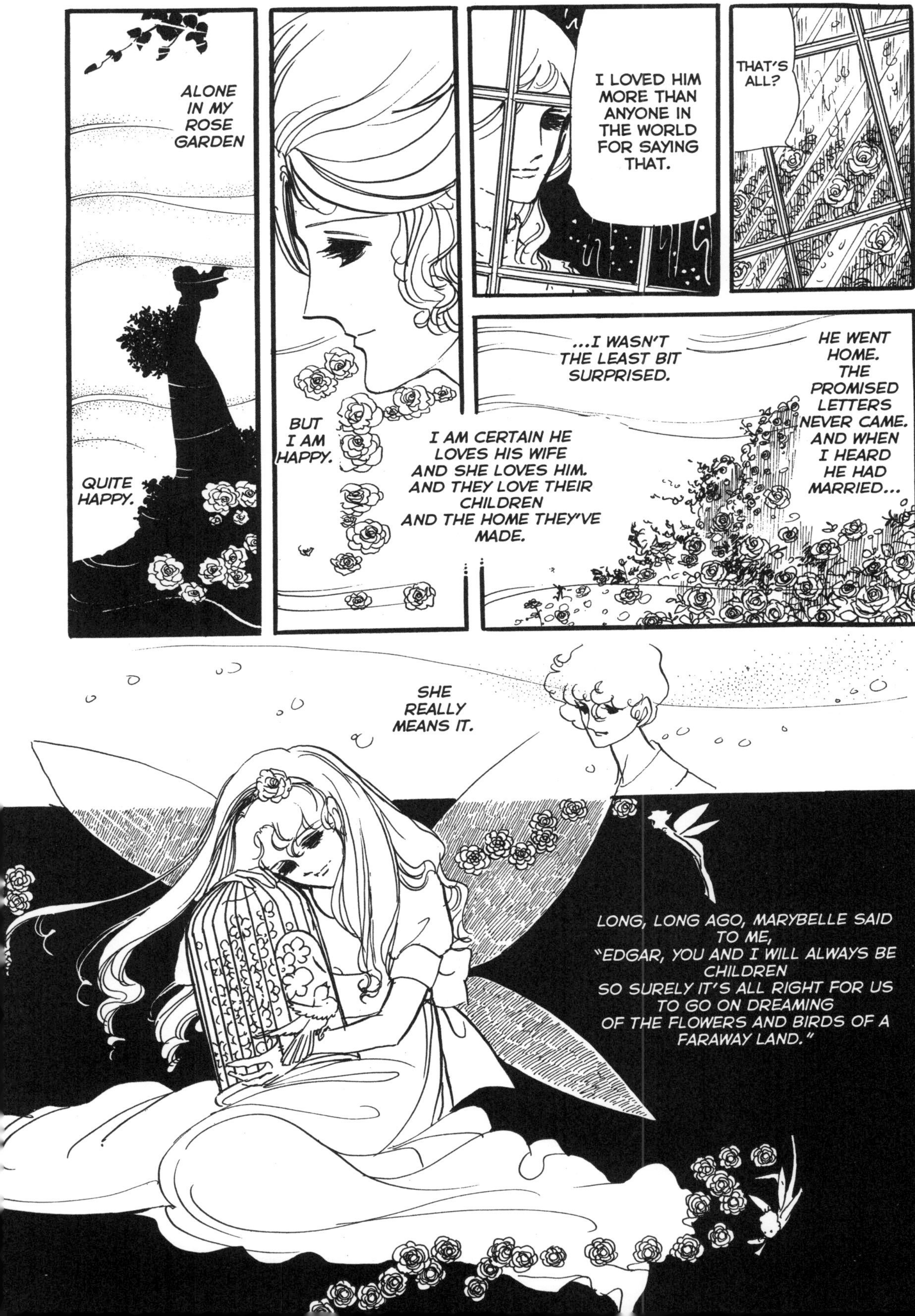

ALONE IN MY ROSE GARDEN
QUITE HAPPY.
BUT I AM HAPPY.

I LOVED HIM MORE THAN ANYONE IN THE WORLD FOR SAYING THAT.

THAT'S ALL?

HE WENT HOME. THE PROMISED LETTERS NEVER CAME. AND WHEN I HEARD HE HAD MARRIED...
...I WASN'T THE LEAST BIT SURPRISED.
I AM CERTAIN HE LOVES HIS WIFE AND SHE LOVES HIM. AND THEY LOVE THEIR CHILDREN AND THE HOME THEY'VE MADE.

SHE REALLY MEANS IT.

LONG, LONG AGO, MARYBELLE SAID TO ME,
"EDGAR, YOU AND I WILL ALWAYS BE CHILDREN
SO SURELY IT'S ALL RIGHT FOR US TO GO ON DREAMING
OF THE FLOWERS AND BIRDS OF A FARAWAY LAND."

DREAMS OF A FARAWAY LAND!? HAH! THAT LADY'S OFF HER ROCKER, SHE IS!

I'D WAGER THAT LOVER OF HER'S DOESN'T EVEN REMEMBER HER!
YET SHE STILL LOVES HIM.

YOU'RE GOING OUT!?
I TOLD HER I'D GO.
ALSO, FREE ROSES.

YOU GO EVERY DAY! IS SHE REALLY SO MARVEL-OUS?
YOU COULD STAY HOME ONCE IN A WHILE.

SO COME WITH ME.
NOT LIKELY!

SHE'S VERY KIND. SHE'D BE THRILLED TO HAVE A NEW MEMBER.

WHAT, AND SING SONGS WITH A SPINSTER AND A BUNCH OF BRATS!?

THEN JUST WAIT HERE ALONE.

RIGHT! WHO CARES A FIG ABOUT ALAN ANYWAY!?
ALAN'S JUST A STAND-IN FOR MARYBELLE!

ELSIE
ELSIE
I LIVE IN
A GARDEN
OF
ROSES
SMACK!
BIRDS
OF LOVE
REFLECTED
IN MY EYES
TMP
HOW CAN
YOU BE
SO HAPPY,
ELSIE?
WITHOUT
THE ONE
YOU LOVE
AT YOUR
SIDE?
ALAN,
I'M
SORRY.
ALAN.

WHERE'S EDGAR?
HE CAME OVER TO MY PLACE
AND BOR-ROWED MY BI-CYCLE.
POST OFFI
HAROLD LEE LIVES ON WYSS ROAD, BUT HE EATS LUNCH EVERY DAY JUST ACROSS THE STREET THERE.
HAROLD LEE?
FLAP
DO YOU KNOW ELSIE?
YES. AND YOU ARE?

YOU! COME BACK!
TMP!
HOLD ON?
BOY!?
CAN'T SAY I DO.
ELSIE?
WHY WOULD HE? A LOVER HE SPENT ONE SUMMER WITH TEN YEARS AGO!
HE DOESN'T REMEMBER HER!
ELSIE ELSIE HAPPY ELSIE
HAPPY, HAPPY ELSIE!

WHO'S THERE?
EDGAR, WHY ARE YOU ABOUT AT THIS HOUR!?
I JUST GOT BACK FROM HOLBEACH.
HOLBEACH! THE TOWN WHERE YOUR LOVER LIVES. I MET YOUR LOVER!
HE... HE...
HOW WAS HE?
CURLY BROWN HAIR AND GREEN EYES?
I HEARD HE WEARS A MOUS-TACHE. DOES IT SUIT HIM?
HE REMEM-BERED YOU.

YOU RESENT HIM, DON'T YOU?

YOU'RE NOT REALLY HAPPY, ARE YOU?

I WONDER IF IT WOULD EVEN BOTHER HER TO KNOW HE DOESN'T REMEMBER HER.

THE TRUTH IS, YOU'RE UNBEARABLY LONELY, AREN'T YOU?
I MEAN... IN POINT OF FACT THE ONE YOU LOVE IS NOT AT YOUR SIDE.

WAKE UP, ELSIE! YOU'RE LIVING IN A DREAM!
EVERYONE HAS TO FACE REALITY. TO FRET. TO HATE. TO GRIEVE. SO WHY!?
HOW CAN YOU ALONE BE SO HAPPY!?

BUT I DON'T WANT TO HATE.
I DON'T WANT TO GRIEVE.

THERE IS NO FARAWAY LAND! IT'S NOT A PLACE REAL PEOPLE CAN LIVE.
ELSIE...

THAT'S WHY I WANT TO JUST GO ON LOVING HIM. IT'S THE ONLY WAY FOR ME TO BE HAPPY.
I LACK THE CAPACITY FOR SORROW OR RESENTMENT. I'M MUCH TOO WEAK TO BEAR SUCH VIOLENT EMOTIONS.
A DISTANT MEMORY A DISTANT MEMORY
THIS IS MY WORLD. A WORLD WHERE I CAN DRIFT AND FLOAT A WORLD ENCLOSED BY HIS LOVE.
SONGS OF LOVE FOREVER ON MY LIPS
I LIVE IN A GARDEN OF ROSES
THINKING EVERY DAY OF THAT GENTLE SOUL
WHERE IS SHE NOW? I CAN'T FEEL HAPPINESS JUST BY THINKING OF HER.
WHERE DID SHE GO? WILL SHE BE BORN AGAIN?
TO BEGIN WITH... MY LITTLE SISTER IS GONE.
SHE'S NOT HERE.
WHY? WHY CAN YOU BE HAPPY?
WHY CAN'T *YOU* BE HAPPY?

WERE THE ROSES FOR YOUR LITTLE SISTER?

THEY WERE FOR A FRIEND. BUT HE'S NOT HER.

THIS IS LOVE. REACH OUT...AND YOU WILL TOUCH THE ONE YOU LOVE.

YOUR LOVE. YOUR LITTLE SISTER'S LOVE.

IT'S GOOD TO HAVE A VESSEL TO RECEIVE YOUR LOVE. IT'S GOOD TO HAVE SOMEONE WHO WILL ACCEPT YOUR ROSES.

EDGAR
EDGAR

THIS IS THE DISTANT LAND... THIS IS THE FAR-AWAY GARDEN.

MY DEAR BROTHER...

KLAK

I CAN RETURN FROM THE LAND OF MEMORY AND HAND HIM A ROSE
BUT SHE... ALL SHE HAS IS THAT WHICH IS IN HER HEART
I WONDER IF SHE'LL EVER WAKE FROM HER DREAM?

I'M SO SORRY.

BOY!
AH!
YOU THERE!
I'LL BE HOME EARLY.
TAKE CARE, DARLING. YOU HAVEN'T BEEN WELL.
WHO COULD HE HAVE MEANT?
I CAN'T GET IT OFF MY MIND.
ELSIE
MRS. GRASSE SAYS SHE'S JUST BEEN TO HAROLD LEE'S FUNERAL!
MISS ELSIE! MISS ELSIE! THERE YOU ARE!

UNTIL A MOMENT AGO, THIS WORLD WAS MY OWN.
HE WAS TRYING TO HELP A BOY WHO'D FALLEN FROM HIS BICYCLE AND WAS RUN OVER BY A CARRIAGE!
I'M SORRY.
THAT'S ALL FOR TODAY, BOYS. I'M AFRAID I CAN'T PLAY THE ORGAN TODAY. I'M SORRY.
TO SLEEP...
AND FROM TOMORROW ONWARDS, I'LL NEVER NEVER WAKE AGAIN.
BY TOMORROW, THE ROSES IN THE GARDEN WILL ALL BE WITHERED.
I DON'T WANT GRIEF. I DON'T WANT RESENTMENT. I JUST NEED TO SLEEP.

EDGAR! THERE'S NO PRACTICE TODAY!
ELSIE'S WHITE AS A SHEET!
WHAT?
HAROLD LEE IS *DEAD!*
THE MAID JUST CAME WITH WORD.
EDGAR?
THE MISTRESS IS RESTING IN HER ROOM! COME BACK!
WHY YOU LITTLE --!
ELSIE !!
BAM
BAM
OPEN UP, ELSIE
ELSIE
ELSIE
BAM

BAM
THE DOCTOR!
FETCH THE DOC-TOR!
GYAHH!!
ELSIE!
ELSIE, WAKE UP!
OPEN YOUR EYES, ELSIE! WAKE UP!
ELSIE!
COME BACK FROM YOUR GARDEN OF DREAMS
COME BACK LITTLE ELSIE

AND YET...
TO THINK SHE...
IT'S A GOOD THING SHE WAS FOUND EARLY. NO NEED FOR WORRY NOW.
THERE, THERE. IT'S ALL RIGHT NOW.
WHEN SHE WAKES UP, ASK HER ABOUT THE CASTLE.
COME AGAIN?
WHEN SHE WAKES AND IS HUMAN AGAIN, THAT IS.
THAT WOMAN NEEDS YOU, DOCTOR. NOW MORE THAN EVER.
HOW PRESUMPTUOUS OF YOU, ELSIE: IMAGINING THAT YOU LIVE FOR YOURSELF ALONE.
THANK GOD SHE'S ALL RIGHT.
SHE SHOULD JUST FORGET THAT LOVER...
...AND MARRY DR. HILLS, IF YOU ASK ME!
I QUITE AGREE.
I QUITE AGREE.

PWEET
THIS IS SUDDEN. THEN AGAIN, IT ALWAYS IS. I'LL GRAB MY COAT.
B-DUM
LET'S GET OUT OF THIS TOWN! RIGHT NOW!
EDGAR!?
BAM
ARE YOU CROSS ABOUT SOME-THING?
DID YOU SAY GOODBYE TO THE WOMAN WITH THE GARDEN?
B-DUM
B-DUM
B-DUM
EDGAR
WHAT IS IT?
WHAT'S WRONG?
B-DUM
B-DUM
B-DUM

I HEAR SHE PASSED, THREE YEARS LATER, OF ILLNESS.

THINKING EVERY DAY OF THAT GENTLE SOUL
SHE WAS THE CITIZEN OF A FARAWAY LAND THAT FLOATED IN A DREAM

THAT SHE DISBANDED THE CHOIR. THAT SHE PASSED EACH DAY SILENTLY WATCHING THE FLOWERS AND THINKING.

I HEAR THAT WHEN THE DOCTOR ASKED HER ABOUT THE CASTLE, SHE MERELY SMILED AND SAID NOTHING.

I LIVE IN A GARDEN OF ROSES

BECOMING HUMAN WAS BEYOND HER CAPACITY.

SONGS OF LOVE FOREVER ON MY LIPS
PERHAPS SHE WAS A FAIRY BY BIRTH.

END OF CHAPTER 6

FIRST PUBLISHED IN **WEEKLY SHÓJO COMIC**, VOLUME 10, NO. 37 (JUNE 7TH, 1975)

CHAPTER 7

HOLMES' HAT

!?
TMP

LONDON, 1934

AH! HOLD THAT BUS!

OH MY.
LOOK AT HIS HAIR.
WHISPER WHISPER
WHISPER WHISPER
HE LOOKS LIKE A WOMAN.
SEEMS A BIT OLD FOR SUCH THINGS.

A SHERLOCK HOLMES' HAT, EH?
HM ...?
YES.
SUCH LONG HAIR. ARE YOU A HUMAN?
NO. I'M A WIZARD!
YES.
I SEE IT.
YOU HAVE A WIZARD'S EYES.
MR. ORBIN! YOU... YOU WANT ME TO *CUT YOUR HAIR!?*
THAT'S RIGHT!
HACK AWAY, BARBER!
TA TA, LAD.
BYE
HM. STRANGE KID.
VRNNN
DECKED OUT IN HIS GRAY TARTAN SUIT.
A WIZARD'S EYES, EH?
WELL, TODAY THE WIZARD HANGS UP HIS WAND.

CUT YOUR HAIR, JOHN ORBIN!
BUT MACK, YOU KNOW LONG HAIR MAKES ONE MORE SENSITIVE TO THE SUPERNATURAL.
MR. GERSON TOLD ME HIS PLANS FOR A NEW MAGAZINE. I'D LIKE YOU TO CONTRIBUTE.
BUT, MACK--
ORBIN. YOU'RE NOT GETTING ANY YOUNGER.
I HEAR CHRABASZCZ SENDS ISOLDE WHITE ROSES EVERY DAY.
SPOO!
THE TIME HAS COME TO CLOSE THE PORTAL TO THE PATH OF DREAMS.
THE OLD TIME HAS PASSED.
W-WELL? WHAT DO YOU THINK?
FINE. IN FACT, IT'S QUITE GOOD.
SNIP SNIP SNIP
FOR EXAMPLE, TO DRAW OUT
AN UNSEEN PRESENCE IN A DARK ROOM
TO SUMMON FORTH A DEMON.
OR TO PLACE A BOWL OF BLOOD IN A PENTACLE
ADONAI

I'M NOT ONE TO COMPLAIN ABOUT A MAN'S CHOICE OF PROFESSION.
I SIMPLY REFUSE TO MARRY A MAN WITH LONG HAIR.
SUCH LOVELY WHITE ROSES, MISS ISOLDE.
TAXI
YES, THEY'RE FROM CASEY CHRABASZCZ.
NOW WHAT'S THIS ABOUT GUESTS THIS EVENING?

JOHN ORBIN! YOU FINALLY DID IT!
RIGHT! OFF TO MR. GERSON'S PLACE!
MY POOR DEMONS
CRUSHED WITH EVERY TURN OF THE WHEELS.
FORGIVE ME, FRIENDS! BUT I MUST WED ISOLDE!
WELL, WELL! IF IT ISN'T JOHN ORBIN!
CHRABASZCZ!
I WASN'T EXPECTING *YOU!*
I'D HEARD YOU'D GONE OFF TO LOCH NESS TO SEARCH FOR THE MONSTER!
MISS ISOLDE!! THE GUESTS ARE MR. MACK, MR. CHRABASZCZ...
...AND MR. JOHN ORBIN!
BUT LISTEN TO THIS! MR. ORBIN HAS *CUT HIS HAIR!!*
HE HAS *WHAT!?*

OH, BUT I'M CERTAIN HE REMEMBERS!
BUT...
...THAT WAS SIX YEARS AGO!
I WILL IF YOU CUT YOUR HAIR.
ISOLDE! ISOLDE! WILL YOU MARRY ME?
ON THAT DAY, HE CHOSE HIS DEMONS OVER ME!
THAT I CANNOT DO.
ISOLDE! ISOLDE!
LOOK AT THIS! CUT IT CLEAN OFF, EH, ORBIN?
YES, SIR. I'VE DECIDED TO SETTLE DOWN, YOU SEE.
I'M TOO OLD TO HAVE TIME FOR SUCH PURSUITS ANYMORE.
I HEARD YOU DREW YOUR ONE HUNDRED AND NINETY-NINTH PENTACLE! DID THE DEMON EVER SHOW?
FLUMP!
MISS ...
THE REASON I BROUGHT YOU TWO HERE THIS EVENING IS TO TALK ABOUT MY NEW MAGAZINE, THE WEIRD & THE FANTASTIC.
BACK OFF, YOU PHONY NECROMANCER!
PZTT!
HMPH! HE HAS DESIGNS ON ISOLDE! HIM AND HIS FAKE MAGIC!

WOOF WOOF WOOF
WHAT WAS THAT!?
SKRSH SKRSH SKRSH
AHHHHH!!
WOOF WOOF
IS IT A BUR-GLAR!?
A BURGLAR!?
BURGLAR!!

THAT GRAY DOUGLAS TARTAN SUIT!
WHA--!?
WHY, YOU'RE THE--!
YOU KNOW THIS BOY!?
WHAT IN BLAZES ARE YOU DOING HERE!?

MY MATE BET I COULDN'T DO IT. I WAITED TILL DARK SO I WOULDN'T BE CAUGHT.
A BET!?
WH... BU...
I SEE THE WIZARD HAS CUT HIS HAIR.
AND WHAT ARE *YOU* DOING HERE?

NO
PAT
WELL--
I WAS CLIMBING THE TREE.

EH-HEM
THIS IS NONE OF YOUR BUSINESS!

JUST A BIT OF CHILDISH MISCHIEF. AHH, ISOLDE! YOUR BEAUTY IS THAT OF A NYMPH, AN ANTHOUSAI OF THE WHITE ROSES I SEND YOU.

YOU MUST BE CHILLED TO THE BONE. DO HAVE A CUP OF TEA WITH US.

DO YOU KNOW WHY HE CUT HIS HAIR?
NO.
BUT I KNOW HE MISSED HIS CHANCE TO GIVE YOU THE ROSES HE BROUGHT.

WELL, HE KEPT ME WAITING SIX YEARS. HE CAN SQUIRM A BIT LONGER.

YOU'RE A FRIEND OF MR. ORBIN? SO NICE TO MEET YOU...
EDGAR.

SO DID YOU WIN YOUR BET?
I'M AFRAID NOT. I WAS CAUGHT BEFORE I GOT TO THE TOP.

FRIEND!? I NEVER SAW HIM BEFORE THIS MORNING!
THE... THE...THE UNBRIDLED CHEEK OF THAT BRAT...!
TSK TSK. LOOKS LIKE YOUR ROSES ARE FOR NAUGHT, ORBIN.

TH--THEY WON'T BE FOR NAUGHT!
LATER I'LL DRIVE THE BRAT HOME AND TELL HIS PARENTS WHAT HE'S BEEN UP TO!

BLAST IT!

SHHH

SHHH

SO, DADDY, WHAT BRINGS THESE GENTLEMEN HERE THIS EVENING?
OUR NEW MAGAZINE, *THE WEIRD & THE FANTASTIC!*
IT'S SURE TO FLY OFF THE SHELVES.
WITH THE HELP OF THESE TWO FINE MEN, OF COURSE!

THAT SOUNDS FUN, DOESN'T IT, JAMES?
HARDLY, MISS ISOLDE. I'M DEATHLY AFRAID OF GHOSTS.

GHOSTS ARE NOTHING TO BE AFRAID OF!
GHOSTS ARE FUN PRECISELY BECAUSE THEY'RE SCARY!

HM!

I'LL HAVE YOU KNOW YOU ARE SPEAKING TO LONDON'S GREATEST MEDIUM!

CASEY CHRABASZCZ, AT YOUR SERVICE!

MAN IS NATURALLY DRAWN TO THE FRIGHTENING. OUR NEW MAGAZINE SHOULD APPEAL TO THAT PSYCHOLOGY!

HAVE YOU EVER SEEN ONE?

SO JUST HOW FRIGHTENING *ARE* THESE GHOSTS?

SNORT!

SO *THE WEIRD & THE FANTASTIC* IS A SCIENTIFIC JOURNAL?

HM!

MINE IS AN AUTHENTICALLY SCIENTIFIC STUDY OF THE SPIRIT REALM!

DEMONS ARE ORBIN'S BUSINESS!

AH, SO YOU SUMMON DEMONS, EH?

SPIRITS ABIDE IN ALL THINGS. FLOWERS, INSECTS, BIRDS, DOGS, AND OF COURSE, MAN. ALL LIVING THINGS.
EHEM
WHEN THE SPIRIT DEPARTS, ALL THAT REMAINS IS LIFELESS FLESH.
I SEE YOU KNOW NOTHING OF SPIRITS.

OF ALL THE --!

MR. ORBIN, YOUR FRIEND SEEMS TO BE A GREAT FAN OF YOURS.
WELL, I NEVER!
OH, MY SIDES HURT!
ISOLDE

ALL HUMANS HAVE SPIRITS!

HAH!
THERE'S NO SUCH THING IN ME.

THIS IS RICH!
HA HA HA HA
BUT I AM NOT A HUMAN.

SURE! AND "I AM NOT HUMAN" WOULD BE A MARVELOUS TITLE, WOULDN'T IT?
NO! IT'S QUARTERLY, AND WE'RE AIMING FOR A CIRCULATION OF FOUR THOUSAND. A THRILL A MINUTE, EH, ORBIN?
IS THE MAGAZINE TO BE A *MOCKERY!?*

I SEE.
SENSATIONALISM! MYSTERY AND THRILLS! THAT'S THE TICKET!
WHY STOP AT FOUR THOUSAND? LET'S AIM FOR FIVE!
TIMES ARE HARD!
WHAT THE PEOPLE NEED IS ENTER-TAINMENT!

I-- I'LL BE WRITING ALL THAT UP IN MY OWN BOOK IN DUE TIME.
I-- I'M NOT GETTING ANY YOUNGER, YOU KNOW!
HEAR, HEAR.
TIME TO SETTLE DOWN. FIND STEADY WORK.
MY, MY. LOOK AT OUR MR. ORBIN, TALKING ABOUT WORK!
TILL NOW
YOU'VE DONE NOTHING BUT RUN AROUND
CHASING KILKENNY CATS AND CHESHIRE CATS
MAN-DRAKES AND CY-CLOPES
NORTH AND SOUTH, OVER LAND AND SEA.
HA HA HA HA HA HA
ENGLAND... THIS TREASURE TROVE OF SONG AND LEGEND
HM
WHY, I JUST SUMMONED A SPIRIT NOT TWO MONTHS AGO.
A CHILD, YOU KNOW. THE MOTHER BURST INTO TEARS.
WHY IS HE...

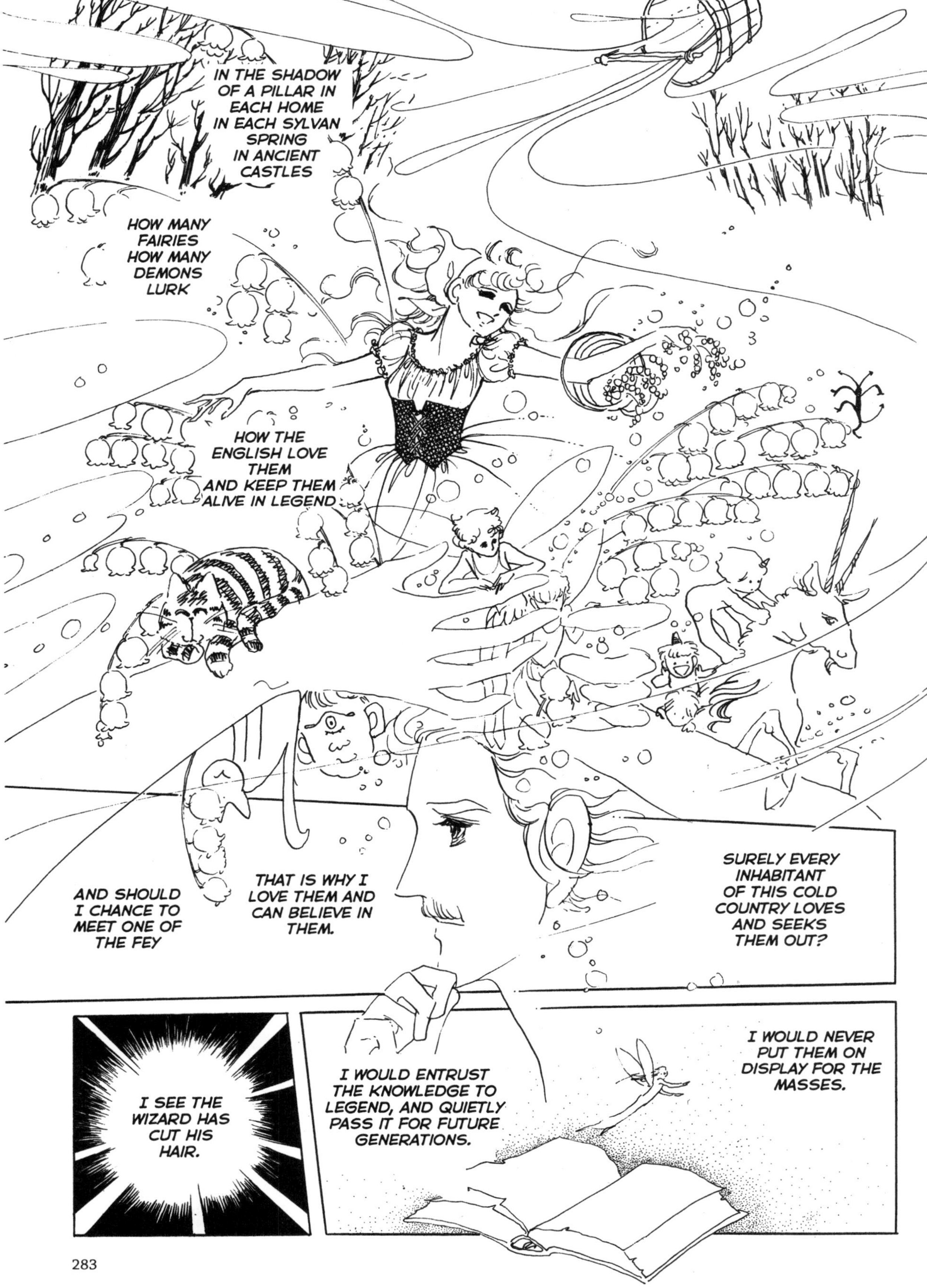
IN THE SHADOW OF A PILLAR IN EACH HOME IN EACH SYLVAN SPRING IN ANCIENT CASTLES
HOW MANY FAIRIES HOW MANY DEMONS LURK
HOW THE ENGLISH LOVE THEM AND KEEP THEM ALIVE IN LEGEND
SURELY EVERY INHABITANT OF THIS COLD COUNTRY LOVES AND SEEKS THEM OUT?
THAT IS WHY I LOVE THEM AND CAN BELIEVE IN THEM.
AND SHOULD I CHANCE TO MEET ONE OF THE FEY
I WOULD NEVER PUT THEM ON DISPLAY FOR THE MASSES.
I WOULD ENTRUST THE KNOWLEDGE TO LEGEND, AND QUIETLY PASS IT FOR FUTURE GENERATIONS.
I SEE THE WIZARD HAS CUT HIS HAIR.

ORBIN! WHO IS THIS... THIS CHILD!?

HM!? COME AGAIN!?
JUST LOOK AT THAT CONDESCENDING EXPRESSION!

I'M NOT CONDESCENDING.
I'M MERELY SAYING THAT NECROMANCY
IS MORE OFTEN THAN NOT SIMPLE SELF-HYPNOSIS.

I AM A TRUE NECROMANCER!!
CHRABASZCZ!
I HAVE THE GIFT!!

THEN SHOW US, CHRABASZCZ!
YES...
WHAT!?
YES! LET'S HAVE A SÉANCE! AND IF A SPIRIT APPEARS, WE'LL MAKE THIS THE COVER STORY OF THE FIRST ISSUE!

A GHOST JOINS THE PLANNING SESSION!
WHY, WE'LL SELL SIX THOUSAND!

SIX THOUSAND!
COVER STORY!
FAME!

FAME!
I ADMIT IT DOES SOUND EXCITING.
WELL, I'M GAME, MR. CHRA-BASZCZ.
THERE GOES JAMES.
I'VE NO MIND TO MEET A GHOST!
AND WITH THAT I BID YOU ALL A GOOD EVENING!

I AM A MEDIUM, AND I AM GOING TO SUMMON FORTH A MEMBER OF YOUR FAMILY.

NOW WHERE ARE YOU OFF TO, LAD?
YOUR PRESENCE IS ESSENTIAL, EDGAR!

SPIRITS MAKE THEIR PRESENCE KNOWN IN MANY WAYS. BY BLOWING OUT A CANDLE, FOR EXAMPLE.

OR BREAKING A CUP. TURNING THE PAGE OF A BOOK. A RUSTLING SOUND.

DO NOT BE ALARMED.

AND HERE'S OUR CANDLE. SILENCE, PLEASE.

NOW. LET'S ALL HOLD HANDS.

EDGAR.

TELL ME THE NAME OF A DECEASED RELATIVE.

I TELL YOU I SHALL SUMMON THEM!
....

EDGAR, NOT SOME DISTANT ANCESTOR. SOMEONE CLOSE TO YOU.
I'M CERTAIN IT'S FUTILE, BUT...
I WAS RAISED BY A WOMAN NAMED OLD HANNAH.
SHE DIED NEARLY TWO CEN-TURIES AGO.

WHEN DID SHE PASS?
AT THE AGE OF THIR-TEEN.

HER NAME?

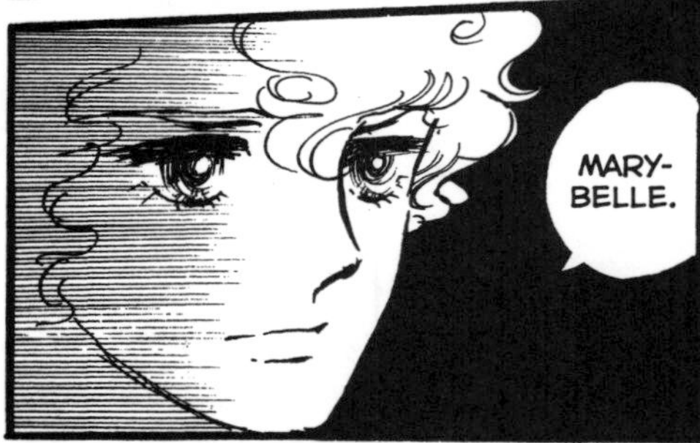
MARY-BELLE.

THEN SUMMON MY LITTLE SISTER.

QUIET. DO NOT LET GO OF YOUR NEIGHBOR'S HAND!
WITH MY POWER I SHALL BRING HER FORTH.
WHEN SHE ARRIVES, YOU SHALL ASK HER QUES-TIONS. IS THAT CLEAR...? IS THAT CLEAR...?

TMP
CASEY CHRABASZCZ
KYAHH!?
FTT

WHERE IS HE!?
I DON'T KNOW! OUTSIDE PERHAPS!?
HE'S GONE!
CHRABASZCZ!
CHRA-BASZCZ!
FASHH!
CASEY CHRABASZCZ!
OF COURSE NOT!
DO YOU SUP-POSE HE REALLY ...?
SOME MEDIUM HE IS!
I'M SURE HE'S JUST PLAYING A NASTY TRICK ON US.

CHRABASZCZ!?
TMP
TMP
MASTER GERSON! UPSTAIRS!
THERE'S SOMEONE IN THE LIBRARY!
BAM!
Y... YOU...
CHR-ABA-SZCZ!
BAM!
LOOK! THEY CAME THROUGH THE TRANSOM WINDOW!
BUT IT'S TOO SMALL! ONLY A CHILD COULD...
WH-- WHY, WE'VE BEEN BURGLED! THE CABINETS ARE ALL OPEN!
WAH!
WHAT'S BEEN TAKEN!? THERE'S NOTHING BUT OUT-OF-PRINT BOOKS IN HERE!

HE CAN'T HAVE GONE FAR!
NO! NO...!
ISN'T HE UPSTAIRS? DID YOU FIND CHRABASZCZ?
WHERE'S EDGAR!?
JUST A MOMENT, JOHN ORBIN.
THIS IS HARDLY THE TIME! CHRABASZCZ HAS DISAPPEARED! AND THE BOY IS A DEMON!!
TELL ME WHY YOU BROUGHT THESE FLOWERS.
JOHN!
JOHN ORBIN!!

YOU HAVE A WIZARD'S EYES.

DID YOU GET THE BOOK?
YES. HERE IT IS. EVERYONE WAS DOWNSTAIRS, SO IT WAS EASY.

OH. TOO BAD.
IT'S NOT ABOUT OUR CLAN.
IT'S JUST A LEGEND ABOUT IMMORTALS.

WHAT!? AFTER ALL THAT WORK!?

WHAT WERE YOU TALKING ABOUT?
NOTHING. WE JUST HAD TEA.

SO WHILE I WAS SQUEEZING THROUGH WINDOWS, YOU WERE SIPPING TEA.

YOUR SERVICE IS APPRECIATED.

WHERE SHALL WE SPEND CHRISTMAS?

IN LONDON.

END OF CHAPTER 7
FIRST PUBLISHED IN
SPECIAL EDITION SHÓJO COMIC,
NOVEMBER 1975

CHAPTER 8

A SINGLE WEEK

ALAN
UNH ...
I FEEL TERRIBLE ALREADY.
I DON'T *WANT* TO GO.
DO YOU WANT ME TO FALL ILL?
YOU *KNOW* THE DAMP DOESN'T AGREE WITH ME.
WE CAN'T BE LATE FOR OUR AP-POINTMENT.
HM? OH, IT'S RAINING. WHAT'S THE RUSH TO LEAVE?
I'LL BE BACK IN A WEEK.
ALONE!?
THEN STAY HERE BY YOURSELF.
....
STAY OUT OF TROUBLE.
BAM

I CAN JUMP ON THE BED ALL I WANT!
I CAN DO WHATEVER I WANT!
ONE WEEK! A WEEK WITHOUT EDGAR'S PESTERING!
HE THINKS I CAN'T BE TRUSTED ON MY OWN.
I CAN RUN AROUND THE HOUSE IN MY NIGHTGOWN!
TMP
TMP
TMP
TMP
ONE WEEK. TODAY'S MONDAY.
What would we have to drink
Monday's child is fair of face
Tuesday's child is full of grace
WHEEEE!
Rain rain go away ......
NOW, IF ONLY
THIS RAIN WOULD STOP.

TUESDAY
SPLASH
Rub-a dub-dub
Alan in a tub
Who do you think they b
WHAT'S THAT?
THANK YOU.
WHERE DID YOU COME FROM?
I'M STAYING AT THE HOUSE OVER THERE WITH MY COUSIN.
DO YOU LIVE ON THE OTHER SIDE OF THE RIVER?
YES.
AHHH
FLIP

I DIDN'T MEAN TO MAKE YOU CRY.
BUT YOU LOOKED LIKE A DOLL
SO I WONDERED IF YOU LOOK LIKE A DOLL UNDER YOUR SKIRT, TOO.
I'M SORRY. PLEASE DON'T CRY.
WH-WH-WH-WHAT DO THINK YOU'RE DOING!?
LOOKING UNDER A GIRL'S SKIRT!
WAHH
SMACK
JUNE!
KAREN! WHAT'S WRONG?
TMP
TMP
TMP
WAHHH
JUNE!

SAY!
YOU'RE THE ONE WHO WAS FRESH WITH KAREN YESTERDAY!
PLINK
Georgie Porgie pudding & pie kissed the girls & made them Cry
CLOP
KAREN!
MY...
SO YOU MUST BE HER COUSIN. PLEASE GIVE HER THESE
WITH APOLOGIES FROM ME.
BYE.
HALLO!
KAREN WANTED TO THANK YOU FOR YESTERDAY'S FLOWERS.
ISN'T THAT RIGHT, KAREN?

HOW LOVELY! LET'S HAVE A PICNIC THERE TOMORROW!
YES! I HOPE THE WEATHER HOLDS.
YOUR NAME'S ALAN?
OH, WE'RE ALL THE SAME AGE!
HAVE YOU ALWAYS LIVED HERE?
WE HAVEN'T BEEN TO THE OTHER SIDE OF THE RIVER YET.
RIGHT, KAREN?
RIGHT, KAREN?
THERE'S A BIG TREE IN FULL BLOOM RIGHT NOW. WANT TO GO AND SEE?
SEE YOU TOMORROW!
YOU DID ALL THE TALKING, JUNE! IT'S NOT FAIR!
THAT'S RIDICULOUS. YOU SHOULD JUST SPEAK UP MORE! OR DON'T YOU LIKE ALAN?
I THINK HE'S GRAND!
BUT... BUT I MET HIM FIRST!
DAREKA
I MET HIM FIRST! AND HE...HE KISSED ME, TOO!
NYAA!
HMPH!
And now Good night
Our play is done

SEE YOU LATER, AUNTIE!
WE'RE HAVING A PICNIC, MUMMY!
MY! AREN'T YOU TWO ALL DRESSED UP!
SPLASH
I'LL GO FETCH SOME WATER!
LET'S SING SONGS THAT BEGIN WITH EACH LETTER.
SUCH DARLING FLOWERS!
ALPHABET COOKIES!
I BAKED THEM MYSELF.
....
JUST WHAT?
YOUR DRESS IS SO STYLISH. IT REALLY SUITS YOU.
REALLY?
WHAT'S WRONG, KAREN? AREN'T YOU ENJOYING OUR PICNIC?
OH, IT'S NOT THAT. IT'S JUST...

I LOOK NICER THAN JUNE?
YES.
YOU MAY KISS ME IF YOU LIKE?
OH?
LOOK! A BABY BIRD!
WHERE COULD IT HAVE COME FROM?
THERE'S A NEST UP THERE. WE'VE GOT TO PUT IT BACK.
OH, ME TOO!
JUNE! THAT'S NOT VERY LADYLIKE! YOU MIGHT FALL!
I'M FINE!
HA HA. I'M A TOMBOY, YOU KNOW. SURPRISED?
I AM.
DO YOU PREFER MODEST GIRLS LIKE KAREN?
OH, SO MANY CHICKS!
YES.
DO YOU LIKE KAREN?
I LIKE YOU, TOO.
DO YOU!?
JUNE!
ALAN!

WHAT DID YOU SAY!?

LA DEE DA
LA LA

DID YOU GIRLS HAVE FUN?
YES, MUMMY.
WE HAD A LOVELY TIME.

When the girls Come out to play
Kissed the girls made them Cry

BUT HE SAID HE PREFERRED ME! HE KISSED ME!
WHAT!? BUT HE SAID THE SAME THING TO ME AND KISSED ME!

THIS IS JUNE'S HORSE.
CAN YOU RIDE?
SURE! SUCH A PRETTY HORSE.
BUT SHE'S A BIT TEMPERAMENTAL.

PLUNK

GOOD MORNING, ALAN!!

NEIGH!
PRAPPP
CLOP
CLOP
CLOP
HUFF
NOW, KAREN!
THIS IS A FINE HORSE!
FLUMP
HA HA
THAT'S WHAT YOU GET FOR TAKING US FOR FOOLS!
YOU RAKE, YOU! USING THE SAME LINES ON BOTH OF US!
AHHH !!
ALAN!?
ALAN!?
ALAN!!

HEE HEE
AH HA HA HA
WHY, YOU LITTLE--!!
AH!

ALAN! CAN YOU HEAR ME!? OH, NO! HE'S DEAD!
NO!
IT CAN'T BE! ALAN! OH, WHAT SHOULD WE DO!?
I'M SO SORRY, ALAN!

BUT WHICH OF US DO YOU *REALLY* LIKE?
BOTH!
OH, YOU'RE INCORRIGIBLE!

HA HA

THE WEEK FLEW BY, THANKS TO THOSE TWO.
SUNDAY! ONE WEEK. EDGAR COMES HOME TOMORROW.

WE'RE GOING TO CHURCH TOMORROW. WILL YOU BE THERE?
NO.

SO WE WON'T SEE YOU UNTIL MONDAY.
SEE YOU THEN!
BYE!

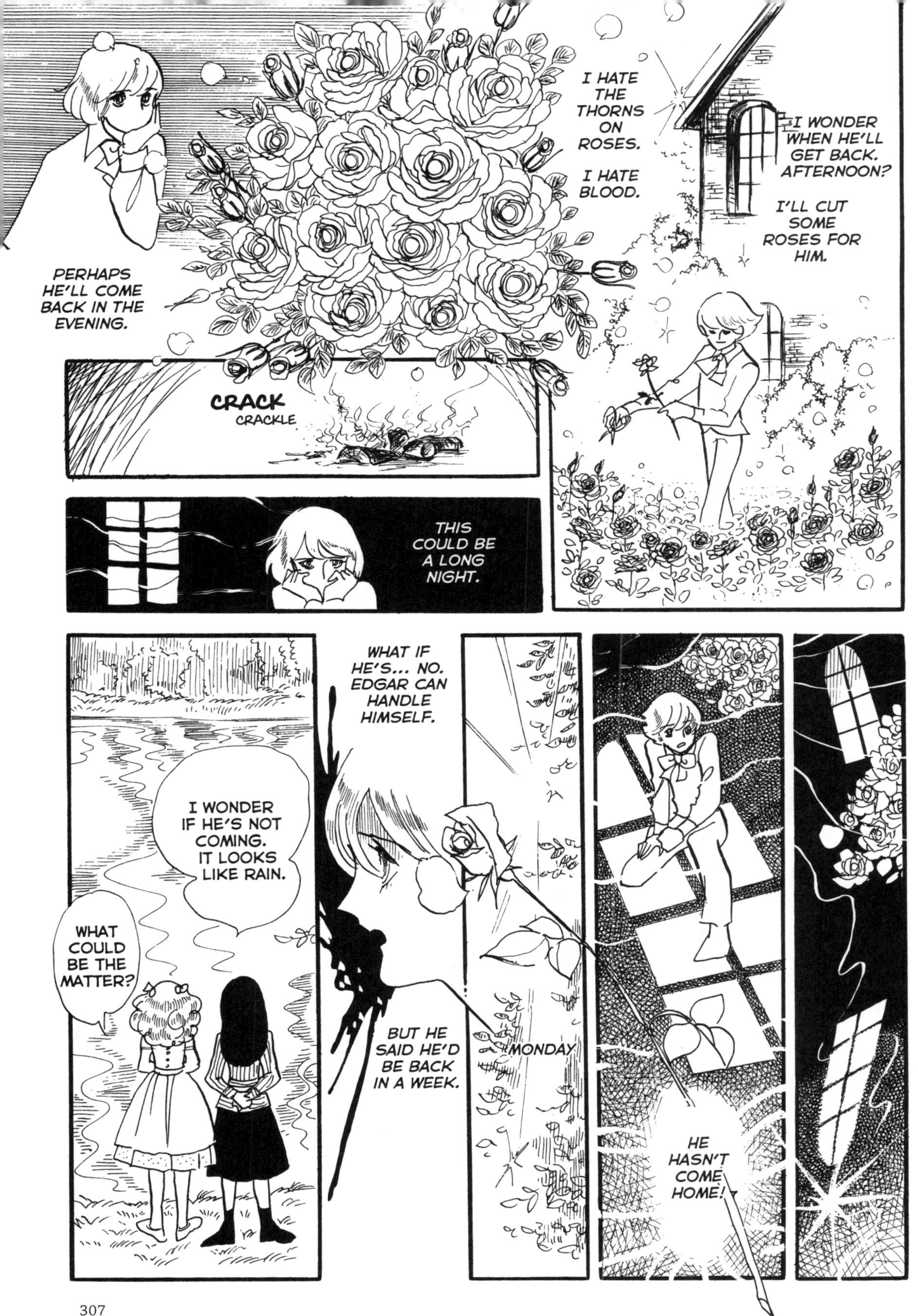
I HATE THE THORNS ON ROSES.
I HATE BLOOD.
I WONDER WHEN HE'LL GET BACK. AFTERNOON?
I'LL CUT SOME ROSES FOR HIM.
PERHAPS HE'LL COME BACK IN THE EVENING.
CRACK
CRACKLE
THIS COULD BE A LONG NIGHT.
WHAT IF HE'S... NO. EDGAR CAN HANDLE HIMSELF.
I WONDER IF HE'S NOT COMING. IT LOOKS LIKE RAIN.
WHAT COULD BE THE MATTER?
BUT HE SAID HE'D BE BACK IN A WEEK.
MONDAY
HE HASN'T COME HOME!

HE SAID HE LIVES ON THE OTHER SIDE OF THE RIVER.
YES.
SOME-THING'S GOTTEN INTO US.
THE MORE I THINK ABOUT IT...
WAS HE... REAL?
HE WAS REAL.
DON'T YOU THINK HE'S SORT OF LIKE A WOODLAND FAIRY? WE ONLY KNOW HIS NAME.
WELL, HE'S SURE TO COME HOME TODAY. HE SAID ONE WEEK.
RAIN ...
I HATE THE DAMP!
BAM
CRACK
I KNOW HE'LL COME HOME TODAY!
KLAK

DID YOU MISS ME?

YES.

END OF CHAPTER 8

FIRST PUBLISHED IN **SPECIAL EDITION SHŌJO COMIC**, DECEMBER 1975

CHAPTER 9

EDITH

O TURN YE, TURN YE, WHEEL OF TIME IN TIME FOR LIFE'S REBIRTH. YE WINDS OF TIME; YE SIGHS
YE DREAMS; O RACE YE, RACE YE T'WARDS YON STILL UNSEEN HORIZON SHINING LIKE THE DAWN

SAY, WHAT'S WITH THE FANCY RIG? YOU--
EDIE!
HEY, EDIE!
AH! I AM SO SORRY!
I THOUGHT YOU WERE A FRIEND OF MINE.
THINK NOTHING OF IT.
KREE
OH! ED! OVER HERE!

YES, THE USUAL BEANS, PLEASE.
OH?
OH! I'M SORRY. I THOUGHT YOU WERE A FRIEND OF MINE.
KREE

HM?
E...
'ULLO, EDITH. THE USUAL COFFEE BEANS?

NOW IT MAKES SENSE.
HA! I THOUGHT THAT GIRL WAS YOU.
SHE HAS MY CURIOSITY PIQUED.

HUH! WE DO LOOK A BIT ALIKE.
BUT HIS FRIEND SEEMS A BIT SCATTER-BRAINED.

IT SEEMS YOUR FRIEND HAS ARRIVED.
CIAO!

I MEAN, WHO KNOWS? SHE MIGHT BE A DISTANT RELATION OF YOURS?
SHE REALLY DOES LOOK LIKE YOU.
HOW SO?
THE HAIR COLOR, THE EYE COLOR...
THE MAN CALLED HER "EDITH."
EDITH!
HULLO!
WELL! WE MEET AGAIN!
BAM!

YOU REMEMBERED! I'VE BEEN HOPING TO SEE YOU AGAIN.
REALLY? WHERE'S YOUR FRIEND TODAY?
ZOOSH

HIS NAME'S EDGAR. I'M ALAN. YOU LIVE NEARBY?
TWO STOPS FROM HERE.
ZOOSH
COME AGAIN?
TWO STOPS FROM HERE.

THE TUBE'S SO LOUD!
YOUR NAME'S EDITH, RIGHT?
YES, EDITH EVANS.
ZOOSH

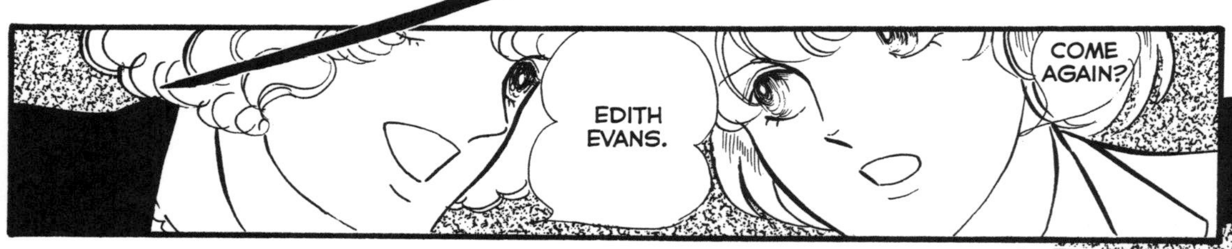
COME AGAIN?
EDITH EVANS.

ZOOSH

... DID...
... YOU HAVE A ... SISTER?
YES.

CHAR-LOTTE ... EVANS?

YES.
BUT SHE DIED WHEN I WAS FOUR.

FOOSH
SKREEE
ALAN?
T-TMP
TMP
I'M HOME.
EVANS ANTIQUES

HOW WAS SCHOOL TODAY, EDITH?
YEAH, I RAN INTO AN ODD BOY.
DID YOU?
HIS NAME'S ALAN.
SAY, HENRY, IS EVANS A WEIRD NAME?
IT'S A FINE NAME. OUR ANCESTORS WERE EARLS.
WE MAY BE HUMBLE ANTIQUES DEALERS TODAY...
...BUT BACK IN THE DAY, YOU'D HAVE BEEN A PRINCESS!
SO WHERE'S OUR CASTLE, ROGER?
THIS IS OUR CASTLE!
A SILVER CANDELABRA, A SILVER SHIP
VELVET GLOVES, A CHINESE VASE, A TURKISH SCREEN!
ROGER! ROGER!
AN OLD DOLL, A MUSIC BOX... AND ALL FOR OUR LITTLE PRINCESS!
MAY I REMIND YOU THAT YOU ARE SURROUNDED BY *FRAGILE ANTIQUES!?*

WHO?
THAT GIRL! GUESS WHO SHE IS!
BAM
EDITH EVANS! THE ONE WHO LOOKS LIKE YOU! SHE'S HER SISTER!
THE SISTER OF CHARLOTTE! THE GIRL WE KILLED!
IT WAS YOU WHO SET THAT FIRE!!
AND I'D HAVE KILLED THEM ALL.
POOR KID.
WE LET THEM LIVE BECAUSE WE KNOW THEY CAN DO NO HARM.
WE BURNED THE MANOR AND THE PAINTINGS.

ALAN ...?
WHERE'S HE GONE OFF TO SO EARLY?
BEE-BEEP
STRATHFORD

ARTHUR! ARE YOU HOME!?

WELL, WELL.
ALAN.
WHAT BRINGS YOU HERE?

I'VE COME FOR THE PAINTING. THE ONE YOU SAID I COULD HAVE.
LAMBTON AMONG FLOWERS.
Y...YOU SAID THAT SINCE I SAVED IT FROM THE FLAMES...

IT'S UP-STAIRS.
STILL IN LONDON?
YES.
TELL EDGAR I'LL VISIT ONE OF THESE DAYS.
I'LL TELL HIM.
CHARLOTTE'S PAINTING.
SHE DIED FOR THIS.
'WHAT'S IT BEEN? TEN YEARS?
HELLO. WHO'S THAT?
THAT BOY'S BEEN STANDING JUST OUTSIDE THE GATE.
AH! HE'S RUN OFF!
IT'S YOUR FAULT FOR STARING LIKE A NINNY!
ALAN!?

I'M HOME.
WEL-COME HOME.
WHY, HELLO, EDITH.
OH! GOOD DAY, MR. ORBIN.

VRRRNN

IT WAS ALAN.
WHAT'S HE UP TO?

WHAT A THING TO SAY ABOUT ONE OF OUR BEST CUSTOM-ERS!
THAT OLD COOT'S BACK AGAIN. WHAT'S HE UP TO NOW?

ROG-ER!
NOW THEN, MR. ORBIN, MAY I INTEREST YOU THIS SET OF SPOONS?

?

UM... CAN I HELP YOU?
N-NO.

THANK YOU, MR. ORBIN. DO COME AGAIN.
HM?

HOW WAS SCHOOL TODAY? READY FOR TEA?
I'LL GRIND THE COFFEE BEANS.
IS SOMEONE THERE?
IT'S NOTHING.
ALAN!
DID YOU COME TO SEE ME?
EDITH.
ALAN!
WE'RE ABOUT TO HAVE TEA. DO JOIN US.

WHAT'S THIS?
I WANT YOU TO HAVE IT.
A PAINTING? FOR ME? BUT WHY?
IT...
IT BELONGED TO CHARLOTTE. SHE WAS QUITE FOND OF IT.
YOU SHOULD HAVE IT.
UM ...
DID YOU KNOW CHARLOTTE?
YEAH.
I BARELY REMEMBER HER MYSELF.
BYE.
OH!
WAIT!
ALAN !!
THANK YOU!

IT'S SO STRANGE. I CAN BARELY REMEMBER CHARLOTTE'S FACE...
...AND YET OUR PATHS ARE INTERSECTING AGAIN. WE'RE BOUND BY SISTERHOOD.

LAMBTON AMONG FLOWERS
APRIL 15, 1889
ARTHUR THOMAS QUENTIN
IT'S QUITE OLD.

TEA'S READY, EDITH.
BE RIGHT THERE.

ALAN... SUCH A CURIOUS BOY. I KNOW NOTHING ABOUT YOU...
...AND YET IT FEELS LIKE WE'RE BECOMING FRIENDS. SUCH A PRETTY PICTURE.

WHA--
HEE HEE. ISN'T IT LOVELY? A FRIEND GAVE IT TO ME.

ROGER!

LAMBTON! JUST AS I THOUGHT!
WHAT ARE YOU DOING!?
THAT CURSED ORBIN!

WELL, HE CAN HAVE IT BACK!!
THAT'S MY PAINTING, ROGER! IT'S MINE!

HOW COULD YOU!? A FRIEND GAVE IT TO ME!

ROG-ER!
HAVE YOU LOST YOUR MIND? STEALING FROM YOUR LITTLE SISTER?

SMACK
LISTEN, HENRY. YOU DON'T KNOW! THIS FELLOW ORBIN IS--

HAVE YOU FORGOT-TEN OUR VOW?

ROGER IS HORRID!
A FRIEND GAVE IT TO ME.
THERE, THERE. IT'S A FINE PAINTING.
NOW BE A LOVE AND WIPE THOSE TEARS AND GO WASH YOUR HANDS.
I'LL GIVE ROGER A PIECE OF MY MIND.

FOURTEEN YEARS AGO, WHEN WE LOST OUR PARENTS, WE SIBLINGS VOWED TO RAISE TO RAISE EDITH OURSELVES, PROVIDING HER NEEDS AND SHOWERING HER WITH LOVE. AND SO, WE HAVE.

AND SOMEDAY WE'LL BUY EDITH HER CASTLE.

NOW THEN. I'VE ARRANGED A DEAL WITH A FENCE FROM CHERBOURG. TAKE A GANDER.
WE'LL MAKE A PRETTY PENNY ON THIS ONE.

BUT LOOK AT YOU. ACTING LIKE A BRAT. ORBIN IS A VALUABLE CUSTOMER.
CHARLOTTE'S DEATH WAS AN ACCIDENT. IT'S BEEN TEN YEARS. MOVE ON.

WAIT, SINCE WHEN DOES EDITH--!?
I'M DYING OF ENVY.
HUH? UM... YEAH. I DID.
BUT...I DIDN'T KNOW ABOUT YOU.
DID YOU USED TO LIVE IN OUR NEIGHBOR-HOOD?
WHAT A FUNNY QUES-TION. YES, I'M HAPPY.
ARE YOU... HAPPY?
OH, EDGAR? NEVER MIND EDGAR.
WHERE'S YOUR BLUE-EYED FRIEND?
I'M FAMOUS FOR MY COOKIES!
UM...
AND YOU?
IT'S LIKE HAVING TWO DADS. ROGER'S QUITE A COOK!
I DON'T HAVE PAR-ENTS...
...BUT I HAVE HENRY AND ROGER. THEY'RE MUCH OLDER THAN ME.

WELL, WELL.
WHAT'S EDITH DOING AT THIS HOUR?
NO IDEA. SHE'S BUSY IN THE KITCHEN.
ROGER!
THEN I'M GLAD I STAYED UP TO TWELVE WORKING ON THEM!!
PHEW
THEY'RE FABU-LOUS!
AH-HA.
HA HA! TRUTH BE TOLD, THESE ARE THE FIRST COOKIES I EVER MADE.
BUT THEY'RE WORTHY OF FAME, AREN'T THEY?

YOU KNOW, ARTHUR SAID...
LET'S STAY A WHILE!
...HE'D COME FROM STRATHFORD TO VISIT.
WHAT?
SO SOON?
IT'S TIME TO LEAVE LONDON.
SO WE'LL VISIT HIM INSTEAD.
...!
AND WHEN, EXACTLY, DID *YOU* VISIT STRATHFORD?

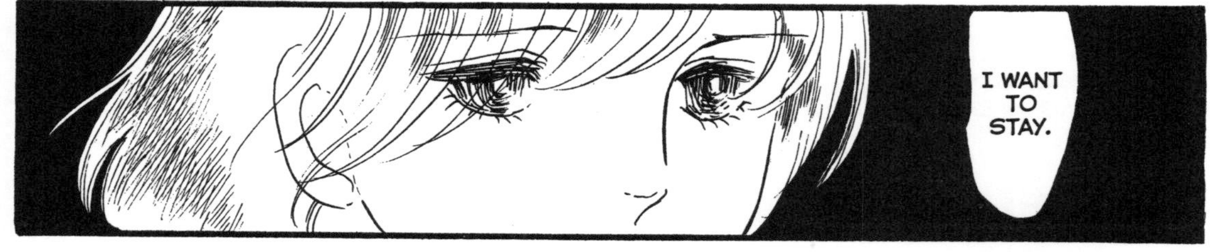

I AM!
I...
I LIKE BEING WITH HER.
SHE'S SO... SUNNY.
YOU'VE GOT IT WRONG.
YOU ARE TRYING TO COMPENSATE FOR FAILING TO SAVE CHARLOTTE.
THAT'S NOT TRUE!
WHEN SHE'S UNHAPPY, YOU'RE UNHAPPY.
YOU ARE WRACKED WITH GUILT.
I HATE TO BREAK IT TO YOU, BUT YOU JUST WANT TO PAY YOUR DEBT TO EDITH.
BUT...
YOU... CAN BE CRUEL.
WE'LL MOVE TO SUSSEX.

I WANT TO SPEND MORE TIME AT HER SIDE.
I WON'T GO TO SUSSEX.
GUILT... COMPENSATION... I DON'T KNOW MYSELF.
BUT...

I'M NOT GOING TO DO ANYTHING.
EDGAR ... YOU WOULDN'T...

LIAR!

EDGAR! IF YOU LAY A FINGER ON HER, I'LL... I'LL NEVER FORGIVE YOU!

I, JOHN ORBIN, WAS BORN IN THE YEAR 1900.

AND SO IT IS THAT I HAVE GROWN AND AGED ALONGSIDE THE TWENTIETH CENTURY.

I AM CURRENTLY SEVENTY-SIX.

THESE RECORDS CARRY A SCENT OF MAGIC.

THE RECORDS OF THE BOYS.

TRANSFER RECORDS FROM GABRIEL SWISS GYMNASIUM. THE PAINTINGS OF LAMBTON, LOST IN THE FIRE. MADAM LYDIA'S TALE. MARSHALL'S TALE. THEO'S TALE. EVANS' WILL.

WHERE IS HE NOW?

I WISH I COULD CATCH HIM, LIKE A BUTTERFLY, PRESS HIM BETWEEN THE PAGES OF A BOOK, AND LOCK THE BOOK AWAY IN A CABINET!

EVER SINCE THE NIGHT... THAT MAGICAL NIGHT IN 1934... I HAVE PURSUED HIM!

I REMEMBER YOU, MR. WIZARD.
I'M SURE YOU'VE FORGOT-TEN ME.
EDGAR... IS IT YOU?
YES...
I MUST BE GOING.

A DREAM?
WHAT A FOOL I AM. OF COURSE, IT WAS A DREAM.
HAVE YOU RUN INTO EDGAR SINCE THEN?
YOUR BLUE-EYED FRIEND? NO.

BLINK BLINK
PROMISE ME YOU'LL KEEP AWAY FROM EDGAR!
!?
BUT LISTEN!
WHA...
WHY DO YOU ASK? YOU'RE ACTING STRANGELY TODAY.
NO, I'M NOT.
EDITH.
OH-H-H, I SEE. YOU'RE AFRAID I'M GOING TO GO RUNNING INTO HIS ARMS, AREN'T YOU? YOU DON'T HAVE TO WORRY ABOUT THAT. NOW YOU PROMISE TO STAY AWAY FROM OTHER GIRLS! PINKIE SWEAR!
I WAS JUST ON MY WAY TO YOUR HOUSE.
OH! GOOD DAY, MR. ORBIN.
RING A RING A PINKIE
HA HA. IS THAT SO?
I'LL HAVE YOU KNOW EVEN I APPRE-CIATE THEIR VALUE!
AS ONE GROWS OLDER, ONE COMES TO APPRECIATE THEIR VALUE.
AND WE ARE GRATEFUL FOR YOUR PATRONAGE. SO, YOU LIKE OLD THINGS, DO YOU?

HERE. ISN'T IT LOVELY?

EDGAR!

YES, I HAVE AN OLD PAINTING. MORE THAN A HUNDRED YEARS OLD.
IT'S CALLED *LAMBTON AMONG FLOWERS* AND WAS PAINTED BY SOMEONE NAMED ARTHUR THOMAS QUENTIN.

HIS NAME'S ALAN, YOU KNOW.

AFTER ALL, IT'S FROM MY BOY-FRIEND!

EDITH! MAY I HAVE THIS PAINTING!?
OH, MY! I CAN'T GIVE YOU MY PAINTING!

EDGAR? YOU MEAN ALAN'S BLUE-EYED FRIEND?
HE'S **SHOWN** HIMSELF!
IF I KEEP AN EYE ON EDITH...
I'LL FIND HIM!

STEPS TO THE ROOF!
TMP
...THEY CERTAINLY HAVE SOME VALUABLE PIECES.
FOR HUMBLE ANTIQUE DEALERS...
HENRY, ROGER-- HAVE EITHER OF YOU SEEN MY HAT?
YOU'RE GOING OUT?
NO, BUT I'LL HELP YOU LOOK FOR IT WHEN I GET BACK.
BE SURE TO LOCK THE DOORS!
I WILL. BYE NOW.
WE'VE COME ACROSS A REAL FIND. WE'LL BE BACK BY ELEVEN.

BUT THE LITTLE KIDS KNEW IT WAS THE WOLF.
"THOU ART NOT OUR MOTHER," CRIED THEY.
"SHE HAS A SOFT, PLEASANT VOICE, BUT THY VOICE IS ROUGH!"
CLAK
IT WAS NOT LONG BEFORE SOMEONE KNOCKED AT THE HOUSE-DOOR AND CRIED, "OPEN THE DOOR, DEAR CHILDREN; YOUR MOTHER IS HERE, AND HAS BROUGHT SOMETHING BACK WITH HER FOR EACH OF YOU."
"OUR MOTHER HAS NOT BLACK FEET LIKE THEE."
VRRNNN
I WONDER WHAT THESE TWO ARE UP TO?
I'M SURE THEY WON'T MIND ME TAGGING ALONG IN THE TRUNK.

RUMBLE
RUMBLE
RUMBLE
RUMBLE
I SMELL THE OCEAN.
WELL, I FOUND EDITH'S HAT.

HALLO?
WE'VE BEEN DRIVING AN HOUR OR MORE.

FOOOOSH
SKREE

WE'RE RIGHT ON TIME. LET'S GO.

TMP
THIS IS WHERE THEIR "FIND" IS?

KNOCK KNOCK

WHERE'S BOBBY? WE ALWAYS WORK WITH HIM.
BOB-BY?

HOW SHOULD I KNOW? MY JOB IS TO EXCHANGE BAGS.

SHE'S AN AMATEUR.
HER FINGERS ARE TREMBLING.

FENCING STOLEN GOODS.
NOW THAT'S A STINGY WAY TO MAKE A LIVING.
OH, HOW MY DESCENDANTS HAVE DESCENDED.

ZOOSH
.....
Z-ZOOSH
VOICES.

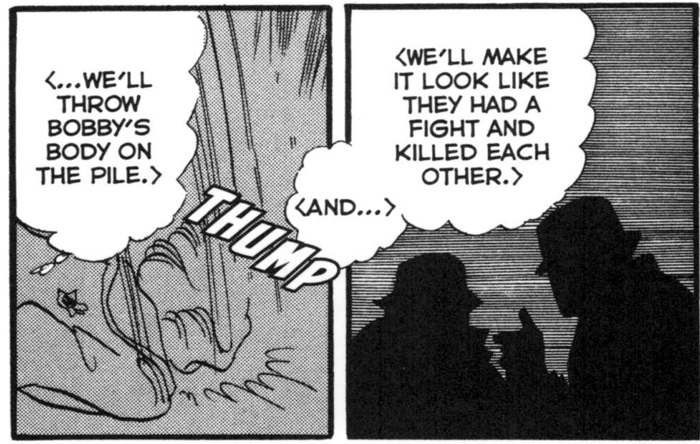

*<> INDICATES FRENCH.

QU'EST ...!?
BLAM! BLAM! BLAM!

THE FUZZ !?
TMP
WHO KNOWS!? COME ON!
TMP
TMP

KRAK

VRNNN
⟨THEY'RE GETTING AWAY!⟩
⟨NEVER MIND! LOOK FOR THE KID! THE KID SAW OUR FACES!⟩

SQUEEEE

I DON'T LIKE IT. NOT ONE LITTLE BIT.

....

YES. I NEEDED THE MONEY.

THIS IS YOUR FIRST DEAL, ISN'T IT? ARE YOU FRENCH?

ARE YOU ALL RIGHT?
PUFF
S-SURE....

SAY, THAT WAS QUI- OH!
OH! HEY! EDITH!

KREEEEE

THIS IS, UM...
... OUR FRIEND WHO JUST ARRIVED IN LONDON AND DOESN'T HAVE A PLACE TO STAY!

OH, GOOD MORNING! I HOPE MY BED WASN'T TOO SMALL FOR YOU.
I SLEPT WELL. THANK YOU.

WHAT A GLORI-OUS MORN-ING!
A PERFECT SUNDAY!

THIS MORNING, IN A BEACH HOUSE FIVE MILES WEST OF MARGATE...
SO, WHAT SHALL WE DO TODAY?

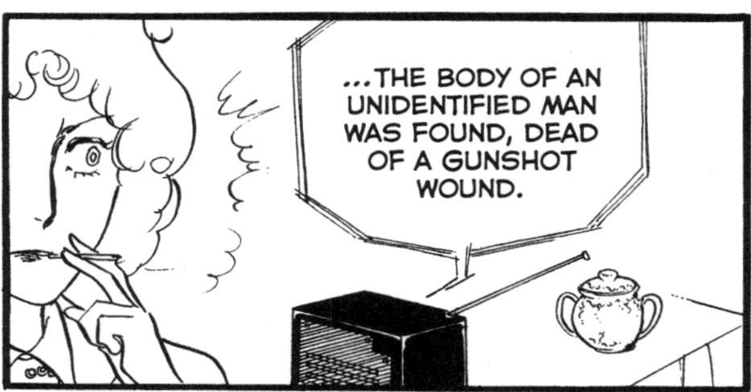
...THE BODY OF AN UNIDENTIFIED MAN WAS FOUND, DEAD OF A GUNSHOT WOUND.

THE POLICE ARE EXAMINING THE FOOTPRINTS AND TIRE TRACKS FOUND AT THE SCENE.
THAT'S... WHERE WE WERE.

HAVE SOME TEA. OR WOULD YOU PREFER COFFEE? SO, YOU'RE FROM FRANCE?
YES.
GOOD MORN-ING.

I'LL BUY YOU A NEW DRESS! THERE'S A GIRL!
YOU LEFT ME ALONE LAST NIGHT AND NOW AGAIN TODAY!?

I'M GOING TO TAKE OUR FRIEND TO A HOTEL. WATCH THE STORE FOR US, WILL YOU?
WH-

HOW HORRID!

I SUGGEST YOU SPEND A FEW NIGHTS AT A HOTEL AND STAY ON YOUR GUARD. IT LOOKS LIKE THINGS ARE GOING TO GET MESSY.

YOUR LITTLE SISTER IS SO SWEET. YOU ARE PLAYING A DANGEROUS GAME, I THINK.
AND YOU'RE *NOT*?

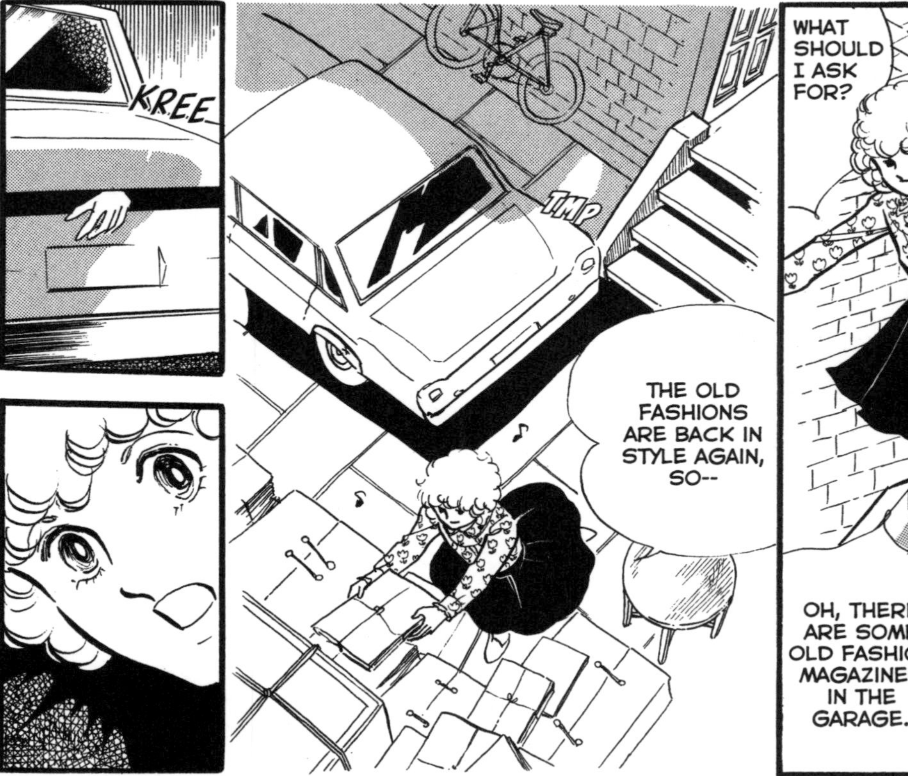
KREE
TMP
THE OLD FASHIONS ARE BACK IN STYLE AGAIN, SO--

NOW THEN!
WHAT SHOULD I ASK FOR?
OH, THERE ARE SOME OLD FASHION MAGAZINES IN THE GARAGE.

ARE YOU ALONE?
ALAN'S... BLUE-EYED...
ED-GAR!
WHAT ON EARTH!?
SORRY. I WAS RESTING HERE. DO YOU HAVE CLOTH I COULD BANDAGE THIS WOUND WITH?
I'LL CALL A DOCTOR!
DON'T. TELL. *ANYONE.*

IT'S NOTHING, REALLY. THE WOUND WILL CLOSE UP SOON.
I'LL GO BUY SOME OINTMENT TO PREVENT INFECTION AND SOME PROPER ELASTIC BANDAGES. AND--
ARE YOU *DAFT!?*

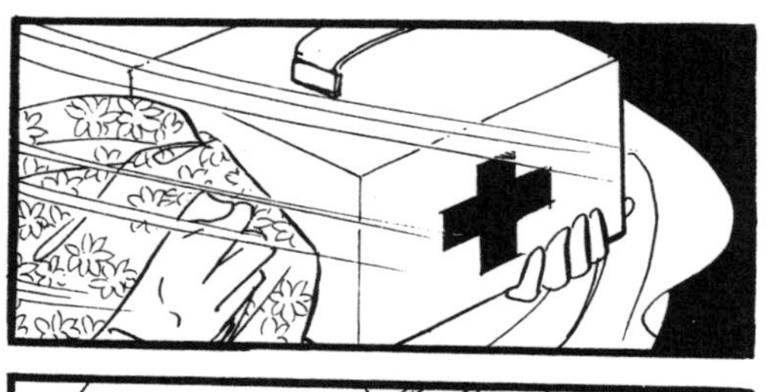

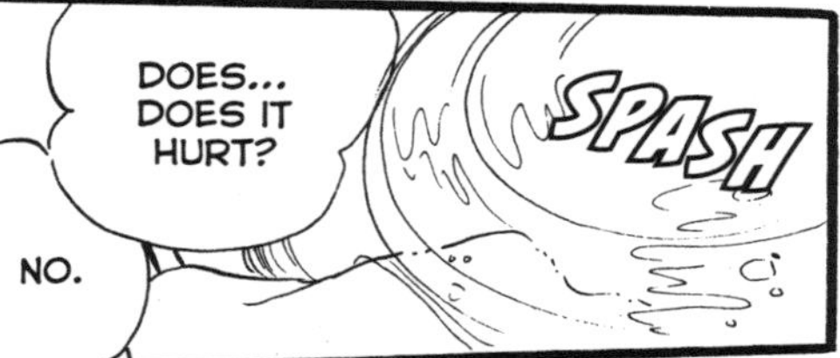
DOES... DOES IT HURT?
NO.
SPASH

I'LL BE BACK IN FIVE MINUTES! YOU STAY RIGHT THERE!

HOW ON EARTH DID YOU GET SUCH A WOUND!? WERE YOU FIGHTING? WHO DID THIS?
REALLY, EDGAR!

JUST WHO IS THAT BOY, ANYWAY?
HURRY HURRY

NOW I SEE. SHE'S A GOOD KID.
NO WONDER HENRY AND ROGER DOTE OVER HER SO.
ALAN WOULD BE A FIFTH WHEEL HERE.

EDITH? HELLO.
OH, MR. ORBIN.

WHUMP

THAT'S NO BRUISE OR SCRATCH.
WHY WAS HE HIDING IN OUR CAR? WAS HE UP TO SOMETHING BAD? IT COULDN'T BE.

NO TIME TO CHAT! GOODBYE!
E- EDITH !!

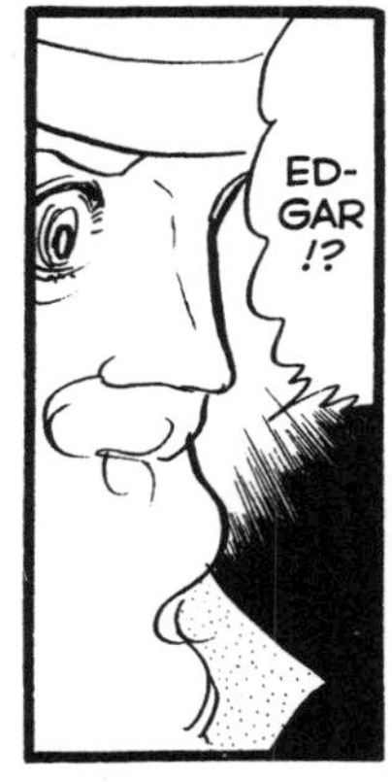
ED- GAR !?

I'M SORRY, I WAS IN A HURRY BECAUSE EDGAR IS... UM...

KREE

TMP
TMP

COME AGAIN!
KUSURI

MR. ORBIN!!

IS SOMEONE INJURED?

NO!

NO, SIR!

THEN WHAT'S THIS?

WHO IS INJURED?

KYAHHH!

GO ON.
DO IT.

LEAVE
NOW.

EDGAR! NO! *NO!*

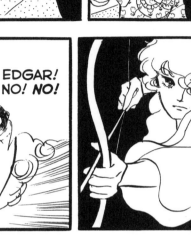

NO!
YOU'RE INJURED! MR. ORBIN, HE'S INJURED!

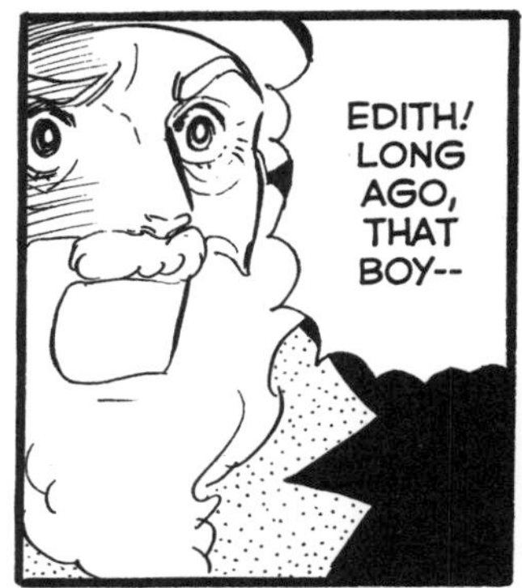
EDITH! LONG AGO, THAT BOY--

JUST LEAVE, MR. ORBIN! *LEAVE!*

EDITH !!
KEEP AWAY FROM HIM!

SPANG
KYAH!
AH!
TUMP!
WHUMP
OH MY! MR. ORBIN! MR. ORBIN! ARE YOU ALL RIGHT!?
EDGAR!!
SEE YOU AROUND, EDITH.
MR. ORBIN!!

I'M LISTENING. SO, I AM HERE TO APOLOGIZE ON EDGAR'S BEHALF, AS WELL.
BUT PLEASE DON'T TREAT MY FRIEND LIKE A MONSTER.
THERE WERE OTHER RECORDS, BUT THEY ALL BURNED IN THE FIRE.
I'M RELIEVED TO SEE THAT YOU WEREN'T BADLY HURT.
EDITH, YOU HAVEN'T HEARD A WORD I'VE SAID.
THIS IS THE LAST WILL AND TESTAMENT OF OSWALD, EARL EVANS.
MR. ORBIN HAS QUITE THE IMAGINATION. HE'S LIKE A CHILD.
VAMPIRNELLA? REALLY!
I COME FACE TO FACE WITH EDGAR FOR THE FIRST TIME IN THIRTY-EIGHT YEARS-- AND LOOK AT ME.
SIGH
BUT EDITH SEEMS FINE, SO PERHAPS THEY ARE GENTLEMEN.
HOW I'VE AGED. LORD, HOW I'VE AGED.
TIME...
...HAS STOPPED....

I'M HOME!
TMPTMPTMPTMPTMPTMP
WEL-COME HOME.

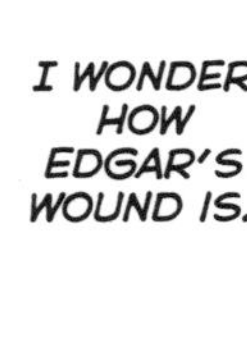
WELL, BUT I HAVEN'T SEEN ALAN IN TWO WHOLE DAYS! WHAT WITH ALL THAT EXCITEMENT.
I WONDER HOW EDGAR'S WOUND IS.

C'EST LA FILLE.
<NO DOUBT ABOUT IT.>

I'M OFF!
TMPTMPTMPTMPTMP
BAM!

SHE NEVER STOPS MOVING.

<SHE ATTENDS THE VALERIE SCHOOL FOR GIRLS. THAT'S THE BLUE-EYED GIRL I SAW THAT NIGHT.>
EDITH

YOU REALLY DIDN'T TRY TO HURT EDITH?
I TOLD YOU I DIDN'T, AND I DIDN'T.

YOU HAVE LOST YOUR TOUCH. GETTING HURT LIKE THAT, AND THEN NEEDING A GIRL TO TAKE CARE OF YOUR INJURY.
BUT NOW YOU KNOW WHAT A GOOD KID SHE IS. CORRECT?
AND YOU'RE KEEPING HER WAITING.

NYA-HH

WELL! IT'S MY MISSING HAT! BUT WHERE--

OH!
IS THIS YOUR HAT?

EXCUSE ME, MISS!

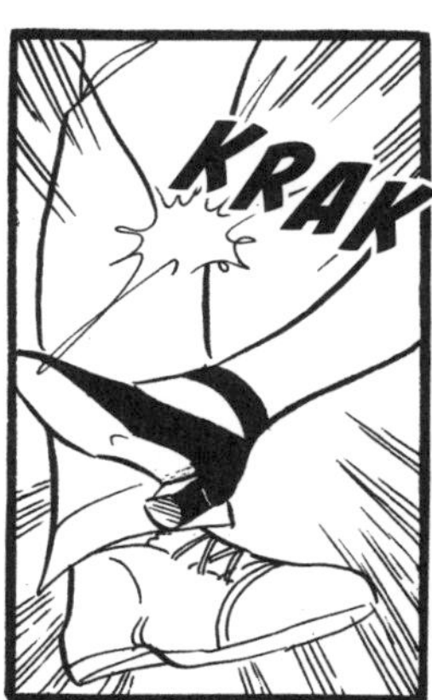
KRAK

SE PRESSER!
U... U...

AIE!
WHACK

UMPH

KIDNAPPERS!!
HFF
HFF
HFF

<WE'LL HAVE TO CREATE AN ACCIDENT! JUMP IN!>

VRRRRNN
KYAH!

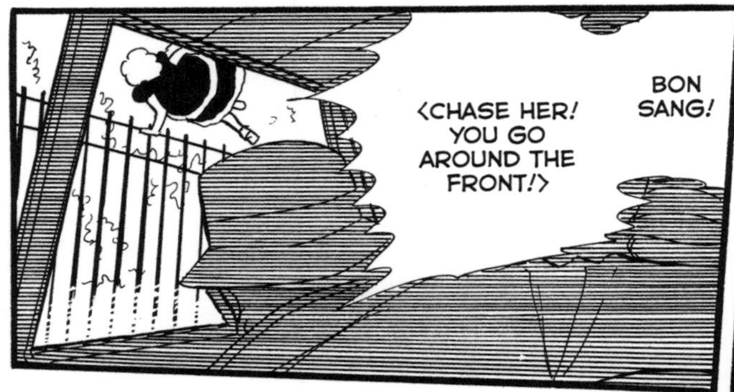
BON SANG!
<CHASE HER! YOU GO AROUND THE FRONT!>

CLANG

CLANG

WHAT SHOULD I DO!?
ALAN
ALAN
HELP!

EDITH

ALAN

COME ON!
SHISH
GET DOWN.
SHISH
THAT GUY?
YEAH.

MEN ARE CHASING ME! THEY TRIED TO PULL ME INTO A CAR!

OKAY
PHEW
THIS IS THE BACK OF THE PARK. OUR HOUSE. YOU'RE SAFE NOW.

SHISH

HOW'S YOUR INJURY!?
IT'S HEALED. LET ME SEE YOUR HAT.
EDGAR! I BROUGHT EDITH. SHE'S BEING CHASED BY STRANGE MEN!
EDGAR!
YOU'VE LOST A POM-POM.
OH! WHEN DID--
WHEN I GOT SHOT.
YOU REMEMBER THE NEWS FROM A COUPLE DAYS BACK? ABOUT AN UNIDENTIFIED MAN MURDERED, NEAR MARGATE?
WELL, I SAW THE KILLERS' FACES.
EDGAR! SO THAT'S HOW YOU--!
WHAT ON EARTH WERE YOU DOING AT THE SCENE OF A MURDER!?
YOU'VE GOT TO GO TO THE POLICE! YOU'RE IN DANGER!
NO, *YOU'RE* IN DANGER.

TAKE YOUR CLOTHES OFF.
WHAT !?
THE KILLERS THINK *YOU* ARE ***ME.***
YES, IT DOES.
RIGHT. WE'LL GO WITH THAT.
DOES YOUR SCHOOL HAVE A DORM?
HIDE ME?
THAT RED DRESS STANDS OUT.
ALAN, BRING SOME OF YOUR SMALLEST CLOTHES.
NOW WHERE CAN WE HIDE YOU?
TELL YOUR BROTHERS YOU HAVE A SHIFT THERE OR SOMETHING.
STAY IN THE DORM AND DON'T GO OUTSIDE.
FOR THREE DAYS.
OH, MY.
MEANWHILE, I'LL WEAR YOUR CLOTHES AND CATCH THE KILLERS.
I NEED A HAT.

YOU'RE RIGHT! THIS IS NO LAUGHING MATTER! IT'S TOO DANGEROUS!
NO LAUGHING.
BONK
TEE HEE
NOT A BIT.
THE PO-LICE.
YES, YES. BUT FIRST WE GET YOU TO THE DORM.
DON'T YOU WORRY ABOUT EDGAR. HE CAN HANDLE HIMSELF.
BUT...
SHE'S SAFELY TUCKED AWAY?
YEAH.

THANKS FOR GOING TO ALL THIS TROUBLE FOR EDITH.
IT'S NOT FOR EDITH.
FAIR ENOUGH.
BUT NOW I CAN'T SEE EDITH FOR THREE DAYS.
THAT FELLOW PUT THREE BULLETS IN ME. I HAVE A SCORE TO SETTLE.
ELLE EST LÀ
HEH

I TELL YE I SAW IT WIT' ME OWN EYES! A LITTLE DEMON IN RED CLOTHES!
IT WUZ WALKIN' ONNA WATER.
IT WAS STANNIN' ONNA ROOF OF THAT CAR WHUT SUNK.

YOU REEK OF AL-COHOL, OLD MAN.
WHAT'S ALL THIS?
AN ACCI-DENT.
CAR FELL IN THE RIVER.
I AIN'T DRUNK!

YES, YES.
A LITTLE RED DEMON, 'OPPIN' ALONG IT WAS
EXAMINE THE BODIES!

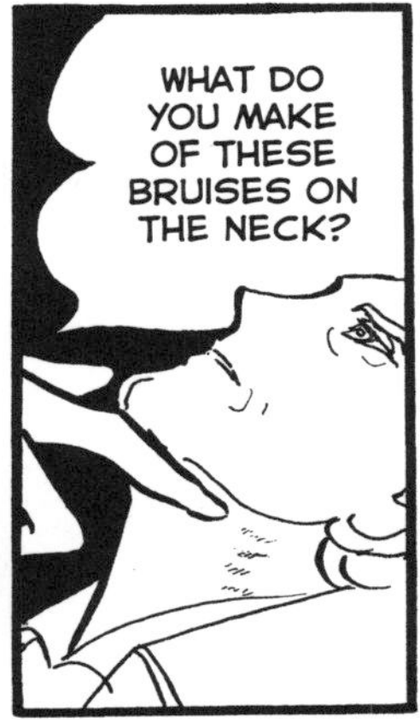

WHAT DO YOU MAKE OF THESE BRUISES ON THE NECK?

THE LEADER OF THE GANG THAT HIRED ME IN FRANCE.
PRINT-EMPS?

WISH I HAD AN ESCORT!

OH, EDITH! IT'S YOUR BOY-FRIEND!

EDITH !!

EDGAR? YOU'RE DRIPPING WET! WHAT HAPPENED.

I SETTLED THE SCORE.

EDGAR! ALAN! HOW DID IT GO?
IT'S SAFE TO GO HOME NOW.
YOU WENT TO THE POLICE?
WHERE?
THE POLICE!
WHAT ABOUT THEM?
THE POLICE.
WHY?
YOU KNOW WHY!
YOU WERE *WOUNDED!*
WOUNDED?
WHERE?
NOT A SCRATCH...
YOU DIDN'T SEE ANYTHING.
YOU DON'T KNOW ANYTHING.
AND NOTHING HAPPENED. IS THAT CLEAR?
!

WELL, I'LL JUST ASK ALAN WHEN EDGAR'S NOT AROUND!
DON'T WORRY? WHAT ARE THEY HIDING?
IT'S FOR YOUR OWN GOOD, EDITH.
DON'T WORRY.
ALAN !!
EDITH !
ROGER! HENRY!
WEL-COME HOME!
TUMP TUMP TUMP
OH! WHAT AN ADORABLE CLOCK!
THE HOUSE WAS DREADFULLY QUIET WITHOUT YOU.
LOOK WHAT I BROUGHT HOME.
IT WILL GO NICELY WITH THE CASTLE WE'LL BUY YOU SOMEDAY.
OH, THANK YOU, HENRY!
SOMETIMES I WISH I COULD GO INSIDE A CLOCK LIKE A LITTLE WOODEN DOLL.
YOU LIKE IT?
WELL, THEN, FOR YOUR SAKE, WE WON'T SELL THIS ONE.

I NOTICED YOU'VE STOPPED COMPLAINING.
ABOUT EDITH.
SURE.
YOU NEED TO DO EVERYTHING YOU CAN TO KEEP EDITH'S MIND OFF THIS INCIDENT.
THE BODIES OF TWO MEN, ALONG WITH THE CAR THEY WERE FOUND IN, HAVE BEEN PULLED FROM THE THAMES.
CRACKLE
BUT YOU SAID YOURSELF SHE'S A GOOD KID!
I'M STILL OPPOSED. THIS IS JUST TILL THINGS SETTLE DOWN.
...
YOUR DOING, NO DOUBT.
I SEE. AND WHEN DO YOU PLAN TO TELL EDITH...
...THAT YOU'RE A MONSTER WHO DOESN'T AGE!?
SHE'S A HUMAN.
DO YOU WANT TO STOP TIME FOR HER?
I'D BEEN THINKING TIME HAD STOPPED FOR EDITH, TOO.
YOU'D FORGOT-TEN, HADN'T YOU?
YES.

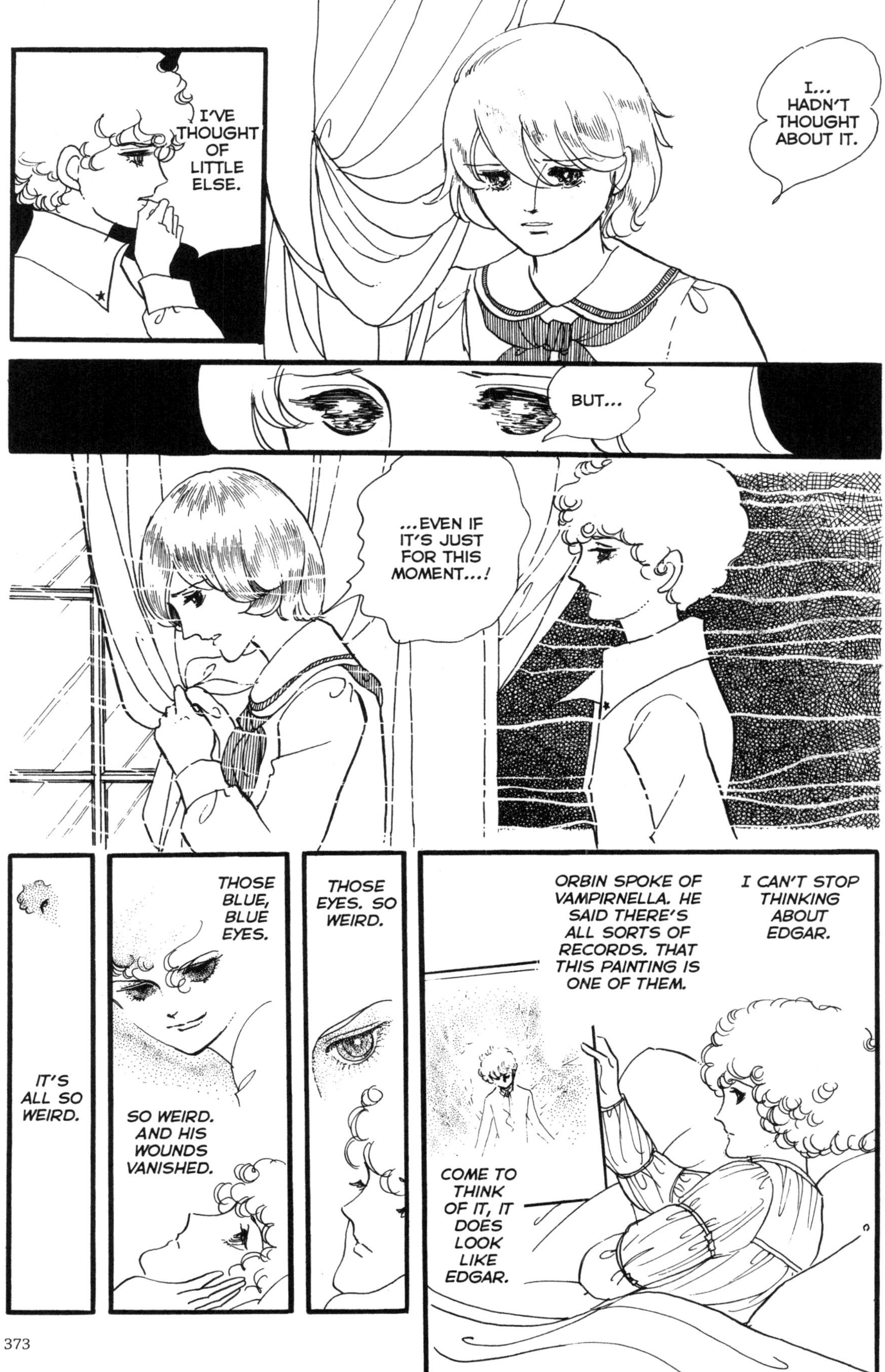
I'VE THOUGHT OF LITTLE ELSE.
I... HADN'T THOUGHT ABOUT IT.
BUT...
...EVEN IF IT'S JUST FOR THIS MOMENT...!
I CAN'T STOP THINKING ABOUT EDGAR.
ORBIN SPOKE OF VAMPIRNELLA. HE SAID THERE'S ALL SORTS OF RECORDS. THAT THIS PAINTING IS ONE OF THEM.
COME TO THINK OF IT, IT DOES LOOK LIKE EDGAR.
THOSE EYES. SO WEIRD.
THOSE BLUE, BLUE EYES.
SO WEIRD. AND HIS WOUNDS VANISHED.
IT'S ALL SO WEIRD.

DAMN!

YOU ARE UNDER ARREST ON SUSPICION OF SMUGGLING STOLEN GOODS AND OF THE MURDERS OF THE TWO MEN FOUND IN THE THAMES!

HENRY AND ROGER EVANS!

HENRY! ROGER!

THIS IS SOME KIND OF MISTAKE!

SEARCH THE HOUSE!

THERE SHOULD BE STOLEN AND SMUGGLED MERCHANDISE HERE!

....

BUT HOW?
THIS IS BAD!

THAT'S EDITH'S!!
MY PAINT-ING!

SORRY, MISS. BUT THEY'LL HAVE TO COME WITH US.
HENRY ....

FRENCH POLICE. I'VE BEEN PURSUING DRUG DEALERS.
THE MEN YOU WERE DEALING WITH ARE BIG PLAYERS.
YOU ...

THAT, TOO.
WE'LL BE RIGHT BACK! I'LL GIVE THE CHIEF OF POLICE A PIECE OF MY MIND FOR THIS!
WE'LL BE RIGHT BACK, EDITH!

COME WITH ME TO MY HOTEL, EDITH.
ROGER! HENRY!
VRRNN
ROG-ER!

IT'S WRONG! IT'S ALL WRONG!
EDITH!

ALAN! EDGAR!
WHERE WAS THE ENTRANCE!?
SKISH
SNIFF
EDITH! EDITH!?
CALM DOWN AND TELL ME WHAT HAPPENED!!
A WHOLE BUNCH OF POLICE CAME AND TOOK MY BROTHERS AWAY.
THEY'RE TURNING THE HOUSE INSIDE OUT. THEY SAID MY BROTHERS ARE KILLERS AND THIEVES.
OF COURSE THEY AREN'T!
EDITH!

BUT IT'S NOT. THEY RAISED YOU.
THAT'S RIGHT! THEY'VE BEEN LIKE PARENTS TO ME! AND...!
IT'S NOT EITHER! MY BROTHERS HAVEN'T DONE ANYTHING!
IT'S SOME KIND OF MISTAKE!!
ED-GAR!
THEY HAD NOTHING TO DO WITH THE MURDERS.
AND THEY HAVE ALIBIS.
ALTHOUGH THE PART ABOUT SMUGGLING IS TRUE.
CALM DOWN. IT'S NOT ALL BAD.
AND THEY FENCED STOLEN ANTIQUES...
...TO FEED YOU AND SEND YOU TO SCHOOL. THEY'RE GOOD BROTHERS.
EDGAR!!
DON'T LISTEN TO HIM, EDITH!
ALL YOU HAVE TO DO IS POST BOND. JUST ASK YOUR BROTHERS.
THERE'S A SECRET ROOM BEHIND THE KITCHEN WHERE THEY HIDE THE STOLEN GOODS.
EDITH!!

YOU'VE HURT HER!!
LET HER GO! SHE HAD A RIGHT TO KNOW!
SMACK!!
IT'S TIME TO STEP BACK!
EDITH!!
IT'S YOU, ALAN!
IT'S YOU WHO'LL BE HURT!
ALAN!

EDITH!
BE CAREFUL!
EDITH!
SKREE!
LOOK OUT!
SHE WON'T TURN AROUND.
EDITH !!
SHE JUST RUNS AND RUNS AND DOESN'T LOOK BACK.
IT WOULD BE A FARCE. A JOKE.
BUT A VAMPIRNELLA CAN'T LOVE A HUMAN.
IF I MADE HER ONE OF US, MAYBE.
EDITH!!
WHEN WILL YOU TELL HER YOU'RE A MONSTER?
I... I CAN'T DO ANYTHING FOR HER!

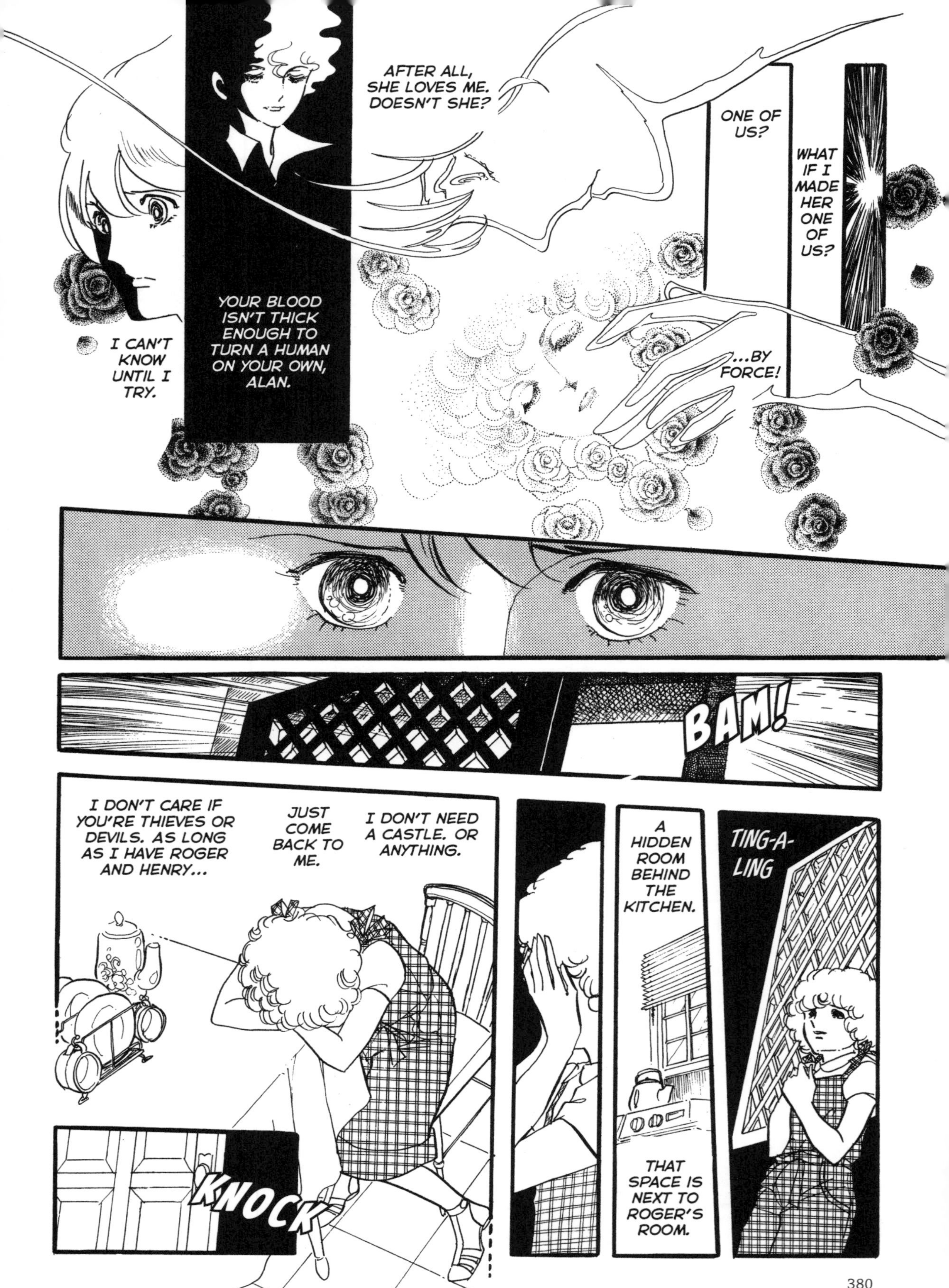

I CAN'T KNOW UNTIL I TRY.

YOUR BLOOD ISN'T THICK ENOUGH TO TURN A HUMAN ON YOUR OWN, ALAN.

AFTER ALL, SHE LOVES ME. DOESN'T SHE?

ONE OF US?

WHAT IF I MADE HER ONE OF US?

...BY FORCE!

BAM!

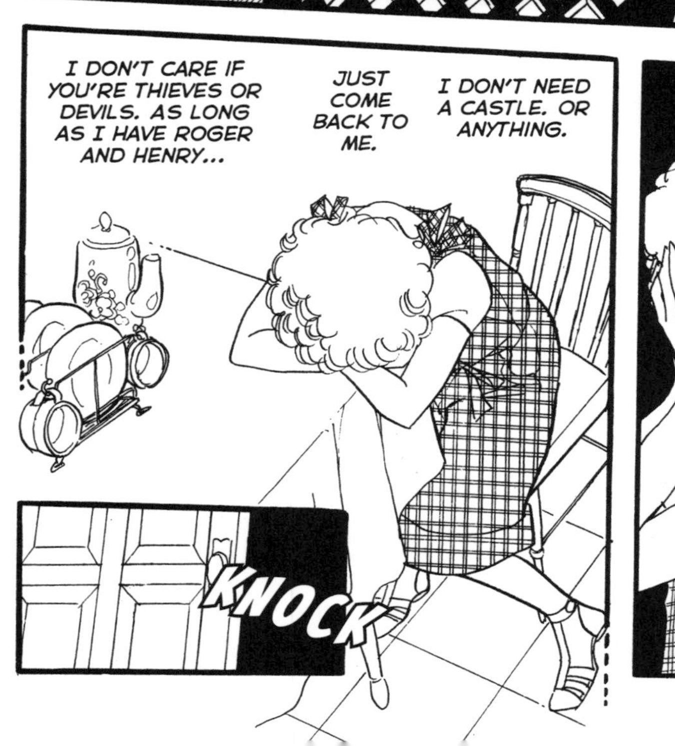

I DON'T CARE IF YOU'RE THIEVES OR DEVILS. AS LONG AS I HAVE ROGER AND HENRY...
JUST COME BACK TO ME.
I DON'T NEED A CASTLE. OR ANYTHING.
KNOCK

A HIDDEN ROOM BEHIND THE KITCHEN.
THAT SPACE IS NEXT TO ROGER'S ROOM.

YES.
I JUST NEED TO POST BAIL! I'LL GO TO THE BANK RIGHT AWAY!

ALAN.

I KNOCKED, BUT THERE WAS NO ANSWER.
COME ON, EDITH. CHEER UP.

WAIT. UM... FIRST I'LL PUT ON SOME TEA.
YES. THEN I'LL GO TO THE POLICE STATION.
KLK
EDITH.

YES! AND THEN WE'LL MOVE AWAY! AND START OVER! ALL THREE OF US.
WE'LL MOVE TO THE COUNTRY. AND PLANT ROSES!
IT WON'T BE FAR. YOU'LL COME TO PLAY, WON'T YOU?

THE COUN-TRY'S NICE.

ALAN !?
SO COME WITH ME.
I'LL LOVE YOU MUCH MORE THAN ROGER OR HENRY DO.

FORGET ABOUT YOUR BROTHERS.
LET GO.
ALAN? STOP, ALAN.

ALAN?
COME WITH ME. ME AND EDGAR.
IT'LL BE FUN.
WE CAN TRAVEL.
AND YOU CAN LIVE FOREVER.

...I NEED ...

...TO HIDE EDITH SOME-WHERE.

I... I SUPPOSE I SHOULD LEAVE THE REST TO EDGAR. BUT WHILE I FETCH HIM...

I DON'T WANT TO FORGET TH-

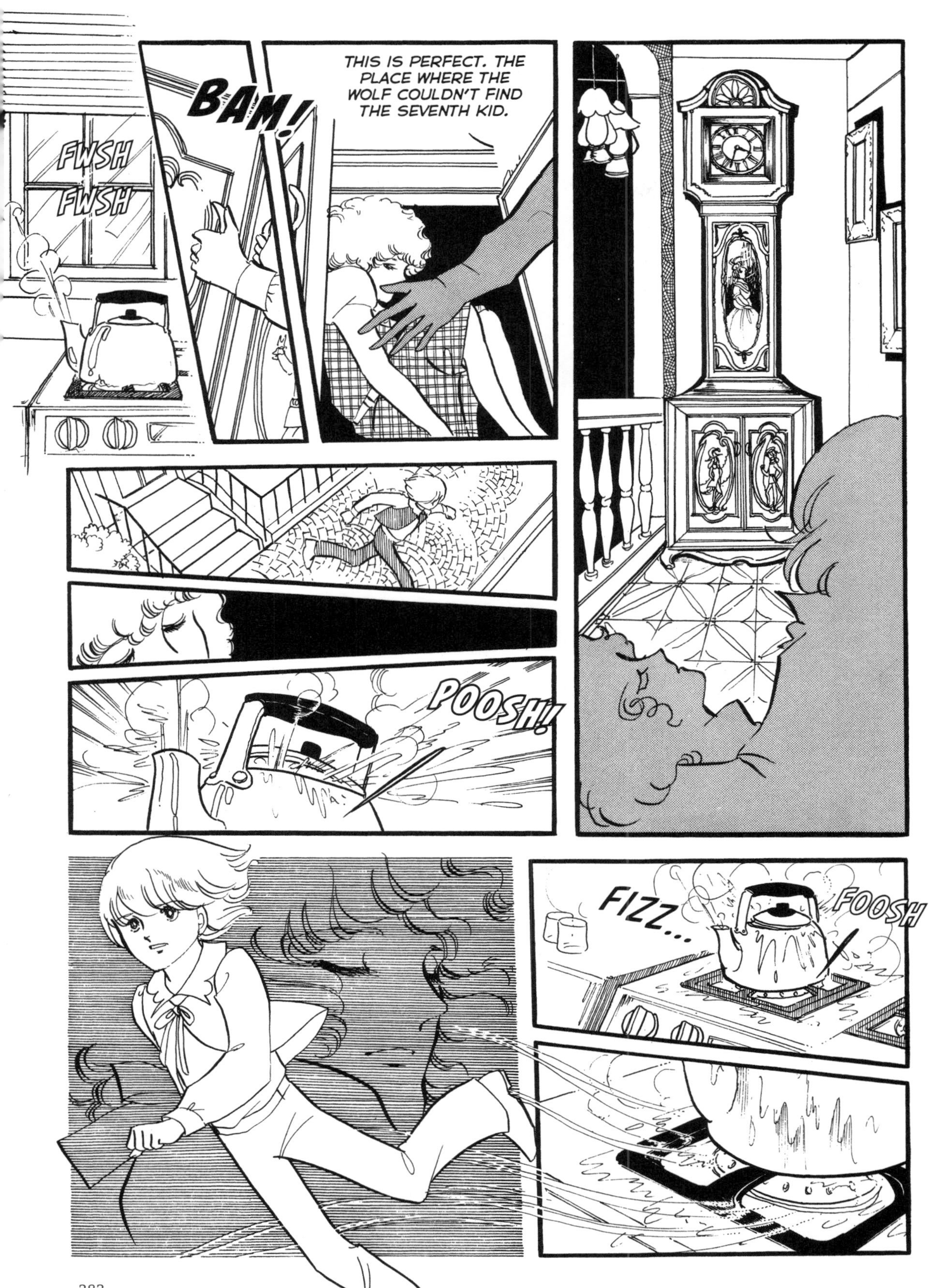
FWSH
FWSH
BAM!
THIS IS PERFECT. THE PLACE WHERE THE WOLF COULDN'T FIND THE SEVENTH KID.
POOSH!!
FIZZ...
FOOSH

EDGAR! COME QUICK! I NEED TO TALK.

IT'S ABOUT EDITH! WE CAN'T TALK HERE.
WE CAN'T TALK HERE?
WE HAVE TO GO TO EDITH'S HOUSE.

WHY?
HURRY! IF SOME-ONE COMES...

HISSSS
...!

WHAT HAVE YOU DONE TO EDITH?

I JUST... KNOCKED HER OUT.

TO TURN HER...

ALAN!!

I LOVE EDITH! AND SHE--

YOU ***DON'T LOVE*** EDITH!!

I-I CALLED TO HER, BUT SHE WOULDN'T TURN AROUND!
SO I... I...
EDGAR
I DO LOVE HER!
LIAR!
AND?
CAN YOU GIVE EDITH HAPPINESS?
YOU CAN TAKE HER FROM ROGER AND HENRY AND HER SCHOOL AND MAKE HER HAPPIER?
WHERE DID YOU LEAVE HER?
IF YOU CARE FOR HER...
IF YOU REALLY LOVE HER...
...THE FRUSTRATION OF BEING UNABLE TO MAKE HER HAPPY WILL EAT YOU UP!
MARYBELLE

TIK
SO WHAT IS EDITH TO ME?
TO EDGAR, I AM A STAND-IN FOR MARYBELLE.
TOK
TUMP
BOOM
AHHH!
KYAHH!

EDITH!
ALAN!
THE ANTIQUE SHOP!
WHAT WAS THAT!?
WHAT WAS...?
THE ANTIQUE SHOP EXPLODED!
SOME-ONE!
CALL THE FIRE DEPART-MENT!
YOU BOYS! STOP! STAY AWAY!
IT COULD BLOW AGAIN!

EDGAR! HELP!
ALAN!

QUICK!

EDITH!
SHE'S IN HERE?

EDITH!

WE'LL ESCAPE THROUGH THE ROOF. THIS WAY.

SNAG
KREEE

EDITH!
SHE'S ALL RIGHT. THE CLOCK PROTECTED HER. SHE'S JUST UNCONSCIOUS.

CRACK
CRACK
CRASH

ALAN
...

LET'S GO HOME
ALAN !
TO THE DISTANT PAST
ALAN ...!
WE'LL TO THE MORROW NO MORE.
MARY-BELLE ...?
ALAN...
ALAN!
HAPPINESS WAITS IN THE PAST
MARY-BELLE ...
SHEILA
LET'S GO HOME LEAP THROUGH TIME
OS-WALD
OLD HANNAH
MOTHER
YOU'RE ALL HERE
HA HA HA
HA HA HA
YOU'RE ALL HERE
ALAN ...!
HA HA HA

EDITH!!

ROGER. HENRY. YOU CAME BACK.
SHE'S ALL RIGHT! SHE'S ALL RIGHT! OH, EDITH!!

WHAT ...?
THE HOUSE BURNED.
WE FOUND YOU SOAKING WET IN THE BATHROOM.

I DON'T REMEMBER.
ALAN WAS THERE.

WHERE'S ALAN?
ALAN ?
YOU WERE THE ONLY ONE FOUND IN THE HOUSE.

FORGET ABOUT YOUR BROTHERS AND COME WITH ME.

ROG-ER

WHY ARE YOU CRYING, ROGER?

COME WITH ME
I'LL LOVE YOU MUCH MORE THAN ROGER OR HENRY DO

LET'S MOVE TO THE COUNTRY.
THAT'S JUST WHAT WE'LL DO.

NOT A CASTLE, BUT A LITTLE COTTAGE.
WE'LL PLANT ROSES... IN THE GARDEN.
THAT SOUNDS WONDERFUL.

SOME-ONE TELL ME WHO THOSE TWO WERE
ALAN
WHERE HAVE YOU GONE?
WHAT WERE YOU?

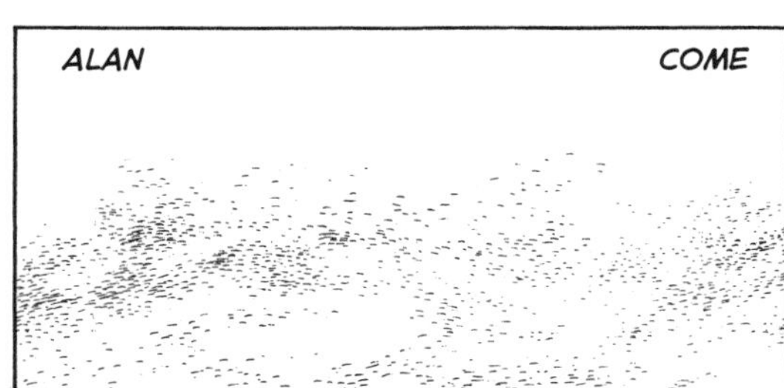
ALAN
COME

THEY LIVED IN THE BACK OF THE PARK. JUST THE TWO OF THEM.
I WONDER IF THEY'VE GONE FAR AWAY.

HERE?

BACK OF THE PARK

BURNED IN THE FIRE. EDGAR... I'LL NEVER SEE HIM AGAIN.

WHAT ARE YOU DOING HERE?

WH... WHO ARE YOU?

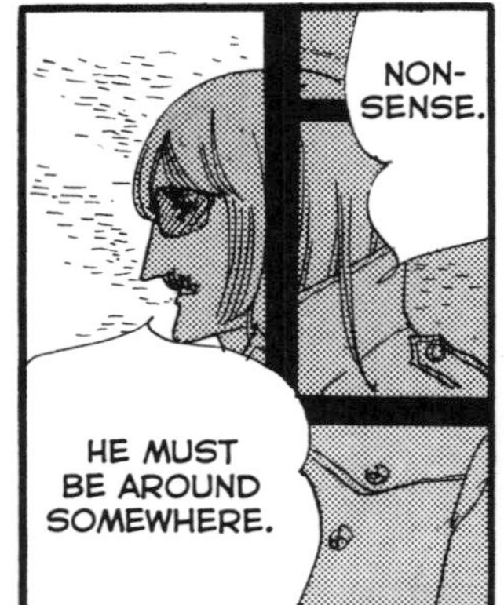

NON-SENSE.
HE MUST BE AROUND SOMEWHERE.

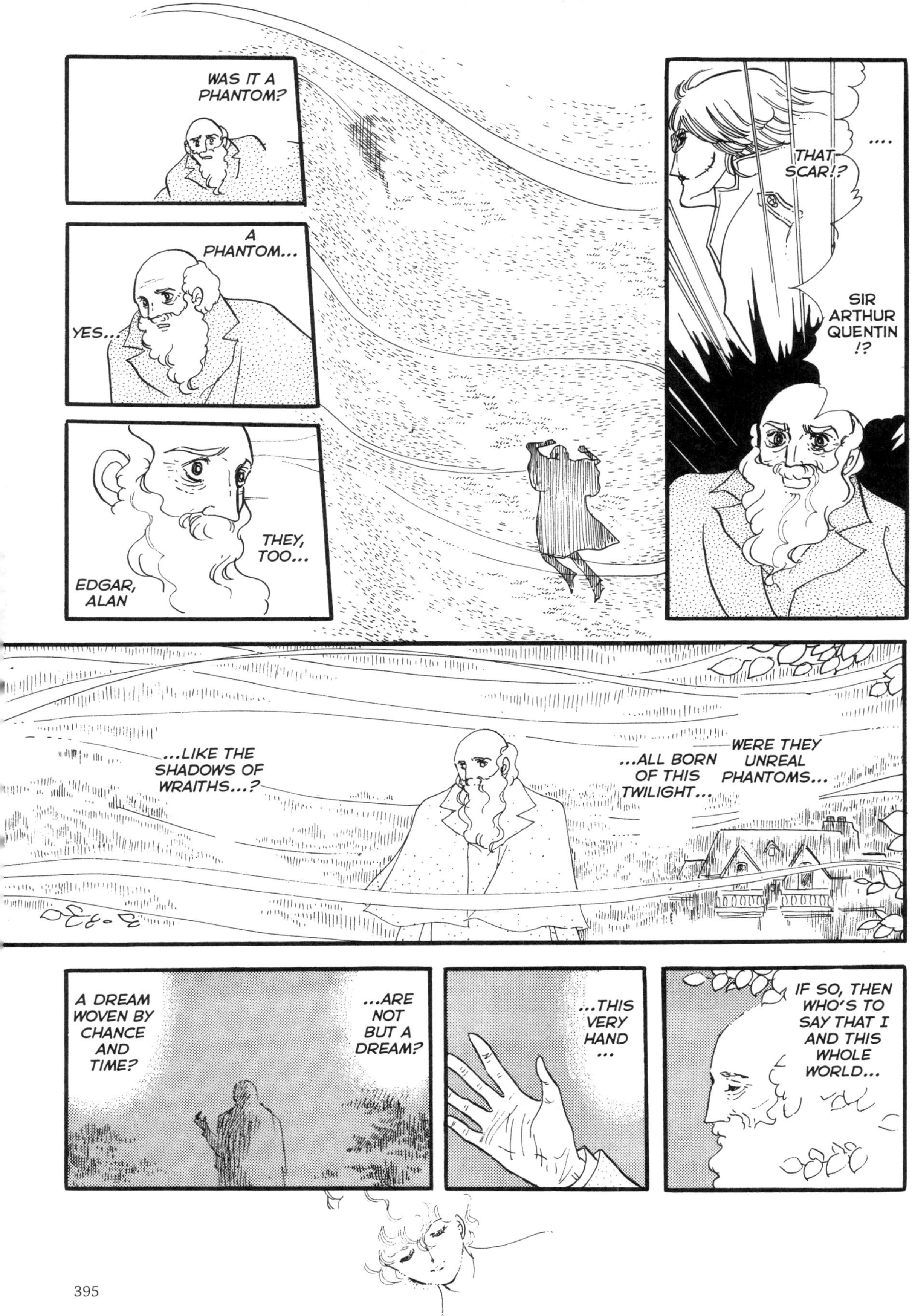

....
THAT SCAR!?
SIR ARTHUR QUENTIN !?
WAS IT A PHANTOM?
A PHANTOM...
YES...
THEY, TOO...
EDGAR, ALAN
WERE THEY UNREAL PHANTOMS...
...ALL BORN OF THIS TWILIGHT...
...LIKE THE SHADOWS OF WRAITHS...?
IF SO, THEN WHO'S TO SAY THAT I AND THIS WHOLE WORLD...
...THIS VERY HAND ...
...ARE NOT BUT A DREAM?
A DREAM WOVEN BY CHANCE AND TIME?

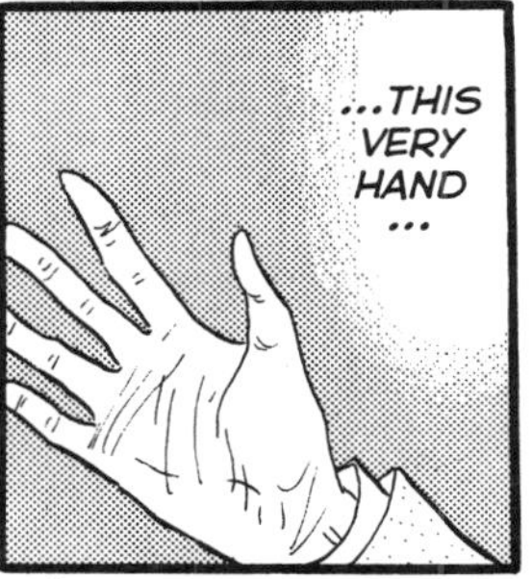

PERHAPS HE NEVER EXISTED.
PERHAPS THE BOYS LOUIS AND THEO AND LYDIA MET WERE JUST ORDINARY BOYS
PERHAPS THERE WAS NOTHING STRANGE ABOUT ANY OF IT.
PERHAPS THEY WEREN'T EDGAR.
NO. THE BOY WAS REAL.
I SEE HIS FORM. HEAR HIS VOICE.
HE EXISTED. I KNOW IT.
MUCH LIKE THIS TWILIGHT
IT'S A SILVER WORLD
WHY, I CAN EVEN SEE THE MORNING OF HIS BIRTH.
A SHADOW SPANNING THE CRACKS BETWEEN DIFFERENT TIMES.

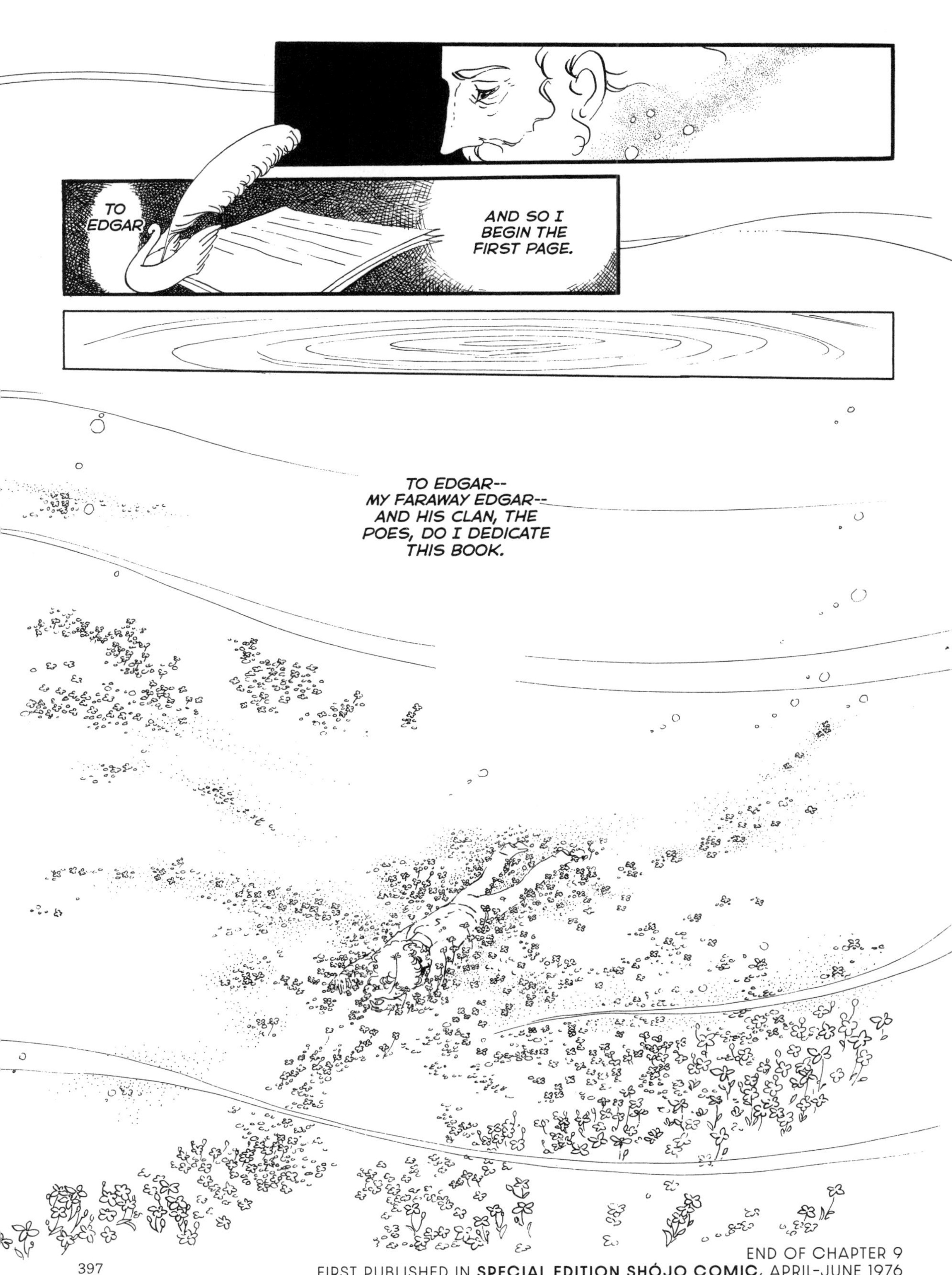
TO EDGAR
AND SO I BEGIN THE FIRST PAGE.
TO EDGAR-- MY FARAWAY EDGAR-- AND HIS CLAN, THE POES, DO I DEDICATE THIS BOOK.

END OF CHAPTER 9

FIRST PUBLISHED IN **SPECIAL EDITION SHÓJO COMIC**, APRIL–JUNE 1976

OTHER FANTAGRAPHICS BOOKS BY

MOTO HAGIO

A Drunken Dream
and Other Stories
$29.99 | ISBN: 978-1-60699-377-4

Otherworld Barbara Vol. 1
$39.99 | ISBN: 978-1-60699-943-1

Otherworld Barbara Vol. 2
$39.99 | ISBN: 978-168396-023-2

BIOS

MOTO HAGIO was born May 12, 1949, in Ōmuta City, Fukuoka Prefecture. She is one of a group of women born that year that broke into the male-dominated manga industry and pioneered the shōjo (girls') movement. Hagio's *Heart of Thomas*, inspired by the 1964 film *This Special Friendship*, was one of the early entries in the shōnen-ai (boys in love) subgenre. Her major works include *A Drunken Dream*, *A,A'*, *They Were Eleven*, and *Otherworld Barbara*. She's won the Japanese Medal of Honor with the Purple Ribbon (the first woman comics creator to do so), received Japan's SF Grand Prize, the Osamu Tezuka Culture Award Grand Prize, and an Inkpot Award, among other accolades. In 2019, she was named a Person of Cultural Merit by the Japanese government. She lives in the Saitama Prefecture.

RACHEL THORN was born May 12, 1965, in Lansdale, Pennsylvania. She is a cultural anthropologist, translator, writer, and teacher. In the English-speaking world, she is known best as a shōjo manga evangelist, a calling she was inspired to follow after reading Moto Hagio's *The Heart of Thomas* at the age of 21. Her translations include Hagio's *They Were Eleven*, *A,A'*, *The Heart of Thomas*, and *The Poe Clan*, as well as Hayao Miyazaki's *Nausicaä of the Valley of Wind*, Rumiko Takahashi's *Mermaid Saga*, and Akimi Yoshida's *Banana Fish*. She is a professor at Kyoto Seika University.

ACKNOWLEDGMENTS
The translator would like to thank the esteemed Charlie Haylock for his invaluable assistance with East Anglian accents; the talented Hayleigh Dunning Joseph for her help with London accents; and the generous Eleanor Goldsmith for singular aid with ... *checks notes* ... British rail routes circa 1951.

PRONUNCIATION GUIDE

VOWELS

a as in "father"
i as in "spaghetti"
u as in "put"
e as in "them"
o as in "pole"

"Long" vowels are usually indicated by a macron ("ō"), circumflex ("ô") or diaeresis ("ö"), although sometimes the vowel is simply repeated. In personal names, a long "o" is sometimes represented as "oh." In cases where one vowel is followed immediately by a different vowel, but is not in the same syllable, they are often separated by a dash or apostrophe to indicate the end of one syllable and beginning of another.

Here are common pairs of vowels that sound to the English-speaker's ear like one syllable (and thus are not separated):

ai as in "my"
ei as in "ray"
oi as in "toy"
ao as in "cow"

CONSONANTS THAT REQUIRE CLARIFICATION

g as in "get" (never as in "age")
s as in "soft" (never like "rise")
t as in "tale" (never like "d")
ch as in "church"

ACCENTS

Most English words have "accented" and "unaccented" syllables. This is generally not the case in Japanese, which is more "flat." When English speakers encounter a new word, they tend to accent the first syllable if it has two syllables, the second if it has three, and after that they wing it. If you can't resist accenting a syllable in a Japanese word, accent the first and you'll be fine.

STOP

The manga in this book is "unflipped," meaning pages run back to front and panels start at the top right and end in the bottom-left. Turn this page and you'll be at the end of the story. Flip the book around for a much more satisfying reading experience.

S0-BCS-850

Android® Application Development

ALL-IN-ONE

3rd Edition

by Barry Burd and John Paul Mueller

Android® Application Development All-in-One For Dummies®, 3rd Edition

Published by: **John Wiley & Sons, Inc.,** 111 River Street, Hoboken, NJ 07030-5774, www.wiley.com

Copyright © 2020 by John Wiley & Sons, Inc., Hoboken, New Jersey

Published simultaneously in Canada

No part of this publication may be reproduced, stored in a retrieval system or transmitted in any form or by any means, electronic, mechanical, photocopying, recording, scanning or otherwise, except as permitted under Sections 107 or 108 of the 1976 United States Copyright Act, without the prior written permission of the Publisher. Requests to the Publisher for permission should be addressed to the Permissions Department, John Wiley & Sons, Inc., 111 River Street, Hoboken, NJ 07030, (201) 748-6011, fax (201) 748-6008, or online at http://www.wiley.com/go/permissions.

Trademarks: Wiley, For Dummies, the Dummies Man logo, Dummies.com, Making Everything Easier, and related trade dress are trademarks or registered trademarks of John Wiley & Sons, Inc. and may not be used without written permission. Android is a registered trademark of Google, LLC. All other trademarks are the property of their respective owners. John Wiley & Sons, Inc. is not associated with any product or vendor mentioned in this book.

LIMIT OF LIABILITY/DISCLAIMER OF WARRANTY: THE PUBLISHER AND THE AUTHOR MAKE NO REPRESENTATIONS OR WARRANTIES WITH RESPECT TO THE ACCURACY OR COMPLETENESS OF THE CONTENTS OF THIS WORK AND SPECIFICALLY DISCLAIM ALL WARRANTIES, INCLUDING WITHOUT LIMITATION WARRANTIES OF FITNESS FOR A PARTICULAR PURPOSE. NO WARRANTY MAY BE CREATED OR EXTENDED BY SALES OR PROMOTIONAL MATERIALS. THE ADVICE AND STRATEGIES CONTAINED HEREIN MAY NOT BE SUITABLE FOR EVERY SITUATION. THIS WORK IS SOLD WITH THE UNDERSTANDING THAT THE PUBLISHER IS NOT ENGAGED IN RENDERING LEGAL, ACCOUNTING, OR OTHER PROFESSIONAL SERVICES. IF PROFESSIONAL ASSISTANCE IS REQUIRED, THE SERVICES OF A COMPETENT PROFESSIONAL PERSON SHOULD BE SOUGHT. NEITHER THE PUBLISHER NOR THE AUTHOR SHALL BE LIABLE FOR DAMAGES ARISING HEREFROM. THE FACT THAT AN ORGANIZATION OR WEBSITE IS REFERRED TO IN THIS WORK AS A CITATION AND/OR A POTENTIAL SOURCE OF FURTHER INFORMATION DOES NOT MEAN THAT THE AUTHOR OR THE PUBLISHER ENDORSES THE INFORMATION THE ORGANIZATION OR WEBSITE MAY PROVIDE OR RECOMMENDATIONS IT MAY MAKE. FURTHER, READERS SHOULD BE AWARE THAT INTERNET WEBSITES LISTED IN THIS WORK MAY HAVE CHANGED OR DISAPPEARED BETWEEN WHEN THIS WORK WAS WRITTEN AND WHEN IT IS READ.

For general information on our other products and services, please contact our Customer Care Department within the U.S. at 877-762-2974, outside the U.S. at 317-572-3993, or fax 317-572-4002. For technical support, please visit https://hub.wiley.com/community/support/dummies.

Wiley publishes in a variety of print and electronic formats and by print-on-demand. Some material included with standard print versions of this book may not be included in e-books or in print-on-demand. If this book refers to media such as a CD or DVD that is not included in the version you purchased, you may download this material at http://booksupport.wiley.com. For more information about Wiley products, visit www.wiley.com.

Library of Congress Control Number: 2020939707

ISBN: 978-1-119-66045-3

ISBN 978-1-119-66043-9 (ebk); ISBN 978-1-119-66046-0 (ebk)

Manufactured in the United States of America

V10019676_070820

Contents at a Glance

Table of Contents

Introduction

As the year 2019 drew to a close, Android ran on 51.8 percent of all smartphones in the United States and on 85 percent of all smartphones worldwide.[1,2] The Google Play Store had 2.57 million apps compared with only 1.84 million in Apple's App Store.[3]

Today, Android is everywhere, and experts predict that Android will dominate the global smartphone market for years to come.[4] So, if you read this book in a public place (on a commuter train, at the beach, on the dance floor at the Coyote Ugly saloon), you can read proudly, with a chip on your shoulder and with your chest held high. Android is hot stuff, and you're cool because you're reading about it.

How to Use This Book

You can attack this book in either of two ways. You can go cover to cover, or you can poke around from one chapter to another. You can even do both (start at the beginning and then jump to a section that particularly interests you). In this book, the basic topics come first, and the more involved topics follow the basics. You may already be comfortable with some basics, or you may have specific goals that don't require you to know about certain topics.

The best advice is as follows:

- » If you already know something, don't bother reading about it.
- » If you're curious, don't be afraid to skip ahead. You can always sneak a peek at an earlier chapter if you really need to do so.

---

[1] See `www.statista.com/statistics/266572/market-share-held-by-smartphone-platforms-in-the-united-states/`.

[2] See `https://hostingtribunal.com/blog/operating-systems-market-share/#gref`.

[3] See `statista.com/statistics/276623/number-of-apps-available-in-leading-app-stores/`.

[4] See `www.idc.com/promo/smartphone-market-share/os`.

Conventions Used in This Book

Almost every technical book starts with a little typeface legend, and this book is no exception. What follows is a brief explanation of the typefaces used in this book:

- New terms are set in *italics*.
- If you need to type something that's mixed in with the regular text, the characters you type appear in bold. For example: "Type **MyNewProject** in the text field."
- You see this `computerese` font for Kotlin code, filenames, web page addresses (URLs), onscreen messages, and other such things. Also, if something you need to type is really long, it appears in `computerese` font on its own line (or lines).
- You need to change certain things when you type them on your own computer keyboard. For instance, the instructions may ask you to type

  ```
  public void Anyname
  ```

  which means that you type **public void** and then some name that you make up on your own. Words that you need to replace with your own words are set in *`italicized computerese`*.

Foolish Assumptions

This book makes a few assumptions about you, the reader. If one of these assumptions is incorrect, you're probably okay. If all these assumptions are incorrect . . . well, buy the book anyway.

The assumptions are as follows:

- You can navigate through your computer's common menus and dialog boxes. You don't have to be a Windows, Macintosh, or Linux power user, but you should be able to start a program, find a file, put a file into a certain folder . . . that sort of thing. Much of the time, when you practice the stuff in this book, you're typing code on your keyboard, not pointing and clicking your mouse.
- You can think logically. That's all there is to application development — thinking logically. If you can think logically, you have it made. If you don't believe that you can think logically, read on. You may be pleasantly surprised.

» You have some programming experience (maybe not a lot). This book should be interesting for experienced programmers, yet accessible to people who don't write code for a living. If you're a programming guru, that's great. If you're a certified Linux geek, that's great, too. But no one expects you to be able to recite the names of Kotlin's concurrency primitives in your sleep, or pipe together a chain of 14 Linux commands without reading the documentation.

By the way, if you have no experience with an object-oriented language, you can get some. Your favorite bookstore has a terrific book titled *Java For Dummies,* 7th Edition, by Barry Burd (John Wiley & Sons, Inc.). The book comes highly recommended.

Icons Used in This Book

Throughout this book, an icon in the margin marks the beginning of a little detour — a fact or tidbit that stands out for one reason or another. The paragraphs marked by icons differ in their degree of importance. Some are valuable reading, others are silly trivia, and many are somewhere in the middle.

What kinds of icons do you find in this book? Here's a list:

TIP

A Tip is an extra piece of information — something helpful that the other books may forget to tell you.

WARNING

A Warning icon describes a mistake that many people make. Don't interpret the icon to mean, "Never make this mistake." That would be unreasonable. Instead, think of the icon as a word of comfort. It says, "Like everyone else, you'll probably make this mistake. When you do, remember that you once read about it here. Return to this section if you feel so inclined."

REMEMBER

Question: What's stronger than a Tip, but not as strong as a Warning?

Answer: A Remember icon.

TECHNICAL STUFF

Each Technical Stuff icon introduces an interesting fact. Some of these facts help you understand the reasoning behind the design of Android. You don't have to read all the Technical Stuff icons, but you may find them useful. They're especially helpful if you plan to read other (geekier) books about Android app development.

Beyond the Book

You've read the *Android All-in-One* book, seen the *Android All-in-One* movie, worn the *Android All-in-One* T-shirt, and eaten the *Android All-in-One* candy. What more is there to do?

That's easy. Just visit this book's website — `www.allmycode.com/Android`. At the website, you can find updates, comments, additional information, and lots of downloadable code. (You can also get there by visiting `www.dummies.com` and searching for *Android Application Development All-in-One For Dummies*, 3rd Edition.

Also on this book's page at `www.dummies.com` is the Cheat Sheet, which provides you with hints you need for nearly every Android app, such as parts of an Android app and the contents of that all important `.apk` file. You also get quick reminders about navigation classes, parts of a notification, and user interface elements.

Where to Go from Here

If you've gotten this far, you're ready to start reading about Android application development. Think of us (this book's authors) as your guides, your hosts, your personal assistants. We do everything we can to keep things interesting and, most important, help you understand.

If you experience any problems at all with this book, please contact either or both of us: Barry (`android@allmycode.com`) or John (`John@JohnMuellerBooks.com`) for assistance. We want you to be truly happy with your purchase and will help in any way we can with book-specific questions. You can also contact Barry on Twitter (`@allmycode`) and Facebook (`www.facebook.com/allmycode`).

Occasionally, we have updates to our technology books. If this book does have technical updates, they will be posted at this book's page at `www.dummies.com` and at `http://allmycode.com/android`.

1 Getting Started with Android Application Development

Contents at a Glance

» A tour of Android technologies

Chapter 1
All about Android

Until the mid-2000s, the word "Android" stood for a mechanical humanlike creature — a rootin' tootin' officer of the law with built-in machine guns, or a hyperlogical space traveler who can do everything except speak using contractions. But in 2005, Google purchased Android, Inc. — a 22-month-old company creating software for mobile phones. That move changed everything.

In 2007, a group of 34 companies formed the Open Handset Alliance. The Alliance's task was (and still is) "to accelerate innovation in mobile and offer consumers a richer, less expensive, and better mobile experience." The Alliance's primary project is *Android* — an open, free operating system based on the Linux operating system kernel.

HTC released the first commercially available Android phone near the end of 2008, but the public's awareness of Android and its potential didn't surface until early 2010. By the mid-2010s, the world had more than 400 Android device manufacturers with 500 mobile carriers using Android and 1.5 million Android activations each day (`https://expandedramblings.com/index.php/android-statistics/`). By mid-2019, more than 2.5 billion active devices ran the Android operating system (`https://venturebeat.com/2019/05/07/android-passes-2-5-billion-monthly-active-devices/`). (We know. By the time you read this book, the year 2019 is old news. That's okay.)

This chapter introduces Android. The chapter examines Android from a few different angles.

The Consumer Perspective

A consumer considers the mobile phone alternatives.

Possibility #1: No mobile phone.

- **Advantages:** Inexpensive. No junk calls. No interruptions. No GPS tracking or snooping by businesses or other agencies.
- **Disadvantages:** No instant contact with friends and family. No calls to services in case of an emergency. No hand-held games, no tweeting, tooting, hooting, homing, roaming, or booping. And worst of all, to break up with your boyfriend or girlfriend, you can't simply send a text message.

Possibility #2: **A feature phone — a mobile phone that's not a smartphone.**

- **Advantages:** Cheaper than a smartphone.
- **Disadvantages:** Not as versatile as a smartphone. Not nearly as cool as a smartphone. Nowhere near as much fun as a smartphone.

There's no official rule defining the boundary between feature phones and smartphones. But generally, a feature phone is one with an inflexible menu of home-screen options. A feature phone's menu items relate mostly to traditional mobile phone functions, such as dialing, texting, and maybe some limited web surfing and gaming. In contrast, a smartphone's home screen provides access to the underlying file system and has icons, customizable skins, and many other features that used to be available only to general-purpose computer operating systems.

Don't write off feature phones. As late as March 2019, Counterpoint Research predicted that people will buy a billion feature phones between 2019 and 2022 (`https://www.counterpointresearch.com/more-than-a-billion-feature-phones-to-be-sold-over-next-three-years/`). This fact may shock you if you live in a country where feature phones are passé. But in 2019, the worldwide feature phone continued to grow.

Possibility #3: An iPhone.

- **Advantages:** Great graphics.
- **Disadvantages:** Little or no flexibility with the single-vendor iOS operating system. Only a handful of different models to choose from. No sanctioned "rooting," "modding," or "jailbreaking" the phone. And then there is the potential cost of an iPhone when compared to Android phones.

Possibility #4: An Ubuntu Touch phone, a Harmony OS phone, or some other non-Android, non-Apple smartphone.

- **Advantages:** Having a smartphone without belonging to a crowd.
- **Disadvantages:** Relatively difficult to get technical support. Not nearly as many apps as Android phones and Apple phones. Smaller selection of hardware to choose from.

Possibility #5: An Android phone.

- **Advantages:** Using an open platform. Using a popular platform with lots of industry support and with powerful market momentum. Writing your own software and installing the software on your own phone (without having to deal with Apple as an intermediary). Access to a broad range of hardware and price points. Publishing software without facing the challenging approval process used by Apple, plus you can choose not to use the Google Play Store (see `https://www.knowband.com/blog/mobile-app/alternatives-for-publishing-android-app-on-google-play-store/` for alternative ideas).
- **Disadvantages:** Security concerns when using an open platform. Confusion about the variety of manufacturers, each with different hardware and with some changes to the Android platform. Dismay when iPhone users make fun of your phone.

Android's advantages far outweigh the possible disadvantages. And you're reading a paragraph from *Android Application Development All-in-One For Dummies*, 3rd Edition, so you're likely to agree.

Having decided to go with an Android phone, the consumer asks, "Which phone?" And the salesperson says, "This phone comes with Android 10." (If you read between the lines, what the salesperson really means is "This phone comes with Android 9, which will eventually be upgraded to Android 10, or so claims the vendor.") So the consumer asks, "What are the differences among all the Android versions?"

The Versions of Android

Android comes with a few different notions of "version." Android has platform numbers, API levels, codenames, and probably some other versioning schemes. (The acronym *API* stands for Application Programming Interface — a library full of prewritten programs available for use by a bunch of programmers. In this case, the "bunch" consists of all Android developers.)

To complicate matters, the versioning schemes don't increase in lockstep. For example, Android 8 (codenamed Oreo) has two API levels — levels 26 and 27. But Android 9 (codenamed Pie) has only one API level — level 28.

An Android version may have variations. For example, you can develop for plain old API Level 29 with an established set of features. To plain old API Level 29, you can add the Google APIs (thus adding Google Maps functionality) and still be using platform API Level 29. You can also add a special set with features tailored for a particular device manufacturer or a particular mobile service provider.

API levels 3 through 28 had tasty dessert codenames, and the names came in alphabetical order. For example, after Lollipop came Marshmallow; after Marshmallow came Nougat. Sad to say, the last-ever Android dessert codename was Pie, released in August 2018. About a year later, Google released a newer version simply named Android 10. The number 10 doesn't taste good the way lollipops and pies do.

Figure 1-1 has a summary of Android's API versions from 2008 to 2019.

A few notes on Figure 1-1 are in order:

- **The platform number is of interest to the consumer and to the company that sells the hardware.** If you're buying a phone with Android 9.0, for example, you might want to know whether the vendor will upgrade your phone to Android 10.0.
- **The API level (also known as the SDK version) is of interest to the Android app developer.** For example, in API level 8.1, the word `Build.SERIAL` stands for the phone's serial number. So, you might be tempted to type **Build.SERIAL** in code that uses API level 9.0. But in API level 9.0, `Build.SERIAL` doesn't help you get a phone's serial number. In API level 9.0, the value of `Build.SERIAL` is `"UNKNOWN"`.
- **The codename is of interest to the creators of Android.** A *codename* (also known as the *version code*) refers to the work done by the creators of Android to bring Android to the next level. Picture Google's engineers working for months behind closed doors on Project Oreo, and you'll be on the right track.

Since 2016, a new version of Android has come roughly once a year. Google released Nougat in 2016, Oreo in 2017, Pie in 2018, and the sugarless Android 10 in 2019. As a developer, your job is to balance portability with feature richness. When you create an app, you specify a minimum Android version. (You can read more about specifying a minimum version in Chapter 4 of this minibook.) The higher the version, the more features your app can have. But the higher the version, the fewer the devices that can run your app.

Year	Platform	API Level	Codename	Features
2008	1.0	1		
	1.1	2		
	1.5	3	Cupcake	
2009	1.6	4	Donut	Maturing app market interface, better voice tools, 800x480
	2.0	5	Eclair	Better user interface, more screen sizes, more camera functionality, Bluetooth 2.1 support, multi-touch support
	2.0.1	6		
	2.1	7		
2010	2.2	8	Froyo	Better performance with just-in-time (JIT) compiler, USB tethering, 720p screen, ability to install apps to the SD card
	2.3	9	Gingerbread	System-wide copy/paste, multi-touch soft keyboard, better native code development, concurrent garbage collection
	2.3.3	10		
	3.0	11	Honeycomb	Designed for tablets, new soft keyboard, tabbed browsing, redesigned widgets, "holographic UI", interface fragments
2011	3.1	12		
	3.2	13		
	4.0	14	Ice Cream Sandwich	Customizable launcher, screenshot capture, face unlock, Chrome browser, near-field communication, Roboto font
	4.0.3	15		
2012	4.1.2	16	Jelly Bean	Audio and accessibility improvements
	4.2.2	17		Expandable notifications, Google Now, smoother drawing, improved voice search
2013	4.3	18		Bluetooth Low Energy, 4K display, right-to-left languages
	4.4	19	KitKat	Immersive mode for apps, WebViews based on Chromium, text messaging management, UI transitions framework
2014	4.4W	20		API for wrist watches (Android Wear)
	5.0	21	Lollipop	Material Design (standards for the look of an app)
2015	5.1	22		Better notification priorities
	6.0	23	Marshmallow	Overhaul of the app permissions scheme, multi-window support, USB-C
2016	7.0	24	Nougat	Doze mode for battery life, new code compiler
	7.1	25		Swipe gestures, new storage manager
2017	8.0	26	Oreo	Notification channels, modular architecture for updates
	8.1	27		Shared memory, cryptography updates
2018	9.0	28	Pie	Optional gesture-based interface, more options for notifications, support for phones with notches
2019	10.0	29	10	Dark theme, support for foldable phones

FIGURE 1-1: Android version history.

This book contains tips and tricks for striking a happy medium between whiz-bang features and universal use, and Google has some nifty tools to help you sort out the differences among Android versions. In Chapter 3 of this minibook, you use Android Studio to create your first app. During the app setup, a drop-down box gives you a choice of Android versions for your app. Beneath that drop-down box is an innocent-looking Help Me Choose link. If you click this link, you see a page with the title Android Platform/API Version Distribution. This interactive page lists several of the most recent Android versions along with the percentage of phones that can run each version. And, when you click one of the Android versions, the page provides information about that version's features.

TECHNICAL STUFF

Storks and fairies don't install updates on your Android devices. The updates come via Wi-Fi or phone service through your carrier or device manufacturer. But by downloading and installing an independently developed Android release, you can break free of the corporate giants. For information about these independently developed releases, visit `http://forum.xda-developers.com/custom-roms`.

The Developer Perspective

Android is a multifaceted beast. When you develop for Android, you use many tool sets. This section gives you a brief rundown of those tool sets.

Java and Kotlin

James Gosling from Sun Microsystems created the Java programming language in the mid-1990s. (Sun Microsystems has since been bought out by Oracle.) Java's meteoric rise in use came from the elegance of the language and the well-conceived platform architecture. After a brief blaze of glory with applets and the web, Java settled into being a solid, general-purpose language with special strength in servers and middleware.

In the meantime, Java was quietly seeping into embedded processors.

TECHNICAL STUFF

An *embedded processor* is a computer chip that's hidden from the user as part of some special-purpose device. The chips in today's cars are embedded processors, and the silicon that powers your photocopier at work is an embedded processor. Pretty soon, the flowerpots on your windowsill will probably have embedded processors. By 2002, Sun Microsystems was developing Java ME (*M*obile *E*dition) for creating *MIDlets* based on the Mobile Information Device Profile (MIDP) to run on mobile phones in a manner similar to applets on a web page (see `https://www.techopedia.com/definition/116/midlet` for details). Java became a major technology in Blu-ray disc players, parking meters, teller machines, and other devices. So, the decision to make Java the primary development language for Android apps was no big surprise.

The trouble was, not everyone agreed about the fine points of Java's licensing terms. The Java language isn't quite the same animal as the Java software libraries, which in turn aren't the same as the *Java Virtual Machine* (the software that enables the running of Java programs). So, in marrying Java to Android, the founders of Android added an extra puzzle piece — the Dalvik Virtual Machine (see the "What is Dalvik" sidebar in Book 2, Chapter 3 for details). And instead of using the official Sun/Oracle Java libraries, Android used *Harmony* — an open-source Java implementation from the Apache Software Foundation. Several years and many lawsuits later, Google and Oracle were still at odds over the use of Java in Android phones.

Programmers always use one kind of software to develop other kinds of software. For several years, programmers had developed Android apps using software named *Eclipse*. In the meantime, a competing product named *IntelliJ IDEA* was growing in popularity. A group of engineers from Google and IntelliJ IDEA's parent company (*JetBrains*) cooperated to create a very lean version of IntelliJ IDEA. Simply put, they removed the features of IntelliJ IDEA that Android developers would never use. From this stripped-down version of IntelliJ IDEA, they created a customized product especially for Android programmers. At its annual developer conference in 2013, Google introduced *Android Studio* — the shiny new tool to help Android developers be more productive.

For everything you need to know about installing Android Studio, see Chapter 2 in this minibook. For instructions on using Android Studio, see Book 1, Chapter 3 and Book 2, Chapter 1.

Also at the aforementioned 2013 developer conference, Google began the process of replacing Dalvik with a new virtual machine named *Android Runtime*, or *ART*. Programs ran faster under ART, plus they consumed less memory and less power, and they were easier to debug. The transition from Dalvik to ART was a first step in the separation of Android from Oracle's proprietary Java technologies. (For more information about the Dalvik Virtual Machine and ART, see Book 2, Chapter 3.)

While Android matured, new programming languages were making improvements on many of Java's long-standing features. Apple was developing Swift to replace the aging Objective-C language. With Swift and other such languages, developers had a natural way of controlling how values may change during the run of a program. Developers could easily extend existing functionality and create code to tame null values — values that expert Tony Hoare had dubbed a "billion-dollar mistake." In newer languages, programmers used built-in features to write code in a *functional style* (a coding technique that expresses computational goals in the form of math functions) — a style that Book 2, Chapter 6 covers in detail.

JetBrains was developing one of these new languages. The language's name — Kotlin — came from the name of an island near St. Petersburg in Russia. Kotlin borrowed many of Java's features and improved on them in significant ways. At its annual developer conference in 2017, Google announced support for creating Android programs using Kotlin.

A year later, 35 percent of all Android programmers were using Kotlin. In 2019, Google officially dubbed Kotlin as the preferred language for Android app development.

Kotlin is fully compatible with Java. So, when you create an Android app, you can borrow pieces of programs written in Java and meld them seamlessly with your Kotlin code. Kotlin also integrates with JavaScript, so developers can write Kotlin programs that drive web pages. Behind the scenes, Kotlin plays nicely with Node.js — a widely used platform that runs on servers around the world. You can even translate Kotlin into native code — code that runs on Windows, macOS, Linux, and other operating systems.

Kotlin is deeply entrenched in the Android ecosystem and in other systems as well. If you already have some Kotlin programming experience, great! If not, you can find a fast-paced introduction to Kotlin in Book 2, Chapters 2 through 4. The time you invest in developing mobile Kotlin-based apps will continue to pay off for a long, long time.

XML

If you find View Source among your web browser's options, you see a bunch of Hypertext Markup Language (HTML) tags that represent the coding for a web page. A *tag* is some text enclosed in angle brackets. The tag describes something about its neighboring content.

For example, to create boldface type on a web page, a web designer writes

```
<b>Look at this!</b>
```

The angle-bracketed `b` tags turn boldface type on and off.

The *M* in HTML stands for *Markup* — a general term describing any extra text that annotates a document's content. When you annotate a document's content, you embed information about the document's content into the document itself. So, for example, in the line of code in the previous paragraph, the content is `Look at this!` The markup (information about the content) consists of the tags `<b>` and `</b>`.

All about Android

The HTML standard is an outgrowth of SGML (Standard Generalized Markup Language). SGML is an all-things-to-all-people technology for marking up documents for use by all kinds of computers running all kinds of software and sold by all kinds of vendors.

In the mid-1990s, a working group of the World Wide Web Consortium (W3C) began developing XML — the eXtensible Markup Language. The working group's goal was to create a subset of SGML for use in transmitting data over the Internet. The group succeeded. Today, XML is a well-established standard for encoding information of all kinds. Java is good for describing step-by-step instructions, and XML is good for describing the way things are (or should be). A Java program says, "Do this and then do that." In contrast, an XML document says, "It's this way, and it's that way." Android uses XML for two purposes:

- **To describe an app's data:** An app's XML documents describe the look of the app's screens, the translations of the app into one or more languages, and other kinds of data.
- **To describe the app itself:** Each Android app comes with an `AndroidManifest.xml` file. This XML document describes features of the app. The operating system uses the `AndroidManifest.xml` document's contents to manage the running of the app.

  For example, an app's AndroidManifest.xml file contains the app's name and the name of the file containing the app's icon. The XML file also lists the names of the app's screens and tells the system what kinds of work each screen can perform.

  For more information about the `AndroidManifest.xml` file and about the use of XML to describe an app's data, see Chapter 4 of this minibook.

Concerning XML, there's bad news and good news. The bad news is, XML isn't always easy to compose. The good news is, automated software tools compose most of the world's XML code. The software on an Android programmer's development computer composes much of an app's XML code. You often tweak the XML code, read part of the code for info from its source, make minor changes, and compose brief additions. But you hardly ever create XML documents from scratch.

REMEMBER

When you create an Android app, you deal with at least two "computers." Your *development computer* is the computer that you use for creating Android code. (In most cases, your development computer is a desktop or laptop computer — a PC, Mac, or Linux computer.) The other computer is something that most people don't even call a "computer." It's the Android device that will eventually be running your app. This device is a smartphone, tablet, watch, or some other cool gadget.

Linux

An *operating system* is a big program that manages the overall running of a computer or device. Most operating systems are built in layers. An operating system's outer layers, such as the applications and the environment in which the user interacts with the applications, are usually right up there in the user's face. For example, both Windows and macOS have standard *desktops* (a paradigm for the interface the user sees, sort of like the physical desktop you use at work). From the desktop, the user launches programs, manages windows, and so on. When you're working with Android, the desktop is represented by the Android Application Framework (shown in Figure 1-2).

An operating system's inner layers are (for the most part) invisible to the user. While the user plays Solitaire, the operating system juggles processes, manages files, keeps an eye on security, and generally does the kinds of things that the user shouldn't micromanage. Figure 1-2 shows the Android version of these inner layers as Libraries and the Android Runtime.

At the very deepest level of an operating system is the system's *kernel.* The kernel runs directly on the processor's hardware and does the low-level work required to make the processor run. In a truly layered system, higher layers accomplish work by making calls to lower layers. So an app with a specific hardware request sends the request (directly or indirectly) through the kernel.

The best-known, best-loved general-purpose operating systems are Microsoft Windows, Apple macOS (which is built on top of UNIX), and Linux (from various vendors). Windows and macOS are the properties of their respective companies. But Linux is open source. That's one of the reasons why the creators of Android based their platform on the Linux kernel. Openness is a good thing!

TECHNICAL STUFF

Rules concerning the use of open-source software come in many shapes and sizes. For example, there's the GNU General Public License (GPL), the Apache License, the GNU Lesser General Public License (LGPL), and others. When considering the use of other people's open-source software, be careful to check the software's licensing terms. "Open source" doesn't necessarily mean "do anything at all for free with this software."

Figure 1-2 is a diagram of the Android operating system. If you'd like a ten-cent tour, read on.

- **At the very top of Figure 1-2 are the applications — the web browser, the contacts list, the games, the dialer, the camera app, and other goodies.** Developers and users interact with this layer. Developers write code to run on this layer, and users see the screens created by apps in this layer.

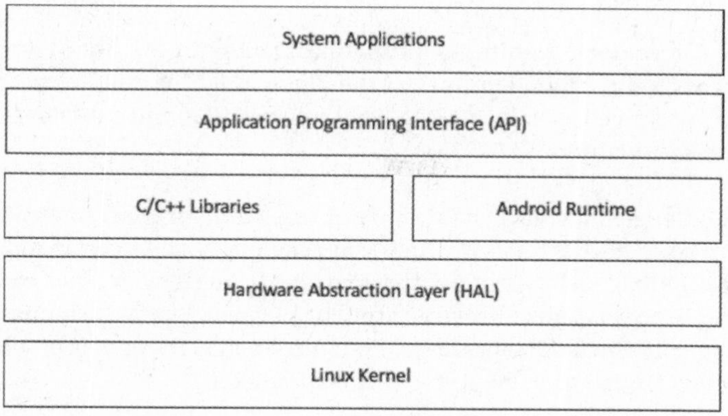

System Applications

Application Programming Interface (API)

C/C++ Libraries | Android Runtime

Hardware Abstraction Layer (HAL)

Linux Kernel

FIGURE 1-2: The Android system architecture.

- **Below the applications layer lies the *Application Programming Interface* (API) layer.** Your Android programs make requests to pieces of code in this API layer. In fact, most of this book's chapters describe ways for you to use Android's API layer.

  As an Android developer, you almost never deal with layers below the API layer. But just this once, you can take a quick peek at those three layers. Here goes . . .

  - **Android's middle layer has two parts: a bunch of code written in the C and C++ programming languages; and the Android Runtime (ART).** The Android Runtime is a workhorse that runs all your Kotlin code. For more on that, see Book 2, Chapter 2.
  - **The Hardware Abstraction Layer (HAL) is a kind of universal translator.** Imagine having guests from many foreign countries and speaking none of their languages. You can learn all their languages, but hiring several translators is easier. That's how HAL works. The Android Runtime runs on many different kinds of hardware, but ART isn't tailored for any particular kind of hardware. Instead, ART hires a HAL for each kind of hardware. Pretty clever!
  - **At the bottom is the Linux kernel, managing various parts of a device's hardware.** The kernel includes a Binder, which handles all communication among running processes. When your app asks, "Can any software on this phone tell me the current temperature in Cleveland, Ohio?" the request for information goes through the kernel's Binder.

As a developer, your most intimate contact with the Android operating system is through the command line, or the *Linux shell.* The shell uses commands, such as `cd` to change to a folder, `ls` to list a folder's files and subfolders, `rm` to delete files, and many others.

The Google Play Store has plenty of free *terminal* apps. A terminal app's interface is a plain text screen in which you type Linux shell commands. And with one of Android's developer tools, the Android Debug Bridge, you can issue shell commands to an Android device through your development computer. If you like getting your virtual hands dirty, the Linux shell is for you. (For a look at the Android Debug Bridge, see Chapter 2 of this minibook.)

The Business Perspective

The creation and selling of mobile phone apps is an enormous industry. The Google Play Store had 2.57 million apps at the end of 2019. By the time you read this book, the number 2.57 million will seem pathetically obsolete. With the marketing potential of alternatives such as the Amazon Appstore for Android and Samsung Galaxy Store, you have many distribution channels for your apps.

Anyone can post an app for approval on the Google Play Store. (The app doesn't actually appear for download until Google reviews and approves it.) You can post free apps, paid apps, and programs with in-app billing. You can test an app with a select group of users before making your app available to everyone. You make a small one-time payment to register as an Android developer. Then you design apps, develop apps, and post apps for the general public.

Book 6 covers the business of posting apps on the Google Play Store and the Amazon Appstore for Android. You may not become a millionaire selling Android apps, but you'll definitely have fun trying.

» Starting the Android Studio IDE

» Working with the Android SDK

Chapter 2

Installing the Software Tools

There are two kinds of people — people who love tools, and people who don't have strong feelings about tools. (As far as we know, no one dislikes tools.) You may be a tool lover because you enjoy the leverage that tools provide. With the right tool, you can easily do things that would otherwise require monumental effort. And you can do these things over and over again, getting better with practice using the tools so that the tasks you're dealing with become easier as time goes on.

Of course, having tool-o-philia isn't always a good thing. You may not be handy with skills like carpentry, car repair, or plumbing, but might not be able to resist buying greasy old screwdrivers and other such tools at garage sales. Some of these tools could be unique. For example, you could have what you think is the world's biggest monkey wrench (bought several years ago for only seven dollars). But your friends and family think you're useless (if not dangerous) using the wrench, so it sits in your attic waiting for your kids to deal with it when, years from now, they inherit your house full of junk.

But software tools are great. They're not greasy; many good tools are free; and if you lose a tool, you can usually find it by searching your computer's hard drive.

Anyway, this chapter is about Android development tools. Enjoy!

REMEMBER

You don't have to type the source code for this chapter manually. In fact, using the downloadable source is a lot easier. You can find the source for this chapter in the `01_02_01` folder of the downloadable source. See the Introduction for details on how to find these source files.

Setting Up the Software

To create an Android application using the least possible effort, you need an *Integrated Development Environment (IDE)* that helps you do things like write code and create screens. Yes, you could play the part of a cave dweller developer and use the command-line tools with a text editor, but no serious developer would actually go that route. The experience would be so painful that it would make going to the dentist seem like having a nice day at the park. The following sections discuss what you need, how to get it, and how to install the IDE used in this book.

Considering the requirements

REMEMBER

This book uses Android Studio version 3.5.1 to perform the task of creating really cool apps. If you use a different version, your screens may not match those in the book and you might find that the book's source code won't compile in precisely the same manner as discussed in the book. It pays to use the right tool for the job in any task. You can currently find the 3.5.1 version of the IDE on the archive Android Studio page at `https://developer.android.com/studio/archive`. If you don't see the version of Android Studio you need for your platform, click Download Options to see other platforms.

Like any other software, you need to have the right environment in which to use Android Studio. This environment varies by platform and by your expectations. If you like drinking lots of coffee, a slower system works just fine, but most developers want to work quickly, so it's important to get a fast system (as described by the Android Studio requirements). Currently, Android Studio supports these platforms:

- Windows 7, 8, or 10 (32-bit or 64-bit)
- Mac OS X 10.10 (Yosemite) to 10.14 (Mojave)
- Linux (Ubuntu 14.04 LTS seems to be your best bet)
- Chrome OS

REMEMBER

Near the bottom of the main Android Studio page, you find all the requirements for each of these platforms. Be sure to look at the particular requirements for each platform. For example, the 32-bit versions of Windows can't run the emulator, making your job considerably harder. And even though you can run the IDE on 4GB of RAM on most systems, you'll find that you get much better results with 8GB. Now that you have some idea of what to get and where to use it, you can look at the particulars for getting what you need.

Downloading the software

You have a number of options for downloading the Android Studio software. The download comes in essentially three parts: Android Studio; Offline Tools; and Command-Line Tools. You must download Android Studio, which includes the Command-Line Tools by default to perform tasks in this book, but the Offline Tools download is optional.

TIP

A good rule of thumb to consider regarding the Offline Tools download and installation is the speed of your Internet connection. The IDE maintains a near constant chatter with online elements when you use it unless you have the Offline Tools installed. If you have a slow Internet connection (anything slower than 200 Mbps or too slow for your tastes when you start to develop an app), installing the Offline Tools will save you lots of time and effort. You can test your actual Internet speed using a tool such as SpeedTest (`https://www.speedtest.net/`). The following steps help you download the software you need:

1. **Visit** `https://developer.android.com/studio`.

   Figure 2-1 shows you what this web page looked like in October 2019 (commonly known as "the good old days") when you visit using a Windows computer.

   TIP

   The page has a big button for downloading Android Studio for the platform the website detects you to be using. Of course, you might not be using this platform for development, in which case clicking the big button would be a mistake. Notice the detected platform indicator under the big button. If this doesn't match your platform, you need to click Download Options and choose one of the other platforms listed, as shown in Figure 2-2.

   The Android Studio download includes everything needed for development, including the Android SDK. However, this download assumes that you want to use a web connection for the Android Gradle Plugin and Google Maven dependencies.

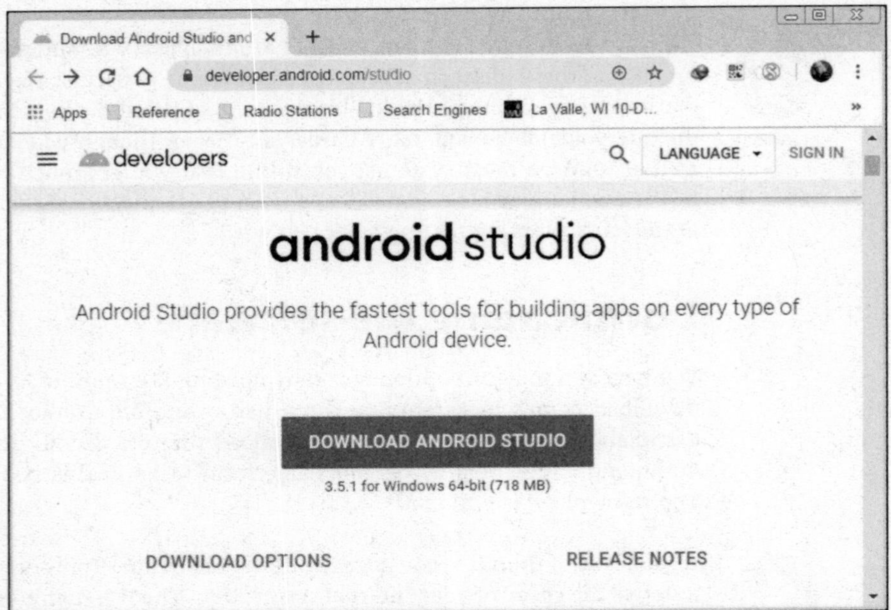

FIGURE 2-1: Downloading Android tools for the default platform.

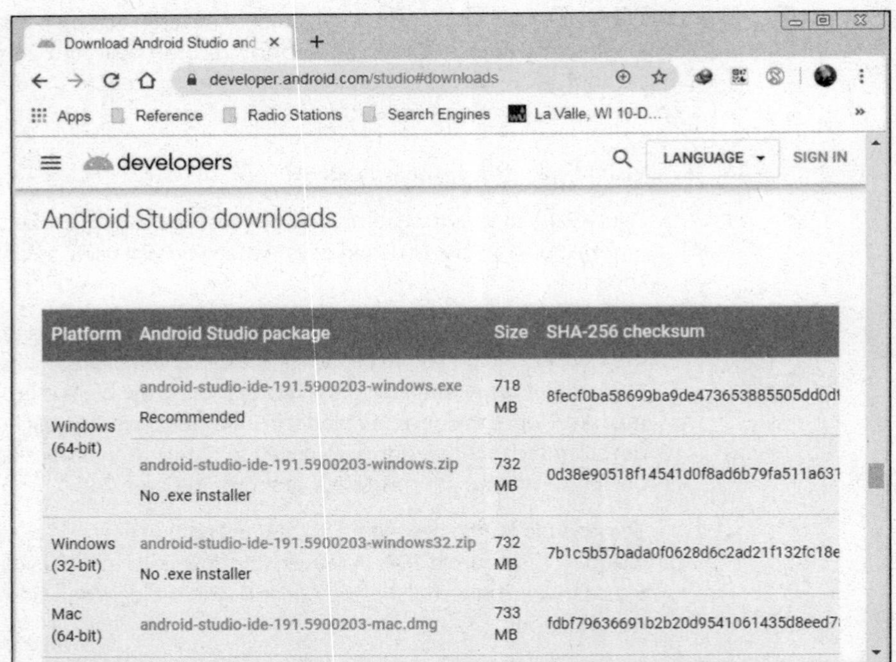

FIGURE 2-2: Downloading Android tools for an alternative platform.

2. **Click the button or link to download Android Studio for your platform.**
3. **Agree to all the legal mumbo-jumbo.**
4. **Save the download to a local drive.**

   The Android Studio download is an `.exe` file (for Windows) unless you specify that you want a `.zip` file instead, a `.dmg` file (for a Mac), a `.tar.gz` file (for Linux), or a `.deb` for Chrome OS. If you don't want to use the offline components, you're done. Otherwise, you need to continue with Step 5.

TIP

   You can perform the Offline Components download later and install it separately if you find that app development lags behind expectations.

5. **Scroll down the page to the Offline Components section.**
6. **Click the Android Gradle Plugin link.**

   No matter what platform you use, you receive a `.zip` file.

7. **Click the Google Maven Dependencies link.**

   Again, you receive a `.zip` file for the download.

Installing the Software Tools

Installing Android Studio

When you download Android Studio, you have an `.exe` file (for Windows) unless you specify a `.zip` file instead, a `.dmg` file (for a Mac), a `.tar.gz` file (for Linux), or a `.deb` for Chrome OS.

- **In Windows:** Double-click the `.exe` file's icon.

  When you double-click the `.exe` file's icon, a wizard guides you through the installation.

- **On a Mac:** Double-click the `.dmg` file's icon.

  When you double-click the `.dmg` file's icon, you see an Android Studio icon (also known as an Android Studio.app icon). Drag the Android Studio icon to your Applications folder.

- **In Linux:** Extract the contents of the `.tar.gz` or `.zip` archive file. (Where you put the extracted contents is up to you.)

  The steps for extracting the file's contents vary from one Linux distribution to another. The best option is to follow the steps for your variant of Linux found in the Linux section of `https://developer.android.com/studio/install`. Make sure to address any special requirements, such as installing some required 32-bit libraries when working with Ubuntu. Fortunately, the installation page gives you a video to watch to get a good install.

- **In Chrome OS:** Before you can install Android Studio on a Chrome OS system, you need to install Linux for Chrome OS using the instructions found at `https://support.google.com/chromebook/answer/9145439`. After you've completed the prerequisites, right-click the `.deb` package and select Install with Linux (Beta). A wizard guides you through the installation.
- After you complete the installation, Android Studio starts automatically. It then asks if you want to use any previous settings. Given that you don't have any, choose Do Not Import Settings and click OK. You see the Android Studio Setup Wizard dialog box. This wizard helps you configure your system with the Android SDK. The "Using the Android Studio Setup Wizard" section, later in this chapter, tells you how to work with this wizard.

While you're still in the mood to follow our advice, note the location on the hard drive where the Android SDK lands. For example, in Figure 2-3, the SDK folder is `\Users\John\AppData\Local\Android\Sdk`. The name used for this home folder in the book is `ANDROID_HOME` folder.

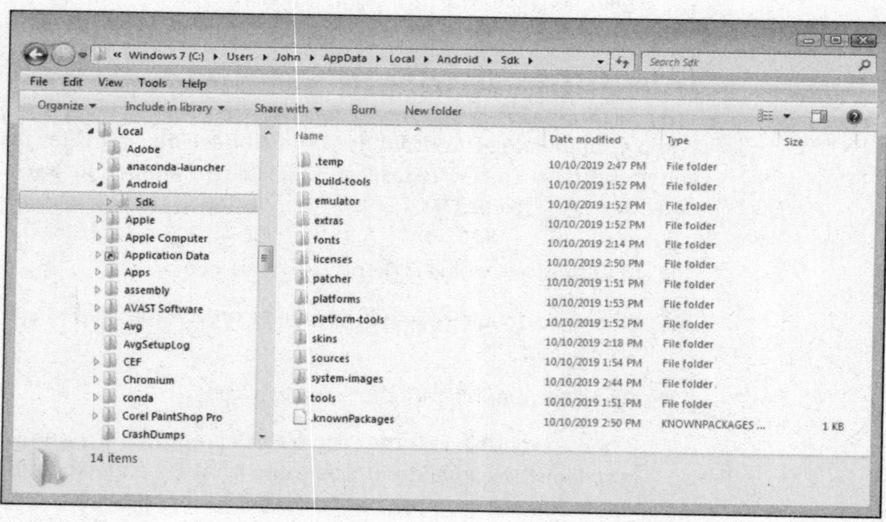

FIGURE 2-3: The ANDROID_HOME folder.

Take a few minutes to browse your `ANDROID_HOME` folder's contents. The folder has folders named `build-tools`, `platform-tools`, `platforms`, `sources`, `tools`, and others. The tools and platform-tools folders contain items that Android developers use all the time.

THERE'S NO PLACE LIKE HOME

This chapter is littered with things that have *home* in their names. If you've been reading every word, you've seen references to the ANDROID_HOME folder. In addition to this _HOME folder, your operating system maintains one or more user home folders — one such folder for each of the computer's users (including administrators and guests).

- To find your user home folder on a Windows computer, run the cmd program and type **set HOMEPATH**.
- To find your user home folder on a Mac, open the Finder and then press Cmd+Shift+H. Alternatively, you can use the Terminal windows and the same command that works in Linux.
- To find your user home folder on a Linux computer, run the Terminal app and type **echo $HOME**.

Unlike the ANDROID_HOME folder, your user home folder is a starting point for subfolders containing your own user files. On most computers, a user's home folder contains subfolders named `Documents`, `Downloads`, and so on.

And here's one more thing to remember: To clearly distinguish the user home folder from the ANDROID_HOME folder, this book refers to this folder by that very name: the user home folder. Other authors simply write home folder (without the extra word *user*). And we might have gotten sloppy and written "home folder" here and there in this book. (Sorry about that!) We tried not to, though.

Installing offline tools

You don't have to download and install the offline tools immediately. In fact, you must start Android Studio at least once to download the Gradle build tool (`https://gradle.org/`). If your Internet connection is fast enough, you may find using the standard configuration easier.

For those of us who like to do something more than look out the window and drink coffee, the offline tool configuration is essential. You can use this method only on

Windows, Mac, or Linux systems. The Mac setup is the same as the Linux setup. The process isn't hard and requires just the few steps shown here:

1. **Create a** `manual-offline-m2` **folder on your system to hold the files you download in the "Downloading the software" section, earlier in this chapter, in one of these locations:**

   - **Windows:** `%USER_HOME%/.android/`
   - **Mac and Linux:** `~/.android/`

   You see a new folder like the one shown in Figure 2-4.

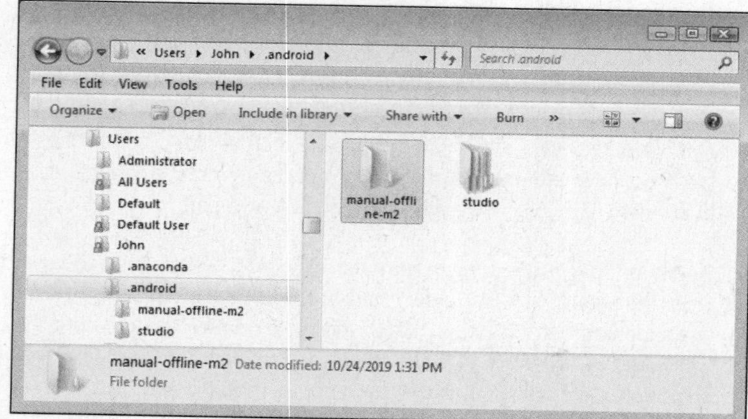

FIGURE 2-4: The manual-offline-m2 folder.

2. **Unzip the contents of the** `offline-android-gradle-plugin-preview.zip` **and** `offline-gmaven-stable.zip` **files to the** `manual-offline-m2` **folder you just created.**

   The extraction process may take a while to complete, depending on the speed of your system. The `manual-offline-m2` folder now contains the folders shown in Figure 2-5.

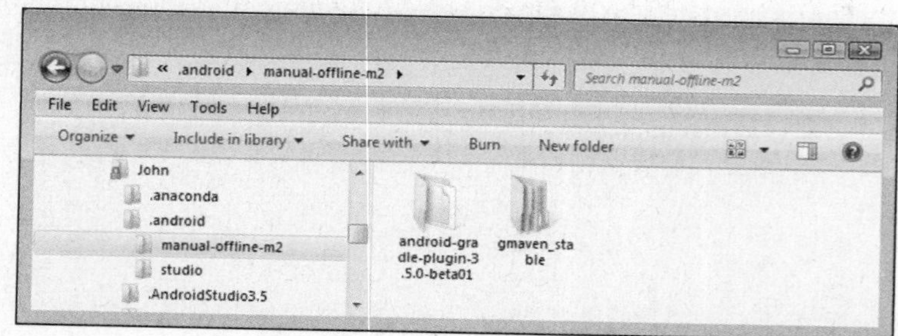

FIGURE 2-5: The offline files used to support Android Studio.

3. **Create an `init.d` folder on your system to hold an initialization file for the Gradle build tool in this location using a method appropriate for your platform (such as Windows Explorer, command prompt, terminal window, or Finder):**

   - **Windows:** `%USER_HOME%/.gradle/`
   - **Mac and Linux:** `~/.gradle/`

4. **Create an empty text file named `offline.gradle` in the `.gradle` folder you just created.**

   Your setup should look like the one shown in Figure 2-6.

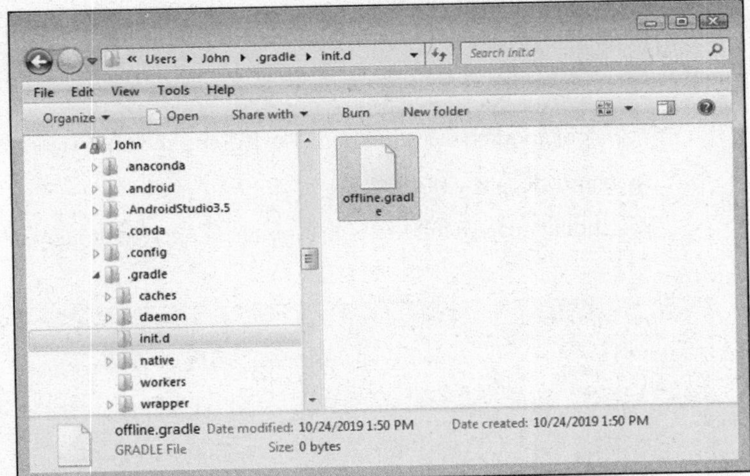

FIGURE 2-6: The Gradle build tool configuration file location.

5. **Add the following information to the `offline.gradle` file (note that the first three lines should all appear on a single line in your file).**

```
def reposDir = new
 File(System.properties['user.home'],
 ".android/manual-offline-m2")
def repos = new ArrayList()
reposDir.eachDir {repos.add(it) }
repos.sort()

allprojects {
  buildscript {
    repositories {
      for (repo in repos) {
```

```
        maven {
          name = "injected_offline_${repo.name}"
          url = repo.toURI().toURL()
        }
      }
    }
  }
  repositories {
    for (repo in repos) {
      maven {
        name = "injected_offline_${repo.name}"
        url = repo.toURI().toURL()
      }
    }
  }
}
```

Your configuration file should look like the one shown in Figure 2-7.

6. **Save and close the file.**

   You should notice a marked improvement in Android Studio's performance.

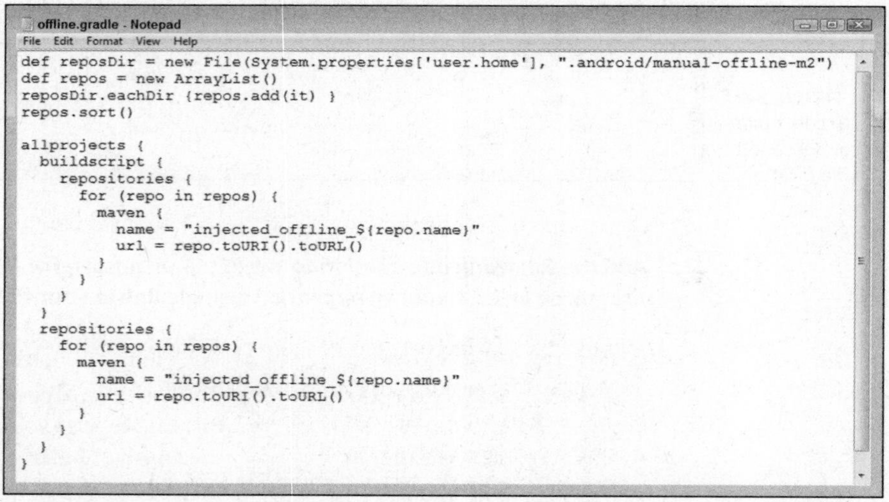

```
offline.gradle - Notepad
File  Edit  Format  View  Help
def reposDir = new File(System.properties['user.home'], ".android/manual-offline-m2")
def repos = new ArrayList()
reposDir.eachDir {repos.add(it) }
repos.sort()

allprojects {
  buildscript {
    repositories {
      for (repo in repos) {
        maven {
          name = "injected_offline_${repo.name}"
          url = repo.toURI().toURL()
        }
      }
    }
  }
  repositories {
    for (repo in repos) {
      maven {
        name = "injected_offline_${repo.name}"
        url = repo.toURI().toURL()
      }
    }
  }
}
```

FIGURE 2-7: The Gradle build tool configuration file.

Launching the Android Studio IDE

The previous sections show you how to download and install Android Studio. Your next task (should you decide to accept it) is to launch Android Studio. This section has the details.

In Windows

When working in Windows, you should see a new Start menu entry for Android Studio. To start Android Studio, follow these steps:

1. **Choose Start⇨All Programs⇨Android Studio⇨Android Studio.**

   The first time you start Android Studio, you see the dialog box shown in Figure 2-8.

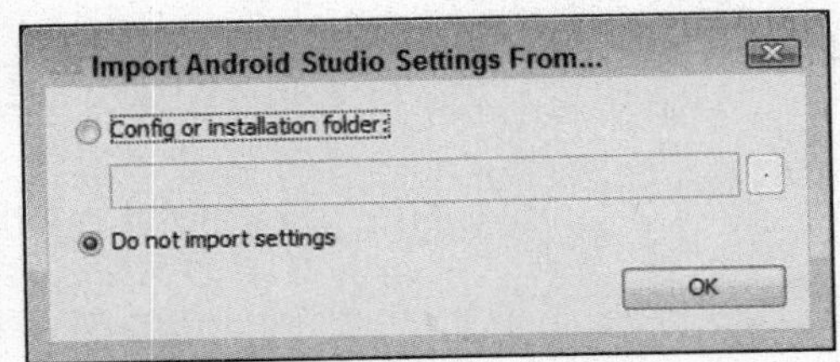

FIGURE 2-8: Importing existing settings.

2. **Choose Do Not Import Settings and click OK.**

   The startup may take a while to start, so be patient. You see the Android Studio Setup Wizard dialog box. This wizard helps you configure your system with the Android SDK. The "Using the Android Studio Setup Wizard" section, later in this chapter, tells you how to work with this wizard.

On a Mac

1. **In a Finder window, visit the Applications folder.**
2. **In the Applications folder, double-click the Android Studio icon.**

   The first time you start Android Studio, you see the dialog box shown in Figure 2-8.

3. **Choose Do Not Import Settings and click OK.**

   The startup may take a while to start, so you have to be patient. You see the Android Studio Setup Wizard dialog box. This wizard helps you configure your system with the Android SDK. The "Using the Android Studio Setup Wizard" section, later in this chapter, discusses how to work with this wizard.

REMEMBER

If your Mac complains that Android Studio is from an unidentified developer, Ctrl-click the Android Studio icon and select Open. When another "unidentified developer" box appears, click the Open button.

In Linux

1. **Open a terminal window.**
2. **Navigate to the** `android-studio/bin/` **folder.**
3. **Type** studio.sh **and press Enter.**

   The first time you start Android Studio, you see the dialog box shown in Figure 2-8.

4. **Choose Do Not Import Settings and click OK.**

   The startup may take a while to start; be patient. You see the Android Studio Setup Wizard dialog box. This wizard helps you configure your system with the Android SDK. The upcoming "Using the Android Studio Setup Wizard" section talks about working with this wizard.

In Chrome OS

Launch Android Studio either from the Launcher or from the Chrome OS Linux terminal by executing `studio.sh` in the `/opt/android-studio/bin/studio.sh` installation folder.

Using the Android Studio Setup Wizard

No matter which platform you use to install Android Studio, you eventually see the Android Studio Setup Wizard dialog box after installation during the first startup. The wizard begins with a Welcome dialog box in which you read the generic message and click Next. The following steps start with the Install Type dialog box, shown in Figure 2-9.

1. **Choose Standard and click Next.**

   You see the Select UI Theme dialog box, shown in Figure 2-10. This book uses the Light theme to make the screenshots easier to see.

2. **Select a UI theme and click Next.**

   The wizard asks you to verify your settings, which include the setup type and the location of the installation folder. You shouldn't have to change either setting unless you used a custom setup rather than the standard setup.

3. **Click Finish.**

   At this point, the components you need start to download and install. It's time for a coffee break!

After everything is done, you may have to click Finish again. Then you see the Android Studio screen, shown in Figure 2-11. Chapter 3 of this minibook takes you through your first Android Studio project.

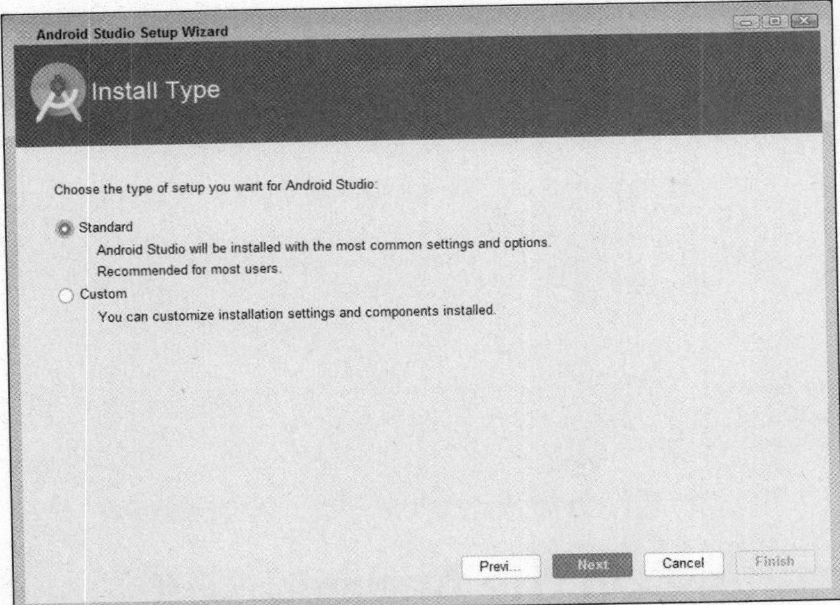

FIGURE 2-9: Starting the SDK installation.

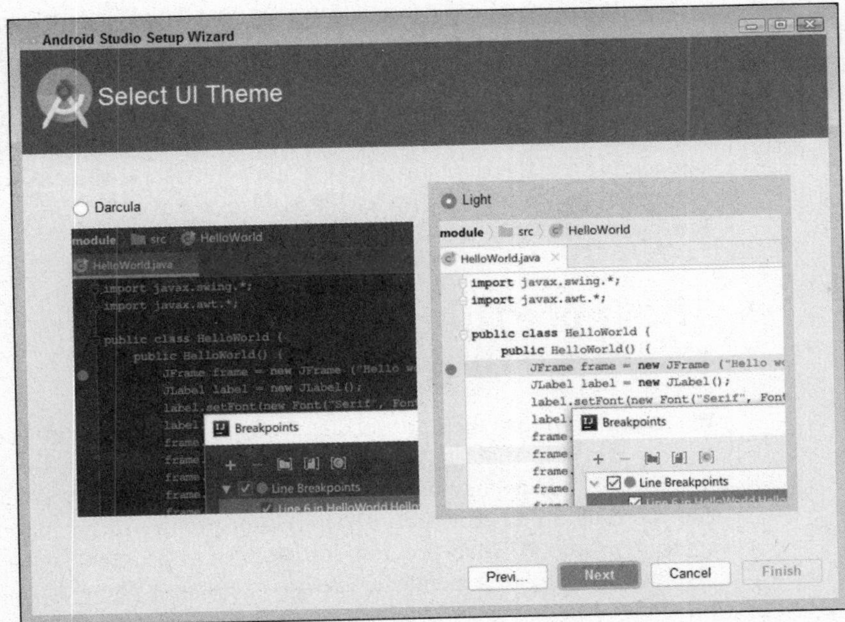

FIGURE 2-10: Choosing a UI theme.

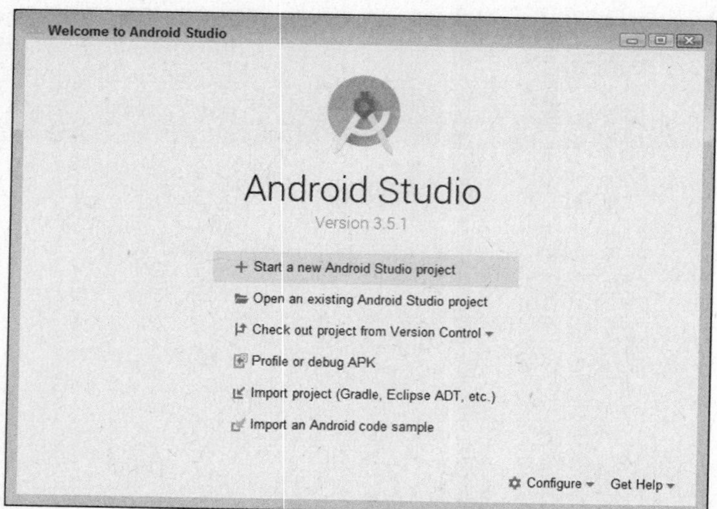

FIGURE 2-11: Finally getting to the initial Android Studio opening screen.

Fattening Up the Android SDK

In the "Using the Android Studio Setup Wizard," earlier in this chapter, you install the part of the Android SDK you need for most tasks. When you create a new project, you determine the level of support you want for that app, the kind of app you want to create, and the devices that app will support. The IDE then addresses any requirements for you before it displays the project, which can mean another trip outside to view the flora and fauna while you wait. At some point in your travels, you may want to install more of the SDK so that you don't have to wait. The following section tells you how.

The more things stay the same, the more they change

When you download the Android SDK, you get the code library (the API) for a particular release of Android. You also get several developer tools — tools for compiling, testing, and debugging Android code. For example, to test your code, you can run the code on an emulator. The emulator program runs on your development computer (your PC, Mac, or Linux computer or a Chrome OS device). The emulator displays a picture of a mobile device (for example, a phone or tablet). The emulator shows you how your code will probably behave when you later run your code on a real phone or tablet.

Another tool, the Android Debug Bridge (ADB), connects your development computer to a device that's executing your new Android code. (The ADB also "connects" your development computer to a running emulator, even though the emulator is running on your development computer.) The ADB is an invaluable tool for testing Android applications.

Neither the basic emulator nor Android's ADB tool change very much over time. But Android's user interface and the features available to Android developers change considerably from one version to another. One month developers work with Android 10.0, codenamed Q. Later that year, developers use Android 8.1, codenamed Oreo. Each version of Android represents a new platform, a new API level, or a new codename depending on the way you refer to the version.

TIP

For more information about Android codenames, tags, and build numbers, visit `https://source.android.com/setup/start/build-numbers`.

To help you juggle the different Android versions, the people at Google have created two tools.

- The Android SDK Manager lists the versions of Android and helps you download and install the versions that you need on your development computer.
- The Android Virtual Device Manager helps you customize the basic emulator so that you can imitate the device of your choice on your development computer.

The next few sections cover these tools in depth.

Installing new versions (and older versions) of Android

When you first install the Android Studio, you can probably skip this section's instructions. Follow this section's instructions when Google releases updated versions of Android, or when you work on a project that requires older versions of Android (versions that you want to install manually). To manage all the Android versions that are available to you (the developer), use the Android SDK Manager. Here's how:

1. **In Android Studio's main menu, choose Tools⇨SDK Manager.**

   After selecting this option, you see a new window — namely, the Android SDK Manager pane of the Settings for New Projects window. (See Figure 2-12.)

In the Android SDK Manager, you see a listing of Android versions and tools. For each item in the tree, the Status column tells you whether you've already installed that item (and, if applicable, that an update is available for the item).

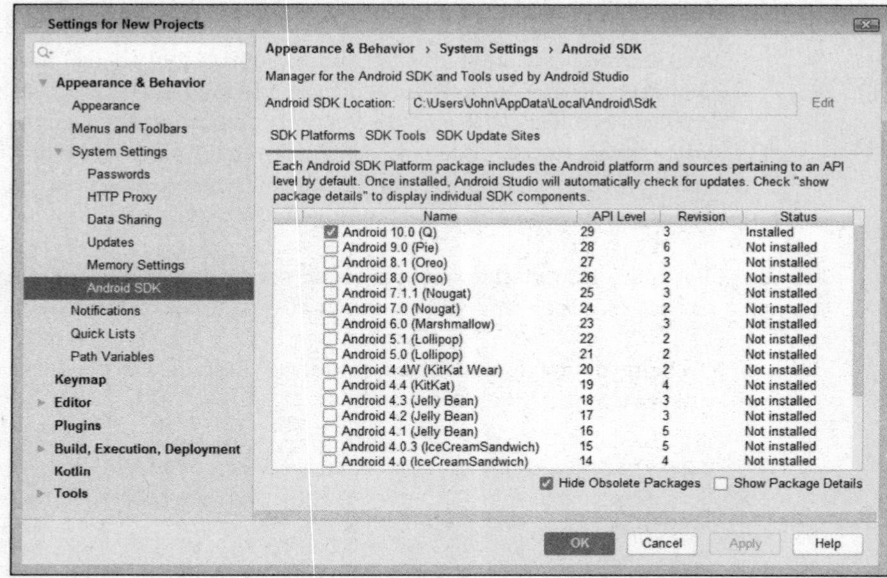

FIGURE 2-12: The Android SDK Manager.

2. **Place check marks next to any items that you want to install, and next to any items that you want to update. (Refer to Figure 2-13.)**

   You can expand parts of the tree so that you can pick and choose from among the items in an Android version. By default, the Android Studio Setup Wizard automatically installs the latest SDK for you, which is likely all you need for this book. If you have lots of space on your hard drive and don't mind waiting a long time for the download to finish, you can select more items.

   REMEMBER

   Notice that the SDK Tools appear on a separate tab. Figure 2-13 shows that the wizard installs only the basic tools for you and that many others are available for your use.

3. **After you check the SDK platforms and SDK tools you want to add to your setup, click Apply.**

   You see a Confirm Change dialog box, which tells you what resources Android Studio will install.

4. **Click OK.**
5. **Do any remaining license accepting and clicking to make the installations begin.**

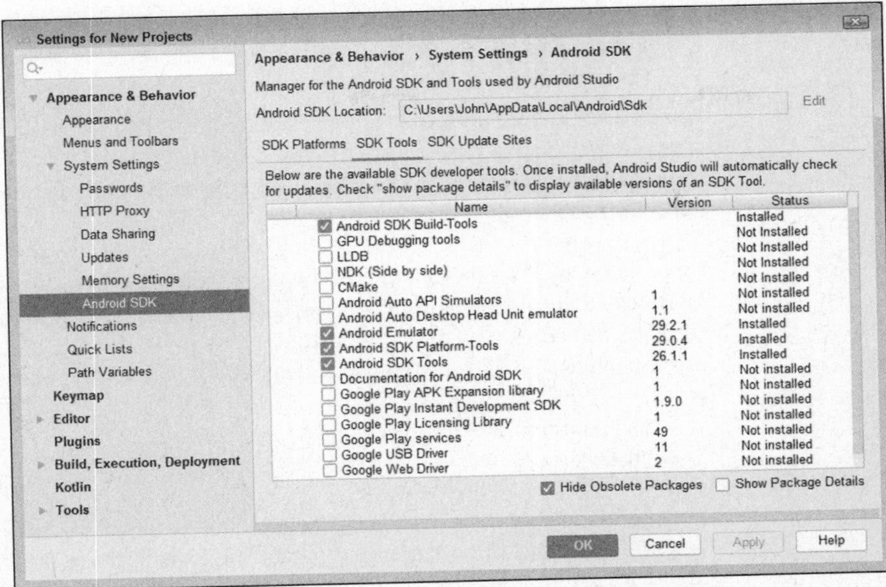

FIGURE 2-13: The Android SDK Tools appear on a separate tab.

Creating an Android virtual device

You might be itching to run some code, but first you must have something that can run an Android program. By "something," we mean either a real Android device (a phone, a tablet, an Android Wear watch, an Android-enabled refrigerator, whatever) or a virtual device. By a virtual device, we mean a program that runs on your development computer and creates a window that looks (and acts) like a real Android device. People call this device an emulator, but in truth, the virtual device has three parts:

- **A system image is a copy of one version of the Android operating system.** A system image provides an Android operating system and any associated functionality normally associated with an operating system. Starting with Android 9, Android Studio uses a Generic System Image (GSI) as described at `https://developer.android.com/topic/generic-system-image`, so you don't have to worry about downloading individual system images for various devices.
- **The emulator bridges the gap between the system image and the processor on your development computer.** You might have a system image for a device that uses Android 9, but your development computer runs a Core i7 processor. The emulator translates instructions that the Android 9 device would need into instructions that the Core i7 processor can execute. You get an emulator when you follow the steps in the section "Installing the software," earlier in this chapter.

STEAL THIS AVD!

You can copy an AVD from someone else's computer. That is, you don't really have to create an AVD. You can use an AVD that's already been created. On your development computer's hard drive, an AVD is an `.ini` file combined with a folder full of configuration information.

For example, if you create your own device (using the instructions in Chapter 3 of this minibook), your computer's `C:\Users\my-user-name\.android\avd\` folder may have files named `Nexus5_4.4.2_API19.ini`, `Tablet_API17.ini`, and so on. When you open `Nexus5_4.4.2_API19.ini` in a text editor, you might see something like this:

```
target=android-19
path=C:\Users\Barry\.android\avd\Nexus5_4.4.2_API19.avd
```

Don't let the dot in the name `Nexus5_4.4.2_API19.avd` fool you. The name `Nexus5_4.4.2_API19.avd` refers to a folder. This folder contains files like `config.ini`, which in turn describes the virtual device's SD card size, RAM size, and so on. Here are a few lines from a config.ini file:

```
hw.lcd.density=480
sdcard.size=1000M
hw.ramSize=512
```

To copy an AVD from someone else's computer, copy the `.avd` folder to your development computer's hard drive. Then create an `.ini` file like my `Nexus5_4.4.2_API19.ini` file. (Don't forget to replace the example target and path values with values that are appropriate for your computer.) Put all this stuff in your user home folder's `.android\avd` folder (or wherever the AVD files are stored).

» **An Android Virtual Device (AVD) is the representation of a real (physical) device's hardware.** The emulator translates Android code into code that your development computer can execute. But the emulator doesn't display a particular phone or tablet device on your screen. The emulator doesn't know what kind of device you want to display. Do you want a camera phone with 800-x-480-pixel resolution, or have you opted for a tablet device with its own built-in accelerometer and gyroscope? All these choices belong to a particular AVD. An AVD is actually a bunch of settings, telling the emulator all the details about the device to be emulated.

  What kind of a processor does the device have? What's the screen resolution of the device? Does the device have a physical keyboard? Does it have a camera? How much memory does it have? Does it have an SD card? All these facts about a virtual device live in an AVD. An AVD runs on a particular system image which, in turn, runs on the emulator.

You create one or more AVDs before testing your code on a development computer. When you tell Android Studio to do a test run of your code, you can choose one of these AVDs.

So before you can run Android apps on your computer, you must first create at least one AVD. In fact, you normally create several AVDs and then use one of them to run a particular Android app.

To create a basic AVD, follow these steps:

1. **In Android Studio's main menu, choose Tools⇨AVD Manager.**

   After selecting this option, you see a new window — namely, the Android Virtual Device Manager window.

2. **Click + Create Virtual Device.**

   You see the collection of devices shown in Figure 2-14. Notice that there are separate categories in the default setup for TV, Phone, Wear OS, and Tablet. You can add other categories by creating a new hardware profile (click New Hardware Profile) or by importing an existing hardware profile (click Import Hardware Profiles).

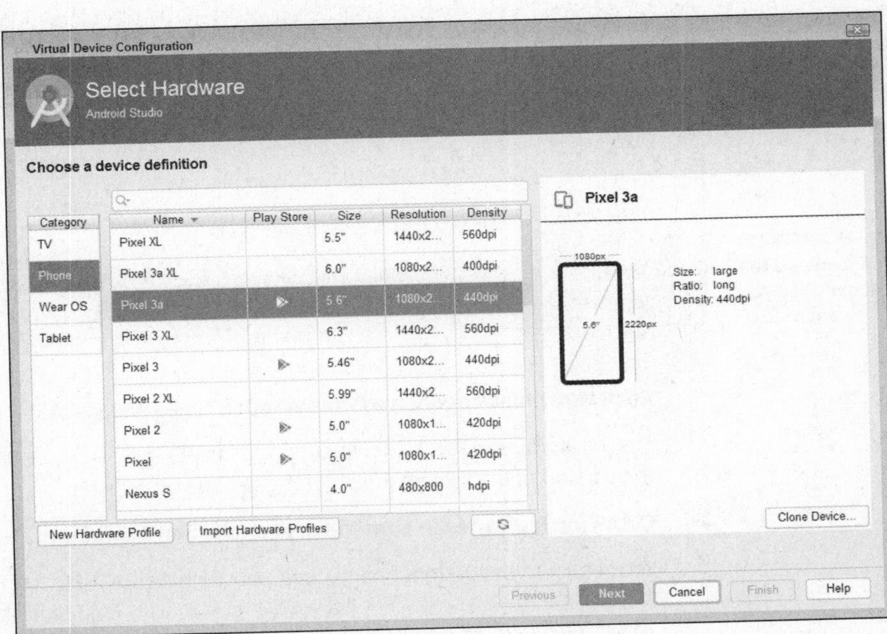

FIGURE 2-14: Choose a category and device that meets your needs.

To create a modified form of one of the default devices, you must first clone it by clicking Clone Device. You can't make changes to the standard device offering.

TIP

Notice that some of the entries contain an icon in the Play Store column. These entries provide access to the Google Play Store so that you can download apps you need for testing. These devices won't allow you to perform tasks that require elevated privileges, so you may end up getting an alternative device from the Android Open Source Project (AOSP) (`https://source.android.com/`).

3. **Choose one of the default devices for now and then click Next.**

   You see options for downloading a system image for the particular device you've selected, as shown in Figure 2-15. If you need more than one system image, you can download them all from this one location.

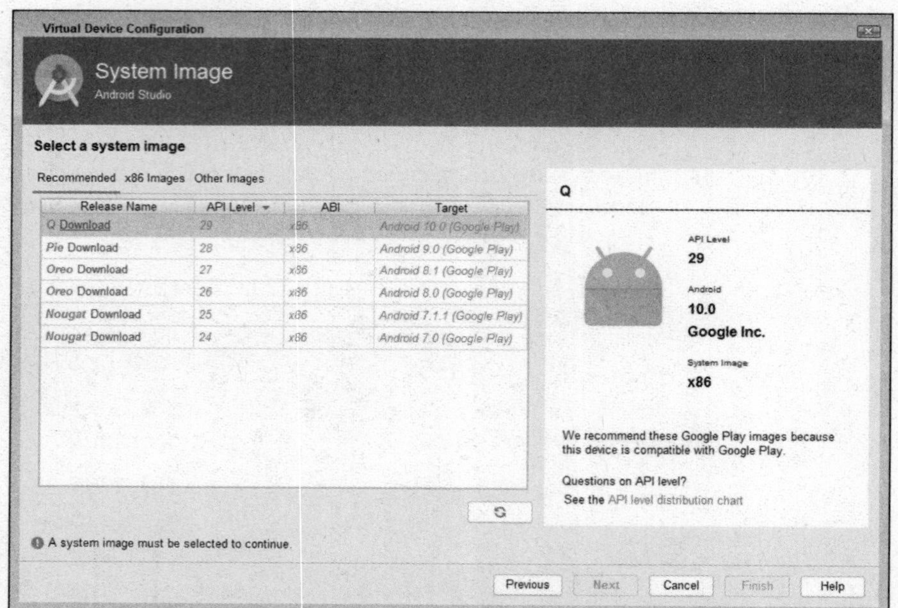

FIGURE 2-15: Download the system image you want to test.

4. **Click Download for each of the system images you want.**

   The wizard automatically downloads and installs the components needed for the version of the system image of the device you selected.

5. **Click Finish after each component installation completes.**

   You return to the System Image page, shown in Figure 2-15.

6. **After you finish downloading all the system images you want, click Next.**

   You see the Verify Configuration page, shown in Figure 2-16. Notice that when you use a standard device, you can't change any of the settings. When working with a cloned or custom device, you have full control over the configuration settings.

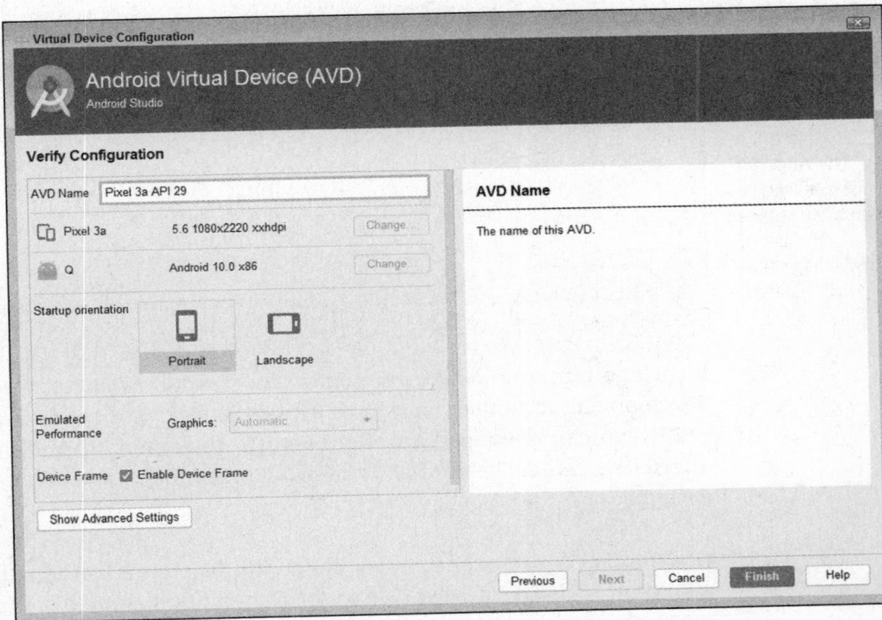

FIGURE 2-16: Download the system image you want to test.

7. **Change the AVD Name, if desired, and then click Finish.**

   You see the virtual device you just created in a list of virtual devices, as shown in Figure 2-17. When running your app, you choose the AVD you want to use for test.

A third-party emulator

Android's standard emulator (the emulator that you download from Google's website) is notoriously messy. The startup is slow, and even after startup, the emulator's response can be painfully sluggish. In Chapter 3 of this minibook, you discover how to test Android code on a real device connected via USB to your computer. The performance on a real device (even on an older Android device) is much snappier than on the standard emulator.

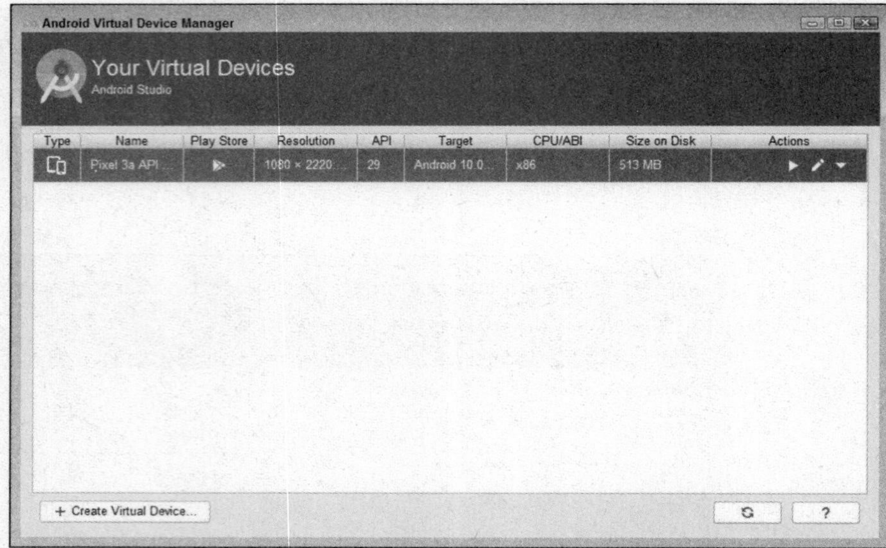

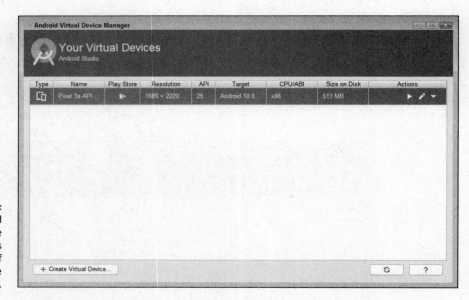

FIGURE 2-17: The Android Virtual Device Manager shows the list of devices you've configured.

If you don't like the standard emulator, and you don't want to attach devices to your development computer, you have a third choice. At `https://www.genymotion.com/`, you can download an alternative to the standard Android emulator. The alternative is available for Windows, Macintosh, and 64-bit Debian-based systems.

Genymotion's emulator is much faster and has more features than the standard emulator. If there's a downside to the Genymotion emulator, it's the cost. Genymotion's product is free for personal use (the download for this version is currently at `https://www.genymotion.com/fun-zone/`) but costs from $136 to $412 for commercial use per year.

If you develop apps only for personal use, or if you have money to spend on a commercial venture, Genymotion's emulator is definitely worth considering.

And that does it! You're ready to run your first Android app. We're sure you're excited about the next step. (We're not watching you read this book, but we're excited on your behalf.) Chapter 3 in this minibook guides you through the run of an Android application. Go for it!

ACTING LIKE A PHONE (WHEN YOU'RE NOT A PHONE)

In computing, the words *emulator* and *simulator* have similar meanings. Some people use the words interchangeably, but if you're being picky, an *emulator* executes each program by doing what another kind of processor would do. In contrast, a *simulator* executes a program any way that's handy and ends up with the same result that an emulator would get. To be even pickier, an emulator mimics your processor's hardware, and a simulator mimics your application's software.

On your development computer's screen, a phone simulator would look like a picture of a phone and would carry out your mobile application's instructions for testing purposes. But on the inside, the simulator would be executing instructions the way your laptop or desktop executes instructions. The simulator would be translating instructions meant for a phone's processor into instructions meant for your laptop's processor. This juggling act (of instructions and processors) works fine on the whole. But in some subtle situations, a simulator doesn't precisely mimic a real phone's behavior.

The goal of precise, reliable mimicry is one reason why the Android crew decided on an emulator instead of a simulator. Android's emulator (the emulator that you download with the SDK starter package) is based on a very popular open-source program named QEMU. On its own, QEMU takes code written for a certain kind of processor (an Intel chip, for example), translates this code, and then runs the code on another kind of processor (an ARM or a PowerPC, for example). The emulator that comes with Android's SDK has add-ons and tweaks to accommodate Android mobile devices. For more information about QEMU, visit `https://www.qemu.org/`.

» Troubleshooting troublesome apps

» Testing an app on an emulator or a real device

Chapter 3

Creating an Android App

In a quiet neighborhood in south Philadelphia, you might find a maternity shop named Hello World. You can find the store on your way to Pat's (to get a delicious Philly cheesesteak). You might even take a picture of the store's sign as a sort of inspiration for the content of this chapter: the Hello World app.

A Hello World app is the simplest program that can run in a particular programming language or on a particular platform. (For an interesting discussion of the phrase Hello World, visit `http://www.mzlabs.com/JMPubs/HelloWorld.pdf`.) Authors create Hello World apps to show people how to get started writing code for a particular system.

So, in this chapter, you make an Android Hello World app. The app doesn't do much. (In fact, you might argue that the app doesn't do anything!) But the example shows you how to create and run new Android projects.

Creating Your First App

A typical gadget comes with a manual. The manual's first sentence is "Read all 37 safety warnings before attempting to install this product." Don't you love it? You can't get to the good stuff without wading through the preliminaries.

REMEMBER

Well, nothing in this chapter can set your house on fire or even break your electronic device. But before you follow this chapter's instructions, you need a bunch of software on your development computer. To make sure that you have this software and that it's properly configured, return to Chapter 2 of this minibook. (Do not pass Go; do not collect $200.)

When at last you have all the software you need, you're ready to launch Android Studio and create a real, live Android app.

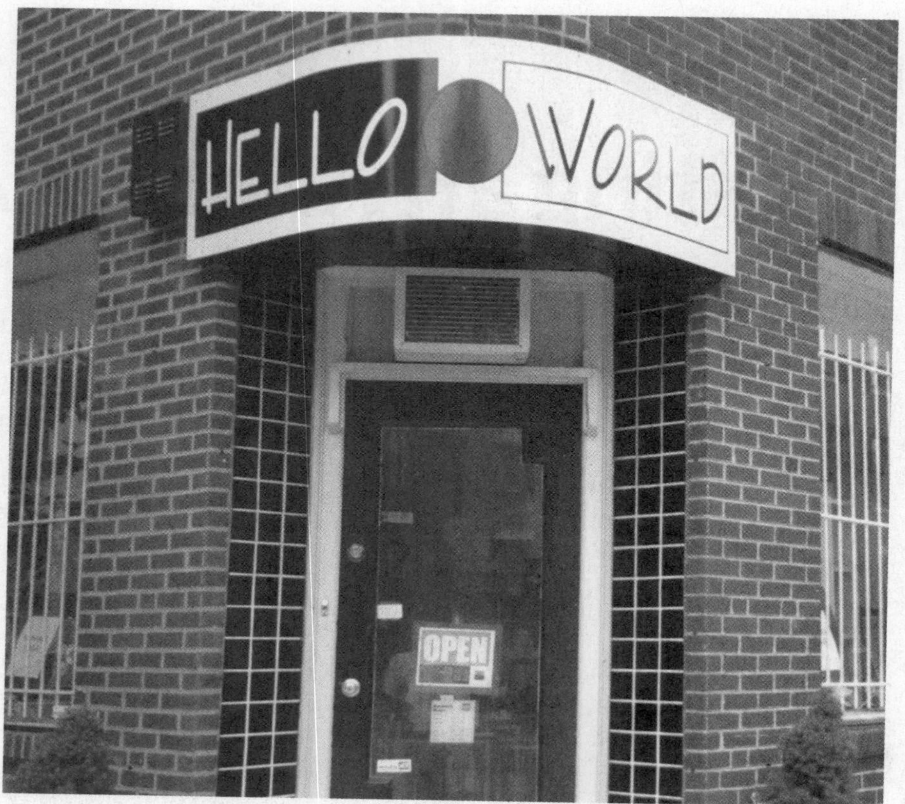

USING THE HANDY TIP OF THE DAY

When you start Android Studio, you see a Tip of the Day dialog box pop up like the one shown here:

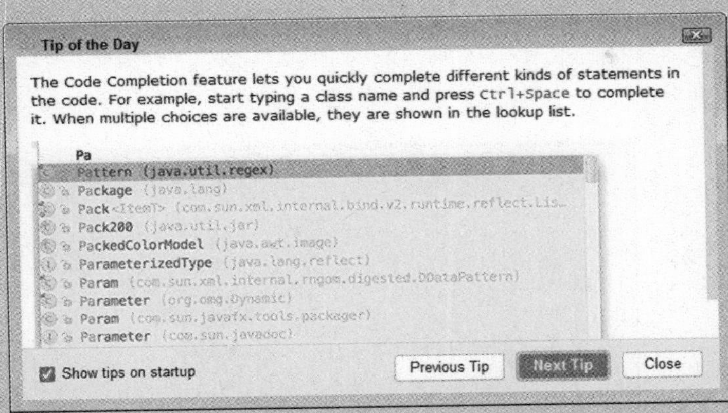

Simply reading these tips every time you start Android Studio can help you become a better developer. You may discover something new or simply have your memory jogged about a wonderful, but forgotten, Android Studio feature.

Of course, you might eventually tire of having to dismiss the Tip of the Day dialog box every time you start Android Studio. It can begin to feel like a haranguing parent reminding you to zip your jacket before leaving the house. Simply clear the Show Tips On Startup check box at the bottom of the dialog box.

If you later decide that you miss the Tip of the Day, choose Help⇨Tip of the Day to display the Tip of the Day dialog box again. Selecting Show Tips On Startup tells Android Studio to display the tips each time you start the IDE again.

Starting the IDE and creating your first app

To start the IDE and create your first app, you start, naturally, at the beginning:

1. **Launch Android Studio.**

   For details on launching Android Studio, see Chapter 2 of this minibook. To find out how to make the most of your Android Studio experience, see Book 2, Chapter 1.

When you launch Android Studio for the first time, you see the Welcome screen. (See Figure 3-1.) The Welcome screen lists any Android Studio projects that you've already created. (Hint: You haven't created any projects yet.) In addition, you see the version of Android Studio you're using, which is 3.5.1 for this book.

The Welcome screen also offers you some Quick Start options, such as Start a New Android Studio Project, Open an Existing Android Studio Project, and so on.

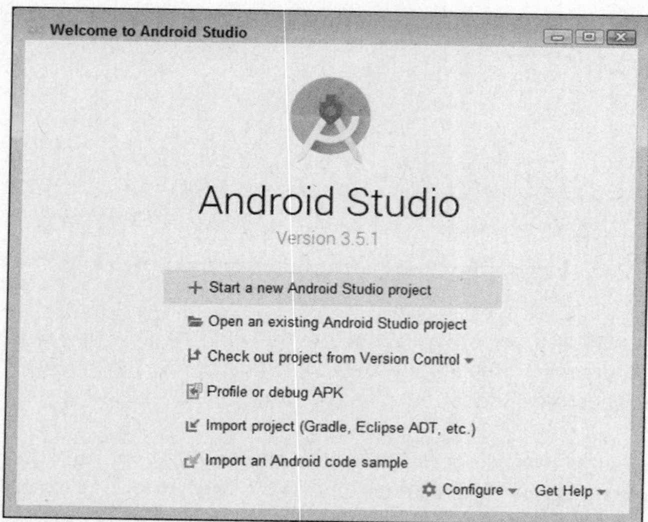

FIGURE 3-1: Welcome to Android Studio.

2. **In the Welcome screen, select Start a New Android Studio Project.**

   The Create New Project dialog box appears, as shown in Figure 3-2. You consider two things when creating a new project:

   - **Device type:** The device types appear across the top of the dialog box, such as Phone and Tablet, Wear OS, TV, Android Auto, and Android Things. Book 5 discusses each of these device types in detail, but for now all you need to know is that you can choose any of them for your app.
   - **Starting point:** A project has a starting point — the elements that the IDE provides for you automatically. The IDE controls what appears in the initial project using a template. If you choose the right starting point, you perform less work when creating an app because you don't have to create all the code manually. The starting points vary by device type. You see the starting points for three Phone and Tablet projects in Figure 3-2, but there are many more. The available templates vary by device.

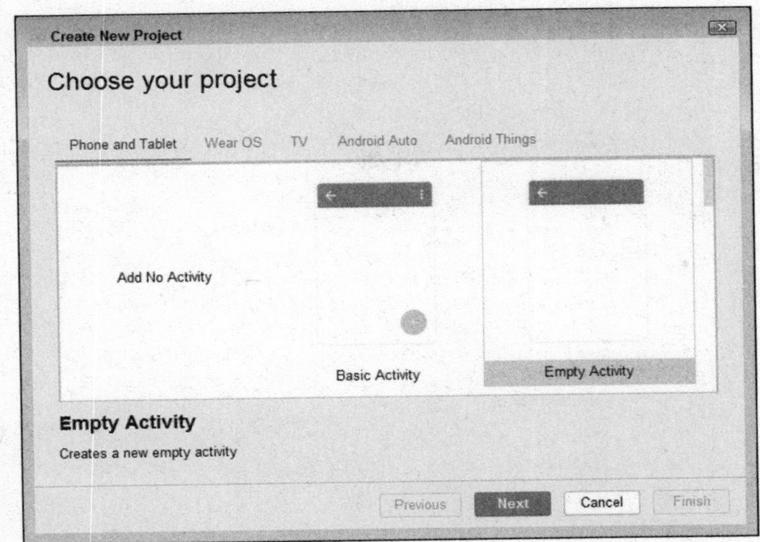

FIGURE 3-2: Select a device and associated starting point (template).

3. **For this example, choose Empty Activity and click Next.**

   You see the Configure Your Project screen, shown in Figure 3-3. This screen is where you tell Android Studio some of the characteristics of your app, such as

   - The app name
   - The name of the package to use to hold your code
   - The location to use to save the project
   - The programming language to use (all apps in this book use Kotlin, but you can also use Java)
   - The Android API level your app requires (the minimum level is 14, which is Android 4.0 [IceCreamSandwich], and the current maximum level is 29, which is Android 10.0 [Q])
   - Whether your app will support instant apps (kind of a micro-app that you can use without installing it)

4. **Type** My First App **in the Name field.**

   Notice that the Package Name and Save Location fields automatically change to match the name of your app. The wizard strips spaces from both the Package Name and Save Location fields because the presence of spaces would create problems when you compile the app and also causes problems when the IDE looks for the app on the hard drive.

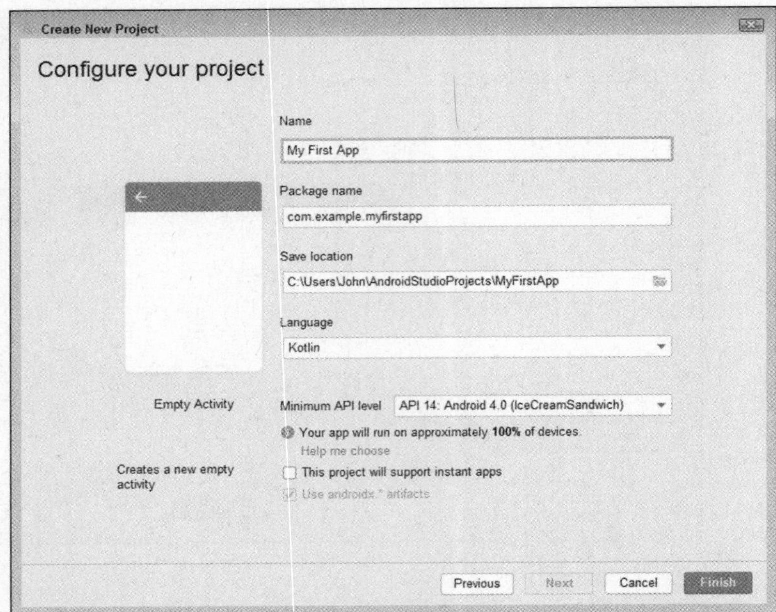

FIGURE 3-3: Define the app configuration.

You don't need to change the other fields for now. However, in a real app, you might. For example, the package name might need to use your domain name instead of `com.example`.

The section "The more things stay the same, the more they change" in Chapter 2 of this minibook tells you about API levels. Newer versions of Android generally have more functionality and sometimes fewer problems than older versions do, but more devices run the older versions. A device that currently has Android 8.0 installed can run apps that require Android 8.0 or older. The Configure Your Project screen shows the percentage of devices that are likely able to run your app based on the Minimum API Level setting that you choose.

5. **Click Finish.**

Android Studio creates a project that has the characteristics you chose. This process can take a while, so you need to be patient (the status bar will keep you informed as to the setup progress, but even the status bar can take a while to update). It's time to play that game of Solitaire you've been wanting for a while now. When the process of creating the project is finished, you see a window similar to the one shown in Figure 3-4. (If you see any informational dialog boxes, you can feel free to dismiss them.)

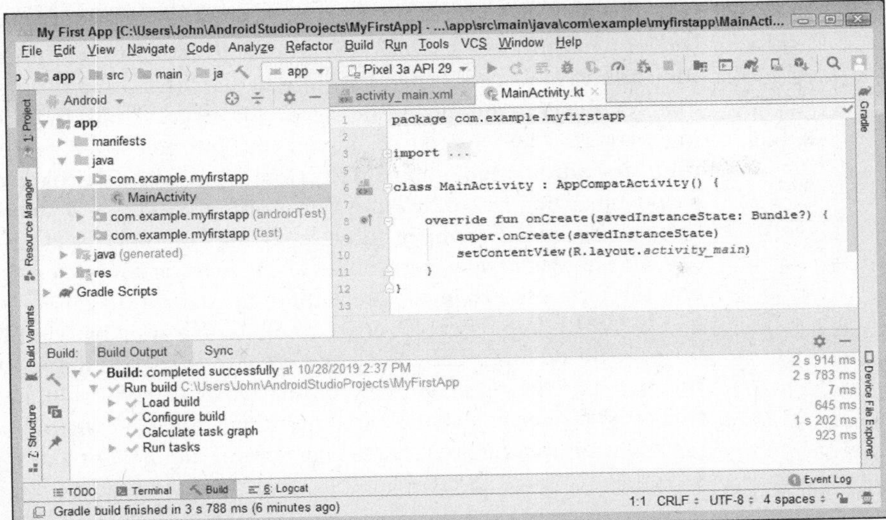

FIGURE 3-4: Your project is ready for editing.

WHAT IS AN INSTANT APP?

The name instant app conjures the image of someone getting a little packet out of a cabinet and adding water. Poof! Out pops an app! In reality, an instant app is a piece of a full-fledged app that a user can request to see how the app works.

You see instant apps in play in many common situations. Say, for example, that you finish a round of a free game and see an ad for another game. The ad shows you all kinds of amazing features for the new game and displays a Try It Now button at the bottom. When you click that button, you see an instant app — a mini version of the actual game. Generally, you get nothing more than a peek; to see more game features, you must install the actual game.

Instant apps are available only with Android 6.0 and higher. The biggest reason to use an instant app is to make your app more discoverable. You don't have to write a game app to take advantage of this technology; many app types can benefit.

You can also employ instant apps for one-time uses. For example, a parking lot could use an instant app to allow a user to scan a parking meter and open a payment page. The user could pay for parking without having to bring out a credit card, and the parking lot owner doesn't have to pay anyone to sit in the payment booth.

WARNING

One of two things can happen the first time you create a project. If you installed the Offline Tools using the procedure in the "Installing offline tools" section of Chapter 2 of this minibook, the setup will progress rather quickly — we're talking seconds. Otherwise, depending on your Internet speed, you can wait a l-o-n-g time for Android Studio to build the Gradle project info (whatever that is). You see a pop-up dialog box indicating that Android Studio is downloading something. The pop-up contains one of those annoying "un-progress" bars — the kind that doesn't show you what percentage of the work is completed. (On some computers, the progress bar looks like a rotating, striped diagonal — the kind you see on old barbershop poles. On other computers, a solid bar simply moves back and forth, back and forth, back and forth. What were they thinking when they designed this pop-up? They probably figured that you'd be more willing to wait as long as this progress bar holds your cat's attention.) Anyway, when Android Studio loads your first project, be prepared to wait several minutes for any signs of life on your screen.

Launching your first app

You've started up Android Studio and created your first project. The project doesn't do much except display Hello world! on the screen. Even so, you can run the project and see it in action. Here's how you start:

1. **Take a look at Android Studio's main window.**

   When Android Studio initially creates your app, you see the `MainActivity.kt` (`.kt` is the Kotlin code file extension) file. For now, you want to see the `activity_main.xml` file, shown in Figure 3-5. Just click its tab (which is left of the `MainActivity.kt` tab).

   In Android Studio, your new app consumes the entire main window. If, for some reason, more than one Android Studio window is open, make sure that the window you're looking at is the one containing your newly created Android app.

2. **In Android Studio's main menu, choose Run⇨Run 'app'.**

   If you see an error message saying "Error running 'app': No target device found," it means that you haven't created an Android Virtual Device (AVD) yet. The steps shown in the "Creating an Android virtual device" section in Chapter 2 of this minibook tells you how to create an AVD. You must have an AVD defined before the emulator will run. The example screenshots (starting with Figure 3-8) show how the app will look in a Google Pixel 3a running Android 10 (Q) with a Portrait startup orientation.

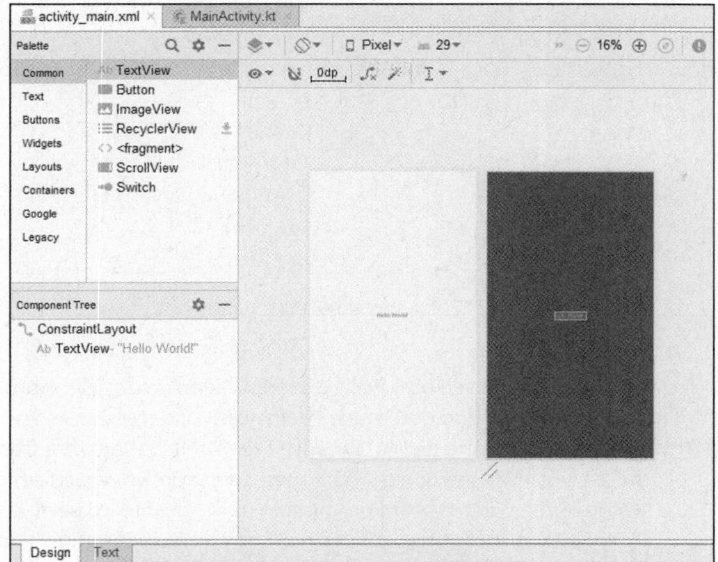

FIGURE 3-5: Look at the design of your new app.

As your application builds, you see messages in the Build Output window, as shown in Figure 3-6. Figure 3-6 actually shows the appearance of this window after the build process completes. Notice that it displays times for each step of the process, a completion message ("Install successfully finished in 10 s 676 ms."), and a total time. You can even drill down into each of the individual steps to obtain further information.

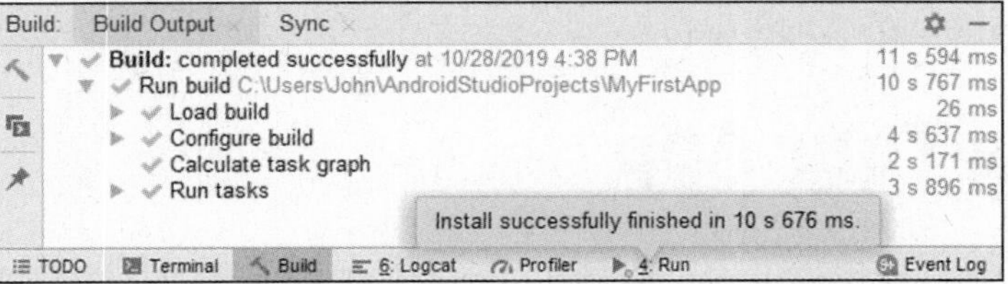

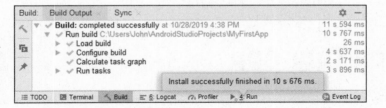

FIGURE 3-6: The Build Output window tells you about the build progress.

REMEMBER

As activity occurs in the various windows, you see an indicator next to them telling you there is more information. In this case, notice that the success message is associated with the Run window.

3. **Click the Run tab.**

   You see a list of run events like those shown in Figure 3-7. Notice that the list tells you which parts of the code are running. This information isn't very useful now, but you'll find it invaluable later when debugging your app.

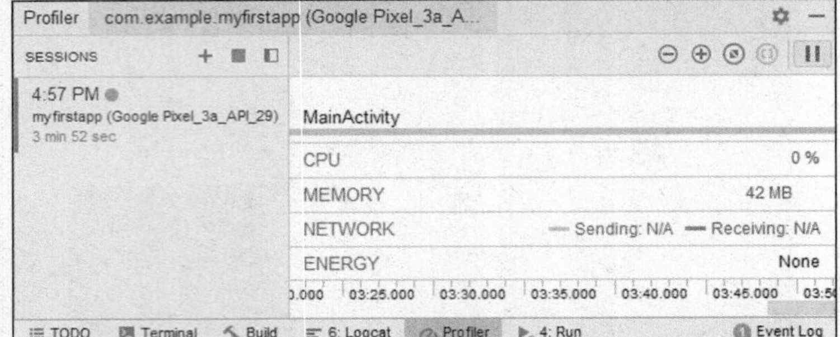

FIGURE 3-7: The Profiler helps you track application resource usage.

TIP

It's also useful to see how well your application is running. A profiler studies your application and determines how well it uses resources and what sort of load it places on the device. Because the profiler is separate from Android Studio, you may see one or more messages from your platform asking whether you want to grant permission to the profiler to perform its task. The next step requires you grant permission, but you can simply skip the next step if desired.

4. **Click the Profiler tab.**

   You see profiling information similar to that shown in Figure 3-7. Because this app is so simple, the CPU usage remains at 0%, for the most part. In this case, the app is using 42.1MB, there is no network activity, and it's not even using enough energy to record.

5. **Click the red square in the Profiler window.**

   Profiling of your app stops.

Running Your App

In this section, you kick your new app's tires and take your app around the block. Here's how:

1. **Launch your app by following the launch instructions in the "Creating Your First App" section.**
2. **Wait for the Android emulator to display a lock screen, a home screen, or an app's screen.**

   What you see depends on the emulator you selected. The process is much like the process used on a real device. You see the initial boot screen, and then a home screen like the one shown in Figure 3-8, and finally the app's screen, which appears in Figure 3-9. Don't worry if you have to squint to see Hello World; it's right there in the center of the screen in incredibly small letters.

FIGURE 3-8: The home screen appears while Android Studio loads the app.

FIGURE 3-9: The app screen appears after the loading process is complete.

TIP

Along with the emulator presentation of the device, you get controls for interacting with that device, as shown in Figure 3-9. Notice that you can turn off the device, mute the sound, rotate it in various ways, and interact with features like the camera and buttons.

3. **We can't overemphasize this point: Wait for the Android emulator to display a lock screen, a home screen, or an app's screen.**

   Android's emulator takes a long time to start. For example, on a system that has a 2.6 GHz processor with 8GB of RAM, the emulator takes a few minutes to mimic a fully booted Android device. Some people blame the fact that it's an emulator instead of a simulator. (See Chapter 2 of this minibook for that argument.) Others claim that the translation of graphics hogs the emulator's time. For whatever reason, you need lots of patience when you deal with Android's emulator.

TIP

   The device loading time seems to decrease after the first time you load it. This is because the emulator saves state information that it uses to load the device again later. The state information consumes more disk space on your system but also reduces loading time, so it's a good trade-off.

4. **Keep waiting.**

   While you're waiting, you might want to visit `https://www.genymotion.com/`. For information on Genymotion's alternative to the standard Android emulator, see Chapter 2 of this minibook.

   Oh! We see that your emulator is finally displaying the lock screen. It's time to proceed . . .

5. **If the emulator displays the lock screen, do whatever you normally do to unlock an Android device.**

   Normally, you perform some sliding or swiping motion.

6. **See your app on the emulator's screen.**

   Figure 3-9 shows the running of Android's Hello World app. (The screen even has Hello World! on it.) Android's development tools create this tiny app when you create a new Android project. Android's Hello World app has no widgets for the user to push, and the app doesn't do anything interesting. But the appearance of an app on the Android screen is a very good start. By following the steps in this chapter, you can start creating many exciting apps.

REMEMBER

Don't close an Android emulator unless you know you won't be using it for a while. The emulator is fairly reliable after it gets going. (It's sluggish, but reliable.) While the emulator runs, you can modify your Android code and tell Android Studio to run the code again. When you do, Android Studio reinstalls your app on the running emulator. The process isn't speedy, but you don't have to wait for the emulator to start. (Actually, if you run a different app — one whose minimum

SDK version is higher than the running emulator can handle — Android fires up a second emulator. But in many developer scenarios, jumping between emulators is the exception rather than the rule.)

When you are finished working with the emulator, click the Close button (the *X* on top of the controls shown previously in Figure 3-9). If you click the Power button, the emulator continues to run; it just emulates the device being turned off.

You Can Download All the Code

Throughout this book, you discover how to create apps that illustrate Android development principles using a simple process. "First, type this code; next, type that code; and so on," says the book. You can follow the instructions in each and every chapter, but you can also bypass the instructions. You can scoop the book's examples from a special website. Here's how:

1. **Visit `http://www.allmycode.com/android` or `https://users.drew.edu/bburd/android/`.**
2. **Click the link to download this book's code.**

   When the download completes, you have a `.zip` file (otherwise known as a compressed archive file).
3. **Unzip the downloaded file.**

   "Unzipping" is the same as "uncompressing" or "expanding." On some computers, this unzipping happens automatically as soon as the download is finished. On other computers, you unzip the file by clicking (or double-clicking) the file's icon. On still other computers, you right-click or Ctrl-click the downloaded file's icon and select an unzip (or uncompress or expand) option in the resulting context menu.

   For more information about `.zip` files, see the sidebar "Compressed archive files."

   After unzipping the file, you have a folder that contains several subfolders. These subfolders have names like `01-05-03`. The folder with the name `01-05-03` contains the third example that appears in Book 1, Chapter 5.
4. **Launch Android Studio.**

   For details, see Chapter 2 in this minibook.

   What you do next depends on what you see when you launch Android Studio.

Creating an Android App

5. **If you see Android Studio's Welcome screen, select Open an Existing Android Project.**

   The Open Project dialog box appears.

   TIP

   You start in your personal folder on most operating systems, so you may have to look around on your hard drive if you placed the `.zip` folder somewhere else.

   If you see Android Studio's main window, choose File➪Open in the main menu.

   The Open File or Project dialog box appears.

6. **In either dialog box, navigate to the folder containing the project that you want to open.**

   For example, to open the third project in Book 1, Chapter 5, navigate to the `01-05-03` folder that's within the unzipped version of the files you downloaded.

7. **Whatever folder you select, look in that folder for a file named `build.gradle`.**

   The `build.gradle` file appears in the project's main folder. Figure 3-10 shows the location of this file for the project you built in the "Starting the IDE and creating your first app" section of this chapter. It will be in the same location for the downloadable source.

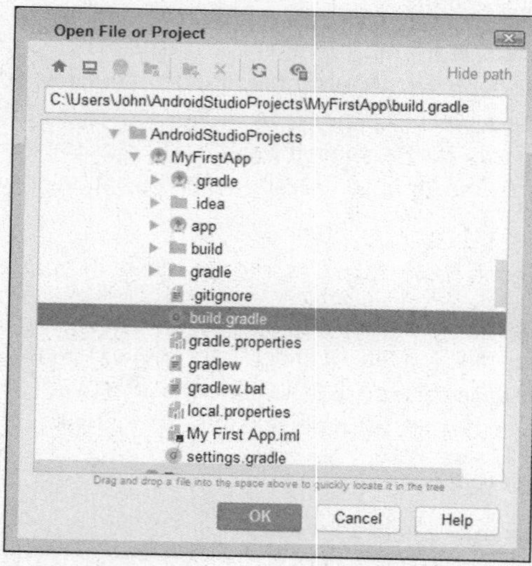

FIGURE 3-10: Locating the `build.gradle` file for a project.

8. **Highlight the `build.gradle` file and click OK.**

Android Studio opens as normal. In the Sync tab, shown in Figure 3-11, you see messages telling you the progress of the import process. As each step completes, you see a green check mark placed next to it.

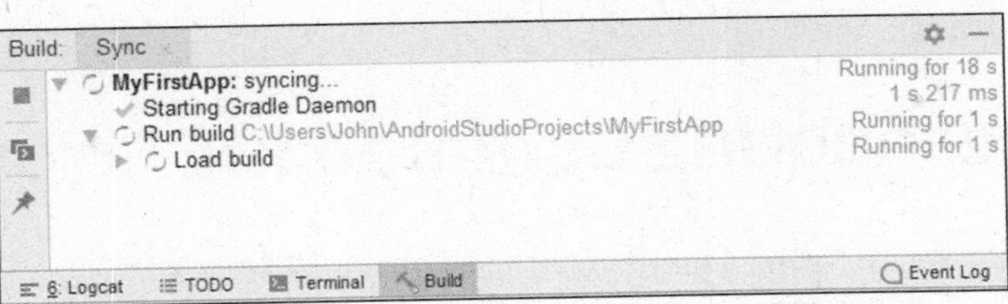

FIGURE 3-11: Syncing Android Studio to the project.

The sync process can take a while to complete, so just watch pet videos while you wait. Android Studio has to download the default Gradle wrapper from the Internet unless you have downloaded and installed the offline tools (see Chapter 2 of this minibook for details). Make sure that you have an Internet connection when you perform this step.

COMPRESSED ARCHIVE FILES

When you visit this book's website, you can download a `.zip` file containing the book's source code. You might also get a `.zip` file when you download Android development tools. A `.zip` file is a single file that encodes a bunch of smaller files and folders. So, for example, the `.zip` file from this book's website encodes a folder named `01-05-03`, `01-06-01`, `03-01-01`, and so on. The `01-05-03` folder contains subfolders named app, `build`, `gradle`, and others. These subfolders contain files and even more subfolders.

A `.zip` file is an example of a compressed archive file. Some other examples of compressed archives include `.tar.gz` files, `.tgz` files, and `.bin` files. Uncompressing or extracting means copying the files from inside the archive to a place on your hard drive. (For a `.zip` file, another word for "uncompressing" or "extracting" is "unzipping.") Uncompressing normally re-creates the folder structure encoded in the archive file. So, after uncompressing this book's examples, your hard drive has folders named `01-05-03`, `01-06-01`, and so on.

When you download a `.zip` file, your web browser may uncompress the file automatically for you. If not, you can see the `.zip` file's contents by double-clicking the file's icon. (In fact, you can copy the file's contents and perform some other file operations after double-clicking the file's icon.)

WARNING

If you're missing something that the project needs on the host system, you see error messages from Android Studio as the import process progresses. It often pays to wait until the process is complete so that you can see all the error messages rather than trying to fix them one at a time.

You can tell everyone that you created the project from scratch. We won't snitch.

Troubleshooting Common IDE Errors

You try to run your first Android app. If your effort stalls, don't despair. This section has some troubleshooting tips.

Error message: Failed to find target

You've created a project with a certain target SDK or told the IDE to compile with a certain API level. But you haven't installed that API level. If Android Studio displays a link offering to Install Missing Platform(s) and Sync Project, click the link. Otherwise, open the Android SDK manager and install that API level. For details, see Chapter 2 in this minibook.

TIP

If you don't want to install a new API level, you can tinker with the SDK version numbers in the project's `build.gradle` file. For details, see Chapter 4 of this minibook.

Error running 'app': No target device found

You must have at least one AVD configured before an app can run. In addition, the AVD must be able to support the app. Use the steps in the "Creating an Android virtual device" section of Chapter 2 of this minibook to fix this problem.

Error message: Android Virtual Device may be incompatible with your configuration

This message probably means that you haven't created an AVD capable of running your project. If Android Studio offers to help you create a new AVD, accept it. Otherwise, open the AVD Manager to create a new AVD. For information about Android Virtual Devices and the AVD Manager, see Chapter 2 of this minibook.

You lose contact with the Android Debug Bridge (ADB)

The Android Debug Bridge (ADB) connects your development computer to a device that's executing your new Android code. (The ADB also "connects" your development computer to a running emulator, even though the emulator is running on your development computer.)

If you see a message that hints of ADB trouble, try restarting your development computer's Android Debug Bridge. Here's how:

1. **Click the Terminal tool button at the bottom of Android Studio's main window.**

   Congratulations! You just opened Android Studio's Terminal tool window. If you're a Mac or Linux user, you see the shell prompt. If you're a Windows user, you see the Windows command prompt.

2. **In the Terminal tool window, go to your** `ANDROID_HOME/platform-tools` **folder.**

   For help finding your `ANDROID_HOME` folder, see the "Installing Android Studio" section in Chapter 2 of this minibook.

3. **In the** `ANDROID_HOME/platform-tools` **folder, type the following two commands:**

   Windows:

   ```
   adb kill-server
   adb start-server
   ```

   Macintosh and Linux:

   ```
   ./adb kill-server
   ./adb start-server
   ```

For more information about the Android Debug Bridge, refer to see Book 1, Chapter 2.

You don't like whatever AVD opens automatically

In Chapter 2 of this minibook, you create an AVD. And, since the old Chapter 2 days, you may have created some additional AVDs. Now, when you launch an app, your computer fires up one of the many AVDs that you created. That's fine, but what if the computer fires up your least-favorite AVD? To get control over which AVD starts up, do the following: In Android Studio's main menu, choose Run⇨Select Device. A context menu like the one shown in Figure 3-12 appears. The menu allows you to choose any of the devices you have created.

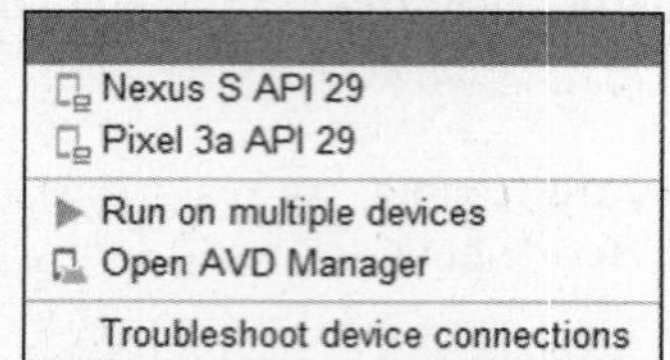

FIGURE 3-12: Choosing a device.

TIP

Notice that you can also choose to run your app on multiple devices. To use this option, you choose Run On Multiple Devices from the context menu, which displays the Select Deployment Targets dialog box, shown in Figure 3-13.

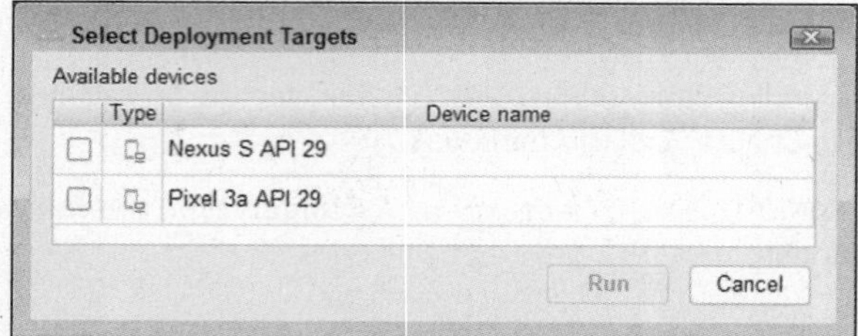

FIGURE 3-13: Running on multiple devices.

If you don't see the device you want to use, perhaps you haven't created it yet or accidentally deleted it. Choose Open AVD Manager in this case to create the device you want to use.

The Troubleshoot Device Connections option sees use only with devices you connect to your system using a USB connection. Selecting this option displays the Connection Assistant, which begins by scanning your system for USB devices that could be Android compatible. Just follow the directions the Connection Assistant provides to ensure that your system can see the device and to install appropriate drivers when it can't.

The emulator stalls during startup

After five minutes or so, you don't see Android's lock screen or Android's home screen. Here are several things you can try:

- **Lather, rinse, repeat.** Close the emulator and launch your application again. Sometimes, the second or third time's a charm. On rare occasions, you may find that your first three attempts fail but the fourth attempt succeeds.
- **Restart the Android Debug Bridge (ADB) server.** Follow the instructions in the earlier section "You lose contact with the Android Debug Bridge (ADB)." And while you're restarting things, it never hurts to restart Android Studio.
- **If you have a more powerful computer, try running your app on it.** Horsepower matters.
- **Run your app on a real Android device.** Testing a brand-new app on a real device makes us queasy. But Android's sandbox is fairly safe for apps to play in. Besides, apps load quickly and easily on real phones and tablets.

  For instructions on installing apps to real Android devices, see the section "Testing Apps on a Real Device," later in this chapter.
- **Try the Genymotion emulator.** For news about Genymotion, see Chapter 2 in this minibook.
- **Switch to an Android Virtual Device with a lower resolution and screen density.** In our experience, older AVDs consume fewer resources on your development computer. So, if an AVD drags you down, follow the instructions in the earlier section "You don't like whatever AVD opens automatically." Then, when you run an app, Android Studio prompts you with a Choose Device dialog box. Pick an AVD with the lowest API level (one that satisfies your app's minimum SDK requirement), and you'll be on your way.

WARNING

You can lower an app's target and minimum SDK version by editing the app's `build.gradle` file. But if your app requires features that aren't available in the lower target or SDK version, you won't be happy with the results. In the best case, Android Studio displays an error message as soon as you make the change. In the worst case, you see no error message until you try to run the app. When you try to run the app, it crashes.

Error message: The user data image is used by another emulator

If you see this message, some tangle involving the emulator keeps Android from doing its job. First try closing and restarting the emulator.

If a simple restart doesn't work, try the following steps:

1. **Close the emulator.**
2. **In Android Studio's main menu, choose Tools⇨AVD Manager.**

3. **In the list of virtual devices, look for the AVD that's causing you trouble.**
4. **In the Actions column, click the tiny downward-pointing arrow associated with that AVD. (See Figure 3-14.)**

   A context menu appears.

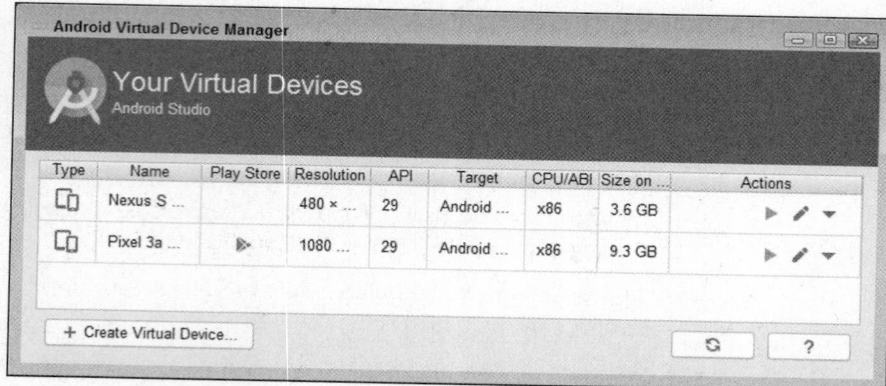

FIGURE 3-14: Using the Actions icons in the AVD Manager.

5. **In the context menu, select Wipe Data.**

   A pop-up dialog box appears. The dialog box asks you to confirm the wiping of the AVD's data.

6. **In the Confirm Data Wipe pop-up dialog box, click Yes.**

   The pop-up dialog box disappears (as you thought it would).

7. **In the Actions column, click the right-pointing arrow (the arrow that looks like a Play button).**

   As a result, Android Studio launches a new copy of the emulator, this time with a clean slate.

To read about the Android Virtual Device (AVD) Manager, see Chapter 2 in this minibook.

If the preceding set of steps doesn't work, take a firmer approach, as follows:

1. **Close the emulator.**
2. **Open whatever file explorer your computer uses to track down files.**
3. **In your user home folder, look for a folder named** `.android` **(starting with a dot).**

   For tips on finding your user home folder, see Chapter 2 in this minibook.

4. **From the `.android` folder, drill down even deeper into the `avd` folder.**

   The avd folder contains a folder for each AVD that you've created.

5. **Drill down one more level to the folder for the AVD that's giving you trouble.**

   For example, if you were running an AVD named Pie1 when you saw the Data Image Is Used by Another Emulator message, navigate to your `Pie1.avd` folder.

6. **Inside your AVD's folder, delete all the files whose names end with `.lock`.**

7. **Return to Android Studio and run your app again.**

Error message: Unknown virtual device name

Android looks for AVDs in your home folder's `.android/avd` subfolder, and occasionally Android's search goes awry. For example, consider that your Windows computer lists the home folder on an `i` drive. The AVDs are in `i:\Users\<user name>\.android\avd`. But Android ignores the computer's home folder advice and instead looks in `c:\Users\<user name>`. When Android doesn't find any AVDs, Android complains.

You can devise fancy solutions to this problem with junctions or symbolic links. But fancy solutions require special handling of their own. To keep things simple, you can simply copy the `i:\Users\<user name>\.android` folder's contents to `c:\Users\<user name>\.android`. That fixes the problem.

The emulator displays a "process isn't responding" dialog box

The formal name for this dialog box is the Application Not Responding (ANR) dialog box. Android displays the ANR dialog box when an app takes too long to do whatever it's supposed to do. When your app runs on a real device (a phone or tablet), the app shouldn't make Android display the ANR dialog box. (Other chapters in this minibook give you tips on how to avoid the dialog box.)

But on a slow emulator, a few ANR boxes are par for the course. When you see the ANR dialog box in an emulator, the best idea is to select Wait. Within about ten seconds, the dialog box disappears and the app continues to run.

Changes to your app don't appear in the emulator

Your app runs and you want to make a few improvements. So, with the emulator still running, you modify your app's code. But after choosing Run⇨Run 'app', the app's behavior in the emulator remains unchanged.

When this happens, something is clogged up. Close and restart the emulator. If necessary, use the Wipe User Data trick that we describe in the section "Error message: The user data image is used by another emulator," earlier in this chapter.

Testing Apps on a Real Device

You can bypass emulators and test your apps on a phone, a tablet, or maybe an Android-enabled refrigerator. To do so, you have to prepare the device, prepare your development computer, and then hook together the two. This section describes the process.

REMEMBER

Your device's Android version must be at least as high as your project's minimum SDK version.

The simplest way to test your app on a real device is to connect the device to your development computer using a USB cable. Not all USB cables are created equal. Some cables have wires and metal in places where other cables (with compatible fittings) have nothing except plastic. Try to use whatever USB cable came with your Android device. If, like us, you can't find the cable that came with your device or you don't know which cable came with your device, try more than one cable. When you find a cable that works, label that able cable. (If the cable always works, then label it stable, able cable.)

To test your app on a real device, follow these steps:

1. **Connect the device you want to use to your computer using the USB cable.**

   You could connect your device later in the process, but doing it now can save you a lot of time and effort when it comes to ensuring that the connection works. If necessary, tell your device that it's okay to connect to the host computer for USB transfer.

2. **On your Android device, find the USB Debugging option:**

   - If your Android device runs version 3.2 or older, choose Settings➪Applications➪Development.
   - If your Android device runs version 4.0, 4.0.3, or 4.1, choose Settings➪Developer Options.
   - If your Android device runs version 4.2 or higher, choose Settings➪About. In the About list, tap the Build Number item seven times. (Yes, seven times.) Then press the Back button to return to the Settings list. In the Settings list, tap Developer Options.

   Now your Android device displays the Development list (a.k.a. the Developer Options list).

3. **In the Development (or Developer Options) list, turn on USB debugging.**

   Your device may display a warning message. For example, here's what a Q device displays when someone messes with this setting:

   ```
   USB debugging is intended for development purposes. Use it
     to copy data between your computer and your device,
     install apps on your device without notification, and
     read log data.
   ```

   The stewards of Android are warning that the USB Debugging option can expose a device to malware.

   Theoretically, you can keep USB Debugging on all the time. But if you're very nervous about security, turn off USB Debugging when you're not using the device to develop apps.

4. **Set up your development computer to communicate with the device.**

   - **On Windows:** As soon as you turn on USB debugging, your system may start installing the required driver. However, if the device driver doesn't install automatically, visit `http://developer.android.com/sdk/oem-usb.html` to download your device's Windows USB driver. Install the driver on your development computer.
   - **On a Mac:** /* Do nothing. It just works. */
   - **On Linux:** Visit `http://developer.android.com/guide/developing/device.html` and follow the instructions that you find on that page. (Don't worry. To connect a device, you don't have to recompile the Linux kernel.)

5. **On your development computer, choose the connected device.**

   To do this, follow the instructions in the earlier section "You don't like whatever AVD opens automatically." The name of your device should appear in the list. However, in some cases, you may see something generic, like Unknown Device or ASUS P027. The point is that the Select Device context menu shown previously in Figure 3-12 will now have another entry in it.

6. **Make sure that your Android device's screen is illuminated.**

   This particular step might not be necessary, but some developers have scraped so many knuckles trying to get Android devices to connect with computers that they want every advantage they can possibly get.

7. **Choose Run⇨Run 'app'.**

   You see the build process proceed as normal, and then the Run tab opens and you see communication occur between Android Studio and your device. Finally, you see the app running on your device (rather than on the emulator).

TIP

Eventually, you want to disconnect your device from the development computer. If you're a Windows user, you dread reading Windows Can't Stop Your Device Because a Program Is Still Using It. To disconnect your device, first issue the `adb kill-server` command, as described in the earlier section "You lose contact with the Android Debug Bridge (ADB)." After that, you get the friendly Safe to Remove Hardware message.

» Assigning names to things

» Choosing API levels

Chapter 4
Examining a Basic Android App

In Chapter 3 of this minibook, you run Android Studio to create a skeletal Android app. The skeletal app doesn't do much, but the app has all the elements you need for getting started with Android. You get a basic activity (a screen full of stuff for the user to look at). You get an elementary layout for your activity. You get an icon or two, and a little text thingy that says Hello World! You can even run the new app on an emulator or on a real Android device.

Unfortunately, this skeletal app contains many, many parts. Your platform likely has a quick way to check how many. For example, on a Windows platform, you can right click the `MyFirstApp` project folder in File Explorer and choose Properties from the context menu. The General tab tells you how many files and folders `MyFirstApp` contains. The test system used to create that example shows a whopping 1,459 files and 417 different directories. All this just to display Hello World! on a mobile device's small screen!

So before you plunge headlong into Android development, you can pause to take a look at this skeletal app. Open Android Studio, make sure that the app from Chapter 3 is showing in the main window, and take this chapter's ten-cent tour of the app.

A Project's Files

Figure 4-1 shows a run of the skeletal app that Android Studio creates for you, and Figure 4-2 shows some of the files in this simple Android project. The tree in Figure 4-2 contains a `manifests` branch, two `java` branches (one for written code and another for code generated during the build process), a `res` branch, and some other stuff.

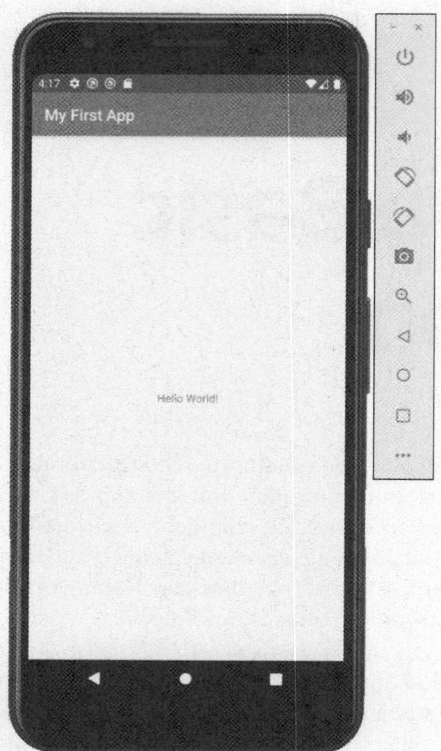

FIGURE 4-1: A run of the app created by Android Studio.

Notice the word Android at the top of Figure 4-2. Under the word Android, you see a tree containing several branches. This tree with its Android title is called the Project tool window. Whenever you look at the Project tool window, you see one of its many views, including the Android view (which is showing in Figure 4-2), the Packages view, and the Project view. You might also see Project Files, Problems, Production, or Tests. (And while you're seeing things, see Figure 4-3.)

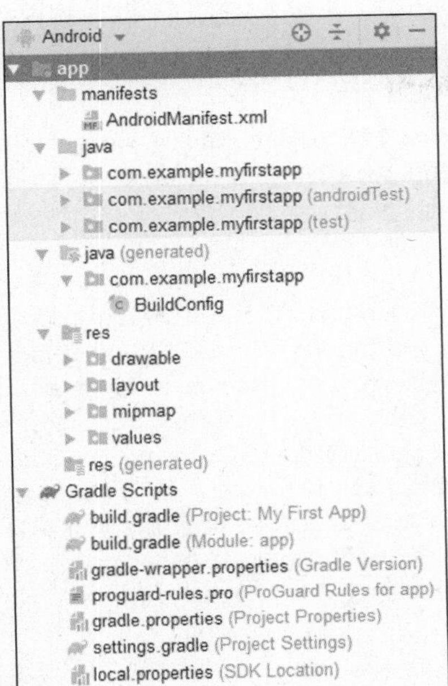

FIGURE 4-2: The structure of a new project in Android Studio.

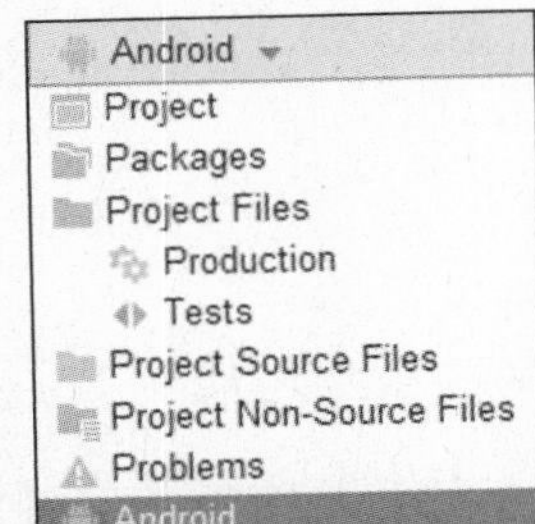

FIGURE 4-3: Options for the Project tool window.

On your own computer screen, look for the word *Android* at the top of the Project tool window. If, instead of Android, you see the word *Project*, the word *Packages*, or some other word, click that word. When you do, you see a drop-down list, as shown in Figure 4-3. In that drop-down list, select the Android option.

For more information about the Project tool window's views, see the sidebar entitled "The many faces of Android Studio," later in this chapter.

The official Android Studio terminology can be confusing. The Project view isn't the only view that belongs to the Project tool window. The next several sections describe the files (and the branches of the tree) in the Project tool window shown previously in Figure 4-2.

TREES, BRANCHES, FILES, AND FOLDERS

The tree shown previously in Figure 4-2 can be misleading. Trees of this kind normally show up in your operating system's File Explorer or Finder. In the File Explorer and the Finder, branches represent either files on your hard drive or directories (also known as folders) containing the files.

This story about files and folders is only partially true of the tree in Figure 4-2. For example, when you create an Android app, the `app\src\main` folder of your hard drive shown below contains a `res` folder, which in turn contains subfolders whose names begin with `drawable`, `layout`, `mipmap`, and `values`. That structure is very much like the tree in Figure 4-2 (albeit more detailed). But unlike the tree in Figure 4-2, your hard drive's `res` folder might have subfolders with extended names, such as `drawable-v24` and `mipmap-hdpi`. And instead of living directly inside an app branch (as in Figure 4-2), the `res` folder on your hard drive appears in the `main` folder, which is inside the `src` (pronounced *source*) folder, which is (finally) inside the app folder.

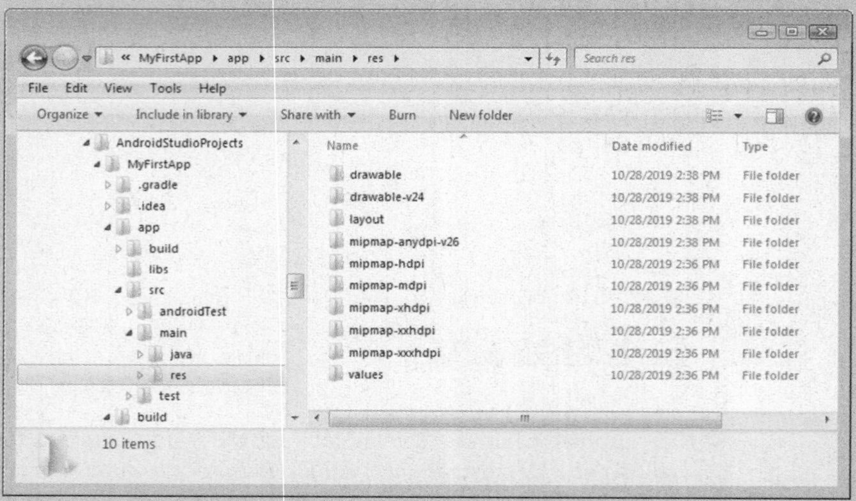

The tree in the Android view presents an abstracted picture of your app's files. You don't see files and folders as you would in Windows File Explorer or Macintosh Finder. Instead, you see a hierarchy that helps you understand the roles of the files in your Android app.

The MainActivity.kt file

Your app can have files named MainActivity.kt, MyService.kt, DatabaseHelper.kt, MoreStuff.kt, and so on. In fact, you can cram hundreds of Kotlin files into a project. But when you create a new project, Android Studio typically creates one activity's .kt (Kotlin) file for you. When you create an Android project in Chapter 3 of this minibook, you accept the default name MainActivity, so Android Studio creates a file named MainActivity.kt. Listing 4-1 shows you the code in the MainActivity.kt file.

LISTING 4-1: Android Studio Creates This Skeletal Activity Class

```
package com.example.myfirstapp

import androidx.appcompat.app.AppCompatActivity
import android.os.Bundle

class MainActivity : AppCompatActivity() {

    override fun onCreate(savedInstanceState: Bundle?) {
        super.onCreate(savedInstanceState)
        setContentView(R.layout.activity_main)
    }
}
```

WARNING

What you see in your editor might be different from the code in Listing 4-1. The code changes to match the specifics of what you select during the initial configuration process, the kind of application you want to create, any updates you've applied, and so on. Rest assured that, here in Chapter 4, the differences don't matter.

An Android activity is one "screenful" of components. Think of an activity as a form — perhaps a form for entering information to make a purchase on a website. Unlike most online forms, Android activities don't necessarily have text boxes — places for the user to type credit card numbers and such. But Android activities have a lot in common with online forms. When you define a class that inherits from AppCompatActivity(), you create a new Android activity. In this case, you create MainActivity.

For more information about Kotlin, see Book 2, Chapters 2 through 6. If you're curious, you can also learn more about AppCompatActivity() at https://developer.android.com/reference/android/support/v7/app/AppCompatActivity.

An Android application can contain many activities. For example, an app's initial activity might list the films playing in your area. When you click a film's title, Android then covers the entire list activity with another activity (perhaps an activity displaying a relevant film review).

Having one activity overlay another activity is typical of small phone screens. But on larger tablet screens, you can display a list of films and a particular film review side by side. Having side-by-side panels is a job for fragments rather than activities. To read about fragments, see Book 5, Chapter 1.

Here's another (possibly surprising) thing to keep in mind: An Android app can invoke an activity belonging to a different app. For example, your app might display a Help button, and clicking Help might open a web page. With the web page housed somewhere on the Internet, your app's button fires up an activity belonging to Android's built-in web browser application. In the Android world, applications don't bogart their activities.

Every Android activity has a lifecycle — a set of stages that the activity undergoes from birth to death to rebirth, and so on. Book 3, Chapter 1 describes the activity lifecycle. But in this chapter, you get a peek at the activity lifecycle with the method `onCreate()` in Listing 4-1.

The onCreate() method

When Android creates an activity, Android calls the activity's `onCreate()` method. This happens much more often than you'd think, because Android destroys and then re-creates activities while the user navigates from place to place. For example, if your phone runs low on memory, Android can kill some running activities. When you navigate back to a killed activity, Android re-creates the activity for you. The same thing happens when you turn the phone from portrait to landscape mode. If the developer doesn't override the default behavior, Android destroys an activity and re-creates the activity before displaying the activity in the other mode.

In Listing 4-1, the `onCreate()` method has things named `savedInstanceState` and `R.layout.activity_main`.

- **The `savedInstanceState` variable stores information about some of the activity's values when the activity was previously destroyed.**

  The statement `super.onCreate(savedInstanceState)` tells Android to restore those previous values. This way, the activity takes up where it last left off.

During what appears to the user to be a continuous run, Android might destroy and re-create an activity several times. An activity's savedInstanceState helps to maintain continuity between destructions and re-creations.

To be precise, the statement super.onCreate(savedInstanceState) calls the parent class's onCreate method. To read more about parent classes in Java, see Book 2, Chapter 5.

- **The setContentView() method parameter R.layout.activity_main is a roundabout way of coding the buttons, text fields, and the way they're all laid out.**

  In Listing 4-1, the call to setContentView() plops these buttons, text fields, images, and other stuff on the activity screen. For more about these activities, check the section "The R.java file", later in this chapter.

Using other templates

The MyFirstApp project uses an Empty Activity template, which is about as simple as you can make things. If you create another app, say Test2, that relies on the Basic Activity template instead, the MainActivity.kt file contains more code, as shown in Listing 4-2.

LISTING 4-2: Different Templates Create Different Activities

```
package com.example.test2

import android.os.Bundle
import com.google.android.material.snackbar.Snackbar
import androidx.appcompat.app.AppCompatActivity
import android.view.Menu
import android.view.MenuItem

import kotlinx.android.synthetic.main.activity_main.*

class MainActivity : AppCompatActivity() {

    override fun onCreate(savedInstanceState: Bundle?) {
        super.onCreate(savedInstanceState)
        setContentView(R.layout.activity_main)
        setSupportActionBar(toolbar)
```

(continued)

LISTING 4-2: *(continued)*

```
        fab.setOnClickListener { view ->
            Snackbar.make(view,
              "Replace with your own action",
              Snackbar.LENGTH_LONG)
                .setAction("Action", null).show()
        }
    }

    override fun onCreateOptionsMenu(
      menu: Menu): Boolean {
        // Inflate the menu; this adds items to the action
        // bar if it is present.
        menuInflater.inflate(R.menu.menu_main, menu)
        return true
    }

    override fun onOptionsItemSelected(
      item: MenuItem): Boolean {
        // Handle action bar item clicks here. The action
        // bar will automatically handle clicks on the
        // Home/Up button, so long as you specify a parent
        // activity in AndroidManifest.xml.
        return when (item.itemId) {
            R.id.action_settings -> true
            else -> super.onOptionsItemSelected(item)
        }
    }
}
```

As Listing 4-2 shows, using a different template creates a different `MainActivity.kt` file. In this case, `onCreate()` now contains a call to `fab.setOnClickListener()`, which adds a Floating Action Button (FAB) to your display. This button triggers the primary action of your app. In addition, you add `onCreateOptionsMenu()` and `onOptionsItemSelected()`. The following sections discuss these two methods.

The onCreateOptionsMenu() method

With a new Android activity comes a new menu. For older Android versions, a separate menu button is somewhere on (or near) the device's screen. But starting with Honeycomb, apps put a menu icon in an action bar. (The activity's menu icon has three vertically aligned dots. The icon appears in the screen's upper-right corner.)

» **In Listing 4-2, the call** `menuInflater.inflate(R.menu.menu_main, menu)` **does the same for the look of your menu items as a call to** `setContentView` **does for the overall look of your activity.**

The call puts items (and perhaps sub-items) in your app's menu.

» **The last statement inside the** `onCreateOptionsMenu()` **method (the** `return true` **statement) tells Android to display your app's menu.**

If, for some reason, you don't want Android to display the menu, change this statement to return `false`.

In Listing 4-2, the `onCreateOptionsMenu()` method creates your activity's menu. That's fine, but what happens when the user taps a menu item? When the user taps an item, Android calls your activity's `onOptionsItemSelected()` method.

The onOptionsItemSelected() method

In Listing 4-2, the `onOptionsItemSelected()` method doesn't do too much.

» **The call to** `return when (item.itemId)` **grabs the code number of whatever item the user tapped.**

For some good reading about Android's use of code numbers, see the section "The R.java file," later in this chapter.

» **When your IDE creates a skeletal app, the app has one menu item named** `action_settings`**. The code in Listing 4-2 checks to find out whether the user tapped this** `action_settings` **item.**

In a real-world app, the code would check to find out which of several menu items the user tapped.

» **Returning** `true` **tells Android that the tapping of this menu item has been handled; no further action is necessary.**

A return value of `false` would mean that some other code should do something in response to the user's tap.

» **Finally, the** `super.onOptionsItemSelected(item)` **call tells Android to do, with this menu item tap, whatever Android normally does by default for any old menu item tap.**

This is no big deal because, by default, Android does almost nothing.

To make use of the code in Listing 4-1, you have to know something about Kotlin. For a big blast of Kotlin, visit Book 2, Chapters 2 through 7.

The res Branch

In this section, you continue exploring the branches in the Project tool window's tree in Figure 4-2. The project's res branch (a branch within the app branch) contains resources for use by the project's Android application. The res branch has sub-branches named drawable, layout, menu, mipmap, and values.

THE MANY FACES OF ANDROID STUDIO

The res branch in the Project tool window displays the contents of a folder on your computer's hard drive. In fact, if you look for this folder in your operating system's File Explorer or Finder, you see a MyApplication/app/src/main/res folder. But if you look at the Project tool window, you may see only a res branch within an app branch. What's going on here?

The Project tool window has several views, including the Android view, the Project view, and the Packages view (there are others). Each view shows (basically) the same stuff, but each view organizes this stuff a bit differently.

- When the Project tool window displays its Android view, the res branch has sub-branches with simple names (such as drawable and values). But the folder on your hard drive has subdirectories named drawable, drawable-v24, mipmap-anydpi-v26, mipmap-hdpi, mipmap-mdpi, and others. In the Android view, the Project tool window presents an abstracted (or developer-centric) view of the files on your hard drive.
- When the Project tool window displays its Packages view, directories such as drawable, drawable-v24, mipmap-anydpi-v26, mipmap-hdpi, and mipmap-mdpi appear immediately inside the app branch of the tree.
- When the Project tool window displays its Project view, you see (more or less) what you'd see in your operating system's File Explorer or Finder. That is, you see a res branch inside a main branch, which is inside a src branch, and so on. You also see sub-branches named drawable, drawable-v24, mipmap-anydpi-v26, mipmap-hdpi, mipmap-mdpi, and so on.

To switch from one view to another, look for the button that appears atop the Project tool window. Click that button and select an option in the resulting drop-down list. (Refer to Figure 4-3.)

The res/drawable branch

The drawable branch contains images, shapes, and other such things. A single drawable item might come in several different sizes, each with its own dpi (dots per inch) level. The sizes include mdpi (a medium number of dots per inch), hdpi (a high number of dots per inch), xhdpi (extra high), and xxhdpi (extra-extra high). You have to wonder how many x's we'll need when Android starts powering digital displays on Times Square!

For more reading about drawables, visit Book 4, Chapter 1.

The res/layout branch

The layout branch contains descriptions of your activities' screens. A minimal app's layout branch contains an XML file describing an activity's screen. (See the activity_main.xml branch in Figure 4-2.) Listing 4-3 shows the code in the simple activity_main.xml file. To see this code in the IDE, you must choose the Text tab at the bottom of the activity_main.xml file display. The default is to use the Design tab, which allows for use of drag and drop to define elements.

LISTING 4-3: A Small Layout File

```
<?xml version="1.0" encoding="utf-8"?>
<androidx.constraintlayout.widget.ConstraintLayout
xmlns:android="http://schemas.android.com/apk/res/android"
    xmlns:app="http://schemas.android.com/apk/res-auto"
    xmlns:tools="http://schemas.android.com/tools"
    android:layout_width="match_parent"
    android:layout_height="match_parent"
    tools:context=".MainActivity">

    <TextView
        android:layout_width="wrap_content"
        android:layout_height="wrap_content"
        android:text="Hello World!"
        app:layout_constraintBottom_toBottomOf="parent"
        app:layout_constraintLeft_toLeftOf="parent"
        app:layout_constraintRight_toRightOf="parent"
        app:layout_constraintTop_toTopOf="parent"/>

</androidx.constraintlayout.widget.ConstraintLayout>
```

An Android app consists of Kotlin code, XML documents, and other stuff. The XML code in Listing 4-3 describes a constraint layout. (In a constraint layout, each element's position is relative to the positions of other elements. So buttons and text fields appear to the right of one another, to the left of one another, below one another, and so on.) Because of its `match_parent` attributes, the layout is large enough to fill its surroundings. Its "surroundings" are the entire screen (minus a few doodads on the edges of the screen).

In Listing 4-2, the only item inside the relative layout is an instance of `TextView` — a place to display text on the screen. Because of the `wrap_content` attributes, the text view is only wide enough and only tall enough to enclose whatever characters it displays.

For more info about layouts, see Book 4, Chapter 1.

TECHNICAL STUFF

Older Android apps you encounter use a relative layout rather than a constraint layout. In both cases, the element positions rely on the relative positions of other elements. However, they have differences that you can read about at `https://developer.android.com/training/constraint-layout`. The important thing to remember is that a constraint layout lets you create an interface using drag and drop alone, rather than having to edit the XML.

The res/menu branch

Each file in the menu branch describes a menu belonging to your app. When creating an app, such as MyFirstApp, which is based on the Empty Activity template, there isn't a menu. However, when you move to Test2, which relies on the Basic Activity template, you do find a menu. A simple Basic Activity template app that your IDE creates contains only one menu. The file to describe that menu is named `menu_main.xml`.

Listing 4-4 contains the bare-bones `menu_main.xml` file.

LISTING 4-4: The menu_main.xml Menu File

```
<?xml version="1.0" encoding="utf-8"?>
<androidx.coordinatorlayout.widget.CoordinatorLayout
xmlns:android="http://schemas.android.com/apk/res/android"
    xmlns:app="http://schemas.android.com/apk/res-auto"
    xmlns:tools="http://schemas.android.com/tools"
    android:layout_width="match_parent"
    android:layout_height="match_parent"
    tools:context=".MainActivity">

    <com.google.android.material.appbar.AppBarLayout
        android:layout_width="match_parent"
        android:layout_height="wrap_content"
        android:theme="@style/AppTheme.AppBarOverlay">
```

```
    <androidx.appcompat.widget.Toolbar
      android:id="@+id/toolbar"
      android:layout_width="match_parent"
      android:layout_height="?attr/actionBarSize"
      android:background="?attr/colorPrimary"
      app:popupTheme="@style/AppTheme.PopupOverlay"/>

  </com.google.android.material.appbar.AppBarLayout>

  <include layout="@layout/content_main"/>

  <com.google.android.material.floatingactionbutton.FloatingActionButton
    android:id="@+id/fab"
    android:layout_width="wrap_content"
    android:layout_height="wrap_content"
    android:layout_gravity="bottom|end"
    android:layout_margin="@dimen/fab_margin"
    app:srcCompat="@android:drawable/ic_dialog_email"/>

</androidx.coordinatorlayout.widget.CoordinatorLayout>
```

The menu begins by defining its layout using a `CoordinatorLayout`, which is a frame for blocking out an area of the app's screen. It's like drawing a box on the screen and telling Android you want to put something in it.

The `AppBarLayout` comes next. It's a box that appears inside the just-created frame that defines things like scrolling actions. It can also contain other controls. In this case, it contains a `Toolbar` holding standard controls that you commonly see in Android apps.

Also within the `CoordinatorLayout` is a `FloatingActionButton`, which is also known as a FAB. A FAB has a special appearance — a circle that floats above the app. A FAB promotes one specific, common, action and has special motion behaviors associated with it.

Notice the line that reads `<include layout="@layout/content_main" />`. This line says to stick the main content in this particular location — between the default menu at the top and the FAB at the bottom.

The res/mipmap branch

The `res/mipmap` branch is like the `res/drawable` branch, except that the `res/mipmap` branch contains your app's icons. The term *mipmap* stands for *multum in parvo* mapping. The Latin phrase *multum in parvo* means "much in little." A *mipmap* image contains copies of textures for many different screen resolutions.

The mipmap folder was introduced in Android 4.3, so you don't see it in older Android apps.

The res/values branch

The files in the values branch describe miscellaneous things that an app needs to know. For example, Listing 4-4 (for Test2 because it contains a menu and MyFirstApp doesn't) contains an entry that describes the AppBarLayout theme: @style/AppTheme.AppBarOverlay. What this is really saying is that Android should look up the selected theme in the styles.xml file. When you open that file, you see the entries shown in Listing 4-5.

LISTING 4-5: The styles.xml Resources File

```
<resources>

    <!-- Base application theme. -->
    <style name="AppTheme"
          parent="Theme.AppCompat.Light.DarkActionBar">
        <!-- Customize your theme here. -->
        <item name="colorPrimary">
          @color/colorPrimary
        </item>
        <item name="colorPrimaryDark">
          @color/colorPrimaryDark
        </item>
        <item name="colorAccent">@color/colorAccent</item>
    </style>

    <style name="AppTheme.NoActionBar">
        <item name="windowActionBar">false</item>
        <item name="windowNoTitle">true</item>
    </style>

    <style name="AppTheme.AppBarOverlay"
         parent="ThemeOverlay.AppCompat.Dark.ActionBar"/>

    <style name="AppTheme.PopupOverlay"
          parent="ThemeOverlay.AppCompat.Light"/>

</resources>
```

When you look at the `AppTheme.AppBarOverlay` entry, you see that it has a `parent` value of `ThemeOverlay.AppCompat.Dark.ActionBar`. This theme gives you the appearance shown previously in Figure 4-1. However, if you change the value to `ThemeOverlay.AppCompat.Light`, you see the appearance shown in Figure 4-4. Notice that Test2 and the associated menu appear in black now, rather than white.

FIGURE 4-4: Themes and styles make customizing your app easy.

Why does the menu_main.xml file contain the following cryptic line?

```
android:theme="@style/AppTheme.AppBarOverlay"
```

Why don't you simply code

```
android:text="ThemeOverlay.AppCompat.Dark.ActionBar"
```

Here's why: Using the XML file makes it easy to change styles without having to recompile the app every time. All you really need to do is change the XML file, and the change simply appears onscreen. In addition, using this approach makes your app more flexible because a user could request a theme change through your app, and the app could simply change the XML file as needed.

In an Android app, resources such as strings, themes, and styles go by many different names. In Listing 4-4, you see `@layout/content_main`. This is the XML file approach to referencing the content for your app. If you were to reference the same content from your Kotlin code, it would appear as `R.layout.content_main`.

To read all about XML documents like the ones in Listings 4-3 through 4-5, see Book 2, Chapter 7.

Other Files in an Android Project

A simple Android app contains dozens of files. Many of these files appear in the Android view (in the Project tool window). Some of the files that don't appear are still worth knowing about.

The build.gradle file

Gradle is a software tool. When the tool runs, it takes a whole bunch of files and combines them to form a complete application. For example, a run of Gradle can use the files shown in Figure 4-2, shown previously, to build a single `.apk` file for posting on Google's Play Store. Gradle can combine files in many different ways, so to get Gradle to do things properly, someone has to provide Gradle with a script of some kind.

A new Android app comes with its own ready-made script. In Figure 4-2, that script appears in the branch labeled `build.gradle (Module: app)`. Listing 4-6 shows the contents of a simple app's `build.gradle` file.

LISTING 4-6: A Little build.gradle File

```
apply plugin: 'com.android.application'

apply plugin: 'kotlin-android'

apply plugin: 'kotlin-android-extensions'

android {
    compileSdkVersion 29
    buildToolsVersion "29.0.2"
    defaultConfig {
        applicationId "com.example.myfirstapp"
        minSdkVersion 14
        targetSdkVersion 29
        versionCode 1
        versionName "1.0"
```

```
        testInstrumentationRunner
          "androidx.test.runner.AndroidJUnitRunner"
    }
    buildTypes {
        release {
            minifyEnabled false
            proguardFiles getDefaultProguardFile(
              'proguard-android-optimize.txt'),
              'proguard-rules.pro'
        }
    }
}

dependencies {
  implementation fileTree(
      dir: 'libs', include: ['*.jar'])
  implementation
 "org.jetbrains.kotlin:kotlin-stdlib-jdk7:$kotlin_version"
  implementation 'androidx.appcompat:appcompat:1.0.2'
  implementation 'androidx.core:core-ktx:1.0.2'
  implementation
    'androidx.constraintlayout:constraintlayout:1.1.3'
  testImplementation 'junit:junit:4.12'
  androidTestImplementation
    'androidx.test.ext:junit:1.1.0'
  androidTestImplementation
    'androidx.test.espresso:espresso-core:3.1.1'
}
```

The section "Your app's API levels," found later in this chapter, covers some `build.gradle` code in more detail. So the following sections describe only a few of the listing's highlights (shown in bold).

An app's versions

In Listing 4-6, the `versionCode` and `versionName` properties have similar (but slightly different) meanings.

- The `versionCode` property is an integer. For publication on the Google Play Store, the `versionCode` must increase from one version of your app to another. The numbers don't have to be consecutive. So your first published version can have `versionCode 47`, and the next published version can be number 63. The app's user doesn't see the `versionCode`.

Examining a Basic Android App

» The versionName can be any string of characters, so this attribute's value is largely cosmetic. The user sees the versionName. Listing 4-6 contains values for an app's compileSdkVersion, minSdk-Version, and targetSdkVersion. To find out what these SDK versions are, see the section "Your app's API levels," later in this chapter.

What is ProGuard?

Obfuscation is a way of making your Kotlin code difficult to understand (which makes the code difficult to steal, difficult to modify, and difficult to infect), and *ProGuard* is a tool that can obfuscate your Kotlin programs. To obfuscate your code, Android Studio needs to configure the ProGuard tool. Listing 4-6 says that this configuration information lives in files named proguard-android.txt and progard-rules.pro. (You can peek at the proguard-rules.pro file by switching to the Project view in the Project tool window and opening the app branch.)

OH! FOR THE GOOD OLD DAYS!

Before Android Studio came along, developers used Eclipse, and Eclipse didn't create build.gradle files. (Oddly enough, there is a Kotlin plug-in for your Eclipse setup; see https://kotlinlang.org/docs/tutorials/getting-started-eclipse.html.) For that matter, Eclipse didn't use the Gradle build tool at all. Consequently, Eclipse's counterpart to the tree in Figure 4-2 looked quite different from what you see there. Eclipse organized files and folders differently from the structure in Figure 4-2. So an Android project built in the Eclipse days doesn't easily fit into the Android Studio IDE.

If you come across an old Eclipse Android project (a project with no build.gradle file) and you need to work with that project, you have two choices:

- You can install Eclipse on your development computer. To do so, visit https://www.eclipse.org/. After installing Eclipse, follow the instructions at https://stuff.mit.edu/afs/sipb/project/android/docs/sdk/installing/installing-adt.html to add the ADT (Android Developer Tools) to Eclipse.
- You can import the Eclipse project into Android Studio. It's not a simple matter of opening a menu option and importing the project, however. Make sure you read about the rather lengthy process required at https://developer.android.com/studio/intro/migrate.

The AndroidManifest.xml file

An app's `AndroidManifest.xml` file describes some of the things a device needs in order to run the app. (See Listing 4-7.)

LISTING 4-7: A Little AndroidManifest.xml File

```
<?xml version="1.0" encoding="utf-8"?>
<manifest
xmlns:android="http://schemas.android.com/apk/res/android"
    package="com.example.myfirstapp">

    <application
      android:allowBackup="true"
      android:icon="@mipmap/ic_launcher"
      android:label="@string/app_name"
      android:roundIcon="@mipmap/ic_launcher_round"
      android:supportsRtl="true"
      android:theme="@style/AppTheme">
      <activity android:name=".MainActivity">
        <intent-filter>
          <action
            android:name="android.intent.action.MAIN"/>

          <category
        android:name="android.intent.category.LAUNCHER"/>
          </intent-filter>
        </activity>
    </application>

</manifest>
```

Each of these elements has a specific purpose. The following sections explain how these elements cause your app to run.

The <application> element

In Listing 4-7, the `application` element has several attributes, including `android:icon` and `android:label`. The user sees the application's icon and label on the device's Apps screen. The application's label (and sometimes the icon) appears when one of the app's activities is in the foreground. (See the words My First App in Figure 4-1, shown previously.)

The <activity> element

The `activity` element can have an `android:label` attribute. An app's activity can have its own icon and label, overriding the app's icon and label.

One way or another, an activity element in an `AndroidManifest.xml` file must have an `android:name` attribute. The `android:name` attribute has either of the following values:

- **The Fully Qualified Name (FQN) of the activity class:**

  The FQN contains the full path (as specified by the package name combined with the entity name in this case) to a particular entity within the Android app. Using an FQN distinguishes `com.example.myapplication.MainActivity` from `com.example2.myapplication.MainActivity`. The FQN for this example is `com.example.myapplication.MainActivity`.

- **The abbreviated activity class name, preceded by a dot:**

  The name `.SomeClass` stands for "the class named `SomeClass` in this project's package." So, in Listing 4-7, the following lines work just fine:

  ```
  package="com.example.myapplication"
  ...
  android:name= ".MainActivity"
  ```

TECHNICAL STUFF

  The manifest element's `package` attribute isn't in the android namespace. In Listing 4-7, you see `package`, not `android:package`. For more information about XML namespaces, see Book 2, Chapter 7.

Within an activity element, an `intent-filter` element describes the kinds of duties that this activity can fulfill. To give you an idea, `action` element `android.intent.action.MAIN` indicates that this activity's code can be the starting point for an app's execution. And the `category` element `android.intent.category.LAUNCHER` indicates that this activity's icon can appear in the device's Apps screen.

REMEMBER

If you create a second activity for your app, you must declare the new activity using an `<activity>` element in the app's `AndroidManifest.xml` file. If you don't, your app will crash with an `ActivityNotFoundException`.

The R.java file

Each Android project has an `R.java` file. Android Studio generates this file and protects it as if the file were made of gold. You, the developer, never create or modify the `R.java` file's text.

TIP

You don't see `R.java` in Figure 4-2, shown previously, because the `R.java` file doesn't appear in the Android view. If you want to see the `R.java` file, switch from the Android window to the Project window. Follow the instructions on switching views in the sidebar "The many faces of Android Studio," earlier in this chapter. When the Project view replaces the Android view, visit the `app/build/generated/not_namespaced_r_class_sources` branch (they really don't want you to find this file, much less mess with it). You may see several branches in this case, depending on the builds you have created, but the default build is a debug build, so that's the one you'll look at now. Within the `debug` branch, you find an `r/com/example/myfirstapp` branch in the tree. Open this branch and you see `R.java`, as shown in Figure 4-5.

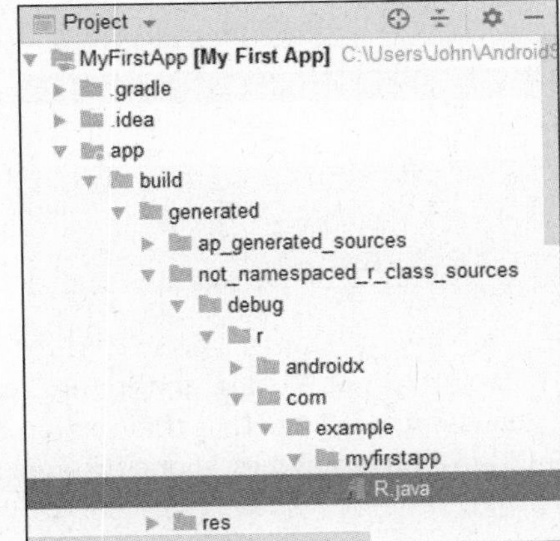

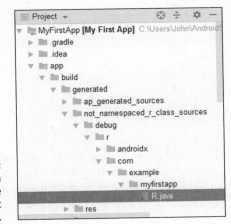

FIGURE 4-5: The very hidden location of the super-secret `R.java` file.

Figure 4-6 shows some of the lines in an `R.java` file.

The hexadecimal values in an R.java file are the jumping-off points for Android's resource management mechanism. Android uses these numbers for quick and easy loading of the things you store in the `res` branch. For example, the code in Figure 4-6 sets the location of the app's animation feature `R.anim.abc_fade_in`, and according to Figure 4-6, `R.anim.abc_fade_in` has the hex value `0x7f010000`.

activity_main.xml × MainActivity.kt × R.java ×

Files under the "build" folder are generated and should not be edited.

```
package com.example.myfirstapp;

public final class R {
  public static final class anim {
    public static final int abc_fade_in=0x7f010000;
    public static final int abc_fade_out=0x7f010001;
    public static final int abc_grow_fade_in_from_bottom=0x7f010002;
    public static final int abc_popup_enter=0x7f010003;
    public static final int abc_popup_exit=0x7f010004;
    public static final int abc_shrink_fade_out_from_bottom=0x7f010005;
    public static final int abc_slide_in_bottom=0x7f010006;
    public static final int abc_slide_in_top=0x7f010007;
    public static final int abc_slide_out_bottom=0x7f010008;
    public static final int abc_slide_out_top=0x7f010009;
    public static final int abc_tooltip_enter=0x7f01000a;
    public static final int abc_tooltip_exit=0x7f01000b;
  }
  public static final class attr {
    /**
     * Custom divider drawable to use for elements in the action bar.
     * <p>May be a reference to another resource, in the form
     * "<code>@[+][<i>package</i>:]<i>type</i>/<i>name</i></code>" or a theme
     * attribute in the form
     * "<code>?[<i>package</i>:]<i>type</i>/<i>name</i></code>".
     */
    public static final int actionBarDivider=0x7f020000;
    /**
     * Custom item state list drawable background for action bar items.
     * <p>May be a reference to another resource, in the form
     * "<code>@[+][<i>package</i>:]<i>type</i>/<i>name</i></code>" or a theme
     * attribute in the form
     * "<code>?[<i>package</i>:]<i>type</i>/<i>name</i></code>".
     */
```

FIGURE 4-6: The `R.java` file contains some interesting entries.

Android's documentation tells you to put `R.java` and its hex values out of your mind, and that's probably good advice (advice that this section breaks). Anyway, here is the most important thing to remember about the role of `R.java` in an Android app:

WARNING

» **You cannot edit `R.java`.**

Long after the creation of a project, your IDE continues to monitor (and, if necessary, update) the contents of the `R.java` file. If you delete `R.java`, Android Studio re-creates the file. If you edit `R.java`, Android Studio undoes your edit.

» **Many of Android's pre-declared methods expect numbers in `R.java` as their parameters.**

This expectation can lead to some confusion. Consider the following (very bad) chunk of code:

```
// THIS IS BAD CODE!
println("42");
println(42);
textView.setText("42");
textView.setText(42);
```

Kotlin's two `println()` calls (rarely used in Android apps) add text to a log file. In the bad code, the first `println()` sends the string `"42"` to the file, and the second `println()` converts the integer value 42 to the string `"42"` and then sends the string `"42"` to the log file. (Kotlin's `println()` is prepared to print a string, an integer, and various other types of values.) So far, nothing is wrong with the code, so you can move on . . .

A text view's `setText()` method accepts a string parameter or an integer parameter. In the bad code, the call `textView.setText("42")` is okay. But here's the gotcha: The integer version of `setText()` doesn't convert the integer 42 into a string. Instead, `textView.setText(42)` looks for a resource with code number 42 (in `R.java`, hex value `0x0000002A`). When Android finds nothing with code number 42 in the `R.java` file, your app crashes. To avoid this whole mess, you'd locate the value you want to print using its `text_view_id`. For example, the following code prints a greeting based on the value contained in `R.string.user_greeting`:

```
final TextView helloTextView = (TextView)
  findViewById(R.id.text_view_id);
helloTextView.setText(R.string.user_greeting);
```

The assets folder

When Android packages an app, a tool named aapt (short for Android Asset Packaging Tool) compiles the stuff in the app's `res` folder. In other words, aapt prepares the `res` folder's items for quick retrieval and use. So your application's access to items in the `res` folder is highly optimized.

But before there was Android, there was plain old Java, and plain old Java has its own ways to fetch images and strings. Using Java's techniques, you generally read byte by byte from the Internet or from a device's file system. To make your Android code grab an image or some other data using Java's standard tricks, put the image or data in the Android project's `assets` folder.

By default, an Android Studio project (the kind of project that's displayed in Figure 4-2) doesn't have an `assets` folder. To create such a folder, do the following:

1. **In the Project tool window (Figure 4-2), right-click the app branch at the top of the tree. (If you're a Mac user, Ctrl-click that branch.)**

   A context menu appears.

2. **In the context menu, choose New⇨Folder⇨Assets Folder.**

   A dialog box appears.

3. **In the dialog box, click Finish.**

   As a result, you see a new assets branch in the Android Project tree.

The android.jar archive

Each Android project's `CLASSPATH` includes Android's pre-declared Java code, and this pre-declared code lives in an `android.jar` archive file.

In Android Studio, you can see `android.jar` by switching to the Project view. Follow the instructions on switching views in the sidebar "The many faces of Android Studio," earlier in this chapter. When the Project view replaces the Android Project view, visit the `External Libraries/Android` API branch of the tree.

TECHNICAL STUFF

A `.jar` file is a compressed archive containing a useful bunch of Java classes. In fact, a `.jar` file is a Zip archive. You can open any `.jar` file with WinZip, StuffIt Expander, or your operating system's built-in unzipping utility. (You may or may not have to change the file's name from `whatever.jar` to `whatever.zip`.) Anyway, an `android.jar` file contains Android's Java classes for a particular version of Android.

The `android.jar` file contains code grouped into Java packages, and each package contains Java classes. (Figures 4-7 and 4-8 show only the tip of the `android.jar` iceberg.) The `android.jar` file contains classes specific to Android and classes that simply help Java do its job. Figure 4-7 shows a bunch of Android-specific packages, and Figure 4-8 displays some all-purpose Java packages.

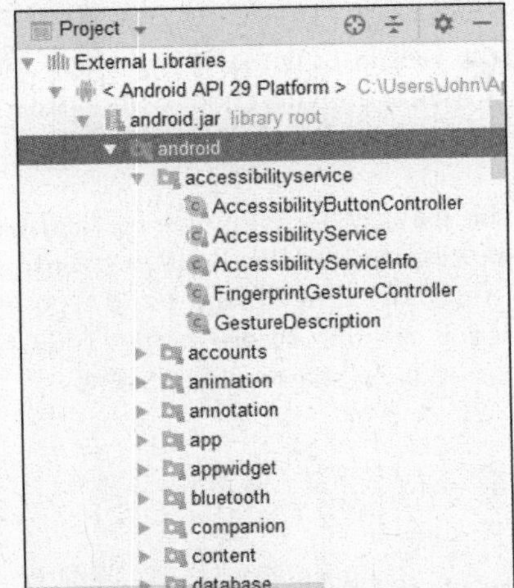

FIGURE 4-7: Some of the packages and classes in `android.jar`.

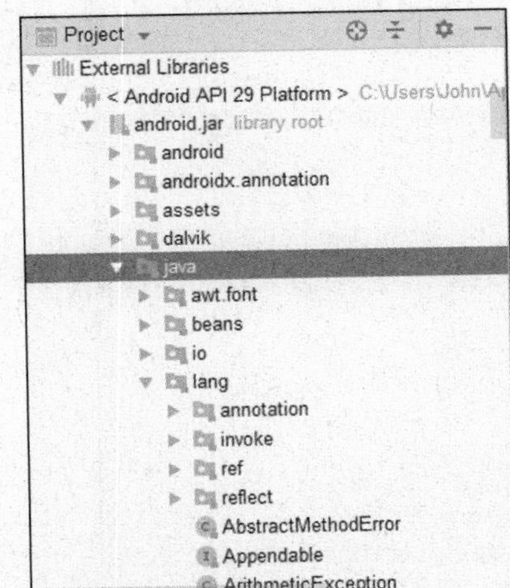

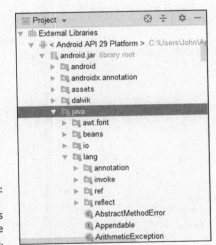

FIGURE 4-8: The `android.jar` file includes general-purpose Java packages.

The APK file

Android puts the results of all its compiling, packaging, and other "ings" into a single file with the `.apk` extension. This *APK* file contains everything a user's device needs to know to run your app. When you install a new app on your Android device, you download and install a new APK file.

An important job of the Gradle tool is to combine your app's file into one APK file. This combining happens each time you choose Run⇨Run 'app' in Android Studio's main menu.

You can find an app's APK file using your Windows File Explorer or Macintosh Finder. For an Android Studio project, the APK file is in the project's `app/build/outputs/apk/<build type>` subfolder. The default build type for Android Studio is a *debug* build, one in which you can find errors in your code. Figure 4-9 shows the debug build location for `app-debug.apk` for MyFirstApp.

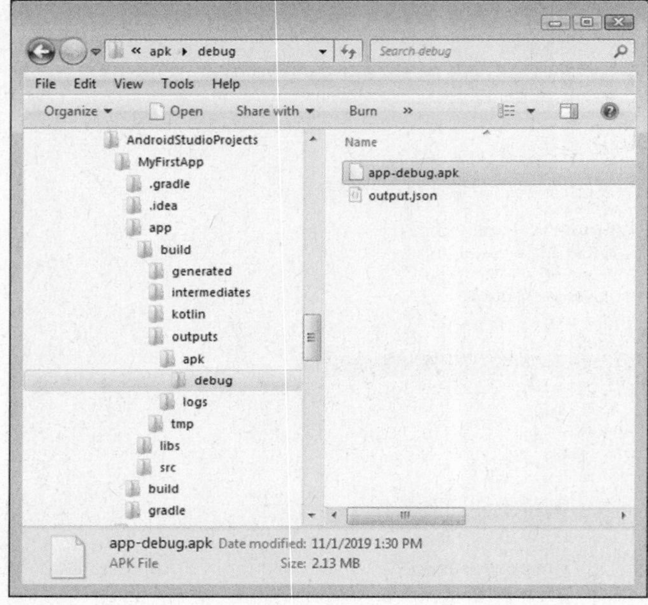

FIGURE 4-9: The debug APK file for MyFirstApp.

The associated `output.json` file contains information about `app-debug.apk`, including the output type, apkData (such as the version code, version name, app filename, and any app properties). Looking into this file can be interesting, but the file is automatically generated, so you don't have to maintain it. You can open this file in Android Studio from the `app\build\outputs\apk\debug` branch. Double-clicking `output.json` displays it in the editor (with a warning not to modify the file). However, what you see is one long line of terribly hard-to-read code. To see it in formatted form, choose Code⇨Reformat Code. You then see a nicely formatted view like the one shown in Figure 4-10.

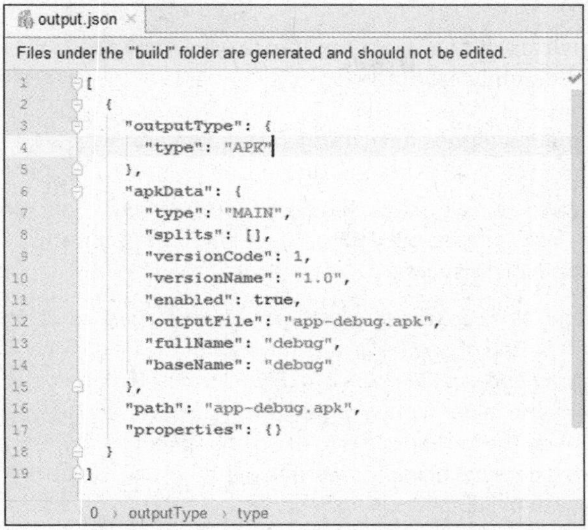

```
output.json
Files under the "build" folder are generated and should not be edited.
[
  {
    "outputType": {
      "type": "APK"
    },
    "apkData": {
      "type": "MAIN",
      "splits": [],
      "versionCode": 1,
      "versionName": "1.0",
      "enabled": true,
      "outputFile": "app-debug.apk",
      "fullName": "debug",
      "baseName": "debug"
    },
    "path": "app-debug.apk",
    "properties": {}
  }
]
0 › outputType › type
```

FIGURE 4-10: A nicely formatted view of `output.json`.

What Did I Agree To?

When you follow the instructions in Chapter 3 of this minibook, you create a new Android project. In doing so, you have a few choices to make. The instructions in Chapter 3 tell you to accept some defaults. This section describes some of the "whys" and "wherefores" concerning those defaults.

What's in a name?

When you create a new application, you assign a bunch of names to things in your application. For example:

- You create an application name and a package name.
- You specify a project location, and in doing so, you name the folder that contains the app on your development computer's hard drive.
- Optionally, depending on template type, you name an activity.

In Chapter 3 of this minibook, when you create your first application, you do give it the somewhat meaningful name of My First App. You also accept the default domain of `example.com` as a company domain and the wizard automatically adds `myfirstapp` to it. In real life, even names that are mildly meaningful to you aren't very helpful to others. Ordinary folks, like Joe and Jane User, will see your application name in the Android device's launcher screen, and the name My First App isn't very inviting. If you're planning to market your app, your app's name should be short, sweet, and descriptive.

Here are some guidelines for naming things:

- When you create a new application, your project and application names may contain blank spaces, but your package name and your activity name must not contain blank spaces.

  In general, blank spaces can gum up the works when your software distinguishes the end of one name and the start of the next name. Consequently, most experienced developers avoid spaces at all costs. For example, in Windows, the folder name Program Files is a never-ending source of angst for developers. The best advice is to use blank spaces only where an app's cosmetics demand blank spaces. If things go wrong, be suspicious of any names with blank spaces.

- For your project name, you can type the name of any valid Kotlin identifier. Make sure to start with a letter and then include only letters, digits, and underscores (_).

  For the scoop on Kotlin identifiers, see Book 2, Chapter 3.

- Your activity is a Kotlin class. So, to adhere to Kotlin's stylistic conventions, start your activity's name with an uppercase letter. In the name, don't include any exotic characters (such as dots, blank spaces, dashes, dollar signs, or pictures of cows).

In Kotlin, as with Java, you normally group a bunch of related classes into a package, and you give the package a name. The name can be almost anything, but Kotlin's rules of etiquette (which are the same as those used with Java) tell you how you should name a package:

- **Reverse your company's domain name.** For example, the domain name for the book's source is `allmycode.com`. So, when the authors create a Kotlin or Java package, they start with `com.allmycode`.

  If you don't have a company, or if your company doesn't have a domain name, you can safely ignore this first rule.

- **Add a word that describes this particular package's purpose.** For example, if the authors were to create a Kotlin program to search for words in the user's input, the code would appear in the `com.allmycode.wordsearch` package.

Android takes Kotlin's package conventions one step further. In the Android world, a package contains the code for one and only one application. For example, in Book 4, Chapter 1, you create a game named Hungry Burds, so the entire Hungry Burds game is in the `com.allmycode.hungryburds` package.

If you create many apps, keeping track of them all can drive you crazy. So it helps if you decide on a formula for naming your apps' packages, and then you stick to that formula as closely as you can.

For the technical story on Java packages and package names, see Book 2, Chapter 3.

Choosing a language

As part of creating a new project, you specify a particular programming language to use: Kotlin or Java. Even though this book relies on Kotlin, you can still use Java for new projects, which is handy if you have existing code you want to use.

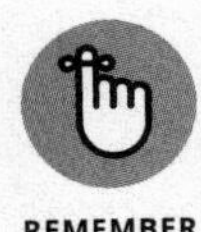
REMEMBER

One of the things to consider when creating new Android apps that rely on Kotlin is that you still have access to your Java code. In the section "The android.jar archive," earlier in this chapter, you see that My First App has access to existing Java packages and classes. You can extend this accessibility to any Java code that you own.

Your app's API levels

In Chapter 3 of this minibook, you create a new app and select a minimum SDK. The acronym SDK stands for the term Software Development Kit. You often see the acronyms SDK and API (application programming interface) used interchangeably. An API level (also known as an SDK version) is a bunch of code that you call upon in your own Android programs. For example, in Listing 4-1, when you write

```
import androidx.appcompat.app.AppCompatActivity
```

you're referring to a bunch of code in Android's SDK. This code is known as Android's `AppCompatActivity` class. In the same listing, when you write

```
setContentView(R.layout.activity_main)
```

you're calling a bunch of code known as the `setContentView()` method. All this code lives in Android's SDK. Now that you have some idea of what an SDK is, the following sections look at what SDK levels mean.

Dealing with updates

From time to time, the stewards of Android introduce improvements in the SDK. When they do, they mark the changes by creating a level number for the new and improved SDK. Level numbers increase as time goes on. That's why, when you create a new project, you select a minimum API level (minimum SDK version) for your new project.

In Chapter 3 of this minibook, when you select a minimum SDK version, Android Studio records your selection in a `build.gradle` file. (Refer to Listing 4-6. In that listing, your selection becomes the `minSdkVersion` number.) If `minSdkVersion` were the only version number in Listing 4-6, life would be simple and this chapter would be finished. But life isn't so simple.

An Android app has several uses for API version numbers. For example, in Listing 4-6, the `minSdkVersion` is API 14, but the `targetSdkVersion` and `compileSdkVersion` numbers are both 29. What's the deal with all these SDK version numbers?

You design an Android app to run on a range of API versions. You can think informally of the minimum SDK (`minSdkVersion`) as the lowest version in the range, and the target SDK (`targetSdkVersion`) as the pinpoint focus of the range. If you select API 14 as the minimum and select 29 as the target, you design your app to run on the following:

- Ice Cream Sandwich (API levels 14 and 15)
- Jelly Bean (levels 16, 17, and 18)
- KitKat (levels 19 and 20)
- Lollipop (levels 21 and 22)
- Marshmallow (level 23)
- Nougat (levels 24 and 25)
- Oreo (levels 26 and 27)
- Oreo (level 28)
- Android 10/Q (level 29)

You also say that your app probably runs on API levels 22, 23, and so on.

These informal notions of "lowest version in the range" and "pinpoint focus" are okay. But what do they mean when the rubber meets the road? And for that matter, why do you even bother specifying a range of SDK versions? Why not say "Every Android user can run my app"?

Here's the story: You can't put any old 1969 car part on a 2019 car, and you certainly can't put most 2019 car parts on an old 1969 car. In the same way, an app is as good as the system it runs on. To extend this line of thinking to computers, consider that you have an old Zenith Supersport computer (ca. 1990) with 5MB of memory and a 6 MHz processor. The Supersport can't run Microsoft Word 2019. And, despite the kinship between older and newer Microsoft operating systems, many of the programs from the Supersport's old disk drive don't run on newer Windows versions.

Considering compatibility

In the old days, a system's underlying software was updated infrequently. When it was, users had to live with whatever consequences were caused by the change. But these days, changes in system software are fast and furious. Your computers and smartphones receive automatic updates over the network. To help you cope, software developers are mindful of compatibility.

At the very least, a system update shouldn't break an existing app. In other words, a system update can add new capabilities, but an update shouldn't mess up older capabilities. (This principle about maintaining older capabilities is called *backward compatibility*. The term emphasizes the direction from new systems back to older software.)

Android's official documentation reports that ". . . new versions of the platform are fully backward-compatible." So an app that runs correctly on API level 21 should run correctly on all levels higher than 21. Of course, the emphasis is on "should run correctly" because in practice, full backward compatibility is difficult to achieve.

Tracking the API level

One of the ways Android keeps track of system updates is with the software's API level. When you look at the Distribution Dashboard at `https://developer.android.com/about/dashboards`, you find that the number of people using an API level varies over time. At the time of this writing, a mere 0.3 percent of people are using API level 10 (Gingerbread), but a healthy 16.9 percent are using API level 23 (Marshmallow). So, no matter what API level you use to compile your app, someone will probably try to run it on a device with a different API level. To face the API levels problem head-on, Android stores several level numbers in your app's files.

Here's what these level numbers mean:

- **The minimum SDK (**`minSdkVersion`**) is the lowest system on which your app is (pretty much) guaranteed to run.** Imagine putting the following code in your app:

  ```
  SharedPreferences prefs =
   PreferenceManager.getDefaultSharedPreferences(this);
  SharedPreferences.Editor editor = prefs.edit();
  editor.putInt("amount", 100);
  editor.apply();
  ```

  In that last line of code, the word *apply* can cause trouble. Android didn't use the word *apply* this way until API level 9. So, when you create your app, you'd better specify level 9 or higher as the minimum SDK.

  If you specify a minimum SDK level of 9, when you then publish your app on the Google Play Store, the store doesn't offer the app to users whose devices run API level 8 or lower.

  An Android project's minimum SDK number is normally in the project's `build.gradle` file. For older projects (created before the Android Studio days), the minimum SDK number appears in the project's `AndroidManifest.xml` file.

- **Another number, the maximum SDK (**`maxSdkVersion`**), is the highest system on which your app is guaranteed to run.** Listing 4-6 has no `maxSdkVersion` and hardly anyone ever specifies a maximum SDK version for an Android project. In fact, the maximum SDK value is a feature that the stewards of Android probably wish they had never created. The Android documentation discourages the use of a maximum SDK version. The docs warn that a maximum SDK version might cause an app to be uninstalled when the app is still usable.

- **The compile SDK (**`compileSdkVersion`**) is the SDK version used to turn your Java code into code that's ready to run.** Put the earlier bullet's `editor.apply()` code in your app, and in the `build.gradle` file, specify a `compileSdkVersion` of 8. Android Studio immediately displays an error message, because the level 8 SDK doesn't understand this use of the `apply()` method. (You're in no danger of running your app on a level-8 device because API level 8 can't even compile your app.)

  Of course, you can try to sneak around the constraints by specifying level 8 as the minimum SDK and some higher level for the compile SDK. But then Android Studio warns you that you're treading on very thin ice. When you test your app on an API level-9 device, everything is ducky. But when you test your app on an API level-8 device, the app crashes.

An Android project's compile SDK version number is in the project's `build.gradle` file. You can change a project's compile SDK version by changing the number in that `build.gradle` file. For an older app (created before Android Studio became part of the picture), you might find the compile SDK number in a `project.properties` or `default.properties` file.

» **The target SDK (`targetSdkVersion`) is the API level of the system on which you intend to test your app.** This notion of intending to test your app is an elusive concept. If you're a thorough developer, you test your app on many devices with many different API levels. Also, if a device or AVD with your app's target SDK isn't available, Android Studio looks for another device that meets your app's minimum SDK requirement.

So the idea of a target SDK remains slippery. Your IDE or your device likely uses this value somewhere in the app's lifecycle, but you shouldn't need to think about the target SDK too much. Most websites devoted to Android tips and techniques tell you to make the target SDK the same as the compile SDK and to leave it at that.

An Android project's target SDK number is in the project's `build.gradle` file.

Considering forward compatibility

In addition to its backward compatibility concerns, Android has some forward-compatibility features. An example of forward compatibility is when a system running API level 4 magically enters a time machine and runs an app that uses fragments — a feature that wasn't created until API level 11.

In reality, forward compatibility in Android comes from things called support libraries. An Android library is an app that can't run on its own. A library exists only to help another app do its duties. A support library is a library that helps an older system deal gracefully with a newer app's features. When you create a new project with fairly disparate minimum and target API levels, Android Studio adds a support library to your code. You often notice this when things named `android.support` and `appcompat` appear without warning as part of your code.

To read more about the ways Android keeps track of its versions, see Chapter 2 in this minibook. For more info on compilers, visit Book 2, Chapter 3.

Divining the buildToolsVersion

As you think about versions, you should look at the `buildToolsVersion` line in Listing 4-6, earlier in the chapter. In spite of what you may see elsewhere, remember that Android Studio is nothing but an IDE — a main window with a bunch of views, panels, tabs, and other visual aids. In its purest form, Android

Studio doesn't create an Android app. Android Studio simply provides an interface to you, the developer. This interface is a go-between to help you work with the real, underlying Android development tools — the tools that actually compose skeletal code, compile the code, run Gradle, bundle up the icons, and package the whole business into a single APK file.

Those underlying tools are the real workhorses of Android development, and the folks at Google strive continuously to improve those tools. That's why, when you go to the main menu and choose Tools⇨SDK Manager, you frequently see a check mark offering to update your Android SDK Build Tools software.

To help maintain compatibility, an Android Studio project keeps a record of the version of the tools that built the project. For the project described in this chapter, the tools are Version 29.0.2. Your own first project is newer than the sample project in this chapter, so the project's build tools version number is likely to be higher. With a different build tools version, you might see some slightly different code. The skeletal Kotlin class in Listing 4-1 might have a few more lines in it. One way or another, Android's basic principles apply to this chapter's example and to your own examples as well.

» Making the app do something

» Finding bugs in your app (not that it has any, of course)

Chapter 5
Conjuring and Embellishing an Android App

When the best developers set out to learn something, they follow a "ready, set, go" approach. They don't "go" right into the detailed technical manuals. Instead, they get ready by examining the simplest example they can find. These developers work with a Hello World scenario like the one in Chapters 3 and 4 of this minibook. Then (and here's where this chapter fits in) they do some probing and poking; they explore some possibilities; they peek around corners; they try some experiments. If you want to learn something new quickly, these initial "ready, set" steps will serve you well.

When the authors are firm on their feet, they do the kind of stuff you do in Books 3 through 6. They "go." If you feel confident, "go" directly to Book 3. But if you want more "ready, set" material, march on into this chapter.

Dragging, Dropping, and Otherwise Tweaking an App

A general guideline in app development tells you to separate logic from presentation. In less technical terms, the guideline warns against confusing what an app does with how an app looks. The guideline applies to many things in life. For example, if you're designing a website, have artists do the layout and have geeks do the coding. If you're writing a report, get the ideas written first. Later, you can worry about fonts and paragraph styles. (Susan, you're this book's copy editor. Do you agree with us about fonts and styles?)

The literature on app development has specific techniques and frameworks to help you separate form from function. But in this chapter, we do the simplest thing: We chop an app's creation into two sets of instructions. The first set is about creating an app's look; the second set is about coding the app's behavior.

Creating the "look"

The process for creating the application's look requires several steps, even for a basic Android app. You start with the basic application and then add components like check boxes, text boxes, and buttons, and finally perform various configuration tasks. The following sections help you through this process.

Defining the app

Before you do anything else, you have to have an app. The following steps perform this task.

1. **Launch Android Studio.**

   If you followed the steps in Chapter 3 of this minibook, you created a skeletal Android project. Maybe you finished by choosing File⇨Close Project, or maybe you simply quit the Android Studio app.

2. **If you didn't choose Close Project (or if you didn't even quit the Android Studio app), you see the project from Chapter 3 in Android Studio's main window. Select File⇨Close Project.**

   The Android Studio's Welcome screen appears.

3. **In the Welcome screen, select** Start a New Android Studio Project **and then follow the remaining steps to create a project, as in the "Starting the IDE and creating your first app" section of Chapter 3.**

ANDROID STUDIO PROJECTS

In Steps 2 and 3, we encourage you to close your existing project and work with the Welcome screen. You can do this over and over again, but you really don't have to. One alternative is to keep the Chapter 3 project open and to enhance that project with the instructions in this chapter. Another alternative is to keep the Chapter 3 project open and to create a second Android project.

With two projects open at the same time, your Android Studio app has two main windows. You can switch between the windows, minimize one of the windows, or do whatever you want with the two windows. One thing you should definitely avoid doing is becoming confused and making changes in the wrong window. That's why we recommend closing any project that you're not actively developing.

To close an existing project, select File⇨Close Project in Android Studio's main menu.

To create a new project without closing one of your existing projects, select File⇨New Project in Android Studio's main menu. (When you do, you see the same Create New Project dialog boxes that you see when you choose New Project in the Welcome screen.)

In this section's listings and figures, you name the app `01_05_01`. Put the app in a package named `com.allmycode.p01_05_01`. The reason you follow this convention is to make your code look as much like the book's code as possible for comparison purposes.

When you're finished creating a brand-new project, it appears in Android Studio's main window.

Adding the components

After you create the basic app and perform any required configuration with it, you add components to it using the following steps:

1. **In the new project's** `app/res/layout` **branch (in the Android view of main window's Project tool window), double-click** `activity_main.xml`**.**

REMEMBER

The Project tool window appears on the left side of Android Studio's main window. The Project tool window has several different views, including the Project view, the Packages view, and the Android view. When you create a new project, the Android view appears by default. So if you're looking for the Project tool window, look for the word Android in a drop-down list in the main window's upper-left corner. The tree that's immediately below this drop-down list is the Project tool window. (If you don't see anything like this, try clicking the 1: Project tool button on the very left edge of the main window.) For more information about working with the Project tool window, see Book 2, Chapter 1.

As a result, Android Studio's Designer tool displays the contents of `activity_main.xml`. The Designer tool has two modes: Design mode for drag-and-drop visual editing, and Text mode for XML code editing. So the bottom of the Designer tool has two tabs — a Design tab and a Text tab.

2. **Click the Design tab.**

   In Design mode, most of the Designer tool is taken up by the palette — a list of layouts, widgets, and other things that you can drag onto your app's screen — and the preview screen. (See Figure 5-1.)

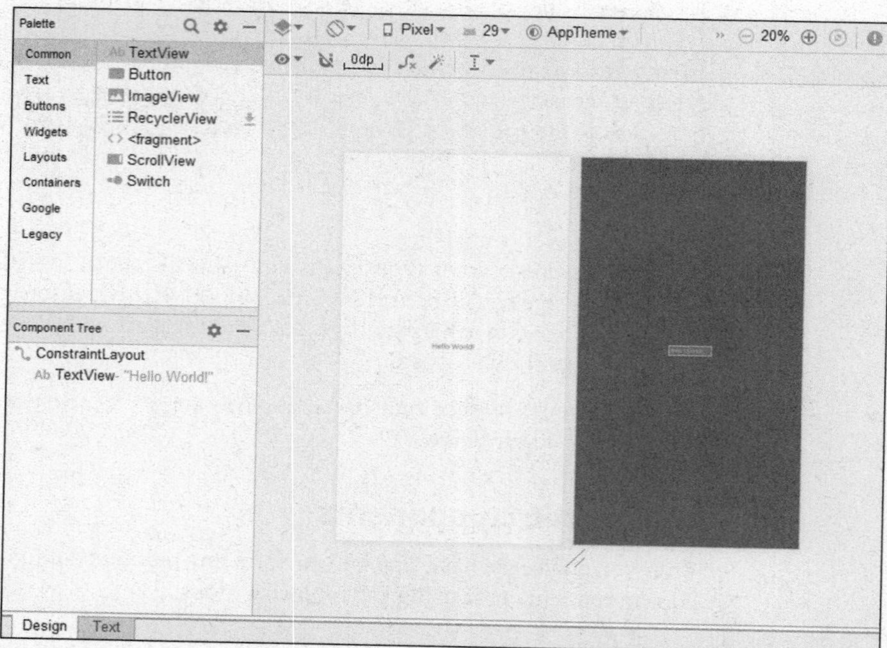

FIGURE 5-1: Design mode allows for drag-and-drop design.

TIP

If you don't see the palette, look for a little Palette button on the left edge of the Designer tool. If you click that button, the palette should appear.

The next several steps guide you through the creation of the app shown in Figure 5-2.

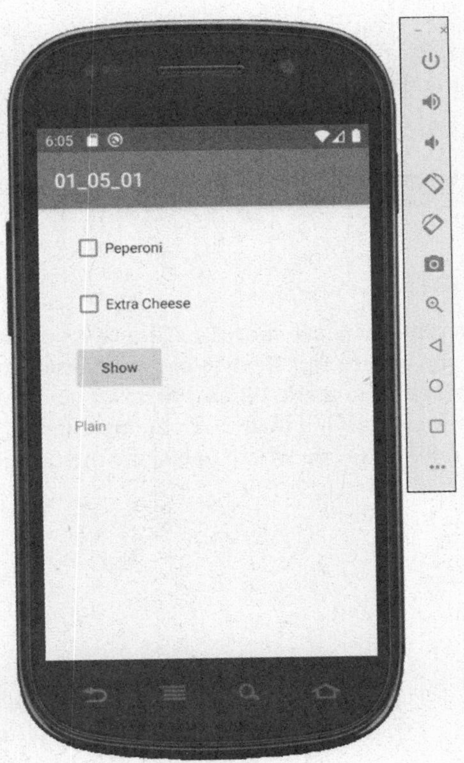

FIGURE 5-2: You want to create this app.

3. **Click the Hello World text view in the Designer and press Delete.**

REMEMBER

You're past Hello World now, so it's time to remove it from the display. To remove any component you don't want, select it and then click Delete. Android Studio then removes all traces of the component from your code.

4. **In the palette's Buttons group, click to select CheckBox.**
5. **Click your mouse in the preview screen.**

A check box appears where you click in the preview screen. (If clicking doesn't work, then use drag-and-drop techniques instead.)

TIP

Instead of clicking twice, you can drag and drop from the palette to the preview screen. You don't need to do two separate clicks.

6. **Repeat Steps 4 and 5.**

Now your app has two check boxes. Don't fuss too much about the positions of the two check boxes. Sure, it's good if the check boxes don't overlap. (If they do, you can drag one of the check boxes within the preview screen, but in our experience, dragging things in the preview screen doesn't always give you what you want.)

With or without dragging, don't put much effort into making the layout look nice. You beautify the layout in Chapter 6 of this minibook.

7. **From the palette's Buttons group, put a Button on the preview screen.**
8. **From the palette's Text group, put a TextView element on the preview screen.**

Adding constraints

Notice the Component Tree window shown in Figure 5-3. You see each of the components added to the app so far. Next to each of these components is a red circle containing an exclamation mark. When you hover your mouse over the circle, you see a pop-up message saying that the component lacks constraints, which is simply a method of telling the app where to display the component onscreen.

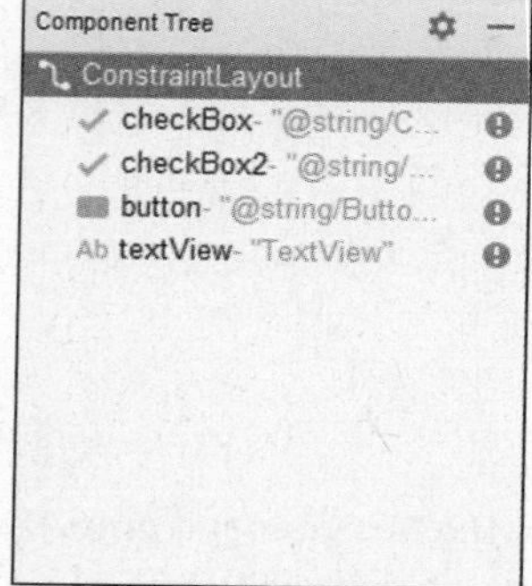

FIGURE 5-3: Each component must have constraints assigned to it.

WARNING

If you try to run your app without defining constraints, all the components will appear in the upper-left corner for the display, one on top of the other. So, all you'll be able to see clearly is the last component that you added to the app, with bits and pieces of the other components showing under it. The following steps help you create constraints for your app:

1. **Click the first check box in the preview screen.**

   You see the settings for this check box in the Attributes window, shown in Figure 5-4. Each component has attributes that you can adjust to create a specific appearance in the final app. Note that there are more attributes than are shown in the figure.

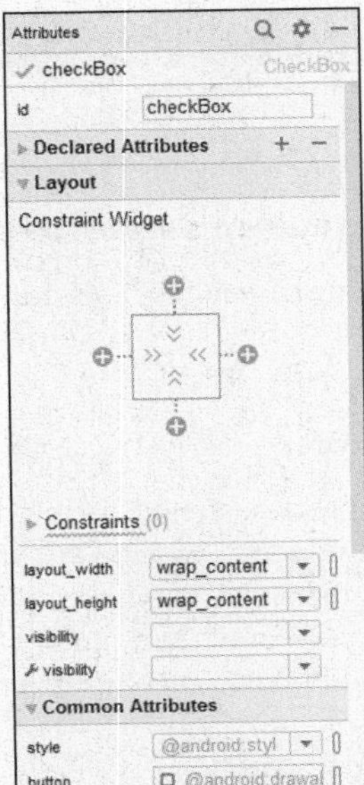

FIGURE 5-4: Changing the properties of a check box.

The Layout tab contains the constraints used to display the component onscreen, as shown in Figure 5-4. You can choose to attach components to each other in various ways using the constraint points — indicated by blue circles with plus signs in them.

2. **Click the constraint point at the top of the Constraint Widget entry.**

   A number appears in a combo box showing the current top margin of the component onscreen (see Figure 5-5). You can choose to keep the current top margin value or select one of the default values. In this case, choose 24 from the drop-down list.

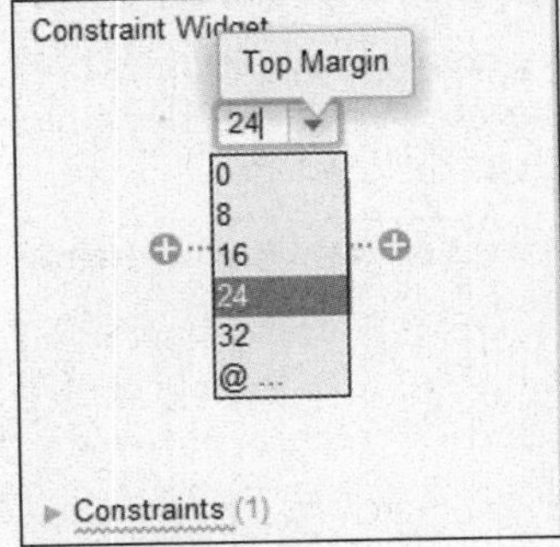

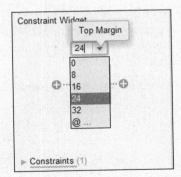

FIGURE 5-5: Constraints position the component onscreen.

3. **Click the constraint point to the left of the Constraint Widget entry.**

   You see another text box appear. In this case, choose 32 from the drop-down list.

4. **Repeat Steps 3 and 4 for the other components in the Component tree.**

   As you change the settings for each of the components, you see the component move in the Design view.

Adding text to each component

The components currently have generic text assigned, which isn't helpful. You can assign text directly to each of the components, which isn't very useful because it makes creating multi-language apps difficult. The best option is to define a resource for each of the text strings that you could then modify without having to recompile the app. The following steps add text to each of the components:

1. **Click the first check box in the preview screen.**

   Notice that the text field has a generic entry of CheckBox in it, as shown in Figure 5-6. Immediately to the right of the text is a little square button, the Pick a Resource button.

Declared Attributes	
layout_width	wrap_content
layout_height	wrap_content
id	checkBox3
text	CheckBox

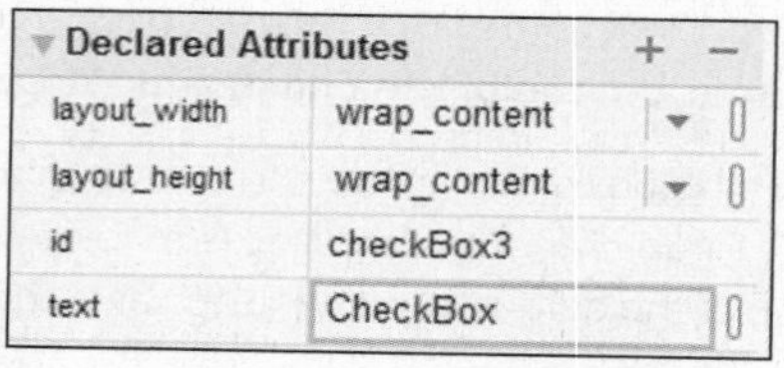

FIGURE 5-6: The text field has a generic value associated with it.

2. **Click the Pick a Resource button next to the text field.**

   You see the Pick a Resource dialog box, shown in Figure 5-7. This dialog box presents a list of the resources that are currently defined for the app. However, no resource is defined for the text for the check box.

3. **Choose New String Value from the Add New Resource drop-down list box.**

   You see the New String Value Resource dialog box, shown in Figure 5-8. This dialog box is where you define the strings used for your components. Notice that the string is automatically stored in `strings.xml` (see the "The res branch" section of Chapter 4 in this minibook for details).

4. **Type** Checkbox1Text **in the Resource Name field and** Pepperoni **in the Resource Value field. Click OK.**

   The first check box's text field now contains a value of `@string/Checkbox1Text`.

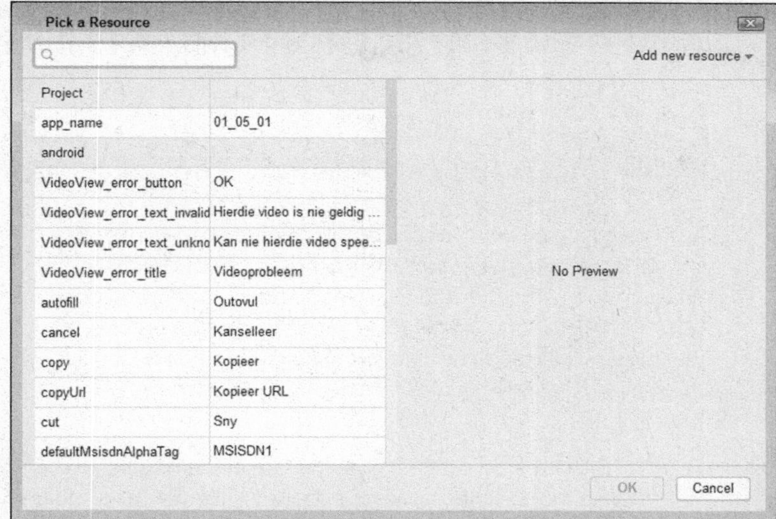

FIGURE 5-7: Obtain access to the currently defined resources.

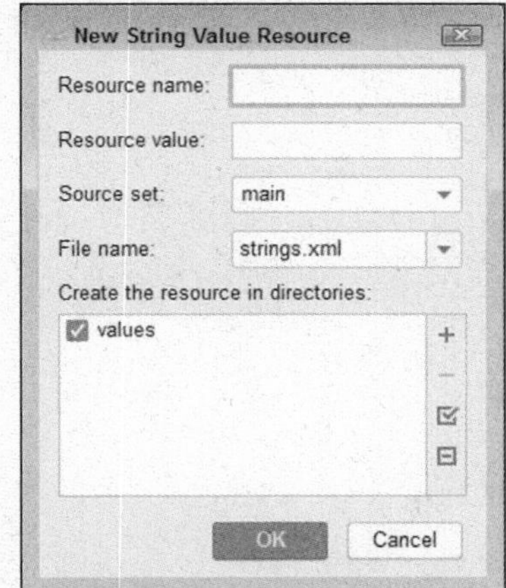

FIGURE 5-8: Create a new string resource.

5. Repeat Steps 2 through 4 for the remaining components to create an app that looks like the one in Figure 5-2 (Listing 5-1 contains precise configuration details to use if you want).

WARNING

You might type Show (with mostly lowercase letters) in the text field for the button. Even so, newer Android devices will display the word SHOW (with all uppercase letters) on the face of the button. Some older devices will display Show. (Refer to Figure 5-2.)

A NOTE ABOUT CODE FORMATTING

When working in your IDE's editor, you have nearly unlimited space to write code on a single line, but this is not so for books, which have a limited number of characters for each line. As a result, the code in this book is formatted to fit your page.

In addition, sometimes code can be slightly different from machine to machine (and still work just fine). The text in Listing 5-1 comes from one of the author's clicking and dragging within Android Studio's preview screen. Your own clicking and dragging might result in some different code. For example, the precise order of entries might differ, but the values will be the same unless you use different values as well.

TIP

To force lowercase letters onto the face of the button, you can switch to Text view in the designer, locate the <Button> element, and add the code shown in bold in the following code:

```
<Button
    android:textAllCaps="false"
    android:id="@+id/button"
    android:layout_width="wrap_content"
    android:layout_height="wrap_content"
    android:layout_marginStart="32dp"
    android:layout_marginLeft="32dp"
    android:layout_marginTop="24dp"
    android:text="@string/Button1Text"
    app:layout_constraintStart_toStartOf="parent"
    app:layout_constraintTop_toBottomOf=
      "@+id/checkBox2"/>
```

6. **Choose File⇨Save All to save your work so far.**

Viewing the result

With this section's steps, you edit your app visually. Behind the scenes, Android Studio is editing the text in your app's `activity_main.xml` document. You can see what changes Android Studio has made to your app's `activity_main.xml` document by selecting the Text tab at the bottom of Android Studio's editor. The `activity_main.xml` document is reproduced in Listing 5-1.

Whenever you want, you can change the look of your app by directly editing the text in `activity_main.xml`.

LISTING 5-1: The activity_main.xml Document

```
<?xml version="1.0" encoding="utf-8"?>
<androidx.constraintlayout.widget.ConstraintLayout
    xmlns:android=
      "http://schemas.android.com/apk/res/android"
    xmlns:app="http://schemas.android.com/apk/res-auto"
    xmlns:tools="http://schemas.android.com/tools"
    android:layout_width="match_parent"
    android:layout_height="match_parent"
    tools:context=".MainActivity">

    <CheckBox
        android:id="@+id/checkBox"
        android:layout_width="wrap_content"
        android:layout_height="wrap_content"
        android:layout_marginStart="32dp"
        android:layout_marginLeft="32dp"
        android:layout_marginTop="24dp"
        android:text="@string/Checkbox1Text"
        app:layout_constraintStart_toStartOf="parent"
        app:layout_constraintTop_toTopOf="parent"/>

    <CheckBox
        android:id="@+id/checkBox2"
        android:layout_width="wrap_content"
        android:layout_height="wrap_content"
        android:layout_marginStart="32dp"
        android:layout_marginLeft="32dp"
        android:layout_marginTop="24dp"
        android:text="@string/Checkbox2Text"
        app:layout_constraintStart_toStartOf="parent"
        app:layout_constraintTop_toBottomOf=
          "@+id/checkBox"/>

    <Button
        android:id="@+id/button"
        android:layout_width="wrap_content"
        android:layout_height="wrap_content"
        android:layout_marginStart="32dp"
        android:layout_marginLeft="32dp"
        android:layout_marginTop="24dp"
        android:text="@string/Button1Text"
        android:textAllCaps="false"
```

(continued)

LISTING 5-1: ***(continued)***

```
            app:layout_constraintStart_toStartOf="parent"
            app:layout_constraintTop_toBottomOf=
              "@+id/checkBox2"/>

        <TextView
            android:id="@+id/textView"
            android:layout_width="wrap_content"
            android:layout_height="wrap_content"
            android:layout_marginStart="32dp"
            android:layout_marginLeft="32dp"
            android:layout_marginTop="24dp"
            android:text="@string/TextView1Text"
            app:layout_constraintStart_toStartOf="parent"
            app:layout_constraintTop_toBottomOf="@+id/button"
/>

</androidx.constraintlayout.widget.ConstraintLayout>
```

In Listing 5-1, you also create resource strings to hold the values for the components. These resource strings appear in the `app\res\values\strings.xml` file. Listing 5-2 shows how these strings appear in the XML file.

LISTING 5-2: **The strings.xml Document**

```
<resources>
    <string name="app_name">01_05_01</string>
    <string name="Checkbox2Text">Extra Cheese</string>
    <string name="Checkbox1Text">Pepperoni</string>
    <string name="Button1Text">Show</string>
    <string name="TextView1Text">Plain</string>
</resources>
```

Coding the behavior

Assuming that you've followed the instructions in the section "Creating the 'look,'" what's next? Well, you want your app to do something, and not just sit there staring at you. To make an app do something, you must provide a series of steps to perform as the result of a user action, like clicking the Show button. The following steps get you started.

1. **Follow the steps in this chapter's "Creating the 'look'" section.**
2. **Make note of the labels on the branches in the Component Tree.**

   The Component tree is on the left side of Android Studio's main window (to the left of the preview screen; refer to Figure 5-1). Notice the labels on the branches of the tree. Each element on the screen has an `id` (a name to identify that element in the Attributes window; refer to Figure 5-4). In Figure 5-3, the ids of the screen's elements include checkBox, checkBox2, button, and textView.

   Android Studio assigns ids automatically, and you can change these ids if you wish. But in this example, it's best to accept whatever you see in the Component Tree. But before proceeding to the next step, make note of the ids in your app's Component Tree. (They may not be the same as the ids in Figure 5-3.)
3. **In the preview screen, select the Show button. (Refer to Figure 5-2.)**
4. **Look for the Attributes window on the right side of the Designer tool. (See Figure 5-9.)**

   To have something happen when you click Show, you need to create a connection between its on`Click` attribute and the code in `MainActivity.kt`. You can perform this task in two ways:

   - Type the name of the function found in `MainActivity.kt` directly.
   - Define a string resource that points to the function found in `MainActivity.kt`.

   Using the string resource approach allows more flexibility and aligns with how Android coding is done today, so that's the approach used in this chapter.

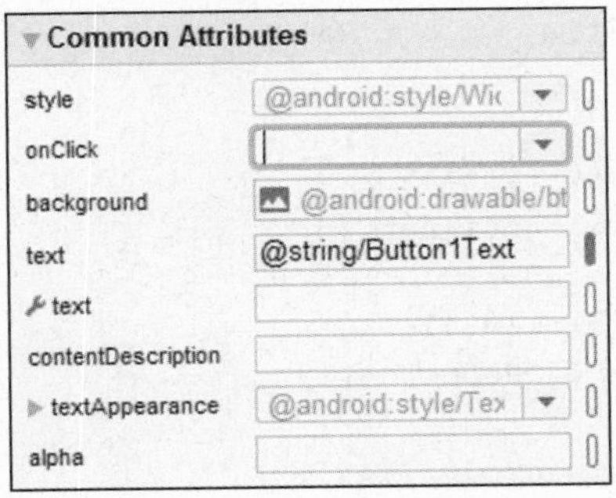

Common Attributes	
style	@android:style/Wic
onClick	
background	@android:drawable/bt
text	@string/Button1Text
text	
contentDescription	
textAppearance	@android:style/Tex
alpha	

FIGURE 5-9: Defining a connection between your form and the code.

5. **Using the same technique found in the "Adding text to each component" section, earlier in this chapter, add a string resource for** `Button1Click` **with a value of** `onButtonClick`**.**

Even though this is text resource, it still creates the required connectivity for you. Using a string resource in this case has the advantage of allowing you to customize click methods as needed.

6. **Inside the** `app/java/com.allmycode.p01_05_01` **branch of the Project tool window, double-click** `MainActivity`.

REMEMBER

In the Project tool window, the `MainActivity` branch is located in a branch that's labeled with your app's package name (`com.example.somethingoro-ther`). That package name branch is directly in the Java branch, which is, in turn, in the app branch.

When you're finished with your double-clicking, the activity's code appears in Android Studio's editor.

7. **Modify the activity's code, as shown in Listing 5-3.**

The lines that you type are set in boldface in Listing 5-3. Listing 5-3 assumes that the branches on your app's Component tree have the same labels as the tree pictured in Figure 5-2, shown previously. In other words, the code assumes that your app's check boxes have the ids `checkBox` and `checkBox2`, and that your `TextView` element has the id `textView`. If your app's widgets have different ids, change the code in Listing 5-3 accordingly. For example, if your first check box has the id `checkBox1`, change `checkBox.isChecked()` to read `checkBox1.isChecked()`.

LISTING 5-3: A Button Responds to a Click

```
class MainActivity : AppCompatActivity() {

    override fun onCreate(savedInstanceState: Bundle?) {
        super.onCreate(savedInstanceState)
        setContentView(R.layout.activity_main)
    }

    fun onButtonClick(view: View){
        val builder = StringBuilder()

        if (checkBox.isChecked()){
            builder.append("Pepperoni")
        }
        if (checkBox2.isChecked()){
            if (builder.length == 0){
                builder.append("Extra Cheese")
            } else {
                builder.append(" and Extra Cheese")
```

```
            }
        }
        if (builder.length == 0){
            builder.append("Plain")
        }

        textView.setText(builder)
    }
}
```

The added code requires some explanation. You could call your function (`fun`) anything, but the standard practice is to start with the word `on`, followed by the name of the control (`button`), followed by the name of action (`click`). Using `onButtonClick()` for your `fun` name makes the code a lot easier to read.

Even though the code makes no use of the `view: View`, you need it as part of the `fun` signature. Without this part of the code, Android can't really tell that your `fun` is an event handler. An Android *view* is a rectangular area of the screen that holds components and performs tasks like drawing them.

REMEMBER

You can't change a Kotlin string; it's immutable. However, you can make modifications to a special kind of object called a `StringBuilder`. The `StringBuilder` provides special properties and methods that make working with strings in Kotlin a lot easier at the expense of a little memory and time. So, `builder` is a `StringBuilder` object that will contain the output to display in `textView`. This way, you can see the options that the app user has selected.

A check box is either checked or it isn't. When something is true or false, it's called a Boolean value. The `checkBox.isChecked()` method asks the app whether the user has checked the first check box. Likewise for `checkBox2.isChecked()`, which checks the second check box. When a user checks a box, it means that the pizza should have this item on it. An `if` statement requires a true value to perform the tasks contained within it.

When checking the first check box, `builder` is always empty, so you can simply call `builder.append("Pepperoni")` when the user checks that box. However, `builder` might not be empty when the code checks the status of the second check box. So, now the code says that if the second check box is checked, but the first check box isn't, call `builder.append("Extra Cheese")`, which places extra cheese but not pepperoni as one of the items on the pizza. To make this determination, the second `if` statement asks `builder.length == 0`, which determines whether `builder` is empty. What if `builder` isn't empty? Well, that's where the `else` clause comes into play. If `builder` already has pepperoni in it, you add cheese to the list as well by calling `builder.append(" and Extra Cheese")` instead.

The final bit of code determines whether the user has selected either pepperoni or extra cheese. If not, the user wants a plain pizza. No matter what happens, the code then shows the result of the user selections by calling `textView.setText(builder)`. Figure 5-10 shows how the application operates.

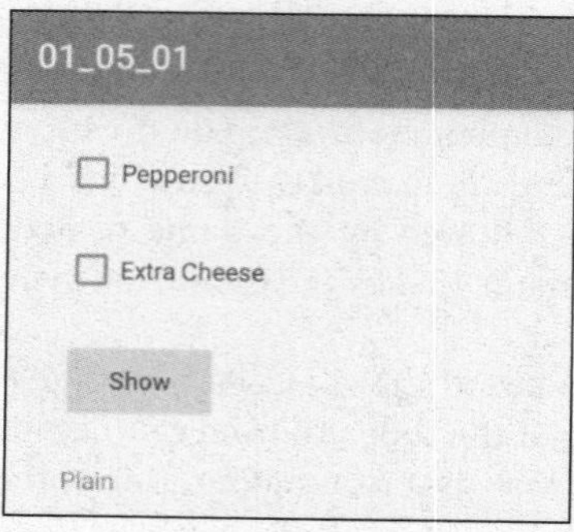

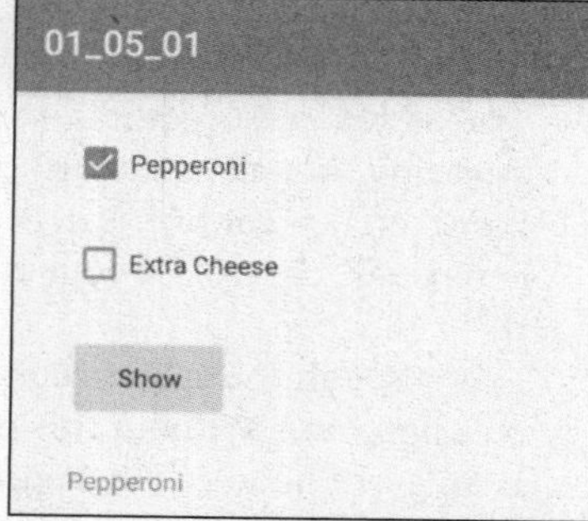

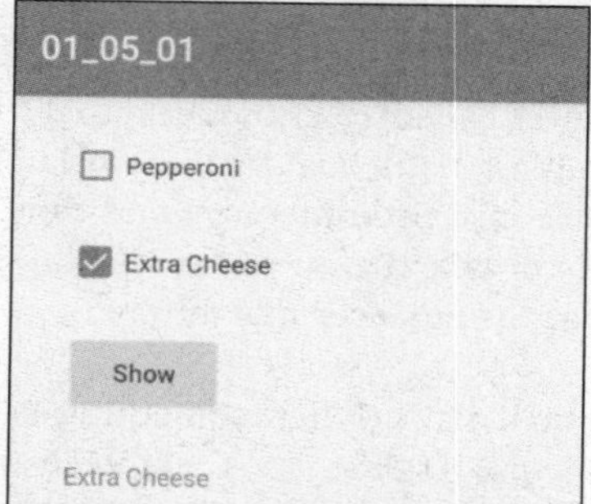

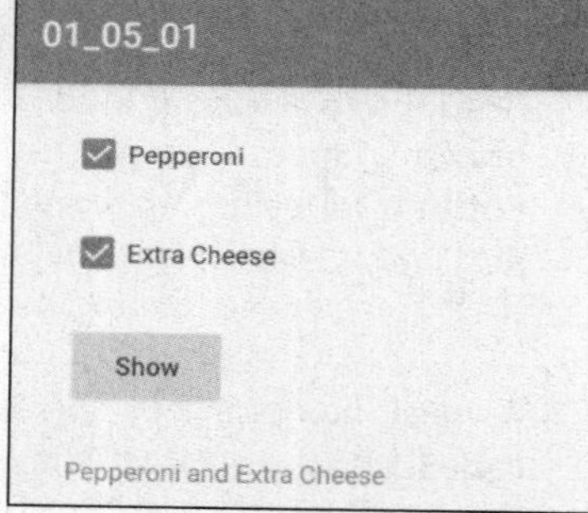

FIGURE 5-10: Running this section's app.

TIP

This chapter contains material that is a little more advanced than you'd probably like to tackle at the moment. Sometimes, it's important to see a little code before you get too far in a book so that you can get an idea of how things go together. Don't worry if you can't make complete sense of it now. If you already know Java and are moving to Kotlin while working through this book, make sure you check out Book 2, Chapter 2 for details of differences between Kotlin and Java. Book 2, Chapter 3 will help you start making sense of the code you're seeing now. Just hang in there; you'll eventually know an amazing amount about working with Kotlin code for Android development!

MAKE ANDROID STUDIO DO THE WORK

To use specific pieces of the Android API, you must import them into your code using the `import` keyword. This example already contains all the imports it needs, as shown here:

```
import androidx.appcompat.app.AppCompatActivity
import android.os.Bundle
import android.view.View
import kotlinx.android.synthetic.main.activity_main.*
```

You can tweak Android Studio's settings so that lines of this kind appear automatically whenever you type words like `View`, `CheckBox`, or `TextView`. Here's how:

1. **If you have a Window's PC, choose File➪Settings. If you have a Mac, choose Android Studio➪Preferences.**

   A dialog box appears. (The dialog box's title is either Settings or Preferences. Whatever!)

2. **In the panel on the left side of the dialog box, expand the Editor\General branch.**

3. **In the Editor\General branch, select Auto Import.**

   Several options appear in the main body of the dialog box. (See the figure.)

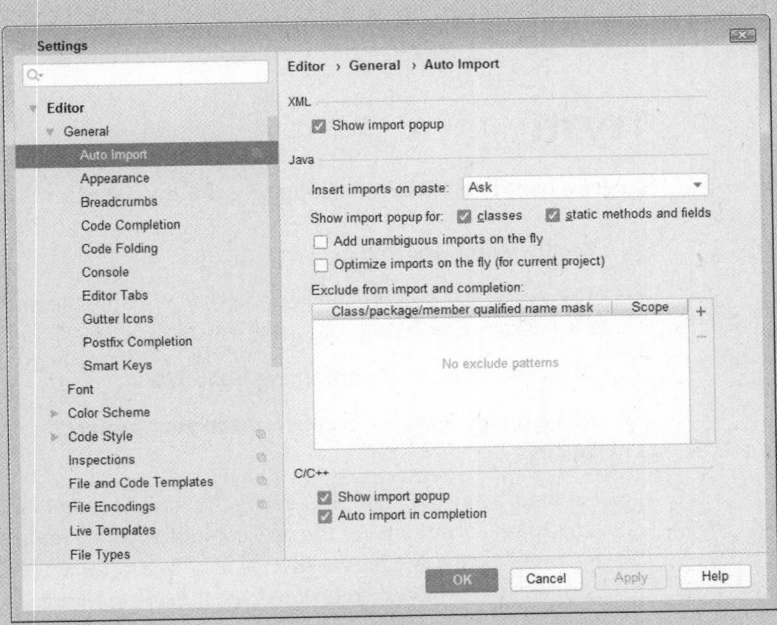

(continued)

4. **In the drop-down list labeled Insert Imports on Paste, select All.**
5. **Put a check mark in the Optimize Imports on the Fly check box.**
6. **Put a check mark in the Add Unambiguous Imports on the Fly check box.**
7. **Click OK to commit these changes.**

   Now, when you type a line of code that requires an import, Android Studio automatically imports the required package for you. That's nice.

8. **Run the app.**

   If you needed an import, Android Studio automatically adds it and then runs the app for you, rather than displaying an error message.

A Bit of Debugging

In a perfect world, you wake up refreshed and energetic every morning. Every app you write runs correctly on the first test. Every word you write in *Android Application Development All-in-One For Dummies*, 3rd Edition, is *le mot juste.*

But the world isn't perfect. And often the first test of a new application forms a disappointing splat on your emulator's screen. So the next few sections contain some useful debugging techniques.

Try it!

To get a handle on Android debugging, follow these instructions:

1. **Create a new Android project.**

   To cook up this section's figures and listings, name the project `01_05_02` and the package `com.allmycode.p01_05_02`.

2. **Delete the `TextView` containing Hello World.**
3. **Add a blank `TextView` component to your project's `activity_main.xml` layout.**

   For details, see the section "Creating the 'look,'" earlier in this chapter. Make sure to set constraints for the new component and create a string resource for it named `textView1Text` with a value of `TextView`. After adding a `TextView` element, the preview screen looks like the one in Figure 5-11, and Android Studio's Component Tree contains a `textView` branch.

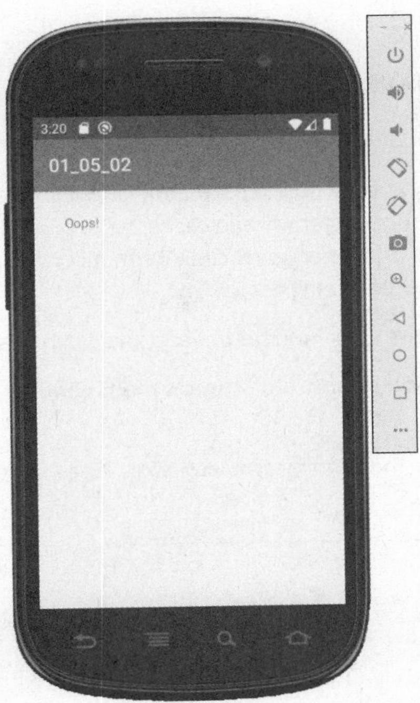

FIGURE 5-11: A layout containing a new text component.

4. **Open the new project's** `MainActivity` **for editing.**

   The activity's `onCreate` method looks like this:

```
override fun onCreate(savedInstanceState: Bundle?) {
    super.onCreate(savedInstanceState)
    setContentView(R.layout.activity_main)
}
```

5. **Add an incorrect statement to the** `onCreate` **method.**

   The statement that you add in Listing 5-4 is set in bold type (along with a comment that is preceded by a // to indicate the bad statement).

LISTING 5-4: A Misguided Attempt to Add a TextView to an Activity

```
override fun onCreate(savedInstanceState: Bundle?) {
    super.onCreate(savedInstanceState)

    // This is bad code!
    textView.setText("Oops!")
    setContentView(R.layout.activity_main)
}
```

6. **Run your app.**

   Your app comes crashing down with a big `01_05_02 Keeps Stopping` message. Two buttons appear: App Info and Close App.

   When you click App Info, you see basic information about your app, such as any notification, the amount of storage and cache the app uses, mobile data and Wi-Fi statistics, and some other advanced information. All this information must be useful sometime, but it isn't useful now.

   You can click the message's Close App button and give up in despair. Or . . .

7. **Look at the lower portion of Android Studio's main window for a Run window.**

   The Run window displays the running emulator's log. (See Figure 5-12.)

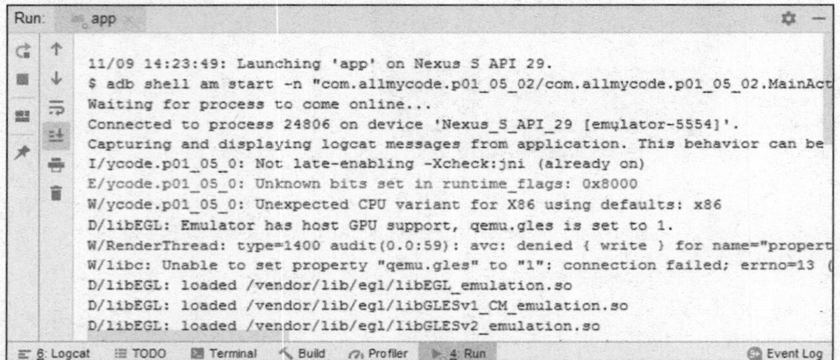

FIGURE 5-12: The Run window.

TIP

If you don't see the Run window, click the Android tool button at the bottom of the main window. Doing so exposes (or hides) the Android tool window. In the Android tool window, click the Run tab. (While you're at it, make a mental note about the Android tool button's having nothing to do with the Android view in the Project tool window!)

REMEMBER

The information you see in Figure 5-12 can also appear in the Logcat window. However, by default, when you run an app, you see the information in the Run window.

The Logcat window is located in the Logcat tab, which is, in turn, part of the Android tool window. (See Figure 5-13.)

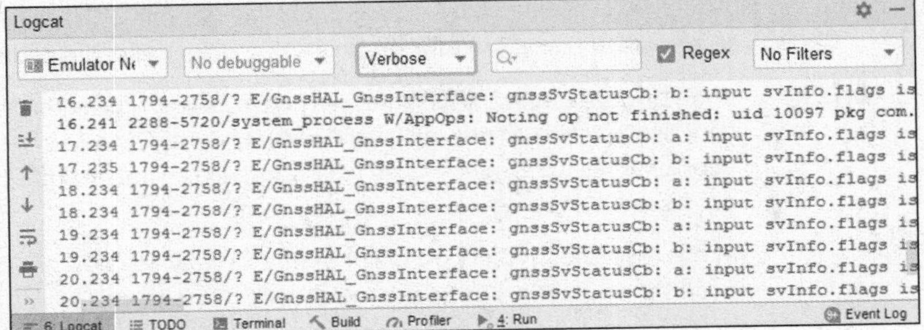

FIGURE 5-13: The Logcat window.

Looking at the two figures should tell you why the emulator's log normally appears in the Run window. The amount of information in the Logcat windows is enormous. The "Filter the output" section, later in this chapter, tells you how to hack away at the excess, but even with filtering, using the Logcat window can be daunting.

8. **In the Run window, look for a Java stack trace.**

   The Java stack trace (plus a few of additional lines in the log) looks like the text shown in Listing 5-5. (The output is reformatted to fit within the confines of the book page.) Note especially the text in bold.

LISTING 5-5: Messages in the Run Window

```
E/AndroidRuntime: FATAL EXCEPTION: main
    Process: com.allmycode.p01_05_02, PID: 24806
    java.lang.RuntimeException: Unable to start activity
     ComponentInfo{
       com.allmycode.p01_05_02/
       com.allmycode.p01_05_02.MainActivity}:
       java.lang.NullPointerException:
         Attempt to invoke virtual method
         'void android.widget.TextView.setText(
         java.lang.CharSequence)'
       on a null object reference
        at android.app.ActivityThread.
          performLaunchActivity(ActivityThread.java:3270)
        at android.app.ActivityThread.
          handleLaunchActivity(ActivityThread.java:3409)
```

A log file always contains more information than you need. But if you look for the most recent bunch of words, you find the trace that you need.

9. **In the stack trace, look for lines relating directly to the code in your app.**

   The stack trace shows which methods were calling which other methods when your app crashed. In this onslaught of details, you find a few lines containing information you recognize from your app, such as the fact that this error occurs when working with a `TextView` component.

   In this case, the problem occurs in `MainActivity.kt`, as a null pointer exception, using the `setText()` method.

10. **In Android Studio's editor, find the offending line in your app's code.**

    In this section's example, the guilty line is `textView.setText("Oops!")` in your code's `MainActivity` class. When you look further down the Logcat output in the Run window, you see this entry:

```
Caused by: java.lang.NullPointerException:
  Attempt to invoke virtual method '
  void android.widget.TextView.setText(
    java.lang.CharSequence)'
  on a null object reference
    at com.allmycode.p01_05_02.MainActivity.onCreate(
      MainActivity.kt:13)
```

TIP

The Run window's text contains hyperlinks. For example, the last two lines contain this information: `MainActivity.onCreate(MainActivity.kt:13)`. Click the `MainActivity.kt:13` link in the Run window, and Android Studio's editor jumps straight to the relevant line of code.

TIP

By default, Android Studio displays line numbers with your code. However, if you don't see the line numbers, right-click the gray area to the left of the code and select Show Line Numbers in the context menu. As an alternative, choose File⇨Settings on Windows or Android Studio⇨Preferences on a Mac. Under Editor⇨General⇨Appearance, put a check mark in the Show Line Numbers check box.

11. **Figure out what part of the offending code might cause the error shown in the stack trace.**

    Unfortunately, this step isn't always easy. You may need to make several guesses, try several possible solutions, or seek advice on some online forums.

    Anyway, like a chef on a cooking show, you can quickly whip out a ready-made solution. When you call `textView.setText()`, you get a `NullPointerException`. So `textView` is `null` (it has no value). The problem in Listing 5-4 is the placement of the call to `textView.setText("Oops!")`.

Until you set the activity's Content view, the app knows nothing about `textView`. So, in Listing 5-4, calling `textView.setText()` before calling `setContentView()` leads to disaster. To fix the problem, swap two statements as follows (in bold):

```
class MainActivity : AppCompatActivity() {

 override fun onCreate(savedInstanceState: Bundle?) {
        super.onCreate(savedInstanceState)

        // This is bad code!
        //textView.setText("Oops!")
        setContentView(R.layout.activity_main)
        // This is the fix.
        textView.setText("Oops!")
    }
}
```

Discovering the secrets of Logcat

Whether you see the emulator's Logcat messages in the Run window or the Logcat window, they're important in helping you determine the source of any application problems. With some clever use of Android's log, you can increase your chances of finding the source of an error.

Read your device's log file

If you connect a device to your development computer, you can see the device's log file in Android Studio's Logcat pane. But sometimes it's more convenient to view the log file right on the device. For example, you might want to debug an app when you're using it on the road.

The Google Play Store has apps to help you view your device's log file. The authors use an app called CatLog, but other apps might work well for you, too.

Filter the output

REMEMBER

There is a good reason to move to the Logcat window in some cases. The Run window doesn't provide any sort of filtering for you. To change this behavior, choose File⇨Settings on Windows or Android Studio⇨Preferences on a Mac. Under Build, Execution, Deployment⇨Debugger, clear the check marks in the Show Application Logcat Messages in Run Console and Show Application Logcat Messages in Debug Console entries. The Logcat output then appears in the Logcat window.

Android's logging has six levels. The levels, in decreasing order of seriousness, are ASSERT, ERROR, WARN, INFO, DEBUG, and VERBOSE. In general, only an ASSERT or ERROR entry is a showstopper. All other entries (WARN, INFO, and so on) are just idle chatter.

Android Studio's Logcat panel has a Log Level drop-down list. (It appears as the third drop-down list box in Figure 5-13 and contains the word Verbose.) You select a level to filter out entries of lesser severity. For example, if you select the Error option, the Logcat pane displays only entries with levels ASSERT or ERROR.

You can filter entries in other ways. For example, to the right of the Log Level drop-down list is a little search field. (Refer to Figure 5-13.) If you type Null in that field, you see only the messages containing the word Null. In particular, you see messages containing the term NullPointerException — a very common error in Kotlin and Java programming.

In the upper-right corner of Figure 5-13, a drop-down list displays the text No Filters, which means you see every message from every source. To see only messages pertaining to your com.allmycode.p01_05_04 package, choose the Show Only Selected Application option instead.

You can also select the drop-down list's Edit Filter Configuration option. When you do, you see a dialog box that offers more choices for filtering messages. (See Figure 5-14.) You can filter by Log Tag, Log Message, Package Name, PID (Process Identifier), and Log Level. You can pile additional criteria on top of existing filters by clicking the plus sign in the upper-left corner of the dialog box.

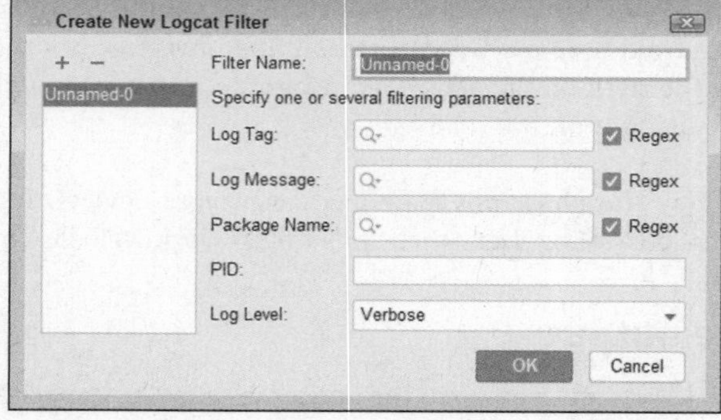

FIGURE 5-14: The Create New Logcat Filter dialog box.

Every Logcat message has a tag. In Listing 5-5, the message's tag is AndroidRuntime. (You get used to finding these tags if you spend enough time staring at Logcat messages.) If you type the letter *a* in the Log Tag field in Figure 5-14, you could see several suggested tags, including `ActivityManager`, `AlarmMessengerService`, `AndroidRuntime`, and `art`.

In addition to its tag, every Logcat message belongs to one of the Android operating system's processes, and every process has its own PID. The PID for the message in Listing 5-5 is 24806. The PID changes every time you run the application. (Once again, filtering by the PID does little good for the text in Listing 5-5. But filtering by PID can, at times, be very useful.)

Write to the log file

What? You don't trust our diagnosis of the problem in Listing 5-4? "Is `textView` really null?" you ask. You can peek at your program's variables with the Debug tool window, but for a quick answer to your question, you can write to Android's log file.

In Listing 5-4, add the following code before the `textView.setText("Oops!")` statement:

```
if (textView == null) {
  Log.i("READ ME!", "textView is null")
} else {
  Log.i("READ ME!", "-->" + textView.getText().toString())
}
```

The `Log` class's static `i` method creates an entry of level `INFO` in Android's log file. In this example, the entry's tag is `READ ME!`, and the entry's message is either `textView is null` or the characters displayed in the `textView`. When you run the app, you see output like this:

```
I/READ ME!: textView is null
```

TIP

By convention, a log entry's tag is the name of the class in which the log is created. For example, if your class's name is `MainActivity`, the first parameter of `Log.i` is the string `"MainActivity"`. This section doesn't follow that formula. But if other developers are involved in your project, coding conventions are very important.

Using the debugger

Debuggers can provide you with a wealth of information — too much information, at times. Because of the overwhelming amount of potential information, some developers don't actually rely on a debugger very often; instead, they use Logcat statements (see the "Discovering the secrets of Logcat" section for details).

Other developers love the amount of detailed information and actually use their debugger as a learning tool, not just for debugging. By following the code around in the debugger, they often discover new programming techniques and even uncover hidden bugs in the underlying packages. There is no set rule as to how you debug an application. The only essential criterion is that the application works when you're finished. The following sections help you get started with the debugger.

Getting started with the debugger

This section of the chapter provides you with a brief overview of some of the essentials of using a debugger for its primary purpose, which is discovering the sources of errors in an app. The following steps get you started.

1. **Follow the steps in the "Try it!" section, earlier in this chapter.**

   When you do, you have a buggy Android app.

2. **With** `MainActivity.java` **showing in the editor, click to the left of the** `textView.setText("Oops!")` **statement (in the editor's border).**

   When you do, Android Studio adds a red circle icon to the editor's border. (See Figure 5-15.) This icon represents a breakpoint — a place where your app will pause its run. During the pause, you can examine variables' values, change variables' values, and do other useful things.

3. **In Android Studio's main menu, choose Run⇨Debug 'app'.**

   When you do, you see all the stuff that you'd see if you had chosen Run 'app'. Choosing Debug instead of Run doesn't change much until execution reaches the statement with the breakpoint. But when execution reaches the `textView.setText("Oops!")` statement, the Debug tool window appears. (See Figure 5-16.)

   WARNING

   Using Run⇨Debug 'app' instead of Run⇨Run 'app' can make your app run very slowly. Don't use Run⇨Debug 'app' routinely. Use Run⇨Debug 'app' only when you need Android Studio's debugging tool.

   In the Debugger tab of the Debug tool window, you see a list of variables in your app's Java code. You may have to fish around for the variable that's giving you trouble. (You might have to expand the `this` branch of the tree in the Variables panel.)

```
activity_main.xml    MainActivity.kt

class MainActivity : AppCompatActivity() {

    override fun onCreate(savedInstanceState: Bundle?) {
        super.onCreate(savedInstanceState)

        // Output information to the Logcat.
        if (textView == null) {
            Log.i( tag: "READ ME!",  msg: "textView is null");
        } else {
            Log.i( tag: "READ ME!",  msg: "-->" + textView.getText().toString());
        }

        // This is bad code!
        textView.setText("Oops!")

        setContentView(R.layout.activity_main)

        // This is the fix.
        //textView.setText("Oops!")
    }
}

MainActivity > onCreate()
```

FIGURE 5-15: A breakpoint.

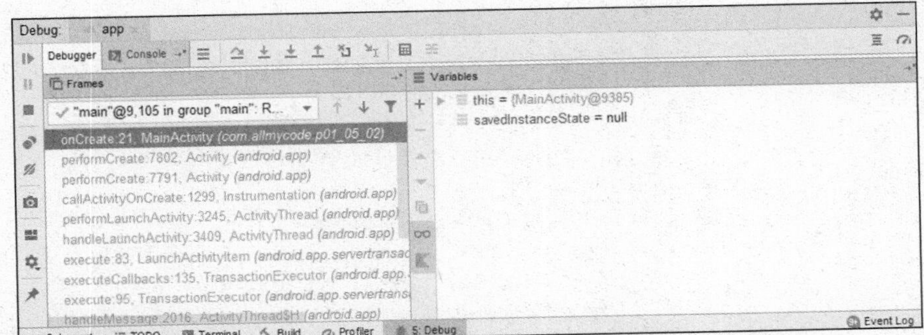

FIGURE 5-16: The Debug tool window.

TIP

You also have the option of hovering the mouse pointer over the variable of interest. The value of that variable will appear in a bubble near the mouse pointer. The value of `textView` is `null`. That's trouble, and it requires correcting. (To find out how to correct this problem, visit the "Try it!" section, earlier in this chapter.)

4. **Choose Run➪Stop 'app' to stop the debugging process.**

   This action allows you to make code changes without stopping the emulator. You can then restart the app using Run➪Run 'app' or Run➪Debug 'app'.

Applying more advanced debugger tricks

While you're on a roll with debugging, it might be time to try a few more tricks. The following steps help you work through some of the more advanced debugger features. You won't use these tricks every time, but they come in handy when you're tracking down certain kinds of errors.

1. **Create a new Android project.**

   To cook up this section's figures and listings, name the project `01_05_03` and the package `com.allmycode.p01_05_03`.

2. **Delete the** `TextView` **containing Hello World.**

3. **Add a blank** `TextView` **component to your project's** `activity_main.xml` **layout.**

   For details, see the section "Creating the 'look.'" Make sure you set constraints for the new component and create a string resource for it named `textView1Text` with a value of `Oops`. After adding a `TextView` element, the preview screen looks like the one in Figure 5-11, and Android Studio's Component Tree contains a textView branch.

4. **Open the new project's** `MainActivity` **for editing.**

5. **Add the code shown in bold to the** `onCreate()` **method:**

```
override fun onCreate(savedInstanceState: Bundle?) {
    super.onCreate(savedInstanceState)
    setContentView(R.layout.activity_main)

    // Perform a calculation
    val i: Int = 7
    val j: Int = plusOne(i)

    // Show the result on screen
    textView.setText("j = " + j.toString())
}
```

6. **Create a new method called** `plusOne()` **after the** `onCreate()` **method, as shown here:**

```
fun plusOne(i: Int): Int {
    val temp: Int = i + 1
    return temp
}
```

7. **Click to the left of the** `val i: Int = 7` **line to add a breakpoint at that line.**

8. **In Android Studio's main menu, choose Run⇨Debug 'app'.**

   The Debug tool window opens and the Variables panel appears in the tool window. The variable `i` doesn't appear in the list because Android hasn't yet executed the statement containing the breakpoint.

   Before proceeding to the next step, notice that the breakpoint statement, `val i: Int = 7`, is highlighted in the editor.

9. **Hover over the icons above the Variables panel. One of these icons displays a small pop-up menu containing the words *Step Over.* Click this icon in order to step to the next statement.**

   In this case, *Step Over* means executing the `val i: Int = 7` statement. If this step included a call to a method, it would step over that method call (executing all the statements that the called method contains) to arrive at the next step. After clicking the icon, the variable `i` appears in the Variables panel. (See Figure 5-17.) The variable's value is 7.

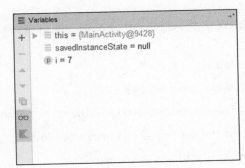

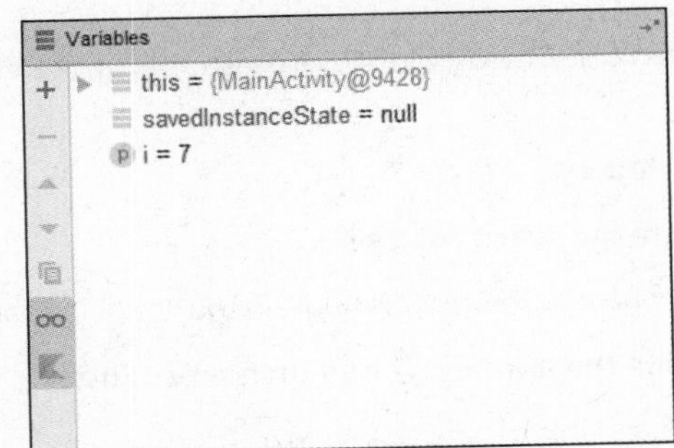

FIGURE 5-17: The variable `i` appears.

   Notice how the statement after the breakpoint, `val j: Int = plusOne(i)`, is highlighted in the editor.

10. **One of the icons above the Variables panel displays a small pop-up menu containing the words *Step Into.* Click this Step Into entry.**

    Step Into means that, if the current statement contains a Java method call, pause the app's execution at the first statement inside the body of that method. The current statement contains a call to the `plusOne()` method, so Android goes into the body of the `plusOne()` method and pauses at the `val temp: Int = i + 1` statement. Notice that the debugger shows you the value of `i` in gray type in the editor, as shown in Figure 5-18. You also see `i` in the Variables panel.

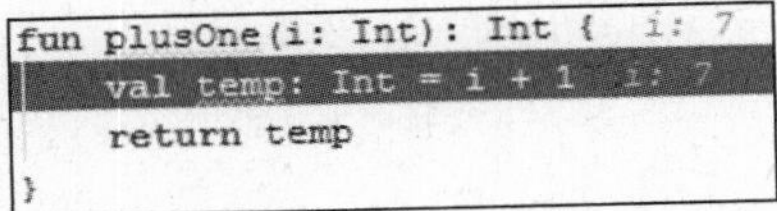

FIGURE 5-18: The debugger supplies the value of `i`.

11. **Click Step Over again.**

    The Variables panel now shows both `i` and `temp`, along with their values. (See Figure 5-19.)

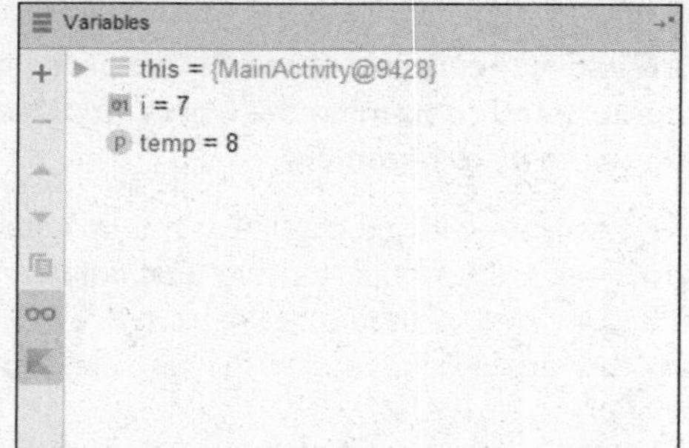

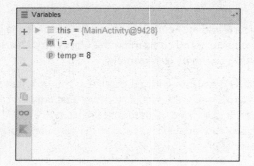

FIGURE 5-19: The variable `temp` appears.

12. **Right-click (or, on a Mac, Ctrl-click) the `temp` variable in the Variables panel.**

    A contextual menu appears.

13. **In the contextual menu, select Set Value.**

    An Edit field appears next to the `temp` variable in the Variables panel.

14. **In the edit field, type the number `42` and then press Enter.**

    As a result, the `temp` variable's value changes to `42`.

15. **One of the icons above the Variables panel displays a small pop-up menu containing the words *Step Out*. Click this Step Out entry.**

    Step Out means to step out of the current method and back into the method that called it.

16. **Click Step Over in the Variables panel.**

    When you do, Android finishes executing the `plusOne()` method and assigns the value returned from the `plusOne()` call (the number `42`) to the variable `j`. The variable `j`, with its value `42`, appears in the Variables panel.

17. **Choose Run⇨Resume Program.**

    This step tells the program to continue running. You see the output in the emulator.

» Helping people in other countries use your app

» Getting your app to communicate with the outside world

Chapter 6
Improving Your App

Face it — the app in Chapter 5 of this minibook is boring! Really boring! Who wants to click a button to see the words *Pepperoni and Extra Cheese* on a device's screen?

In this chapter, you improve on the app that you created in Chapter 5. We can't promise instant excitement, but with modest effort, you can add features to make the app more interesting. (We confess: In this chapter, the *real* reason for making the app interesting is to show you some additional Android developer tricks. Anyway, read on . . .)

Improving the Layout

In addition to being boring, the app in Chapter 5 is ugly. You can improve an app's look in two ways: the way it looks to a user and the way it looks to another developer. In this section, you do both. When you're done, you have a layout like the one in Figure 6-1.

Before creating the layout's code, you should make some observations about the layout in Figure 6-1:

- The button is below the pair of check boxes.
- The check boxes are side by side.

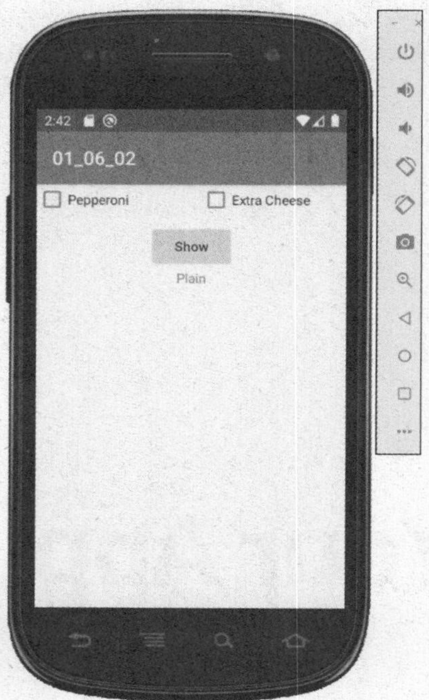

FIGURE 6-1: Your mission, should you decide to accept it.

- The pair of check boxes is centered (side by side) on the screen.
- The button is centered on the screen.
- Taken as a group, the check boxes and the button don't fill the entire screen.
- Using a different layout will provide better results.

You may wonder why you should make these six observations and not others. If so, read on.

Changing the layout

You can use the various layouts either singularly or in groups to make designing your app easy. How you use the layouts will determine how your app appears onscreen — how the components align themselves. Think about organizing your closet. If you use a combination of shelves and clothes racks, you get one appearance. However, you might have tons of shoes and other small items, so cubbies might be useful. Drawers might come in handy for tiny items. If you need long-term storage, you might add some covered trays. Just as with a closet, you use Android layouts to provide specific results when working with components:

» **ConstraintLayout:** Allows you to position components anywhere within the area defined by the `ConstraintLayout` by defining a constraint for it. This is the default layout and often acts as a container layout for other layouts (as you see in this chapter).

» **Guideline:** Works with a `ConstraintLayout` to provide horizontal or vertical alignment for a group of components. Think about it as drawing a line on the screen for positioning the items you need. You don't see the `Guideline` when viewing the app.

» **LinearLayout:** Groups components vertically or horizontally into a single column or row. You combine `LinearLayout` components to get specific component organizations.

» **FrameLayout:** Blocks out an area of the screen for a specific component. The idea is to ensure that the component resides in one specific area and uses a specific amount of screen real estate.

» **TableLayout and TableRow:** Creates an environment akin to that used by web pages that rely on tables for organization. The `TableLayout` is the entire table, while a `TableRow` is a single row within that table.

» **Space:** Defines a space between components. You combine this component with any other layout to provide a view that isn't cramped. The components can breathe. (Imagine that!)

» **Other:** There are other layouts in the Legacy group of the Palette. In general, you want to avoid these layouts because they don't match the current Android design guidelines. In addition, they may not work well with new layouts.

Defining the project

Understand that the layouts described in this section aren't exclusive of each other. You might start with a `ConstraintLayout` to organize the screen as a whole, use a `LinearLayout` for some overview information, and have a `TableLayout` for details. The layouts nest inside each other to give you precise control over your app's appearance on any device. Using layouts means that the organization of your app will change to meet the constraints of a device automatically, so you don't have to worry about a smartphone being overwhelmed by an app that is usually used on a tablet. Of course, everything has limits, and you still need to test whether a layout is successful in creating a useful app. The following steps help you change the layout for this example:

1. **Launch Android Studio and create a new Android project with an app name of `01-06-01` and a package name of `com.allmycode.p01_06_01`.**

   For details on creating a new project, see Chapter 3 of this minibook.

2. **In the Designer tool's preview screen, select the Hello World!** `TextView` **and press Delete.**

   The Hello World! `TextView` is deleted.

3. **Drag a** `LinearLayout (Vertical)` **from the Layouts group of the Palette window to the location under the** `ConstraintLayout` **in the Component Tree.**

   The `LinearLayout (Vertical)` automatically indents under the `ConstraintLayout`, showing that it's nested within the parent layout.

REMEMBER

   Notice the yellow triangle next to the LinearLayout (Vertical) entry. This triangle currently tells you that the layout is useless because it has no children. Of course, you'll make it happy by adding children later.

   Not noted is that you still have to provide constraints for a layout. If you don't provide the constraints, the designer will complain later.

4. **Set all four contraints of the** `LinearLayout (Vertical)` **to** `0` **using the Layout section of the Attributes window, as described in the "Adding constraints" section of Chapter 5 of this minibook.**

5. **Click the Design button.**

   Note that the Component Tree now shows a `LinearLayout` in addition to the `ConstraintLayout`, as shown in Figure 6-2. The `ConstraintLayout` is now acting as a container for the `LinearLayout`, but the `LinearLayout` is actually controlling the appearance of the components onscreen. The yellow triangle is in place because we still haven't added children.

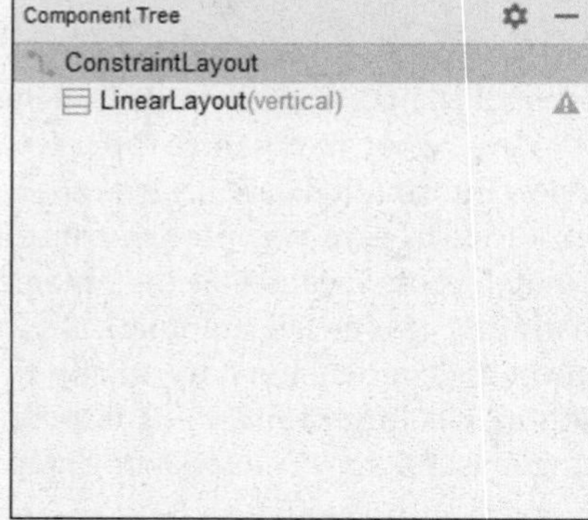

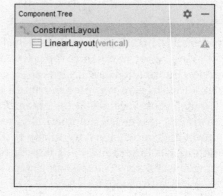

FIGURE 6-2: This app uses a `LinearLayout` for component layout, rather than a `Constraint Layout`.

REPLACING A LAYOUT

Previous layouts have an effect on current layouts, as you see as the chapter progresses. So, in some situations, you may not want to keep the default ConstraintLayout. For example, you might want a LinearLayout unbounded by constraints. For that matter, if you need a legacy layout as a starting point to maintain compatibility with an existing look, you might replace the ConstraintLayout with a RelativeLayout (which is the layout used the previous edition of this book).

Unfortunately, you can't simply drag and drop a new high-level layout onto the designer. Give it a try; we'll wait. To change the top-level layout in the Component Tree, you must replace the existing layout with the new layout in the Text tab rather than the Design tab. You delete everything but the XML declaration and then start over with a new layout. The new layout must include all the namespaces used to create a layout in Android. Here is an example of a LinearLayout (Vertical) used to replace a ConstraintLayout:

```
<LinearLayout
    xmlns:android="http://schemas.android.com/apk/res/android"
    xmlns:app="http://schemas.android.com/apk/res-auto"
    xmlns:tools="http://schemas.android.com/tools"
    android:layout_width="match_parent"
    android:layout_height="match_parent"
    android:orientation="vertical"
    tools:context=".MainActivity">

</LinearLayout>
```

Look carefully and you see that the namespaces are the same, so you could simply copy and paste them between layouts. The android:layout_width and android:layout_height entries also tend to be the same between layouts.

The only difference between a vertical LinearLayout and a horizontal LinearLayout is the android:orientation="vertical" attribute. If you change this value to horizontal, the layout becomes horizontal instead.

It's also essential to provide a tools:context entry that associates the layout with a particular activity. In this case, the context is associated with the MainActivity.

Adding project components

It's time to add components to the new layout. The most important thing you notice is that the layout process is different from that used for the examples in the previous chapters of this minibook. The results you see onscreen are different as well, and components like buttons suddenly have different attributes — all because you changed layouts!

To add components, follow these steps:

1. **Drag a `Button` component from the Buttons group of the Palette window onto the `LinearLayout (Vertical)` component in the Component Tree.**

   Voilà! Your app has a button. However, notice that the button consumes the entire width of the app. You'll fix this problem later so that the button looks like the one in Figure 6-1.

   Next, you want something that aligns objects horizontally so that the check boxes are side by side.

2. **Drag a `LinearLayout (Horizontal)` component from the Layouts group of the Palette window directly under the `Linear Layout (Vertical)` in the Component Tree.**

   Try to place the horizontal linear layout component above the button. The `LinearLayout (Horizontal)` and `Button` components should be at the same level as shown in Figure 6-3. The IDE will try to place the button within the `LinearLayout (Horizontal)` branch, but you should drag it back to its correct position.

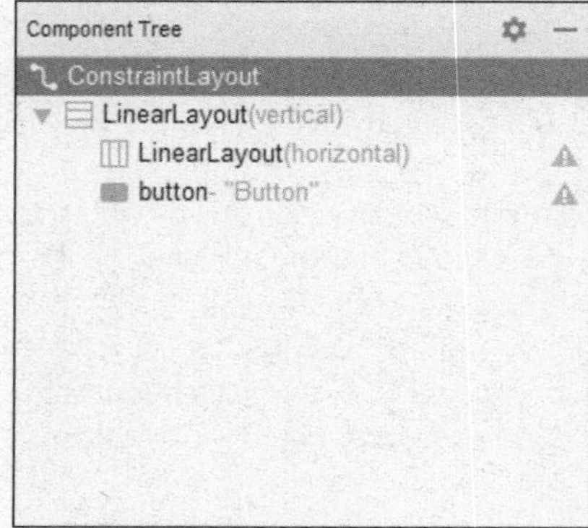

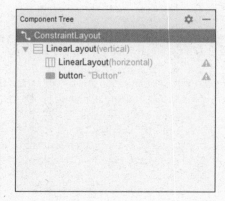

FIGURE 6-3: Place the various components at the correct levels to obtain the desired layout.

TIP

It pays to look at the two yellow triangles currently in the Component Tree. The first tells you that the `LinearLayout (Horizontal)` component is useless because it lacks children. The second tells you that you should use a string resource for the `Button` component. Later steps address both issues. (Notice also that the yellow triangle next to the `LinearLayout (Vertical)` component is gone.)

Oddly enough, the button will seem to have disappeared — it actually appears under the horizontal linear layout. Because the horizontal linear layout is currently using the entire display area, the button appears off screen below it. You'll fix this problem later as well.

Next, you put the check boxes into your horizontal linear layout.

3. **Drag a** `CheckBox` **component from the Palette window's Buttons group to the horizontal linear layout element in the preview screen.**

   If you have trouble dragging the component inside the horizontal linear layout, place the check box anywhere on the preview screen. Then, in the Component Tree, drag the `checkBox` component so that it's subordinate to the `LinearLayout (Horizontal)` branch.

4. **Drag another** `CheckBox` **component from the Buttons group of the Palette window to the horizontal linear layout element in the preview screen.**

   Like the first check box, this second check box is inside your horizontal linear layout. The two components are side by side. Perhaps they're uncomfortable being that close and need a little space.

5. **Drag a** `Space` **component from the Layouts group of the Palette window to place it between** `checkBox` **and** `checkBox2`**.**

   Ahhh! Able to breathe again.

Configuring the project components

As things stand now, you can see the two check boxes with a space between them, but the button seems to have disappeared. Yes, it's still there — just hiding. To make the layout useful, you need to make a few adjustments, including getting rid of those yellow triangles.

To make the needed adjustments, follow these steps:

1. **In the Component Tree, select the** `LinearLayout (Vertical)` **component.**

   You can try selecting this element in the preview screen but, for an element with nothing but a border, doing the selecting in the Component tree is easier.

2. **In the Attributes window, locate the** `gravity` **entry in the All Attributes group. Expand this entry to reveal the underlying settings and select the** `center_horizontal` **entry.**

   The value will change to `true`. This attribute controls the positioning of components that don't take up the entire width of the parent area. If you don't select this attribute, the components will appear on the left side of the app.

3. **In the Component Tree, select your** `LinearLayout (Horizontal)` **component.**

4. **In the Attributes window, locate the** `layout_height` **entry in the Declared Attributes group and set it to** `wrap_content`**.**

   Okay, there's that pesky button. However, it takes up the entire width of the app and is too close to the two check boxes.

5. **In the Component Tree, select the button.**

6. **In the Attributes window, locate the** `layout_width` **entry in the Declared Attributes group and set it to** `wrap_content`**.**

   The button is now centered onscreen and the right size. However, it's still too close to the check boxes.

7. **In the Attributes window, locate the** `layout_margin` **entry in the All Attributes group. Expand this entry and type** 10dp **in the** `layout_marginTop` **entry.**

   The button is now a respectable distance from those check boxes.

TECHNICAL STUFF

   You may wonder what the `10dp` business is all about. It means to set the start of the button to ten density-independent pixels (dp) from the bottom of the previous component. Mobile device designers use the dp because different displays have different densities. For example, the Samsung Galaxy S5, S6, and S7 all have 360 x 640 dp displays, even though the actual resolution of the S5 is 1080 x 1920 pixels and the S6 and S7 both are 1440 x 2560 pixels. Using dp simplifies design and ensures that each display shows whatever you have created in the same manner. If you really want to know more, the article at `https://medium.com/mockingbot/why-ui-designers-are-using-dp-instead-of-pixel-as-unit-to-design-mobile-app-2c080f90936b` covers this issue in significantly more detail.

8. **Change the text on the check boxes and the button so that it matches what you see in Figure 6-1 by clicking the box in the text attribute in the Attributes window. Make sure you use a string resource as described in the "Adding text to each component" section of Chapter 5 of this minibook.**

   Don't worry about the word *Plain* in Figure 6-1. You work on that in the section "Reusing a layout," later in this chapter.

When setting the button text, be sure to add the `android:textAllCaps="false"` entry by switching to Text mode as described in Chapter 5.

9. **Set the `onClick` property of the `button` (found in the Attributes window) to a resource string named `Button1Click` with a value of `onButtonClick`.**

   For help setting the `onClick` property, see Chapter 5 of this minibook. Figure 6-4 shows how the Component Tree should appear at this point.

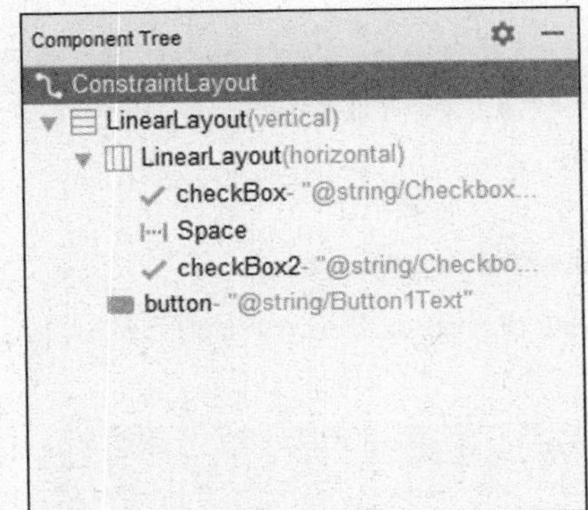

FIGURE 6-4: The Component Tree (what you have so far, anyway).

Creating a reusable layout

The check boxes and the button in Figure 6-1 are useful in more than one situation. You might place these widgets in an app with a confirmation word (such as the word *Plain* in Figure 6-1). You might use the same widgets in a different app with a picture of a pizza below the widgets. One way or another, it's worth your while to save the layout containing these widgets. You save these widgets in a new layout resource document (a *`blahblah`*`.xml` document in the `res/layout` folder). This section tells you how to do that.

1. **Open the project that you create in the "Improving the Layout" section, earlier in this chapter.**
2. **In the Component Tree, right-click `Linear Layout (Vertical)` and choose the Refactor submenu.**

   Make sure that you see the outline of the layout that contains both check boxes and the button.

   A context menu containing the Style and Layout options shown in Figure 6-5 appears. If you don't see this list of options (or if they're different in some way), you may not have the right item selected.

Improving Your App

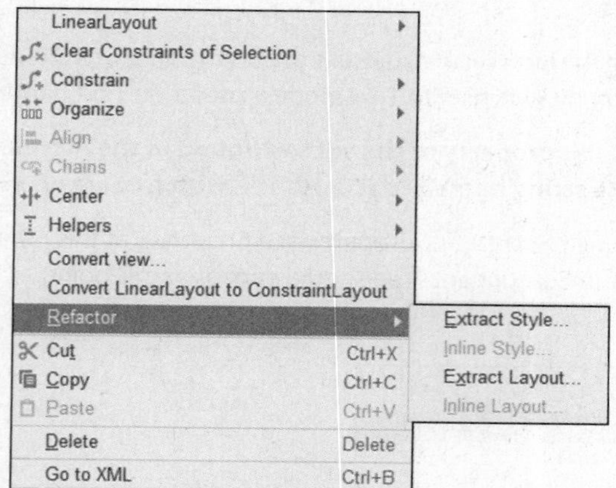

FIGURE 6-5: A list of refactoring options.

3. **In the context menu, select Extract Layout.**

   The Extract Android Layout dialog box shown in Figure 6-6 appears.

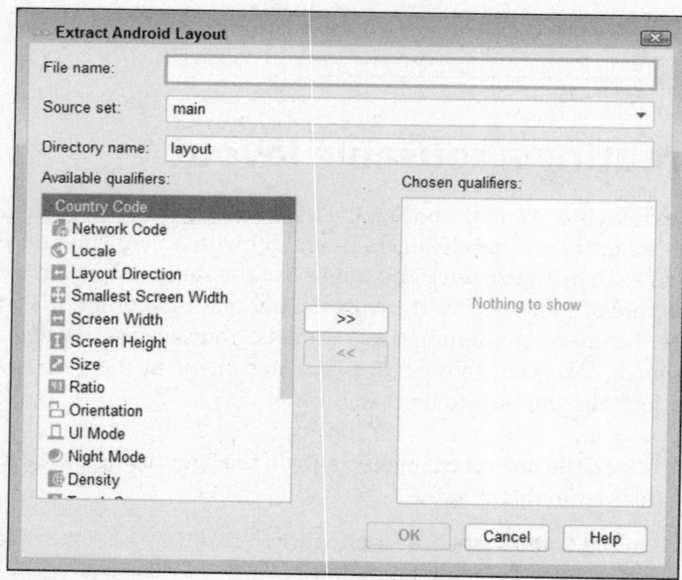

FIGURE 6-6: Extracting your style for future use.

4. **In the dialog box's File Name field, type the name of your new resource document.**

   The example uses **reusable_layout.xml**.

WARNING

The names of Android's resource files must not contain capital letters. You can use lowercase letters and underscores. You cannot use Java's or Kotlin's customary "camelCase" naming convention with names like `reUsableLayout.xml`. And, yes, a layout filename must end with the extension `.xml`.

5. **Click OK to close the dialog box.**

   The `app/res/layout` branch in the Project tool window now has a new item. If you named the file as described in Step 4, the branch is labeled `reusable_layout.xml`.

6. **Double-click the `reusable_layout.xml` branch in the Project tool window.**

   Android Studio displays the Designer tool for the `reusable_layout.xml` file.

7. **Make sure that the Designer tool is in Design mode (as opposed to Text mode).**

   In Design mode, you can see the Component Tree.

8. **Make note of the labels on the branches in the Component Tree.**

   Look for names like `checkBox`, `checkBox2`, and `button`. (See Figure 6-7.) You use these names (these id values) in the code that you write later in this chapter.

TIP

To change an element's id, select the component in the Component Tree. Change whatever is entered in the `id` text field in the Attributes window.

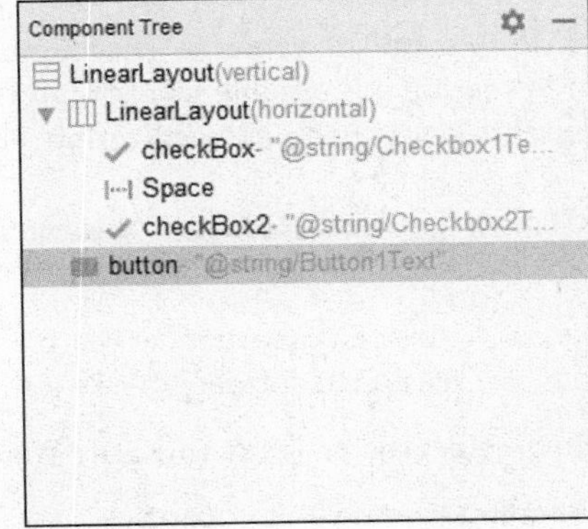

FIGURE 6-7: The saved layout Component Tree.

Your current app automatically uses the layout you just saved. Look in the Text tab of `activity_main.xml` and you see that the code has changed to look like this:

```
<?xml version="1.0" encoding="utf-8"?>
<androidx.constraintlayout.widget.ConstraintLayout
    xmlns:android="http://schemas.android.com/apk/res/android"
    xmlns:app="http://schemas.android.com/apk/res-auto"
    xmlns:tools="http://schemas.android.com/tools"
    android:layout_width="match_parent"
    android:layout_height="match_parent"
    tools:context=".MainActivity">

    <include layout="@layout/reusable_layout"/>
</androidx.constraintlayout.widget.ConstraintLayout>
```

The `<include layout="@layout/reusable_layout" />` element places the layout you just saved in the specified place on the app screen. Congratulations! You have a group of widgets that you can use and reuse.

Reusing a layout

In the preceding section, "Creating a reusable layout," you create a layout with check boxes and a button. You can reuse this layout in many of this chapter's examples. Here's how:

Copying the initial project's files

The first thing you need to do is copy the required files from the initial project (from the earlier section "Creating a reuseable layout") to the new project in which you plan to use the reusable layout in a new application. Follow these steps:

1. **Follow the steps in the "Creating a reusable layout" section if you haven't already done so.**

   If you're impatient, you can skip a few of that section's steps, but be sure to create a `reusable_layout.xml` file and to populate the file with a few widgets.

2. **In the Project tool window, select the project's `reusable_layout.xml` file.**
3. **In Android Studio's main menu, choose Edit ⇨ Copy.**

   You don't see much happening, but now your Clipboard contains a copy of the `reusable_layout.xml` file.

4. **Without closing the existing project, start a new Android project by choosing File⇨New⇨New Project.**

   Give the new project the name `01_06_02` and a package name of `com.allmycode.p01_06_02`. Make sure you delete the Hello World `TextView` component as well.

5. **In the new project's Project tool window, select the** `app/res/layout` **branch.**

6. **In Android Studio's main menu, choose Edit ⇨ Paste.**

   You see the Copy dialog box, shown in Figure 6-8.

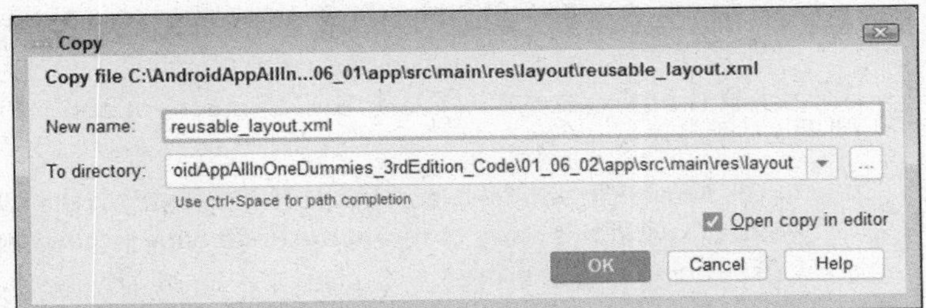

FIGURE 6-8: Place a copy of a layout or other file in your current project.

7. **Click OK.**

   Now the `app/res/layout` branch contains a `reusable_layout.xml` file. In addition, Android Studio automatically opens a copy of the file for you.

8. **Perform Steps 5 through 7 for the** `strings.xml` **file located in the** `app/res/values` **branch of the initial project. However, in this case, rename the file** `copied_strings.xml` **in the new project by typing the new name in the New Name field of the Copy dialog box.**

   The reusable layout you created relies on resource strings you defined. To keep the layout functional, you need to provide a source for those strings in the new application.

TIP

   Using a separate file keeps the reusable layout string resources separate from those used for the current project. This approach makes it easier to locate specific strings when you need to.

9. **Open** `copied_strings.xml` **and delete** `<string name="app_name">01_06_01</string>`.

   If you leave this particular string resource in place, the compiler complains about a duplicate resource. Plus, the app name will be wrong!

Adding components to the reusable layout

Now that you have the required files, you can use the reusable layout to create the beginnings of an app and then complete the app using other components.

1. **Open your project's** `res/layout/activity_main.xml` **file.**

   When you do, you see your new project's preview screen (which is mostly empty).

2. **Delete the Hello World** `TextView`**.**

   This project is going to be stacking components, so you need a `LinearLayout (Vertical)` component to hold the components.

3. **In the Layouts group of the Palette window, drag the** `LinearLayout (Vertical)` **component under the** `ConstraintLayout` **in the Component Tree window.**

4. **Select the** `LinearLayout (Vertical)` **component and set the four constraints to** `0`**.**

5. **In the Attributes window, locate the** `gravity` **entry in the All Attributes group. Expand this entry to reveal the underlying settings and select the** `center_horizontal` **entry.**

   At this point, your `LinearLayout (Vertical)` component is ready to receive the reusable layout and the `TextView` you need to show the selections.

6. **In the Containers group of the Palette window, drag the** `<include>` **item to below the** `LinearLayout (Vertical)` **in the Component Tree.**

   When you do this, a Resources dialog box appears, as shown in Figure 6-9.

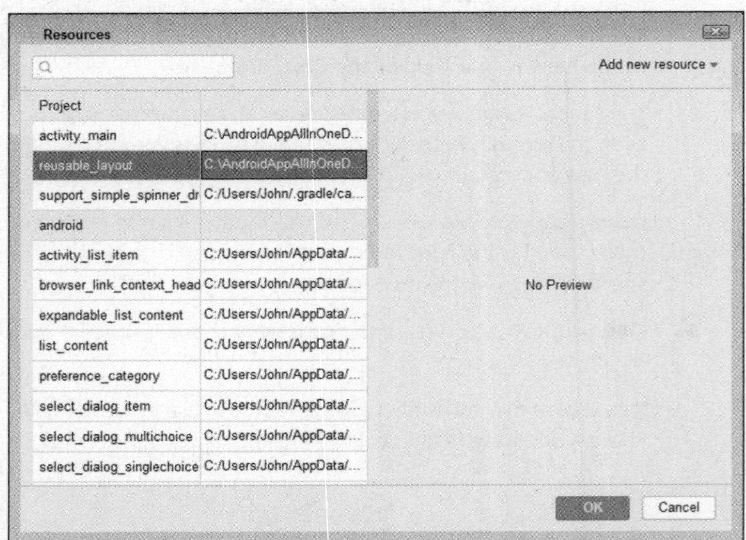

FIGURE 6-9: The Resources dialog box.

7. **In the Resources dialog box, select your reusable layout — the one you named `reusable_layout.xml`; then click OK.**

   The Resources dialog box closes.

8. **Click `include` in the Component Tree.**

   As if by magic, the stuff that you created in the "Creating a reusable layout" section appears on the preview screen. (Well, anyway, it looks like magic to us.) This stuff appears as one group.

9. **In the Declared Attributes group of the Attributes window, choose `match_parent` in the `layout_width` field and `wrap_content` in the `layout_height` field.**

   These settings ensure that the reusable layout takes up the appropriate amount of space in the upper portion of the screen.

   If all goes well, your layout looks like the stuff in Figure 6-1.

   In the next step, you add the word *Plain* to your app's screen. (Refer to Figure 6-1.)

10. **From the Palette window, drag a `TextView` component to a location under the `include` component in the Component Tree.**
11. **Select `textView` in the Component Tree.**
12. **In the Declared Attributes group of the Attributes window, choose `wrap_content` in both the `layout_width` and the `layout_height` fields.**

    The `textView` should appear in the middle of the screen directly under the reusable layout.

13. **Replace the `textView` placeholder text with a resource string named `TextView1Text` that has a value of `Plain`.**
14. **(Optional) If you're very ambitious, follow the steps in Chapter 5 of this minibook for coding your app's behavior. Then run your app.**

    Ambitious or not, you have a decent-looking layout with a reusable component. Nice work!

Improving Your App

Starting Another Activity

As we mention in Chapter 4 of this minibook, an Android *activity* is one "screenful" of components. So juggling activities is a major endeavor for Android developers. This section's example does the simplest thing you can do with an activity — namely, make it run.

1. **Launch Android Studio and create a new project.**

   This example uses an app name of `01_06_03` and a package name of `com.allyourcode.p01_06_03`.

2. **Follow the instructions in the earlier section "Reusing a layout" to include** `reusable_layout` **on your new app's screen.**

   You have two check boxes and a button. When a user clicks the button, you want Android to display a different activity's screen. So you have to create another activity.

   Let's get cracking . . .

3. **In the Project tool window, right-click or (on a Mac) Ctrl-click your project's** `app/java/`*`your.package`* **branch.**

   In Listing 6-1, the package name is `com.allyourcode.p01_06_03`. If you used the same package name, you'd right or Ctrl-click your project's `app/java/com.allyourcode.p01_06_03` branch.

4. **In the context menu that appears, choose New ➪ Activity ➪ Empty Activity.**

   The Configure Activity dialog box, shown in Figure 6-10, appears. (You see this dialog box whenever you create a new, blank activity.)

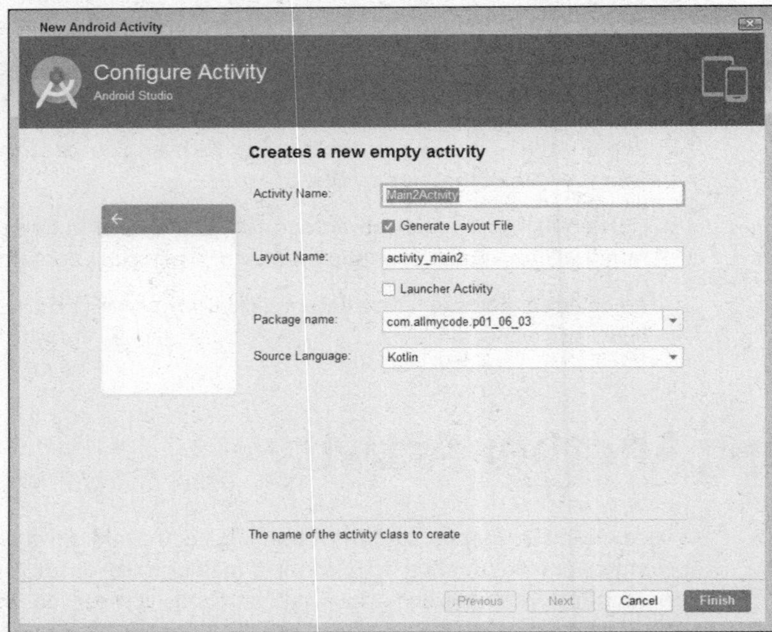

FIGURE 6-10: The Configure Activity dialog box.

5. **In the dialog box, fill in the Activity Name and Layout Name fields.**

   Listings 6-1 and 6-2 refer to `OtherActivity` and `other_layout`. So, if you're following along letter for letter with these instructions, type **OtherActivity** in the Activity Name field, and type **other_layout** in the Layout Name field. You can accept the defaults for all the other fields in the dialog box.

6. **Click Finish to close the dialog box.**

   Your new `other_layout` now appears in Android Studio's Designer tool. (You may need to click the other_layout tab to see the layout.)

7. **(Optional, but worth doing.) In this step, you don't have to do anything. Just look at something! In your project's** `app/manifests/AndroidManifest.xml` **file, notice the following code:**

```
<activity android:name=".OtherActivity">
</activity>
```

   Android Studio adds this `<activity>` element when you create `OtherActivity` in Steps 3 through 6.

   Each activity in your application must have an `<activity>` element in the `AndroidManifest.xml` file. In an `<activity>` element, the `android:name` attribute points to the name of the activity's Kotlin class. In this step, the attribute's value is `".OtherActivity"`. The initial dot refers to the application's package name (the name `com.allyourcode.p01_06_03` from Step 1). The rest of the attribute refers to the class name in Listing 6-2.

REMEMBER

   Each activity in your application must have an `<activity>` element. If you're missing an `<activity>` element, the app can't start that activity. (Instead, the app crashes, and you see an *Unable to find explicit activity* message in the Logcat panel.)

8. **With** `other_layout.xml` **showing in the preview screen, drag a** `TextView` **component from the Palette onto** `other_layout`.

   Now, `other_layout` has a `TextView` element.

9. **Configure the** `TextView` **component as you have in the past by setting constraints for it and using a string resource to set the default text to** `Plain`.

REMEMBER

   Your project has two activities (two Java files) and a layout for each activity (two XML files in the Project view's `app/res/layout` branch). In addition, your project has a `reusable_layout` that's included inside your main activity's layout. You can switch back and forth between the two activities and their layout files, but try to be mindful of the switching. Try not to become confused by editing the wrong Java code or the wrong layout file.

10. **Look for your new `TextView` element in the Component tree.**

Make note of the label on that element's branch of the tree. In the example's version of the app, the label is `textView`.

TECHNICAL STUFF

If you switch momentarily to the Designer tool's Text mode, you see the attribute `android:id="@+id/textView"` inside the `TextView` tag. The `id` of this element is `textView`.

TIP

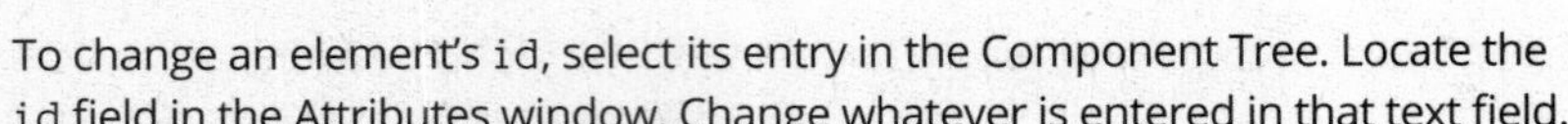

To change an element's `id`, select its entry in the Component Tree. Locate the `id` field in the Attributes window. Change whatever is entered in that text field.

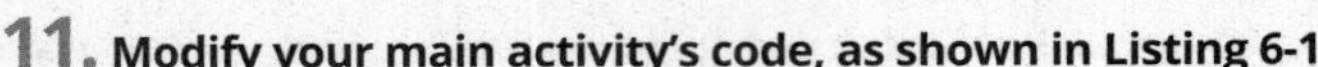

11. **Modify your main activity's code, as shown in Listing 6-1.**

The listing shows the code to be added in boldface type.

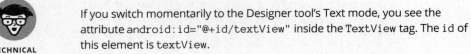

REMEMBER

Double-check the expressions `R.id.checkBox` and `R.id.checkBox2` in Listing 6-1 against the names in the Component tree at the end of the "Creating a reusable layout" section. If the Component tree's labels aren't `checkBox` and `checkBox2`, change your Listing 6-1 code appropriately.

In the `MainActivity` (Listing 6-1), you have code that starts up the `OtherActivity`. You don't start an activity by calling the activity's methods. Instead, you create an intent. An *intent* is like an open-ended method call. In Listing 6-1, you create an *explicit intent* — an intent that invokes a specific class's code, as follows:

- The intent in Listing 6-1 invokes the code in a class named `OtherActivity` (or whatever you name your app's second activity).
- The intent in Listing 6-1 has two extra pieces of information. Each "extra piece" of information is a name/value pair. For example, if the user selects the Pepperoni box, `checkBox.isChecked()` is `true`, so the intent contains the extra pair `"Pepperoni", true`.
- In Listing 6-1, the call `startActivity(intent)` invokes the `OtherActivity` class's code.

Next up, your `OtherActivity` should have some code that responds to the fact that `OtherActivity` was started.

12. **In your new `OtherActivity` class, add the code in Listing 6-2.**

The listing shows the code to be added in boldface type.

WARNING

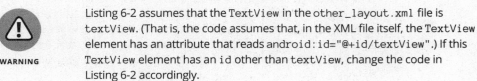

Listing 6-2 assumes that the `TextView` in the `other_layout.xml` file is `textView`. (That is, the code assumes that, in the XML file itself, the `TextView` element has an attribute that reads `android:id="@+id/textView"`.) If this `TextView` element has an `id` other than `textView`, change the code in Listing 6-2 accordingly.

In Listing 6-2, by calling `intent.getBooleanExtra()`, the `OtherActivity` discovers the values of `checkBox.isChecked()` and `checkBox2.isChecked()` from Listing 6-1. For example, the call

```
intent.getBooleanExtra("Pepperoni", false)
```

returns `true` if the value of `checkBox.isChecked()` in Listing 6-1 is `true`. The call returns `false` if the value of `checkBox.isChecked()` in Listing 6-1 is `false`. The call's second argument is a default value. So, in Listing 6-2, the call to `intent.getBooleanExtra("Pepperoni", false)` returns `false` if the intent created in Listing 6-1 doesn't have an extra named `"Pepperoni"`.

13. **Run your app.**

When you click the app's button, you see a new activity like the one pictured in Figure 6-11.

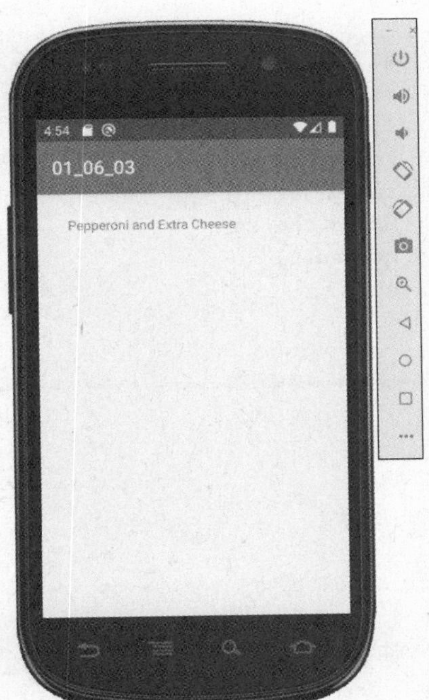

FIGURE 6-11: A new activity appears on the device's screen.

LISTING 6-1: Starting OtherActivity from the MainActivity

```
package com.allmycode.p01_06_03

import android.content.Intent
import androidx.appcompat.app.AppCompatActivity
import android.os.Bundle
import android.view.View
import kotlinx.android.synthetic.main.reusable_layout.*

class MainActivity : AppCompatActivity() {

    override fun onCreate(savedInstanceState: Bundle?) {
        super.onCreate(savedInstanceState)
        setContentView(R.layout.activity_main)
    }

    fun onButtonClick(view: View){
        val intent = Intent(this,
            OtherActivity::class.java)
        intent.putExtra("Pepperoni",
            checkBox.isChecked())
        intent.putExtra("Extra cheese",
            checkBox2.isChecked())
        startActivity(intent)
    }
}
```

LISTING 6-2: The OtherActivity

```
package com.allmycode.p01_06_03

import androidx.appcompat.app.AppCompatActivity
import android.os.Bundle
import kotlinx.android.synthetic.main.other_layout.*

class OtherActivity : AppCompatActivity() {

    override fun onCreate(savedInstanceState: Bundle?) {
        super.onCreate(savedInstanceState)
        setContentView(R.layout.other_layout)

        val builder = StringBuilder()
```

```
            if (intent.getBooleanExtra("Pepperoni",
                    false)){
                builder.append("Pepperoni")
            }
            if (intent.getBooleanExtra("Extra cheese",
                    false)){
                if (builder.length == 0) {
                    builder.append("Extra Cheese")
                } else {
                    builder.append(" and Extra Cheese")
                }
            }
            if (builder.length == 0) {
                builder.append("Plain")
            }

            textView.setText(builder)
        }
    }
```


Localizing Your App

Words, words, words. The apps in this chapter have so many words. `"Pepperoni"` here; `"Extra cheese"` there! It's a wonder a developer can keep this stuff straight. It's too easy to type a word one way in one part of the code and misspell the word in a different part.

The example application currently supports just one language, likely English. In a world where the United States ranks third of all countries where cellphones are used (see `https://www.infoplease.com/science-health/cellphone-use/cell-phone-usage-worldwide-country` or `https://en.wikipedia.org/wiki/List_of_countries_by_number_of_mobile_phones_in_use` for details), you don't want to make assumptions about your audience.

Fortunately, you already have a good start on solving this problem because the example application relies on string resources rather than hard-coded text. Even so, you still need to add the text for the languages you want to support in your app. Here's what you do:

1. **Right-click (or, on a Mac, Ctrl-click) the `strings.xml` file in your project's `res/values` folder in the Project tool window.**

2. **In the context menu that appears, select Open Translations Editor.**

   The Translations Editor appears in place of the Designer tool. (See Figure 6-12.)

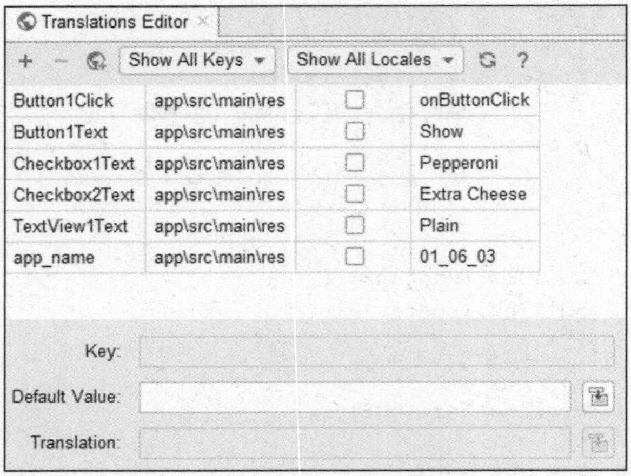

FIGURE 6-12: The Translations Editor.

3. **Near the top of the Translations Editor, click the globe icon.**

   A list of language locales appears. (See Figure 6-13.)

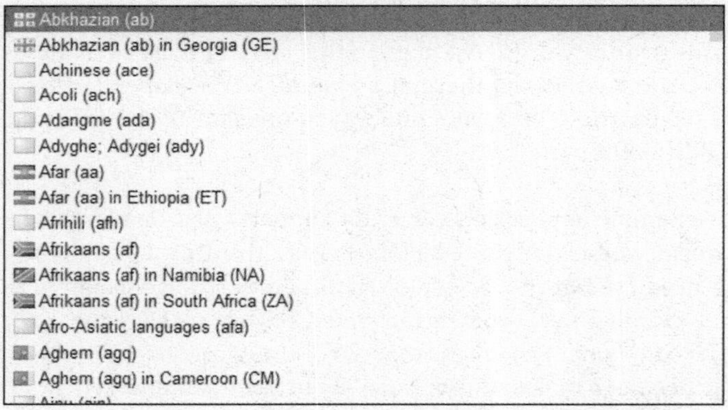

FIGURE 6-13: Select a language.

4. **Select a language locale from the list.**

   For this exercise, we select *Italian (it)*. (We'd be disloyal to our buddies Steve and Luca if we did otherwise.) For the full scoop on language locales, visit `https://www.iso.org/iso-3166-country-codes.html`.

   As a result, the `strings.xml` branch in the Project tool window now has two sub-branches. Both sub-branches sport the label `strings.xml`, but the new sub-branch's icon is a tiny picture of the flag of Italy. (See Figure 6-14.)

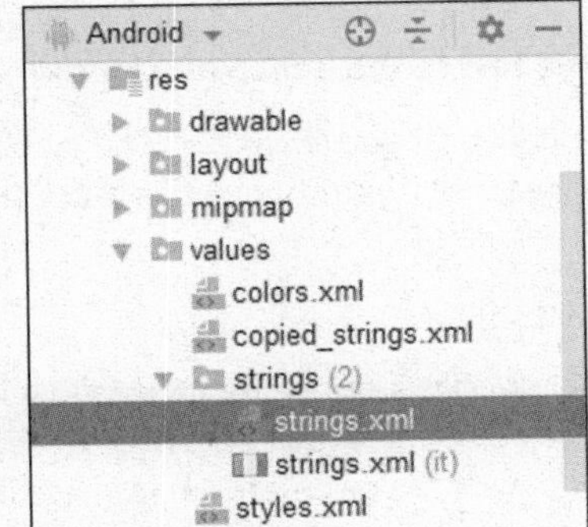

FIGURE 6-14: Look! You have two `strings.xml` files.

Temporarily change the Project tool window from Android view to Project view. Your project's app/`src/main/res` folder now has a `values` subfolder and a `values-it` subfolder. The `values-it` subfolder contains its own `strings.xml` file. (Okay, you can go back to the Android view now!)

In the Translations Editor, the term `extra_cheese` is in red because you haven't yet translated `extra_cheese` into Italian. The same is true for other terms that you haven't yet translated.

5. **Click the Italian (it) column in the** `Checkbox2Text` **row. In that column, type** `Con più formaggio` **and then press Enter.**

   (Sorry. The Translations Editor doesn't do any translating for you. The Translations Editor only adds code to your project when you type in the translations of words and phrases.)

6. **Repeat Step 4 for the** `app_name`**,** `Checkbox1Text`**,** `Button1Text`**, and** `TextView1Text` **rows.**

   If your Italian is a bit rusty, copy the text from the `res/values-it/strings.xml` file in Listing 6-3.

ELENCO 6-3: Benvenuto in Italia!

```
<?xml version="1.0" encoding="utf-8"?>
<resources>
    <string name="app_name">Il mio secondo progetto Android</
  string>
    <string name="Checkbox2Text">Con più formaggio</string>
    <string name="Checkbox1Text">Merguez</string>
    <string name="TextView1Text">Semplice</string>
    <string name="Button1Text">Mostra</string>
    <string name="Button1Click">onButtonClick</string>
</resources>
```

7. **Copy the `Button1Click` value row to the Italian (it) column.**

   The viewer will never see the native language value of `onButtonClick` in this row, but Android won't react well if you change this particular string to Italian.

8. **Test your app.**

   As with most devices, the emulator has a setting for Language & Input. How you access this setting depends on the particular emulator, but in some cases you must add the language you want to use before you can use it, as shown in Figure 6-15. In addition, you usually have to set the language you want to use as the primary language.

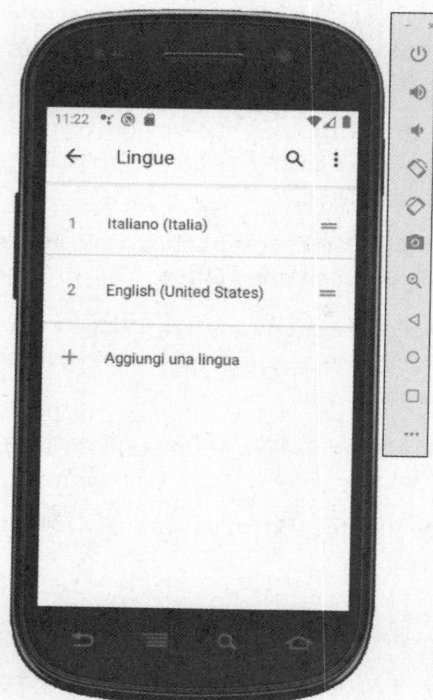

FIGURE 6-15: Add the required language support to your emulator.

9. **Change the language setting of your emulator to Italiano (Italia).**

   Suddenly, your app looks like the display in Figure 6-16.

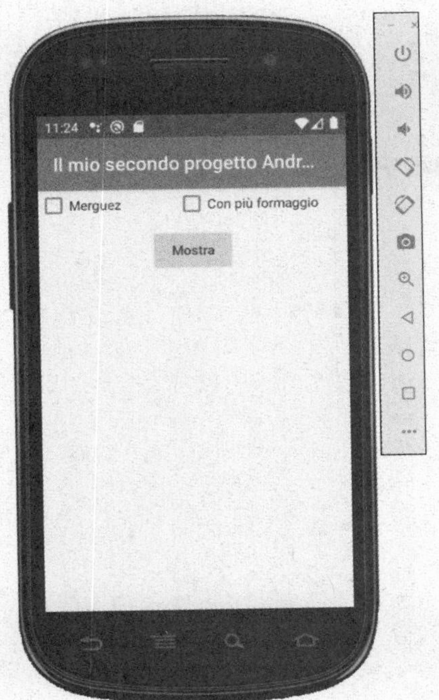

FIGURE 6-16: *Buongiorno!*

Responding to Check Box Events

Why click twice when you can do the same thing by clicking only once? Think about the example in the previous section. Your app responds to the contents of check boxes when the user clicks a button. In a streamlined scenario, your app might respond as soon as the user selects a box. Figure 6-17 shows a variation of the app you've been using, but this one is missing the Show button. It does, however, have the two check boxes and the text box, which is configured the same as the Show button it replaces. The setup for this app is the same as the one used for the reusable layout (see the "Changing the layout" section, earlier in this chapter, for details), just without the Show button.

REMEMBER

After you have the appearance just right, you need to create `onClick` (found within the All Attributes group of the Attributes window) string resources for both check boxes. In fact, the second check box uses the same string resource as the first one does — imagine that! Give the single string resource a name of `CheckboxClick` and a value of `onCheckboxClick`. To assign the resource string to the `onClick` field, you must actually type **@string/CheckboxClick** in the field.

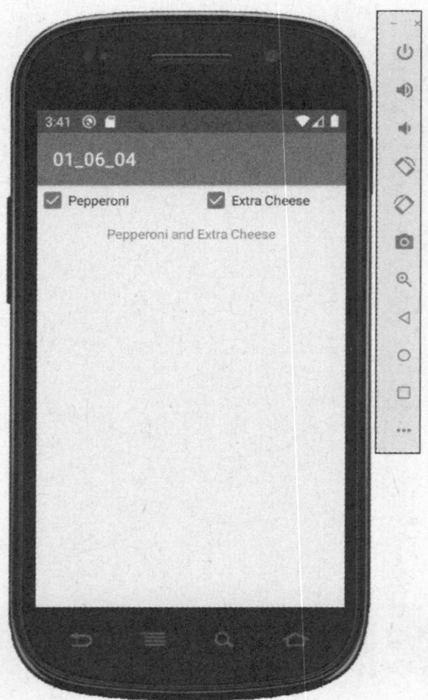

FIGURE 6-17: A reduced number of control versions of the previous examples.

Listing 6-4 shows you how to make this happen. Just add `onCheckboxClick()` to your `MainActivity.kt` file. You can also find this example in the `01_06_04` folder of the downloadable source.

LISTING 6-4: Responding to CheckBox Events

```
fun onCheckboxClick (view: View)
{
    val builder = StringBuilder()

    if (checkBox.isChecked()){
        builder.append("Pepperoni")
    }
    if (checkBox2.isChecked()){
        if (builder.length == 0){
            builder.append("Extra Cheese")
        } else {
            builder.append(" and Extra Cheese")
        }
    }
    if (builder.length == 0){
```

```
        builder.append("Plain")
    }

    textView.setText(builder)
}
```

Like a button, each check box listens for `onClick` events. So you can write this section's code very much like the code in Listing 5-3 in Chapter 5. As with that example, you must declare a single input argument, `view: View`. The output text appears within a `StringBuilder()`.

TECHNICAL STUFF

The only real difference between a standard `Button` and a check box is that the check box is a `CompoundButton`, so there are other ways you could track the button state, such as by using a listener. (The technique shown in the example is by far the easiest, and you should use it whenever possible.) A `CompoundButton` is a widget with checked and unchecked states. The `CheckBox` class is a subclass of `CompoundButton`. Other subclasses of `CompoundButton` are `Switch`, `RadioButton`, and `ToggleButton`. A `ToggleButton` is that cute little thing that lights when it's in the checked state. The `Switch` is the slider type button that you see in many Android apps today.

Displaying Images

After designing an app and its variations in the previous sections, you may decide that your app needs some flair. How about designing your app so that when a user clicks a button, your app displays a picture of the pizza being ordered? The Show button in Figure 6-1 is perfect for this.

Android has all kinds of features for drawing images and displaying bitmap files. Here is one possible approach:

1. **Launch Android Studio and create a new project.**

   The example in this section uses a project name of `01_06_05`, and a package name of `com.allmycode.p01_06_05`.

2. **Copy the `reusable_layout.xml` file from "Creating a reusable layout" section, earlier in this chapter, to your new project's `app/res/layout` branch in the Project tool window.**

3. **Include** `reusable_layout.xml` **and** `copied_strings.xml` **files in your project.**

   For details, see the "Reusing a layout" section of the chapter.

4. **Find four images — one for plain, one for pepperoni, one for extra cheese, and one for pepperoni with extra cheese.**

   Android's official documentation recommends the `.png` format for images. If you don't have `.png` images, Android's docs call the `.jpg` format "acceptable." If you don't have `.png` or `.jpg`, the docs tell you to hold your nose and use `.gif`. But remember that in this section, you're creating a practice application, not a work of art. Your images don't have to look good. They don't even have to look like pizzas. Besides, you can download our silly-looking drawings of pizzas from this book's website at `www.allmycode.com/Android`. (You can also get there by visiting `www.dummies.com` and searching this book's title.)

   In creating this project, the example uses the filenames `plain.png`, `pepperoni.png`, `extracheese.png`, and `pep_extracheese.png`.

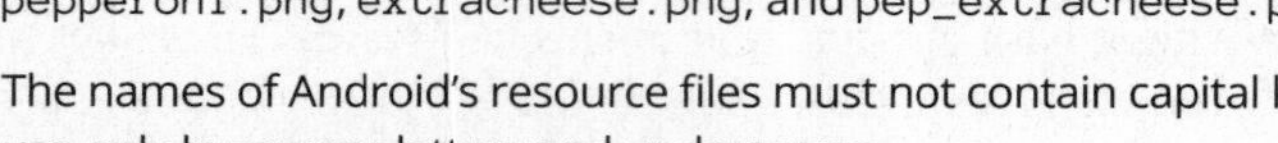

REMEMBER

   The names of Android's resource files must not contain capital letters. You can use only lowercase letters and underscores.

TIP

   For working with image formats, the program IrfanView works well. You can get this Windows program at `https://www.irfanview.com/`. The program is free for noncommercial use. Free alternatives to IrfanView for the Mac are Picasa (`https://picasa-mac.en.softonic.com/mac`) or Preview (`https://support.apple.com/guide/preview/welcome/mac`).

5. **In your operating system's File Explorer or Finder, select the image files. Then, in the main menu, choose Edit ⇨ Copy.**

6. **In Android Studio's Project tool window, select the** `app/res/drawable` **branch.**

7. **In the main menu, choose Edit ⇨ Paste.**

   The Choose Destination Directory dialog box, shown in Figure 6-18, appears.

8. **In the Choose Destination Directory dialog box, select the** `drawable` **branch, as shown in Figure 6-18, and then click OK.**

   You see a Copy dialog box that contains a verification of the directory to use in the To Directory field.

   In a real-life app, you use the `drawable-dpi` directories (such as `drawable-v24`, shown in Figure 6-18) as alternatives for devices with high, medium, extra-high, and extra-extra-high screen densities. But in this practice app, a default `drawable` folder is the easiest to use.

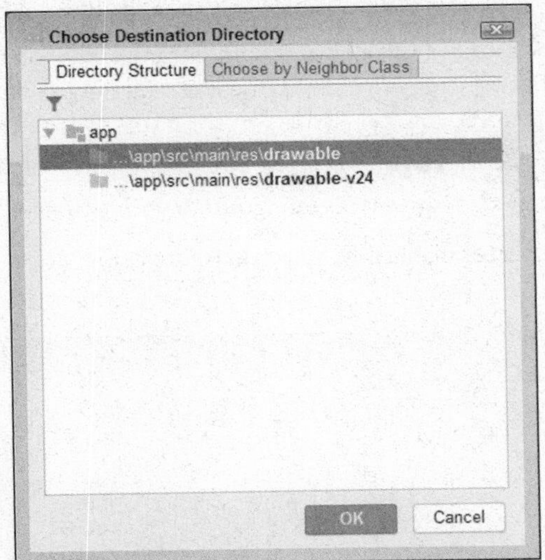

FIGURE 6-18: Be sure to choose the correct destination for the files.

The letters *dpi* stand for *dots per inch.* Android senses a device's screen density and uses the resources in the most appropriate `drawable-?dpi` folder. To find out what Android considers "most appropriate," visit `https://developer.android.com/guide/practices/screens_support.html`.

9. **Click OK.**
10. **Right-click (on Windows) or Ctrl-click (on a Mac) the** `app/res/drawable` **branch.**
11. **In the menu that appears, choose New ➪ File.**

    Once again, the Choose Destination Directory dialog box rears its ugly head.

12. **Select the** `drawable` **branch, and then click OK.**

    A New File dialog box appears. This dialog box has only one field — a field for the name of your new file.

13. **In the New File dialog box's field, type** levels.xml**.**
14. **Click OK to dismiss the New File dialog box.**
15. **Use Android Studio's editor to populate your** `levels.xml` **file with the code in Listing 6-5.**

    A *level-list* is a list of alternative drawables for a single image component to display. At any moment during an app's run, the image component has an integer level. You set the component's level using the `setImageLevel` method.

When your app calls `setImageLevel`, Android starts at the top of the level-list and looks for the first item whose `android:maxLevel` is greater than or equal to the new image level. You can also assign an `android:minLevel` attribute to an item. But in most situations, `android:maxLevel` is all you need.

16. **Add an `ImageView` from the Widgets group to your activity's layout.**

    You see the Resources dialog box, shown in Figure 6-19.

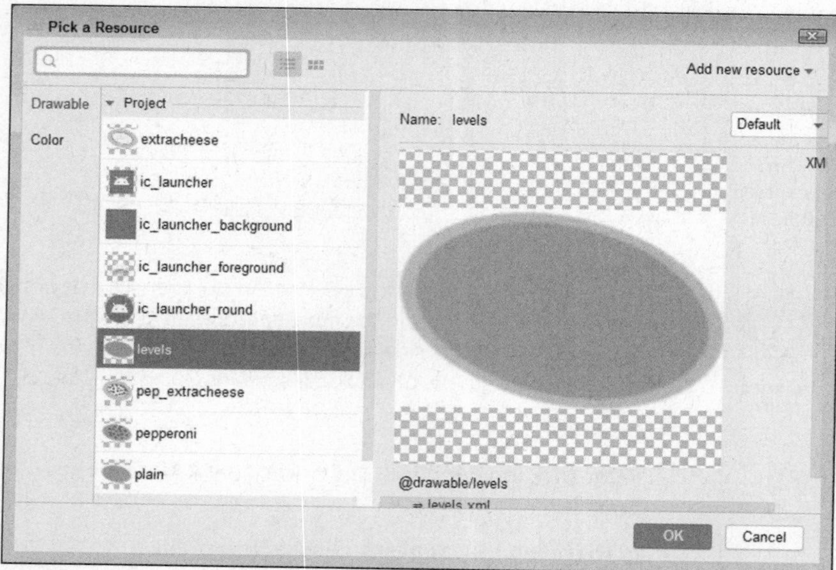

FIGURE 6-19: Use the Resources dialog box to configure the `ImageView`.

17. **Open the Project drop-down list and choose levels from the list.**

    You see the plain pizza displayed in the right pane, as shown in Figure 6-19.

18. **Click OK.**

    You see the plain pizza image added to the `ImageView` component in the preview area.

19. **Select the `ImageView` component and set the `layout_marginTop` field found in the All Attributes group of the Attributes window to `20dp`.**

20. **Add the `onButtonClick()` method shown in Listing 6-6 to your `MainActivity.kt` file.**

In Listing 6-6, the `onButtonClick()` method calls the `setImageLevel()` method. The method parameter's value depends on the states of the activity's check boxes.

21. Run the app.

The results, along with the beautiful drawing of the selected pizza with toppings, are shown in Figure 6-20.

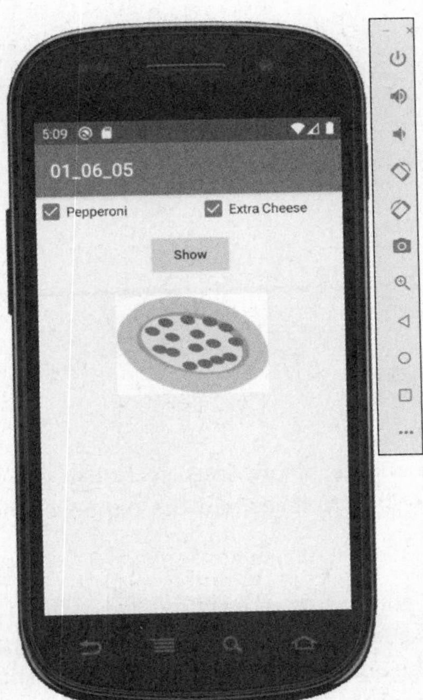

FIGURE 6-20: What a lovely drawing!

LISTING 6-5: A Level-List Document

```
<?xml version="1.0" encoding="utf-8"?>
<level-list xmlns:android="http://schemas.android.com/apk/res/android">
    <item android:drawable="@drawable/plain" android:maxLevel="0"/>
    <item android:drawable="@drawable/pepperoni" android:maxLevel="1"/>
    <item android:drawable="@drawable/extracheese" android:maxLevel="2"/>
    <item android:drawable="@drawable/pep_extracheese" android:maxLevel="3"/>
</level-list>
```

LISTING 6-6: Changing Images

```
fun onButtonClick(view: View) {
    if (checkBox.isChecked()) {
        if (checkBox2.isChecked()){
            imageView.setImageLevel(3)
        } else {
            imageView.setImageLevel(1)
        }
    } else {
        if (checkBox2.isChecked()){
            imageView.setImageLevel(2)
        } else {
            imageView.setImageLevel(0)
        }
    }
}
```

Sending in Your Order

If you've read any of this chapter's previous sections, you're probably very hungry. An app with nothing but pictures and the names of pizza toppings is a real tease.

So you'd better add some purchasing power to this chapter's example. Real e-commerce functionality is the subject of several other books. But in this book, you can get a small taste of the online pizza-ordering process (pun intended). You can submit your choice of toppings to an existing web server — Google's search engine, to be precise. It's not as good as biting into a tasty pizza, but the example shows you one way to send information from a mobile device.

In a real application, you might program your own server to respond intelligently to users' requests. For passing money back and forth, you might use the Google Play Store's in-app billing facilities.

Programming web servers isn't an Android-specific topic. To read all about servers, check out *PHP & MySQL: Server-side Web Development*, by Jon Duckett (Wiley).

1. **Launch Android Studio and create a new project.**

   In this section's listing, we call the project `01_06_06`, and we use the package `com.allmycode.p01_06_06`.

2. **Include the `reusable_layout.xml` and `copied_strings.xml` files in your project.**

   For details, see the "Reusing a layout" section of the chapter.

3. **Drag a `WebView` component from the Widgets group of the Palette to your app's preview screen.**

   A WebView is a mini web browser that you can add to an existing activity. It doesn't set an `id` value when you drag it to the screen, so you must perform this task separately.

4. **Select the `WebView` in the Component Tree and change the `id` field in the Attributes window to `myWebView`.**

5. **Code your project's activity file as in Listing 6-7.**

6. **Add the following element to your project's `AndroidManifest.xml` file:**

   ```
   <uses-permission android:name="android.permission.
     INTERNET"/>
   ```

   Make this `uses-permission` element a direct sub-element of the document's `manifest` element by pressing Enter and typing the code.

   The `uses-permission` element grants your app permission to access the Internet. Access to the Internet will appear in the list the user sees before installing your app.

REMEMBER

   When you create an app, don't forget to add the appropriate permissions to the app's `AndroidManifest.xml` file. In a recent survey of *For Dummies* book authors, all respondents reported that they frequently forget to add permissions to their apps' manifest files. (Survey sample size: one.)

7. **Run your app. Click Show.**

   You might have to wait for the web page to load. When the page loads, your app looks something like the screen in Figure 6-21.

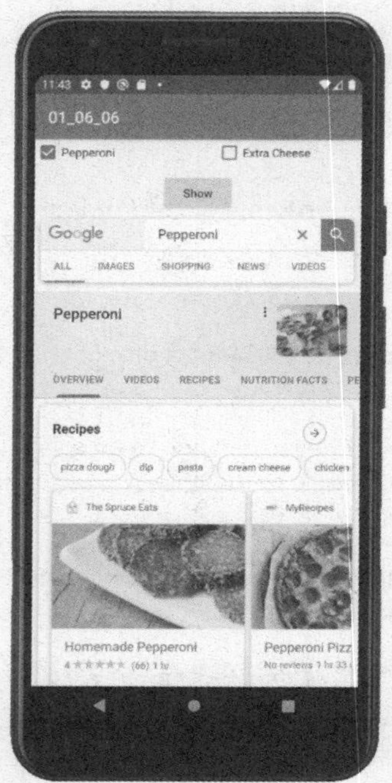

FIGURE 6-21: Your app sends stuff to a web server.

LISTING 6-7: Sending Info to a Server

```
fun onButtonClick(view: View){
    val builder = StringBuilder()

    if (checkBox.isChecked()){
        builder.append("Pepperoni")
    }
    if (checkBox2.isChecked()){
        if (builder.length == 0){
            builder.append("Extra Cheese")
        } else {
            builder.append(" and Extra Cheese")
        }
    }
    if (builder.length == 0){
        builder.append("Plain")
    }

    val thisView: WebView = findViewById(R.id.myWebView)
    val mySettings: WebSettings = thisView.settings
```

```
    mySettings.setAppCacheEnabled(true)
    mySettings.cacheMode = WebSettings.LOAD_CACHE_ELSE_NETWORK
    mySettings.javaScriptEnabled = true
    mySettings.loadWithOverviewMode = true

    thisView.loadUrl("https://www.google.com/search?q="
            + builder.toString())
}
```

WARNING

You should note a few things about this example. First, it won't run on all emulators. For example, it runs fine on the Pixel 3a but not on the Nexus S. (Your results may vary from ours.) The Nexus S will report `ERR_ACCESS_DENIED` even if you add the `<uses-permission android:name="android.permission.INTERNET" />` permission to `AndroidManifest.xml`. So, if your example reports errors, try a different emulator.

The second item to note is that the settings used for this example appear to work on most emulators and most devices. However, you may have to locate any special settings for your particular device on vendor sites. For example, some devices may require an addition `config.xml` file that isn't covered as part of this example because it's a special file.

Of the settings shown, `javaScriptEnabled` and `loadWithOverviewMode` are the most important. Many sites won't load properly, or sometimes not at all, unless you have JavaScript support enabled. The overview mode zooms the content out so that it fits on the device you're using. Otherwise, you might not see anything, even though the page is loaded, because you've zoomed in on a particular page component.

2 Android Background Material

Contents at a Glance

» **Getting the most out of Android Studio**

Chapter **1**

Using Android Studio

When you develop software, you have two options:

» **Be tough and use only command-line tools.** Edit programs with plain-text editors, such as UNIX vi, GNU Emacs, Windows Notepad, or Macintosh TextEdit. Issue commands to the Windows command prompt or in the Macintosh Terminal window.

» **Be wimpy and use an integrated development environment (an IDE).** Execute commands by clicking menu items. Edit programs with a full-featured editor — an editor customized for whatever programming language you use. Change object values with code-aware property sheets. Create forms by dragging widgets from a palette to a visual layout.

We admire toughness, but wimpiness is more efficient. Being wimpy makes you more productive and less prone to error. Also, being wimpy helps you to concentrate on the app that you're creating instead of having to focus on the commands to create the app.

Don't get us wrong. Tough command-line tools are great in a pinch. When your IDE covers up subtle (but important) details, you need command-line tools to show you what's going on behind the scenes. But for most developers, most of the time, IDEs are great time-savers.

REMEMBER

With or without Android, IntelliJ IDEA (the backbone of Android Studio) is a mature platform, with tools for Kotlin development, Java development, C/C++ development, PHP development, modeling, project management, testing, debugging, and much more. In fact, the listing of languages at `https://www.jetbrains.com/help/idea/supported-languages.html` is worth a look because you might be able to use this IDE for more than just Android development.

So this chapter covers Android Studio. It (naturally enough) focuses on features that help you build Android apps, but keep in mind that Android Studio has hundreds of general-purpose software development features and many ways to access each feature.

Good to Know versus Need to Know

Several chapters in this minibook contain instructions for using Android Studio. Here are some highlights:

- In Book 1, Chapter 2, you install Android Studio.
- In Book 1, Chapter 3, you create and run an app using Android Studio.
- In Book 1, Chapter 3, you download this book's code examples and open them in Android Studio.
- In Book 1, Chapter 5, you create the look of your app using Android Studio's Designer tool.

Many other chapters contain all the need-to-know Android Studio features. But some very useful things aren't need-to-know things. You can live a full life without knowing that Android Studio can fix your code's indentation. (You can fix the indentation yourself.) You can develop top-selling apps without knowing about the Project tool window's Floating mode.

For information about the need-to-know Android development tasks, skip to other chapters. But for the useful-to-know items (things that aren't absolutely required for getting the work done — the handy tricks that help you work more efficiently), check out this chapter.

Getting a Feel for the Big Picture

Each Android app belongs to a project. A project can contain several modules. For example, an app that runs on Android Wear (an Android-enabled wristwatch) will have at least two modules. One module contains code that runs on a watch; the other module contains supporting code that runs on the user's smartphone (assuming that you check Pair with Empty Phone App when you create the project). Figure 1-1 shows the structure of a project that contains two modules — a mobile module (for the smartphone) and a wear module (for the watch).

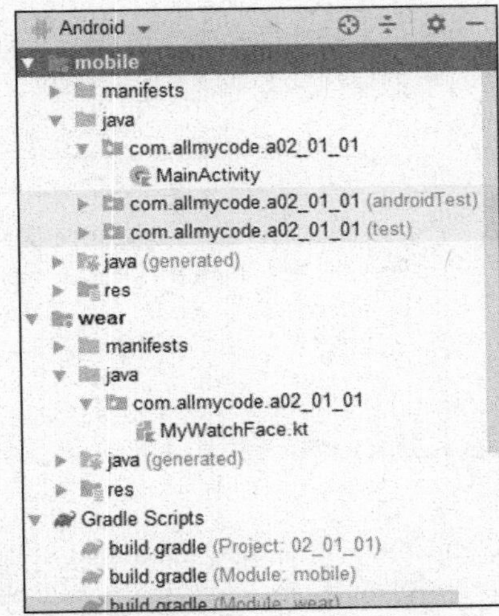

FIGURE 1-1: A project with two modules.

Most of this book's examples live in simple, one-module projects.

You can have dozens of projects on your computer's hard drive. When you run Android Studio, each of your projects is either *open* or *closed*. An open project appears in a window (its own window) on your computer screen. A closed project doesn't appear in a window.

Several of your projects can be open at the same time. You can switch between projects by moving from window to window. Each open project uses a chunk of your computer's precious RAM (random access memory). So, if you're not actively working on a particular project, it's best to close that project.

TECHNICAL STUFF

The book often refers to an open project's window as Android Studio's *main window*. This can be slightly misleading because, with several projects open at one time, you have several main windows open at the same time. None of these windows is more "main" than the others. However, the book is referring to the main window of the current project — the one that you're focusing on at the moment.

If Android Studio is running, and no projects are open, Android Studio displays its Welcome screen. (See Figure 1-2.) The Welcome screen displays some recently closed projects. You can open a project by clicking its name on the Welcome screen. For an app that's not on the Recent Projects list, you can click the Welcome screen's Open an Existing Android Studio Project option.

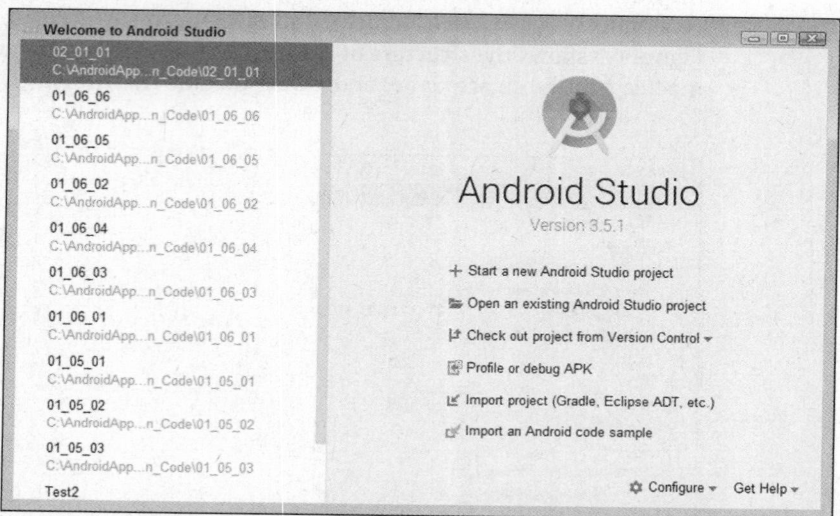

FIGURE 1-2: The Welcome screen.

If you have any open projects, Android Studio doesn't display the Welcome screen. In that case, you can open another project by choosing File ➪ Open or File ➪ Open Recent in an open project's window. To close a project, you can choose File ➪ Close Project, or you can do whatever you normally do to close one of the windows on your computer. (On a PC, click the X in the window's upper-right corner. On a Mac, click the little red button in the window's upper-left corner.)

TIP

Android Studio remembers which projects were open from one run to the next. If any projects are open when you quit Android Studio, those projects open again (with their main windows showing) the next time you launch Android Studio. You can override this behavior (so that only the Welcome screen appears each time you launch Android Studio). To do so on a Windows computer, start by choosing File ➪ Settings and then selecting Appearance and Behavior/System Settings in the Settings dialog box. On a Mac, choose Android Studio ➪ Preferences and then select Appearance and Behavior/System Settings in the Settings dialog box. In either case, deselect the Reopen Last Project on Startup check box.

The main window

The main window is divided into several areas. Some of these areas can appear and disappear on your command. What comes next is a list of the areas, going from the top of the main window to the very bottom. (You can follow along in Figure 1-3.)

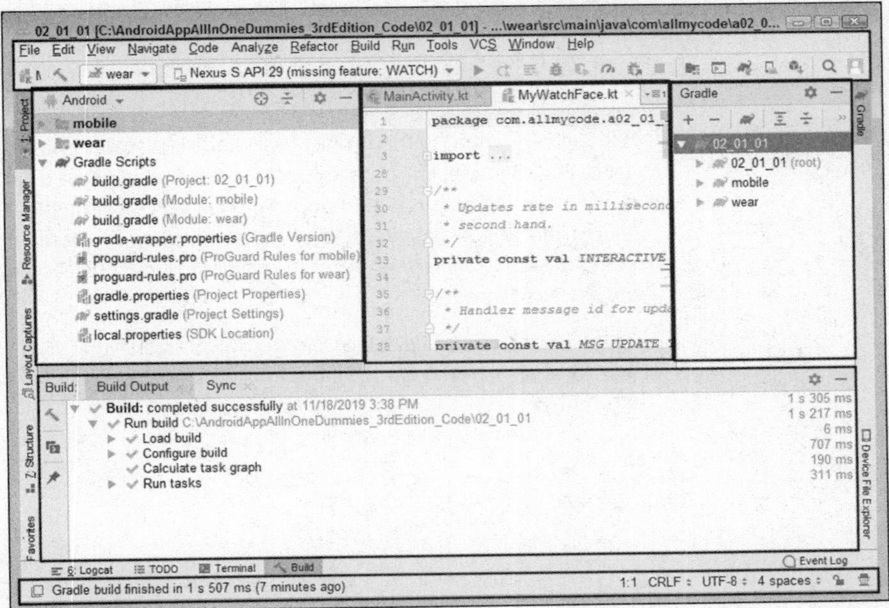

FIGURE 1-3: The main window has several areas.

- The topmost area contains the main menu and the toolbars.
- Below the main window and the toolbars, you see as many as three different areas:
  - The leftmost of these areas contains the Project tool window.

    You use the Project tool window to navigate from one file to another within your Android app.
  - The middle area contains the editor.

    The editor can have several tabs. Each tab contains a file that's open for editing. To open a file for editing, double-click the file's branch in the Project tool window. To close the file, click the little *x* next to the file's name in the editor tab.

TECHNICAL STUFF

- The rightmost area contains the Gradle tool window.

  Gradle is a tool for orchestrating the building of software projects (the combining of dozens of project files into one `.apk` file suitable for installation on a user's device). Gradle instructions are written in a language called Groovy.

  Android Studio creates Gradle scripts for each of your projects and executes these scripts as you develop your projects. If you have special requirements for a particular project, you can specify these requirements in the Gradle window. (None of this book's examples requires that kind of customization.)

At any given moment, the Project tool window displays one of several possible views. For example, in Figure 1-3, the Project tool window displays its Android view. Figure 1-4, shows what happens when you click the drop-down list to select the Project view (instead of the Android view). Notice that this view makes it easy to drill down into actual files. For example, you can actually peer into `Android.jar`.

Figure 1-5 shows the Packages view. (The Packages view displays many of the same files as the Android view, but in the Packages view, the files are grouped differently.)

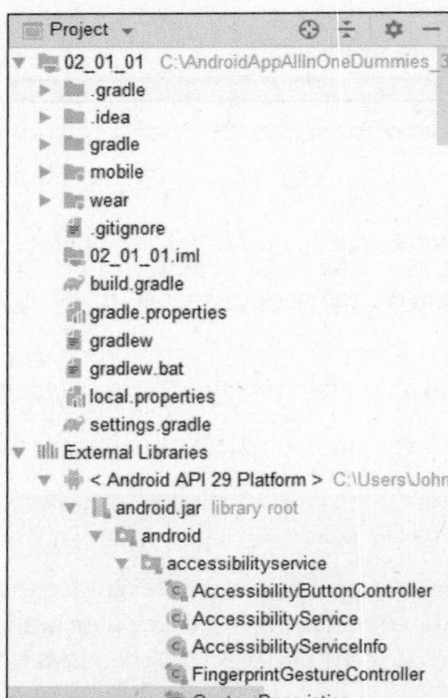

FIGURE 1-4: Selecting the Project view.

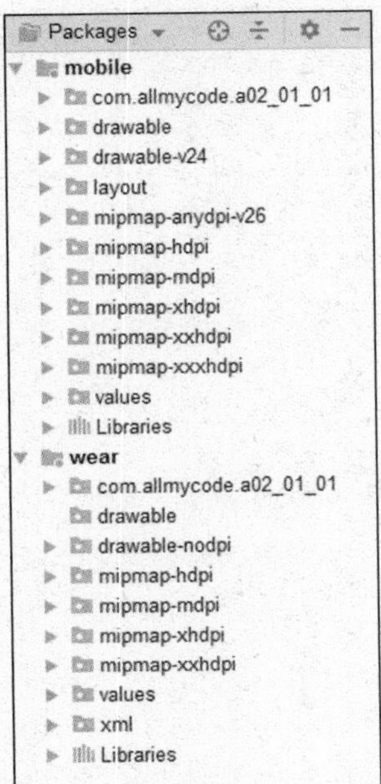

FIGURE 1-5: The Packages view.

In Figure 1-3, shown previously, a Tool Window bar appears to the left of the Project tool window. The Tool Window bar can contain tool window buttons labeled "1: Project," "Resource Manager," "Layout Captures," "7: Structure," "2: Favorites," and "Build Variants." If the Project tool window is showing and you click the 1: Project tool button, the entire area consumed by the Project tool window disappears. (See Figure 1-6.) If you click the 1: Project tool button again, the area reappears with the Project tool window inside.

TIP

You can move a tool window from one area to another by right-clicking the toolbar (you can also click the gear icon) and choosing one of the following options from the context menu that appears. Try it!

- Choose View Mode and select the Undock, Float, or Window options.
- Choose Move To and select one of the location options on the submenu, such as Left Bottom.

Using the default setup, if the Project tool window is showing and you click the 7: Structure tool button, the Structure tool window appears below the Project tool window in the leftmost area. (See Figure 1-7.)

The same kind of thing happens when you click any of the tool buttons using the default layout:

- If the clicked tool button's window is showing, the window disappears, and its area shrinks to nothing.

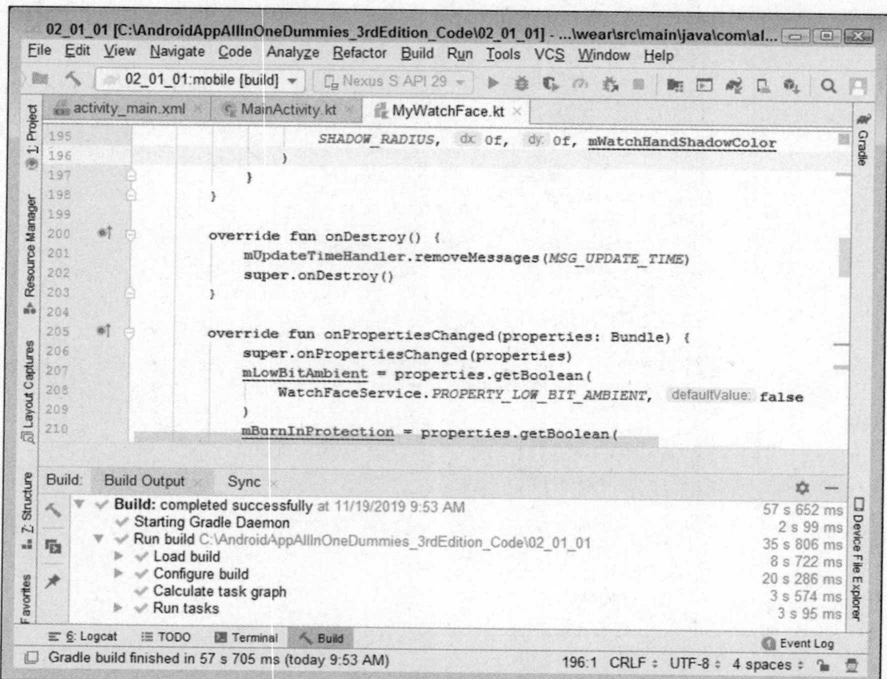

FIGURE 1-6: Look! No Project tool window!

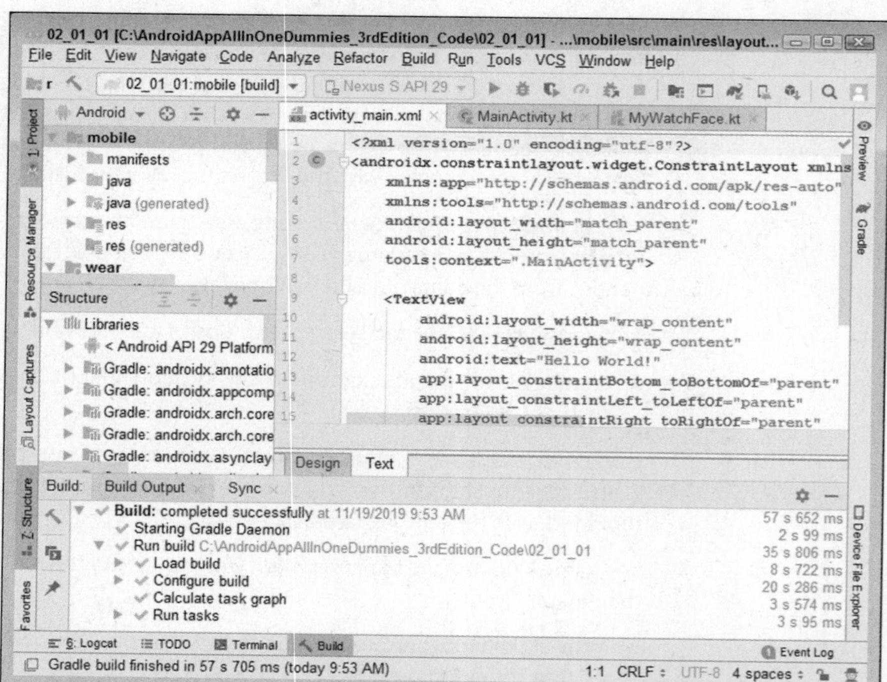

FIGURE 1-7: The Structure tool window.

- If the clicked tool button's area isn't showing, the area appears with the corresponding tool window inside it.
- If the clicked tool button's area is displaying a different tool window, the clicked button's tool window appears either above or below the tool window that is being displayed (according to the hierarchy of tool buttons on the left side).

To continue your tour of the areas in Figure 1-3:

» Below the middle three areas (that is, below the Project tool window, the editor, and the Gradle tool window) is another area that contains several tool windows:

- The Terminal tool window displays a PC's Windows command prompt, a Mac's Terminal app, or some other text-based command screen that you specify. (See Figure 1-8.)
- The Run tool window displays information about the launching of an Android app. (In Figure 1-9, a phrase such as `Waiting for process to come online...` refers to the process of moving and starting the app on the emulator or physical device.)

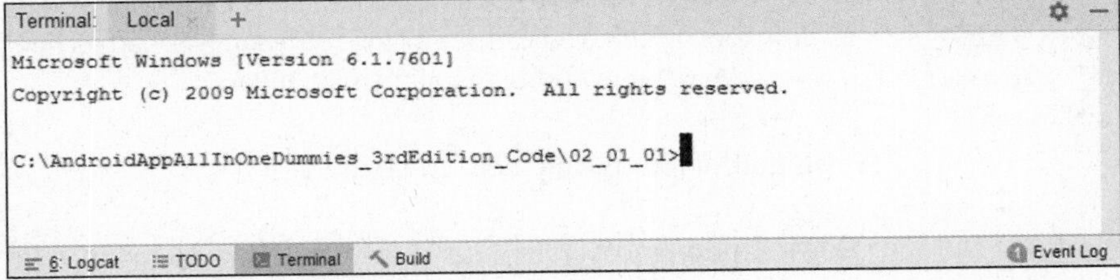

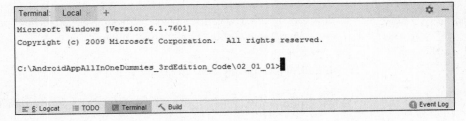

FIGURE 1-8: The Terminal tool window on a PC.

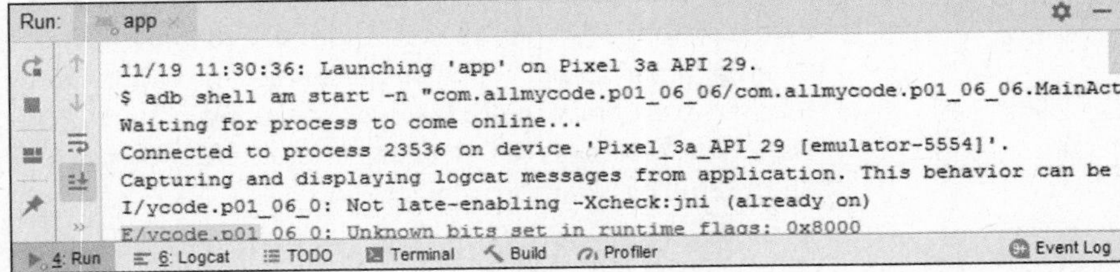

FIGURE 1-9: The Run tool window.

The Run tool window appears automatically when you tell Android Studio to launch one of your projects.

- The Android tool window displays information about the run of an Android app. This tool window appears automatically (replacing the Run tool window) when your app starts running on an emulator or a connected physical device.

  The Android tool window has several different panes — the Logcat pane, the Profiler pane, and possibly others. (Notice the tabs with these labels back in Figure 1-3.) The pane that many developers find most useful is the Logcat pane. In the Logcat pane, you see all the messages being logged by the running emulator or physical device. If your app isn't running correctly, you can filter the messages that are displayed and focus on the messages that are most helpful for diagnosing the problem.

- The Debug tool window appears in this area when you invoke Android Studio's debugger.

  For details on the use of the Logcat panel, the Debugger, and other nice toys, see Book 1, Chapter 5.

You can force any of these tool windows to appear by clicking the corresponding tool button.

REMEMBER

A particular tool button might not appear when you can't do anything with it. For example, if you're not trying to run an Android app, you might not see the Run tool button. You can see all the tool windows' names by choosing View ⇨ Tool Windows in Android Studio's main menu.

Finishing the tour of the areas in Figure 1-3:

» The bottommost area contains the status bar.

  The status bar tells you what's happening now. For example, if your cursor is on the 37th character of the 11th line in the editor, you see *11:37* somewhere on the status line. When you tell Android Studio to run your app, you see `Gradle: Executing Tasks` on the status line. When Android Studio has finished executing Gradle tasks, you see `Gradle Build Finished` on the status line. Messages like these are helpful because they confirm that Android Studio is doing what you want it to do.

In addition to the areas that mentioned in this section, other areas might pop up as the need arises. You can dismiss an area by clicking the area's Hide icon. (See Figure 1-10.)

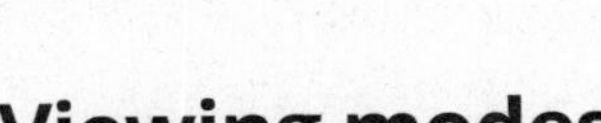

FIGURE 1-10: The icon for hiding areas.

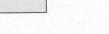

Viewing modes

The behavior described in the previous section reflects tool windows in pinned, docked modes. You can change this behavior (and make other changes in the way tool windows behave) by clicking the gear icon in a tool window's upper-right corner. (See Figure 1-11.)

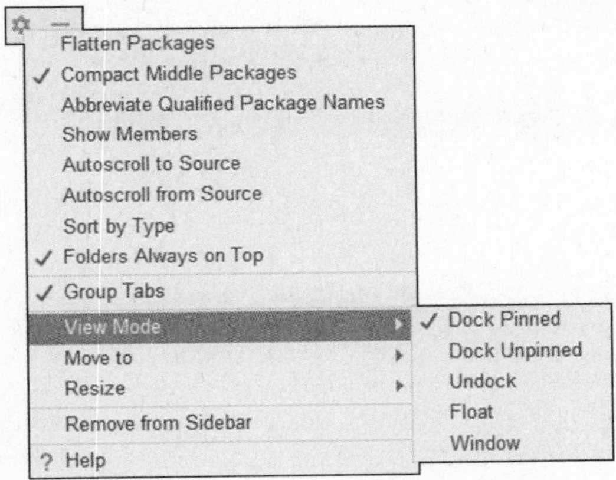

FIGURE 1-11: Selecting viewing modes.

There are five viewing modes: Dock Pinned; Dock Unpinned; Undock; Float; and Window. For a particular tool window at a particular moment, you select one of the five available modes.

REMEMBER

The view setting for one tool window doesn't affect the view setting for another tool window. For example, if you select the Undock view mode for the Project tool window, the setting doesn't affect the Resource Manager tool window. Being able to set each tool window individually makes it easier to customize your setup.

Here's the meaning of each mode:

- **Dock Pinned:** This is the default mode, in which the window stays precisely where it is and you can't move it. This mode is helpful because you don't have to worry about stray mouse clicks or other events changing the appearance of your display. A stable IDE is a thing of beauty.

- **Dock Unpinned:** The window is still docked in a specific location. However, it hides from view until you click one of the toolbar buttons. Instead of having to click a button a second time or clicking the Hide button, the window just hides when not needed.
- **Undock:** The window usually takes a specific area of the IDE. When undocked, it can overlap the other windows while you're using it and then automatically hides when you're done. Look at Figure 1-12 to see how this works with the Project tool window.

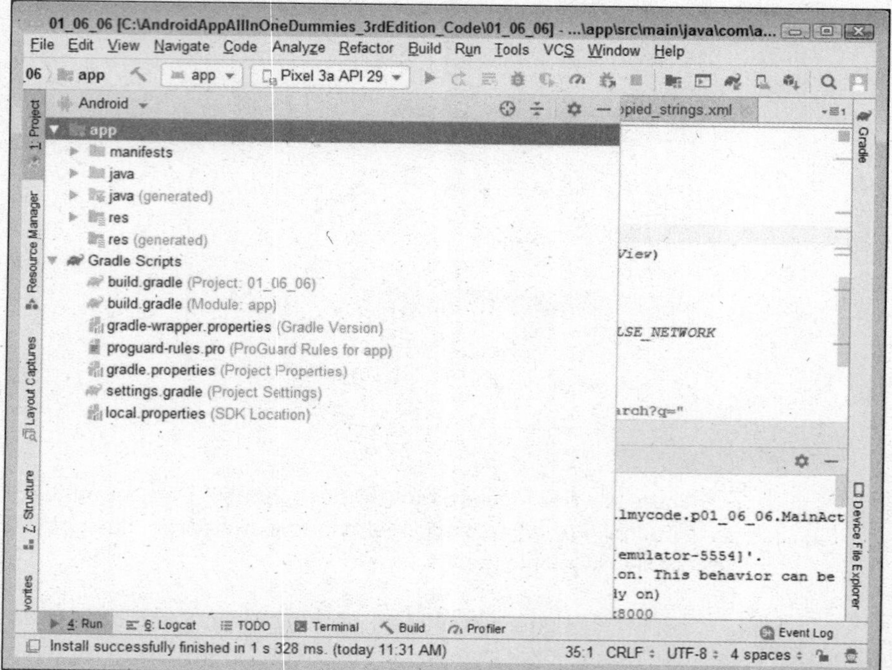

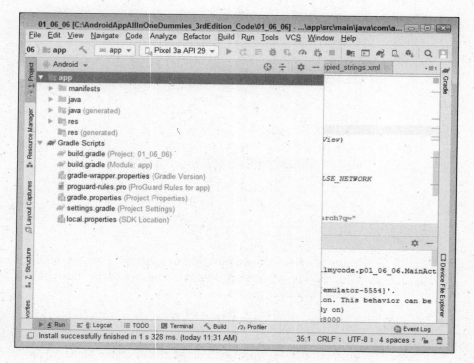

FIGURE 1-12: Seeing the Project window undocked.

- **Float:** You use float mode to remove the tool window from the IDE, as shown in Figure 1-13. Now you can put the tool window wherever you want — on another screen, under the IDE, or in the corner. Just don't misplace it.
- **Window:** Instead of looking like a pane in the IDE, the tool window now appears as an actual window, as shown in Figure 1-14. When working with Windows, you see the individual tool window listed on the taskbar so that you can select just that window, rather than the IDE as a whole.

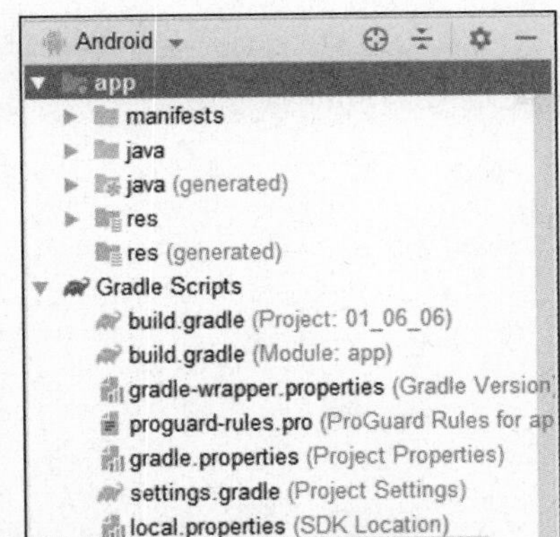

FIGURE 1-13: Use the float mode to move windows somewhere outside the IDE.

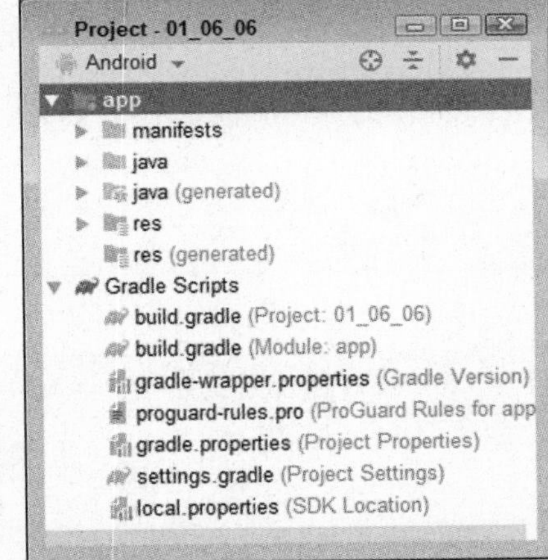

FIGURE 1-14: Window mode is similar to float mode, except you see a taskbar entry.

The Designer tool

When you edit a layout file (for example, the `activity_main.xml` file in the `res/layout` folder), Android Studio displays its Designer tool. The Designer tool has two modes: Design mode for drag-and-drop visual editing, and Text mode for XML code editing. (See Figures 1-15 and 1-16.) So the bottom of the Designer tool has two tabs — a Design tab and a Text tab.

In Design mode, you edit the layout by dragging and dropping widgets onto the Designer tool's Preview screen or onto the Component Tree. In Text mode, you edit the same widgets by typing text in the XML file. When you use the Design mode's Preview screen, Android Studio automatically updates the XML file. And it works both ways. When you edit the XML file, Android Studio keeps the Preview screen up to date.

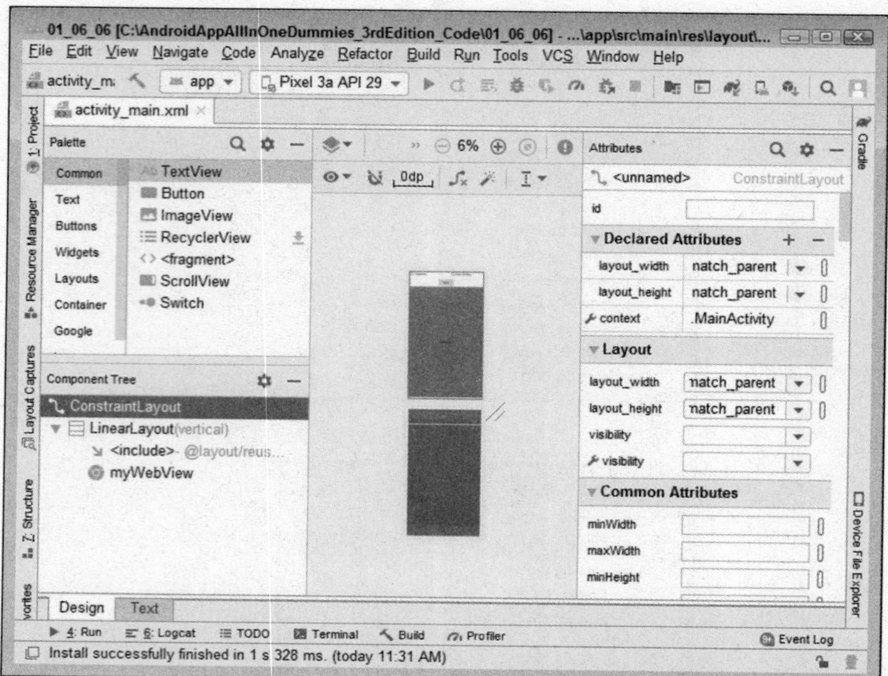

FIGURE 1-15: The Designer tool's Design mode.

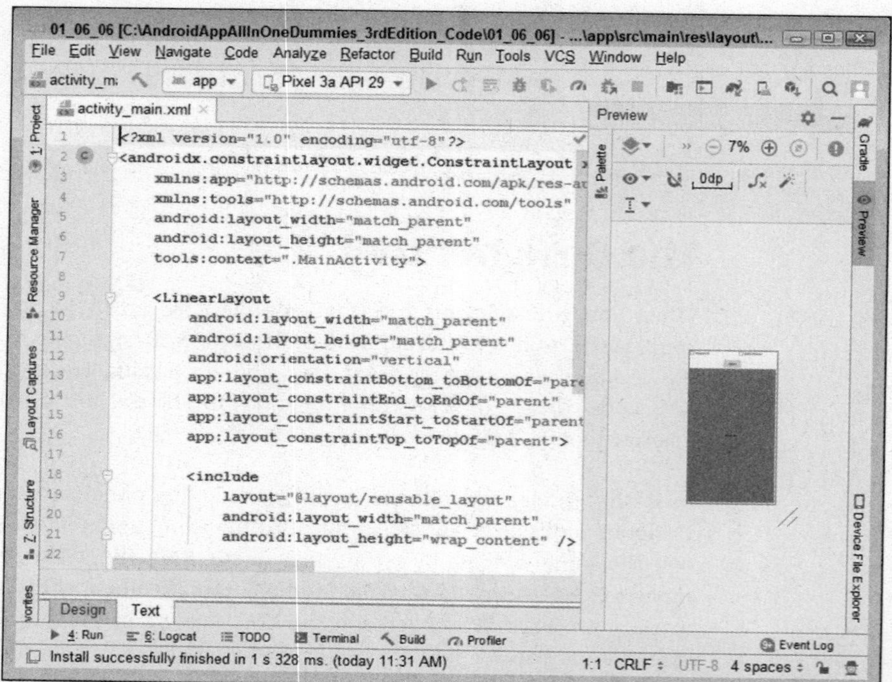

FIGURE 1-16: The Designer tool's Text mode.

In Design mode, the Designer tool has four parts:

- » The Preview screen in the middle is a place to drag and drop widgets. (Refer to Figure 1-15.)
- » The Palette on the upper left is a place to get the widgets that you drop onto the Preview screen or Component Tree.
- » The Component Tree on the lower left shows the layout of your app using an outline format.
- » The Attributes pane on the right display facts about your activity's layout. You can change your layout by modifying the values that you find here.

You can hide the Palette, Component Tree, and Attributes windows by clicking their respective Hide icons. (These icons look like the one in Figure 1-10.) When you hide one of these parts, Android Studio creates a little tool button along the side of the Designer tool. Click the tool button to unhide one of the Designer tool's parts.

The Palette, Component Tree, and Attributes windows also support viewing modes. So if one of these windows is taking up too much space on one monitor, you can move them to another and continue working on your design. See the "Viewing modes" section of the chapter for details on viewing modes.

Look carefully at the Preview screen in Figure 1-15. Notice that there are actually two views of the layout that you use for two different purposes (you can't see the colors in the book, but you can see them onscreen):

- » **Design (upper, in gray):** Shows the actual presentation of the app. For example, when working with example `01_06_06` from Book 1, Chapter 6, you see the two check boxes, button, and `WebView` in this view.
- » **Blueprint (lower, in teal):** Shows the elements used to create the app's presentation. For example, when working with example `01_06_06` from Book 1, Chapter 6, you see that the upper part of the app relies on an `include`, while the lower part of the app has an element with an `id` of `myWebView`.

The default is to display both the Design and Blueprint views. However, you can click the Select Design Surface button on the left side of the Preview window to select the view you want. The same drop-down list contains an option for forcing a refresh of the layout after you make a change.

Locating particular items can be difficult, and you don't want to spend a lot of time doing it, so the Palette and Attributes windows also have a Search icon, which looks like a little magnifying glass. When you click this icon, you see a search box like the one shown in Figure 1-17. As you type the name of the item you want to find, the display changes to show just the items that meet the search criteria. Click the X at the rightmost end of the search box to clear the search criteria.

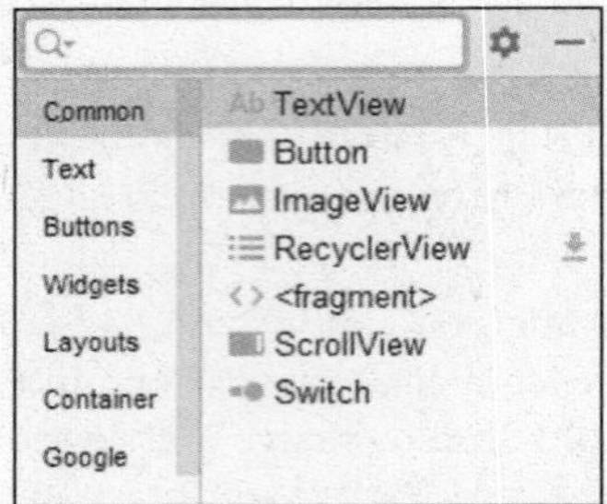

FIGURE 1-17: Locate the components or attributes you want to work with using the search box.

When the Designer tool is in Text mode, Android Studio doesn't display a Preview tool window. (Refer to Figure 1-16.) The Preview tool window (in Text mode) looks a lot like the Preview screen (in Design mode). The difference is that the Preview tool window is only a viewer. It's not an editor. You can't modify the layout by dragging and dropping things in the Preview tool window.

TIP

If Android Studio's Designer tool is in Text mode, and you don't see the Preview tool window, click the Preview tool button. You'll find that button on the right-most edge of the main window.

For details on using the Designer tool, see Book 1, Chapter 5.

When you go to the Project tool window and double-click a file that's not a layout file, Android Studio dismisses the Designer tool and replaces it with the plain old editor area.

Discovering What You Can Do

Android Studio has thousands of useful features. A typical developer uses a small percentage of all these features. This section covers some of the features that most developers use every day.

Finding things

You're probably familiar with a document editor's Find facilities. Using Pages, Microsoft Word, or some similar software, you search through a document to find a word or a phrase. Searching through a text document is a big job, but searching an entire Android project is even bigger. After all, an Android project has many folders, and each folder contains many files. It's a complicated bundle of data. But along with this complexity comes great opportunity. Each file has a known structure, and each word in each file has a very well-defined meaning. The potential for intelligent search is enormous.

Choosing Edit ⇨ Find in Android Studio's main menu gives you some hints about Android Studio's Find capabilities. (See Figure 1-18.)

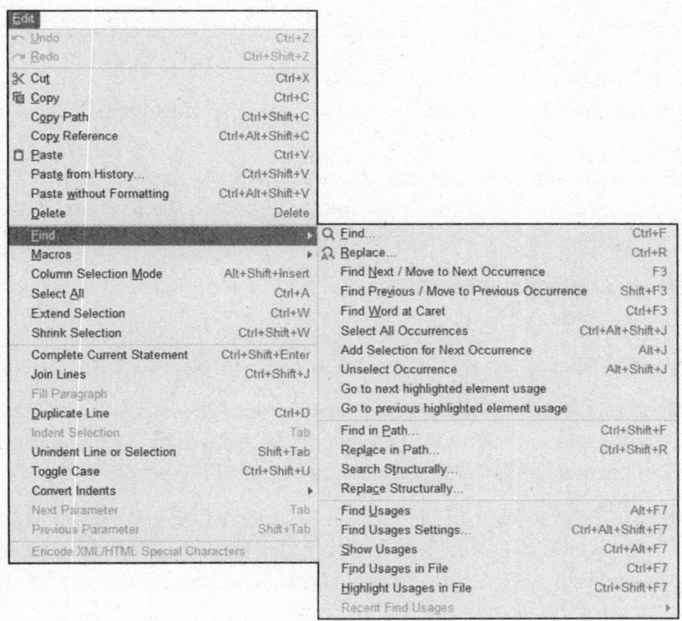

FIGURE 1-18: Finding a Find option.

The Find menu in Figure 1-18 has more than a dozen options. A long list describing the use of each option would be tedious for you to read. (What's more, it would be really boring for us to write!) So, in this section, we describe a few favorite options. If you want, you can set aside some time to poke around and explore the other options. When you do, you'll probably stumble on some favorites of your own.

Using plain old Find

With the old Edit ➪ Find ➪ Find standby, you search for text in the current file (whatever file is currently visible in the editor). And, of course, when you choose Edit ➪ Find ➪ Replace, you replace occurrences of a word or phrase with another word or phrase.

TIP

Even if you're not big on memorizing keyboard shortcuts, you should use shortcuts for this simple version of Find. It's Ctrl+F on Windows and Cmd+F on a Mac. For the corresponding Replace action, it's Ctrl+R on Windows and Cmd+R on a Mac.

When you select the plain old Find option, you get a Find panel. (See Figure 1-19.) This Find panel has some nice options to help you customize your search.

FIGURE 1-19: The Find panel.

Starting from left to right, you have access to these special features:

- **Search box:** This is where you type the text you want to find. In this case, the search is for the term CheckBox, and you can see that two matches are found (as shown on the right side of the panel).
- **Up and Down arrows:** Let you find the previous or next occurrence of a search term.
- **Find All:** Locates all the entries for the search term in all project files.
- **Select Next, Unselect Next, and Select All:** Instead of just finding the search term, these options actually select the text within the document. It's as if you individually highlighted each occurrence of the search term.
- **Show Filter Popup:** Displays a pop-up in which you choose where to search: Anywhere; In Comments; In String Literals; Except Comments; Except String Literals; and Except Comments and String Literals. Using a filter helps you reduce the number of hits for common terms.
- **Match Case:** Performs searches based on case. Consequently, CheckBox becomes different from checkbox.
- **Words:** Locates only whole words. Consequently, you would find CheckBox if the search was for CheckBox, but not CheckBox2.
- **Regex:** Relies on a regular expression to perform a search. The question mark next to this entry provides you with a list of regular expression constructs.

Look at Regex in more detail because it gives you a great deal of flexibility. Here are some examples:

- **A character followed by an asterisk matches zero or more of those characters.** For example, if you search for `o*ps!`, you find `ps!`, `ops!`, `oops!`, `ooops!`, and so on.
- **A character followed by a plus sign matches one or more of those characters.** For example, if you search for `o+ps!`, you find `ops!`, `oops!`, and `ooops!`. But you don't find `ps!`.
- **A dot matches any single character.** The pattern `b.t` finds `bat`, `bet`, `bit`, `bot`, `but`, `bbt`, `bct`, `b@t`, `b.t`, and so on.
- **A backslash followed by a dot matches a single dot character.** The pattern `b\.t` finds `b.t`, but it doesn't find `bat`, `but`, `b..t`, or `b\t`.
- **A dot followed by an asterisk matches any sequence of zero or more characters.** For example, `b.*t` matches `bt`, `bat`, `boat`, and the characters `binge wat` in the phrase `binge watching`.
- **A bunch of characters enclosed in square brackets matches any one of the characters.** For example, `b[aeiou]t` finds `bat`, `bet`, `bit`, `bot`, `but`. It doesn't find `bt`, `boat`, or `bbt`.

For the authoritative description of Android Studio's regular expression syntax, visit `https://www.jetbrains.com/help/idea/regular-expression-syntax-reference.html`.

Searching several files at one time

When you choose Edit ⇨ Find ⇨ Find in Path, you get the dialog box shown in Figure 1-20. This is useful for finding all occurrences of a particular word in the following:

- **Project:** The current project in its entirety.
- **Module:** A particular module within the project. You choose the module you want to search using a drop-down list box containing the module names.
- **Directory:** Any directory on your system. All you need to do is specify its location (a browse button makes this task easier by displaying a Select Path dialog box that you can use to find the location you want).
- **Scope:** A particular file location and type: All Places; Project Files; Project and Libraries; Project Source Files; Project Production Files; Project Test Files; Scratches and Consoles; and Open Files.

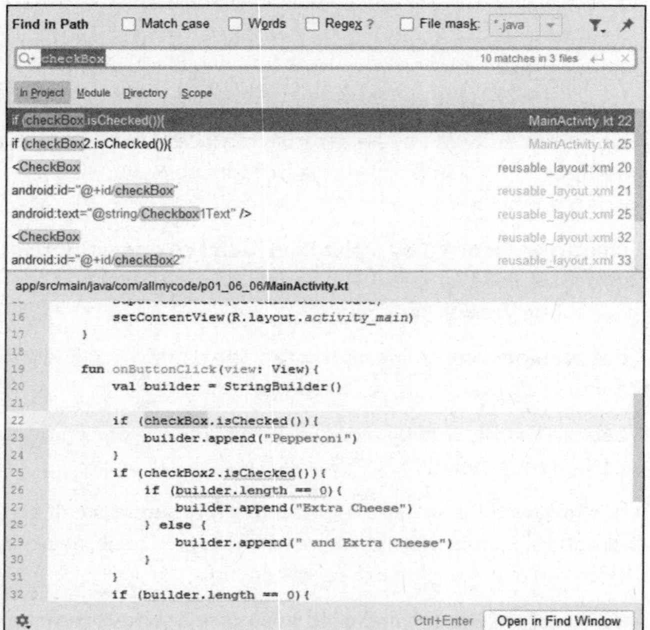

FIGURE 1-20: The Find in Path dialog box.

Imagine that the name checkBox occurs somewhere in a project containing 100 .kt files. You can find all files that mention checkBox using the Find in Path dialog box. As with a standard search, you can look for a particular case, or only whole words, and you can use regular expressions to define the search term. You can also choose to search files with a specific extension, such as .kt.

REMEMBER

Note that the dialog box in Figure 1-20 only finds instances of a search term. To perform replacements as well, you must choose Edit ⇨ Find ⇨ Replace in Path instead.

Highlighting usages

You want to find all occurrences of a variable named button1 in your activity. You can do an ordinary Find, but there's a better way. On a PC, choose File ⇨ Settings to display the Settings dialog box. In the Settings dialog box, choose Editor/General. (On a Mac, choose Android Studio ⇨ Preferences to display the Settings dialog. In the Settings dialog, choose Editor/General.) Look for the check box labeled Highlight Usages of Element at Caret. Put a check mark in that check box. (Note that the default setting has this option checked.)

When you return to the editor, select any occurrence of a common variable, such as builder or button1. In response, the editor highlights all occurrences of that variable, with the selected highlight appearing darker than the other highlights. (See Figure 1-21.)

```
activity_main.xml   MainActivity.kt

fun onButtonClick(view: View){
    val builder = StringBuilder()

    if (checkBox.isChecked()){
        builder.append("Pepperoni")
    }
    if (checkBox2.isChecked()){
        if (builder.length == 0){
            builder.append("Extra Cheese")
        } else {
            builder.append(" and Extra Cheese")
        }
    }
    if (builder.length == 0){
        builder.append("Plain")
    }

    val thisView: WebView = findViewById(R.id.myWebView)
    val mySettings: WebSettings = thisView.settings

    mySettings.setAppCacheEnabled(true)
    mySettings.cacheMode = WebSettings.LOAD_CACHE_ELSE_NETWORK
    mySettings.javaScriptEnabled = true
    mySettings.loadWithOverviewMode = true

    thisView.loadUrl( url: "https://www.google.com/search?q="
            + builder.toString())
}
MainActivity › onButtonClick()
```

FIGURE 1-21: The editor highlights occurrences of the selected variable field.

The Kotlin file in Figure 1-21 is so small that highlighting a few words hardly matters. But even in this tiny example, you can see how smart the highlighting feature is. The code in Figure 1-21 has eight occurrences of the text `builder`, so if you were to do an ordinary Find for `builder`, you'd get eight hits.

TIP

Normally, when you select a name in your code, Android Studio highlights all usages of that name in the file and removes the highlighting from previously highlighted names. You can override this behavior so that the highlighting of a name persists, even when you're no longer selecting an occurrence of that name. To do so, select a name in the editor. Then, in Android Studio's main menu, choose Edit ➪ Find ➪ Highlight Usages in File. All occurrences of that name will remain highlighted until you press Esc.

Navigating from place to place in your project

A method named `computePrice` gives you an answer that you don't expect. You're staring at the call to `computePrice` wondering why it gives you that answer. It would help to look at the declaration of the `computePrice` method. You can shuffle through your project's files to find the method's declaration, but it's easier to select the method call and then choose Navigate ➪ Declaration. Android Studio jumps instantly to the declaration of the `computePrice` method. This works for methods, variables, and other names in Android's SDK, as well as for names that you declare in your own project.

The navigation trick has many variations. Consider the statement

```
builder.append("Pepperoni")
```

If you select `builder` and choose Navigate ➪ Declaration, Android Studio jumps to a line of the following kind:

```
val builder = StringBuilder()
```

But, if you select `builder` and choose Navigate ➪ Type Declaration, Android Studio jumps to the declaration (in the SDK) of the `StringBuilder` class. If you select `MainActivity` and choose Navigate ➪ Super Method, you jump immediately to the declaration of the `AppCompatActivity` class.

You can even jump quickly to the Android documentation. Select a name in your code in Android Studio's editor. Then choose View ➪ Quick Documentation in the main menu. When you do, a pop-up menu appears. The pop-up menu contains a summary of the Javadoc for that name. The summary contains links. So, within the pop-up menu, you can go from `MainActivity` to `AppCompatActivity` to `FragmentActivity` and beyond.

Fixing code

In the previous section, you look but you don't touch. You find things in your project's code, but you don't make any changes. But this section is different. In this section, Android Studio helps you make changes to your code.

Using intention actions

You're minding your own business, typing code, having a good time, and suddenly you see some commotion in the Editor window. A yellow light-bulb icon appears. The icon signals the presence of *intention actions* — proposals to make small changes to your code. In response to the icon's appearance, you press Alt+Enter. Doing so makes a pop-up menu appear. The pop-up menu contains a list of suggested changes. If you scroll to a list item and press Enter, Android Studio makes the change.

Figure 1-22 shows just such a pop-up menu. (The items you see on such a menu vary by the object selected.)

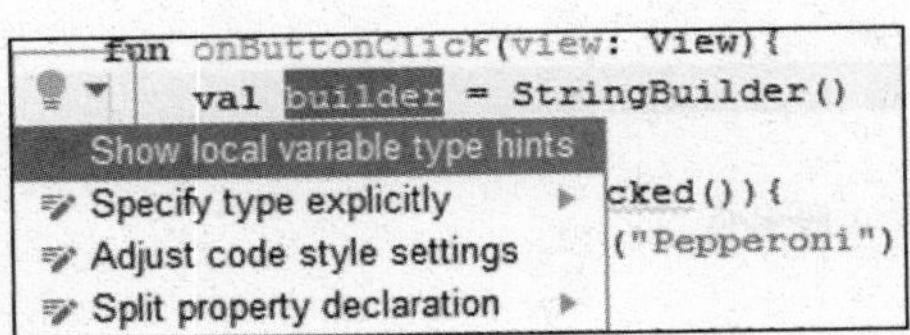

FIGURE 1-22: A list of intention actions.

TIP

» **If you select Show Local Variable Type Hints:**

You see additional documentation for variables that tells you the type of the variable. When you declare a variable as `val myVar = checkBox.text`, the IDE will tell you that the type of `checkBox.text` is `CharSequence` in grayed-out text next to `myVar`, as if you had explicitly declared `myVar` of that type.

Oddly enough, Android Studio doesn't provide a quick means to turn the feature off later. To turn it back off on a PC, choose File ➪ Settings to display the Settings dialog box. (On a Mac, choose Android Studio ➪ Preferences to display the Settings dialog.) In the Settings dialog box, choose Editor/General/Appearance. Click Configure next to the Show Parameter Name Hints setting to display the Configure Parameter Name Hints dialog box, shown in Figure 1-23. Select Kotlin in the Language field and then select the options for the parameter name hints you want to see in the IDE (or deselect those that you don't).

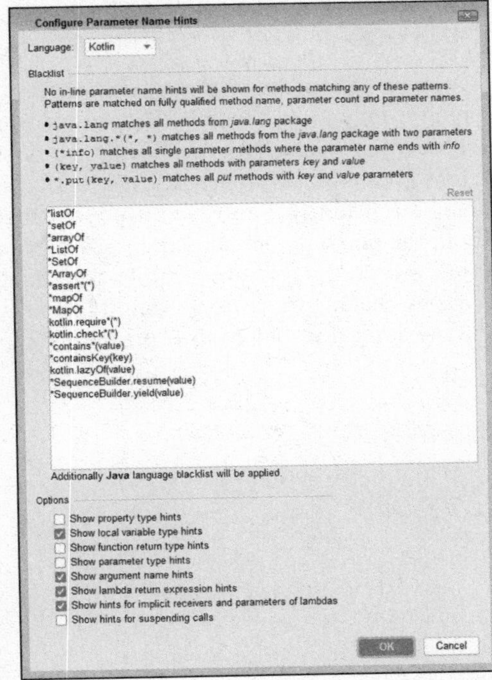

FIGURE 1-23: Configuring the parameter name hints.

Using Android Studio

» **If you select Specify Type Explicitly:** You see a submenu in which you can choose to edit the setting or disable it. When enabled, you explicitly declare the type of each variable. The IDE helps you perform this task with helpful pop-ups. A declaration of `val builder = StringBuilder()` becomes `val builder: StringBuilder = StringBuilder()`.

» **If you specify Adjust Code Style Settings:** You see a little dialog box like the one shown in Figure 1-24, in which you can define how the code appears onscreen.

» **If you specify Split Property Declaration:** The declaration of a variable becomes separate from its initialization. For example, `val builder = StringBuilder()` becomes:

```
val builder: StringBuilder
builder = StringBuilder()
```

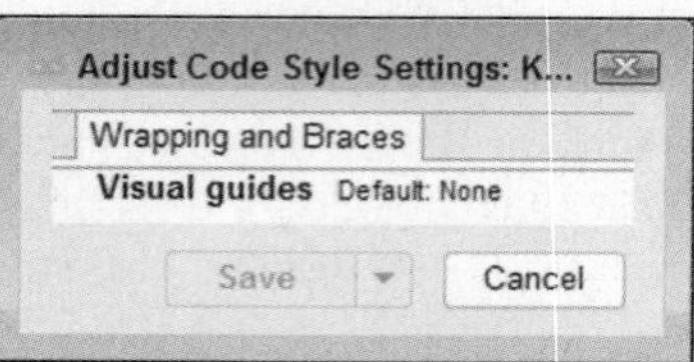

FIGURE 1-24: Defining the appearance of code onscreen.

Using code completion

When you type code in Android Studio, the editor guesses what you're trying to type and offers to finish typing it for you. In Figure 1-25, you see what happens when you type the letters **Log.** (ending with a dot). Android Studio reminds you that the `Log` class has static methods named `d`, `e`, `getStackTraceString`, and so on. You can select one of these by double-clicking the entry in the pop-up menu. Alternatively, you can select an entry in the pop-up menu and then press Enter or Tab. In most cases, you see the options ordered by relevance, rather than in alphabetical order. You can change the order by clicking the little pi icon in the lower-right corner of the list and choosing a new order from the context menu that appears.

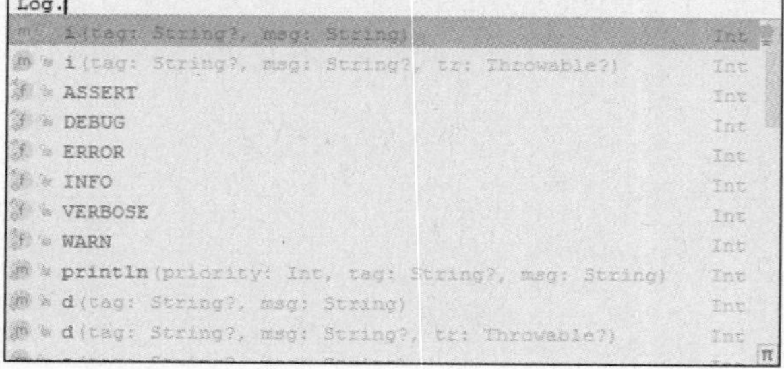

FIGURE 1-25: Android Studio displays the Log class's static members.

If you press Enter, the selected item goes after the dot. For example, if you select the first `i` entry in Figure 1-25, you see `i()` appear onscreen. The caret will appear between the opening and closing parentheses. A bubble will appear to remind you of what to type, as shown in Figure 1-26. As a minimum, you must supply a tag and a message in this case.

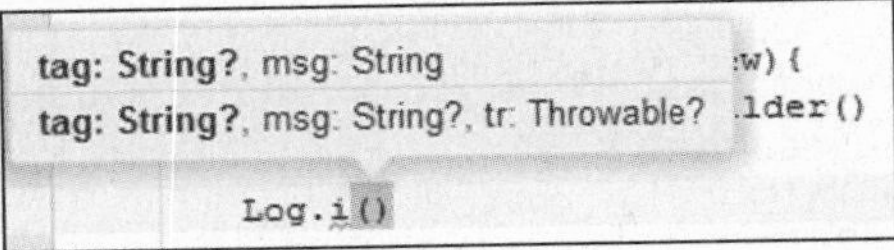

FIGURE 1-26: Android Studio suggests the variables to type.

As you type, the IDE automatically provides the entry type, unless you specifically provide it, as shown in Figure 1-27. What you end up with is a clearly defined call that requires a minimum of typing on your part.

```
Log.i( tag: "MyTag",  msg: "MyMessage")
```

FIGURE 1-27: The IDE automatically provides the type.

Optimizing imports

In Book 1, Chapter 5, you discover a way to make Android Studio write all your import declarations. (On a PC, you put check marks in check boxes after choosing File ➪ Settings ➪ Editor ➪ General ➪ Auto Import. On a Mac, you do the same, but you start by choosing Android Studio ➪ Preferences.) When you follow the instructions, Android Studio automatically adds and removes import declarations as you type. That can be a good thing. But sometimes, you want a bit more control.

So what happens if you ignore the instructions from Book 1, Chapter 5? You still need import declarations, so you type all the import declarations yourself. But typing import declarations is a big pain. You might not remember the package names for all the classes and methods that you use in your code. Even if you remember these names, you have better things to do with your time than to type a bunch of import declarations.

To help you generate import declarations, Android Studio has several tricks. Here are two stories to illustrate some of the tricks:

- You type the name **Toast** (a name from the Android API). You haven't typed the required import declaration at the top of the Kotlin file, so the name Toast appears in red letters. If you hover over the name, Android Studio says *Unresolved reference: Toast.* (See Figure 1-28.)

  Finally, you click the word `Toast`. When you do, Android Studio suggests a fully qualified name. (See Figure 1-29.)

  When you press Alt+Enter, you see a list of potential fixes, as shown in Figure 1-30. The first option on this list is Import. Highlight this entry and press Enter to automatically create the required `import` statement.

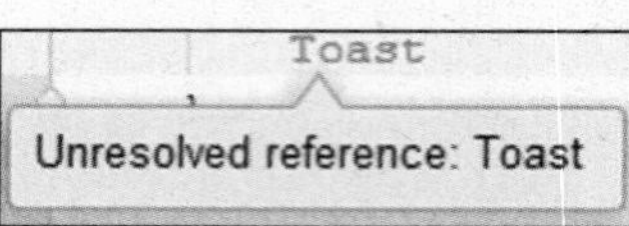

FIGURE 1-28: Cannot resolve reference.

FIGURE 1-29: Do you mean `android.widget.Toast`?

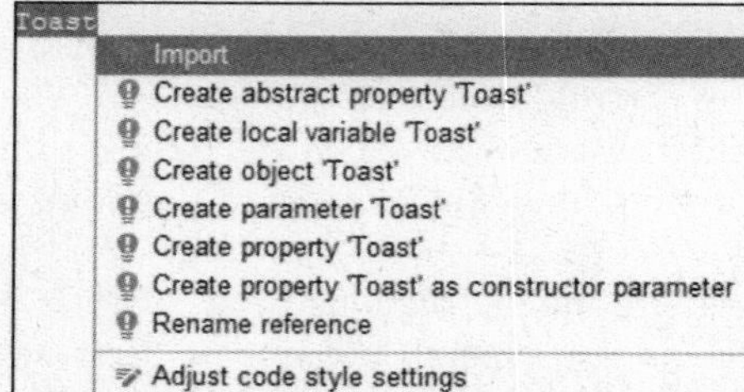

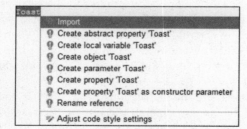

FIGURE 1-30: You don't see just one potential fix for the `Toast` issue.

» You use the name Random, and (one way or another) you add `import kotlin.random.Random` to your code.

```
import kotlin.random.Random
...
val random = Random(5)
```

Sometime later, you change your mind and decide not to create an instance of the Random class. You delete the declaration of `random`, but you don't remove the `import` declaration. Android Studio changes the color of the `import` declaration from blue and black to a light gray.

You can delete the `import` declaration yourself, but you might have several other declarations to delete. You can delete all the unused `import` declarations in one fell swoop by choosing Code ➪ Optimize Imports in Android Studio's main menu.

Reformatting code

In these busy days, who isn't in a hurry sometimes? You're rushing to write code, and you type it in a sloppy fashion.

```
inner class MyClass {
internal var textView: TextView? = null
fun onButtonClick(view: View) {
textView!!.text = "Hello"
}}
```

You figure you'll fix the indentation later, when you're not so pressed for time. But "later" keeps slipping away. Eventually, you have to bottle up your code and publish it on the Google Play Store. No worries! The code's poor formatting has no impact on its run.

But there's a big problem. The next time you look at this code (and that time will definitely come), you'll have trouble understanding what you wrote. Poorly formatted code is difficult to read. And code that's difficult to read is costly to maintain. What's even worse, hard-to-read code is annoying!

So how do you fix this quickly and easily? One solution is to avoid ever writing poorly formatted code. To some extent, Android Studio helps you in this goal. As you create new code, the editor positions your lines where they're supposed to go. Of course, you can override this automatic positioning. (Sometimes, you override the positioning without intending to do so.)

The good news is that Android Studio has a magic bullet. Click your mouse inside the editor. Then, in the main menu, choose Code ⇨ Reformat Code. *Et voilà!* Android Studio fixes your code's indentation.

```
inner class MyClass {
    internal var textView: TextView? = null
    fun onButtonClick(view: View) {
        textView!!.text = "Hello"
    }
}
```

Of course, you might not like the way Android Studio reformats code. We certainly don't. We have to squeeze long lines of code onto narrow, 58-character-wide printed pages. For most of the book examples, we need two-character indenting instead of four-character indenting. And we need spaces instead of tab characters because, on the printed page, spaces are more predictable.

Here's another example. Some people prefer the Allman style for positioning curly braces. In the Allman style, each brace has a line of its own:

```
inner class MyClass
{
    internal var textView: TextView? = null
    fun onButtonClick(view: View)
    {
        textView!!.text = "Hello"
    }
}
```

Can Android Studio help you with that?

Yes, it can. On a PC, choose File ⇨ Settings to display the Settings dialog. (On a Mac, do the same, but start with Android Studio ⇨ Preferences.) In the Settings dialog box, choose Editor/Code Style/Kotlin. When you do, you see hundreds (maybe thousands) of options for adjusting the way Android Studio formats your code. Change your code's line length, change the indentation, change the positioning of curly braces, and change so many other things.

In addition to all of its check boxes and drop-down menus, this dialog box shows you some sample Kotlin classes. So when you make a change, you see immediately how the change affects the sample code. If you like the change, you can click Apply. If not, you can keep experimenting.

Commenting and uncommenting

Your source may have several lines of code that you don't particularly like. You want to experiment to find out what happens if these lines are gone. You can select these lines and press Delete, but you might not like the results of the experiment. You might want the lines back in your code. Instead of deleting these lines, you can turn them (perhaps temporarily) into comments.

Kotlin has a few different kinds of comments, including block comments and end-of-line comments. (The language also has KDoc comments, but you probably wouldn't use a KDoc comment to temporarily disable lines of code.) To turn one or more statements into a comment, start by selecting those statements. Then, in the main menu, choose Code ➪ Comment with Line Comment or Code ➪ Comment with Block Comment. Whichever option you choose, Android Studio obliges by commenting out the lines that you selected. This trick is a lifesaver if you want end-of-line comments on many lines. But it also helps when you want to create a block comment.

Android Studio's commenting trick works both ways. Imagine that you've turned several statements into end-of-line comments, and you want to change them back to ordinary statements. (That is, you want to *uncomment* these lines.) First, select the lines. Then, in the main menu, choose Code ➪ Comment with Line Comment. The name of the option is a bit misleading. (You want to uncomment, not to comment.) Nevertheless, Android Studio sees that you've selected commented lines and removes the comment markers as you wish.

Generating code

Consider the humble Kotlin class that is reformatted in a previous section.

```
inner class MyClass {
    internal var textView: TextView? = null
    fun onButtonClick(view: View) {
        textView!!.text = "Hello"
    }
}
```

With your cursor positioned somewhere inside that class, choose Code ➪ Generate. When you do, you see the pop-up menu shown in Figure 1-31.

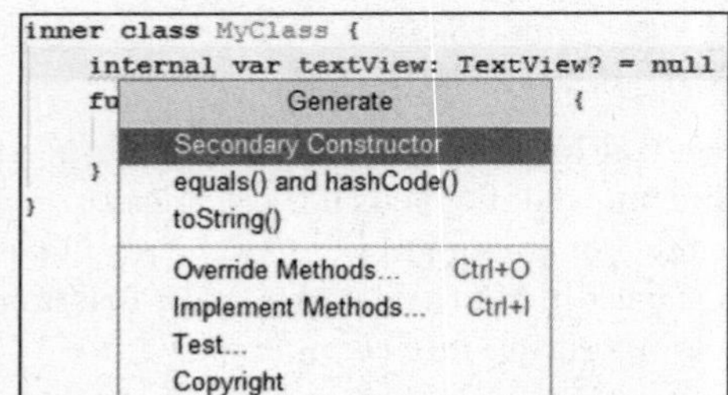

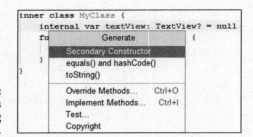

FIGURE 1-31: Several options for generating code.

If you select Secondary Constructor in the pop-up menu, you get another dialog box. (See Figure 1-32.) This little `MyClass` example has only one field — namely, the `textView` field. So you can either select or deselect that `textView` field. If you select the field, Android Studio adds this constructor to your code:

```
constructor(textView: TextView?) {
    this.textView = textView
}
```

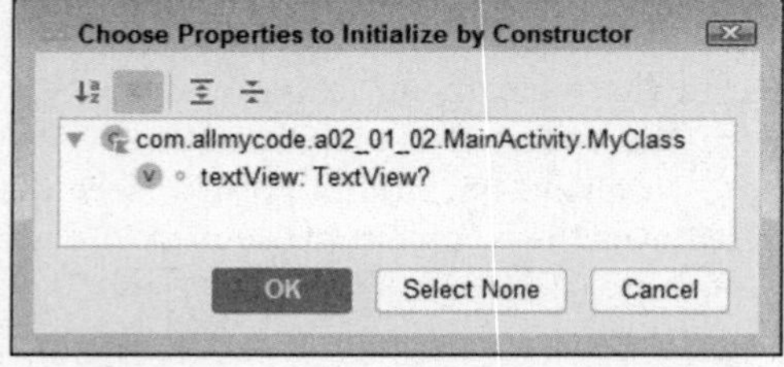

FIGURE 1-32: Choose fields to initialize.

If you don't select the `textView` field, you get the empty constructor:

```
constructor()
```

You can repeat the procedure to get as many constructors as you like.

Other options in Figure 1-31 include generating the `equals()`, `hashCode()`, and `toString()` methods. You can also override or implement methods, generate test code, or create a copyright statement. As with the constructors, what you get depends on the options you select. For example, here is what the `toString()` method looks like when you select the `textView` field:

```
override fun toString(): String {
    return "MyClass(textView=$textView)"
}
```

Refactoring

In the parlance of computer programming, *refactoring* means improving the internal structure of your code without changing the code's behavior. Along with this concept come several *refactoring patterns*. Each pattern is a recipe for taking code that's structured a certain way and turning it into code that's structured differently.

For example, you're developing a game and writing several lines of code to make a ball bounce.

```
class Ball {
    fun dropTo(drop: Int) {
    }
    fun riseTo(height: Int) {
    }
    var elasticity = 0
}

fun doALot(backgr: Background, sprite: Sprite, ball: Ball)
    if (backgr.isCity()) {
        val steps: Int = getSteps()
        sprite.move(steps)
        if (sprite.isNear(monster)) {
            sprite.changeFace(Sprite.PANIC)
            sprite.release(ball)
            val ballHeight: Double = sprite.handHeight

            while (ballHeight > 0) {
                val g: Double = 9.807
                val timeToDrop: Double =
                    Math.sqrt(2 * ballHeight / g)
                val rebound: Double =
                    ballHeight * ball.elasticity
                ball.dropTo(0)
                ball.riseTo(rebound)
            }

        }
        val seconds: Int = getLevel() + 2
        showCar(seconds)
        makeNoise()
    }
}
```

At some point, you realize that you'll be making balls bounce in other parts of your program. So you want to create a general `bounceBall` method with parameters such as `ball` and `ballHeight`.

You don't write the `bounceBall` method from scratch. Instead, you apply the Extract Method refactoring pattern. In the previous code sample, you select all the lines set in boldface. (These are the lines that make the ball bounce.) You move these lines outside the method that currently houses them. You surround the lines with a method header and a closing brace. Then you write a method call where the lines used to live.

You can do all this work manually, but it's easier (and less error prone) if you get Android Studio to do the work for you. Here's how:

1. **Select the statements that will form the body of your new method.**
2. **In Android Studio's main menu, choose Refactor ➪ Extract ➪ Function.**

   An Extract Function dialog box appears. (See Figure 1-33.)

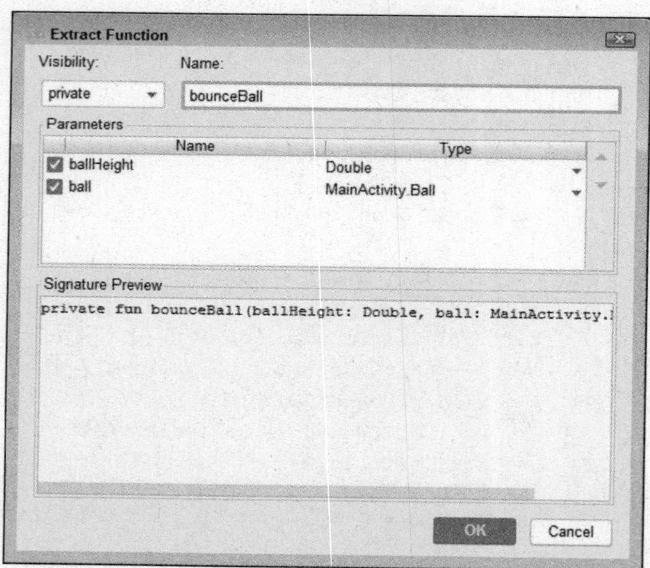

FIGURE 1-33: The Extract Function dialog box.

3. **In the dialog box's Name field, type a name for your new method.**

   In Figure 1-33, you type **bounceBall**.

4. **Click OK.**

As a result, Android Studio rewrites your code. For the bouncing ball example, the new code looks like this:

```
fun doALot(backgr: Background, sprite: Sprite, ball: Ball) {
    if (backgr.isCity()) {
        val steps: Int = getSteps()
        sprite.move(steps)
        if (sprite.isNear(monster)) {
            sprite.changeFace(Sprite.PANIC)
            sprite.release(ball)
            val ballHeight: Double = sprite.handHeight

            bounceBall(ballHeight, ball)

        }
        val seconds: Int = getLevel() + 2
        showCar(seconds)
        makeNoise()
    }
}

private fun bounceBall(ballHeight: Double, ball: Ball) {
    while (ballHeight > 0) {
        val g: Double = 9.807
        val timeToDrop: Double =
            Math.sqrt(2 * ballHeight / g)
        val rebound: Double =
            ballHeight * ball.elasticity
        ball.dropTo(0)
        ball.riseTo(rebound)
    }
}
```

Android Studio supports about 30 refactoring patterns. You can find descriptions of these patterns almost anywhere on the web, so the book doesn't describe all the patterns here. But we can't end this chapter without writing about our favorite pattern — the *Rename pattern*. Here's the story:

You're working with this section's game code and you want to change a name. It could be a variable name, a method name, or any other name in the project. For the purpose of this example, imagine replacing the method name `dropTo()` with the new name `dropFrom()`. To make the change manually, you have to edit the method header and then replace the name in each of the project's `dropTo()` method calls. If there are many such method calls, the change can take a long time.

So, instead of doing it manually, you select any occurrence of the method name `dropTo()` in your project. (The occurrence that you select doesn't have to be the one in the method header.) Then choose Refactor ⇨ Rename. You can choose the quick rename method or you can press Shift+F6 to see the Rename dialog, shown in Figure 1-34.

Start typing to replace the current name. After you type the new name, select the boxes to indicate where you want it changed. When you click Refactor, the renaming occurs and all your `dropTo()` occurrences are now `dropFrom()` occurrences. It's simple. It's consistent. And it's free from manual typing errors. It's great!

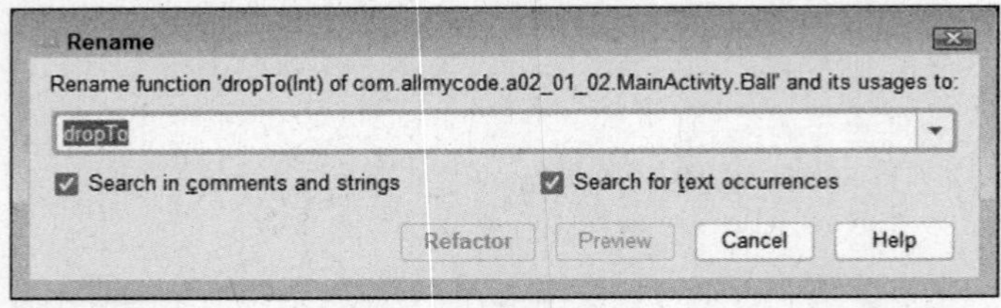

FIGURE 1-34: Renaming a method.

» Considering the things that Kotlin fixes (or doesn't fix)

» Understanding that Kotlin adds significant new functionality

Chapter 2
Kotlin for Java Programmers

You're already behind schedule, and now you find out that you need to learn another new language to keep up to date with Android development. What could be worse? After all, Java isn't so bad. You've used it all these years. The thing is, languages evolve to match the needs of the people using them. Sometimes a language can't quite evolve enough, though, to address all the issues that people have brought up without breaking everything that came before, which is definitely something you want to avoid. So, the main purpose of creating Kotlin is to address Android development needs that people have brought up without destroying what came before in Java. At least, that's how we look at it in this chapter. You may have a different take.

Fortunately, if you know Java, you already have some great starting knowledge about how Kotlin works as well because Java is still lurking under the hood. The projects you worked on in Book 1 have allowed you to peek at the Java lurking under the Kotlin from time to time. In this chapter, you discover the differences between the two and consider why they're important. More important, you see that Java isn't completely out of the picture, even if you use Kotlin for your development needs.

It would be nice to say that Kotlin fixes every issue. The problem is that not everyone sees the issues in the same way, so a one-size-fits-all-fix is nearly impossible. Plus, trying to come out with everything in one lump sum would prove so time consuming that we'd need to create another new language before Kotlin would ever get released. So, this chapter also helps you understand the Kotlin warts — things that everyone hopes to fix someday after everyone can agree to a particular fix and come up with the time to make it.

Using Kotlin or Java for Development

To begin, be aware that there are no perfect programming languages, but only languages that work particularly well for a given need. A *need* is defined as a means to meet a development requirement, but you can also define it more personally, as in the need to use a language you like. Even though Google has officially announced that Kotlin is the preferred development language for Android (see the article at `https://techcrunch.com/2019/05/07/kotlin-is-now-googles-preferred-language-for-android-app-development/` for details); you can cling to Java for now. Android Studio makes Java available as a second language for development, as shown in Figure 2-1. All you need to do is choose it as a language option. So, you don't have to make the move from Java to Kotlin today, but sooner is likely better than later because Google plans to offer all the new Android functionality it provides in Kotlin first.

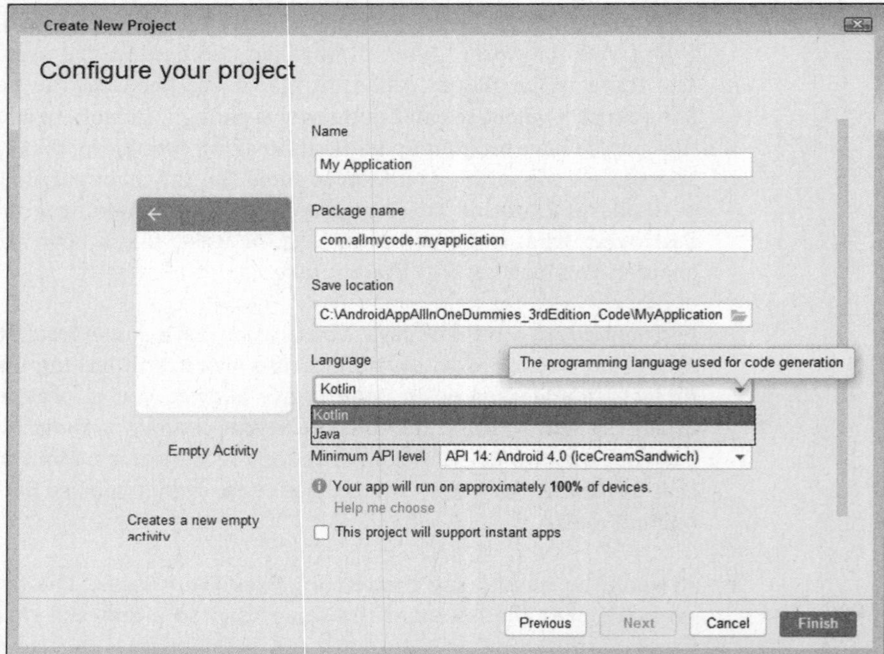

FIGURE 2-1: You can still choose to develop in Java.

REMEMBER

If you were to state the one reason to use Kotlin over Java, it's the fact that you can accomplish tasks in Kotlin using less code than Java. The less code you write, the fewer chances you have to make mistakes and the less time you spend performing maintenance and testing tasks. Still, it has a learning curve, and some developers may want to put it off as long as possible. Chapter 3 of this minibook offers a tutorial on Kotlin that will help ease the pain, so take solace in the fact that we're here to help.

Another consideration is that you may not focus exclusively on Android development. Perhaps you have a life that's just a little more varied than that. When you look at the Tiobe Index (`https://www.tiobe.com/tiobe-index/`), you find that Java is still the number one programming language in the world; Kotlin ranks about 35 as of this writing. (The Tiobe Index is considered one of the most accurate indicators of language popularity available today.) So, if you wanted to become proficient in a programming language that would open as many doors as possible, Java seems to be the better choice of the two. On the other hand, you might choose to believe surveys like the one on Stack Overflow more (see `https://insights.stackoverflow.com/survey/2019#most-loved-dreaded-and-wanted`), which places Kotlin above Java, at least when it comes to being most loved.

Productivity is the focus behind using Kotlin. Not only do you write less code because Kotlin is concise, but you also write less *boilerplate* (repetitive) code. Here is an example of an extremely simple calculator function written in Java:

```
public static double calculate (double a, String op,
 double b) throws Exception {
   switch (op) {
      case "add":
         return a + b;
      case "subtract":
         return a - b;
      case "multiply":
         return a * b;
      case "divide":
         return a / b;
      default:
         throw new Exception();
      }
   }
}
```

Kotlin for Java Programmers

Here is the same function written in Kotlin:

```
fun calculate (a: Double, op: String, b: Double): Double {
    when (op) {
        "add" -> return a + b
        "subtract" -> return a - b
        "multiply" -> return a * b
        "divide" -> return a / b
        else -> throw Exception()
    }
}
```

The two functions provide the same output, but the Kotlin function requires about half the number of lines of code. However, in order to achieve that succinctness, some developers would say that the Kotlin version is less readable. There is no free lunch; everything comes with trade-offs — even conciseness.

Kotlin also supports mixed language development and gives you modern development features, such as support for *functional programming* (a method of using math functions for development, as explained in Book 2, Chapter 6). The point is to make you as efficient as possible when creating Android applications so that some of that time spent learning a new language is repaid by less time spent writing new applications. The advantages are significant enough that companies like Pinterest, Twitter, Netflix, Uber, Airbnb, Trello, and Evernote are making the switch to Kotlin.

As you continue through the chapter, you discover that Kotlin does have a lot to offer and fixes some serious problems, such as getting rid of the dreaded `NullPointerException` by providing built-in null safety. Because the support for null safety comes as part of the Kotlin package, a developer doesn't have to continually write workarounds for the issue.

REMEMBER

The point of this section is that you should move forward with the idea that you'll likely find that Kotlin makes your development experiences simpler, more productive, and less error prone. However, many developers still see Java as a viable Android development option because it still has features to offer that Kotlin doesn't (see the "Nothing's Perfect: Kotlin Is Missing Features, Too" section of the chapter for details). Even if you choose to continue to use Java for your development language, you should learn at least the basics of Kotlin because you'll encounter it at some point when working with other people's code.

Defining the Java Issues That Kotlin Fixes

There aren't any perfect programming languages. Part of the problem is that no one can agree on what constitutes perfect. People like to fight about things, including programming language features. With this in mind, you might feel sorry for Java as the victim of mean-spirited finger pointing by those who just don't like the language. However, as the following sections point out, Java has some real issues that Kotlin attempts to fix. Whether you agree with the fixes is a matter for you to decide, of course.

Improving control over null references

A *null reference* describes an object that points to nothing. It's sort of like having a mailbox on a post outside of an empty lot. Yep, there is a mailbox there, but no one will ever get the mail. The mailbox, the object, seems to point to something, but when you investigate it, you find that it doesn't point to anything at all —the lot is empty. When you try to access an object that points to null in Java, you get the dreaded `NullPointerException`. Of course, the first thing on your mind is determining what happened to the house that's supposed to appear on that empty lot.

Unfortunately, we've been dealing with the null reference since 1965, when Tony Hoare decided to add it to ALGOL W. He calls it his billion-dollar mistake during the 2009 QCon London presentation (see `https://www.infoq.com/presentations/Null-References-The-Billion-Dollar-Mistake-Tony-Hoare/`). When the inventor of a method of doing something says it was a horrid mistake, getting rid of it seems like a good idea. But getting rid of the null reference would mean breaking a lot of Java code, so that's where Kotlin comes into play.

REMEMBER

Kotlin doesn't actually remove null references entirely, but it does help you control them better. For example, the following code results in a compilation error in Kotlin:

```
var a: String = "abc"
a = null
println(a)
```

A `String` is a non-nullable type. (Chapter 5 of this minibook explores nullable types.) The type system ensures that you can't place a `null` value in `a` for any reason. Consequently, `a` can never experience a `NullPointerException`.

VAL VERSUS VAR

You see both `val` and `var` used in Kotlin programming for variable declaration. The essential difference between the two is that `val` is final and you can't reassign its value, but `var` is mutable, so you can reassign its value.

Generally, you want to use `val` when you can because it provides some significant advantages in Kotlin, especially when it comes to functional programming techniques that include extremely efficient multiprocessor applications. When working with `val`, you receive these advantages no matter what sort of programming you do. When working with a multithreaded applications, all objects are thread safe by default. You don't have to worry about *race conditions* (where two parts of the code try to access the data at the same time); there are no *concurrency problems* (where multiple parts of the code executed simultaneously and possibly out of order cause inaccurate output); and you never need to sync values. Using immutable variables created with `val` also changes how you write code, making you significantly more conscious about when and how you change values, and reducing errors as a result.

However, sometimes you use `var` because you really do need to stick with the object-oriented view of changing values to write code that is easy to explain. Several of the examples in this chapter would need additional lines of code to write using `val`. You just want to use `var` as seldom as possible.

Of course, there must be allowances. You can tell Kotlin to allow null values in specific cases by using a special operator. The following code defines a nullable `String` and will compile:

```
var a: String? = "abc"
a = null
println(a)
```

However, when you print `a`, what you see is the value `null`, not a `NullPointerException`. Consequently, the null value is still safe. However, it comes with limits. For example, when using the following code, you get an output value of `3`.

```
val a: String = "abc"
println(a.length)
```

The limitation comes when you make `String` nullable. The following code produces a compilation error saying that only safe calls are allowed on nullable `String` objects.

```
val a: String? = "abc"
println(a.length)
```

You still might want to check the length of a. Kotlin has a workaround for this issue as well. The following code first determines whether a is null and, if it isn't, returns length:

```
val a: String? = "abc"
println(a?.length)
```

TIP

What if you want to assign a potentially null value to another variable? In this case, you rely on the Elvis operator (?:). The following code safely assigns that length of a to b, unless a is null, in which case, b receives a value of 0:

```
val a: String? = "abc"
val b = a?.length ?: 0
println(b)
```

It seems that Kotlin is quite determined not to allow you to produce a NullPointerException in your code. If you're equally determined to produce one, you can use the not-null assertion operator (!!), as shown in the following code:

```
val a: String? = null
println(a!!.length)
```

TECHNICAL STUFF

Kotlin goes only so far to protect you from yourself. You can still see a NullPointerException in these situations:

- The throw NullPointerException() being specifically called by the code.
- The use of the non-null assertion operator (!!), described earlier.
- A data inconsistency that results from improper initialization:
  - The this object found in a constructor is passed to some other code (called a "leaking this" problem).
  - A superclass constructor calls on an open member that is supposed to be initialized in a derived class, but isn't (see https://kotlinlang.org/docs/reference/classes.html#derived-class-initialization-order for details).
- Your code calling Java code that produces a NullPointerException. Unfortunately, Kotlin can't protect you from Java.

Kotlin for Java Programmers

Removing raw data types

A *raw data type* occurs when you create a generic Java type without specifying a data type as part of the declaration. For example, here is a raw data type in Java:

```
List names = Arrays.asList("John", "Mia", "Herb", "Ann");
```

This code will compile in Java. The problem with this code is that you have no idea what data type `names` contains; it could be anything. More important, the compiler now has to guess what data type to use, and forcing the compiler to guess is always a bad idea. Plus, to use the values in `names`, you must now cast the individual entries, such as

```
Iterator iter = stars.iterator();
while(iter.hasNext()) {
  String name = (String) iter.next(); //cast needed
  println(name);
}
```

Kotlin can use Java types. In fact, you can interoperate with Java successfully using the techniques described at `https://kotlinlang.org/docs/reference/java-interop.html`. However, to use `names` in Kotlin, you must specifically declare a type, as shown here:

```
val names: List<String> =
   Arrays.asList("John", "Mia", "Herb", "Ann")

for (name in names){
    println(name)
}
```

Notice that using Java types in Kotlin is a little different from how you use them in Java. However, the basic principle is the same. You define `names` as type `List<String>` and then assign it names using `Arrays.asList("John", "Mia", "Herb", "Ann")`. The point is that you can't use raw data types because the compiler will display an error.

Using invariant arrays

When working with Java, you can copy an array of a specific type, such as `String`, to an array of type `Object`. You can then manipulate the items in the `Object` array as desired. Consequently, code like this will compile without problem in Java:

```
String[] stuff = {"Tom", "Sam", "Ann"};
Object[] moreStuff = stuff;
```

You can do things this way because arrays are *covariant* in Java. `String` is subclassed from `Object`, so an `Object` can contain a `String`. However, when you're able to do things like this, you can encounter problems. Consider the following code:

```
String a = stuff[0];
System.out.println(a);
String b = moreStuff[0];
System.out.println(b);
```

This code won't compile because Java loses track of the type of the data in `moreStuff`. It now views element `0` as an `Object`, not a `String`, so it can't make the second assignment to `b`. Of course, you can overcome this issue by using a cast: `String b = (String)moreStuff[0];`. However, now that you've fixed one problem, you have another. Look at this code:

```
String a = stuff[0];
System.out.println(a);
moreStuff[0] = 5;
String b = (String)moreStuff[0];
System.out.println(b);
```

You now get a runtime error because you can't cast an `Integer` (the changed type of `moreStuff[0]`) to a `String`. Java overcomes this problem by using generics, which are *invariant* (objects must be of the same type when you set one equal to the other). This code won't compile because converting a `String` to an `Object` isn't possible.

```
List<String> stuff = Arrays.asList("Tom", "Sam", "Ann");
List<Object> moreStuff = stuff;
```

Generics are invariant in Java. Likewise, arrays are invariant in Kotlin. Consequently, this Kotlin code won't compile for the same reason that generics won't compile in Java:

```
val stuff: Array<String> = arrayOf("Tom", "Sam", "Ann")
val moreStuff: Array<Any> = stuff
```

Working with proper function types

The term *proper function types* refers to the kind of programming performed using lambda functions in a functional programming way (see Book 2, Chapter 6 for an explanation of functional programming principles). Most Java developers aren't really familiar with functional programming because functional programming is historically difficult to implement in Java, and addressing all the tenets of functional programming isn't possible. However, Java developers can perform functional programming after a fashion by using techniques such as Single Abstract Method (SAM) conversions. To give you some idea of how functional programming differs from Java programming, here are the basic tenets:

- Creating functions that are first-class objects
- Using pure functions
- Employing higher-order functions
- Relying on a lack of function state
- Depending on an absence of side effects
- Using immutable variables
- Favoring recursion over looping

As you can see, trying to implement most of these requirements in Java would be impossible, or at least nearly so. However, the article at `http://tutorials.jenkov.com/java-functional-programming/index.html` demonstrates that some of them are possible and that there are distinct benefits to using this functional programming approach. For example, here's an example of a Java pure function:

```
public class performSum{

    public int sum(int a, int b) {
        return a + b;
    }
}
```

The function doesn't have state, it doesn't use any sort of member variables, and it relies only on the input variables. Because of this, you can be sure that every call to this function with a given set of inputs will have precisely the same result every time.

Java's lambda functionality relies on SAM, which is an interface version (also called a functional interface) of the pure function. Here's an example of SAM:

```
public interface OnClickListener {
    void onClick(View v);
}
```

A SAM conversion occurs when Java converts the SAM interface into functional code. Here is the lambda expression for the SAM interface:

```
myView.setOnClickListener((view) -> logger.debug(
    "View Clicked!"));
```

TIP

Unlike Java, Kotlin provides first-class support for lambda functions. You don't have to create an interface specification in Kotlin to achieve the desired result — all you need is a signature specification provided as part of your function. Consequently, the Kotlin version of the Java example looks like this:

```
fun setOnClickListener(listener: (view: View) -> Unit) {
   // ...
}
```

Notice that the listener is defined as part of the function signature. The signature defines the callable parameters and the resulting output. More important, a callable parameter can be just about anything, including a function. This is an extremely quick overview of a more complex process. Chapter 6 of this minibook tells you more about the functional programming capabilities found in Kotlin.

TECHNICAL STUFF

The main issue to consider when working with the Kotlin form of lambda expressions is that the Kotlin form is essentially incompatible with the Java form, making interop a lot more difficult to deal with. You can use the Java form of lambda expressions in Kotlin when working with Java code. However, when working with Kotlin code, you must use the Kotlin form instead, which means that you now have to know two ways of making lambda expressions work.

Getting rid of the checked exceptions

Checked exceptions may have seemed like a good idea at first because the developer is forced to ensure that code using particular methods also checks for exceptions that can occur as a result of relying on that method. Over the years, however, developers have found that checked exceptions don't necessarily create robust code and that they do waste a lot of time. Here are some resources to consider:

- **Anders Hejlsberg:** `https://www.artima.com/intv/handcuffs.html`
- **Rod Waldhoff:** `http://radio-weblogs.com/0122027/stories/2003/04/01/JavasCheckedExceptionsWereAMistake.html`

The point of these articles is that checked exceptions were an experiment that didn't work. Languages that follow the Java example don't use them for a good reason. When you look at C# and Ruby, you don't see checked exceptions, so it's hardly a surprise that Kotlin eliminates them, too.

Nothing's Perfect: Kotlin Is Missing Features, Too

Whenever you create a new language and seek to get rid of problems in an older language, you end up weighing the pros and cons of each change. Sometimes you throw out features used by the older language that will cause users of the new language woe during code updates. Whether you consider the following omissions from Java in Kotlin a problem depends on how you use Java. Perhaps they aren't an issue, but you still need to know about them.

Considering primitive types that are not classes

A *primitive type* is one that a language represents in the same form as that which the processor sees (which is only numbers). In times past, primitive types could result in significant processing speed improvements and storage efficiency benefits. A primitive type `int` requires only four bytes of storage space, fits easily in a 32-bit register in the processor, and requires no special fiddling to work with the processor. A Java `int` can hold any value between −2,147,483,648 to 2,147,483,647, but it doesn't offer any functions beyond those that the processor offers. To obtain modern functionality, you must place the primitive type within an object in a process called `boxing`. The object takes more memory, runs slower, and doesn't look the same as what the processor works with, but it's also more functional.

Kotlin doesn't offer primitive types. Every number is an object that has a storage capacity that corresponds to those processor registers of old, but it's only for convention. Because the numbers are objects, you could actually create them to be in any form. However, conventions are important. Consequently, a Kotlin `Int` is still 32-bits in size and still has a range of −2,147,483,648 to 2,147,483,647.

Losing static members

A *static member* is one that a subclass doesn't inherit from a superclass; instead, the static member exists essentially outside the class and is just an inclusion within the class code. You can access static members without creating an instance of the class. When working with a static variable, you can access the value of that variable without creating an instance of the class, such as the use of `java.lang.Math.PI`, which provides access to the value of pi in Java. Likewise, when using a static method, you access the method without creating an instance of the class. For example, `java.lang.Math.abs()` returns the absolute value of a number.

TIP

Kotlin does have equivalent functionality. For example, `kotlin.math.PI` returns the value of pi in Kotlin. The difference is in the implementation. When working with Kotlin, you use a companion object in place of a static member. Here's an example of a companion object implementation for both a variable and a function:

```
class Secrets {
  companion object {
    val secretNumber = 52
    fun getPhrase():String { return "The Secret Phrase" }
  }
}
```

To call these companion objects, you could use code like this:

```
println(Secrets.secretNumber)
println(Secrets.getPhrase())
```

So, it would seem as if static members and companion objects are the same, but they aren't. A companion object is part of the class and can inherit from other classes. Unlike static members, companion objects are flexible and relatively easy to test because they are part of the host class.

Eliminating non-private fields

Java can use *non-private fields* (essentially a kind of variable) within classes to hold values, which can be problematic because the field can become corrupted in all sorts of ways without checks. Because the field is non-private, an entity outside the class can access it, which results in a lack of control.

A better solution is to use properties. A *property* has a getter and a setter that are used to access a private field. The getter and setter can contain code to validate any change to the field before the change happens, making access controlled and less prone to errors.

Kotlin uses only properties. A property declared using `val` is read-only (has only a getter), while a property declared using `var` is read-write (has both a getter and a setter). The default getter and setter are empty, which means no actual checks are made, but you can define code to perform whatever checks are needed. Chapter 5 of this minibook fills you in on the details of working with classes in Kotlin.

Reducing confusion by eliminating wildcard-types

In Java, a *wildcard type* is a type that isn't known at the time of writing a generic type function. You represent it using the question mark (?). The problem with a wildcard type is the fact that incompatibilities exist between instantiations of generic types. Even though the following Java code works, the ambiguity of the generic type can become problematic because you could call `sum()` with something that's not compatible.

```
public static void main(String []args){
   List<Integer> list1 = Arrays.asList(1, 2, 3);
   System.out.println("Total sum is:"+sum(list1));

   List<Double> list2 = Arrays.asList(1.1, 2.2, 3.3);
   System.out.print("Total sum is:"+sum(list2));
}

private static double sum(List<?> list)
{
    double sum=0.0;
    for (Object i: list)
    {
        double addend = ((Number)i).doubleValue();
        sum+=addend;
    }

    return sum;
}
```

To see why this particular code is such a serious problem (and you typically wouldn't write it this way, but this is an example, after all), try calling `sum()` with the following code:

```
List<String> list3=Arrays.asList("A", "B", "C");
System.out.print("Total sum is:"+sum(list3));
```

Obviously, you can't add three `String` values together using `sum()`, but the code still compiles. Java actually supports a number of wildcard implementations, all of which have potential compatibility issues.

Kotlin uses a different approach to working with generics. In this case, you'd probably replace the `sum()` method with the following `sum()` function in Kotlin:

```
fun main(args: Array<String>) {
    val list1: Array<Number?> = arrayOf(1, 2, 3)
    println("Total sum is: "+sum(list1))
    val list2: Array<Number?> = arrayOf(1.1, 2.2, 3.3)
    println("Total sum is: "+sum(list2))
}

fun sum(list: Array<Number?>) : Double {
    var sum: Double = 0.0
    for (i in list){
        sum += i!!.toDouble()
    }
    return sum
}
```

Because this code has less ambiguity, it has fewer chances to create potential problems. Code such as `val list3: Array<Number?> = arrayOf("A", "B", "C")` won't even compile with the Kotlin version.

Abandoning the ternary-operator a ? b : c

The Java ternary-operator is essentially a short if . . . then . . . else statement. It's a handy notation to use when you need to make a quick decision. The condition appears first, followed by a question mark with the true output, and then a colon with the false output. Here's an example in Java:

```
Integer value = 22;
System.out.println(
    (value > 10) ? "Big Number" : "Small Number");
```

The problem with this terse bit of code is that it can become hard to read, so Kotlin doesn't provide it. However, there is a short form of the Kotlin if . . . then . . . else statement that can appear on a single line, yet remain easy to read. Here is the equivalent version in Kotlin:

```
val value: Int = 22
println(
    if (value > 10) "Big Number" else "Small Number")
```

Looking at What Kotlin Adds to the Picture

When you build a new language, you want to add all the features that you felt were missing in the language you used before. It's just like buying a new car or appliance: You expect to see all the latest gizmos in it. Why buy an old-technology refrigerator when the new one will automatically order everything you use for you? Likewise, it's not surprising that Kotlin contains an interesting array of new features that you won't find in Java. The sections that follow tell you about those new features.

Considering higher order functions and lambdas

Chapter 6 of this minibook considers the issue of higher-order functions and lambda expressions in detail. However, from an overview perspective, a *higher-order function* is one that is able to accept functions as input. A higher-order function can also return a function as output. Consequently, you see higher order functions being used to manipulate collections or perform certain kinds of analysis.

A lambda expression provides an elegant way to define an operation in a simple manner. You assign what amounts to an anonymous function to a variable like this:

```
val sum: (Int, Int) -> (Int) = {x: Int, y: Int -> x + y}

println(sum(1, 2))
```

The benefit of using lambda expressions is that they provide a convenient method of passing input to a higher order function. Of course, they're quite handy all on their own as well.

Refining object orientation using extension functions

Extension functions make it possible to add functionality to an existing class without having to inherit from the class or use design patterns such as Decorator. What you do instead is to define an extension function like the one shown here:

```
fun Int.name(): String{
    return "Extension Function"
}

fun main(args: Array<String>) {
    val myInt: Int = 22

    println(myInt.name())
}
```

Obviously, you wouldn't normally extend a class in this manner, but this example offers a simple illustration of an extension function. The extension function adds a new method, `name()`, to `Int` using a special declaration. The example outputs `"Extension Function"`, as you might expect.

TIP

This feature has some interesting applications, such as the ability to extend a third-party class even when you don't have the source code for it. You can even create generic extension functions when needed.

REMEMBER

Chapter 5 of this minibook discusses Kotlin object orientation in depth, but an important thing to remember about extension functions is that you aren't actually modifying the original class. Nor are you creating a new class. This means that you can't do things like override the member functions of the existing class. If your extension class has the same name as a member function, the member function always wins.

You can also create extension properties using techniques similar to those used to create extension functions. An extension property has the same limits as an extension function does, but you'll find them incredibly useful in some cases. Chapter 5 of this minibook also discusses extension properties.

Relying on smart casts

The Kotlin compiler spends a great deal more time looking over your shoulder, which helps it perform casts in a smart way much of the time. You don't have to cast a variable to a particular type when the compiler can detect the type in context. For example, consider this code:

```
fun printIt(input: Any){
    if (input is String){
        print("Input length is: " + input.length)
    } else if (input is Int){
        print("Input Byte value is: " + input.toByte())
    } else {
```

```
        print("Input is not a string or integer.")
    }
}

fun main(args: Array<String>) {
    val myString: String = "Hello There!"
    val myInt: Int = 220220
    val myBool: Boolean = true

    printIt(myString)
    println()
    printIt(myInt)
    println()
    printIt(myBool)
}
```

Even though the type of `input` in `printIt()` starts as `Any`, the compiler performs the appropriate cast automatically to perform the expected tasks of the required type. For example, when the detected type is `String`, `input` automatically is cast as a `String`, you don't have to do it manually. The smart cast makes the appropriate methods and properties available for the given type, such as `length` when working with a `String` or `toByte()` when working with an `Int`.

TIP

You can still specifically cast one type to another. In addition, Kotlin provides support for unsafe casts, safe nullable casts, and unchecked casts. Chapter 3 of this minibook tells you more about these and other type-related topics.

Employing string templates

String templates make it easier to present formatted text onscreen. A string template begins with a dollar sign (`$`), followed by an expression. Having a `$` by itself doesn't constitute a template; you must follow it with an expression of some sort. Complex expressions can appear in curly braces (`{}`). In addition, you can use string templates inside raw strings. Here are some examples of string templates:

```
val amount: Double = 9.99
val greeting: String = "Hello There!"
val complex: String = """${'$'}$amount"""

println("The amount is: $$amount.")
println("The greeting has a length of: " +
       "${greeting.length}.")
println("The complex value is: $complex.")
```

Looking at the first output, you see that the first $ appears alone, so it isn't a string template. However, the second $ is followed by an expression, so it is a string template.

The second output uses curly braces because the expression is somewhat complex: You're accessing a property rather than a value. As with any other string, you can break strings with string templates across multiple lines of code.

The third output contains a raw string. Notice how the string is constructed in this case. The first string template contains a string literal and the second string template contains an expression. Here is the result of these three `println()` calls:

```
The amount is: $9.99.
The greeting has a length of: 12.
The complex value is: $9.99.
```

Understanding primary constructors

When creating a class, you can define one primary constructor and one or more secondary constructors. The *primary constructor* appears as part of the class declaration and contains no code. Rather, you use a series of initializers to define the default state of any object instantiated using the class. The point is that a class will always have a primary constructor, even if you don't define one. The default constructor is public and blank. It's the default constructor used when working with the class.

A *secondary constructor* appears within the class code. It begins with the word *constructor*, provides a unique signature, and contains a block with initialization code. You aren't required to create any secondary constructors for a class. They serve only to provide a different behavior from the primary constructor. Secondary constructors must delegate to the primary constructor either directly or indirectly through another secondary constructor when the class has a primary constructor defined.

Chapter 5 of this minibook contains more information about how the two types of constructors work, along with examples of their construction.

Implementing first-class delegation

Kotlin relies on the delegation pattern (`http://best-practice-software-engineering.ifs.tuwien.ac.at/patterns/delegation.html`) instead of implementation inheritance. The *delegation pattern* lets a class present methods and properties as being part of the class implementation, even when it delegates that implementation to another class. Unlike some other implementations, the Kotlin implementation manages all this without requiring you to write a ton of boiler-plate code — you simply express the delegated connections, as shown here:

```
interface Base {
    val message: String
    fun printMessage()
    fun printValue()
}

class BaseImpl(val value1: Int) : Base {
    override val message = "The value is $value1."
    override fun printMessage() {println(message)}
    override fun printValue() {println(value1)}
}

class Derived(value2: Int) : Base by BaseImpl(value2) {
    override val message = "Derived value is ${value2/2}"
    override fun printMessage() {println(message + ".")}
}

fun main(args: Array<String>) {
    val value3 = 10
    BaseImpl(value3).printMessage()
    Derived(value3).printMessage()
    Derived(value3).printValue()

    val derived = Derived(20)
    derived.printMessage()
    derived.printValue()
}
```

The `BaseImpl` class begins by implementing all the requirements of the `Base` interface. `Derived` delegates some of the `Base` interface implementation to `BaseImpl` using `Base by BaseImpl(value2)`. You can still call `printValue()` from `Derived`, no matter how you interact with it. However, `Derived` also has unique implementations of both message and `printMessage()`. Notice that the `Derived` version of `message` lacks a period, so it gets added later. When you run this example, you see the following output:

```
The value is 10.
Derived value is 5.
10
Derived value is 10.
20
```

Chapter 5 of this minibook contains more information about how the delegation pattern works in Kotlin.

Using ranges of values

Kotlin has a nice feature for working with ranges of values. You can specify the range by simply separating the starting and ending point with a range operator (..). For example, to print the numbers 1 through 4, you could use code like this:

```
for(i in 1..4) print(i)
```

It's also possible to print the numbers in reverse using this code:

```
for(i in 4 downTo 1) print(i)
```

Notice that you use `downTo` in place of `..` in this case. If you want to display only certain numbers, you can apply a `step` value, like this:

```
for(i in 1..8 step 2) print(i)
```

In addition to the standard ranges you might expect, you can also apply filtering and mapping to ranges. For example, the following code shows the effects of a filter first, followed by a map:

```
val intRange = 1..20
println(intRange.filter { it % 3 == 0 })
println(intRange.map {it -> it * it})
```

The filter displays only the values that are divisible by 3: `[3, 6, 9, 12, 15, 18]`. The map displays the square of all the values in the range: `[1, 4, 9, 16, 25, 36, 49, 64, 81, 100, 121, 144, 169, 196, 225, 256, 289, 324, 361, 400]`.

TIP

Don't get the idea that ranges work only for numbers. You can also use them for other data types, such as characters:

```
for (chr in 'a'..'f') print(chr)
```

However, to use ranges in this manner, your data type must provide an iterator. So, the native Kotlin support won't support iterating a date range in this manner, although you can use it for other purposes. Fortunately, developers are already working on a date iterator (see `https://gist.github.com/elye/5c107e9c8e9121d785f4ddfa103f5808`).

Creating data classes

It often happens that a class is used exclusively to hold data. Writing a lot of code to make this happen seems like a waste of effort. The data class makes things easy. All you need to do is define your data class using the `data` keyword, as shown here:

```
data class Point(val x: Int = 0, val y: Int = 0)

fun main(args: Array<String>) {
    val myPoint: Point = Point(2, 4)
    println(myPoint.toString())
}
```

The output you receive from `toString()` is `Point(x=2, y=4)`. You can also access specific data members using properties, such as `myPoint.x`, which in this case outputs a value of 2. When needed, you can override the default `copy()`, `equals()`, `hashCode()`, and `toString()` functions.

TIP

The data class shown in this example provides default values for `x` and `y` of `0`. This means that `x` and `y` will always have a value, even if the caller doesn't provide them.

The difference between `val` and `var` is important here because the example shown won't allow changes to `x` and `y`. If you want to make changes, you need to declare `x` and `y` as `var`.

You can also add properties and methods to a data class. See Chapter 5 of this minibook for more information about the specifics of data classes.

Overloading operators

The previous section discusses the data class. Sometimes you need to create a specific implementation of operators for your data class, and Kotlin provides a convenient method for doing so. Here is an example of the Point class from the previous section modified to allow a unary minus operator:

```
data class Point(var x: Int = 0, var y: Int = 0)

operator fun Point.unaryMinus() = Point(x - 1, y - 1)

fun main(args: Array<String>) {
    val myPoint: Point = Point(2, 4)
```

```
    println(myPoint)
    println(-myPoint)
}
```

Notice that the second `println()` call includes a unary minus operator. Consequently, the output from this example is

```
Point(x=2, y=4)
Point(x=1, y=3)
```

Developing asynchronous code using coroutines

Asynchronous programming allows apps to scale and to be fully responsive to user needs by offloading a request and immediately returning to the main app. At some point, the offloaded request responds and the main app can do something with it. A full discussion of asynchronous programming and the use of coroutines won't fit in this chapter. Kotlin provides coroutines for the purpose of making asynchronous programming relatively easy. In general, you won't use this form of programming for Android development because of how Android apps are designed (they're naturally asynchronous). You can read more about this methodology at `https://kotlinlang.org/docs/reference/coroutines-overview.html`.

IN THIS CHAPTER

» How computers, phones, and other devices run Kotlin programs

» The parts of a typical Kotlin program

Chapter 3 Kotlin for Everyone

You might have noticed in Chapter 2 of this minibook that Kotlin starts with a Java base but ends up doing a lot more. In fact, it borrows features from Groovy, Scala, C#, and Python as well. Kotlin and Java have many similarities, and you can still write code in Java-style, with limits. However, to realize the full potential of Kotlin, you really need to stick to Kotlin-specific methodologies, which is something that Chapter 2 brings up. Still, there is the question of just how Kotlin and Java compare when it comes to developing and executing applications, which is part of what this chapter will tell you.

Although this chapter focuses on Android development issues, you have quite a bit more to discover with Kotlin. For example, you aren't limited to interacting with just Java. You can also interact with other language files, such as native code C/C++ files (see `https://developer.android.com/studio/projects/add-native-code` for details). You can also compile your code in several ways, such as by creating JavaScript output (see `https://kotlinlang.org/docs/tutorials/javascript/kotlin-to-javascript/kotlin-to-javascript.html` for details). But to do these other amazing things, you need an IDE other than Android Studio.

This chapter, along with Chapters 4, 5, and 6, gives you an overview of the Kotlin language as it applies to Android development, which is to say that we're just covering the basics here. If you want to become a Kotlin expert, you'll actually need to read several books as well as most of the online documentation, plus you'll need to experience all the development environments in which

Kotlin works. For example, you can also use Kotlin for data science apps (see `https://towardsdatascience.com/introduction-to-kotlin-statistics-cdad3be88b5`). The point is that Kotlin is an amazing language within certain realms and well worth the effort to learn.

Moving from Development to Execution with Kotlin

Modern computer languages and development strategies insulate developers from the computer hardware, but a process has to occur from the time you write words that a human can understand to the time the computer executes those instructions as machine code. This process varies by language, but some parts are similar across all computer languages, such as the requirement to perform some type of translation. Keep reading for a brief overview of this process as it applies to Kotlin.

What is a compiler?

At one time, computer scientists worked with computers using machine code. You can check out a demonstration of using a switch panel to create an app for a PDP-8 using machine code at `https://www.youtube.com/watch?v=yUZrn7qTGcs`. When you watch this video, you wonder how computer scientists got anything useful done, but they did. Most computers use the concept of an *opcode,* a number that changes the switch positions within the computer, and an *operand,* the data used to perform a task. The combination of opcode and operand form a *computer instruction* — a single unit of execution. For example, an opcode might tell the computer to add the values (the operation part) found in two locations (the operands) and to put the result back into the first location. (Other opcodes perform the actual task of moving the data. Computers don't actually do anything automatically.)

Of course, developers didn't continue to use the switch panel. They went through a whole series of steps that occurred to move from using the switch panel to working with assembler, a language that somewhat translates machine code into something a little more human by substituting words for the opcodes used to provide computer instructions (see the list of Intel opcodes at `http://sparksandflames.com/files/x86InstructionChart.html`).

Assembly language (`https://www.cs.virginia.edu/~evans/cs216/guides/x86.html`) is much easier to work with than a series of numbers, but not much. To turn those words into numbers, a developer used an *assembler,* which is a special application designed to perform a translation between what developers can understand and what the machine understands. The resulting executable file contains a combination of opcodes, operands, and data in numeric form that looks similar to the display in Figure 3-1.

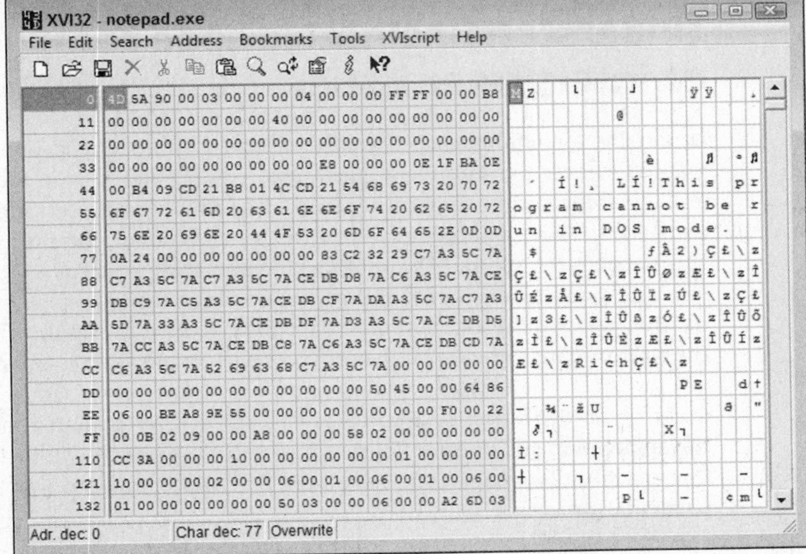

FIGURE 3-1: The contents of an executable file look like nothing more than a series of numbers.

REMEMBER

Assemblers work only when a one-to-one correspondence exists between the human-like words and the machine code. *Compilers* can create multiple lines of machine code for each human word. For example, simply asking the computer to add two numbers infers the move operations as well because the compiler adds them for you. Consequently, modern languages all rely on compilers when creating executable code.

Another form of translation can also occur in the form of an interpreter. An *interpreter* works with the human words in real time, rather than performing the task all at one time as a compiler would. The result is the same, but the difference is when the translation occurs. At one time, developers avoided interpreters for the most part, because they suffered a speed penalty when compared to compiled, native-language code. However, computers are so fast today that it can be hard to tell the difference between compiled and interpreted code unless you perform incredibly complex tasks.

REMEMBER

Whether you use a compiler or an interpreter to directly translate human language into machine code, the result is what developers call *native code.* Native machine code is specific to a particular processor, and it really can't work any other way when you think about it. An Intel processor can't suddenly become fluent in ARM processing instructions, for example.

Understanding native code compiler or interpreter issues

Originally, a single processor would execute a single application at a time. If you wanted to execute multiple applications, you needed to stop the first application and allow the second application to work (switching between the two applications as needed). Early computers went through all sorts of odd machinations to make this happen, but ultimately, multitasking operating systems enabled computers to seemingly do a whole bunch of things at the same time. The operating system takes control over vital resources while appearing to give the application full control of the system. This *virtual environment* gives each application a separate place to run.

Creating an operating system to wrest control over resource management from the application still doesn't address the problem presented in the previous section. The machine language code generated by early compilers was still specific to a particular processor.

A *runtime* can eliminate the problem of processor differences. The runtime interprets an intermediate form of compiled code, called *bytecode,* and performs the final, machine-specific interpretation. That's why your Android app can execute equally well on a smartphone, tablet, local PC, or other device you want to use. The runtime on each device interprets common bytecode and performs the final stage of creating machine language.

You can see how the runtime works for yourself if you have Java installed on your system and you created the examples in Book 1, Chapter 6 (or downloaded the source). Open a command prompt or terminal window and locate the `\01_06_06\app\build\tmp\kotlin-classes\debug\com\allmycode\p01_06_06` folder on your system. In that folder, you find the `MainActivity.class` file. Type **javap -c MainActivity** and press Enter. This act opens the class file and prints the Java bytecode so that you can see it, as shown in Figure 3-2 (which is cropped to fit in the book).

Of course, now you're confused. Aren't you using Kotlin to write the example? The Kotlin compiler produces Java bytecode. It's possible to execute this code directly on the Java Virtual Machine (JVM), or, with addition translation, you can use it on an Android device, within a browser, or create a native code application for your favorite processor. The icons at `https://kotlinlang.org/` tell you all about it.

```
C:\Windows\system32\cmd.exe
C:\AndroidAppAllInOneDummies_3rdEdition_Code\01_06_06\app\build\tmp\kotlin-classes\debug\com\allmy
Warning: Binary file MainActivity contains com.allmycode.p01_06_06.MainActivity
Compiled from "MainActivity.kt"
public final class com.allmycode.p01_06_06.MainActivity extends androidx.appcompat.app.AppCompatAc
  protected void onCreate(android.os.Bundle);
    Code:
       0: aload_0
       1: aload_1
       2: invokespecial #9                  // Method androidx/appcompat/app/AppCompatActivity.onC
       5: aload_0
       6: ldc           #10                 // int 2131296284
       8: invokevirtual #14                 // Method setContentView:(I)V
      11: return

  public final void onButtonClick(android.view.View);
    Code:
       0: aload_1
       1: ldc           #23                 // String view
       3: invokestatic  #29                 // Method kotlin/jvm/internal/Intrinsics.checkParamete
       6: new           #31                 // class java/lang/StringBuilder
       9: dup
      10: invokespecial #35                 // Method java/lang/StringBuilder."<init>":()V
      13: astore_2
      14: aload_0
      15: getstatic     #41                 // Field com/allmycode/p01_06_06/R$id.checkBox:I
      18: invokevirtual #45                 // Method _$_findCachedViewById:(I)Landroid/view/View;
      21: checkcast     #47                 // class android/widget/CheckBox
      24: invokevirtual #51                 // Method android/widget/CheckBox.isChecked:()Z
      27: ifeq          37
      30: aload_2
```

FIGURE 3-2: The bytecode created for MainActivity.kt.

REMEMBER

The most important thing to discover about Figure 3-2 is that you can actually follow the bytecode instructions and compare them to your original code. Notice that you can find the declaration for `onButtonClick()` without problem. If you look a little further down, you see that Kotlin is indeed part of this method in its call to `kotlin/jvm/internal/Intrinsics.checkParameterIsNotNull()`. Directly below this call, you see some Java interaction with a call to `java/lang/StringBuilder."<init>":()`. Although reviewing the bytecode isn't necessary, it can be interesting because doing so helps you understand how things work under the covers.

Considering the Android Runtime (ART)

A runtime environment can take multiple forms. The form used by Android is a virtual machine. A *virtual machine* is essentially an emulation of the runtime that allows multiple apps to run in their own copy of the environment, combining platform independence with a multitasking operating system. The Android Runtime (ART) virtual machine enables you to have multiple apps open simultaneously without allowing those apps to interfere with each other except through specific rules.

Virtual machines create order from the chaos of working with multiple devices that could have any number of Android versions installed on them and rely on various processors. Each virtual machine performs the tasks required to make a given set of bytecodes work.

The ART translates your Kotlin code into something that it can understand; it goes through several translation steps, as shown in Figure 3-3. Dalvik refers to the previous virtual machine used for Android (see the "What is Dalvik?" sidebar for details), and the process keeps it in place for backward compatibility. However, any new apps you create rely on ART for execution, so that's what you should focus on.

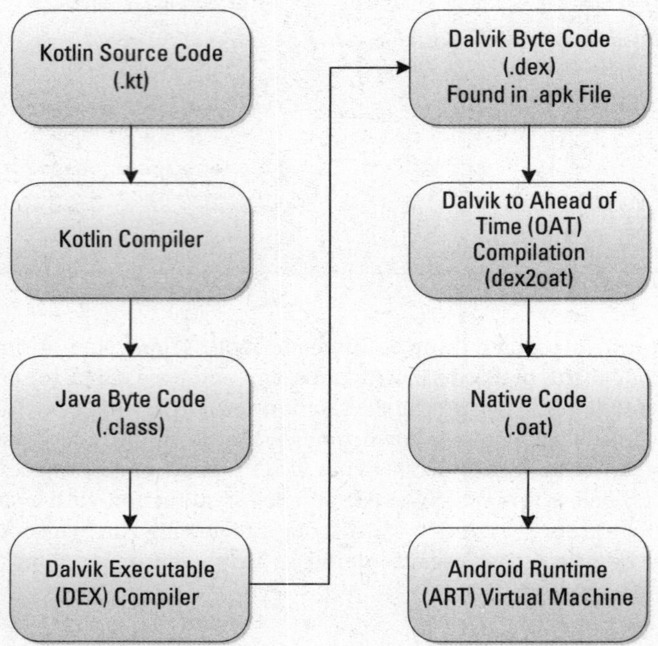

FIGURE 3-3: The translation process for an Android app.

You see how the first several steps of this process work in the "Understanding native code compiler or interpreter issues" section, earlier in this chapter. To understand the use of the Dalvik Executable (DEX) compiler, you need to look inside the Android Package (APK) file generated as part of the project. This is the file that you upload to the device in order to install your app. Fortunately, you can easily see and analyze the `.apk` file by choosing Build⇨Analyze APK. . . from the Android Studio menu. What you see is a list of the `.apk` file contents, as shown in Figure 3-4.

As you can see, the file contains a lot more than just the classes used to run your app. Here's a quick rundown on the various entries shown in Figure 3-4:

- **classes.dex:** The compiled classes for the DEX version of your application code. This bytecode won't match the Java bytecode you saw in Figure 3-2. To see the difference for yourself, click the `classes.dex` entry to display the list of classes shown in Figure 3-5.

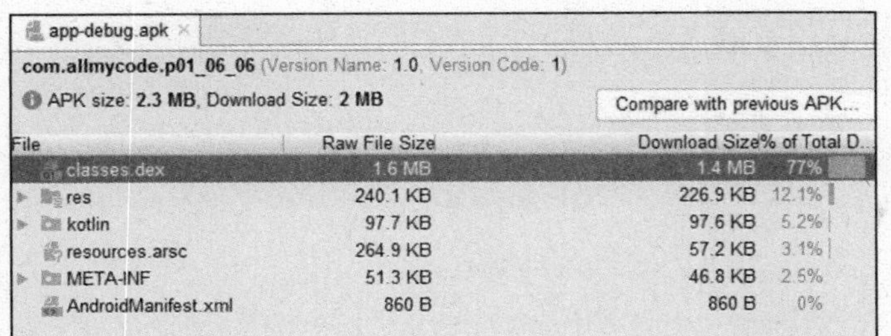

app-debug.apk

com.allmycode.p01_06_06 (Version Name: 1.0, Version Code: 1)

APK size: 2.3 MB, Download Size: 2 MB

Compare with previous APK...

File	Raw File Size	Download Size	% of Total D...
classes.dex	1.6 MB	1.4 MB	77%
res	240.1 KB	226.9 KB	12.1%
kotlin	97.7 KB	97.6 KB	5.2%
resources.arsc	264.9 KB	57.2 KB	3.1%
META-INF	51.3 KB	46.8 KB	2.5%
AndroidManifest.xml	860 B	860 B	0%

FIGURE 3-4: Seeing the content of the .apk file.

Load Proguard mappings... nes 2383 classes with 19324 methods, and references 25616 methods.

Class	Defined Methods	Referenced Methods	Size
kotlin	7469	8286	920.3 KB
android	19	3225	80.4 KB
java		989	24.1 KB
org	23	39	3.3 KB
com	22	24	31.4 KB
allmycode	22	24	31.4 KB
p01_06_06	22	24	31.4 KB
MainActivity	5	7	802 B
<init>()	1	1	56 B
void _$_clearFindViewByIdCache()	1	1	58 B
android.view.View _$_findCachedViewById(int)	1	1	125 B
void onButtonClick(android.view.View)	1	1	360 B
void onCreate(android.os.Bundle)	1	1	76 B
android.view.View findViewById(int)		1	26 B
void setContentView(int)		1	26 B
java.util.HashMap _$_findViewCache			11 B
BuildConfig	2	2	237 B

FIGURE 3-5: Classes in the `classes.dex` file.

Figure 3-2 shows the Java bytecode for the `onButtonClick()` method. Right-click this same method for the DEX bytecode and choose Show Bytecode from the context menu. You see the DEX bytecode in Figure 3-6, which you can now compare to the Java bytecode (should you want to do so).

REMEMBER

The differences are quite noticeable and should tell you that each virtual machine speaks its own language. For example, `new #31` in Java bytecode translates to `new-instance v0, Ljava/lang/StringBuilder` in DEX.

- **res:** Uncompiled resources for your app, such as images.
- **kotlin:** Contains a list of Kotlin classes that aren't compiled into the `classes.dex` file. Rather, they're mapped to existing types on the target platform.
- **resources.arsc:** Contains the compiled resources for your app. When you choose this entry, you can see the list of resources and drill down into them to see specific entries, such as the `Checkbox1Text` entry shown in Figure 3-7.
- **META-INF:** Contains the manifest file, signature, and a list of resources in the .apk file.
- **AndroidManifest.xml:** Describes the name, version, and contents of the .apk file. You can read all the details of this file in the "The AndroidManifest.xml file" section of Book 1, Chapter 4.

DEX Byte Code for void onButtonClick(android.view.View)

```
.method public final onButtonClick(Landroid/view/View;)V
    .registers 7
    .param p1, "view"    # Landroid/view/View;

    const-string v0, "view"

    invoke-static {p1, v0}, Lkotlin/jvm/internal/Intrinsics;->checkParameterIsNotNull(Ljava/lang/Object

    .line 20
    new-instance v0, Ljava/lang/StringBuilder;

    invoke-direct {v0}, Ljava/lang/StringBuilder;-><init>()V

    .line 22
    .local v0, "builder":Ljava/lang/StringBuilder;
    sget v1, Lcom/allmycode/p01_06_06/R$id;->checkBox:I

    invoke-virtual {p0, v1}, Lcom/allmycode/p01_06_06/MainActivity;->_$_findCachedViewById(I)Landroid/v

    move-result-object v1

    check-cast v1, Landroid/widget/CheckBox;

    invoke-virtual {v1}, Landroid/widget/CheckBox;->isChecked()Z

    move-result v1

    if-eqz v1, :cond_1d
```

FIGURE 3-6: Viewing the DEX bytecode.

Package: com.allmycode.p01_06_06

Resource Types: anim, attr, bool, color, dimen, drawable, id, integer, layout, mipmap, string, style

There are **46** string resources across **86** configurations

ID	Name	default	ca	da
0x7f0b0000	Button1Click	onButton...		
0x7f0b0001	Button1Text	Show		
0x7f0b0002	Checkbox1Text	Pepperoni		
0x7f0b0003	Checkbox2Text	Extra Ch...		
0x7f0b0004	abc_action_bar_home_description	Navigate ...	Navega a...	Naviger hj...
0x7f0b0005	abc_action_bar_up_description	Navigate up	Navega c...	Naviger op
0x7f0b0006	abc_action_menu_overflow_description	More opti...	Més opci...	Flere mul...
0x7f0b0007	abc_action_mode_done	Done	Fet	Luk
0x7f0b0008	abc_activity_chooser_view_see_all	See all	Mostra'ls ...	Se alle
0x7f0b0009	abc_activitychooserview_choose_applic...	Choose a...	Seleccio...	Vælg en ...
0x7f0b000a	abc_capital_off	OFF	DESACTI...	FRA
0x7f0b000b	abc_capital_on	ON	ACTIVAT...	TIL

FIGURE 3-7: Seeing the list of compiled resources for your app.

After you install the `.apk` file on an Android device, another series of translations takes place. DEX provides a convenient method of working with all Android devices. However, the bytecode still isn't specific to one particular device. The dex2oat compiler takes a generic `.dex` file and compiles it into a device-specific native code `.oat` file (which, oddly, stands for Of Ahead of Time, or OAT; this book uses the natural word order, which is Ahead of Time). It's this code that the ART virtual machine actually runs on a particular device. Wow! All that work just to say Hello World.

WHAT IS DALVIK?

Before there was ART, Android relied on Dalvik as a runtime. Back in 2007, along with Dalvik bytecode, the folks at Google created a Dalvik virtual machine. This virtual machine runs Android apps on devices running Cupcake, Donut, and all the desserts up to and including KitKat. But in 2013, Google announced a replacement for Dalvik called ART. ART still uses Dalvik bytecode of the kind shown in Figure 3-2. (Despite what you read in the tabloids, Dalvik hasn't gone away entirely.) But after your code is translated to Dalvik bytecode, ART takes advantage of the enhanced horsepower in newer smartphones. In general, an app that's executed with ART runs much faster than the same app executed with Dalvik. By default, every app created for the Android Lollipop (and beyond) target runs on the newer ART virtual machine.

One of the big differences between the Dalvik and ART virtual machines is the time when a final translation step takes place. The Dalvik machine uses just-in-time (JIT) compilation, which means that the final translation takes place as needed while the app runs on a user's device. But wait! Doesn't that final translation take up time during the run? Doesn't the user notice slower performance while the phone does a last translation step on the code? Yes! JIT compilation slows down the run of an app. In contrast to Dalvik's JIT compilation, ART uses ahead-of-time (AOT) compilation. With AOT, an app's final translation takes place when the app is being installed on a device. By the time a user runs the app, the app's code has already been translated. That's one of the reasons why ART's virtual machine is faster than Dalvik's.

Grasping Kotlin Code

When you create a new Empty Activity project, Android's tools create a small, no-nonsense Kotlin class. (Other project templates create classes that are more complicated.) Listing 3-1 shows this class.

LISTING 3-1: A Minimalistic Android Activity Class

```
package com.example.myfirstapp

import androidx.appcompat.app.AppCompatActivity
import android.os.Bundle

class MainActivity : AppCompatActivity() {

    override fun onCreate(savedInstanceState: Bundle?) {
```

(continued)

LISTING 3-1: ***(continued)***

```
        super.onCreate(savedInstanceState)
        setContentView(R.layout.activity_main)
    }
}
```

This chapter covers the Kotlin language features used in Listing 3-1. So in this chapter, `androidx.appcompat.app.AppCompatActivity` (from the second line of Listing 3-1) is only the name of something to import — nothing more. To read about the meaning of the word `Activity` and the word's implications for Android, see Book 3, Chapter 3.

Nearly everything begins with an expression

Kotlin embraces functional programming, and one of the tenets of functional programming is that everything is an expression or a declaration, rather than a statement, as is used for imperative programming. However, Kotlin bends the functional programming paradigm rules by allowing statements too, but they're used in a slightly different manner.

TIP

When working with other languages, such as Java, you rely on statements to perform every task (even tasks that could be viewed as expressions, as noted later in this section). However, in Kotlin, nearly everything begins with an expression, but you can use expressions to form statements in some cases. (If you want to play with the code that follows and in other areas of this chapter without having to start Android Studio, you can use an online interpreter, such as the one at `https://try.kotlinlang.org/`.) Here are the definitions of essential terms:

- **Expression:** A combination of one or more explicit values, constants, variables, operators, or functions used to compute another value. An expression always returns a value. In Kotlin, if a function doesn't explicitly return a value, it returns `Unit` instead, so it always returns something. An expression can also contain other expressions. Here are examples of Kotlin expressions:

```
fun greater(a: Int, b: Int) = if(a > b) a else b
1 + 1
sum(1, 2, 3)
sum(1, 2, (1 * 3))
```

- **Declaration:** The creation of a new entity. A declaration always returns an object of some type. However, declarations can also include expressions. Here are some examples of declarations:

```
val myVal = "Hello"
val myVal2 = 5 * 10
class myClass {}
```

- **Statement:** An action that the application carries out as part of an overall process. Each statement in Java ends with a semicolon, but you use semicolons in Kotlin only when placing multiple statements on a single line. Still, the idea is that a statement corresponds to an action of some sort. Statements can contain expressions. Here are some examples of Kotlin statements:

```
println("Hello World")
for (i in 2..6) {println(i)}
print(sum(1, 2, 3))
```

- **Expression Statement:** A stand-alone expression that performs an action when executed. In most cases, this designation is limited to expressions that don't return a value other than `Unit` and would appear as a statement in imperative languages, such as Java. Here is an example of an expression statement:

```
performUpdate(User)
```

The designations in this list are important because they define how Kotlin interacts with code, and you need them to clearly express how the code works. There are also differences between Java and Kotlin when it comes to describing the meaning of code. For example, Kotlin uses declarations to create and assign values to variables, while Java uses expressions. When performing an assignment in Java, the assignment returns a value and is therefore also an expression. The following statement is legal in Java but not in Kotlin:

```
a = b = 2
```

As another example, Java works with control structures such as `if` and `switch` statements. Kotlin views control structures as expressions. For example, this code is legal in Kotlin:

```
val a = 2
val b = 4
val larger = if(a > b) a else b
println(larger)
```

The Kotlin class

You have to remember that Kotlin is a functional language, not necessarily an object-oriented programming (OOP) language. You can program in an OOP manner, but you can program in other ways, too, and they all work fine. Consequently, you could define a package level function like this:

```
fun main(args: Array<String>) {
     if (args.size > 0) {
          for (arg in args){
               println(arg)
          }
     } else {
          println("There are no arguments!")
     }
}
```

However, when working with Android, you rely on classes, just as you do when working with Java. Listing 3-1, shown previously, shows a Kotlin class declaration. The keyword `class` declares a public class (meaning that everyone can see it, which is the default visibility) named `MainActivity` that inherits from `AppCompatActivity`. Android Studio automatically defines the class name for you in this case, but you can use other class names. The class names within a package must be unique.

`MainActivity` is an *identifier* — it identifies a class. A Kotlin identifier can be any word containing only letters, digits, and underscores (_). An identifier must not begin with a digit. Other than that, there are no restrictions. Words like `MainActivity`, `LaFong3`, and `a_b_c` are valid Kotlin identifiers. A word like `1Mississippi` isn't valid because it begins with a digit. A phrase like `my activity` isn't valid because it contains a blank space. A string like `one~two` isn't valid because the tilde (~) isn't a letter, a digit, or an underscore.

WARNING

tHE kOTLIN PROGRAMMING LANGUAGE IS cASe-sEnsITiVE. iF YOU CHANGE A lowercase LETTER IN A WORD TO AN UPPERCASE LETTER, YOU CHANGE THE WORD'S MEANING.

A single Kotlin file can contain any number of classes. You also don't have any limitation on the filename, except as required by the platform you're using. However, a best practice is to use filenames that match the requirements for Kotlin identifiers to avoid any strange behavior by the IDE that you use. In fact, when you perform Android programming using Android Studio, the filename will match the class name. Consequently, you find the `MainActivity` class in the `MainActivity.kt` file.

Classes and objects

You can use classes and object in Kotlin, and you normally will when writing Android code. However, what, precisely, is a class? Here's an analogy: A chair has a seat, a back, and legs. Each seat has a shape, a color, a degree of softness, and so on. These are the properties that a chair possesses. What these properties describe is *chairness* — the notion of something being a chair. In object-oriented terminology, they describe the `Chair` class.

REMEMBER

The preceding paragraph refers to the `Chair` class, not to the `chair` class. Even though many Kotlin developers use either form, Java developers normally use initial caps to begin class names. It pays to humor them when you can, so starting your Kotlin class names using initial caps is a good idea, at least when developing for Android, as you are now. With a class name such as `chair`, your code does what you want it to do, but you're committing a stylistic faux pas as far as Java developers are concerned. Real Java developers start the names of their classes with uppercase letters.

Now peek over the edge of this book's margin and take a minute to look around your room. (If you're not sitting in a room right now, fake it.)

Several chairs are in the room, and each chair is an object. Each of these objects is an example of that ethereal thing called the `Chair` class. So that's how it works — the class is the idea of chairness, and each individual chair is an *object*.

REMEMBER

A class isn't quite a collection of things. Instead, a class is the idea behind a certain kind of thing. When you contemplate the class of chairs in your room, you're thinking about the fact that each chair has legs, a seat, a color, and so on. The colors may be different for different chairs in the room, but the specific color doesn't matter; the fact of having color does. When you talk about a class of things, you're focusing on the properties that each of the things possesses.

It makes sense to think of an object as being a concrete instance of a class. In fact, the official terminology is consistent with this thinking. If you write a Kotlin program in which you define a `Chair` class, each actual chair (the chair that you're sitting on, the empty chair right next to you, and so on) is called an *instance* of the `Chair` class.

Here's another way to think about a class. Imagine a table displaying three bank accounts. (See Table 3-1.)

TABLE 3-1 A Table of Accounts

Name	Address	Balance
Barry Burd	222 Cyberspace Lane	24.02
John Q. Public	140 Any Way	–471.03
Jane Dough	800 Rich Street	247.38

Think of the table's column headings as a class, and think of each row of the table as an object. The table's column headings describe the `Account` class.

According to the table's column headings, each account has a name, an address, and a balance. Rephrased in the terminology of object-oriented programming, each object in the `Account` class (that is, each instance of the `Account` class) has a name, an address, and a balance. So, the bottom row of the table is an object with the name `Jane Dough`. This same object has the address *800 Rich Street* and a balance of *247.38*. If you opened a new account, you would have another object, and the table would grow an additional row. The new object would be an instance of the same `Account` class.

Kotlin types

What does "six" mean? You can have six children, but you can also be six feet tall. With six children, you know exactly how many kids you have. (Unlike the average American family, you can't have 2.5 kids.) But if you're six feet tall, you could really be six feet and half an inch tall. Or you might be five feet eleven-and-three-quarter inches tall, and no one would argue about it.

A value's meaning depends on the value's *type*. If you write

```
val numberOfChildren: Int = 6
```

in a Kotlin program, 6 means "exactly six." But if you write

```
val height: Double = 6.0
```

in a Kotlin program, 6.0 means "as close to six as you care to measure." However, note that in Kotlin, you can't simply use 6 by itself when working with the Double type, you must instead use 6.0. And if you write

```
val keystroke: Char = '6'
```

in a Kotlin program, `'6'` means "the digit that comes after the 5 digit."

REMEMBER

In a Kotlin program, every value has a *type*. However, unlike many languages, Kotlin doesn't support primitive data types (see the "Considering primitive types that are not classes" section of Chapter 2 of this minibook). In addition, it doesn't support raw data types (see the "Removing raw data types" section of Chapter 2 of this minibook). Rather, all data types are true objects in Kotlin, and Kotlin places strict limits on the kinds of conversions you can perform between types.

Table 3-2 displays Kotlin's numeric data types (all of which are declared using the approach shown earlier in this section).

TABLE 3-2 Kotlin's Numeric Data Types

Type	Size	Range
Double	64	-1.8×10^{308} to 1.8×10^{308}
Float	32	-3.4×10^{38} to 3.4×10^{38}
Long	64	-9223372036854775808 to 9223372036854775807
Int	32	-2147483648 to 2147483647
Short	16	-32768 to 32767
Byte	8	-128 to 127

TIP

When working with numbers, Kotlin provides a number of convenient aids. For example, when working with a `Long`, you can add an *L* to the end of the number, such as `val longVal = 22L`. The *L* tells the compiler that the value 22 is of type `Long`. The same technique works with the `Float` type, except you add an *f* or an *F* to the end of the value.

Large numbers can prove difficult to deal with in your code, so you can use underscores in place of commas. For example, `val longVal: Long = 123_456_789` is easier to read than `val longVal: Long = 123456789`. You can also use binary and hexadecimal notation, such as `val longVal: Long = 0b0001_0100_0101_1001` or `val longVal: Long = 0x001_459`. Scientific notation works for the `Double` and `Float` types: `val floatVal: Float = 1_234.5e6f`. Spending a little extra time to discover the various presentation methods will help you write clearer code.

Kotlin has other basic types, all of which are objects. Table 3-3 shows these basic types with examples and notes.

TABLE 3-3 Kotlin's Other Basic Types

Type	Value Range	Example
Char	Any single character found in any code page declared using single quotes	`val keystroke: Char = 'a'`
Boolean	`true` or `false`	`val question: Boolean = true`
String	An array of characters enclosed in double quotes	`val myString: String = "This is a string."`
Array	A collection of data values of a particular type. Shortcut types include `IntArray`, `ShortArray`, and `ByteArray`	`val numbers: Array<Int> = arrayOf(1, 2, 3, 4)` `val numbers: IntArray = intArrayOf(1, 2, 3, 4)`
Mutable Collection	One of any editable collection types in Kotlin	`val numbers: MutableList<Int> = mutableListOf(1, 2, 3)`
Immutable Collection	One of any non-editable collection types in Kotlin	`val numbers: List<Int> = listOf(1, 2, 3)`
Range	A sequential collection of values with a starting and ending point and a specific step between values	`val numRange: IntRange = 1..5`

A *literal* is an expression whose value doesn't change from one Kotlin program to another. For example, the expression `42` means "the int value 42" in every Kotlin program. Likewise, the expression `'B'` means "the second uppercase letter in the Roman alphabet" in every Kotlin program, and the word `true` means "the opposite of false" in every Kotlin program.

When considering the concept of data as objects, you need to know that all data in Kotlin is an object and that the classes you create or use can be a type of data. To start simply, the following code obtains the type of a Float value:

```
val floatVal: Float = 1_234.5e6f
println(floatVal.javaClass.kotlin)
```

Running this code produces an output of: `class kotlin.Float`, which tells you that a `Float` is an object created from a specific class. When viewing the code in Listing 3-1, earlier in the chapter, you see these classes that create objects and act as data types as well:

- androidx.appcompat.app.AppCompatActivity
- android.os.Bundle
- MainActivity

Because every class is a type, and because your newly declared `MyActivity` type is a class, you can add a line such as:

```
val anActivity = MyActivity()
```

to the code in Listing 3-1. This new line declares that the name `anActivity` is a placeholder for a value (a value whose type is `MyActivity`). In case this idea muddies your mind, Listing 3-2 has another example.

LISTING 3-2: A Class Is a Type

```
fun main(args: Array<String>) {
    val myAccount = Account()
    val yourAccount = Account()

    myAccount.name = "Burd"
    yourAccount.name = "Dough"
    myAccount.balance = 24.02

    println(myAccount.toString())
    println(yourAccount.toString())
}

class Account {
    var name: String = ""
    var address: String = ""
    var balance: Double = 0.0
}
```

Listing 3-2 declares a class named `Account`. This blueprint for an account has three fields. The first field — the `name` field — refers to a Kotlin `String` (a bunch of characters lined up in a row). The second field — the `address` field — refers to another Kotlin `String`. The third field — the `balance` field — stores a `Double` value. (Refer to Table 3-2.)

In Listing 3-2, you see two instances of the Account class. The variable `myAccount` refers to an `Account` object, and the variable `yourAccount` refers to another `Account` object. The `myAccount.balance = 24.02` statement in Listing 3-2 assigns the value `24.02` to the balance field of the object referred to by `myAccount`.

When working with Kotlin, you also have access to the data class, which has certain rules and certain features. For example, the output from the example in Listing 3-2 might look like this:

```
Account@28a418fc
Account@5305068a
```

which is pretty much useless. You can take a look at a data class version of the same example in Listing 3-3.

LISTING 3-3: Using a Data Class

```
fun main(args: Array<String>) {
    val myAccount = Account("Burd")
    val yourAccount = Account("Dough")

    myAccount.balance = 24.02
    yourAccount.balance = 9.99

    println(myAccount.toString())
    println(yourAccount.toString())
}

data class Account (val name: String,
                    var address: String = "",
                    var balance: Double = 0.0)
```

This code is actually safer than the previous example because you can't create an object that lacks some sort of identification. You could have done this with the previous class, but a data class enforces the idea by making it impossible to create the class without at least one primary constructor variable. In this case, `name` is also unchangeable after you create the object, so there is less chance that someone can simply modify it without thinking. However, the most noticeable difference is the output, which looks like this:

```
Account(name=Burd, address=, balance=24.02)
Account(name=Dough, address=, balance=9.99)
```

REMEMBER

As you can see, data classes in Kotlin tend to be more useful than standard classes, but you have to remember to use them. When creating a class specifically to hold data, always use a data class to ensure that your application runs efficiently and experiences fewer errors.

Performing casts

A magician is supposed to pull a rabbit out of a hat, yet ends up with a chicken instead. Hmmm . . . That didn't work out so well. Then, in a puff a smoke, the chicken turns into a rabbit. The crowd goes wild! Data can be like that. You may have data in one form, but you really need it in another form. Would it surprise you to know that you can also perform a bit of magic in some cases? The magic is a *cast*, which turns one sort of data into another sort of data, but within limits. You have already seen that Kotlin provides more than a little magic in the form of special features like the data class. The following sections tell how you can use the special features to your advantage in turning one sort of data into another.

Understanding casts

The fact that Kotlin doesn't have any primitive types affects how it performs casting, especially when compared to other languages that do support primitive types. For example, to convert one type to any other type, you normally need to specify the kind of conversion you want. In addition, you can't simply compare the values of two types without using the appropriate means. Even if an `Int` and a `Long` have precisely the same value, you can't compare them without performing some type of cast or using a function that performs the cast for you. The following example gives you an idea of how this approach works:

```
val intValue: Int = 1
val longValue: Long = intValue.toLong()

println(intValue.toLong() == longValue)
println(intValue.equals(longValue))
println(intValue.compareTo(longValue))
```

As shown in the code, you can't simply assign an `Int` value to a `Long` — the compiler will display an error message if you do. The call `toLong()` ensures that the developer is aware of the type conversion taking place.

When you want to compare values, you must also perform a type conversion. If you try to compare an `Int` to a `Long` without explicitly performing a cast, the compiler will display an error message. In this case, `intValue.toLong() == longValue` outputs `true` because the two values are equal.

You also have access to two functions to help you perform comparisons. The `equals()` function outputs false in this case because an `Int` isn't a `Long`. Even if the values are equal, the objects themselves aren't. However, `compareTo()` succeeds by outputting a value of `0`, which indicates the two values are equal, even if the objects aren't.

TIP

The compareTo() function is especially handy because it doesn't just measure value equality, as using intValue.toLong() == longValue does. If intValue is less than longValue, the output is -1, while the output is 1 when intValue is more than longValue.

Using smart casts

Kotlin includes features to avoid the dreaded NullPointerException as described in the "Improving control over null references" section of Chapter 2 of this minibook. One of these features actually tracks variable content to ensure that the variable isn't null (empty). Of course, you can't make a variable null unless it's a nullable type, which is another safety feature. Here is an example using a variable of type Any, which means it can contain any data except a null:

```
val obj: Any? = "This is a string."

if (obj is String){
   println("The string is ${obj.length} characters long.")
}
```

The length property is available in this context only with a String. For example, if you had instead assigned obj a value of 22, it wouldn't be a String, and the length property wouldn't be available. The if statement and the use of the keyword is forces the runtime to review the actual content of obj to ensure that using length is doable.

REMEMBER

You can perform the same sort of check using the !is (not is) operator. This operator simply checks to ensure that the variable isn't of the type that you specify.

Considering the safe, nullable cast

Sometimes you need to make an object nullable. Perhaps you have cases when the object simply won't contain any data. To make any object nullable, you add the question mark (?) operator. For example, to make a String nullable, you use String?. In looking at Listing 3-1, you see that Bundle? is nullable. If this is the first run of your app, savedInstanceState will contain a null, rather than any data.

However, now you have a problem because the object could contain nothing, which means that properties and methods associated with the object will return a NullPointerException when used. The call to super.onCreate() in Listing 3-1, earlier in the chapter, will have to deal with the nullable nature of savedInstanceState. Rather than delve into the mysteries of the Android libraries, take a look at a simple example. The following code shows how you perform a safe cast to verify that the variable contains something:

```
val obj: String? = null

if (obj != null){
    println("String is ${obj.length} characters long.")
} else {
    println("String is Empty")
}
```

REMEMBER

The Kotlin compiler raises an error when you call `obj.length` unless you perform this check because `obj` is a nullable `String?`. Even though `obj` is of the right type, the fact that it's nullable means that you must make additional checks in your code.

Employing an unsafe cast

Sometimes you must perform a cast that you aren't sure will work because you don't know what the variable might contain. The unsafe cast operator is `as`. You tell Kotlin that you want to try to cast a variable as a particular type. For example, the following code shows an unsafe cast:

```
val obj: Any? = "A String"
val aString: String = obj as String

println(aString)
```

This particular example works because `obj` does indeed contain a String. However, this code raises a `ClassCastException` because the unsafe cast didn't work:

```
val obj: Any? = "A String"
val anInt: Int = obj as Int

println(anInt)
```

You would need to work with `anInt` within a `try...catch` block to catch the exception when using this approach. To avoid the exception, you can use a nullable type and a safe cast form of the `as?` operator, as shown here:

```
val obj: Any? = "A String"
val anInt: Int? = obj as? Int

println(anInt)
```

After attempting to cast `obj` as an `Int`, `anInt` contains `null` instead of raising a `ClassCastException`. You can then use a smart cast to determine how to work with `anInt` afterward. The safe cast approach is preferred because you don't risk raising an exception that might go unhandled.

Dealing with type erasure and unchecked casts

All the casting information described so far in this section deals with basic types. It also applies to any classes you use or create. However, in working with Kotlin in Android development, you also deal with generics at times, and casting can work differently in this case because a generic cast is checked only at compile time, not at runtime, which means that your code could generate unexpected exceptions and you need to take precautions by using `try...catch` blocks. The loss of information about the generic type is called *type erasure*. For example, consider this use of a generic:

```
val obj: List<Any> = listOf(1, 2, 3)
val numbers: List<Int> = obj as List<Int>

for (value in numbers) {
    println(value)
}
```

This code will compile and run. However, you receive an `Unchecked Cast` warning message from the Kotlin compiler because verifying the cast from `List<Any>` to `List<Int>` at runtime isn't possible. The following code shows how things can go wrong, resulting in a `ClassCastException`:

```
val obj: List<Any> = listOf(1, 2, 3)
val letters: List<String> = obj as List<String>

try {
    for (value in letters) {
        println(value)
    }
} catch (e: ClassCastException) {
    println(e.message)
}
```

The output of this example is `java.lang.Integer cannot be cast to java.lang.String`, which simply means that you can't turn an `Int` into a `String`. The point is that the `try...catch` block handles the exception in this case, which is the only method available to handle casting errors.

The Kotlin function

You hear multiple terms for a package of code found in an easily callable form. For example, a *procedure* is a set of operations executed without calculating any return value. In Java, you hear about the *method*, because methods are associated with objects. Java is focused on objects, so the most appropriate term is *method* — a method of working with that object in some meaningful way. In Kotlin, you find functions.

A *function* is a set of operations that don't necessarily link to an object but always return a value. If a Kotlin function doesn't provide a specific return value, it returns a value called `Unit`. Consequently, you never use the term *procedure* when working with Kotlin because the procedure doesn't exist (although you could make the argument that procedures do exist in Java). Here is an example of the `Unit` return value:

```
val result = println("A String")

if (result is Unit) {
    println("result is of type Unit")
    println(result)
}
```

You wouldn't expect `println()` to return a value, and it doesn't, but it does return `Unit`. Because `println()` is a stand-alone call not associated with an object, you always call it a function.

In looking at Listing 3-1, earlier in the chapter, you see the `onCreate()` function, which is part of the `MainActivity` class. Because `onCreate()` exists as part of a class in this case, you can also call it a method. The `onCreate()` method exists as a part of objects instantiated from `MainActivity`. Chapter 5 of this minibook exposes you to more of the object-oriented features of Kotlin, but for now, remember that a function that appears as part of a class is more specifically called a method, even though it's also a function.

Some ambiguity exists in other languages that use the static method, which is part of a class but is not called as part of an object. Some people argue that these methods are really functions. Kotlin gets rid of the ambiguity by using companion objects in place of static methods in classes. The "Losing static members" section of Chapter 2 of this minibook explains companion objects and their significance in more detail. The point is that they really are methods in Kotlin because they're members of the associated singleton object.

Kotlin functions have certain characteristics, as shown in the following code:

```
fun main(args: Array<String>) {
    println(monthlyPayment(10_000.00, 5.25, 30))
    println(monthlyPayment(10_000.00, 5.00, 15))
}

fun monthlyPayment(principle: Double,
                   percentageRate: Double,
                   years: Int): Double {

    val numPayments: Int = 12 * years
    val rate: Double = percentageRate / 100.00
    val effectiveRate: Double = rate / 12

    return (principle * effectiveRate /
            (1 - Math.pow(1 + effectiveRate,
                          -numPayments.toDouble())))
}
```

When you run this example, you receive the expected monthly payments given a $10,000 loan, certain percentage rates, and the number of years that someone will make payments. The functions used in this example have certain characteristics:

- **The names of the two functions are `main()` and `monthlyPayment()`.**
- **In the body of the `monthlyPayment()` function declaration, the processor computes the monthly payments on a mortgage.** You can follow this description of functions and function parameters without understanding anything about the calculations.
- **The body of the `monthlyPayment()` function uses certain names as placeholders.** For example, in the body of the `monthlyPayment()` function, the name `years` stands for the number of years in the mortgage's term. Likewise, the name `principal` stands for the total amount borrowed.
- **Some placeholders appear in parentheses at the beginning of the function's declaration.** The names `principal`, `percentageRate`, and `years` are the function's *parameters.* Each parameter is destined to stand for a particular value. But a parameter doesn't stand for a value until an app executes a function call.

  The `main()` function contains a call to `monthlyPayment(10_0000.00, 5.25, 30)` that gives the function's first parameter (namely, `principal`) the value `10000.00`. That same call gives the function's second parameter (percentageRate) the value 5.25. Finally, that function call gives the method's third parameter (years) the value 30.

The next function call in main() gives the monthlyPayment() function's parameters different values (again 10000.00 for principal, but 5.00 for percentageRate and 15 for years). Each time you call a function, you supply values for the function's parameters.

- **The types of parameters in a function call must match the types of the parameters in a function declaration.** The declaration of function monthlyPayment() has a Double parameter (principal), another Double parameter (percentageRate), and an Int parameter (years). Accordingly, the first function call has two Double parameters (10000.00 and 5.25) followed by an Int parameter (30). The second function call also has two Double parameters followed by an Int parameter.

TECHNICAL STUFF

You can declare the same function more than once, as long as each declaration has a different parameter list. For example, another monthlyPayment() function declaration might have the same name monthlyPayment but only two parameters: principle: Double and percentageRate: Double. To call this alternative monthlyPayment() function, you write something like monthlyPayment(10_000.00, 5.00). In this situation, the body of the alternative monthlyPayment() method probably contains a statement like val years: Int = 30. You don't call this two-parameter method unless you know that the mortgage's term is 30 years.

- **A function call might stand for a value.** The first function call in main() stands for the Double value 55.22 (or a value very close to the number 55.22). The value 55.22 comes from all the calculations in the body of the monthlyPayment() function when the principal is 10000.00, the percentageRate is 5.25, and the number of years is 30. Near the end of the monthlyPayment() function body, the formula

```
principle * effectiveRate /
(1 - Math.pow(1 + effectiveRate,
          -numPayments.toDouble()))
```

has the value 55.22, and the word return says "send 55.22 back to the statement that called this method." So, the end of the monthlyPayment() function body effectively says

```
return 55.22
```

and the associated println() statement in main() effectively says

```
println(55.22)
```

Similarly, the second `println()` function call in `main()` outputs the value `79.08`. Because of the second function call's parameter values, the end of the `monthlyPayment()` function body effectively says

```
return 79.08
```

and the last line in the listing effectively says

```
println(79.08)
```

- **A function's declaration can end with the name of the return type.** The `monthlyPayment()` function declaration begins with the keyword `fun` (which is short for function), followed by the function name, `monthlyPayment`, a list of parameters in parentheses, and finally the keyword `Double`. That's good because the value returned at the end of the method's body (either `55.22` or `79.08`) is of type `Double`.

Objects and their constructors

A *constructor* is a special kind of method within a class that defines how to create (instantiate) objects defined by that class. Kotlin provides for two kinds of constructor:

- **Primary:** Initializes the class, including the class members. There is never more than one primary constructor. You can define the primary constructor at the class header level.
- **Secondary:** Augments class initialization by providing additional logic as needed. Secondary constructors are optional, but a class can have more than one. You always define secondary constructors as part of the class code using the `constructor` keyword.

Listings 3-2 and 3-3, earlier in the chapter, show two different versions of the `Account` class. In both cases, you see `name`, `address`, and `balance` initialized to particular values — either by default or through assignment. You previously discovered that using a data class has certain advantages, but here's a look at a Kotlin form of a standard class with a primary constructor:

```
fun main(args: Array<String>) {
    val myAccount = Account("Burd")
    val yourAccount = Account("Dough", balance=19.99)

    myAccount.balance = 24.02

    println(myAccount.toString())
```

```
    println(yourAccount.toString())
}

class Account(val name: String,
              var address: String = "",
              var balance: Double = 0.0) {
}
```

This example has some interesting differences from the previous ones. For example, you must provide the name argument as part of creating an instance of the class because it has no default value. In addition, you can't change name later because name is a val rather than a var.

TIP

Notice also that you can use *positional arguments* (name appears first, so you don't have to specifically provide it) or *named arguments* (balance is assigned without assigning a value to address first by specifically naming it in the arguments). This form of the Account class doesn't provide a useful implementation of toString(), so you get gibberish in the output. Here's an updated version with a secondary constructor and an implementation of toString(). The toString() function is one of the most common additions you make to a standard class:

```
class Account(val name: String) {

    var address: String = ""
    var balance: Double = 0.0

    constructor (name: String,
                 address: String = "",
                 balance: Double = 0.0): this(name) {
        if (address == ""){
            this.address = "N/A"
        }
        this.balance = balance
    }

    override fun toString()  = "Name: " + name +
                               "\nAddress: " + address +
                               "\nBalance: " + balance
}
```

This version shortens the primary constructor to just the name argument. So, when the code calls val myAccount = Account("Burd"), it uses the primary constructor directly. Because of this change to the primary constructor, you must now include two fields within the class to hold address and balance. You must initialize these local variables or Kotlin will raise an error during compilation.

REMEMBER

The secondary constructor begins with the word *constructor.* Notice that it isn't followed by a name but rather by a list of fields similar to those found in the primary constructor. You can't declare these fields as either `val` or `var`, however; they're all `val` because they're local to the constructor. The `this(name)` part of the secondary constructor declaration calls the primary constructor. The arguments you supply must match those required by the primary constructor. The `val yourAccount = Account("Dough", balance=19.99)` call contains more than just a name, so it uses this secondary constructor.

The secondary constructor performs some additional processing. If `address == ""`, then the code calls `this.address = "N/A"`. When you reference `address` alone, it refers to the `address` value passed to the secondary constructor. When you refer to `this.address`, it represents the field within the class. You must also assign the secondary constructor `balance` value to `this.balance` or it won't appear as part of the object.

To create a useful `toString()` function, you must override the default `toString()` found in the `Any` class. This example simply defines a new string with the three field values and headings. The output looks like this:

```
Name: Burd
Address:
Balance: 24.02
Name: Dough
Address: N/A
Balance: 19.99
```

Notice that the first set of fields lacks a value for `address`. That's because the first set of fields relies on the primary constructor. The second set of fields shows `address` as `N/A`. The secondary constructor adds this value for you.

Classes grow on trees

In Listing 3-1, you see `class MainActivity : AppCompatActivity()`. This means that `MainActivity` uses the features found in `AppCompatActivity`; `MainActivity` *inherits* from `AppCompatActivity`, so `AppCompatActivity` is above `MainActivity` in the class hierarchy. The easiest way to view class hierarchies in Kotlin is to see them as trees, with `MainActivity` being a leaf and `AppCompatActivity` being a twig holding the leaf.

When you review the documentation for `androidx.appcompat.app.AppCompatActivity` at `https://developer.android.com/reference/kotlin/androidx/appcompat/app/AppCompatActivity`, you find that this class inherits from a number of other classes:

- `FragmentActivity`
- `AppCompatCallback`
- `TaskStackBuilder.SupportParentable`
- `ActionBarDrawerToggle.DelegateProvider`

TIP

If you check out each of these other classes (made easy by the links on the web page), you find that each of them also inherits from other classes. It doesn't take long to determine that there really is a tree-like structure of classes in place and that you can trace back through them to better understand how Android works.

At times, you also want to see the actual code used to create a particular parent class. In this case, right-click the class you want to review, such as `AppCompatActivity` and choose Go To➪Declaration from the context menu. A new file opens that contains the required source, as shown in Figure 3-8.

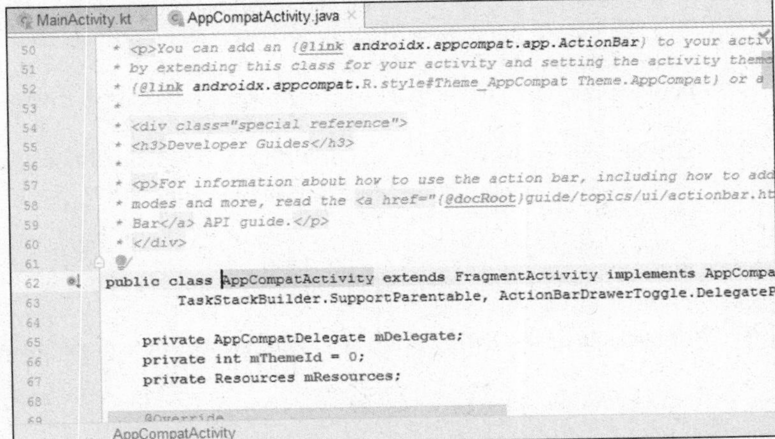

FIGURE 3-8: Viewing the source for a parent class in Android Studio.

The Kotlin package

Kotlin has a feature that lets you lump classes into groups of classes. Each lump of classes is a package. The class in Listing 3-1 belongs to the `com.example.myfirstapp` package because of the listing's first line of code.

In the Kotlin world, developers customarily give packages long, dot-filled names. For instance, because this book's source relies on the registered domain name `allmycode.com`, most examples name a package `com.allmycode.samples` or `com.allmycode.whatever`. The Kotlin API is actually a big collection of packages.

The Java API, with which Kotlin interacts, has packages with names like java.lang, java.util, java.awt, javax.swing, and so on. The Android SDK is also a bunch of packages, with package names such as android.app, android.view, and android.telephony.gsm.

An import declaration starts with the name of a package and ends with either of the following:

- » The name of a class within that package
- » An asterisk (indicating all classes within that package)

For example, in the declaration

```
import androidx.appcompat.app.AppCompatActivity
```

androidx.appcompat.app is the name of a package in the Android SDK, and AppCompatActivity is the name of a class in the androidx.appcompat.app package. The dotted name androidx.appcompat.app.AppCompatActivity is the fully qualified name of the AppCompatActivity class. A class's fully qualified name includes the name of the package in which the class is defined.

With an import declaration, you don't have to repeatedly use a class's fully qualified name. For example, in Listing 3-1, you could write

```
class MainActivity :
    androidx.appcompat.app.AppCompatActivity()
```

but because of the listing's import declaration, you can get away with plain old

```
class MainActivity : AppCompatActivity()
```

In a declaration such as

```
import androidx.appcompat.app.*
```

the asterisk refers to all classes in the androidx.appcompat.app package. With this import declaration at the top of your Kotlin code, you can use abbreviated names for all classes in the androidx.appcompat.app package — names like ActionBar, ActionBarDrawToggle, AlertDialog, AppCompatDelegate, and many others.

Considering Kotlin visibility rules

All classes, methods, fields, and packages can receive a visibility modifier. The default visibility for everything in Kotlin is `public`, so you can always access whatever you need. You don't have to declare a class or other entity as being public; it's automatically public. Consequently, in Listing 3-1, earlier in the chapter, `MainActivity` is public. To make things clearer to users of other languages, you can add the `public` keyword to a declaration, but its use is superfluous. Kotlin defines three other levels of visibility:

- `private`: The entity is visible only within the immediate scope. For example, in the following code:

  ```
  fun main(args: Array<String>) {
      val greetObj = Greeting()
      greetObj.name = "Sally"
      greetObj.sayHello()
  }

  class Greeting {
      private var name: String = ""
      fun sayHello() {
          if (name.length == 0){
              name = "George"
          }
          println("Hello " + name)
      }
  }
  ```

  `greetObj.name = "Sally"` will raise an error because name is `private` to class `greeting`. However, `name = "George"` will set the value of name because the call is made within the class.

- `protected`: This visibility modifier isn't available to top-level entities. For example, you can't protect a package or a top-level class like `MainActivity` in Listing 3-1. You can protect members inside a class, which makes the member visible only to the class itself and to subclasses of the class (unlike `private`, where the member is also hidden from subclasses).

- `internal`: Any entity can be defined as internal. An internal entity is accessible only within the current package (or within the current module when defining a package as internal). Consequently, the following code works without error because name is now defined as internal, rather than private, as it was earlier in this list:

```
fun main(args: Array<String>) {
    val greetObj = Greeting()
    greetObj.name = "Sally"
    greetObj.sayHello()
}

class Greeting {
    internal var name: String = ""
    fun sayHello() {
        if (name.length == 0){
            name = "George"
        }
        println("Hello " + name)
    }
}
```

Defying your parent

In families, children often rebel against their parents' values. The same is true in Java. The `MainActivity` class (in Listing 3-1, earlier in the chapter) is a child of the `AppCompatActivity` class. So at first glance, `MainActivity` should inherit the `onCreate()` method declared in the `AppCompatActivity` class's code.

But both the `AppCompatActivity` and `MainActivity` classes have `onCreate()` method declarations. And the two `onCreate()` declarations have the same parameter list. In this way, the `MainActivity` class rebels against its parent. The `MainActivity` class says to the `AppCompatActivity` class, "I don't want your stinking `onCreate()` method. I'm declaring my own `onCreate()` method."

So when you fire up an app, and your phone creates a `MainActivity` object, the phone executes the `MainActivity` version of `onCreate()`, not the parent `AppCompatActivity` version of `onCreate()`.

TECHNICAL STUFF

Like all rebellious children, `MainActivity` can't break completely from its parent class's code. The first statement in the `MainActivity` class's `onCreate()` method is a call to `super.onCreate()`. The statement `super.onCreate()` calls the parent class's `onCreate()` method. So, before the `onCreate()` method in Listing 3-1 does anything else, the processor runs the `AppCompatActivity.onCreate()` method. (The creators of Android rigged things so that your `onCreate()` method must call `super.onCreate()`. If you forget to call `super.onCreate()`, Android displays a blunt, annoying error message.)

Kotlin comments

A *comment* is part of a program's text. But unlike declarations, method calls, and other such things, a comment's purpose is to help people understand your code. A comment is part of a good program's documentation.

The Kotlin programming language has two kinds of comments:

- **Block comments:** A *block* comment begins with `/*` and ends with `*/`. Everything between the opening `/*` and the closing `*/` is for human eyes only. No information between `/*` and `*/` is translated by the compiler.

  A block comment can span across several lines. For example, the following code is a block comment:

  ```
  /* This is my best
  Android app ever! */
  ```

- **End-of-line comments:** An *end-of-line* comment starts with two slashes and goes to the end of a line of type. So in the following code snippet, the text `// A required call` is an end-of-line comment:

  ```
  super.onCreate(savedInstanceState); // A required call
  ```

  Once again, no text inside the end-of-line comment gets translated by the compiler.

WHERE IS JavaDoc?

Java developers have likely used JavaDoc comments to generate documentation for their applications. A *JavaDoc* comment begins with a slash and two asterisks (`/**`), such as `/** Called at the end of each month */`. However, JavaDoc works only with Java classes. You still have access to the JavaDoc feature in Android Studio, but if you try to use it on your Kotlin code, what you see is an error message stating, "Error running 'JavaDoc'. Selected scope contains no Java classes." There is no standard replacement for JavaDoc in Android Studio, but if you need to automatically generate comments from your code, you can look at alternatives such as Dokka (`https://github.com/Kotlin/dokka` and `https://github.com/Kotlin/dokka/issues/352`), which actually works with Java as well, so it's perfect for mixed Kotlin and Java projects. To create Dokka-compatible comments, you use KDoc, as specified at `https://kotlinlang.org/docs/reference/kotlin-doc.html`.

» Repeating actions with Kotlin statements

» Adding exception handling

Chapter 4 What Kotlin Does (and When)

Human thought centers on nouns and verbs. Nouns are the "stuff," and verbs are the stuff's actions. Nouns are the pieces, and verbs are the glue. Nouns are, and verbs do. When you use nouns, you say, "book," "room," or "stuff." When you use verbs, you say "Do this," "Do that," "Hoist that barge," or "Lift that bale."

Kotlin also has nouns and verbs. Kotlin's nouns include `String`, `List`, and `Array`, along with Android-specific things such as `AppCompatActivity`, `ActionBar`, and `Bundle`. Kotlin's verbs involve assigning values, choosing among alternatives, repeating actions, and other courses of action.

This chapter covers some of Kotlin's verbs. In Chapter 5 of this minibook, you bring in the nouns.

Making Decisions (Kotlin if Statements)

When you're writing computer programs, you're constantly hitting forks in roads. Did the user correctly type his or her password? If yes, let the user work; if no, kick the bum out. So the Kotlin programming language needs a way of making a program branch in one of two directions. Fortunately, the language has a way: It's called an `if` statement. The use of an `if` statement is illustrated in Listing 4-1. (If you want to play with the code that follows and in other areas of this chapter without having to start Android Studio, you can use an online interpreter, such as the one at `https://try.kotlinlang.org/`.)

LISTING 4-1: Using an `if` Statement

```
fun main(args: Array<String>) {
    val a = 2
    val b = 4

    if (a > b) {
        print("a is greater")
    } else {
        print("b is equal or greater")
    }
}
```

An `if` statement checks a condition, such as whether `a` is greater than `b`. In this case, `b` is greater, so the output is `"b is equal or greater"`.

An `if` statement has the following form:

```
if (condition) {
    statements to be executed when the condition is true
} else {
    statements to be executed when the condition is false
}
```

In Listing 4-1, the condition being tested is

```
(a > b)
```

The condition in an `if` statement must be enclosed within parentheses. The condition must be a `Boolean` expression — an expression whose value is either `true` or `false`. (See Chapter 3 of this minibook for information about Java's primitive types, including the `Boolean` type.) So, for example, the following condition is okay:

```
if (numberOfTries < 17) {
```

But the strange kind of condition that you can use in languages such as C++ is not okay:

```
if (17) { //This is incorrect.
```

REMEMBER

You can omit curly braces when only one statement comes between the condition and the word `else`. You can also omit braces when only one statement comes after the word `else`. For example, the following code is okay:

```
if (a > b)
    print("a is greater")
else
    print("b is equal or greater")
```

An `if` statement can also enjoy a full and happy life without an `else` part. So the following code forms a complete `if` statement:

```
if (a > b)
    print("a is greater")
```

Kotlin also has an `if` expression. An `if` expression differs from an `if` statement in the way that you create and use it. Instead of performing an action within the `if` statement, you place the result in the variable output of the `if` expression and then use it as needed. Listing 4-2 shows an example of an `if` expression.

LISTING 4-2: Using an `if` Expression

```
fun main(args: Array<String>) {
    val a = 2
    val b = 4

    val max = if (a > b) {
        print("a is greater")
        a
    } else {
        print("b is equal or greater")
        b
    }

    print("\nThe value of max is ${max}.")
}
```

In this case, max receives the output of the if expression. When a is greater, it receives the value of a. Likewise, when b is greater, it receives the value of b. However, the output expression need not be a number. For example, you could change the code to make max a Boolean, a Double, or a String, as shown here:

```
val max: String = if (a > b) {
    print("a is greater")
    a.toString()
} else {
    print("b is equal or greater")
    b.toString()
}
```

TIP

An if expression is more useful than an if statement when you need to use the result of a comparison in multiple locations or you need additional flexibility in the outcome of the comparison. Rather than perform the comparison multiple times, especially one in which a conversion is made, you can perform it just once and then use the result as often as needed. Comparisons require computer time, so anytime you can save time by not performing a comparison, you help your application run faster and use resources more efficiently.

Testing for equality

Kotlin has several ways to test for equality ("Is this value the same as that value?"). None of these ways is the first thing you'd think of doing. In particular, to find out whether variable a is equal to variable b, you *don't* write `if (a = b)`. Instead, you use a double equal sign (==). You write `if (a == b)`. In Kotlin, the single equal sign (=) is reserved for *assignment.* So `val n = 5` means "Let n stand for the value 5."

Comparing two strings is yet another story. When you compare two strings with one another, you don't want to use the double equal sign. Using the double equal sign would ask, "Is this string stored in exactly the same place in memory as that other string?" That's usually not what you want to ask. Instead, you usually want to ask, "Does this string have the same characters in the same order in it as that other string?" To ask the second question (the more appropriate question), Kotlin's String type has a method named equals:

```
if (response.equals("yes")) {
```

The equals method compares two strings to see whether they have the same characters in them. In this paragraph's tiny example, the variable response refers to a string, and the text "yes" refers to a string. The condition response.

`equals("yes")` is true if `response` refers to a string whose letters are `'y'`, and then `'e'`, and then `'s'`.

Like most programming languages, Kotlin has the usual complement of comparison operators (such as `<` for "less than") and logical operators (such as `&&` for "and"). For a list of such operators, visit `https://kotlinlang.org/docs/reference/keyword-reference.html`.

TECHNICAL STUFF

There are times when you do want to verify that two variables point to the same object, a condition called referential equality. In this case, you use the `===` operator (or the `!==` operator if you want to verify that they don't point to the same object). For example, in the following code, `a` and `b` point to the same object, so the output of the referential equality comparison is `true`:

```
fun main(args: Array<String>) {
    val a: String = "A String Value"
    val b = a
    println(a === b)
}
```

Because Kotlin spends so much time ensuring that `null` values appear only in the right place, you also use a special `!!` operator to verify that a nullable object isn't equal to `null`. This particular kind of check is called an assertion. Kotlin *asserts* whether `a` is equal to `null`. You use this operator before performing a task that would fail with a `null` value, such as obtaining the length of a string, as shown here:

```
fun main(args: Array<String>) {
    val a: String? = "A String Value"
    println(a!!.length)
}
```

This particular form will raise an exception when `a` equals `null`. If you don't want to raise an exception, you use the Elvis operator (`?:`) form, shown here:

```
fun main(args: Array<String>) {
    val a: String? = null
    println(a?.length ?: 0)
}
```

In this case, Kotlin first checks whether `a` equals `null`. If so, it outputs a value of `0`, rather than trying to obtain the length of `a`.

Choosing among many alternatives (Kotlin when statements)

We'll bet you were expecting something about the switch statement here. Most languages use some type of switch statement to choose from many alternatives, but a switch statement can be extremely limited. What a switch statement does is replace a series of if...else statements with a single statement. You compare a single value with one or more constants, and there is only one word for the situation: boring. A when structure is so much more flexible, for these reasons:

- You can use it as an expression or a statement (returning a value or not).
- The design is safer in that it's harder to have unexpected outcomes (such as leaving out a break clause).
- The conditions can be expressions rather than just constants.
- You have no need for an argument if you don't have one to provide.

Here's a basic when statement:

```
fun main(args: Array<String>) {
    val a = 5

    when (a) {
        0, 1, 2, 3, 4 -> println("Less than 5")
        5 -> println(5)
        else -> print("Greater than 5")
    }
}
```

The code begins by providing an argument, a, which equals 5. It then checks a against the values 0 through 4 and the precise value 5, and it includes a clause to use when all else fails: else. If you have worked with other languages and relied on a switch statement, you immediately notice that

- The when statement is more concise.
- You can separate multiple choices using a comma.

The when statement isn't limited to constants. This version of the previous example uses an expression (a range) in place of individual constants. It also checks to determine whether the argument is an Int:

```
when (a) {
    in 0..4 -> println("Less than 5")
```

```
        is Int -> println("It's an Int")
        5 -> println(5)
        else -> print("Greater than 5")
    }
```

WARNING

You might expect multiple outputs in this case because two of the conditions are `true`, but you see only the first one, `"It's an Int"`, as output. The order of branches in your `when` statement is important when it's potentially possible for multiple conditions to be `true` under certain circumstances. The ability to have multiple true conditions can also lead to bugs, so you need to structure your `when` structures carefully.

The expression form of `when` works much like the expression form of `if`, except you're looking at multiple conditions:

```
fun main(args: Array<String>) {
    val a = 5

    val result: Any = when (a) {
        in 0..4 -> "Less than 5"
        5 -> 5
        else -> false
    }

    println(result)
}
```

Depending on the value of `a`, result could contain a `String`, `Int`, or `Boolean`. The use of the `Any` type enables you to receive the most appropriate value type. Type casting would let you convert the value to what you need in given situations.

REMEMBER

The expression form of `when` always requires an `else` clause unless the compiler can determine that the other clauses cover every contingency. For example, this expression form of `when` doesn't require an `else` clause:

```
fun main(args: Array<String>) {
    val a = false

    val result = when (a) {
        true -> "The value is true."
        false -> "The value is false."
    }

    println(result)
}
```

The expression form of `when` can also appear as part of a function. Consider this example in which the expression form of `when` forms the body of a function used to check data type:

```
fun main(args: Array<String>) {
    println(checkType(3))
    println(checkType(true))
    println(checkType("Hello"))
    println(checkType(arrayOf(1, 2, 3)))
}

fun checkType(x: Any) = when (x) {
    is String -> "Value is a String."
    is Int -> "Value is an Int."
    is Boolean -> "Value is a Boolean."
    else -> "Value isn't a usable type."
}
```

Another use of `when` is to check various conditions without an argument, which is quite frankly mind boggling. You use it to choose an action based on likely conditions, with the most likely or most desirable conditions first in the list. Here is a basic example:

```
fun main(args: Array<String>) {
    val a = 5
    val b = "Goodbye"
    val c = true

    when {
        a - 1 > 5 -> println("a is greater than 5")
        b == "Hello" -> println("Hello There!")
        c is Boolean -> println("c is ${c}")
        else -> println("None of the conditions is true.")
    }
}
```

In this case, no argument is supplied because none is needed. The code checks each condition in turn and provides the desired output. Note that you can include math or other kinds of expressions as part of the conditions. Kotlin will perform the required manipulation before it determines the truth value of a particular condition. The only real requirement is that the condition eventually valuate to a `Boolean`.

Repeating Instructions Over and Over Again

In 1966, the company that brings you Head & Shoulders shampoo made history. On the back of the bottle, the directions for using the shampoo read, "Lather, rinse, repeat." Never before had a complete set of directions (for doing anything, let alone shampooing your hair) been summarized so succinctly. People in the direction-writing business hailed this as a monumental achievement. Directions like these stood in stark contrast to others of the time. (For instance, the first sentence on a can of bug spray read, "Turn this can so that it points away from your face." Duh!)

Aside from their brevity, the thing that made the Head & Shoulders directions so cool was that, with three simple words, they managed to capture a notion that's at the heart of all instruction-giving — the notion of repetition. That last word, *repeat,* took an otherwise bland instructional drone and turned it into a sophisticated recipe for action.

The fundamental idea is that when you're following directions, you don't just follow one instruction after another. Instead, you take turns in the road. You make decisions ("If HAIR IS DRY, then USE CONDITIONER"), and you go into loops ("LATHER-RINSE and then LATHER-RINSE again"). In application development, you use decision-making and looping all the time.

REMEMBER

Looping is somewhat different in Kotlin than other languages you might have used. Kotlin does provide a traditional `while` loop that you use to repeat pieces of code. Kotlin doesn't provide a true `for` looping mechanism like that found in Java and other languages. Instead, it relies on *iterators,* objects that provide sequential access to collection elements without exposing the underlying collection structure. Kotlin also supports looping through *recursion,* which is when a function calls itself until it reaches a basic form of a problem (the functional language approach to looping). The result of using the iterator and recursive approaches is the same as using loops, but the techniques differ. The following sections discuss Kotlin loops in specific. Chapter 6 of this minibook tells you about the use of recursion to solve problems using the functional programming method in more detail.

Kotlin while statements

A `while` statement has the following form:

```
while (condition) {
    statements to be executed
}
```

You can omit the curly braces when the loop has only one *statement to be executed.*

A traditional `while` statement performs a task while a condition remains `true`. The following loop counts down from 5 through 1:

```
fun main(args: Array<String>) {
    var a = 5

    while (a > 0) {
        println(a)
        --a
    }
}
```

Each time the loop executes, the `--a` statement reduces the value of `a` by `1`. Note that this is a prefix form; you could also use `a-=1` to reduce the value by 1. You don't see a `0` in the output because the condition is `a > 0`, and the condition is checked before the `println(a)` statement is executed. The `while` statement has no expression form, so you won't ever see a variable made equal to a `while` statement as you can with the `if` or `when` expressions.

In an Android app, a content provider feeds a *cursor* to your code. You can think of the cursor as a pointer to a row in a table. In Listing 4-3, each table row has three entries: an `_id`, a `name`, and an `amount`. Supposedly, the `_id` uniquely identifies a row, the `name` is a person's name, and the `amount` is a huge number of dollars owed to you by that person.

LISTING 4-3: A `while` Loop

```
cursor.moveToFirst()

while (!cursor.isAfterLast()) {
    val _id: String = cursor.getString(0)
    val name: String = cursor.getString(1)
    val amount: String = cursor.getString(2)
    textViewDisplay.append(_id + " " +
                           name + " " + amount + "\n")
    cursor.moveToNext()
}
```

A cursor's `moveToFirst` method makes the cursor point to the first row of the table. Regardless of the row a cursor points to, the cursor's `moveToNext` method makes the cursor point to the next row of the table. The cursor's `isAfterLast` method returns `true` when, having tried to move to the next row, it finds that there is no next row.

In Kotlin, an exclamation point (`!`) means "not," so `while (!cursor.isAfterLast())` means "while it's not true that the cursor has reached past the table's last row . . ." So the loop in Listing 4-3 repeatedly does the following:

```
As long as the cursor has not reached past the last row,
    get the string in the row's initial column and
        make _id refer to that string,
    get the string in the row's middle column and
        make name refer to that string,
    get the string in the row's last column and
        make amount refer to that string, and
append these strings to the textViewDisplay, and then
move the cursor to the next row in preparation
        for returning to the top of the while statement.
```


Imagine that a particular cursor's table has 100 rows. Then a processor executes the statements inside Listing 4-3's `while` loop 100 times. Using the official developer lingo, the processor performs 100 loop *iterations.*

TECHNICAL STUFF

In Listing 4-3, the characters `\n` form an *escape sequence.* When you put `\n` inside a string, you're escaping from the normal course of things by displaying neither a backslash nor a letter `n`. Instead, `\n` in a Java string always means "Go to the next line." So in Listing 4-3, `\n` puts a line break between one `_id`, `name`, `amount` group and the next.

Kotlin do statements

Kotlin provides a second form of the `while` statement called the `do` statement. Unlike the `while` statement, which may execute only once, a `do` statement will always execute at least one time because the condition is checked at the end of the loop, rather than at the beginning of the loop. A `do` statement has the following form:

```
do {
    statements to be executed
} while (condition)
```

The following example shows how the do statement works by setting a variable to a value that won't meet conditions.

```
fun main(args: Array<String>) {
    var a = 0

    do {
        println(a)
        --a
    } while (a > 0)
}
```

The example outputs a 0 but then stops. Even though the value of a at the outset doesn't meet the condition while (a > 0), the loop executes once anyway.

To find a particular row of a cursor's table, you normally do a *query*. (For straight talk about queries, see Book 4.) You almost never perform a do-it-yourself search through a table's data. But just this once, look at a loop that iterates through row after row. The loop is in Listing 4-4.

LISTING 4-4: Leap Before You Look

```
cursor.moveToFirst()
name: String = ""

do {
    val _id: String = cursor.getString(0)
    name = cursor.getString(1)
    val amount: String = cursor.getString(2)
    textViewDisplay.append(_id + " " +
                            name + " " + amount + "\n")
    cursor.moveToNext()
} while (!name.equals("Burd") && !cursor.isAfterLast())
```

In Listing 4-4, you're looking for a row with the name *Burd*. (After all, the bum owes you lots of money.) When you enter the loop, the cursor points to the table's first row. Before checking a row for the name *Burd*, you fetch that first row's data and add the data to the textViewDisplay where the user can see what's going on.

Before you march on to the next row (the next loop iteration), you check a condition to make sure that another row is worth visiting. (Check to make sure that you haven't yet found that Burd guy, and that you haven't moved past the last row of the table.)

TECHNICAL STUFF

To get the code in Listing 4-4 working, you have to move the declaration of `name` outside the `do` statement. A declaration that's inside a pair of curly braces (such as the `_id`, `name`, and `amount` declarations in Listing 4-3) cannot be used outside curly braces. So, in Listing 4-4, if you don't move the `name` declaration outside the loop, Java complains that `!name.equals("Burd")` is incorrect.

Also note the use of the `&&` (AND) operator. The `while (!name.equals("Burd") && !cursor.isAfterLast())` expression has two conditions: `!name.equals("Burd")` and `!cursor.isAfterLast()`. Both conditions must be `true` for the `do` loop to continue processing. If you had used the `||` (OR) operator instead, the loop would continue to run as long as one of the two conditions was `true`.

Arrays in Kotlin

An *array* is a bunch of values placed in a single object. When working with a Kotlin array, what you're really doing is working with a class that stores information, not a primitive construct as found in other languages. Kotlin arrays are extremely flexible depending on how you declare them. For example, here's a basic Kotlin array containing mixed types:

```
fun main(args: Array<String>) {
    var myArray = arrayOf(1, 2, true, false, "Hello")
    println(myArray[1])
}
```

The object `myArray` now contains five members: two `Int` values, two `Boolean` values, and a `String`. To access a particular element in the array, you provide the array name, followed by an index in square brackets. The output of this example is 2 because Kotlin arrays are zero-based. So, `myArray[1]` is actually the second array element.

An array can also accept input from expressions. Here is an example that fills the variable `byThree` with the values 1 through 3 and then repeats the process.

```
fun main(args: Array<String>) {
    var byThree = Array(6) {i -> (i % 3) + 1}
    println(byThree[3])
}
```

The output is `1` in this case. The example uses a lambda expression, which you find explained in detail in Chapter 6 of this minibook. The value `i` is the current index, starting with 0 and going through 5. Therefore, `(i % 3) + 1` is the remainder of the index divided by 3 and with 1 added.

Now that you have a basic idea of what arrays are, you can look at a few details. The following sections give some specifics that you'll find handy while creating your Android apps.

Understanding what *invariant* means

Being able to place anything in an array might seem nice at first, but you might want to limit an array to a specific type. To make this happen, you must define the type as part of the array by placing the type in angle brackets, as shown in the following example:

```
fun main(args: Array<String>) {
    var words: Array<String> = Array<String>(6) {String()}
    println("Content of words[0] ${words[0]}")
    words[0] = "Hello"
    println("Content of words[0] ${words[0]}")
}
```

Notice that you must define a size for the array or that the initialization arguments must imply a size. Kotlin arrays can't change size after you create them. To make a larger array, you must first create a new array and then move the current content to the new one. The `String` array, `words`, begins with empty strings, which you verify by printing the array content at index 0.

The `words` array is *invariant,* which means that it accepts only one kind of input, a `String`. If you tried to add a line of code like `words[1] = 2`, the compiler would complain that the entry is of the wrong type. Creating an invariant array means that you can depend on the array to contain a specific type of information, which makes working with the array easier and less error prone.

TECHNICAL STUFF

Note that you might need an array of a certain size and able to hold a specific type, but you might not have content to fill it immediately. If this is the case, you can create a nullable version of the array and fill the missing entries with null values to make it easier to determine when an element contains useful information, as shown here:

```
fun main(args: Array<String>) {
    var words: Array<String?> = Array<String?>(6) {null}
    words[0] = "Hello"
    words[1] = "Goodbye"
    println("Content of words[0] ${words[0]}")
    println("Content of words[1] ${words[1]}")
    println("Content of words[2] ${words[2] == null}")
}
```

Because this is a nullable array, as signified by Array<String?>, you can set the initializer to {null}. Until you specifically assign a value to an element, its entry equals null. In this case, words[2] == null returns true because you haven't specifically set words[2] to a String value.

Working with Kotlin arrays

Kotlin arrays have many marvelous features that you can access through functions or properties. The complete list of these functions and properties appears at https://kotlinlang.org/api/latest/jvm/stdlib/kotlin/-array/index.html. However, here is an example showing some of the more interesting functions that are at your disposal when working with numeric arrays:

```
fun main(args: Array<String>) {
    var numbers: Array<Int> = arrayOf(1, 2, 4, 8, 3, 7, 4, 5)
    println(numbers.all({i -> i > 0}))
    println(numbers.any({i -> i == 8}))
    println(numbers.contains(3))
    println(numbers.find({i -> i > 4}))
    println(numbers.findLast({i -> i > 4}))

    println(numbers.distinct())
    numbers.sort()
    println(numbers.distinct())

    println(numbers.average())
    println(numbers.distinct().count())
    println(numbers.max())
    println(numbers.min())
    println(numbers.sum())
}
```

The functions are grouped into three categories: search, list manipulation, and math. When you need to look for things, you may not always need to look for a specific value, but simply know that the value exists, which is where numbers.all({i -> i > 0}) and numbers.any({i -> i == 8}) come in. These functions help you determine whether all the values meet a minimum criteria or at least one of the values does. The lambda expression {i -> i > 0} says that for each element in the array, compare the element to 0 and if the element is greater than 0, return true. The numbers.contains(3) function looks for a specific value. If you need to find the element where a value appears, you can use functions like `numbers.find({i -> i > 4})` and `numbers.findLast({i -> i > 4})`. Here are the outputs from this section.

```
true
true
true
8
5
```

The array functions include a lot of list-manipulation features — possibly more than you can use in a lifetime. However, the ability to find distinct values and to sort the array so that the values are in order are high on the list. Fortunately, you don't have to come up with any odd lambda expressions to use these functions. Here are the outputs:

```
[1, 2, 4, 8, 3, 7, 5]
[1, 2, 3, 4, 5, 7, 8]
```

The math functions let you perform statistics on the array. Statistics are useful for all sorts of things, like determining whether item one or item two is a better value in your shopping app. You also use statistics for games and to determine whether fraud is occurring. In some cases, you can combine functions to get unique results, such as `numbers.distinct().count()`, which counts only the unique entries in a list. Here is the output from this part of the code:

```
4.25
7
8
1
34
```

Using Kotlin arrays for primitive types

Because you need to interoperate with Java at times, it would be handy to have an array type that works with primitive variables without the *boxing overhead* (the time needed to place a primitive variable into an object). In this case, you rely on a specific kind of array that has nothing to do with the standard Kotlin `Array` object. These primitive arrays take the following form:

```
var numbers: IntArray = intArrayOf(1, 2, 3, 4)
```

You can also initialize these arrays to a specific size and specific content using any of these methods:

```
val numbers1 = IntArray(5)
val numbers2 = IntArray(5) {-1}
val numbers3 = IntArray(5) {i -> i + 1}
```

In the first case, you get an array of five elements containing zeros. The second case gives you five elements filled with −1. The third case uses a lambda expression to fill the elements with values from 1 through 5.

REMEMBER

The primitive arrays don't cover things like `String` values because these values are already reference types in Java and wouldn't create any boxing overhead. You can obtain primitive arrays in the following types:

- `ByteArray`
- `ShortArray`
- `IntArray`
- `LongArray`
- `FloatArray`
- `DoubleArray`
- `BooleanArray`
- `CharArray`

Kotlin's for statements

Kotlin doesn't have a `for` statement of the type used with other programming languages in which you define a variable to keep track of a specific number of loop iterations. When the variable meets a certain criterion, the loop stops, so basically you can say, "Execute this loop five times and then stop." Instead, Kotlin relies on a `for` statement that uses an iterator, as described in the introduction to this section. Essentially, an iterator makes it easy to access members of an object one item at a time, but you don't have to know how many times at the outset. As with a standard `for` loop, however, the loop executes a fixed number of times and then stops. The following sections describe how the Kotlin `for` statements work.

Defining the iterator

A Kotlin `for` statement has this form:

```
for (item in collection) print(item)
```

A collection is any object that provides an iterator. To qualify, the object must possess these features:

- Have a member or extension function called `iterator()`. The return type of the `iterator()` function must provide access to these elements:
  - A `next()` member or extension function that obtains the next item.
  - A `hasNext()` member or extension function that returns Boolean indicating whether there is a next item to obtain.
- All three functions — `iterator()`, `next()`, and `hasNext()` — need to be marked as `operator`.

REMEMBER

The term *collection* could refer to a `Collection`, `MutableCollection`, `List`, `Set`, or `Map`, which are collections in the general sense. A collection can also refer to a range, progression, or sequence. In fact, *collection* refers to any object that implements the `Iterable` interface. You can see an example of a custom color range iterator at `https://www.baeldung.com/kotlin-custom-range-iterator`.

Working with ranges, progressions, sequences

A collection is a generic sort of grouping of items into a single object using the `Iterable` interface. However, you can get more specific with certain kinds of collections because they follow a particular pattern. Here are three kinds of Kotlin collections normally associated with numeric data that follow a particular pattern:

- **Range:** A closed interval in a mathematical sense where the range is defined by a starting and an ending point. The collection is an ordered object for comparable types, such as integers, that implement the `Comparable` interface. Not all ranges implement the `Iterable` interface, which means that you can't use them in a `for` statement without modification. For example, the following code will raise an error if you try to use `versionRange` in a `for` loop:

```
fun main(args: Array<String>) {
    val versionRange = KotlinVersion(1, 11)..KotlinVersion(1, 30)
    println(KotlinVersion(0, 9) in versionRange)    // Displays false
    println(KotlinVersion(1, 14) in versionRange)   // Displays true
}
```

- **Progression:** A special kind of numeric range for types, such as `Int`, `Long`, and `Char`, that provides a starting point, ending point, and non-zero step between values.

» **Sequence:** An alternative to iterable collections in which processing occurs *lazily,* only as needed. There is little difference between an iteration and a sequence for simple collections, but when you're working with collections that require multiple processing steps, using a sequence can improve app performance.

Ranges take all sorts of forms, and you'll use a lot of them in Android development. However, the simplest ranges are found when working with numbers. The following example shows a range of `Int` values from 1 through 10 and two methods of printing that range:

```
val numbers = 1..10

for (number in numbers) println(number)
numbers.forEach({println(it)})
```

REMEMBER

The standard `for` loop method lets you work with the individual values in a structured way and works best for complex processing. The `forEach()` function approach lets you perform simple tasks using extremely concise code. Both forms make it easy to iterate through a range of numbers or any other collection.

Progressions specify a step between values in a range. You can define them using a number of methods. Here are two methods of creating a progression as a variable:

```
val numbers = 2..10 step 2
val numbers = IntProgression.fromClosedRange(2, 10, 2)
```

In both cases, you specify a starting value, ending value, and a step value. You can also create a progression as part of the `for` loop:

```
val numbers = 2..10

for (number in numbers step 2) println(number)
numbers.forEach({i -> if (i % 2 == 0) println(i)})
```

In the first case, you specify a `step` value as part of the `for` loop condition. When working with the `forEach()` function, you need to specify the step value as part of a lambda expression, as shown here, or use some other method of filtering values. The lambda expression used here selects even values by obtaining the result of the current value mod 2.

You can turn any range into a sequence by using the `asSequence()` function. Using a sequence can reduce processing steps when working with a multiple-step process. However, after you turn a range into a sequence, you can't work with it as a progression, which means that you can't specify a `step` value as part of a `for` loop. Instead, you need to resort to techniques such as filtering, as shown here:

```
val numbers = (2..10).asSequence()

for (number in numbers.filter({it % 2 == 0})) {
    println(number)
}
numbers.forEach({i -> if (i % 2 == 0) println(i)})
```

Sometimes you need to resort to clever programming or tricks to get the result you want. For example, even though a `KotlinVersion` range doesn't allow direct iteration, you can use the following code to obtain a list of major and minor values:

```
fun main(args: Array<String>) {
    val versionRange = KotlinVersion(1, 11)..KotlinVersion(1, 30)

    val start = versionRange.start
    val end = versionRange.endInclusive

    for (major in start.major..end.major) {
        for (minor in start.minor..end.minor) {
            println("$major.$minor")
        }
    }
}
```

Iterating indexes

When working with a standard `for` loop, you have an index value you use to access each member of the collection. However, using the iterator approach means that you either need to create a counter or simply do without an index value in Kotlin using its approach. Fortunately, you have two methods to work with indexes in Kotlin:

- `withIndex()`
- `forEachIndex`

These two functions produce about the same results and should have the same performance characteristics. The only difference is in how you implement them. Use the method that works best for you. Here's an example of `withIndex()`:

```
val numbers = 2..10

for ((index, number) in numbers.withIndex()) {
    println("The value $number is at index $index.")
}
```

You don't have to do anything special with the range. The only changes are your addition of `withIndex()` to the range and output values to two variables: `index` and `number`. The index is always the first variable, and the value is always the second variable in the output.

The `forEachIndex` approach does rely on a lambda expression. It looks like this:

```
val numbers = 2..10

numbers.forEachIndexed{index, number ->
    println("The value $number is at index $index.")}
```

The results are the same as before, but the technique used to obtain them differs. In this case, `index` and `number` act as inputs to the lambda expression, but otherwise the code looks the same.

Looping using Kotlin recursion

When working with standard loops, each iteration of the loop depends on the previous iteration. Consequently, it's difficult to perform looping in a multiprocessing environment because of the element of *state*, the recording of loop conditions, in each iteration. One of the goals of functional programming is to enable you to split up everything in an app so that each part can execute on a different processor. Although this might not seem a very laudable goal with the kinds of examples you see in this book, it's an essential element of higher-end apps that perform machine learning or deep learning tasks (among other things). In these environments, developers often use GPUs instead of CPUs to perform processing, and some of the GPU cards used contain hordes of processors. (The NVidia Titan V contains 5,120 CUDA core; see `https://www.nvidia.com/en-us/titan/titan-v/`.) Consequently, you need another way to perform looping, which is where recursion comes into play. However, even in an Android app, the ability to break up a problem into very small pieces for execution on separate processors can be important, especially when it comes to games.

Chapter 6 of this minibook delves more deeply into recursion, but for now, take a look at a simple example:

```
fun main(args: Array<String>) {
    val numbers = (2..10)

    LoopIt(numbers, numbers.count() - 1)
}

fun LoopIt(range: Iterable<Any>, posit: Int) {
    if (posit >= 0) {
        LoopIt(range, posit - 1)
        println(range.elementAt(posit))
    } else {
        println("All elements visited!")
    }
}
```

The actual display of values occurs in the `LoopIt()` function. The idea is that you can't display multiple range values — you can display only one range value using `println(range.elementAt(posit))`. So, you must work through the range until you get to the first element and then display each single element in turn until you reach the end. The `LoopIt(range, posit - 1)` call keeps calling `LoopIt()` one element position at a time until it reaches the beginning of the range: element 0.

The amazing thing is that each of these calls is separate and the variables are `val`, which means they can't change. Until the code reaches element 0, the `LoopIt(range, posit - 1)` call doesn't return; instead, it keeps moving forward in a circle until it reaches its destination. When the code does reach element 0, it prints the message `"All elements visited!"`. What you see as output is

```
All elements visited!
2
3
4
5
6
7
8
9
10
```

Working with break and continue

Sometimes a loop condition that you didn't expect or want to avoid will occur. The condition isn't necessarily an error, but it's just not what you wanted. In this case, you need to perform a structural jump. Kotlin provides three such jumps:

- `continue`: The loop stops at its current point of processing and continues with the next loop iteration. This type of jump allows processing to continue, even if you want to avoid a particular condition.
- `break`: The loop exits at its current point of processing and continues with the next statement in the current function. You use this kind of jump when a condition will make further loop processing pointless, but you want to continue with the current processing instructions.
- `return`: The loop exits at its current point of processing and returns to the caller. You use this kind of jump when a condition will prevent further processing in a called function, but the condition isn't necessarily an error — it's just unexpected or unwanted.

You use `continue` or `break` in any loop, whether the code exists in the current function or in a called function. Here's an example of using `continue` and `break` in a `for` loop:

```
fun main(args: Array<String>) {
    val numbers = (2..10)

    for (number in numbers) {
        if (number == 3) continue
        if (number == 8) break
        println(number)
    }
    println("The loop has ended.")
}
```

The output from this example is

```
2
4
5
6
7
The loop has ended.
```

REMEMBER

Notice that the `println(number)` call doesn't occur for 3 because the loop continues with the next iteration: `if (number == 3) continue`. Even though the loop could continue processing values beyond 7, the loop ends at 7 because of the call to `if (number == 8) break`. Always remember that `break` implies that you want to break out of the loop and `continue` implies that you want to continue processing the loop.

The `return` jump works a bit differently from `continue` or `break`. Here's an example of `return`:

```
fun main(args: Array<String>) {
    val numbers = (2..10)

    processData(numbers)
    println("The call has returned.")
}

fun processData(numbers: IntRange) {
    for (number in numbers) {
        if (number == 8) return
        println(number)
    }
    println("The loop has ended.")
}
```

In this case, the jump occurs in a called function, `processData()`. You see the values 2 through 7 output, but when the value reaches 8, the code calls `return`. The example never displays `"The loop has ended."`, as it would when `break` is called. Instead, the entire `processData()` function ends and the call returns to `main()`.

WARNING

If the `return` call had happened in `main()`, the app would have stopped, which would be confusing to your user, so you should avoid using `return` unless absolutely necessary.

Jumping Away from Trouble

The Kotlin programming language has a mechanism called *exception handling*. With exception handling, a program can detect that things are about to go wrong and respond by creating a brand-new object. In the official terminology, the program is said to be *throwing* an exception. That new object, an instance of the `Exception` class, is passed like a hot potato from one piece of code to another until some piece of code decides to *catch* the exception. When the exception is caught, the program executes some recovery code, buries the exception, and moves on to the next normal statement as if nothing had ever happened (at least in theory).

The whole thing is done with the aid of several Kotlin keywords. These keywords are as follows:

- `throw`: Creates a new exception object.
- `try`: Encloses code that has the potential to create a new exception object. In the usual scenario, the code inside a `try` clause contains calls to methods whose code can create one or more exceptions.
- `catch`: Deals with the exception, buries it, and then moves on.
- `finally`: Sometimes you need to execute some code regardless of whether an exception occurs. For example, you might need to perform some cleanup so that when the program recovers because of your exquisite error handling, it doesn't immediately throw another exception.
- `Nothing`: This is a special type used to tell the Kotlin compiler what a particular function never returns. It's an end point when something too terrible for words occurs. When the compiler sees `Nothing`, it assumes that the app won't continue. Here's an example:

```
fun appFailure(message: String): Nothing {
    throw IllegalArgumentException(message)
}
```

TECHNICAL STUFF

If you have worked with Java, you know that Java also supports a `throws` keyword for checked exceptions. Kotlin doesn't support checked exceptions, so you won't see the `throws` keyword used (see the "Getting rid of the checked exceptions" section of Chapter 2 of this minibook for details).

Kotlin spends a good deal of time looking over your shoulder, so you'll encounter fewer exceptions as you write apps. However, it's a good idea to make preparations to handle them anyway. In the following example, the code attempts to convert a `String` value to an `Int` value:

```
val myIntStr: String = "Hello"

try {
    val myInt = myIntStr.toInt()
    println("Success: $myInt!")
} catch (e: NumberFormatException) {
    println("myIntStr is in the wrong format.")
```

```
} finally {
    println("Try another int conversion?")
}
```

Obviously, a value of "Hello" will never convert to an Int value, so the toInt() function throws a NumberFormatException, which the code catches and then displays "myIntStr is in the wrong format.". However, if you change "Hello" to "2", the conversion does take place and you see "Success: 2!" instead. No matter what happens, however, you always see the final output of "Try another int conversion?".

Now the problem is in trying to determine which exceptions to catch. The Kotlin documentation includes an Exceptions section for each of the functions it supports. So, for example, when you look at the toInt() function documentation at https://kotlinlang.org/api/latest/jvm/stdlib/kotlin.text/to-int.html, you see that the only exception it throws is NumberFormatException.

Unlike other languages, try isn't a statement; it's an expression. So you can use it as part of any expression you create. Here's an example of performing an Int conversion that relies on an expression:

```
val myIntStr: String = "Hello"

val myInt: Int = try { myIntStr.toInt() }
    catch (e: NumberFormatException) {
        println("myIntStr is in the wrong format.")
        0
    }

println(myInt)
```

Because this is an expression, you must return a value to myInt, even if the conversion fails. You could handle this in several ways. The example simply sets the output to 0. However, you could also make myInt nullable and set the output to null, or you could use a special value such as -1 (when no negative values are expected).

Working with Kotlin Collections

A *collection* is a grouping of items in a specific kind of container. Some containers, such as List, are simple; others, such as Map, are more complicated. The container you choose depends on the complexity of the app environment — that is, how the data in the container will get used. The following sections take a brief look at Kotlin containers.

KOTLIN ARRAY VERSUS LIST

A Kotlin `Array` isn't in the same boat as a Kotlin collection. You need to know that an `Array` is implemented differently from any of the collections, and using a collection is preferable to an `Array` because collections provide more flexibility and adhere to a strong set of constraints. Here are some differences to consider between `Array` and `List`:

- An `Array` consumes a fixed amount of memory and has a specific implementation, while a `List` is dynamically allocated and relies on an interface, so its implementation depends on the data stored.
- An `Array` is always mutable, but you must use a special `List` type to provide mutability.
- An `Array` has a fixed size, so you must copy the `Array` to change its size. A mutable `List` can grow or shrink as needed.
- An `Array` is optimized for use with basic (primitive) types.
- An `Array` is invariant on `T` (`Array<Int>` is not `Array<Number>`), while `Lists` are covariant on `T` (`List<Int>` is `List<Number>`).

There are other differences, but these are the most important to remember. The bottom line is that you can view an `Array` as a kind of collection, but programmatically, it's not one.

Considering the collection types

Kotlin doesn't actually support many native collection types. You have three choices, as described here:

- `List`: An ordered collection of items in which item values can appear more than once and each value is accessed by a unique index. You would use a `List` to hold the individual words in a sentence, for example, when order is important.
- `Set`: A collection of unique items in which each value is accessed by an index, but the order of the items is unimportant. You would use a `Set` to hold the letters of the alphabet or the numbers 0 through 9, for example.
- `Map`: A collection of key and value pairs in which the keys are ordered and unique, while the values need not be unique. Each key points to a specific value, even when that value is the same as some other value in the `Map`. Another term for a `Map` is a dictionary. You often see a `Map` used to store logical connections between items, such as locations on a map or the hierarchy in an organization.

However, these three choices aren't the extent of your options. Kotlin provides Java interoperability, so this is one place where you may need to go the Kotlin version of the Java route to make things work. With this idea in mind, you also have these Java-specific options:

ArrayList	LinkedList	Vector
Stack	Queue	PriorityQueue
Deque	ArrayDeque	HashSet
LinkedHashSet	SortedSet	TreeSet

REMEMBER

Using a Kotlin-specific implementation when possible is always preferable. In fact, the compiler often warns you when you attempt to use a Java collection when a Kotlin version is available. The Kotlin implementation provides additional flexibility and more safeguards than the Java version. Here is a Kotlin implementation of a `Map`:

```
val myMap = mapOf("Yellow" to 1, "Green" to 2, "Blue" to 3)

for ((Key, Value) in myMap) {
    println("The value $Value is associated with $Key.")
}
```

Notice that when you create a `Map`, you must associate a key, such as `"Yellow"`, with a value, such as `1`. Likewise, when iterating through a Map, you obtain both a key and a value for each loop.

As previously mentioned, sometimes you need to use a Java collection when Kotlin doesn't provide what you need. One of the most common Java collections you use is the `Stack`. A `Stack` pushes new values into the collection and pops them back off the top, which makes this is a last-in/first-out (LIFO) collection. Here is an example of a Java `Stack` implemented in Kotlin:

```
import java.util.Stack

fun main(args: Array<String>) {
    val myStack = Stack<String>()

    myStack.push("Hello")
    myStack.push("Goodbye")
    myStack.push("Yesterday")

    println(myStack.count())
    println(myStack.pop())
}
```

The example begins by importing the proper collection from `java.util`, which is a `Stack` in this case. You use the standard Kotlin approach to creating a new `Stack`, but you must make sure to specify the data type that will appear in the `Stack` or the compiler will complain. Theoretically, you can use the `Any` type with a Java collection.

To add a new item to `myStack`, you call the `push()` function with whatever value you want to add. You determine the number of items on the stack by calling `count()`. To remove an item, you call `pop()`, and the value is provided as a return.

Differentiating between read-only and mutable collections

By default, Kotlin collections are *immutable*, meaning read-only. After you create the collection, you can't add, subtract, or change values. For example, the documentation for `List` at `https://kotlinlang.org/api/latest/jvm/stdlib/kotlin.collections/-list/index.html` contains all sorts of methods for searching, selecting, and otherwise stretching the `List` in every conceivable direction, but the data remains the same. You can obtain part of the data and put it into a new `List`, but the current `List` is immutable.

REMEMBER

Making a collection immutable lets you work with the collection in ways that aren't possible when you use a mutable collection. If you know that the collection won't ever change, you can offload processing to a bunch of processors and not really care which processor does what. When working with huge datasets, the ability to use multiple processors outweighs almost every other consideration. Even with smaller apps of the sort you create for Android, the speed difference of using an immutable collection can be noticeable, but there is the penalty of never being able to change the collection content to pay. Of course, this may be a non-issue if the data you've collected, such as a list of states in the U.S., isn't likely to change. Here's an example of an immutable `List`:

```
val myList = listOf(1, 2, 3, 4, 5)
for (item in myList) println(item)
```

TIP

Oddly enough, using an immutable `List` is also more secure than using the mutable version. Because no one can modify the `List` content, it becomes harder for someone to suddenly decide to make your life interesting with unauthorized changes.

A MutableList offers the flexibility of being able to grow or reduce the size of the collection and to change collection items. When you look at the documentation for MutableList at https://kotlinlang.org/api/latest/jvm/stdlib/kotlin.collections/-mutable-list/index.html, you see all sorts of functions to modify the list content. Here is an example of a MutableList:

```
val myList = mutableListOf(1, 2, 3, 4, 5)
myList.add(6)
myList.set(2, 20)
myList.remove(0)
for (item in myList) println(item)
```

Here is the output from this example:

```
1
2
20
4
5
6
```

All the changes that the code made are shown in the output, as expected. Even with this sort of list, you have limits on what you can do unless you create your code correctly at the outset. For example, myList.add("Hello") would fail with myList in this case. To make it possible to add a string, you'd need to declare myList like this:

```
val myList: MutableList<Any> = mutableListOf(1, 2, 3, 4, 5)
```

Notice that the myList is now defined as being of type MutableList<Any>. As you work through your Android app, you have to choose the correct methods of interacting with app data to make your app secure, efficient, and fast. The collection choices that Kotlin provides let you make good choices more easily.

» Working with Kotlin's classes and interfaces

» Being part of Kotlin's inner circle

» Putting your eggs (your file, that is) in a basket

Chapter 5 Object-Oriented Programming in Kotlin

Kotlin can work in the object-oriented programming (OOP) paradigm, much as Java does. It's not limited to OOP, though. If your heart so desires, you can use it as a functional programming language, too. Chapter 3 in this minibook covers the highlights of both functional and OOP in Kotlin. That chapter focuses on the object-oriented nature of Android development, though, because that's the topic of this book.

There are significant differences between Java and Kotlin in OOP implementation, so even if you're familiar with Java OOP, read this chapter to prepare for future chapters on Android programming using Kotlin. This chapter covers some of object-oriented programming's finer points.

Static Fields and Methods

Listing 5-1 reproduces a small portion of the source code of Android's `Toast` class from `Toast.java`. (To open the file in Android Studio, right-click any `Toast` entry in your code and choose Go To⇨Declaration from the context menu.) This class relies on Java even when you're using it from Kotlin, so the underlying class uses

Java principles. Using the class differs in Kotlin when compared to Java. (For comparison purposes, you can read about the Kotlin version of this class at `https://developer.android.com/reference/kotlin/android/widget/Toast.html` and the Java version of this class at `https://developer.android.com/reference/android/widget/Toast.html`.)

LISTING 5-1: An Unrepresentative Sample of Android's Toast Class Code

```
public class Toast {


  public static final int LENGTH_LONG = 1;


  public static Toast makeText(Context context,
                               CharSequence text,
                               int duration) {
    Toast result = new Toast(context);

    LayoutInflater inflate = (LayoutInflater) context.
      getSystemService(Context.LAYOUT_INFLATER_SERVICE);
    View v = inflate.inflate
      (com.android.internal.
      R.layout.transient_notification, null);
    TextView tv = (TextView)v.findViewById
      (com.android.internal.R.id.message);
    tv.setText(text);

    result.mNextView = v;
    result.mDuration = duration;

    return result;
  }

  public void show() {
    if (mNextView == null) {
      throw new RuntimeException
        ("setView must have been called");
    }

    INotificationManager service = getService();

    String pkg = mContext.getPackageName();

    TN tn = mTN;
```

```
    try {
      service.enqueueToast(pkg, tn, mDuration);
    } catch (RemoteException e) {
      // Empty
    }
  }
}
```

According to the code in Listing 5-1, the Toast class has a static field named LENGTH_LONG and a static method named makeText. Anything that's declared to be static belongs to the whole class, not to any particular instance of the class. When you create the static field, LENGTH_LONG, you create only one copy of the field. This copy stays with the entire Toast class. No matter how many instances of the Toast class you create — one, nine, or none — you have just one LENGTH_LONG field.

REMEMBER

Kotlin doesn't support static fields (as described in Chapter 2 of this minibook). However, you can create an equivalent of a static field when necessary. Here is the equivalent of the LENGTH_LONG field in Kotlin:

```
companion object {
    const val LENGTH_LONG = 1
}
```

Contrast this situation with the one in Chapter 3 of this minibook. In that chapter, the Account class has fields called name, address, and balance. The fields aren't static, so every instance of the Account class has its own name, its own address, and its own balance. One instance has name Barry Burd and balance 24.02, and another instance has name John Q. Public with balance -471.03. To refer to Burd's balance, you may write something like

```
val myAccount = Account()

myAccount.name = "Burd"
myAccount.address = "222 Cyberspace Lane";
myAccount.balance = 24.02
```

To refer to a non-static member of a class, you write the name of an object (such as myAccount), followed by a dot and then the name of the member (such as balance).

But the Toast class's LENGTH_LONG field is static. When you create a Toast instance, you don't create a new LENGTH_LONG field. The Toast class has one LENGTH_LONG field, and that's that. Accordingly, you refer to LENGTH_LONG by prefacing the field name with the Toast class name, followed by a dot:

```
Toast.LENGTH_LONG
```

In fact, a typical use of `Toast` in an Android app refers to the static field `LENGTH_LONG` and the static method `makeText`:

```
Toast.makeText
  (getApplication(), "Whoa!", Toast.LENGTH_LONG).show();
```

A call to the `Toast` class's `makeText` method returns an actual object — an instance of the `Toast` class. (You can verify this by referring to the first line of the `makeText` method in Listing 5-1, earlier in the chapter.) So in an Android app, an expression such as

```
Toast.makeText
  (getApplication(), "Whoa!", Toast.LENGTH_LONG)
```

stands for an object. And (again, according to Listing 5-1) each object created from the `Toast` class has its own non-static `show()` method. That's why you normally follow a `Toast.makeText` call with `.show()`.

Here's one final word about Listing 5-1: In addition to being `static`, the `LENGTH_LONG` field is also `final`. A `final` field is one whose value cannot be changed. In other words, when you declare `LENGTH_LONG`, you can initialize its value to `1` (as in Listing 5-1). But elsewhere in the code, you can't write `LENGTH_LONG = 2`. (For that matter, you can't even write `LENGTH_LONG = 1` elsewhere in the code.)

TECHNICAL STUFF

Many programming languages, including Kotlin, use the word *constant* (or the abbreviation `const`) to refer to a variable whose value cannot be changed.

Interfaces and Callbacks

Because you'll be looking at both Kotlin and Java interfaces when working through your Android code, this section presents both. Listing 5-2 contains a snippet from Android's pre-declared Java code. The listing contains a Java *interface*.

LISTING 5-2: Android's `OnClickListener` Interface

```
public interface OnClickListener {
    void onClick(View v);
}
```

The Kotlin version of this same interface (which you won't find in the underlying libraries) looks like this:

```
interface OnClickListener {
    fun onClick(View v)
}
```

An interface is like a class, but it's different. (So, what else is new? A cow is like a planet, but it's quite a bit different. Cows moo; planets hang in space.) Anyway, when you hear the word *interface*, you can start by thinking of a class. Then, in your head, note the following things:

- **A class doesn't extend an interface; instead, a class *implements* an interface.** Later in this chapter, you can see the following line of code:

  ```
  class MyListener implements OnClickListener
  ```

  To implement the same interface using Kotlin, you use

  ```
  class MyListener: OnClickListener
  ```

- **A class can extend only one parent class, but a class can implement more than one interface.** For example, if you want `MyListener` objects to listen for long clicks as well as regular clicks, you can write

  ```
  class MyListener implements OnClickListener,
                              OnLongClickListener {
  ```

  A long click is what nondevelopers would probably call a touch-and-hold motion.

  TECHNICAL STUFF

  Kotlin doesn't allow true multiple inheritance, so you can still inherit from just one parent class. However, by using a fancy feature called *class delegation,* in which you delegate handling of inherited features to another class, you can create something that looks a lot like multiple inheritance but doesn't come with the problems that multiple inheritance can create. Covering class delegation is outside the scope of this book, but you can read about it at `https://sites.google.com/a/athaydes.com/renato-athaydes/posts/solutionstomultipleinheritanceinkotlin` if you really want to know how to do something fancy.

  As with Java, you can implement multiple interfaces in Kotlin with ease. Here is the Kotlin version of the Java example that appeared earlier in this bullet:

  ```
  class MyListener: OnClickListener, OnLongClickListener {
  ```

- **An interface can extend another interface.** For example, in the following line of code, a homegrown interface named `SomeListener` extends Android's built-in `OnClickListener` interface:

  ```
  public interface SomeListener extends OnClickListener {
  ```

  The Kotlin version of the same code looks like this:

  ```
  interface SomeListener: OnClickListener {
  ```

- **An interface can extend more than one interface.**
- **An interface's methods have no bodies of their own.** In Listing 5-2, the `onClick` method has no body — no curly braces and no statements to execute. In place of a body, there's just a semicolon (just the function declaration in Kotlin).

  A method with no body, like the method defined in Listing 5-2, is an *abstract method.*

  Starting with Java 8, a method declared inside an interface can have a body. A method of this kind is called a *default method.* As an Android developer, you can use these features, but only when you configure your project correctly. To do this, you update your `build.gradle (Module:app)` by adding a `compileOptions` block as well as `JavaVersion.VERSION_1_8`, as shown here:

  ```
  compileOptions {
      sourceCompatibility JavaVersion.VERSION_1_8
      targetCompatibility JavaVersion.VERSION_1_8
  }
  ```

  When working with Kotlin, you don't have to worry about any changes to support default methods.

- **When you implement an interface, you provide bodies for all the interface's methods.** That's why the `MyListener` class in Listing 5-3 has an `onClick()` method. By announcing that it will implement the `OnClickListener` interface, the `MyListener` class agrees that it will give meaning to the interface's `onClick()` method. In this situation, *giving meaning* means declaring an `onClick()` method with curly braces, a body, and maybe some statements to execute.

LISTING 5-3: Implementing Android's `OnClickListener` Interface in Java

```
package com.allmycode.samples;

import android.app.Activity;
import android.os.Bundle;
```

```
import android.view.View;
import android.view.View.OnClickListener;
import android.widget.Button;

public class MyActivity extends Activity {

    Button button;

    @Override
    public void onCreate(Bundle savedInstanceState) {
        super.onCreate(savedInstanceState);
        setContentView(R.layout.main);

        button = ((Button) findViewById(R.id.button1));

        button.setOnClickListener(new MyListener(this));
    }
}

class MyListener implements OnClickListener {
    Activity activity;

    MyListener (Activity activity) {
        this.activity = activity;
    }

    @Override
    public void onClick(View arg0) {
        ((MyActivity) activity).button.setBackgroundColor
                             (android.graphics.Color.GRAY);
    }
}
```

Listing 5-3 doesn't illustrate the most popular way to implement the `OnClickListener` interface, but the listing presents a straightforward use of interfaces and their implementations. The Kotlin version of the same `MyListener` class looks like this:

```
package com.example.myfirstapp

import androidx.appcompat.app.AppCompatActivity
import android.os.Bundle
import android.view.View
import kotlinx.android.synthetic.main.activity_main.*
```

Object-Oriented Programming in Kotlin

```
class MainActivity : AppCompatActivity() {

    override fun onCreate(savedInstanceState: Bundle?) {
        super.onCreate(savedInstanceState)
        setContentView(R.layout.activity_main)

        button.setOnClickListener(MyListener())
    }
}

class MyListener : View.OnClickListener {
    override fun onClick(v: View?) {
        v!!.setBackgroundColor(android.graphics.Color.GRAY)
    }
}
```

When you override the function `onClick()` in Kotlin, you must set `v` as nullable. This means that you must use a `!!` operator to access the `v` members. Fortunately, the IDE automatically addresses this issue for you, but it's something to be aware of because of Kotlin's handling of `null` values.

When you announce that you're going to implement an interface (as in `class MyListener implements OnClickListener` or class `MyListener : View.OnClickListener`), the compiler takes this announcement seriously. In the body of the class, if you fail to give meaning to any of the interface's methods, the compiler yells at you.

Fortunately, Android Studio tells you about any missing implementations. It displays messages telling you which methods to implement. As an alternative, you can choose Code⇨Implement Methods to tell the IDE to implement the methods for you automatically.

You can think of an interface as a kind of contract. When you write

```
class MyListener implements OnClickListener
```

or (for Kotlin):

```
class MyListener : View.OnClickListener
```

you're binding `MyListener` to the contract described in Listing 5-2. That contract states, "You, the implementing class, hereby agree to provide a body for each of the abstract methods declared in the interface and to indemnify and hold harmless this interface for any damages, mishaps, or embarrassments from wearing pocket protectors."

As a member of society, you have exactly two biological parents, but you can enter into agreements with any number of companies. In the same way, a Java class has only one parent class, but a class can implement many interfaces. Likewise, even though Kotlin has some tricky ways to get around implementing just one parent class, the reality is that you can implement only one parent class, in the strictest sense, and implement as many interfaces as you want.

The interface-implementing hierarchy (if you can call it a "hierarchy") cuts across the class-extension hierarchy. Figure 5-1 illustrates this idea, showing class extensions vertically and displaying interface implementations horizontally. (Android's `KeyboardView` class lives in the `android.inputmethodservice` package. Both `KeyboardView` and the homegrown `MyListener` class in Listing 5-3 implement Android's `OnClickListener` interface.)

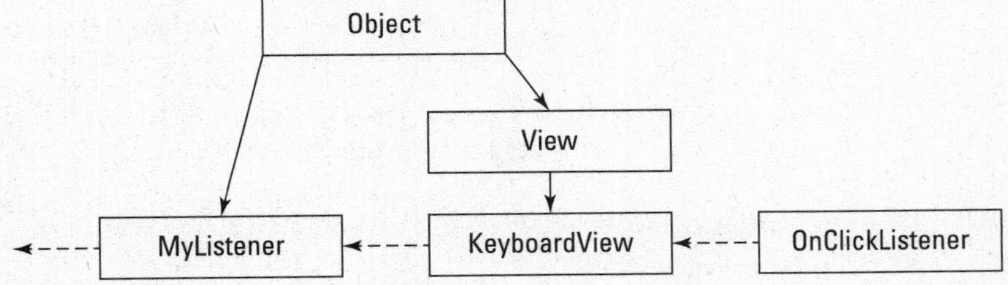

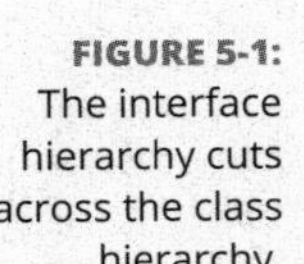

FIGURE 5-1: The interface hierarchy cuts across the class hierarchy.

Event handling and callbacks

The big news in Listing 5-3, shown in the preceding section, is the handling of the user's button click. Anything the user does (such as pressing a key, touching the screen, or whatever) is an *event*. The code that responds to the user's press or touch is the *event-handling* code.

TECHNICAL STUFF

Some things that the user doesn't do are also events. For example, when you turn on a device's GPS sensor and the sensor gets its first fix, Android calls the `onGpsStatusChanged` event handler.

Listing 5-3 deals with the click event with three parts of its code:

- The `MyListener` class declaration says that this class implements `OnClickListener`.
- The activity's `onCreate()` method sets the button's click handler to a new `MyListener` object.
- The code for the `MyListener` class has an `onClick()` method.

Taken together, all three of these tricks make the `MyListener` class handle button clicks. Figure 5-2 illustrates the process. (The details are for Java, but the Kotlin details are similar.)

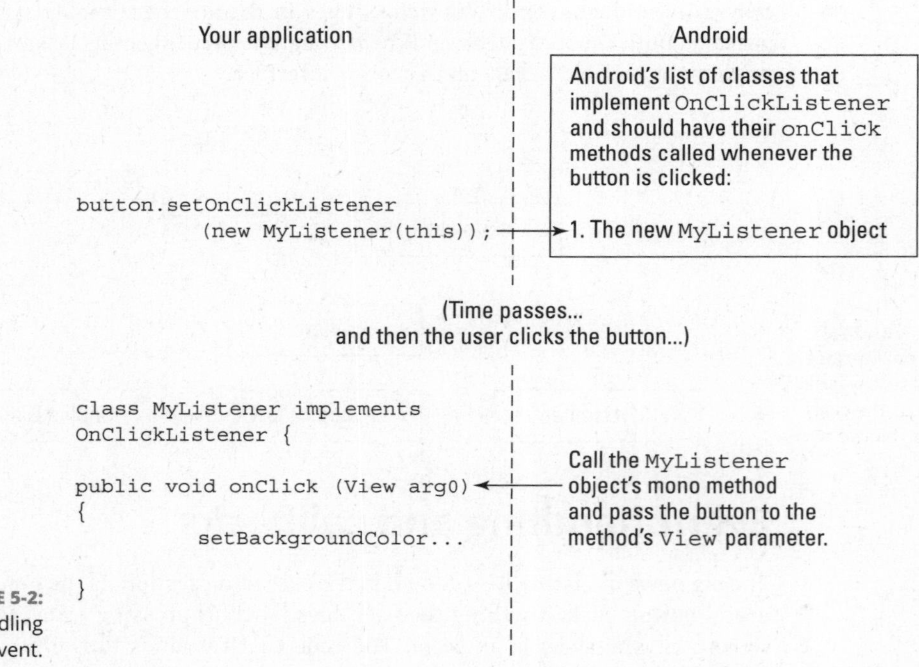

FIGURE 5-2: Handling an event.

When the user clicks the button, Android says, "Okay, the button was clicked. So, what should I do about that?" And the answer is, "Call an `onClick()` method." It's as if Android has code that looks like this:

```
OnClickListener object1;
if (buttonJustGotClicked()) {
    object1.onClick(infoAboutTheClick);
}
```

Of course, behind every answer is yet another question. In this situation, the follow-up question is, "Where does Android find `onClick()` methods to call?" And there's another question: "What if you don't want Android to call certain `onClick()` methods that are lurking in your code?"

Well, that's why you call the `setOnClickListener()` method. In Listing 5-3, the call

```
button.setOnClickListener(new MyListener(this));
```

or (for Kotlin)

```
button.setOnClickListener(MyListener())
```

creates a new `MyListener` object. You tell Android, "Put the new object's `onClick` method on your list of methods to be called. Call this object's `onClick()` method whenever the button is clicked."

And in response to this request, Android asks, "Oh, yeah? How do I know that your `MyListener` object has an `onClick()` method that I can call?" And before you can answer the question, Android notices that your `MyListener` class implements the `OnClickListener` interface. So (because of the code in Listing 5-2), your `MyListener` object has an `onClick()` method.

TECHNICAL STUFF

Of course, Android doesn't really ask, "How do I know that your `MyListener` object has an `onClick()` method?" For one thing, Android doesn't say anything because Android doesn't have a mouth. And for another thing, Android's code to call `onClick()` declares the object containing the `onClick()` method to be of type `OnClickListener()`. So, if your `MyListener` method doesn't implement `OnClickListener`, the compiler notices a type inconsistency (and the compiler complains vigorously).

So here's the sequence of events (follow along in Figure 5-2): Your app registers a listener with Android. Then your app goes about its business. When a relevant event takes place (such as the clicking of a button), Android calls back to your app's code. Android calls the `onClick()` method inside whatever object you registered.

Android calls back to your app's code, so the term *callback* describes the mechanism that Android uses to handle events.

TIP

Starting with version 1.6 (also known as *Donut* or *API Level* 4), Android provides a way to respond to button clicks, keystrokes, and other things without all the complicated code in this chapter's listings. That is, you can handle certain events without implementing the `OnClickListener` interface. Even so, you can't write Kotlin or Java code without understanding events and callbacks. At many points in your Android development life, you have to write the kind of code that you find in this chapter.

For more information on handling events without implementing `OnClickListener`, see Book 1, Chapter 5.

An object remembers who created it

This section is Java-specific. If you're not interested in how Java works because you don't plan to go into the library code, you can skip it. Kotlin still does the things that this section discusses, but it does them in the background (hence the shortness of the Kotlin version of the example code found in Listing 5-3).

When you're working with Java code, the preceding section raises several questions about the interaction between your app and Android's callback. But that section misses one of the questions, which is, "In the `onClick()` method of Listing 5-3, how does the code know what `button` means?" Listing 5-3 contains two classes — `MyActivity` and `MyListener`. Without jumping through some hoops, one class doesn't know anything about another class's fields.

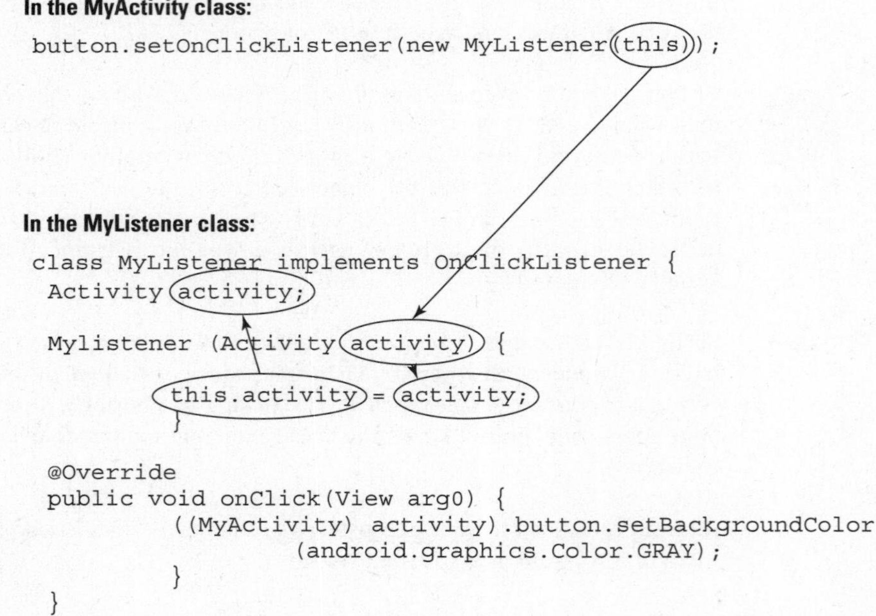

In the MyActivity class:
button.setOnClickListener(new MyListener(this));
In the MyListener class:
class MyListener implements OnClickListener {
Activity activity;
Mylistener (Activity activity) {
this.activity = activity;
}
@Override
public void onClick(View arg0) {
((MyActivity) activity).button.setBackgroundColor
(android.graphics.Color.GRAY);
}
}

FIGURE 5-3: How a listener remembers its creator.

In Listing 5-3, the keyword `this` sits inside the code that defines the `MyActivity` class:

```
button.setOnClickListener(new MyListener(this));
```

In Java, `this` refers to "the object that contains the current line of code." So, in Listing 5-3, the word `this` refers to an instance of `MyActivity` — the activity that's being displayed on the device's screen. The current `MyActivity` instance has a button. So far, so good.

Later in Listing 5-3, the `MyListener` constructor tucks a reference to the current activity into one of its fields. (See Figure 5-3.)

Looking again at Figure 5-3, `MyListener` refers to an `activity`, and that activity contains a button. When Android calls the `onClick()` method, the method executes an instruction that's very much like this one:

```
activity.button.setBackgroundColor(android.graphics.Color.GRAY);
```

The instruction takes the referenced activity's button and sets the button's background color to gray. To make things work properly, you have to do some casting in the `onClick()` method of Listing 5-3. For example, when you see the statement:

```
button = ((Button) findViewById(R.id.button1));
```

what you're telling the compiler is that the output of `findViewById()` needs to be turned into a `Button` object, so that it matches the type of `button`. Otherwise, the assignment could result in an error.

A less wordy way to implement an interface

If you read the preceding section and then you read this section, you'll probably want to send us a nasty email message. The preceding section describes an admittedly convoluted way to make a listener remember which activity's button to tweak. You need to know how Listing 5-3 works, but if you modify Listing 5-3 so that the activity is its own listener, things become much simpler. Listing 5-4 shows you how to do it.

LISTING 5-4: An Activity Eats Its Own Dog Food

```
package com.allmycode.samples;

import android.app.Activity;
import android.os.Bundle;
import android.view.View;
import android.view.View.OnClickListener;
import android.widget.Button;

public class MyActivity extends Activity
                        implements OnClickListener {

    Button button;

    @Override
    public void onCreate(Bundle savedInstanceState) {
        super.onCreate(savedInstanceState);
        setContentView(R.layout.main);

        button = ((Button) findViewById(R.id.button1));

        button.setOnClickListener(this);
    }

    @Override
    public void onClick(View arg0) {
        button.setBackgroundColor
                             (android.graphics.Color.GRAY);
    }
}
```

The combination of automation in Android Studio and the concise nature of Kotlin make things even easier. Here is the Kotlin version of the same upgrade:

```
package com.example.myfirstapp

import androidx.appcompat.app.AppCompatActivity
import android.os.Bundle
import android.view.View
import kotlinx.android.synthetic.main.activity_main.*

class MainActivity : AppCompatActivity() {
```

```
    override fun onCreate(savedInstanceState: Bundle?) {
        super.onCreate(savedInstanceState)
        setContentView(R.layout.activity_main)
    }

    fun onClick(v: View) {
        button.setBackgroundColor(android.graphics.Color.GRAY)
    }
}
```

The earlier section starts with a question: "In the onClick() method, how does the code know what button means?" In this section, that question goes away just as your lap goes away when you stand up.

In Listing 5-4, both the button and the onClick() method are members inside the activity. So the onClick() method has free-and-easy access to the button. You don't need an Activity field as in Listing 5-3, and you don't need any fancy casting from Activity to MyActivity.

When working with Java, you have to remind Android that MyActivity contains an onClick() method, and you do that by adding implements OnClickListener to the declaration of MyActivity. You must also remind Android to notify the current MyActivity object whenever the button gets clicked. You do this reminding by writing

```
button.setOnClickListener(this);
```

which, roughly speaking, translates to "Hey, Android! When someone clicks the button, call the onClick() method that's inside the this object (a MyActivity object, which fortunately implements OnClickListener)." All this connectivity takes place in the background when working with Kotlin, but it still takes place.

The pattern in Listing 5-4 (having an Activity implement whatever interface it requires) is a very common application-programming idiom.

Classes That Must (and Must Not) Be Extended

Java and Kotlin take very different views on extensions. For example, in Kotlin, all classes are final by default. To inherit a class in Kotlin, you must open the class. Having all classes final by default adds a level of security and makes some tasks faster. However, it also means that you have to perform additional work just to override behaviors in an existing class. The following sections compare Java and Kotlin with regard to extensions. You need to know both when working with Android because many of the underlying library classes take the Java approach (given that they're written in Java).

The need to override

Suppose you want to add functionality to an existing Java class. You like Android's `Activity` class, but the pre-declared `Activity` class displays nothing on the screen. Do you rewrite Android's `Activity` class? No.

Instead of rewriting an existing class, you extend the class. Even in a do-nothing Android "Hello" application, you write

```
public class MyActivity extends Activity
```

Then, in the `MyActivity` class's declaration, you write

```
@Override
public void onCreate(Bundle savedInstanceState) {
    super.onCreate(savedInstanceState);
    setContentView(R.layout.main);
}
```

Your `MyActivity` class creates new functionality by extending most of Android's `Activity` functionality while overriding the `Activity` class's brain-dead `onCreate()` method.

REMEMBER

When working with a Java class in Kotlin, you can override the functions just as if you were programming in Java. This is the reason that the Kotlin version of the code can also override the `onCreate()` method.

Java's final classes

In object-oriented programming, extending a class is the noblest thing you can do.

But some classes aren't meant to be extended. Take, for example, Java's `String` class. A `String` is a `String` is a `String`. You don't want somebody's `MyString.length` method to return the length of time it takes to scramble a string's characters. To prevent someone from doing something unexpected, unconventional, or unusual with a string's methods, the creators of Java made the `String` class final:

```
public final class String
```

Some of Android's pre-declared classes are also final, including the `Telephony` and `MediaStore` classes.

Kotlin's open classes

As previously mentioned, all classes in Kotlin are final by default. To create a class that you can override, you must declare the class as being open. In addition, you must declare all functions, fields, and other elements that you want to override as being open. Here is an example of the Kotlin open classes:

```
fun main(args: Array<String>) {
    val primary: MySaying = MySaying()
    val secondary: YourSaying = YourSaying()

    primary.printSaying()
    secondary.printSaying()
}

open class MySaying {
    open fun printSaying() {
        println("This is my saying.")
    }
}

class YourSaying: MySaying() {
    override fun printSaying() {
        println("This is your saying.")
    }
}
```

You still have to initialize `MySaying` when extending `YourSaying`, which is why it appears as `MySaying()`. To override `printSaying()`, you must also include the `override` keyword.

Kotlin extensions

Unlike with Java, you can extend classes in Kotlin by using a special kind of function, the extension function. An *extension function* adds something new to a class without changing anything about the existing class. For example, you might want a new way to work with a `List` that Kotlin doesn't currently provide. Instead of creating an entirely new `List` class, you simply add the required functionality. Here's an example of working with an extension in Kotlin:

```
fun main(args: Array<String>) {
    val doSaying: MySaying = MySaying()

    doSaying.printSaying()
    doSaying.printSaying("My custom saying.")
}

class MySaying {
    fun printSaying() {
        println("This is my saying.")
    }
}

fun MySaying.printSaying(saying: String){
    println(saying)
}
```

The extension function uses the form *class_name.function_name*. This extension adds a version of `printSaying()` to the original class that accepts a String argument. This extension method works with final classes (the default), so you can make a kind of modification to Kotlin final classes without having to write everything from scratch.

REMEMBER

As long as the function declaration is different, you can add just about anything you want. However, you can't override existing functionality by declaring a new function with the same *signature* (the same name and parameter list) as an existing function. The two functions must be different.

Abstract classes

Both Kotlin and Java provide abstract classes, and they work just about the same for both languages. Although a final class hates to be extended, an *abstract class* insists on being extended. Android's `ViewGroup` is an example of an abstract class. (See Listing 5-5.)

LISTING 5-5: A Small Part of Android's `ViewGroup` Class

```
public abstract class ViewGroup {

    public void bringChildToFront(View child) {
        int index = indexOfChild(child);
```

```
        if (index >= 0) {
            removeFromArray(index);
            addInArray(child, mChildrenCount);
            child.mParent = this;
        }
    }

    protected abstract void onLayout(boolean changed,
                int l, int t, int r, int b);
}
```

Android's `ViewGroup.java` file is more than 3,700 lines long. So Listing 5-5 has only a tiny fraction of the file's code. But you can see from Listing 5-5 how a class becomes abstract. To no one's surprise, the word `abstract` precedes the word `class`. But the word `abstract` also starts the declaration of some methods belonging to the class. (Kotlin abstract classes and functions also begin with the word `abstract`.)

The founders of Android decided that the idea of a `ViewGroup` is useful. They were correct because your favorite Android layouts (`LinearLayout`, `RelativeLayout`, and so on) are subclasses of `ViewGroup`. They also understood that from one kind of `ViewGroup` to another, some functionality doesn't change. For example, Listing 5-5 defines a `bringChildToFront()` method, and subclasses of `ViewGroup` inherit this method.

But the founders also realized that some aspects of a `ViewGroup` make no sense unless you work with a particular kind of group. For example, a `LinearLayout` positions things one after another, and a `RelativeLayout` positions things above, below, and to the side of one another. So Listing 5-5 doesn't have a full-blown `onLayout()` method. The `onLayout()` declaration in Listing 5-5 has no method body. But Android requires each subclass of the `ViewGroup` class to declare its own `onLayout()` method. Both Kotlin and Java enforce this requirement when (as in Listing 5-5) you declare method `onLayout()` to be `abstract`.

As a developer, you can't create an object from an abstract class. If you write

```
ViewGroup group = new ViewGroup();
```

or (for Kotlin)

```
val group: ViewGroup = ViewGroup()
```

the compiler tells you that you're behaving badly. To do something useful with the ViewGroup class, you need a subclass of the ViewGroup class. The subclass has a concrete version of each abstract method in the ViewGroup class:

```
package com.allmycode.samples;

import android.content.Context;
import android.view.ViewGroup;

public class MyLayout extends ViewGroup {

    public MyLayout(Context context) {
        super(context);
    }

    @Override
    protected void onLayout(boolean changed,
                int l, int t, int r, int b);
    }
}
```

Here's the Kotlin version of this code:

```
class MyLayout: ViewGroup(context) {
    override fun onLayout(changed: Boolean, l: Int,
                          t: Int, r: Int, b: Int) {

    }
}
```

Inner Classes

Here's big news! You can define a class inside another class! Most classes don't live inside another class, and most classes don't contain other classes. But when the idea behind one class screams out to be part of another class, feel free to create a class within a class. Oddly enough, this is one area in which Kotlin and Java work alike.

Named inner classes

For the user, Listing 5-6 behaves the same way as Listings 5-3 and 5-4. But in Listing 5-6, the MyActivity class contains its own MyListener class.

LISTING 5-6: A Class within a Class

```
package com.allmycode.samples;

import android.app.Activity;
import android.os.Bundle;
import android.view.View;
import android.view.View.OnClickListener;
import android.widget.Button;

public class MyActivity extends Activity {

    Button button;

    @Override
    public void onCreate(Bundle savedInstanceState) {
        super.onCreate(savedInstanceState);
        setContentView(R.layout.main);

        button = ((Button) findViewById(R.id.button1));

        button.setOnClickListener(new MyListener());
    }

    class MyListener implements OnClickListener {

        @Override
        public void onClick(View arg0) {
            button.setBackgroundColor
                          (android.graphics.Color.GRAY);
        }
    }
}
```

Here is the Kotlin version:

```
package com.example.myfirstapp

import androidx.appcompat.app.AppCompatActivity
import android.os.Bundle
import android.view.View
import kotlinx.android.synthetic.main.activity_main.*
```

```
class MainActivity : AppCompatActivity() {

    override fun onCreate(savedInstanceState: Bundle?) {
        super.onCreate(savedInstanceState)
        setContentView(R.layout.activity_main)

        button.setOnClickListener(MyListener())
    }

    class MyListener : View.OnClickListener {
        override fun onClick(v: View?) {
            v!!.setBackgroundColor(android.graphics.Color.GRAY)
        }
    }
}
```

The `MyListener` class in Listing 5-6 is an *inner class*. An inner class is a lot like any other class. But within an inner class's code, you can refer to the enclosing class's fields. For example, the `onClick()` method inside `MyListener` uses the name `button`, and `button` is defined in the enclosing `MyActivity` class.

Listings 5-4 and 5-6 are very similar. In both listings, you circumvent the complexities described in the section "An object remembers who created it," earlier in this chapter. For this chapter's example, the choice of Listing 5-4 or Listing 5-6 is largely a matter of taste.

Anonymous inner classes

Notice that the code in Listing 5-6 uses the `MyListener` class only once. (The only use is in a call to `button.setOnClickListener`.) So, do you really need a name for something that's used only once? No, you don't. You can substitute the entire definition of the inner class inside the call to `button.setOnClickListener`. When you do this, you have an *anonymous inner class*. Listing 5-7 shows you how it works.

LISTING 5-7: A Class with No Name (Inside a Class with a Name)

```
package com.allmycode.samples;

import android.app.Activity;
import android.os.Bundle;
import android.view.View;
```

```
import android.view.View.OnClickListener;
import android.widget.Button;

public class MyActivity extends Activity {

    Button button;

    @Override
    public void onCreate(Bundle savedInstanceState) {
        super.onCreate(savedInstanceState);
        setContentView(R.layout.main);

        button = ((Button) findViewById(R.id.button1));

        button.setOnClickListener(new OnClickListener() {

            @Override
            public void onClick(View arg0) {
                button.setBackgroundColor
                        (android.graphics.Color.GRAY);
            }
        });
    }

}
```

Here's the Kotlin version of the same code:

```
package com.example.myfirstapp

import androidx.appcompat.app.AppCompatActivity
import android.os.Bundle
import android.view.View
import kotlinx.android.synthetic.main.activity_main.*

class MainActivity : AppCompatActivity() {

    override fun onCreate(savedInstanceState: Bundle?) {
        super.onCreate(savedInstanceState)
        setContentView(R.layout.activity_main)
```

```
        button.setOnClickListener(object: View.OnClickListener {
            override fun onClick(v: View?) {
                v!!.setBackgroundColor(android.graphics.Color.
GRAY)
            }
        })
    }
}
```

Inner classes are good for things like event handlers, such as the `onClick()` method in this chapter's examples. The most difficult thing about an anonymous inner class is keeping track of the parentheses, the curly braces, and the indentation. So our humble advice is to start by writing code without any inner classes, such as the code in Listing 5-3 or Listing 5-4. Later, when you become bored with ordinary classes, experiment by changing some of your ordinary classes into inner classes.

functional programming

» Considering the requirements of functional programming

» Performing essential tasks in functional programming

» Using functional programming for Android development

Chapter 6 Functional Programming in Kotlin

Early Android applications relied entirely on Java to perform tasks. However, Google has now embraced Kotlin as the right language to use for Android development, and with good reason — it's often easier than Java. Throughout this book, we compare Kotlin with Java using a mix of examples to show you that Kotlin does make things easier in most cases. You can still use Java, of course, but the one thing about Kotlin that Java can't replicate is functional programming.

This chapter isn't about a specific programming language (even though it uses Kotlin to present examples). Instead, it's about a programming paradigm (which, in this case, is functional programming). A *paradigm* is a framework that expresses a particular set of assumptions, relies on particular ways of thinking through problems, and uses particular methodologies to solve those problems. Other programming paradigms you may use are imperative, procedural, object-oriented, and declarative.

This chapter focuses on the problems you need to solve. Initially, the chapter explains how the functional programming paradigm accomplishes this problem solving, and then you see how functional programming differs from other paradigms you may have used. Later, you look at essential functional programming methods. And finally, the chapter relates functional programming techniques to Android development so that you can use this paradigm to good effect in making your code more secure, highly efficient, and easier to work with in a multiprocessing environment.

Throughout this chapter, you consider why you'd want to use functional programming at all. The math orientation of functional programming means that you might not create the essential elements of an application using it; you might instead solve straightforward math problems or devise what-if scenarios to test. As you find out in Chapter 3 of this minibook, a compiler translates every bit of code you write into machine code for execution. So, using a particular programming paradigm is a matter of making you, the developer, more efficient and better able to write code with few (or any) errors.

Defining Functional Programming

Functional programming has somewhat different goals and approaches than other paradigms do. *Goals,* the accomplishment of a development task in a particular manner, define what a programming paradigm is trying to do in forging the approaches used by languages that support it. For example, when working with functional programming, you express everything using mathematically based functions. Likewise, when you work with Object-Oriented Programming (OOP), the goal is to encapsulate everything in objects that reflect real-world objects as often as is possible. However, the goals of a programming paradigm don't specify a particular implementation; doing that is within the purview of the individual languages. The following sections tell you how the functional programming paradigm differs from other paradigms in its pure state. Being in a pure state means that the language follows the paradigm guidelines precisely. As you discover later, Kotlin is an *impure* language, which means that it incorporates functional programming with other paradigms, such as OOP.

Differences from other programming paradigms

The main difference between the functional programming paradigm and other paradigms is that functional programs use math functions rather than statements to express ideas. So instead of writing a precise set of steps to solve a problem, you use math functions, and you don't worry about how the language performs the task. In some ways, this approach makes languages that support the functional programming paradigm similar to applications such as MATLAB, which is used to perform various kinds of high level, complex math computations. With MATLAB, you get a user interface, which reduces the learning curve. But you pay for the convenience of the user interface with a loss of power and flexibility, which functional languages do offer. Using the functional approach to defining a problem relies on the *declarative programming* style, which you see used with other paradigms and languages, such as Structured Query Language (SQL) for database management.

In contrast to other paradigms, the functional programming paradigm doesn't maintain state. The use of *state* enables you to track values between function calls. Other paradigms use state to produce *variant results* (output that changes) based on environment, such as to determine the number of existing objects and to do something different when the number of objects is zero. But because functional programs don't maintain state, calling a functional program function always produces the same result when you have a particular set of inputs. Functional programs are therefore more predictable than those that support state.

Because functional programs don't maintain state, the data they work with is also *immutable*, which means that you can't change it. To change a variable's value, you must create a new variable. Again, this feature makes functional programs more predictable than other approaches and could make functional programs easier to run on multiple processors.

Understanding its goals

Imperative programming, the kind of programming that most developers have done until now, is akin to an assembly line, where data moves through a series of steps in a specific order to produce a particular result. The process is fixed and rigid, and the person implementing the process must build a new assembly line every time an application requires a new result. Object-oriented programming (OOP) simply modularizes and hides the steps, but the underlying paradigm still works on that assembly-line idea. Even with modularization, OOP often doesn't allow rearrangement of the object code in unanticipated ways because of the underlying interdependencies of the code.

REMEMBER

Functional programming gets rid of the interdependencies by replacing procedures with pure functions, which require the use of immutable state. The assembly line is no more. An application can manipulate data using the same means as those used in pure math. The seeming restriction of immutable state lets anyone who understands the math of a situation also create an application to perform the math.

Using pure functions creates a flexible environment in which code order depends on the underlying math. That math models a real-world environment, and as the human understanding of that environment changes and evolves, the math model and functional code can change with it — without the usual problems of brittleness that cause imperative code to fail. Modifying functional code is faster and less error prone than using other paradigms because the person implementing the change must understand only the math; there's no need to know how the underlying code works. In addition, learning how to create functional code can be faster as long as the person understands the math model and its relationship to the real world.

Functional programming also embraces a number of unique coding approaches, such as the capability to pass a function to another function as input. This capability enables you to change application behavior in a predictable manner that isn't possible using other programming paradigms.

Understanding Pure and Impure Languages

Languages that support functional programming fall into two categories: pure and impure. A *pure language* allows only functional programming techniques and fully implements the functional programming paradigm. An *impure language* allows the use of other programming techniques and may only mostly implement the functional programming paradigm. Both pure and impure languages have specific advantages and disadvantages, as described in the sections that follow.

Using the pure approach

Programming languages that use the pure approach to the functional programming paradigm rely on lambda calculus principles, for the most part. In addition, a pure-approach language allows the use of functional programming techniques only, so the result is always a functional program. Haskell is probably the most popular pure language because it provides the purest implementation and is generally a relatively popular language, according to the TIOBE index (`https://www.tiobe.com/tiobe-index/`). Other pure-approach languages include Lisp, Racket, Erlang, and OCaml.

When considering functional programming, especially in the pure sense, a language must meet these requirements:

- **It uses pure functions.** A pure function always produces precisely the same result for a given set of inputs. Also, a pure function doesn't modify any global variables or any input arguments. Pure functions are extremely easy to debug because they have no side effects; nothing is hidden. Plus, a compiler can do things like memorize the results of a pure function call because such calls never change, and the compiler can wait to calculate results until they're actually needed. When working with a pure function, you can

- Remove the function if no other functions rely on its output.
- Reverse the order of calls to different functions without any change to application functionality.
- Process the function calls in parallel without any consequence.
- Evaluate the function calls in any order, assuming that the entire language doesn't allow side effects.

» **It relies on recursion.** There are no for, while, do, or any other sort of looping mechanisms in a functional language. Instead, a functional language relies on recursion because recursion doesn't require state (a counter variable as a minimum) to complete a looping task.

» **It uses referential transparency.** The language uses no assignment statements. The value of a variable is replaceable with its actual value at any point in the program. If a new value needs to be stored, the environment creates a new variable to do it.

» **Its functions are first class and can be higher order.** A first-class function can act as a variable and you can pass it to any function requiring an argument. In addition, a function can return a first-class function instead of a value. Higher-order functions can accept other functions as input and output functions as results.

» **Its variables are immutable.** The value of something can't change, so you can always rely on it to be the same value. This means you can create a variable in one place and use its value in another place without ever worrying about the value of the variable changing.

WARNING

As with many elements of programming, people have strong opinions about whether a particular programming language qualifies for pure status. For example, many people consider JavaScript to be a pure language, even though it's untyped. Others feel that domain-specific declarative languages such as SQL and Lex/Yacc qualify for pure status even though they aren't general programming languages. Simply having elements of functional programming doesn't mean that a language adheres to the pure approach.

Using the impure approach

Many developers have come to see the benefits of functional programming. However, they also don't want to give up the benefits of their existing language, so they use a language that mixes functional features with one of the other programming paradigms (as described in the "Comparing the Functional Paradigm" section that follows). For example, you can find a few functional programming features in languages such as C++, C#, and Java.

WARNING

Adding functional features to an existing language rarely results in a good mix of functional features because the additions have too many compromises. When you work with an impure language, you need to be careful because your code won't work in a purely functional manner, and the features that you might think will work in one way actually work in another. For example, you can't pass a function to another function in some languages, but doing so is a requirement for functional programming.

TIP

Languages such as Kotlin and Python are designed from the outset to support multiple programming paradigms. In fact, some online courses make a point of teaching this particular aspect of Kotlin as a special benefit (see `https://functionalkotlin.com/`). The use of multiple programming paradigms makes Kotlin quite flexible but also leads to complaints and apologists. This chapter relies on Kotlin to demonstrate the impure approach to functional programming because it's both popular and flexible, plus it's easy to learn.

Comparing the Functional Paradigm

You might think that only a few programming paradigms exist besides the functional programming paradigm explored in this chapter, but the world of development is packed with them. That's because no two people truly think alike. Each paradigm represents a different approach to the puzzle of conveying a solution to problems by using a particular methodology while making assumptions about things like developer expertise and execution environment. You can find entire sites that discuss the issue, such as the one at `https://cs.lmu.edu/~ray/notes/paradigms/`. Oddly enough, some languages (such as Kotlin and Python) mix and match compatible paradigms to create an entirely new way to perform tasks based on what has happened in the past. Here's a progression to think about as you work with impure functional languages:

- **Imperative:** Imperative programming takes a step-by-step approach to performing a task. The developer provides commands that describe precisely how to perform the task from beginning to end. During the process of executing the commands, the code also modifies application state, which includes the application data. The code runs from beginning to end. An imperative application closely mimics the computer hardware, which executes machine code. *Machine code* is the lowest set of instructions that you can create and is mimicked in early languages, such as assembler.

- **Procedural:** Procedural programming implements imperative programming, but adds functionality such as code blocks and procedures for breaking up the code. The compiler or interpreter still ends up producing machine code that runs step by step, but the use of procedures makes it easier for a developer to follow the code and understand how it works. Many procedural languages provide a disassembly mode in which you can see the correspondence between the higher-level language and the underlying assembler. Examples of languages that implement the procedural paradigm are C and Pascal.
- **Object-oriented:** The procedural paradigm does make reading code easier. However, the relationship between the code and the underlying hardware still makes it hard to relate what the code is doing to the real world. The object-oriented paradigm uses the concept of objects to hide the code, but the more important aim is to make modeling the real world easier. A developer creates code objects that mimic the real-world objects they emulate. These objects include properties, methods, and events to allow the object to behave in a particular manner. Examples of languages that implement the object-oriented paradigm are C++ and Java.

REMEMBER

Languages that implement the object-oriented paradigms also implement both the procedural and imperative paradigms. The fact that objects hide the use of these other paradigms doesn't mean that a developer hasn't written code to create the object using these older paradigms. Consequently, the object-oriented paradigm still relies on code that modifies application state, but could also allow for modifying variable data.

- **Declarative:** Functional programming actually implements the declarative programming paradigm, but the two paradigms are separate. Other paradigms, such as logic programming, implemented by the Prolog language, also support the declarative programming paradigm. The short view of declarative programming is that it does the following:
  - Describes what the code should do, rather than how to do it
  - Defines functions that are referentially transparent (without side effects)
  - Provides a clear correspondence to mathematical logic

Using Kotlin for Functional Programming Needs

Remember that functional programming is a paradigm, which means that it doesn't have an implementation. The basis of functional programming is lambda calculus (`https://brilliant.org/wiki/lambda-calculus/`), which is actually a math abstraction. So when you want to perform tasks by using the functional programming paradigm, you're really looking for a programming language that implements functional programming in a way that meets your needs. In fact, you may even be performing functional programming tasks in your current language without realizing it. Every time you create and use a lambda function, you're likely using functional programming techniques (in an impure way, at least).

Kotlin has significantly more functional features than Java does, but Kotlin still shows its Java roots. For purists, the Java connection is a problem because Kotlin code can look too much like Java code (as shown in Chapter 5 of this minibook). Developers often look at languages based on need, rather than on strict adherence to a set of principles. Still, you can find discussions online that say Kotlin isn't quite as functional as Python and not nearly as functional as languages such as Haskell. These theoretical discussions don't actually matter in the real world. You want to use Kotlin for Android development when functional programming is important because Kotlin

- Is suitable for Android and possibly system development, whereas Python focuses on data science and machine learning needs
- Can execute relatively quickly, even on devices that have less robust processors
- Uses a smaller number of lines of code when compared to Java due to the ability to use functional techniques
- Is easier to read than Java code
- Is easier to learn than Java, but not as easy as Python
- Offers multi-statement lambdas
- Has relatively compact collection comprehensions, which improve readability of collection manipulations
- Uses receivers to create complex code manipulations with simple names
- Has access to inline functions that actually do place the function into the surrounding code, making the application run faster (at the cost of size)
- Includes special functions to handle potentially `null` input

With Kotlin, you gain all these features that require some level of functional programming without losing access to the Java libraries. Because Java libraries are important for Android development, an Android developer should see Kotlin functional capabilities as being more useful than Java.

TIP

When working with Kotlin, you also get a bonus for Android development; you can use C++ libraries, too. The articles at `https://yalantis.com/blog/android-ndk-the-interaction-between-kotlin-and-c-c-plus-plus/` and `https://developer.android.com/studio/projects/add-native-code` tell how to use these libraries. Given how Kotlin works, you can use C++ to augment your applications in a number of ways, especially when it comes to obtaining the last bit of speed from your application.

Defining the Role of State

Application *state* is a condition that occurs when the application performs tasks that modify global data. An application doesn't have state when using functional programming. The good news about the lack of state is that any call to a function will produce the same results for a given input every time, regardless of when the application calls the function. But here's the bad news: The application now has no memory. When you think about state, think about the capability to remember what occurred in the past, which, in the case of an application, is stored as global data.

Kotlin naturally works to keep the role of state in applications to a minimum; although state does sometimes make an appearance in Android programming. For example, creating views without some sort of state information would be hard. The way Android handles events also makes managing state necessary, but you can still reduce the amount of state management in your applications and obtain a better result than using OOP or procedural techniques alone. Here are some things to consider:

- Variables can be made immutable by default, and this is actually the preferred method of creating them.
- Variables are non-nullable by default, which means that they always have a result to provide.
- Classes are final by default, making it possible to depend on specific class behaviors.
- *Currying* allows you to change complex functions that require multiple arguments into a series of simple functions that require just one argument each.

» Data structures are immutable by default, which means that you can depend on them to remain the same after creation.

» Working with data using pure functions is not only possible but also efficient and concise.

REMEMBER

State is unavoidable for many reasons in real-world applications. For example, you can't stream data without creating both state and side effects. This is where functional programming falls short of providing a complete solution. If you want to stream your favorite music using an app you create, your app will have to store and manipulate state.

Using Recursion to Perform Calculations

The "Looping using Kotlin recursion" section of Chapter 4 of this minibook tells you how you can use recursion to perform looping tasks. The main benefit of this approach is that you can create loops that have no state. Also, recursion can be an elegant way to solve certain problems. Still, using recursion can be like bending your head around a hole in time and space — it's not particularly easy because it takes a different mindset to perform.

The more common way to use recursion is to perform calculations. In fact, some very common math problems, such as the calculation of factorial (n!) and the Fibonacci sequence (Fn) are solved using recursion. Kotlin supports two forms of recursion for solving problems: standard and tail recursion. The following sections discuss both kinds of recursion.

Relying on standard recursion

When using recursion to solve a problem, you normally start with something complex that can be divided into a simple case. For example, when you calculate a factorial, 1!, is the simplest case because it has a value of `1`. So, this simple case is `n = 1`. The next case is a little harder; now you must multiply `1 * 2` to obtain the result, so this next case is `n = 1 * 2`. Instead of just one step, you now have two steps. Each case becomes progressively more difficult, with 3 being the next case: `n = 1 * 2 * 3`. So, recursion rests on dividing the problem into simple steps until you reach the simplest case.

The reason recursion works for the factorial problem is that you can create this reduction in complexity by having the function call itself as often as needed to reach the simplest case of `n = 1`. (If you want to play with the code that follows and in other areas of this chapter without having to start Android Studio, you can use an online interpreter, such as the one at https://try.kotlinlang.org/.) Here is the Kotlin code to perform this task:

```
fun main(args: Array<String>) {
    println(factorial(5))
}

fun factorial(n: Int): Int {
    if (n == 1){
        println("Ended")
    } else {
        println("Handling n = $n")
        var value = n * factorial(n - 1)
        println("Value = $value")
        return value
    }

    return n
}
```

This code contains a number of println() statements so that you can better understand how the recursion works. Normally, this code could be extremely short:

```
fun fact(n: Int): Int {
    return if (n==1) n else n * fact(n - 1)
}
```

You could even make it shorter still, but really, it's short enough. The output from the wordy version looks like this:

```
Handling n = 5
Handling n = 4
Handling n = 3
Handling n = 2
Ended
Value = 2
Value = 6
Value = 24
Value = 120
120
```

The factorial() function keeps calling itself until it reaches the simplest case, n == 1. However, it doesn't finish anything. It doesn't get to the next step, which is var value = n * factorial(n - 1). At each step, the code pushes the current iteration onto the stack (think of a stack of pancakes, except we're talking memory here) and then it calls the next iteration and finally reaches n == 1. This is why you see each of the Handling n = statements as output without any value statements.

At this point, the procedure for n == 1 finishes and this iteration, n == 1, is popped from the stack, which means the next iteration, n == 2 * 1, can complete. This is why you see an output of Value = 2. Each iteration completes and is popped from the stack in turn, until, finally, nothing is left to return and the factorial() function returns the value of n == 5 * 4 * 3 * 2 * 1, which is 120.

REMEMBER

The main benefit of this approach to recursion is that it works on every kind of problem. Developers have used this form of recursion for years with every language imaginable, so it's hardly an earth-shaking approach to dazzle your friends. Consider this the tried-and-true approach to recursion.

Relying on tail recursion

You might wonder why someone would need a second form of recursion given that standard recursion will work on every problem. The fact is that standard recursion has certain problems that you can solve using this second form, which is called *tail recursion* because there is nothing to do after the last step of the recursion process. Using tail recursion has these advantages:

- It executes faster because it doesn't rely on stack pushes and pops to maintain the previous iteration.
- Recursion can occur infinitely because no stack resources are used (so there is no chance of running out of memory due to the recursion).
- It eliminates the potential for StackOverflow exceptions.

You have a few ways to handle tail recursion. Some don't work with every problem, but you can take a look at a general approach before delving into other approaches. Here is a version of the factorial problem using tail recursion (use the main() function from the "Relying on standard recursion" section to execute both factorial2() and factorial3()):

```
fun factorial2(n: Int, acc: Int = 1): Int {
    if (n == 1) {
        println("Ended with n = $n, acc = $acc")
        return acc
    }
```

```
    println("Handling n = $n, acc = $acc")
    return factorial2(n - 1, acc * n)
}
```

In this case, the code relies on an accumulator, `acc`, to track the current value. Notice that the recursive call occurs at the tail — the end — of the process. The actual process is similar, but you won't encounter stack problems using this approach. Here is the output from this version of the example:

```
Handling n = 5, acc = 1
Handling n = 4, acc = 5
Handling n = 3, acc = 20
Handling n = 2, acc = 60
Ended with n = 1, acc = 120
120
```

REMEMBER

The only problem with `factorial2()` is that it hasn't been optimized to use tail recursion. You won't actually see this optimization as part of the code (you write it the same way), but you need to tell Kotlin to perform the optimization for you using the `tailrec` keyword. Here is a final version that won't suffer from stack overflows and works quite fast:

```
tailrec fun factorial3(n: Int, acc: Int = 1): Int {
    return if (n == 1) acc else factorial3(n - 1, acc * n)
}
```

WARNING

The only problem with tail recursion is that it won't work with every problem. You need to validate the results of any recursion you perform using this approach to ensure that you're getting the correct output.

Using Function Types

Creating a function that acts as a type is one of the tenets of functional programming. Kotlin provides a number of methods to use function types. Naturally, first you have to start with one or two functions that you want to use, such as these shown here:

```
fun doAdd(a: Int, b: Int): Double = a.toDouble() + b
fun doSub(a: Int, b: Int): Double = a.toDouble() - b
```

There really isn't anything special about these functions except they output a `Double` as the result of `Int` math. However, they serve well to demonstration how function types could be helpful in Android programming.

The first way to use these functions as types is to create a variable that is equal to the function. You can then invoke the variable, as shown in the following example:

```
val f = ::doAdd
println(f(1, 2))
```

Notice the function reference (`::`) operator. This operator tells Kotlin to reference the function in variable `f`. You can then invoke `f(1, 2)` as part of a `println()` call. However, you can use `f` anywhere that you use a variable. For example, you can place the value into another variable, as shown here:

```
val myNum = f(1, 2)
println("${myNum::class.qualifiedName}")
```

The output type of `myNum` is a `Double`, as you'd expect, not a function. You can use `f` anywhere you need a `Double`, but because of the nature of `f`, the value you receive depends on the inputs you provide.

You can also use a function type as input to another, higher-order, function. For example, consider this higher-order function:

```
fun doMath(MathType: (a: Int, b: Int) -> Double ,
           a: Int, b: Int): Double {
    return MathType(a, b)
}
```

The first argument, `MathType`, relies on a function input with a particular signature, one that matches the two example functions. You place the input arguments within parentheses as usual, followed by `->`, and then the output type. The `doMath()` function accepts any function that has the correct signature, so you can do this in your code:

```
println(doMath(::doAdd, 2, 1))
println(doMath(::doSub, 2, 1))
```

REMEMBER

The output you receive depends on the function you provide as input. Notice that you must use the function reference operator in this case as well or the compiler will complain.

Understanding Function Literals

A function literal is an extremely compact type of function that you can supply directly to functions as an argument. Unlike most languages, Kotlin allows multistatement function literals, but the final statement must always provide the return value. There are two kinds of function literal: lambda expressions and anonymous functions. The following sections explore both forms.

Lambda expressions

A lambda expression is an expression that you assign to a variable. You can make the assignment directly, or you can make the assignment to a function argument. Here's an example of a lambda expression assigned to a variable:

```
val doAdd = {a: Int, b: Int -> a.toDouble() + b}
println(doAdd(1, 2))
```

You can also supply a lambda expression as input to a function that expects a function as input. Consider these string manipulation examples:

```
fun main(args: Array<String>) {
    val repeat: String.(Int) -> String =
        {times -> this.repeat(times)}
    val part: String.(Int) -> String =
        {len -> this.take(len)}

    println(changeString(repeat, "A String ", 4))
    println(changeString(part, "A String ", 4))
}

fun changeString(function: (String, Int) -> String,
                 string: String, number: Int): String {
    return function(string, number)
}
```

TIP

This example has two different string manipulation lambda functions with an important change from the previous example. Notice the `String.(Int)` part of the declaration. The `String` is referenced as the `this` argument in the lambda function. So, `this.repeat` or `this.take` refers to the `String` that is supplied as input. Using this technique can make your coding easier at times.

Another difference is that this example provides an expression signature so that it's clear what the expression requires as input. Normally, the compiler automatically detects the signature, but defining one doesn't hurt. The `repeat` signature of `String.(Int) -> String` states that the expression needs a `String` that is used for `this`, along with an `Int`, and it outputs a `String`.

REMEMBER

Notice that only the `Int` appears as an argument to the expression in the form of `times: {times -> this.repeat(times)}`. When working with a lambda expression of this sort, developers have a tendency to provide too many or too few inputs to the expression.

The function, `changeString()`, works differently depending on the lambda expression you provide. Using this approach means that you can write a single function that performs what is essentially a boilerplate task of manipulating a string, but it can change the behavior of the function based on what you need at any given time. As long as the signature of the function matches the signature of the lambda expression, the function will work as anticipated.

Anonymous functions

An anonymous function is simply a function that lacks a name. You use anonymous functions in many of the same places as you do lambda expressions. In many cases, the choice between the two comes down to a combination of personal preference and clarity of expression. Even though the two forms of expression obtain the same result in most cases, the way you construct the expression differs, so one form might be clearer in some cases than the other is.

REMEMBER

Aside from the need to declare an anonymous function as a function (despite it acting like an expression), an anonymous function also differs from a lambda expression in one important way: You can provide a return type with an anonymous function.

The previous section shows how to use multiple lambda expressions with a single function, `changeString()`. You can perform the same task using an anonymous function, as shown here:

```
fun main(args: Array<String>) {
    val repeat = fun(inStr: String, times: Int): String {
        return inStr.repeat(times)
    }
    val part = fun(inStr: String, len: Int): String {
        return inStr.take(len)
    }
```

```
    println(changeString(repeat, "A String ", 4))
    println(changeString(part, "A String ", 4))
}

fun changeString(function: (String, Int) -> String,
                 string: String, number: Int): String {
    return function(string, number)
}
```

Notice that `changeString()` hasn't changed at all, and this is the amazing thing about being able to use either a lambda expression or an anonymous function. The function receiving either form doesn't change, which means that even when you provide expressions to Kotlin or Android functions, you still have a choice as to which form to use for your particular need.

The anonymous function looks like any other function you might have created in the past, except for the lack of a name. You can create a function body of any size needed to complete the task, so anonymous functions often work better than lambda expressions when performing a complex set of steps within the function body.

Defining the Function Types

When using functional programming techniques in Kotlin, you discover that Kotlin has some built-in function types. Each of these function types reduces the code needed to perform a task, while also making the code clearer and easier to understand. The following sections discuss the most important function types and demonstrate how to use them. These functions can be quite important in Android programming in helping manipulate data for various purposes.

Comprehensions

A *comprehension* is a kind of manipulation you perform on a `List`, `Set`, or `Map` to understand it in a certain way. These comprehensions are listed as part of the extension functions for a collection, such as those shown for `List` at `https://kotlinlang.org/api/latest/jvm/stdlib/kotlin.collections/-list/index.html`. To differentiate a comprehension from another sort of extension function, look at the input, which is normally a predicate or transform, and the output, which is normally a subset of the current `List`.

A comprehension begins with the original `List`, followed by the dot-separated list of comprehension functions. Here's an example of a numeric comprehension that returns only the values that meet a specific criterion and transforms them into strings:

```
val numbers = listOf(1, 2, 3, 4, 5)
val selection = numbers
    .filter {it >= 3}
    .map {"Value = $it"}

selection.forEach({println(it)})
```

TIP

Placing each comprehension on its own line tends to make the entire expression easier to read. In this case, the `filter()` function returns only those `numbers` elements that are equal to or greater than `3`. It then calls on `map()` to transform the numbers into a specifically formatted string. Each function works on the input `List` in the order in which it appears, so order is important in defining how the comprehension works.

REMEMBER

Whenever you work with comprehensions, `it` represents the collection as it appears from the previous step. So, in `.filter {it >= 3}`, `it` represents the original `List` found in `numbers`. However, in `.map {"Value = $it"}`, `it` represents the modified `List` from the filter step. Here's the output from this example:

```
Value = 3
Value = 4
Value = 5
```

Receivers

A *receiver* is a kind of member addition to a class made outside the class proper. You use a receiver as the start of an extension function that makes the class able to do more than it otherwise could without actually modifying the class itself or creating a new subclass. The receiver consists of a signature followed by a lambda expression. Here is a simple example:

```
class Name (val aName: String)

fun main(args: Array<String>) {
    val greet: Name.() -> String =
        {"Hello ${this.aName}!"}
```

```
    val person = Name("George")

    println(person.greet())
}
```

The example begins with the Name class, which takes a String argument, aName, as part of its primary constructor. The receiver, greet, references the Name class and provides an extension to it (as designated by the period) that requires no arguments (as shown by the empty parentheses). The lambda expression outputs a string that includes the content of aName. Note that you must reference aName using this.aName.

To use the extension, you create a new object, person, and provide a value of "George" to aName. The call to println() displays the greeting Hello George! by calling person.greet().

You can further extend this example by providing a specific greeting, rather than simply Hello. This update allows the addition of a greeting:

```
val greet: Name.(String) -> String =
    {"$it ${this.aName}!"}

val person = Name("George")

println(person.greet("Good morning"))
```

REMEMBER

In this case, you specify a String input argument for greet(). A receiver can only have one input parameter. You reference this input argument using it within the lambda expression code. In addition, when calling greet(), you must now supply the input argument. Consequently, this version of the code outputs: Good morning George!.

One of the reasons that knowing how to use receivers and extension functions is so important is that some Kotlin classes and functions use them. For example, even though you're usually not likely to write code like this, you could create a complex StringBuilder object using this approach:

```
    val aGreeting = StringBuilder("Hello ")
        .apply {
            append("there ")
            append("from Kotlin!")
        }.toString()

    println(aGreeting)
```

The apply() inline function accepts a series of inputs to modify the original StringBuilder input using the append() extension function. You can see a list of other StringBuilder extension functions at https://kotlinlang.org/api/latest/jvm/stdlib/kotlin.text/-string-builder/index.html. The output of this example is Hello there from Kotlin!.

Inline

When you create lambda expressions, anonymous functions, standard functions, and other kinds of modularized code, the code resides in a separate area of memory. To use the code, the compiler must create a connection to it, which adds overhead to the application. If you call this modularized code many times, the overhead can significantly slow your application, but at the same time, because the code exists in just one place, you don't use any additional memory. On the other hand, if you were to repeat the modularized code everywhere you need it, application performance would improve, but at the cost of memory. (Not only that, but by repeating the code all over the place you make code modifications a nightmare!)

REMEMBER

A way around the performance issue is to use the inline keyword to tell the compiler to inline the code — that is, to place the compiled version of the code directly where the application needs it. For example, you could inline this code:

```
fun main(args: Array<String>) {
    val repeat = fun(inStr: String, times: Int): String {
        return inStr.repeat(times)
    }
    val part = fun(inStr: String, len: Int): String {
        return inStr.take(len)
    }

    println(changeString(repeat, "A String ", 4))
    println(changeString(part, "A String ", 4))
}

inline fun changeString(function: (String, Int) -> String,
                        string: String, number: Int): String {
    return function(string, number)
}
```

When you inline the code like this, the `println()` calls change. What the compiled version does looks like this:

```
println(("A String ").repeat(4))
println(("A String ").take(4))
```

Utility

Kotlin provides a number of utility functions that make dealing with potentially null values a lot easier. In some cases, you use them to manipulate values in such a manner that potentially null results aren't a problem. Here is a list of utility functions that you should keep in mind:

- `run()`: Enables you to work with potentially null values and pass non-null values to functions that can't accept a null value. Here's an example of `run()` in use:

```
fun main(args: Array<String>) {
    val myInt: Int? = null
    val result = myInt?.run {greaterThan(this)}
    println(result)
}

fun greaterThan(x: Int): Boolean {
    return x > 5
}
```

  In this case, `run()` will place a value of `null` in `result` because `myInt` is `null`. However, if `myInt` hadn't been `null`, `result` would contain the `Boolean` comparison provided by `greaterThan()`.

- `let()`: This is a syntactical variation of `run()`, except that you can use it with a series of normal functions rather than function types with receivers. A difference between `run()` and `let()` is in the passing of values. You'd need to change the call in the previous example from `this` (an object) to `it` (a value), like this:

```
val result = myInt?.let {greaterThan(it)}
```

- `with()`: Performs one or more operations on a non-null variable. To modify the previous example to use `with()`, you need to make `myInt` non-null, like this:

```
val myInt: Int = 5
val result = with(myInt) {greaterThan(this)}
```

- `apply()`: Applies extension functions when provided with a non-null value. If the value is null, the output is null as well. This form uses the object `this` to pass values to the functions.
- `also()`: Applies normal functions when provided with a non-null value. If the value is null, the output is null as well. This form uses the object `it` to pass values to the functions.
- `takeIf()`: Performs a conditional comparison and, if the comparison is `true`, passes value to a lambda expression. Here's an example:

  ```
  val myInt: Int = 5
  val result = myInt.takeIf {it > 4} ?.let {it * it}
  println(result)
  ```

  In this case, the code determines whether `myInt` is greater than `4`. If so, the code returns the square of the value in `myInt`. The variable being compared can't be `null`. When the comparison fails, the output is a `null` value.
- `takeUnless()`: Performs the opposite of `takeIf()`. The result is non-null when the comparison fails.

Using Functional Programming for Android Apps

Throughout this chapter you have discovered what functional programming is and how to perform tasks using it, which is nice, but it's not helpful if you don't have a practical use for it when building an Android app. The world is packed with interesting technologies that don't necessarily work well or aren't practical. Some are just downright useless, even though they started out looking like a promising approach, like the `NullPointerException` (see Chapter 3 of this minibook for a discussion of this particular issue). From a general perspective, using functional programming techniques has these advantages in nearly any environment in which you use Kotlin:

- Reduction of code size
- Easier to debug
- Faster in most cases
- Less prone to side effects
- Easier to read and understand

» More flexible
» Less potential for data loss or corruption
» Reduction of security issues
» Fewer errors because of better compiler support

However, you haven't really seen functional techniques used for any of the book examples so far because the book examples have focused on the essential Android environment where the Java influence is felt quite strongly. The examples in this chapter give you a start by showing various techniques, but they're outside the Android environment. As you move into more complex examples, such as those found in Book 4, you start to see the potential for using functional programming techniques.

TIP

You can also view some detailed articles online, such as "A Functional Approach to Android Architecture using Kotlin," by Jorge Castillo, at `https://academy.realm.io/posts/mobilization-2017-jorge-castillo-functional-android-architecture-kotlin/`. In this article, you discover how functional programming techniques help fix some of the issues that Java developers encountered when writing code for apps like games. The example code looks at a simple task — fetching a hero — and explores the serious problems involved in doing it in Java and even in Kotlin without functional programming approaches.

Comparing languages is always an opinionated process because developers simply like particular languages, sometimes for no apparent reason except that the language of choice is familiar. Looking at use cases, however, could make it easier to determine how to use Kotlin and functional programming techniques to make your next app a success. The article "Kotlin vs. Java: Which Programming Language to Choose for Your Android App," by Maria Redka, at `https://mlsdev.com/blog/kotlin-vs-java` takes a use-case approach to comparing the two languages and the techniques they rely on to get the job done.

WARNING

Functional programming may not work well for every development team, especially if you're already heavily invested in Java. However, you can find case studies online, such as "Why we choose Kotlin for creating Android apps," by Dima Kovalenko, at `https://hackernoon.com/why-we-choose-kotlin-for-creating-android-apps-46030b10d19c`. This article discusses experiences in moving from Java to Kotlin. The article writer isn't shy in saying that some things simply didn't work at the outset. Reviewing articles of this sort can help you understand whether functional programming techniques will work in your particular case (something that would be very tough to do in a book).

- What goes into an XML document
- How XML handles the names of things

Chapter 7
A <brief> Look at XML

As described in the "Comparing the Functional Paradigm" section of Chapter 6 of this minibook, modern software takes on several forms, and Kotlin can express a number of them in a similar manner as other languages like Python do. One way or another, a development platform should use the best software for the job. That's why the Android platform uses both procedural and declarative software.

- Android's *procedural* Kotlin code tells a device what to do.
- Android's *declarative* XML code describes a layout, an application, a set of strings, a set of preferences, or some other information that's useful to a mobile device.

A typical Android application is a mix of Kotlin code (with Java underpinnings), XML code, and a few other things. So when you develop for Android, you write lots of Kotlin code and you mess with XML code.

What? You "mess with" XML code? What does that mean?

The truth is, XML code is painful to type. A typical XML file involves many elements, each requiring very precise wording and all looking very much alike at first glance. So in the Android world, most XML files are generated automatically. You don't type all the file's angle brackets. Instead, you drop widgets from a palette onto a preview screen. You let Android Studio create the XML code on your behalf.

So, in many situations, you don't have to compose XML code. But you can encounter situations in which you want to bypass Android Studio's tools and tweak the XML code yourself. Maybe the tools don't readily provide an option that you want to use in your XML code. Or maybe your app isn't behaving the way you want it to behave, and you read over the XML code to check for subtle errors.

For these reasons and others, you're best off understanding the fundamentals of XML. So this chapter covers XML basics.

XML Isn't Ordinary Text

You may already be familiar with *Hypertext Markup Language* (HTML) because HTML is the universal language of the World Wide Web. Choose View⇨Source in your favorite web browser, and you'll see a bunch of HTML tags — tags like `<head>`, `<title>`, `<meta>`, and so on. An HTML document describes the look and layout of a web page.

An XML document is something like an HTML document. But an XML document differs from an HTML document in many ways. The two most striking ways are as follows:

- An XML file doesn't describe only look and layout. In fact, very few XML files describe anything visual at all. Instead, most XML files describe data: a list of stock trades; a hierarchical list of automobile makes and models; or a nested list of movements, measures, and notes in a Beethoven symphony.
- Certain rules describe what you can and cannot write in an HTML or an XML document. The rules for HTML are very permissive. The rules for XML are very strict.

  In HTML, a missing character or word often goes unnoticed. In XML, a missing character or word can ruin your whole day.

The formal definitions of an XML document's parts can be daunting. But you can think of an XML document as a bunch of elements, with each element having one or two tags.

Of tags and elements

Tags and elements are the workhorses of XML. Here's the scoop:

- **A tag is some text surrounded by angle brackets.** For example, Listing 7-1 contains a basic `AndroidManifest.xml` file. In this file, `<intent-filter>` is a tag; `</intent-filter>` (which comes a bit later in the file) is another tag. Text such as `<application ... android:icon="@mipmap/ic_launcher" android:label="@string/app_name" ...>` is also a tag.

LISTING 7-1: An `AndroidManifest.xml` File

```
<?xml version="1.0" encoding="utf-8"?>
<manifest xmlns:android="http://schemas.android.com/apk/res/android"
    package="com.allmycode.p01_05_01"
    android:versionCode="1"
    android:versionName="1.0" >

    <uses-sdk
        android:minSdkVersion="14"
        android:targetSdkVersion="29"/>

    <application
        android:allowBackup="true"
        android:appComponentFactory="androidx.core.app.CoreComponentFactory"
        android:debuggable="true"
        android:icon="@mipmap/ic_launcher"
        android:label="@string/app_name"
        android:roundIcon="@mipmap/ic_launcher_round"
        android:supportsRtl="true"
        android:testOnly="true"
        android:theme="@style/AppTheme" >
        <activity android:name="com.allmycode.p01_05_01.MainActivity" >
            <intent-filter>
                <action android:name="android.intent.action.MAIN"/>

                <category android:name="android.intent.category.LAUNCHER"/>
            </intent-filter>
        </activity>
    </application>

</manifest>
```

Not everything with angle brackets qualifies as an XML tag. For example, the text `<This is my application.>` violates many of the rules of grammatically correct XML. For more about what an XML tag can and cannot contain, read on.

TECHNICAL STUFF

An XML document is *well formed* when its text obeys all the rules of grammatically correct XML.

» **An XML document may have three different kinds of tags.**

- A *start tag* begins with an open angle bracket and a name. The start tag's last character is a closing angle bracket.

  In Listing 7-1, `<intent-filter>` is a start tag. The start tag's name is `intent-filter`.

- An *end tag* begins with an open angle bracket followed by a forward slash and a name. The end tag's last character is a closing angle bracket.

  In Listing 7-1, `</intent-filter>` is an end tag. The end tag's name is `intent-filter`.

- An *empty element tag* begins with an open angle bracket followed by a name. The empty element tag's last two characters are a forward slash followed by a closing angle bracket.

  In Listing 7-1, the text

```
<action android:name=
"android.intent.action.MAIN"/>
```

  is an empty element tag. The tag's name is `action`.

WARNING

  In this bullet's empty element tag, the text `android:name` isn't the tag's name! It's the name of an *attribute,* but the letters `name` in `android:name` have nothing to do with its being a name. For details about XML attributes, read on in this section.

The next several paragraphs discuss tags in more detail. But in the meantime, it's important to describe an XML element.

» **An XML element either has both a start tag and an end tag, or it has an empty element tag.** The document in Listing 7-1 contains several elements. For example, the document's `intent-filter` element has both a start tag and an end tag. (Both the start and end tags have the same name, `intent-filter`, so the name of the entire element is `intent-filter`.)

In Listing 7-1, the document's `action` element has only one tag — an empty element tag.

» **The names of XML elements are not cast in stone.** In an HTML document, a `b` element creates boldface text. For example, the text `<b>Buy this!</b>` in an HTML document looks like **Buy this!** in your web browser's window.

In an HTML document, the element name `b` is cast in stone. But in XML documents, names like `manifest`, `application`, `activity`, and `intent-filter` are not cast in stone. An XML document has its own set of element names, and these names are likely to be different from the names in most other XML documents. You can create your own well-formed XML document as follows:

```
<pets>
    <cat>
        Felix
    </cat>
    <cat>
        Sylvester
    </cat>
</pets>
```

If your goal is to store information about kitty cats, your XML document is just fine.

WARNING

The text in an XML document is case sensitive. An element named `APPLICATION` doesn't have the same name as another element named `application`.

» **A non-empty XML element may contain *content*.** The content is stuff between the start tag and the end tag. For example, in Listing 7-1, the `intent-filter` element's content is

```
<action android:name=
            "android.intent.action.MAIN"/>
<category android:name=
            "android.intent.category.LAUNCHER"/>
```

An element's content may include other elements. (In this example, the `intent-filter` element contains an `action` element and a `category` element.)

An element's content may also include ordinary text. For example, in Listing 7-2, the `resources` element contains five `string` elements, and each `string` element contains ordinary text.

LISTING 7-2: **An Android `strings.xml` File**

```
<resources>
    <string name="app_name">01_06_04</string>
    <string name="Checkbox1Text">Pepperoni</string>
    <string name="Checkbox2Text">Extra Cheese</string>
    <string name="TextView1Text">Plain</string>
    <string name="CheckboxClick">onCheckboxClick</string>
</resources>
```

You can even have mixed content. For example, between an element's start and end tags, you may have some ordinary text, followed by an element or two, followed by more ordinary text.

Oddly enough, the generated `strings.xml` file in Listing 7-2 doesn't contain an XML declaration, the `<?xml version="1.0" encoding="utf-8"?>` at the beginning of the code, as you see in Listing 7-1. The declaration is an optional part of XML 1.0 files, but it's a mandatory part of XML 1.1 files. You usually provide an XML declaration in all XML files by convention. The declaration defines the XML version and how the file is encoded to make processing easier. Some of your other Android Studio XML files also omit the declaration, such as `styles.xml`. When an XML file omits the declaration, the file processor assumes that the file is an XML 1.0 file. (See the "Other things you find in an XML document" section, later in this chapter, as well as `https://www.w3resource.com/xml/declarations.php` for more details about XML declarations.)

- **In some cases, two or more elements may have the same name.** In Listing 7-2, five distinct elements have the name `string`. To find out more about the names used in an XML file, see the nearby sidebar "What element names can you use?"
- **Elements are either nested inside one another or they don't overlap at all.** In Listing 7-1, the `manifest` element contains an `application` element. The `application` element contains an `activity` element, which in turn contains an `intent-filter` element, and so on.

```
<manifest>

   This code demonstrates element nesting.
   This code is NOT a real AndroidManifest.xml file.

   <application>

      <activity>
         <intent-filter>
            <action/>
            <category/>
         </intent-filter>
      </activity>

   </application>

</manifest>
```

In Listing 7-1 (and in the fake listing inside this bullet) the `action` and `category` elements don't overlap at all. But whenever one element overlaps another, one of the elements is nested completely inside the other.

For example, in Listing 7-1, the `intent-filter` element is nested completely inside the `activity` element. The following sequence of tags, with overlapping and not nesting, would be illegal:

```
<activity>
   <intent-filter>
      This is NOT well-formed XML code.
</activity>
   </intent-filter>
```

TECHNICAL STUFF

The start of this chapter announces that the rules governing HTML aren't as strict as the rules governing XML. In HTML, you can create non-nested, overlapping tags. For example, the code `<b>Use <i>irregular</b> fonts</i> sparingly` appears in your web browser as

Use *irregular* *fonts* sparingly

with "Use irregular" in bold and "irregular fonts" italicized.

TIP

Web browsers, such as Chrome, Firefox, and Microsoft Internet Explorer, are decent XML viewers. When you visit an XML document with most web browsers, you see a well-indented display of your XML code. The code's elements expand and collapse on your command. And if you visit an XML document that's not well-formed (for example, a document with overlapping, non-nested tags), the browser displays an error message. To display an XML file in your browser, the file must possess an XML declaration, so you can display `AndroidManifest.xml` in your browser, but you can't display `strings.xml` in your browser.

- **Each XML document contains one element in which all other elements are nested.** In Listing 7-1, the `manifest` element contains all other elements. That's good. The following outline would not make a legal XML document:

```
<manifest>
   <application>
   </application>
      This is NOT a well-formed XML document
      because another element comes after the
      following manifest end tag:
</manifest>

<manifest>
   <application>
   </application>
</manifest>
```

In an XML document, the single element that encloses all other elements is the *root* element. The only element that doesn't appear in the root element is the XML declaration, which always appears as the first element in the file and always appears alone.

- **Start tags and empty element tags may contain *attributes*.** An *attribute* is a name-value pair. Each attribute has the form

  ```
  name="value"
  ```

  The quotation marks around the value are required.

  In Listing 7-1, the start tags and empty element tags contain many attributes. For example, in the `manifest` start tag, the text

  ```
  package="com.allmycode.p01_05_01"
  ```

  is an attribute. In the same tag, the text

  ```
  xmlns:android=
      "http://schemas.android.com/apk/res/android"
  ```

  is an attribute. Later in Listing 7-1, the `application` start tag has nine attributes, the `activity` start tag has one attribute, the empty element `action` tag has one attribute, and the empty element `category` tag has one attribute. Finally, the poor, lonely `intent-filter` start tag has no attributes. Sorry about that!

WHAT ELEMENT NAMES CAN YOU USE?

In HTML, the tags `<b>` and `</b>` surround text that appears in bold type. That's the way web pages are encoded.

But in XML, tags like `<cat>` and `</cat>` might represent a Windows security catalog, catenary-shaped wire hanging down from telephone poles, or a pet who's climbing on your computer keyboard (while you write *Android Application Development All-in-One For Dummies,* 3rd Edition, we might add).

How do you know whether the names in your XML document are meaningful?

The short answer is, "Meaning is as meaning does." (Whatever that means!) An element's name is meaningful as long as a computer program can do the things that you intend programs to do with that element. For example, a program that checks security catalogs to distinguish trustworthy from malicious downloads probably does nothing useful with an element like

```
<cat name="Felix" age="7" breed="calico"/>
```

On the other hand, a security catalog program may include instructions to deal with the following element:

```
<cat name="Firefox" verified="true" publisher="mozilla.org"
   version="7.0.1"/>
```

Even so, the XML specs provide two ways to describe the names in a document. The older way is with a *DTD* (*D*ocument *T*ype *D*efinition). A DTD looks something like this:

```
<!ELEMENT CatThoughts (Image, Thought+)>
<!ATTLIST CatThoughts frequency CDATA #REQUIRED>
<!NOTATION JPEG SYSTEM "image/jpeg">
<!ENTITY CuteCat SYSTEM "weelie.jpg" NDATA JPEG>
<!ELEMENT Image EMPTY>
<!ATTLIST Image source ENTITY #REQUIRED>
<!ELEMENT Thought (#PCDATA)>
<!ENTITY meow "Feed me">
```

A DTD describes the names that you can use in a particular XML document (or in a bunch of XML documents) and describes the order in which you can use those names. But a DTD doesn't describe all the fine points of element-naming (like the fact that a name must refer to an integer value or to a date). So the newer way to describe the names in a document is with a *schema.* A schema looks something like this:

```
<?xml version="1.0"?>
<!-- Children.xsd -->
<xsd:schema xmlns:xsd="http://www.w3.org/2001/XMLSchema">
   <xsd:element name="Children" type="xsd:integer"/>
</xsd:schema>
```

This schema says that a certain XML document (or a bunch of XML documents) uses the element name `Children`, and that the value stored in the `Children` element must be an integer. (A family can't have 2.5 children.) Even better, a schema is itself an XML document (with start tags, end tags, and everything else), so all the tools that you apply to ordinary XML documents can be applied to schema documents as well. (A DTD may look something like an XML document, but in a DTD, the exclamation points and the lack of end tags break the grammar rules of an XML document.)

Not every XML document is connected to a DTD or to a schema — and even if an XML document has a DTD or a schema, that document may or may not be valid. A *valid* XML document is a document whose names obey the rules described in the document's DTD or schema.

To test the validity of an XML document, use the online test application at `https://www.w3schools.com/xml/xml:validator.asp`.

Other things you find in an XML document

There's more to life than tags and elements. This section describes all the things you can look forward to.

- **An XML document begins with an XML declaration.** The declaration in Listing 7-1 is

  ```
  <?xml version="1.0" encoding="utf-8"?>
  ```

  The question marks distinguish the declaration from an ordinary XML tag.

  This declaration announces that Listing 7-1 contains an XML document (big surprise!), that the document uses version 1.0 of the XML specifications, and that bit strings used to store the document's characters are to be interpreted with their meanings as Unicode Transformation Format, 8-bit (UTF-8) codes (a standard method of encoding text in a file).

  In practice, you seldom have reason to mess with a document's XML declaration. For a new XML document, simply copy and paste the declaration in Listing 7-1.

  The `version="1.0"` part of an XML declaration may look antiquated, but XML hasn't changed much since the initial specs appeared in 1998. In fact, the only newer version is XML 1.1, which developers seldom use. This reluctance to change is part of the XML philosophy — to have a universal, time-tested format for representing information about almost any subject.

- **An XML document may contain comments.** A comment begins with the characters `<!--` and ends with the characters `-->`. For example, the lines

  ```
  <!-- This application must be tested
  very, very carefully. -->
  ```

  form an XML comment. A document's comments can appear between tags (and in a few other places that aren't worth fussing about right now).

  Comments are normally intended to be read by humans. But programs that input XML documents are free to read comments and to act on the text within comments. Android doesn't normally do anything with the comments it finds in its XML files, but you never know.

- **An XML document may contain processing instructions.** A processing instruction looks a lot like the document's XML declaration. Here's an example of a processing instruction:

  ```
  <?chapter number="x" Put chapter number here ?>
  ```

A document may have many processing instructions, and these processing instructions can appear between tags (and in a few other places). But in practice, most XML documents have no processing instructions. (For reasons too obscure even for a Technical Stuff icon, the document's XML declaration isn't a processing instruction.)

Like a document's XML declaration, each processing instruction begins with the characters `<?` and ends with the characters `?>`. Each processing instruction has a name. But after the processing instruction's name, anything goes. The processing instruction near the start of this bullet has the name `chapter` followed by some free-form text. Part of that text looks like a start tag's attribute, but the remaining text looks like a comment of some sort.

REMEMBER

You can put almost anything inside a processing instruction. Most of the software that inputs your XML document will simply ignore the processing instruction. (As an experiment, you can add chapter-processing instruction to the file in Listing 7-1. This change will make absolutely no difference in the running of your Android app.)

So what good are processing instructions, anyway? Well, if you stumble into one, you don't want to mistake it for a kind of XML declaration. Also, certain programs may read specific processing instructions and get particular information from these instructions.

For example, a *style sheet* is a file that describes the look and the layout of the information in an XML document. Typically, an XML document and the corresponding style sheet are in two different files. To indicate that the information in your `pets.xml` document should be displayed using the rules in the `animals.css` style sheet, you add the following processing instruction to the `pets.xml` document:

```
<?xml-stylesheet href="animals.css" type="text/css"?>
```

» **An XML document may contain entity references.** We poked around among Android's official sample applications and found the following elements (spread out among different programs):

```
<Key android:codes="60" android:keyLabel="&lt;"/>
<Key android:codes="62" android:keyLabel="&gt;"/>
<Key android:codes="34" android:keyLabel="&quot;"/>
<string name="activity_save_restore">
   App/Activity/Save &amp; Restore State
</string>
```

The first element contains a reference to the < entity. You can't use a real angle bracket just anywhere in an XML document. An angle bracket signals the beginning of an XML tag. So, if you want to express that the name three-brackets stands for the string "<<<", you can't write

```
<string name="three-brackets"><<<</string>
```

The extra brackets will confuse any program that expects to encounter ordinary XML tags.

So, to get around XML's special use of angle brackets, the XML specs include the *entities* < and >. The first, <, stands for an opening angle bracket. The second, >, stands for the closing angle bracket. So to express that the name three-brackets stands for the string "<<<", you write

```
<string name="three-brackets">&lt;&lt;&lt;</string>
```

In the entity <, the letters lt stand for "less than." And after all, an opening angle bracket looks like the "less than" sign in mathematics. Similarly, in the entity >, the letters gt stand for "greater than."

What's in a Namespace?

The first official definition of XML was published in 1998 by the World Wide Web Consortium (W3C). This first standard ignored a sticky problem. If two XML documents have some elements or attributes with identical names, and if those names have different meanings in the two documents, how can you possibly combine the two documents?

Here's a simple XML document:

```
<?xml version="1.0" encoding="utf-8"?>
<banks>
   <bank>First National Bank</bank>
   <bank>Second Regional Bank</bank>
   <bank>United Trustworthy Trusty Trust</bank>
   <bank>Federal Bank of Fredonia (Groucho Branch)</bank>
</banks>
```

And here's another XML document:

```
<?xml version="1.0" encoding="utf-8"?>
<banks>
   <bank>Banks of the Mississippi River</bank>
```

```
    <bank>La Rive Gauche</bank>
    <bank>La Rive Droite</bank>
    <bank>The Banks of Plum Creek</bank>
</banks>
```

An organization with seemingly limitless resources aims to collect and combine knowledge from all over the Internet. The organization's software finds XML documents and combines them into one super, all-knowing document. (Think of an automated version of Wikipedia.)

But when you combine documents about financial institutions with documents about rivers, you get some confusing results. If both First National and the Banks of Plum Creek are in the same document's `bank` elements, analyzing the document may require prior knowledge. In other words, if you don't already know that some banks lend money and that other banks flood during storms, you might draw some strange conclusions. And unfortunately, computer programs don't already know anything. (Life becomes really complicated when you reach an XML element describing the Red River Bank in Shreveport, Louisiana. This river bank has teller machines in Shreveport, Alexandria, and other towns.)

To remedy this situation, members of the XML standards committee created XML namespaces. A *namespace* is a prefix that you attach to a name. You separate the namespace from the name with a colon (`:`) character. For example, in Listing 7-1, almost every attribute name begins with the `android` prefix. The listing's attributes include `xmlns:android`, `android:allowBackup`, `android:icon`, and more.

So to combine documents about lending banks and river banks, you create the XML document in Listing 7-3. What you're seeing is one method you could use to combine the two XML documents from earlier in this section using namespaces to differentiate between the two.

LISTING 7-3: A Document with Two Namespaces

```
<?xml version="1.0" encoding="utf-8"?>

<banks xmlns:money=
            "http://schemas.allmycode.com/money"
       xmlns:river=
            "http://schemas.allmycode.com/river">

<money:bank>First National Bank</money:bank>
<money:bank>Second Regional Bank</money:bank>
<money:bank>
    United Trustworthy Trusty Trust
```

(continued)

LISTING 7-3: *(continued)*

```
</money:bank>
<money:bank>
    Federal Bank of Fredonia (Groucho Branch)
</money:bank>

<river:bank>
    Banks of the Mississippi River
    </river:bank>
    <river:bank>La Rive Gauche</river:bank>
    <river:bank>La Rive Droite</river:bank>
    <river:bank>The Banks of Plum Creek</river:bank>

</banks>
```

TECHNICAL STUFF

In a name such as `android:icon`, the word `android` is a *prefix*, and the word `icon` is a *local name*.

At this point, the whole namespace business branches into two possibilities:

- **Some very old XML software is not namespace aware.** The original XML standard had no mention of namespaces. So the oldest XML-handling programs do nothing special with prefixes. To an old program, the names `money:bank` and `river:bank` in Listing 7-3 are simply two different names with no relationship to each other. The colons in the names are no different from the letters.
- **Newer XML software is namespace aware.** In some situations, you want the software to recognize relationships between names with the same prefixes and between identical names with different prefixes. For example, in a document containing elements named `consumer:bank`, `investment:bank`, and `consumer:confidence`, you may want your software to recognize two kinds of banks. You may also want your software to deal with two kinds of consumer elements.

  Most modern software is namespace aware. That is, the software recognizes that a name like `river:bank` consists of a prefix and a local name.

To make it easier for software to sort out an XML document's namespaces, every namespace must be defined. In Listing 7-3, the attributes

```
xmlns:money=
   "http://schemas.allmycode.com/money"
xmlns:river=
   "http://schemas.allmycode.com/river"
```

define the document's two namespaces. The attributes associate one URL with the `money` namespace and another URL with the `river` namespace. The special `xmlns` namespace doesn't get defined because the `xmlns` namespace has the same meaning in every XML document. The `xmlns` prefix always means, "This is the start of an XML namespace definition."

In Listing 7-3, each namespace is associated with a URL. So, if you're creating a new XML document, you may ask, "What if I don't have my own domain name?" You may also ask, "What information must I post at a namespace's URL?" And the surprising answers are "Make up one" and "Nothing."

The string of symbols doesn't really have to be a URL. Instead, it can be a URI — a *Universal Resource Identifier*. A URI looks like a URL, but a URI doesn't have to point to an actual network location. A URI is simply a name, a string of characters "full of sound and fury" and possibly "signifying nothing." Some XML developers create web pages to accompany each of their URIs. The web pages contain useful descriptions of the names used in the XML documents.

But most URIs used for XML namespaces point nowhere. For example, the URI `http://schemas.android.com/apk/res/android` in Listing 7-1 appears in almost every Android XML document. If you type that URI into the address field of your favorite web browser, you get the familiar `cannot display the webpage` or `Server not found` message. (Trying the URI to see what you can find is always interesting; some actually do point to websites.)

REMEMBER

An *unbound prefix* message indicates that you haven't correctly associated a namespace found in your XML document with a URI. Some very old software (software that's not namespace aware) doesn't catch errors of this kind, but most modern software does.

The package attribute

In Listing 7-1, the attribute name `package` has no prefix. So you might say, "What the heck! I'll change the attribute's name to `android:package` just for good measure." But this change produces some error messages. One message reads `Unknown attribute android:package`. What's going on here?

In an `AndroidManifest.xml` file, the `package` attribute has more to do with Kotlin and Java than with Android. (The `package` attribute points to the Kotlin package containing the application's Kotlin code.) So the creators of Android decided not to make this `package` attribute be part of the `android` namespace.

TECHNICAL STUFF

Each Android platform, from Cupcake onward, has a file named `public.xml` among the files you get when you download the Android SDK. Android Studio performs these downloads for you automatically. If you open a `public.xml` file in a text editor, you see a list of names in the `android` namespace. The precise location of this file on your system varies by platform, but on a Windows system, you can find the file at `\Users\`*`<Your User Name>`*`\AppData\Local\Android\Sdk\platforms\android-29\data\res\values`.

The style attribute

The same business about not being an `android` name holds for `style` and `package`. A *style* is a collection of items (or *properties*) describing the look of something on a mobile device screen. A style's XML document might contain Android-specific names, but the style itself is simply a bunch of items, not an Android property in its own right.

To see how this works, imagine creating a very simple app. The XML file describing the app's basic layout may look like the code in Listing 7-4, with the style attribute in bold.

LISTING 7-4: Using the `style` Attribute

```
<?xml version="1.0" encoding="utf-8"?>
<LinearLayout xmlns:android=
  "http://schemas.android.com/apk/res/android"
    android:orientation="vertical"
    android:layout_width="match_parent"
    android:layout_height="match_parent"
    >
<TextView
    android:layout_width="match_parent"
    android:layout_height="wrap_content"
    android:text="@string/callmom"
    style="@style/bigmono"
/>
</LinearLayout>
```

In Listing 7-4, all attribute names except `style` (and the name android itself) are in the `android` namespace. The value `"@style/bigmono"` points Android to an XML file in your app's `res/values` folder. Listing 7-5 contains a very simple file named `styles.xml`.

LISTING 7-5: A File with Style

```
<?xml version="1.0" encoding="utf-8"?>
<resources>
    <style name="bigmono">
        <item name="android:textSize">50dip</item>
        <item name="android:typeface">monospace</item>
    </style>
</resources>
```

Again, notice the mix of words that are inside and outside the `android` namespace. The words `android:textSize` and `android:typeface` are in the `android` namespace, and the other words in Listing 7-5 are not.

The style in Listing 7-5 specifies a whopping 50 density-independent pixels for the size of the text and monospace (traditional typewriter) font for the typeface. When Android applies the style in Listing 7-5 to the layout in Listing 7-4, you see the prominent message in Figure 7-1.

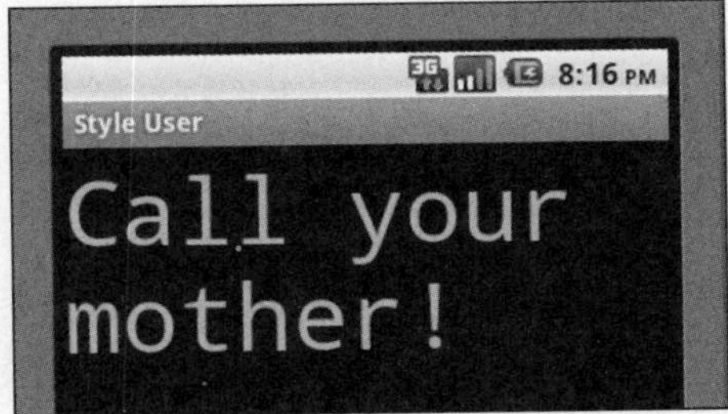

FIGURE 7-1: Be a good son or daughter.

3
The Building Blocks

Contents at a Glance

» Defining the Jetpack elements

» Working with the AndroidX package

» Interacting with lifecycle-aware components

Chapter 1
Getting an Overview of Jetpack

Jetpack is all about making things simpler, and who doesn't like that idea? Book 2 tells you about how Kotlin makes things easier when compared to Java, yet Kotlin also provides new ways of doing things. You use Jetpack to make things easier and perform new tasks by

- Reducing the amount of boilerplate code
- Ensuring that your app follows best practices more often than is possible through hand coding so that you don't end up with horrid errors that are impossible to find
- Modularizing the development environment so that it's easier to understand
- Unbundling the `androidx.*` packages from the API to improve backward compatibility and ensure that you have the latest updates
- Helping you manage the life span of your app so that it doesn't end up being some sort of Franken-app

Of course, you keep hearing about such features, but they never seem to be fully realized in most products. Jetpack does have some warts, too. This chapter helps you understand the benefits of using Jetpack, understand the various Jetpack components, look into the details of the `android.*` packages, and gain insights into this whole thing about lifecycle management. As you discover all the really amazing things about Jetpack, you're also introduced to a few of the less lovely aspects as well.

Understanding the Benefits of Jetpack

Development environments of all sorts are moving toward the elimination of coding that has nothing to do with what you want to do. Android is no different. For example, you do want to display the prices for your new product, The Amazing Widget, onscreen so someone can buy it and make you incredibly rich. You don't want to worry about managing the memory used to display the text. The first is what you want to do (display text); the second is what you want to avoid (managing memory). The combination of Kotlin and Jetpack is designed to help you avoid doing any more work than you really have to in order to complete a task. Achieving this goal means eliminating activities like

- Background task management
- Navigation
- Lifecycle management
- Memory management
- Configuration change management

None of these activities has anything to do with what you want to do with your app, but they're important in making your app work. Look at Jetpack as a helper that takes all these obscure burdens off your back and lets you focus on the main event: writing that game app or creating a fraud detector.

REMEMBER

To make it easy for you to perform tasks without worrying about whether you're using the latest code, best practices, or coding techniques, Jetpack gets updated more often than the rest of Android. This means that you can ensure that your code is always current without expending much effort. However, because Jetpack is packaged separately, you can also choose to use an older version for backward compatibility. So, you get the best of both worlds: the latest code and the ability to support existing apps with less trouble.

Eliminating boilerplate code

Of all the Jetpack benefits, the one that developers like most is the reduction or elimination of boilerplate code. *Boilerplate code* is simply glue code that you use to explain how to do something to the compiler. Here's an example of Kotlin code without Jetpack to automatically perform tasks in the background:

```
view.viewTreeObserver.addOnPreDrawListener(
    object : ViewTreeObserver.OnPreDrawListener {
        override fun onPreDraw(): Boolean {
            viewTreeObserver.removeOnPreDrawListener(this)
            actionToBeTriggered()
            return true
        }
    })
```

The code spends a great deal of time explaining things like what to create and where to add it. Here's the same code with the boilerplate elements eliminated:

```
view.doOnPreDraw { actionToBeTriggered() }
```

That's it! You don't have to do anything more than say what you want to do, which is to tell Android that when it is about to draw a *view tree* (a listing of elements to draw when an activity receives focus in your app), it should perform the actions specified by the `actionToBeTriggered()` function first. Eliminating the boilerplate code makes your code a lot easier to write now and read later. Of course, a lot of automation makes this happen, and you need to be aware of the consequences of using automation when writing code (see "The effects of automation" sidebar, later in this chapter). You can see more examples of how elimination boilerplate code is useful at `https://jakewharton.com/https:/android-developers.googleblog.com/2018/02/introducing-android-ktx-even-sweeter.html`.

Managing background tasks

Background tasks are those tasks that you can perform asynchronously without the user monitoring them, such as downloading a document from online storage. Well-designed apps use background tasks so that the user doesn't just sit there, looking at the screen and hoping that something will eventually happen. When a task does need to complete before the user can move on, you use a `ForegroundService`, which isn't deferrable. Otherwise, you can use one of the background task services:

- `DownloadManager`: Downloading data requires time that the user won't want to wait. Using the `DownloadManager` allows you to perform this task in the background to any destination, even if the destination is outside the app process. The download request can survive changes in connectivity and even device reboots. You must configure any required permissions, including `Manifest.permission.INTERNET`, to use this service.

- AlarmManager: In some cases, you need to perform tasks at a specific time. The AlarmManager waits for the time you set and immediately begins running the task in the background, which can be disruptive when used inappropriately. If the host device is asleep when the alarm goes off, AlarmManager can wake the device to perform the task. In addition, you can set it so that the host device can't go to sleep until the task completes. An alarm won't survive a device reboot.
- WorkManager: You use this service when you need to perform tasks in the background in a manner that won't slow the host system down. The WorkManager considers issues like network and battery resources as it completes the tasks you assign to it. It's possible to configure the WorkManager to complete tasks even if the host app terminates unexpectedly or the device reboots. You typically use WorkManager to perform tasks such as sending logs or analytics to backend servers or to sync app data with a server. The "Performing Background Tasks Using WorkManager" section of Book 3, Chapter 3 tells you more about working with this background task service.

Navigating between activities and fragments

Each *activity* (full-screen user interface element) or *fragment* (self-contained partial-screen user interface element) in your app is a separate element. To move between them, the user clicks something or some piece of automation performs the move on the user's behalf. The act of moving between activities or fragments is called *navigation*, and it's essential that the navigation works correctly. Every activity or fragment that a user can navigate to is a *destination*. *Actions* determine when and how the navigation occurs. Three elements comprise navigation in Android:

- **Navigation graph:** An XML file that contains all the navigation information. This information includes the destinations you define, along with all the paths a user can take to reach those destinations.
- **NavHost:** An empty container that displays all the destinations defined in the navigation graph. It also contains a NavHost implementation that supports *destination fragments,* which are self-contained parts of an activity that have their own user interface that you might want to use as a destination in some cases. Destination fragments rely on a NavHostFragment rather than a NavHost.

» **NavController:** An object that manages navigation within a `NavHost` or `NavHostFragment`. This is the app element that actually swaps app content as the user moves through the app. You provide the `NavController` with a path to take through the app (such as when you want the user to perform specific steps) or a destination to move directly from one place to another.

TECHNICAL STUFF

As the user moves through an app, the navigation elements automatically update the *back stack*, which is a last-in/first-out structure that tracks where the user has been. The back stack normally starts with a single entry: the main activity for your app where all the user activities begin. When the user clicks the Back button, the navigation elements automatically pop the previous destination off the back stack and display it. However, the display isn't static; you see any updates that occur as a result of navigating to the new destination. For example, in an email app, a message might appear as unread until a user clicks it. Clicking the Back button would show that the message is now read. You discover more about how navigation works in the "Providing for Navigational Needs" section of Book 3, Chapter 3.

TIP

The navigation elements actually do a lot of work for you. In addition to managing the navigation between destinations, the navigation elements perform these tasks:

» Handle fragment transactions, such as displaying common elements for all activities in your app.

» Process Up and Back actions correctly by default. For example, clicking Up should never exit the application (removing the main activity from the back stack), and the navigation elements know about this requirement.

» Use standardized resources for animations and transitions so that what the user sees onscreen won't look odd or cause other problems.

» Implement and control *deep linking*, which is the method a user can employ to access a specific activity in an Android app directly. Deep linking implies that there is no back stack because the user accesses the activity directly. Consequently, the Up and Back actions have no effect.

» Provide helpers that help you employ Navigation UI patterns, such as navigation drawers and bottom navigation, with minimal additional work.

» Ensure type safety when navigating and passing data between destinations using Safe Args — a Gradle plug-in.

» Create a `ViewModel` object for a navigation graph to share UI-related data between the graph's destinations. For example, you need a `ViewModel` to ensure that the display remains consistent when the user rotates the device.

As with many elements of Android design, you use a special graphical editor to create a navigation graph. Figure 1-1 shows a simple sample consisting of a main activity and an output data fragment.

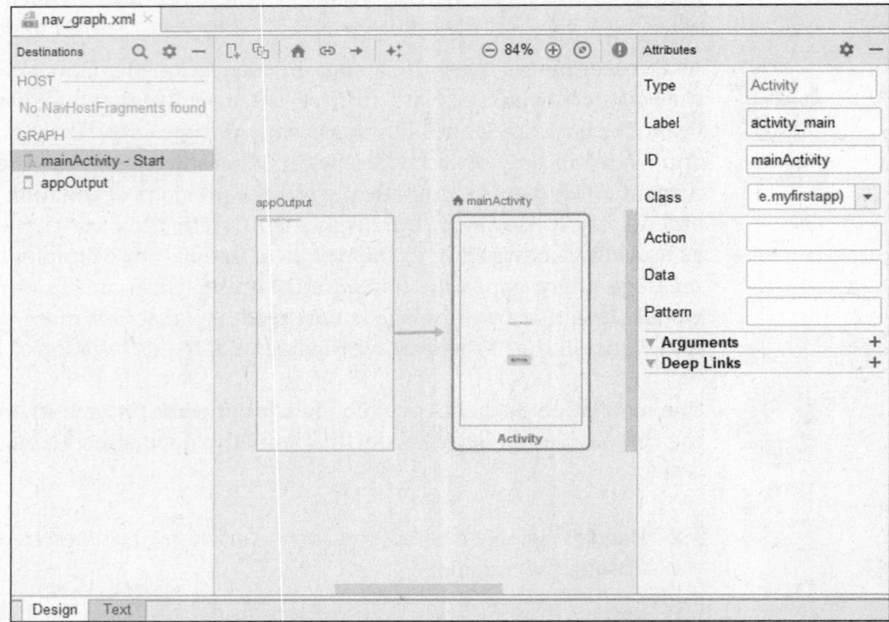

FIGURE 1-1: Using a graphical editor to create a navigation graph.

Managing memory

Mobile devices typically don't have huge amounts of memory, especially RAM, which means that memory is at a premium. In addition, the Android platform runs on the premise that free memory is wasted memory, so it tries to use as much available memory as it can at all times, as described at `https://developer.android.com/topic/performance/memory-management`. Android also doesn't create a swap file in storage to increase the apparent size of RAM because doing so tends to cause solid-state memory failures.

REMEMBER

With all these factors in mind, keeping *memory leaks* (a failure to release unused objects in memory) to a minimum is essential if you want your app to perform well. If you're really interested in precisely how memory leaks occur, the article at `https://proandroiddev.com/everything-you-need-to-know-about-memory-leaks-in-android-d7a59faaf46a` details them. You don't really need to know this information to use this book, but it's interesting to delve into later.

Kotlin already helps you prevent memory leaks, and some people are frankly amazed at how well it does (see the article at `https://proandroiddev.com/how-kotlin-helps-you-avoid-memory-leaks-e2680cf6e71e` for details). By adding Jetpack to the mix, you create applications with less code and a consistent style that tends to reduce memory leaks as well. So memory issues that you've dealt with in the past when working with Android apps are likely to be greatly reduced.

To see how your app uses memory, you can use the profiler accessed with Run➪Profile 'app' in Android Studio. Starting your app will seem to take an enormously long time because the profiler slows things down quite a lot. When you select MEMORY from the profiler's drop-down list, you see a graph of memory usage similar to the one in Figure 1-2. The "Benchmarking Your Application" section of Chapter 2 of this minibook gives more details on how this process works.

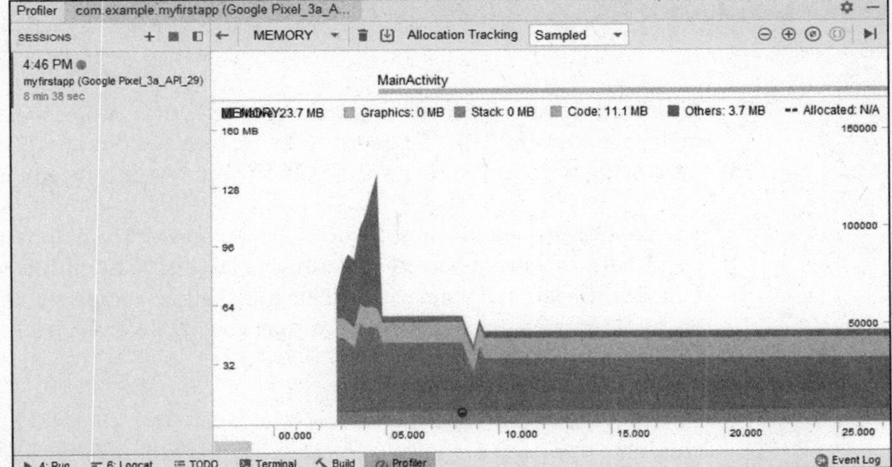

FIGURE 1-2: Checking memory usage in your app.

Performing configuration changes

Configuration changes can ruin your app's day by making the device environment unstable. A device configuration change occurs because of these types of actions:

- » The user changing the screen orientation
- » A keyboard being added or removed
- » Device features like multiwindow mode being enabled

THE EFFECTS OF AUTOMATION

Automation has its pros and cons. When the automation works, which is fortunately most of the time with Jetpack, amazing things happen, such as you get home in time for dinner. In addition, because the automation performs those tasks you really don't want to hear about in a best-practices manner, your app users also see fewer crashes and better memory use. Happy users are a wonder because they promote your app for you and make you look really good to the boss.

Except, the automation doesn't always work. Because you don't understand what's going on under the hood, finding the mind-numbingly complex bugs can have you ripping out your hair. The automation provided by Jetpack hides details from view, but those details are still present, so you sometimes need to think about details in order to find problems in your app. All this said, look at the videos, and you'll find that most Android developers have full heads of hair, so the automation must work most of the time.

Android responds by restarting the activity. It first calls `onDestoy()` to stop the activity and then calls `onCreate()` to restore the activity. The problem is the destroying part. Any state information in your app is now gone.

Fortunately, `ViewModel` automatically saves state information for your UI, so you don't have to worry about re-creating the user interface from scratch. The problem is with your app's data state. This information requires boilerplate code using `onSaveInstanceState()` to ensure that your app comes back up into the same state that the user left it in.

REMEMBER

By using the Saved State module for `ViewModel` that comes with Jetpack, you can eliminate the need for most, if not all, of this boilerplate code and the inherent errors that such code produces. The difference is that your `ViewModel` now receives a `SavedStateHandle` object that contains the saved instance data for your app. You no longer have to deal with restoring the data by hand. The article at `https://developer.android.com/topic/libraries/architecture/viewmodel-savedstate` provides some additional details about using the Saved State module.

Considering the Jetpack Components

Jetpack is a relatively large package, but you can easily divide it into four component areas: foundation, architecture, behavior, and UI. These component areas address specific application needs, such as benchmarking your application code or navigation to a particular destination. The following sections talk about each of these component areas and provide a quick overview of what each of them contains.

Foundation

The foundation components are sort of like the basement of a house. You might not find them that interesting at first, but like a house, you really need a basement or at least a foundation for your Android app. The foundation components provide various kinds of low-level support and enable you to create exciting apps. Here's a quick overview of each of the foundation components.

- **Android KTX (`https://developer.android.com/kotlin/ktx.html`):** Provides a set of special Kotlin extensions that help you create concise code using these Kotlin features:
  - Extension functions
  - Extension properties
  - Lambdas
  - Named parameters
  - Parameter default values
  - Coroutines

  You use these features to perform tasks such as animation, content management, database access, graphics, user location management, network access, OS access, and so on. The point is that you write less code, and the code you do write is smaller, so it creates less chance for experiencing errors. The "Working with Android KTX" section of Chapter 2 of this minibook provides you with additional details.

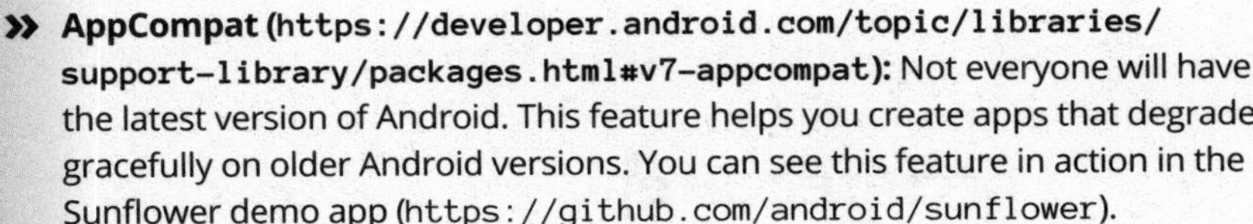

- **AppCompat (`https://developer.android.com/topic/libraries/support-library/packages.html#v7-appcompat`):** Not everyone will have the latest version of Android. This feature helps you create apps that degrade gracefully on older Android versions. You can see this feature in action in the Sunflower demo app (`https://github.com/android/sunflower`).
- **Car (`https://developer.android.com/cars`):** Helps you create apps for your car. Book 5, Chapter 4 talks about how to use this feature in more detail.
- **Benchmark (`https://developer.android.com/studio/profile/benchmark.html`):** This feature lets you determine how well your app actually runs. It allows you to check things like CPU and memory usage to create a more efficient app that users will like using. You can see a short version of this feature in action in the "Managing memory" section, earlier in this chapter. A fuller treatment appears in the "Benchmarking Your Application" section of Chapter 2 of this minibook.

- **Multidex (`https://developer.android.com/studio/build/multidex.html`):** Sometimes an app requires fancy packaging to make it work. The "Considering the Android Runtime (ART)" section of Book 2, Chapter 3 contains a description of the Dalvik Executable (DEX) file, which contains the compiled classes for your app. This enables you to bundle multiple DEX files within a single app. The main reason for using this feature is that your app has exceeded the 65,536 methods Android limit.
- **Security (`https://developer.android.com/topic/security/data`):** Every app requires security to keep data safe. Of course, data includes things like your identity, so you have a vested interest in making sure that your app is secure. The main reason to use this feature is to enhance the security of your app using security best practices developed by people who likely sit around and act paranoid all day. When it comes to security, paranoid is good. The "Addressing Security Issues" section in Chapter 2 of this minibook talks about security in detail.
- **Test (`https://developer.android.com/topic/libraries/testing-support-library/index.html`):** Most platforms today include some sort of testing framework to make app testing easier. This is the testing framework for Android. The "Testing Application Functionality" section of Chapter 2 of this minibook talks about testing issues in more detail.
- **TV (`https://developer.android.com/tv`):** Helps you create apps for your smart television. Book 5, Chapter 3 talks about how to use this feature in more detail.
- **Wear OS by Google (`https://developer.android.com/wear`):** Helps you create apps for your wearable device. Book 5, Chapter 2 talks about how to use this feature in more detail.

Architecture

Architecture components tend to give you access to data or help you manage program elements better. These components contribute directly to the app, but aren't really the main event because the user rarely sees them directly. The user would feel the effect if these components failed to function, but invisibility is the focus of these components. We tell you about some of these components, such as `ViewModel` and `WorkManager`, earlier in the chapter, and here are some others:

- **Data binding (`https://developer.android.com/topic/libraries/data-binding/`):** Unless you want to spend a lot of time individually coding data fields in your app, data binding is the best solution for making data available to the user. *Data binding* is the process of moving data from a source to a UI element so that the user can see and possibly modify it. Chapter 4 of this minibook provides additional information about using data in these ways:

- Storing and restoring user preferences
- Accessing the media player
- Interacting with the camera
- Sharing data with others

» **Lifecycles (`https://developer.android.com/topic/libraries/architecture/lifecycle`):** Manages the lifecycles of both fragments and activities. You can discover more about this topic in the "Working with Lifecycle-Aware Components" section, later in this chapter.

» **LiveData (`https://developer.android.com/topic/libraries/architecture/livedata`):** Databases store information that changes; otherwise, they wouldn't be particularly useful. This component detects database changes and provides notifications that lets you update the user information with the new data. This method of working with databases has the following advantages over using other component types:

- Automatically updates the data state of your app so that you don't spend a lot of time writing boilerplate code to do so
- Eliminates memory leaks by automatically cleaning up after itself
- Performs updates only when the activity is able to receive them
- Automatically performs lifecycle management for you
- Updates components that become active again after being inactive
- Manages configuration changes for you so that a device configuration change, such as a data rotation, also includes a data update
- Allows sharing of resources

» **Navigation (`https://developer.android.com/topic/libraries/architecture/navigation.html`):** Provides the functionality needed for in-app navigation. The "Navigating between activities and fragments" section, earlier in this chapter, discusses this component in more detail.

» **Paging (`https://developer.android.com/topic/libraries/architecture/paging/`):** Gradually loads information from a data source into your app to make data management more efficient. By loading only the information that the app needs at any given time, the app uses fewer resources and makes better use of resources like network bandwidth.

- **Room (`https://developer.android.com/topic/libraries/architecture/room`):** This component simplifies SQLite database access. It also creates a cache of app data to make accessing previously used data faster and easier.
- **ViewModel (`https://developer.android.com/topic/libraries/architecture/viewmodel`):** Manages the UI-related data in your app in a lifecycle-conscious way. You find the `ViewModel` discussed throughout this chapter and in many of the chapters to come.
- **WorkManager (`https://developer.android.com/topic/libraries/architecture/workmanager`):** Provides the means for creating Android background jobs. You can discover more about background processing techniques in the "Managing background tasks" section, earlier in this chapter.

Behavior

How an app behaves is important because it has to interact with the rest of Android. These components help your app interact correctly with standard Android services like notifications, permissions, sharing, and the Assistant.

- **CameraX (`https://developer.android.com/training/camerax`):** Enables your app to interact with the camera (or cameras) supported by a device. Cameras aren't just used for selfies. You can use them for all sorts of things, like reading barcodes on products or obtaining information based on visual cues. What makes this component different is that it relies on a use-case approach, and it's lifecycle aware. You also don't need to worry about differences in device capabilities because this component addresses them for you automatically. The "Adding Camera Support Using CameraX" section of Chapter 4 of this minibook tells you more about this component.
- **Media and playback (`https://developer.android.com/guide/topics/media-apps/media-apps-overview.html`):** Allows the playback of video and audio digital media. The component provides controls that let the user control the playback and optionally display the player state. You have two options when working with media:
  - `MediaPlayer`: Offers functionality for basic playback situations using the most common audio/video data formats and data sources. You can discover more about using the `MediaPlayer` in the "Working with MediaPlayer" section of Chapter 4 of this minibook.
  - `ExoPlayer`: Allows you to create a custom player by using the low-level Android audio APIs. The `ExoPlayer` supports high-performance features such as Dynamic Adaptive Streaming over HTTP (DASH) and HTTP Live Streaming (HLS). This book doesn't discuss the use of `ExoPlayer`.

- **Notifications (`https://developer.android.com/guide/topics/ui/notifiers/notifications.html`):** A *notification* is a message that Android displays from your app. It could tell you about an appointment you need to make or remind you about something you need to do. When you tap the notification, Android opens the app so that you can see any additional details the app can provide. This component also provides support for wearable devices and interactions with your automobile. The "Working with Notifications" section of Chapter 4 of this minibook tells you more about this component.
- **Permissions (`https://developer.android.com/guide/topics/permissions/index.html`):** Your interactions with your device are private. However, to perform certain tasks, you must interact with others in a manner that might reduce your privacy. A *permission* is a method of allowing the interaction to take place. You use permissions to allow access to your private data, such as emails and contacts, and to provide access to device features, such as your camera or the device's file system. Your app must also have permission to access certain data sources, such as the Internet.

REMEMBER

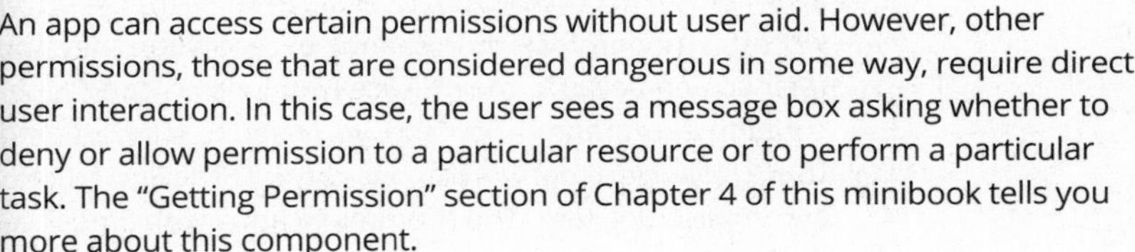

An app can access certain permissions without user aid. However, other permissions, those that are considered dangerous in some way, require direct user interaction. In this case, the user sees a message box asking whether to deny or allow permission to a particular resource or to perform a particular task. The "Getting Permission" section of Chapter 4 of this minibook tells you more about this component.

- **Preferences (`https://developer.android.com/guide/topics/ui/settings`):** This component helps you maintain user configuration information for your app. The "Complying with User Preferences" section of Chapter 4 of this minibook tells you more about this component.
- **Sharing (`https://developer.android.com/training/sharing/shareaction`):** You use this component to send and receive data from other apps. The "Sharing with Others" section of Chapter 4 of this minibook tells you more about this component.
- **Slices (`https://developer.android.com/guide/slices`):** A *Slice* is Android's latest approach for building interactive remote content into your app. For example, you could use a Slice to display the results of a Google search based on what the user is doing with your app at any given moment. A Slice appears as a template in your app that you use to define how the slice should appear and interact with the user. The "Using Slices" section of Chapter 4 of this minibook tells you more about this component.

UI

The UI components are the components that the user will see and interact with the most. *Widgets* (components that add functionality) and *helpers* (components that enable interactions indirectly) reduce the coding you have to perform and give your app the same feel as other apps on the user's device (making the app easier and more predictable to use). The following list tells about the widgets and helpers in this category.

- **Animation and transitions (`https://developer.android.com/training/animation/`):** These aren't animations like those found in Saturday cartoons. Rather, an *animation* gives feedback to the user when there is a change in your app's layout. When the layout also includes modifying the layout hierarchy, you can use a *transition* to make the change more natural for the user. The "Using Animations and Transitions" section of Chapter 5 of this minibook tells you more about this component.
- **Emoji (`https://developer.android.com/guide/topics/ui/look-and-feel/emoji-compat`):** Users love *emoji* (those pictures used to replace words in modern communication), except when they appear as squares on their screen because their device hasn't downloaded the latest emoji. If you're creating a communication app, you need to support emoji. We can't have users relying on real words now, can we? The `EmojiCompat` library helps you accomplish this task. The "Communicating with Emoji" section of Chapter 5 of this minibook tells you more about this component.
- **Fragment (`https://developer.android.com/guide/components/fragments`):** *Fragments* let you take a LEGO-like approach to developing activities. The "Navigating between activities and fragments" section, earlier in this chapter, offers an overview of fragments. The "Working with fragments" section of Chapter 3 of this minibook tells you more about this component.
- **Layout (`https://developer.android.com/guide/topics/ui/declaring-layout`):** In its most basic form, a *layout* simply describes what a user sees when using the app. The layout isn't the presentation of widgets or data, but what order Android presents those elements onscreen. You see how to create single-activity layouts in a number of examples in Books 1 and 2. However, a layout also defines the precise hierarchy of elements in your app, which is what the "Creating a Great Layout" section of Chapter 5 of this minibook discusses in detail.
- **Palette (`https://developer.android.com/training/material/palette-colors`):** Not everyone knows which colors to use to create a visually appealing presentation. Of course, if the user isn't wowed by the

first screen, it's possible that no one will see the second. The Palette library provides aids in choosing the right colors for your app based on things like the images you use so that you can wow the user. The "Employing Color and Texture" section of Chapter 5 of this minibook tells you more about this component.

- **ViewPager2 (`https://developer.android.com/training/animation/vp2-migration`):** Essentially, this element helps you create an environment that lets a user use swipes to move between pages of your app. The `ViewPager2` component provides improvements to make working with various layouts easier.

Getting an Overview of the AndroidX Package

In the beginning, there was the Android Support Library, but it proved inconsistent and unmanageable, so people started looking for an alternative. That's where the AndroidX package comes into play. It gives you features that make working with Android easier:

- **Consistent namespace:** All the packages in AndroidX appear within the `androidx` namespace. Any remaining Android Support Library packages are mapped to the `androidx` namespace as well. This means that you can find everything you need under one roof. Of course, mapping an old library to a new namespace can turn into a problem because any existing code will be looking in the wrong place. Look here to find the mappings you need:
  - **Artifacts:** `https://developer.android.com/jetpack/androidx/migrate/artifact-mappings`
  - **Classes:** `https://developer.android.com/jetpack/androidx/migrate/class-mappings`
- **Separate maintenance:** One of the issues with the Android Support Library was having to update the entire library every time a change took place. AndroidX packages are separately maintained and updated so that you get changes faster and the update is a lot less painful. The packages also use semantic versioning (see `https://semver.org/` for a description), which brings the version numbers in line with what everyone else is using.

WARNING

The last release of the Android Support Library is 28.0.0. You won't see any additional updates, which means that every day your app waits to use AndroidX is another day that it falls behind with needed changes. All new features will appear as part of the `androidx` namespace.

It's important to realize that AndroidX adds to app features. So, if you're use an `ActionBar` in your app, you rely on the `androidx.appcompat.app.AppCompatActivity` class, which appears in all the examples so far in the book. However, you still need other imports, like these:

```
import android.os.Bundle
import android.view.View
```

REMEMBER

You use `android.os` (`https://developer.android.com/reference/android/os/package-summary`) to provide access to basic operating system services, message passing, and interprocess communication. Likewise, `android.view` (`https://developer.android.com/reference/android/view/package-summary`) provides basic user interface classes. You use them to interact with the user and display information onscreen. Both of these appear as part of the underlying API, not as part of the Android Support Library.

The example code also includes support for Kotlin extensions:

```
import kotlinx.android.synthetic.main.activity_main.*
```

Again, these extensions aren't part of the Android Support Library. You don't need to worry that they're outdated pieces of code hanging around your modern app (see `https://kotlinlang.org/docs/tutorials/android-plugin.html` for additional details).

Working with Lifecycle-Aware Components

A *lifecycle* is the current state of a particular component and the range of those states while the component is in use. For example, a component might be: initialized, created, stopped, started, paused, resumed, or destroyed. An event triggers a change in state. When you call `onStart()`, a component will likely start doing something, like processing data. The lifecycle begins when the component is initialized and ends when the component is destroyed.

When creating activities for your app, you place components within each activity, and those components interact. If they interact in a random manner or react at the wrong time, you could find that your app crashes, causes memory leaks, or has other problems. A *lifecycle-aware* component is simply one that monitors other components before it begins performing a task.

Now that you have a basic idea of what a lifecycle and a lifecycle-aware component are all about, it's time to view them in more detail. Keep reading for a good overview of how a lifecycle management strategy works.

Focusing on activities

When your app runs, a new activity begins in which components interact with each other. An activity might do something like display your current location based on the location service input. In order to do that, a component would need to access the location service, obtain the location information, and then disconnect from the location service. In other words, the process would have a distinct start and stop.

Now consider another component in the same activity. This component contacts a map service and displays your location on the map. However, if this second component tries to display the location before the first component actually obtains it, the app could act in a strange manner, provide incorrect results, or simply crash the app. Consequently, the second component must first ask the first component about its state, which is done using the `getLifecycle()` method of the first component's `LifecycleOwner` interface.

In short, components often interact with each other, and the state of one component might depend on the state of another. Consequently, you often see Android app activities that are simply packed with code designed to keep one component from doing something before another component finishes its task.

REMEMBER

Rather than create a huge mess within your activity code, you can instead rely on lifecycle-aware components that contain code allowing them to monitor the app and react as needed. Because the dependent component can monitor the lifecycle of the monitored component directly, the code is smaller, easier to manage, and less likely to contain errors. More important, the app as a whole is better organized and more modular, so you can reuse code with greater ease. You find the classes and interfaces used to create lifecycle-aware components in the `androidx.lifecycle` package.

Using lifecycle-aware components can also decrease problems like *race conditions*, where one component tries to start a task before another component comes to a complete stop (or vice versa). Using lifecycle-aware components also reduces crashes caused by resource contention and memory leaks that develop when resources are used incorrectly.

Understanding events and states

When working with lifecycle-aware components, the `Lifecycle` class object resides in a component and provides interaction with other components that depend on the host component. The information appears in two enumerations:

- **Event:** The action that triggered a change in state. These events map to the callbacks found in other components.
- **State:** The current status of the component.

When an *observer*, the component that wants to know the status of another component, calls `getLifecycle()`, it receives a `Lifecycle` object (`https://developer.android.com/reference/androidx/lifecycle/Lifecycle.html`) back. The `Lifecycle` object contains the two enumerations with the events and states. In addition, this object provides the `addObserver()` function, which tells the `LifecycleOwner`, the first component, to provide the observer with event notifications, such as `Lifecycle.Event.ON_START`, and state information, such as `Lifecycle.State.STARTED`.

» Developing apps that perform well

» Performing app testing

Chapter 2
Building a Foundation for Your App

Creating a good foundation for your app depends on knowledge of what the API and various tools can do for you. For example, extension functions and extension properties help you add features to existing classes. The idea is that you don't want to spend a lot of time writing the code that someone else has already written. With this in mind, you need to consider what Android KTX is all about because it's your main tool in developing a good app using Kotlin. The first part of this chapter provides you with a great overview of Android KTX.

As you start building your app with Android KTX, you also want to be sure that the app is secure and that it runs fast. The two issues go hand in hand because users won't work with apps that run slow, but they won't thank you if your app releases all their personal information, either. You must have a balance between security and speed. The second part of this chapter provides best-practice approaches to including security in your apps, while the third part of this chapter shows how to perform app benchmarking so that you can ensure that users will enjoy using your app.

Working with Android KTX

The goal of Android Kotlin Extensions (KTX) is to make development easier. KTX provides a layer over the underlying Java functionality so that you can write apps using the Kotlin approach, rather than trying to adapt Kotlin to Java. You don't necessarily get any new features with KTX, just easier access to existing ones along with a few additions that make working with the Java API easier. Keep reading for some details about what KTX contains.

Getting a feel for KTX features

KTX enables you to write code faster and with greater ease. Kotlin's ability to add new functionality to an existing class without inheriting from the class comes from *extensions*, which play a major role in making KTX possible. To make writing Android code easier, KTX relies on using the following Kotlin features to make the underlying Java libraries more accessible for the Kotlin developer:

- **Extension functions:** An extension function lets you add a new function to an existing class. The new function may simplify a task or reduce the code needed to implement a repetitive task. For example, the following extension function adds to the Int class without modifying the actual class in any way.

  ```
  fun Int.squared(): Int {
      return this * this
  }

  fun main(args: Array<String>) {
      var result = 10.squared()
      println(result)
  }
  ```

  You can add the `squared()` function without modifying `Int`. In this example, `this` is the underlying value of the object, which is `10`.

- **Extension properties:** An extension property works much like an extension function, except for properties. You add a new property to an existing class without modifying the class. Here's an example of an extension property:

  ```
  val String.specialSub
      get() = this.substring(0, 5)

  fun main(args: Array<String>) {
      var myString = "Hello There"
  ```

```
    if (myString.specialSub.compareTo("Hello") == 0)
        println("It's special!")
}
```

TECHNICAL STUFF

Note that this example doesn't offer a setter and that you create it as a `val`. You can find examples of using setters with extension properties online, but doing so is difficult because extension properties can't have backing fields, which means you can't set the value of `this`. When using a setter, the extension property must appear as a `var`, rather than a `val`, because you're setting a value (the property must be mutable). The discussion at `https://stackoverflow.com/questions/55314687/kotlin-extension-property-setter-for-mutable-subclass` is one such example of attempting to create a setter for an extension property.

- **Lambdas:** A lambda expression is an anonymous function that you can pass as arguments to first-class functions, or you can return them from a first-class function call. You use lambda expressions throughout the book, but they're used regularly in Book 2, Chapter 6, which considers functional programming techniques. Here's a simple example of using a lambda to interact with a string:

```
var myString = "Hello There"
var specPrint = {s: String ->
                     println(s.toUpperCase())}
specPrint(myString)
```

- **Named parameters:** Providing named parameters makes your code clearer and reduces errors. A named parameter is one that you can provide when calling a function. In the following example, the output is correct, despite the fact that the parameters appear in reverse order:

```
fun div(value1: Int, value2: Int): Int {
    return value1 / value2
}

fun main(args: Array<String>) {
    println(div(value2 = 3, value1 = 6))
}
```

» **Parameter default values:** Giving parameters a default value, when possible, makes your code clearer. You can call a function with no parameters when the defaults are acceptable. In fact, the inclusion of a parameter emphasizes that the parameter isn't the default value. Here's an example of using default parameter values where `value1` defaults to `2` and `value2` defaults to `1`:

```
fun div(value1: Int, value2: Int): Int {
    return value1 / value2
}

fun main(args: Array<String>) {
    println(div(value2 = 3, value1 = 6))
}
```

» **Coroutines:** A *coroutine* is a sort of light threading mechanism in Kotlin. You use it to offload work while the main thread continues to work. There are a number of built-in coroutine classes, including `CoroutineScope`, `MainScope`, and `GlobalScope`. The essential difference between the three is the context in which they create threads. Threads have a big job to do in Android development because they not only offload tasks but also help you manage component lifetimes and provide desirable UI functionality. Here's a simple example of a coroutine in action:

```
import kotlinx.coroutines.*

fun main(args: Array<String>) {
   println("Start")

   GlobalScope.launch {
      delay(1000)
      println("Hello")
   }

   println("Stop")
   Thread.sleep(2000)
}
```

In this case, the code prints `"Start"` first, launches the `GlobalScope` thread next, prints `"Stop"`, and then prints `"Hello"`. The reason you need to use `Thread.sleep(2000)` is to keep the app alive long enough to see the thread results.

In reality, KTX adds another layer to your app. However, the benefit is that it makes things easier, clearer, and shorter. For example, if you want to process a Uniform Resource Identifier (URI) in standard Kotlin, you use code like this:

```
val uri = Uri.parse(myUriString)
```

Even though the KTX form isn't much shorter, it is clearer:

```
val uri = myUriString.toUri()
```

When using KTX, you avoid the ambiguity of what `parse()` means in this instance. Instead, you simply state that you want to turn `myUriString` into a URI by calling `toUri()`. Most of this functionality relies on the use of extension functions to add features to existing classes.

As another example, say you want to modify shared preferences. When working with pure Kotlin code, you use something like this:

```
sharedPreferences.edit()
            .putBoolean(key, value)
            .apply()
```

When working with KTX, you can use this code instead:

```
sharedPreferences.edit {
    putBoolean(key, value)
}
```

This code is not only shorter but clearer as well. It also relies on using an expression to perform the required task. You don't have to call `apply()` because the application of the change occurs by default.

Book 2, Chapters 1 and 5 talk about the `Toast` class, which provides a method of displaying a message onscreen. In the "Static Fields and Methods" section of Book 2, Chapter 5, you see this code:

```
Toast.makeText
   (getApplication(), "Whoa!", Toast.LENGTH_LONG).show();
```

However, KTX can make that code a lot shorter. Here's the KTX version:

```
toast("Whoa!")
```

Using KTX in your project

By default, your Android Studio projects automatically give you a basis to rely on KTX. If you want to verify this fact, look in the `build.gradle` file for your project (the one in the root of the project folder) and verify that you see `google()` as one of the repositories, as shown here (in bold):

```
allprojects {
    repositories {
        google()
        jcenter()
    }
}
```

REMEMBER

In addition to making sure that Android Studio can find KTX (which you normally get by default when you create the project), you must also specify which of the KTX features to include. You do this by adding dependencies to the `build.gradle` file for your app (the one in the `app` folder of your project). By default, your project will have support for the `Core` module, which provides essential KTX functionality (see the "Considering the modules" section of the chapter for additional details). You add a specific module to your project by providing an `implementation` entry in the `dependencies` element, as shown here (in bold):

```
dependencies {
  implementation fileTree(dir: 'libs', include: ['*.jar'])
  implementation"org.jetbrains.kotlin:kotlin-stdlib-
    jdk7:$kotlin_version"
  implementation 'androidx.appcompat:appcompat:1.1.0'
  implementation 'androidx.core:core-ktx:1.1.0'
  implementation
    'androidx.constraintlayout:constraintlayout:1.1.3'
  testImplementation 'junit:junit:4.12'
  androidTestImplementation
    'androidx.test.ext:junit:1.1.1'
  androidTestImplementation
    'androidx.test.espresso:espresso-core:3.2.0'
}
```

So if you want to provide other KTX modules, you can add them by adding a new module dependency. For example, if you want `Fragment` support, you use this entry:

```
implementation 'androidx.fragment:fragment-ktx:1.1.0'
```

Considering the modules

Just as including the entire Android API in your app doesn't make sense, including all of KTX doesn't make sense, either. When you create a new project, you automatically get the Core module. You can add more modules as needed, with the following modules seeing the most use for developers:

- **Core:** Provides extensions for the common libraries that are part of the Android framework. You don't need to add any Java libraries to work with this module. Here are the packages you find within this module:
  - `androidx.core.animation`
  - `androidx.core.content`
  - `androidx.core.content.res`
  - `androidx.core.database`
  - `androidx.core.database.sqlite`
  - `androidx.core.graphics`
  - `androidx.core.graphics.drawable`
  - `androidx.core.location`
  - `androidx.core.net`
  - `androidx.core.os`
  - `androidx.core.text`
  - `androidx.core.transition`
  - `androidx.core.util`
  - `androidx.core.view`
  - `androidx.core.widget`
- **Collections:** Provides access to Android's memory efficient collections, including `ArrayMap`, `LongParseArray`, and `LruCache`. This module makes use of Kotlin's operator overloading functionality to simplify common tasks. For example, you can combine two `ArraySets` into one using the following code:

TIP

```
val added = arraySetOf(1, 2, 3) + arraySetOf(4, 5, 6)
```

You can also add single numbers to `ArraySets` using code like this:

```
val newSet = added + 7 + 8
```

» **Fragment:** Makes working with the fragment API easier. For example, you can simplify working with `fragmentManager()` by using lambda expressions:

```
fragmentManager().commit {
   addToBackStack("...")
   setCustomAnimations(
           R.anim.enter_anim,
           R.anim.exit_anim)
   add(fragment, "...")
}
```

In addition, you can bind to a `ViewModel` using the `viewModels` and `activityViewModels` property delegates, like this:

```
val viewModel by viewModels<AViewModel>()
val viewModel by activityViewModels<AViewModel>()
```

» **Palette:** Reduces the work required to create a color scheme for your app that actually looks nice. Using a simple two-step process, you can create a custom palette based on the graphics you use in your app. Here is the basic technique:

```
val palette = Palette.from(bitmap).generate()
val swatch = palette[target]
```

» **SQLite:** Provides access to a SQLite database using greatly simplified syntax. This is a relational database offering, which gives you a lot of power with respect to how the data is stored and accessed. Unfortunately, relational databases are also known for the amount of space they consume and the sometimes slow access they provide. However, using KTX makes working with SQLite a lot easier. For example, by using the `transaction` extension, you can make working with database data as easy as a few simple calls, like this one:

```
db.transaction {
    // insert data
}
```

TIP

In addition to these common modules, you might also need to use these modules because they provide added functionality:

» **Lifecycle:** Makes it easier to create and manage component interactions through the use of lifecycles, as described in the "Working with Lifecycle-Aware Components" section of Chapter 1 of this minibook. When working with lifecycles, KTX creates a `LifecycleScope` (another type of coroutine class) for each Lifecycle object. When the Lifecycle terminates, any coroutines for that Lifecycle also terminate.

Listing 2-1 shows a simple example of lifecycle management for a fragment. It doesn't look much different from the onCreate() function used with the MainActivity examples shown earlier in the book except for the viewLifecycleOwner.lifecycleScope.launch entry. This entry defines a coroutine that accepts a number of parameters and precomputed text to use with the coroutine.

LISTING 2-1: Using KTX to Manage a Fragment

```
class MyFragment: Fragment() {
  override fun onViewCreated(view: View,
    savedInstanceState: Bundle?) {
      super.onViewCreated(view, savedInstanceState)
      viewLifecycleOwner.lifecycleScope.launch {
        val params =
          TextViewCompat.getTextMetricsParams(textView)
        val precomputedText =
          withContext(Dispatchers.Default) {
            PrecomputedTextCompat.create(longTextContent,
                                         params)
        }
        TextViewCompat.setPrecomputedText(textView,
                                          precomputedText)
      }
    }
}
```

Building a Foundation for Your App

» **LiveData:** As we describe in the "Architecture" section of Chapter 1 of this minibook, LiveData detects database changes and provides notifications that let you update the user information with the new data. What KTX contributes is a LiveData builder function that makes working with the user data easier and reduces the amount of code you need to write as well. While it's retrieving the data, the builder also calls a suspend function until the data is read into memory. Here's an example that shows how to load user data:

```
val user: LiveData<User> = liveData {
    val data = database.loadUser()
    emit(data)
}
```

In this example, `loadUser()` is a suspend function. It waits until the data is ready for use. The `emit()` function then makes the data accessible to the app.

» **Navigation:** Allows navigation between destinations as described in the "Navigating between activities and fragments" section of Chapter 1 of this minibook. Unlike other modules that require just one dependency reference, however, Navigation requires three:

```
androidx.navigation:navigation-runtime-ktx:2.1.0
androidx.navigation:navigation-fragment-ktx:2.1.0
androidx.navigation:navigation-ui-ktx:2.1.0
```

REMEMBER

You eventually see some fancier ways to navigate in the book, but working with KTX can make navigation quite simple. All you really need is an `Intent`, some settings, and then to start the `Intent` using `startActivity()`, as shown here (from example p01_06_03 from Book 1, Chapter 6):

```
fun onButtonClick(view: View){
    val intent = Intent(this,
        OtherActivity::class.java)
    intent.putExtra("Pepperoni",
        checkBox.isChecked())
    intent.putExtra("Extra cheese",
        checkBox2.isChecked())
    startActivity(intent)
}
```

You can use an intent in a number of ways:

- Start an activity
- Start a service
- Broadcast a message

There are common intents you can use to perform a variety of tasks, such as for creating an alarm or timer (see `https://developer.android.com/guide/components/intents-common`). When working with a destination, you rely on a `NavController` to perform various navigation tasks for you in the background. Navigation differs from using an intent in that you rely on centralized management of various destinations, which is critical when working with complex projects. A navigation graph provides a listing of all the destinations and how they interact so that you can get to anywhere from anywhere without constantly recoding your app, as you'd have to with intents. The "Providing for Navigational Needs" section of Chapter 3 of this minibook shows how to use navigation techniques in your app.

- **ReactiveStreams:** Provides a `ReactiveStreams` implementation of `LiveData`, which is a method of working with a data stream. A `ReactiveStream` consists of four elements:
  - Publisher
  - Subscriber
  - Subscription
  - Processor

  Normally, you use another tool to assist you in working with `ReactiveStreams` because implementing the four elements on your own can be daunting in the best of times. So, for example, you might create a database for your users and then rely on RxJava (a publisher) to display the data in your app. RxJava can go further in helping you perform other tasks as well, such as retrieving a list of database users by using code like this:

  ```
  val fun getUsersLiveData() : LiveData<List<User>> {
    val users: Flowable<List<User>> = dao.findUsers()
    return LiveDataReactiveStreams.fromPublisher(users)
  }
  ```

- **Room:** Creates an interface over SQLite to reduce the work of making your app persistent. The goal is to use `create` to make a local data cache containing app data that your app can use to restore state and address other persistence needs even when the device doesn't have access to an Internet connection. You can use Room in combination with RxJava to create a `ReactiveStream` to handle app data needs.
- **ViewModel:** Creates an easier use version of `CoroutineScope` named `viewModelScope` that helps you create coroutines for your app that interact with the `ViewModel`. A `CoroutineScope` is attached to the `Dispatchers.Main`, which means that it gets cleared when the `ViewModel` is cleared. You can use a single `viewModelScope` for all your `ViewModel` needs. The coding techniques you use for a `viewModelScope` are the same as those used for any other coroutine scope. The "Performing Background Tasks Using WorkManager" section of Chapter 3 of this minibook tells you more about performing tasks in the background.
- **WorkManager:** Allows interaction with `CoroutineWorker` and `Worker` to give you the means to perform long-term tasks that survive system crashes and device down time. The emphasis is on long-term jobs — the ones you don't need to get done on any particular schedule. The "Performing Background Tasks Using WorkManager" section of Chapter 3 of this minibook tells you more about performing tasks in the background.

DATABASES USED WITH ANDROID

This section of the chapter discusses three databases that have KTX modules: SQLite, Room, and Firebase. Of course, these aren't the only databases used for mobile development. In fact, the top five databases are: SQLite, Oracle Berkeley DB, OrmLite, Realm, and Couchbase Lite.

In some cases, you need to consider functionality over convenience when it comes to database use. For example, the article at `https://db-engines.com/en/system/Oracle+Berkeley+DB%3BRealm%3BSQLite` compares SQLite, Oracle Berkeley DB, and Realm. It doesn't take long to see that they're very different offerings.

Unfortunately, the road to the ultimate database is often lined with potholes and terrifyingly complex instructions. For example, Chapter 4 of the instructions at `https://docs.oracle.com/database/bdb181/html/installation/index.html` tell how to build the Oracle Berkeley DB, install it on Android, and then move from SQLite to Oracle Berkeley DB. The point is that you often have to make hard decisions when it comes to database support for your app, so take the time to consider just how difficult the database is to use versus the features it provides.

You aren't limited to the modules that come with AndroidX. Add other KTX modules is possible simply by referencing them in your `build.gradle` file and performing the required installation. Here are examples of these popular external KTX modules:

- **Firebase:** Provides access to a real-time database named Firebase. To use the Firebase module associated with the Firebase database, you must install the database into your project using the instructions at `https://firebase.google.com/docs/android/setup`, which involves the Firebase console. After you have Firebase installed (both module and database), you can begin working with it as described at `https://firebase.google.com/docs/database/android/start`.
- **RxJava:** Gives you a way to interact with a data source in a number of ways. For example, you could use it to create a publish/subscribe model. In many cases, you create three elements: `Observable` (the data source); `Operator` (a kind of data translator to ensure that the data is in the correct format); and a, `Observer` (the part of the app that requires the data). Here's a short example of what this code might look like in Kotlin:

```
Observable.just("Hello World")
    .subscribe { value -> println(value) }
```

The call to `just()` converts the string `"Hello World"` to an `Observable`, which is then consumed by `subscribe`, where the string is printed out. You normally use something a little more complex than a string as a data source, but the example gets the idea across.

- **Play Core:** Allows monitoring of the current app state. The emphasis is on one-shot, short-term requests for information that you plan to act on immediately. You react to state changes by adding extension functions to `SplitInstallManager` and `AppUpdateManager` in the Play Core library.

Addressing Security Issues

No safe havens exist anywhere in the computing world. The fact that users seem to be completely unaware of this fact places a burden on developers to create the most secure apps possible. Oddly enough, many developers feel that having their app in the Google Play Store and using a new, supposedly bulletproof language like Kotlin will fix the issue. According to the article at `https://www.zdnet.com/article/android-security-first-kotlin-based-malware-found-in-google-play-store/`, the first Kotlin app in the Google Play Store with malware has already appeared on the scene. So, it's still up to you to create the most secure app you can.

Kotlin does contain a lot of security features, and you're safer using it than you might be when working with Java or another language. This safety relies on your actually employing the safety features, though, plus it assumes that someone doesn't find a way into your app through the underlying Java. Here are some tips for adding security to your app without a lot of additional programming:

- **Avoid overflows.** Book 2, Chapter 6 talks about recursion in Kotlin. When you use standard recursion, a hacker can cause a `StackOverflow` exception in a number of ways. By causing your app to fail in specific ways, the hacker can gain access to the underlying app. The best way to avoid this problem is to use tail recursion, as described in the "Relying on tail recursion" section of that chapter whenever possible. Because tail recursion doesn't rely on the stack, it can't generate a `StackOverflow` exception.
- **Pay attention to warnings.** When you see an exception or your app crashes, you know that you have a problem, and you fix it. However, hackers don't look for obvious things; they look for hidden things. For example, when a signed integer overflows, your app ends up with an incorrect value. Unfortunately, Kotlin continues to use the incorrect value, which may have serious consequences for app security. Fortunately, Android Studio does detect a majority

of integer overflow problems, but it only displays a warning for them. In some cases, the fix for these issues is incredibly easy. You just use a `Long` in place of the integer. To avoid the hidden security breach, pay attention to every warning and potentially treat it as an error instead.

- **Sanitize input.** Many developers know that sending code along with the data when an app asks for input is possible. Kotlin is safer than most languages when it comes to input, but the wrong input still has a real chance to do all sorts of nasty things to your app. Consequently, you want to make use of Kotlin features to validate any input that your app receives. One of the easiest starting points is to validate input data length using the `android:maxLength="*Length*"` attribute in any text boxes you create. Better yet, avoid text boxes whenever possible by using safer controls, such as check boxes. You can also do other things:
  - Rely on regular expressions to validate the form of the data.
  - Perform range checking to ensure that values like numbers are in the correct range.
  - Remove suspect characters from filename data, including dots and slashes that may give a hacker to a directory other than the one you want the app to use.
  - Look for unexpected nulls in input because they can hide all sorts of things, like code used to change settings.
  - Escape special characters as needed, especially when working with HTML, XML, and JSON data.
- **Interact with data sources safely.** The reason to create most apps is to manipulate data, some of which will appear on sources that are prone to security problems. For example, if you interact with SQLite, your app is open to a SQL injection attack, which happens when someone sends data that looks like data, but really isn't. (You can read more about SQL injection attacks and methods for preventing them at `https://www.malwarebytes.com/sql-injection/`.) When working with Kotlin, one of the easiest ways to provide minimal prevention is to strip suspect characters from the input using code like this:

```
var inputStr = myDataInput.text.toString()
inputStr = inputStr.replace("\\", "")
    .replace(";", "").replace("%", "")
    .replace("\"", "").replace("\'", "")
```

- **Look for data that isn't data at all.** Sometimes a photo isn't a photo. You might allow someone to upload their picture as part of the input, only to find that the JPEG file they supplied was really something else. Use every means possible to validate files that could be something else. For example, when you work with the JPEG format, the first two bytes are always `FF D8` and the last two bytes are always `FF D9`.

- **Validate stored data.** The data stored on the host device may seem as though it should be safe, but it might not be. One way to infect one app using another is to modify the stored data in some way. Make sure you check for things like added nulls, which can hide malevolent code. Ensure that the format of the file is what you expect and that the object data contained within the file is in the correct form. Some methods that prove helpful during validation include:
  - `Char.isLetterOrDigit()`
  - `Char.isLetter()`
  - `Char.isDigit()`
  - `String.length`

  In other words, Kotlin includes properties and methods that you can employ to ensure that the data you think you're reading from disk is the data you were expecting. These functions and methods come in handy for all sorts of data validation tasks as well.

TIP

- **Hide error information.** Detailed error information can tell a hacker a lot about your app, the underlying data, data sources, the host server, and all sorts of other things. A television set that displays an error message saying something unexpected happened isn't giving out any information that a hacker could use to hack the underlying Android app. The best way to handle detailed error information is to send it in encrypted form to your server for analysis by your developers.

TECHNICAL STUFF

- **Keep interoperability with other languages safe.** Kotlin can interact with other languages, such as Java and C/C++. Some of these other languages, however, use unsafe methodologies, such as pointers, to get the job done. When working with these other languages, you have to use the same techniques that developers who regularly use those other languages use to keep things safe. For example, when working with pointers, you need to
  - Bounds check any incoming data to ensure that it is within the proper range.
  - Avoid saving pointers for later; instead get rid of them as soon as you can.
  - Don't use unsafe operations, such as `.reinterpret()`, `.toLong()`, and `.toCPointer()` methods when working with C/C++.

SECURITY BY OBSCURITY

Some security professionals can behave like ostriches with their heads stuck in the sand. They feel that if they can't see you, you probably can't see them either. Unfortunately, this technique doesn't work. Someone can see them. So, how does this attitude get reflected in security by obscurity? If your main method of hiding security holes in your app is by obscuring the code, someone will almost certainly crack your app and cause you all kinds of woe. Too many talented hackers out there just love a good challenge. The only way to create a secure app is to create it that way and then keep digging around for potential security holes, and you're bound to find some because there aren't any perfect apps out there. The article at `https://www.nowsecure.com/blog/2019/07/11/think-twice-before-adopting-security-by-obscurity-in-kotlin-android-apps/` provides a lot of help in understanding why security by obscurity doesn't work.

Even with this long list, this section has just barely scratched the surface of all the terrible things that can happen to your app. You need to keep looking for vulnerabilities because the hackers certainly will. In some respects, a developer is in a constant race with someone who wants to make the app into something it isn't. Today, hackers aren't just trying to make the developer look bad; they want to gain access to things like user identity in order to make money, which can be a powerful incentive for anyone.

Benchmarking Your Application

Users are impatient. *Really* impatient. Unless your app spends most of its time waiting for the user, the user will see it as way too slow. Any time the user has to wait is an opportunity for the user to either complain or find another app that works faster. So creating apps that run as fast as possible is critical if you want the user to actually work with your app in some significant way. You have three methods of checking app performance:

- **Profiling:** Generates a visual presentation of resource usage, such as memory and CPU use. Knowing how and when your app uses resources can help you determine whether some devices may work slowly due to resource starvation. Tuning your app to use fewer resources can make a big difference.
- **Tracing:** Generates log files that describe how and when methods in your app are called. In some cases, you might see patterns that indicate how you can improve app performance by reducing unneeded calls. There are two kinds of tracing, only one of which is useful for performance tuning:

- **Debug:** Provides you with precise control over how and when logs are generated in an effort to reduce the work required to locate problems in your app. This form of tracing isn't useful for performance tuning.
- **CPU Profiler:** You can start and stop trace logs within the CPU Profiler. Doing so gives you a record of how the app calls methods when in a release configuration. Even though this approach creates a small drag on performance, that drag isn't significant enough to reduce this method's effectiveness as a performance tuning aid.

» **Benchmarking:** Generates a visual presentation of the time spent performing various tasks. This output helps you locate areas of your app that could benefit from tuning the code to work more efficiently.

Read on to find out various ways to view app performance.

Removing barriers to correct results

Before you profile or benchmark your app, you need to turn off debugging and compile a release build. The reason is simple. Having debugging turned on is akin to doing time trials on a race car with the brake on. The debugger helps you locate faults in your app, but it also slows your app considerably.

The simulators that you use to create the app can also impede correct results. A simulator is unlikely to run as fast as a real device, so you should perform profiling and benchmarking on the device you actually plan to target with your app, if possible. If you plan to target a lot of devices, try profiling and benchmarking the app on the slowest and the fastest of the devices so that you get a range of results.

Determine what is important to benchmark. For example, unless you want to see how long it takes your app to start, benchmarking the startup code isn't useful because it runs only once during each session. What you want to benchmark is the code that users will rely on throughout a session.

Removing the effects of various built-in performance enhancers can also be helpful. For example, code that runs in a loop is optimized by the system when you rely on the same parameters each time. In fact, in some cases, the code may not run at all, and the system may simply provide a result based on the output in prior loops. To avoid this problem, you need to use different parameters for each loop when you can.

Creating a test app

The chapters in Book 1 lead you through a series of simple app modifications. You view various ways to start an app and add a few components to it. The following steps create an app that performs a simple task in a loop so that you can use it to understand profiling, tracing, and benchmarking.

1. **Launch Android Studio and create a new Android project with an app name of** `03_02_01` **and a package name of** `com.allmycode.p03_02_01`**. Set the minimum API level to 24, rather than the default of 14.**

   For details on creating a new project, see Book 1, Chapter 3. Select the Empty Activity project type in the Phone and Tablet category.

2. **In the Designer tool's preview screen, select the Hello World!** `TextView` **and press Delete.**

   The Hello World! `TextView` is deleted.

3. **Drag a** `TextView` **and a** `Button` **from the Common group to the location under the** `ConstraintLayout` **in the Component Tree.**

4. **Drag a** `ProgressBar (Horizontal)` **from the Widgets group to the location under the** `ConstraintLayout` **in the Component Tree.**

   You see all three components under the ConstraintLayout, as expected.

5. **Set the constraints for the three components as follows:**
   - `textView`**: top:** `24`**, left:** `24`
   - `button`**: top:** `60`**, left:** `24`
   - `progressBar`**: top:** `120`**, left:** `24`

6. **Create resource strings for the** `textView` **and the button as follows:**
   - `textView`: `textView_Text` = `0`
   - `button`: `button_Text` = `"Click Me"`

7. **Create a string resource for** `button.onClick` **of** `button_onClick` = `button_onClick`.

8. **Set the** `progressBar` **properties to**
   - `max`: `100`
   - `progress`: `0`

- layout_height: 40dp
- layout_width: 200dp

Your layout should look like the one shown in Figure 2-1.

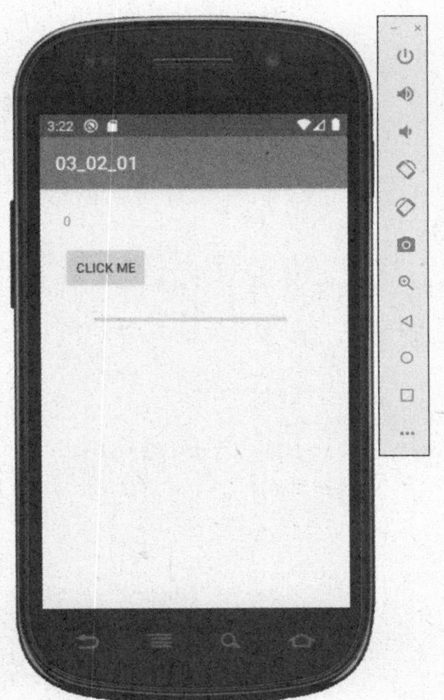

FIGURE 2-1: Creating a simple app for profiling, tracing, and benchmarking.

Now you need to add some code to test. Because this example relies on a progress bar and you want to see the progress bar do something, you need a `Handler`. Essentially, a `Handler` sends messages to the components onscreen telling them to update themselves. To use a `Handler`, you must add the following `import` statement:

```
import android.os.Handler
```

You could place all the code for this example in one function. However, to make it more interesting to profile, trace, and benchmark, the example uses two functions. Oddly enough, using two functions also makes the process of updating `textView` and `progressBar` easier to understand. Listing 2-2 shows the code needed to make the example work.

LISTING 2-2: Updating a Text Box and Progress Bar

```
fun button_onClick(view: View) {
    textView.setText("0")
    progressBar.setProgress(0)

    Thread( Runnable {
        for (i in 0..9) {
            updateData(i)
            Thread.sleep(200)
        }
    }).start()
}

private var handler = Handler()

fun updateData(i: Int){
    for (j in 1..10){
        handler.post(Runnable {
            textView.setText((i*10+j).toString())
            progressBar.setProgress(
                i*10+j, true)
        })
        Thread.sleep(100)
    }
}
```

The code in Listing 2-2 begins by resetting `textView` and `progressBar` as needed in `button_onClick()` each time you click Click Me. Otherwise, you'd click once and not really see the whole process after that.

The `button_onClick()` function creates a separate thread for interacting with `textView` and `progressBar`. If you don't create this separate thread, you won't see any updates. The updates occur outside the main thread. During each `for` loop from 0 through 9, the code calls `updateData()` with the current loop value and then sleeps for 200 milliseconds using `Thread.sleep()`.

Within `updateData()`, the function creates another `for` loop that counts from 1 to 10. So, at the minimum, the value of `textView` and `progressBar` is `1` and at the maximum the value is `100`. The call to `handler.post()` sends a message to each component telling it what new value to use. Because `progressBar` has a maximum value of `100`, you see the bar turn completely red by the end of the run. After each update, the code sleeps again, but this time for only 100 milliseconds, so there are noticeable jumps between each group of ten updates.

Profiling your app

Profiling your app is straightforward. All you need to do is choose Run➪Profile '*Element Name*' (where the default element is app) or Run➪Profile to start the process. You see your app start as normal, but it will run slower than normal because Android Studio is checking its performance. After the app is up, you see a Profile window like the one shown in Figure 2-2.

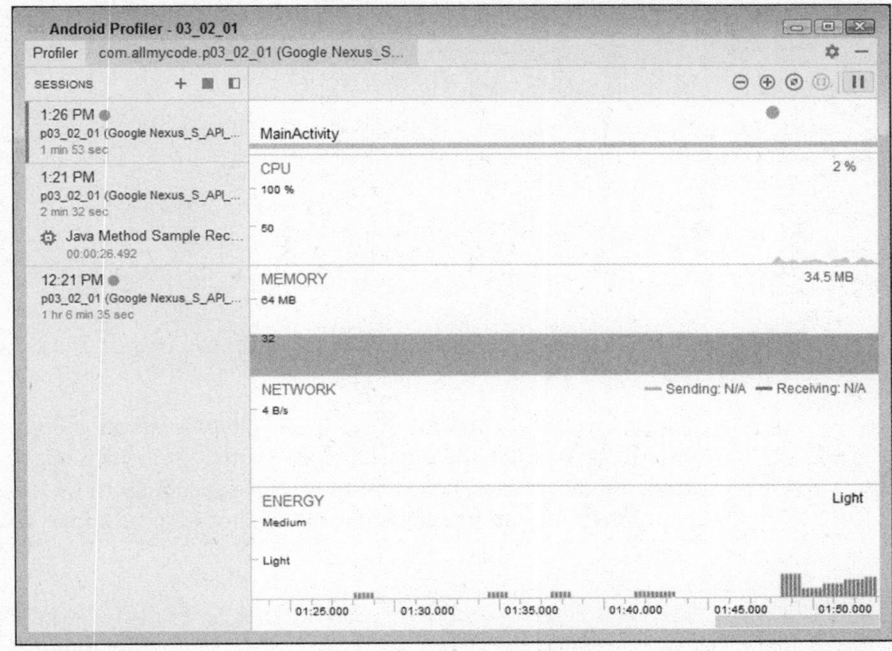

FIGURE 2-2: Android Studio provides a visualization of your app's use of resources.

The initial display shows four categories of information: CPU, Memory, Network, and Energy. To see a particular category in more detail, click its entry. Figure 2-3 shows the CPU category. You see the level of CPU use over time in this case.

REMEMBER

The profile won't display much with your app doing nothing. To see any changes, you need to work with your app performing various tasks. As you make app changes, you can see how resource usage is affected and potentially find useful patterns for the tuning process. When working with the example app, you must click Click Me to see changes to the CPU activity.

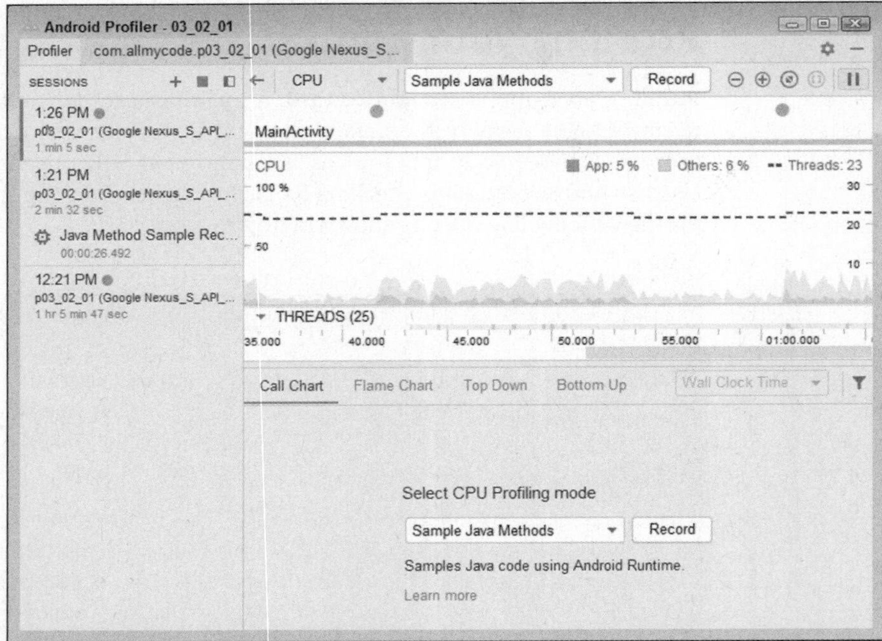

FIGURE 2-3: View the use of various resource categories.

Also important is choosing what to profile. When you choose Run⇨Profile, you see a dialog box like the one shown in Figure 2-4, which lets you choose what to profile. In most cases, you want to profile a specific activity to see the most detail about how your app functions instead of choosing the app as a whole.

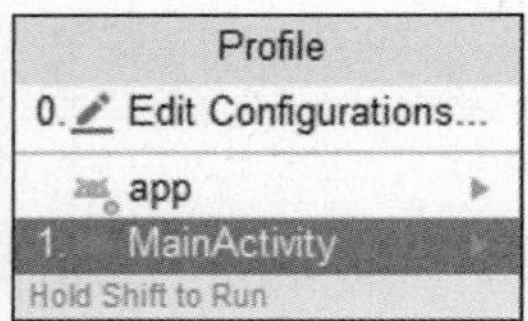

FIGURE 2-4: Choose the specific element of your app that you want to monitor.

Figures 2-2 and 2-3 show the activity you see when profiling the MainActivity, rather than app. If you try app instead (the default), you likely won't see anything.

Tracing your app

This section tells you about the CPU Profiling approach to creating an app trace. To begin this process, you choose a trace option in the drop-down list box at the top of the CPU Profiling window and click Record. As you interact with your app,

Android Studio records the results for you. You have these options when tracing an app:

REMEMBER

- **Sample Java Methods:** Captures the app's call stack at regular intervals as you interact with it. The profiler looks at each of the captures for potential patterns and tells you more about how the underlying Java execution is working.

  This approach to tracing your app has the advantage of not burying you in excess data. In addition, it has only a small impact on performance, so it tends to produce better results in most cases. However, it has the disadvantage of not capturing everything. If the app enters and leaves a method between captures, the method doesn't appear in the trace. One way around this issue is to rely on a Debug trace as mentioned earlier in the chapter. You can also use an instrumented trace, as described in the next bullet.
- **Trace Java Methods:** Creates an instrumented trace of your app, which means that you see every method call, no matter how quickly the method executes. The main issue of using this approach is that you quickly get buried in data, which may actually hide the information you want to see. Also, because of the huge amount of data collected, the trace file may fill and exceed its capacity in a short time.
- **Sample C/C++ Functions:** Captures sampled traces of the low-level calls that your app makes. Your device must be running Android 8.0 (API level 26) as a minimum to make this feature work. This particular tracing method is useful only when you want to understand the native mode operation of your app, and you should generally avoid using it.
- **Trace System Calls:** Provides extremely detailed information on how your app interacts with the system, including helping you see how threads access various CPUs. This kind of trace can generate a huge amount of data, depending on how you configure it. The use of custom trace events helps control the amount and kind of data you receive. This trace is especially helpful with multithreaded apps to ensure that you're using CPU resources effectively.

When working with the example app, you can start the recording right before you click Click Me and then stop it again after the progress bar is full. Figure 2-5 shows the CPU activity during this time frame. Below it, you see the results of the trace, which also appear in a trace file. The trace files appear on the left side of the display (there are two of them: one for 1:26 p.m. and another for 1:21 p.m.). To see the live display again, you click the bottom entry.

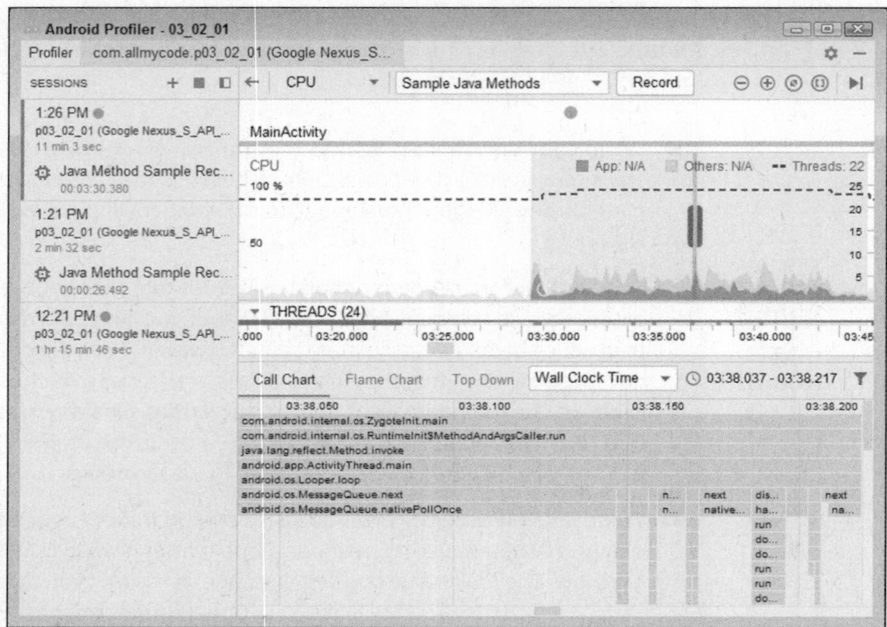

FIGURE 2-5: The results of creating a trace log for the example app.

Notice the bar displayed in the CPU area. This bar reflects the data you see in the lower half of the display. By making the bar wider (using the two gray handles), you see a summary of more of the data in the CPU area. Figure 2-5 shows the Call chart, which tells you about the underlying Java calls. The Flame Chart tells you about the most used calls (so that you can better tell where your app spends most of its time). Figure 2-6 shows the Top Down display, which gives you a sequence of events that comes close to matching the process used by your app. (You can match it to your Kotlin code.)

Checking for benchmarking module support

This chapter describes how to create a benchmark module for your app. Before you can add a benchmark module, though, you need access to it. Older versions of Android Studio (anything before 3.6) will need a special module addition made. The following steps can get you started with benchmarking for an older version of Android Studio:

1. **Choose Help➪About.**

   You see an About dialog listing the Android Studio version number. If the number is 3.6 or above, you can skip this part and move on to the next section, "Benchmarking the app."

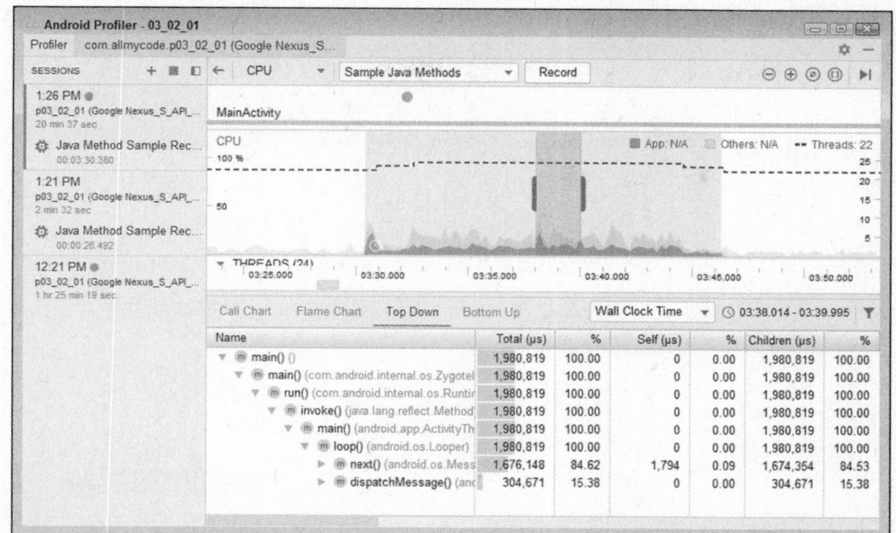

FIGURE 2-6: Looking at a trace log in detail.

2. **Choose Help⇨Edit Custom Properties.**

   Android Studio may display a dialog box like the one shown in Figure 2-7. If so, click Create.

   You see `idea.properties` file open in the editor.

3. **Type** npw.benchmark.template.module=true **and save the file.**

4. **Restart Android Studio.**

   You're ready to work with the benchmarking module.

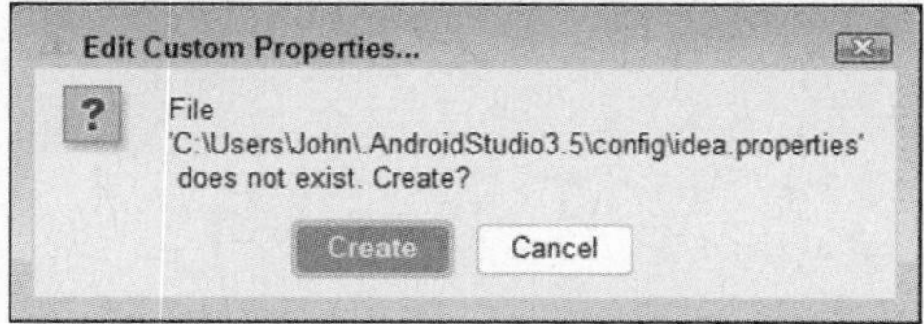

FIGURE 2-7: Creating the custom properties file.

Benchmarking the app

In this section, you add a benchmark to your app. To do this, you're creating a new Kotlin class file to hold the benchmark code by following these steps:

1. **Right-click the App entry and choose New⇨Module from the context menu.**

   You see the New Module dialog box, shown in Figure 2-8.

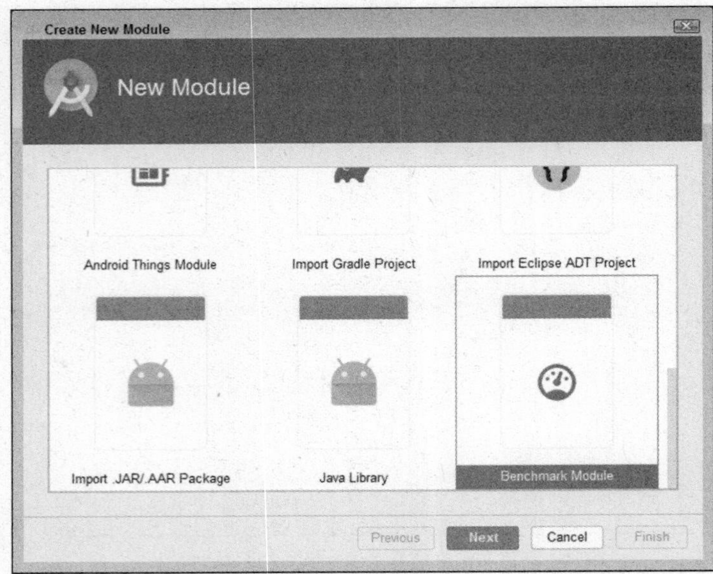

FIGURE 2-8: Creating a new module.

2. **Select Benchmark Module and click Next.**

   Android Studio asks how you want to configure the benchmark module, as shown in Figure 2-9. The default setup will work fine in this case.

3. **Click Finish.**

   Android Studio creates the new module for you.

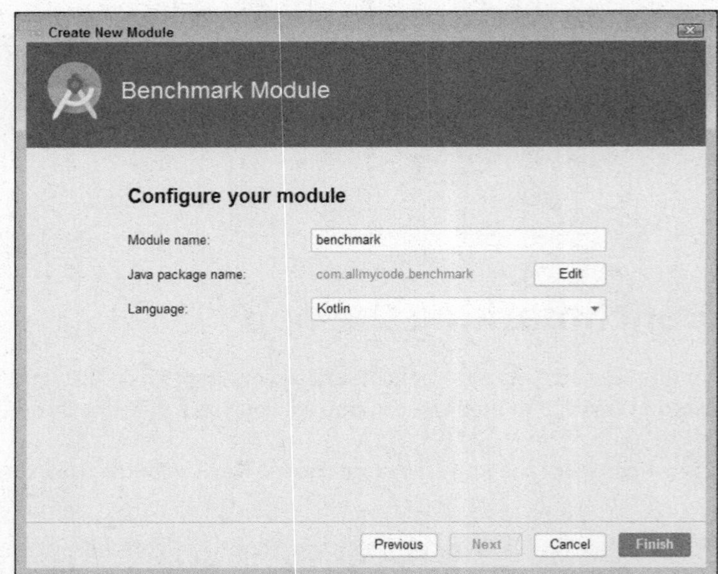

FIGURE 2-9: Define the module name and package.

WARNING

You need to rebuild your project by choosing Build⇨Make Project. If Android Studio asks about syncing Gradle to your project, make sure you perform the sync as well. In some cases, you see the following error message after you accomplish these tasks:

```
Detected usage of the testInstrumentationRunner,
  androidx.benchmark.AndroidBenchmarkRunner, in project
  benchmark, which is no longer valid as it has been moved
  to androidx.benchmark.junit4.AndroidBenchmarkRunner.
```

To fix this error, open the `build.gradle (Module: benchmark)` file (rather than the other two `build.gradle` files). In the `defaultConfig` section of the file, replace

```
testInstrumentationRunner
  'androidx.benchmark.AndroidBenchmarkRunner'
```

with

```
testInstrumentationRunner
  'androidx.benchmark.junit4.AndroidBenchmarkRunner'
```

Rebuilding your project and performing any required synchronization will clear the error. To run the benchmark, you right-click `benchmark/java/com.allmycode.benchmark/ExampleBenchmark` in Android view (see Figure 2-10) and choose Run 'ExampleBenchmark' from the context menu. The file contains a default test that demonstrates how the benchmarking works.

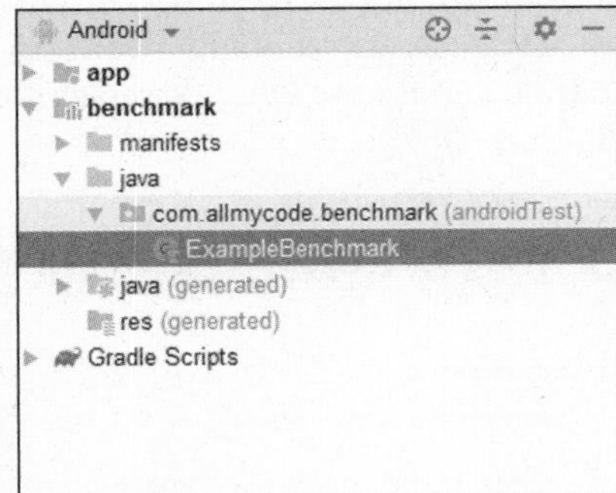

FIGURE 2-10: Locating the benchmark.

Testing Application Functionality

Normally, you test application functionality using a combination of manual and automated testing. The automated testing usually focuses on whether functions return a specific value given specific inputs. The manual testing focuses on issues of whether the app performs as intended. Android studio provides access to two test types: instrumented and unit. This section focuses on the unit testing.

When you create your project, you get an `ExampleUnitTest.kt` file with it. Open this file and you see that it contains a default test:

```
@Test
fun addition_isCorrect() {
    assertEquals(4, 2 + 2)
}
```

The test will pass because 2 + 2 does indeed equal 4. The example doesn't currently contain code that you can test in this way, so add the following function to the `MainActivity.kt` file.

```
fun doAdd(value1: Int, value2: Int): Int {
    return value1 + value2
}
```

Now you can add a unit test to the `ExampleUnitTest.kt` file.

```
@Test
fun doAdd_isCorrect() {
    val main = MainActivity()
    assertEquals(4, main.doAdd(2, 2))
}
```

You have to create an instance of `MainActivity` to test it. The code should pass in this case as well. The unit test currently contains two tests. To run it, right-click `ExampleUnitTest` in Android and choose Run 'ExampleUnitTest'. You see the expected output shown in Figure 2-11.

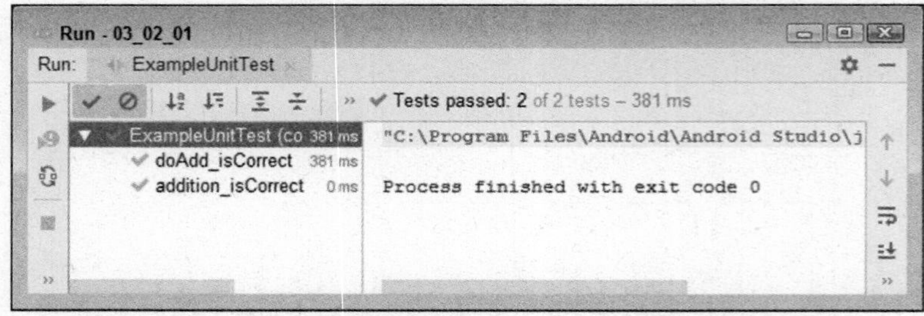

FIGURE 2-11: Seeing the test result.

» Obtaining data

» Displaying data

Chapter 3
Creating an Architecture

The entirety of your app, from a design perspective, must meet certain organizational requirements or it won't work properly. It would be like trying to find something in a library with books shelved just anywhere. The content would be there, but you wouldn't be able to find it unless you just happened to stumble upon the right shelf. Your app is all about presenting content in some way and if you want anyone to make any sense of it, you must organize it. An *architecture* is a means of describing the elements of your app (the shelving), how they interact (the library layout), and how they present and manage data (the content your patrons want). So, this chapter is about organizing your app in a specific way.

Managing Application Activities

Every app developed to this point in the book contains an activity: the main activity. Up to this point in the book, except for one of the examples, only a main activity of limited dimensionality has been presented. Most apps contain a number of activities, and these activities can perform a wide range of tasks based on their current state. The following sections describe activities at a level of detail that will help you create more complex apps as the book progresses.

Defining an activity

Mobile apps and desktop applications operate differently. When you start an application on the desktop, some `main()` method starts the whole thing off until the user sees your application onscreen. A user may not need all of an app and may not even start it in the same location each time. The user is interested only in performing a specific task — an activity. Even if your widget app normally begins with the main activity showing a menu of things the user can do, the user may only need to perform one of those items and may not want to see the menu. Using an activity approach means that the user can start the activity in question without even seeing the menu.

REMEMBER

Other apps may also call specific activities in your app. For example, if your widget app provides the means for looking up items in a company catalog as one activity, any other app that needs to perform catalog searches will likely call on that particular activity in your app. Mobile devices need to save resources, so using just one activity every time makes sense. In addition, using this approach means that every app that needs to perform a catalog search presents a consistent interface because only one interface exists. (Book 1, Chapter 4 has details about the actual layout of an app, including information about the manifest.) Activities have these common features:

- **Activity class:** Every activity inherits from the `Activity` class (or another activity that inherits from the `Activity` class). The `Activity` class ensures that your activity behaves like every other activity.
- **Single screen:** When creating an activity, the activity usually supports just one screen. When you need another screen, you create another activity.
- **Loosely bound:** Activities form a sort of cooperative, where each activity can stand alone, yet each activity contributes to the app as a whole to produce a cohesive experience.
- **Registration required:** Each activity must appear in the app manifest if you want to use it.
- **Permissions:** If you want to call one activity from another activity, both activities must have the same permissions. For example, if you want to use the SMS functionality in another activity, both activities need the `<uses-permission android:name="android.permission.SEND_SMS"/>` permission entry in the manifest.

WARNING

Android considers some permissions dangerous because they can affect device health or expose the user's personal information (among other things). Even if both apps have the correct permissions listed, the user still gets involved in granting final permission for any dangerous activities. The user sees a dialog box appear that tells about the permission needed. The user must then click Grant to allow the activity.

Getting an overview of intent filters

In Book 1, Chapter 6, example 3, you create a simple app that has two activities: Main and Other. The Main activity is the one that gets called when the app starts. You access the Other activity only through the Main activity. The app manifest reflects this fact, as shown here:

```
<application
  ... Some Stuff Removed ...>
  <activity android:name=".OtherActivity"></activity>
  <activity android:name=".MainActivity">
    <intent-filter>
      <action android:name="android.intent.action.MAIN"/>
      <category
        android:name="android.intent.category.LAUNCHER"/>
    </intent-filter>
  </activity>
</application>
```

Notice that `MainActivity` includes an `<intent-filter>`. This filter specifies an action, which is to interact with the main entry point, and a category, which is to launch the app. These are standard intent filter entries. You can see a wealth of other activities, such as `ACTION_VIEW` (display some information), `ACTION_EDIT` (change some information), and `ACTION_DIAL` (dial a phone number), at `https://developer.android.com/reference/android/content/Intent.html`. When you see these actions in a manifest, they always appear in the form `action.MAIN`, `action.VIEW`, `action.EDIT`, or `action.DIAL`.

REMEMBER

To make any activity in your app accessible to other apps or implicitly by your own app, you must define an intent filter. The intent filter must contain the `<action>` element as a minimum; however, most contain the `<category>` and sometimes the `<data>` elements as well.

Considering the activity lifecycle

An activity has a specific lifecycle. As a minimum, you must create a lifecycle as part of creating an app. In fact, the `onCreate()` method is the only lifecycle method that the example apps provide so far. The following list provides you with a more detailed view of the callback methods that you can override in your activity to provide specific lifecycle handling:

» `onCreate()`: You must implement this callback method because it configures the essential app functionality. It also provides code to display the initial interface and restores previous configuration information.

After the `onCreate()` callback completes, Android calls `onStart()`. You see `onCreate()` called only once for each app session.

- `onStart()`: This callback method lets you perform additional setup tasks after the app becomes visible to the user, but before the user begins interacting with it. For example, this might be where you would place a startup animation or perform other setup tasks you want the user to see. Android calls `onResume()` next, even if the app isn't actually resuming anything.
- `onResume()`: At this point, the app is visible to the user and is receiving user input. The app isn't quite fully online at this point, but it's nearly so. For example, the app is at the top of the activity stack. This is where you implement much of the app's core functionality. The app remains in this state until the user wants to do something else. When the user wants to leave to do something else or end the app, Android calls `onPause()`.
- `onPause()`: When the user clicks the Back or Recents buttons, the app enters the paused state. The app is still visible to the user, but it generally isn't doing anything; it's waiting. The user could decide to give the app the focus back, which would mean calling `onResume()`, or decide to end the app, which would mean calling `onStop()`. This isn't the place to perform tasks like saving the user's data — the app is merely paused at this point.

TIP

Pausing the app, disallowing any user input, doesn't mean that your app stops doing everything. If your app is playing music when it gets paused, the user will want it to continue playing music. The only difference is that the user won't select a new album while the app is paused. When the app runs out of music to play, it simply waits until the user provides more input.

- `onStop()`: When the app is no longer visible to the user, Android calls this method. While in this method, your app should discontinue performing tasks like updating the display, even if the user might ordinarily expect it to continue updating, because the user can no longer see the display. However, nonvisual tasks that the user expects to continue running, such as playing music, should continue as before. If the user decides to go back to the app, Android calls `onRestart()`. However, when the user decides to end the app, Android calls `onDestroy()`.
- `onRestart()`: If your app has stopped, you may need to perform some updates to the data before it can start again. That's the purpose of this callback method — to prepare your app to start again. After this method exits, Android calls `onStart()` to bring the app back to full functionality.
- `onDestroy()`: This is the last callback method that Android calls when the user decides to stop using the app. You use this method to perform tasks like releasing resources. The resources in question are generally not those within your app, such as strings you create, but rather those that are outside your app, such as a database connection where you need to do things like flush the database cache.

REMEMBER

This list contains only the basics. For example, Android may decide to pause or stop an app when a higher-priority app requires resources. Your app needs to respond to all sorts of inputs on an activity level, rather than an app-wide level. Each activity must operate as a separate entity.

Understanding the backstack

A *task* is a collection of activities presented in an order that results in a certain output, like answering your email or updating a social media site. Even though each activity is independent, you call them in a certain order to achieve the result you want. These activities are stacked together onto a *backstack*, as shown in Figure 3-1. In this case, you see three activities, with Activity 1 being started first and Activity 3 being started last. When you press the Back button, the activity at the top of the stack, Activity 3, is destroyed, and the next activity on the stack, Activity 2, is resumed. When all the activities are popped off the backstack, the task ends.

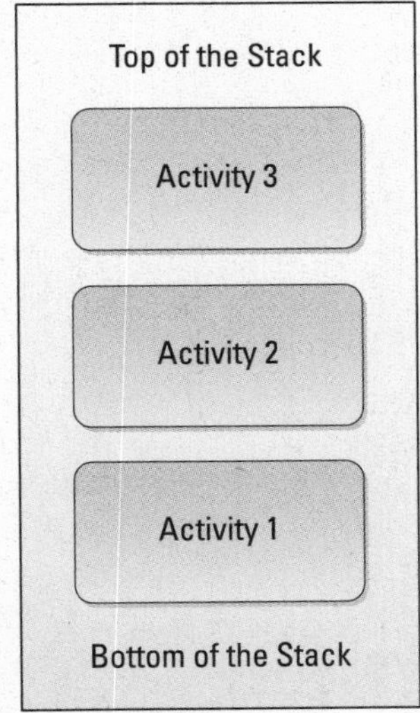

FIGURE 3-1: A view of the backstack with activities.

REMEMBER

Android manages the tasks for each window separately. Consequently, when the user runs in a multiwindowed environment, each window has its own backstack. Using multiple backstacks means that the user won't face the odd situation of moving from window to window when clicking Back. However, if one app launches an activity found in another app, the activity ends up in that app's backstack. The backstack is task based, not activity based.

WARNING

Remember that the user may end up running so many tasks that memory becomes an issue. Android will destroy background tasks (those that aren't running) to recover memory when necessary. As a result, the ability to resume a particular task is lost. (Normally it's the one that has been in the background the longest.)

The default behavior for tasks is to add the activity to the backstack each time the user invokes it, as shown in Figure 3-2. In some cases, you don't want this behavior because it would prove confusing to the user. By using various flags in the application manifest or when you call `startActivity()`, you can tell Android to use the backstack differently, perhaps even clearing everything except the main activity when the task loses focus. Because taking this approach can be risky, including the risk of potential data or state loss, you should use it only as a last resort when attempting to create a good app flow.

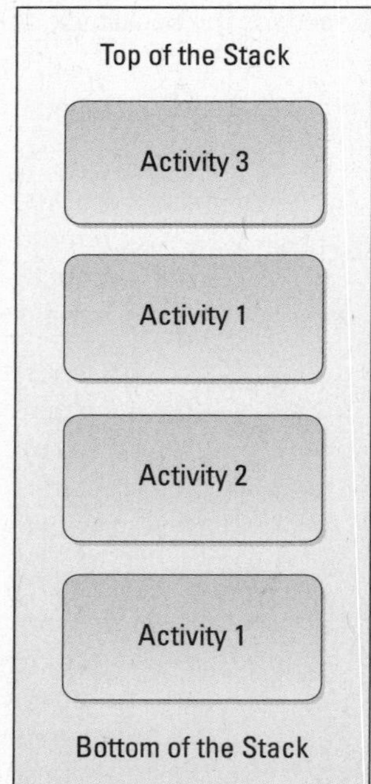

FIGURE 3-2: A backstack with multiple invocations of Activity 1.

Here are some of the attributes you can use to manage your tasks (you can find more activity attributes at `https://developer.android.com/guide/topics/manifest/activity-element.html`):

- `taskAffinity`: An *affinity* is a natural attraction. Normally, all your activities have the same affinity. However, you can give them a different affinity, and activities with a like affinity will group together in the backstack. In short, this attribute can affect the backstack ordering.

* `launchMode`: Determines how the task is launched. The `standard` behavior is to create a new instance of the activity every time it's invoked. Here are other modes:
  * `singleTop`: Tells Android to retain just the current invocation of the activity when the activity is already at the top of the call stack. The existing activity receives any invocation data. If the activity is somewhere else on the call stack, Android creates a new instance.
  * `singleTask`: Allows only one invocation of the activity, no matter where it appears in the call stack. The existing activity receives any invocation data.
  * `singleInstance`: Creates a task where the activity is the only member. There is never a second instance of the activity, so the sole activity receives all invocation data.
* `allowTaskReparenting`: Normally an activity remains with the same task for its entire lifetime. However, this attribute tells Android to place the activity in a new task (a new parent) when another activity that has the same affinity is launched. The action ensures that like activities remain together under the same parent.
* `clearTaskOnLaunch`: Normally a tasks retains a list of activities even if a user starts another task and works with it for a while before returning. This attribute tells Android to clear the task of all activities except the main activity whenever the user relaunches the task from the home screen.
* `alwaysRetainTaskState`: Normally, Android maintains task state unless certain things happen, like a low memory condition or the task remaining in the background for a long time (say, 30 minutes). When any of these normal events happen, Android clears the task of activities except the main activity. This attribute forces Android to always maintain task state until the user ends the task.

TIP

This particular attribute can be helpful with certain application classes, such as a browser that has many tabs open. The user won't want to come back later and find all the tabs closed. Likewise, you might use this attribute with mission-critical apps that the user may rely on throughout the day off and on, and a loss of state would require a major time investment on the user's part to recover.

* `finishOnTaskLaunch`: Specifies that the activity should end every time the user places it in the background. If you use this attribute with `allowTaskReparenting`, this attribute takes precedence. The activity is always ended rather than reparented when a task with an activity with the same affinity starts.

TIP

You use this attribute for times when the user is unlikely to want to continue the previous activity. For example, if the user is playing a time-based game, waiting for a while before restarting to play would ruin the user's score anyway — the user would want to start again to achieve a better score.

In addition, you can further modify behavior using the following intent flags (you can find additional flags at `https://developer.android.com/reference/android/content/Intent.html#FLAG_ACTIVITY_BROUGHT_TO_FRONT`):

» `FLAG_ACTIVITY_NEW_TASK`: Creates a new task using the specified activity within the current backstack. You use this flag with launcher-type activities, when the activity is meant to stand alone or to act as the beginning of an entirely new task.

» `FLAG_ACTIVITY_CLEAR_TOP`: Clears older activities from the task, with the target activity appearing at the top. For example, if you have a task with activities A, B, C, and D on it, and D calls on activity B, Android will destroy activities C and D and give B the focus at the top. The stack would then consist of activities A and B.

TIP

This flag is useful for returning from deep within an app without forcing the user to click Back an unimaginable number of times. If you know that the user will always want to return to activity B after working with activity D, using this flag makes sense.

» `FLAG_ACTIVITY_SINGLE_TOP`: Prevents the activity from running when it already appears at the top of the stack.

Working with fragments

Fragments are the LEGOs of the Android world. You place them within an activity to perform part of an activity. They can appear in multiple activities so that you don't end up writing the same code multiple times. Figure 3-3 shows a call stack with two activities. Activity 2 contains two fragments. These fragments exist outside Activity 2 in that they are self-contained, but they do rely on Activity 2 as a container.

REMEMBER

Android originally introduced fragments to help support larger devices, such as tablets. By using fragments, you can adjust the layout of your app to meet a particular device's needs. For example, a tablet might show an overview in one pane and a selected detail in another. A smartphone might show the overview as the whole screen. When you click an item in the overview, the detail appears on the whole screen. Clicking the Back button removes the detail fragment and displays the overview again.

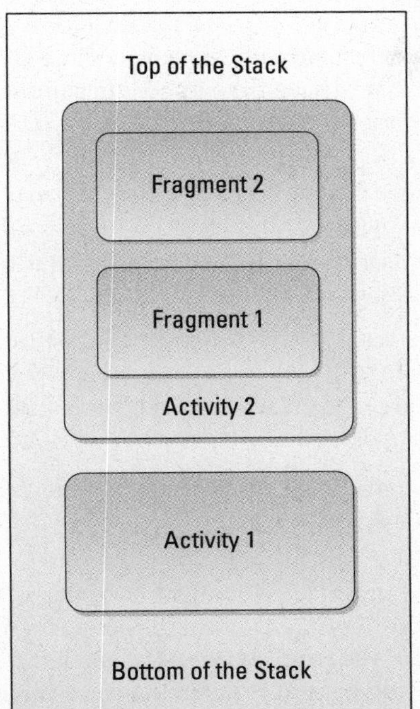

FIGURE 3-3: An activity that contains two fragments.

As with activities, fragments rely on the call stack. When you invoke an activity that supports fragments, each of the fragments is part of the same call stack. If a fragment is added to the activity as a separate step, popping the fragment from the backstack separately using the Back button is also possible. Popping a fragment doesn't end the activity. Only after popping all the fragments off the call stack does another click of the Back button end the activity as well. However, when the activity ends, so do all the fragments that the activity hosts.

To create a fragment, you create a class that inherits from the `Fragment` class (`https://developer.android.com/reference/androidx/fragment/app/Fragment.html`). The `Fragment` class looks and acts a lot like an activity, but with the caveat that the fragment must exist within an activity. As with an activity, you can explicitly create a fragment using an intent (as you do for example 3 of Book 1, Chapter 6), or you can implicitly create it, which requires app manifest settings similar to those used with an activity.

Creating an Architecture

TIP

In addition to standard fragments, Android gives you some specialty fragments. You use these special fragments to save time in adding common functionality to your app:

- `DialogFragment`: Displays a floating dialog box that you can use for notifications and other purposes. Unlike activity dialog box helpers, a `DialogFragment` appears on the backstack, which means that the user can rely on the standard buttons to interact with them.
- `ListFragment`: Displays a list of items from which the user can choose (as in a master/detail configuration). You control the presentation by the adapter you choose, such as `SimpleCursorAdapter`. Overriding the `onListItemClick()` callback lets you respond to click events.
- `PreferenceFragmentCompat`: Displays a hierarchy of preference items as a list, allowing the user to configure your app.

Working with a fragments user interface is similar to working with a user interface for an activity, except now you're doing it within the activity's scope. The Android Studio automation does a lot of the required work for you, but you're still responsible for actually adding the fragment to the activity's user interface. The following sections address this issue using two methods: XML and programmatically.

Adding a fragment to an activity using XML

When using the XML approach, you work with a fragment much as you would any other component. In fact, you can use the designer to help make things easier. As with a component, you place the fragment within some sort of container, as shown here:

```
<?xml version="1.0" encoding="utf-8"?>
<androidx.constraintlayout.widget.ConstraintLayout
xmlns:android="http://schemas.android.com/apk/res/android"
    xmlns:app="http://schemas.android.com/apk/res-auto"
    xmlns:tools="http://schemas.android.com/tools"
    android:layout_width="match_parent"
    android:layout_height="match_parent"
    tools:context=".MainActivity">

    <fragment
      android:name="com.allmycode.p03_01_01.MyFragment"
      android:id="@+id/list"
      android:layout_weight="1"
```

```
        android:layout_width="0dp"
        android:layout_height="match_parent"/>

</androidx.constraintlayout.widget.ConstraintLayout>
```

The fragment has many of the same settings as a component. The only difference is that the `android:name` attribute must provide the fully qualified name of the fragment, which is `"com.allmycode.p03_01_01.MyFragment"`, in this case.

TIP

You normally use this approach for design-time additions of fragments. Using this approach is easier than trying to code a dynamic addition during the app `onCreate()` function call.

Programmatically adding a fragment to an activity

You can attach and detach fragments anytime you want during normal app activity. To do so, however, you must programmatically attach or detach the fragment, which means paying attention to details that you might not ordinarily have to consider, such as the effect of the fragment's UI on the activity's layout. To start the process, you must create a `FragmentManager` and associated `FragmentTransaction`, as shown here:

```
val fragmentManager = supportFragmentManager
val fragmentTransaction =
    fragmentManager.beginTransaction()
```

After you have a transaction started, you can add the fragment, as shown here:

```
val fragment = MyFragment()
fragmentTransaction.add(R.id.fragment_container, fragment)
fragmentTransaction.commit()
```

The fragment you create will have its own class and associated constructor, so you create an instance of the fragment just as you would create an instance of a component. The `fragmentTransaction.add()` function consists of two arguments, the `ViewGroup` used to hold the fragment and the fragment you want to add to it. The call to `fragmentTransaction.commit()` actually adds the fragment to the `ViewGroup`. Note that you can use this approach to add, remove, and replace fragments as needed.

Considering the fragment lifecycle

The lifecycle of a fragment is similar to the lifecycle of an activity. You find a few more callbacks than with activities, and a few of them work slightly differently, but the essential concepts are the same. Here are the callbacks you commonly use to control a fragment lifecycle.

- `onAttach()`: This is the first function called when a fragment attaches to an activity. It provides you with a `Context` in which the fragment will appear. You use this callback to perform any setup required to interact with a particular activity. Android calls `onCreate()` when this function exits.
- `onCreate()`: Works precisely the same as the activity equivalent, except on a fragment scale. The capability to create objects, for example, is limited by the capabilities of the activity.
- `onCreateView()`: A fragment doesn't actually draw its own view. What it does is create a `View` that it passes as a result when this function ends. The activity then interacts with the `View` to present the fragment onscreen. Some fragments don't actually display anything onscreen, in which case you return `null`. Android calls `onActivityCreated()` after this function exits.
- `onActivityCreated()`: A fragment must be aware of the state of its host activity. This callback lets the fragment know that the activity has been created and that it should perform any tasks required to restore state or re-create a view.
- `onStart()`: This callback is called immediately after the activity's `onStart()` callback exits. It serves the same purpose as the activity `onStart()`.
- `onResume()`:This callback is called immediately after the activity's `onResume()` callback exits. It serves the same purpose as the activity `onResume()`.
- `onPause()`: This callback is called immediately before the activity's `onPause()` callback. It essentially works the same as an activity `onPause()` with one exception: This is the place to save any user data because you don't know whether the user is coming back and the fragment might see use in another activity.
- `onStop()`: This callback is called immediately before the activity's `onStop()` or if the activity intends to detach the fragment. It serves the same purpose as the activity `onStop()` callback.
- `onDestroyView()`: This callback is called before the activity's `onDestroy()` or in other cases where the fragment needs to destroy the current view. When the app needs a new view, Android will call `onCreateView()` to create it. The main emphasis of this call is that the fragment is likely to be detached from the activity.

» onDestroy(): This callback works similarly to the activity onDestroy(), except Android may also call it when the fragment will be detached from the activity. This callback doesn't necessarily indicate that the activity will be destroyed, but it's always called before the activity onDestroy() callback. The onDetach() callback is called after this function exits.

» onDetach(): This is the last callback method that Android calls when the user decides not to use the fragment any longer. The fragment is detached from the activity, but the activity may continue to run (and could eventually attach a new copy of the fragment).

REMEMBER

The essential methods for a fragment are onCreate(), onCreateView(), and onPause(). You should always implement these callbacks as a minimum to ensure that your fragment works properly.

Seeing activities and fragments in action

It helps to play with activities and fragments a bit to understand how the whole process of using explicit and implicit intents to load either an activity or fragment works. To begin this section, create a test app named 03_03_01 using the same techniques in Book 1, Chapter 3. Use an Empty Activity as a starting point and a minimum API level of 14.

Creating an app with multiple activities

You need at least three activities to truly see the backstack in action, starting with the main activity. You wouldn't actually create an app like the one in this section; the approach used is to help you see how everything works together without creating a lot of UI code. The following steps get you started.

1. **Right-click** app\java\com.allmycode.p03_03_01 **and choose New⇨Activity⇨Empty Activity.**

   You see the Configure Activity dialog box, shown in Figure 3-4.

2. **Type** FirstActivity **in the Activity Name field and click Finish.**

   Android Studio creates a new activity for you.

3. **Perform Steps 1 and 2 again to create** SecondActivity.

Creating an Architecture

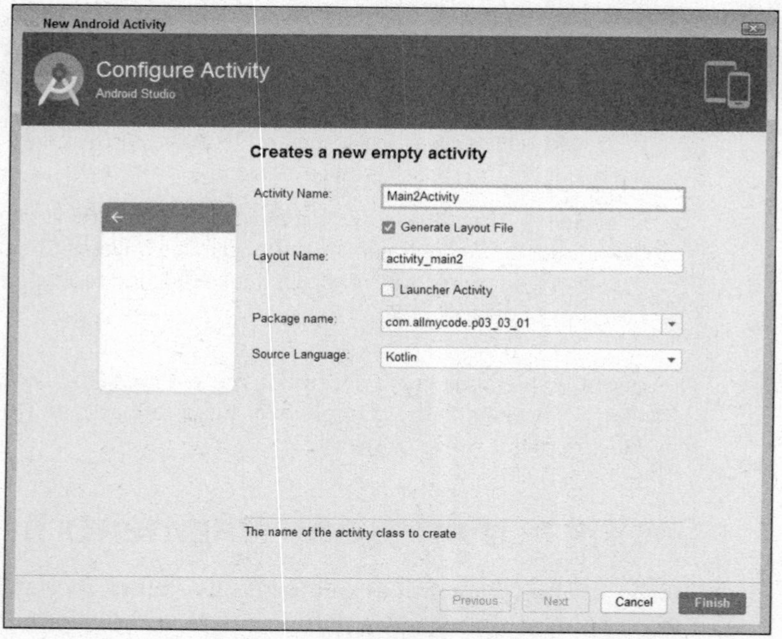

FIGURE 3-4: Configure a new activity.

At this point, you have two new activities, and you could use an explicit intent to interact with them, but you want to see both implicit and explicit intents at work, so open the `AndroidManifest.xml` file. You need to add intent filters to both of these new entries so that they look like this:

```
<activity android:name=".SecondActivity">
  <intent-filter>
    <action
      android:name= "android.intent.action.SECOND"/>
    <category
      android:name="android.intent.category.DEFAULT"/>
  </intent-filter>
</activity>
<activity android:name=".FirstActivity">
  <intent-filter>
    <action
      android:name=" android.intent.action.FIRST"/>
    <category
      android:name="android.intent.category.DEFAULT"/>
  </intent-filter>
</activity>
```

REMEMBER

Notice that both of the activities belong to the DEFAULT category, so you can access them implicitly but you can't use them to launch the app. If you had wanted to allow these activities to launch the app, especially from an external app, you'd need to use the LAUNCHER category instead.

Each activity also has its own unique <action> property that starts with the package name and includes a special action name of FIRST or SECOND, depending on the activity. If either activity had been performing a common task, you could have used one of the common actions found at https://developer.android.com/guide/components/intents-common instead.

All three activities will have the same interface: a TextView and two Button components, as shown in Figure 3-5. Assign the components id values of Caller, FirstLoc, and SecondLoc, respectively. You also need to create onClick entries of FirstLocClick and SecondLocClick. The Caller text field begins empty, so you can't see it in the display when you first start the app.

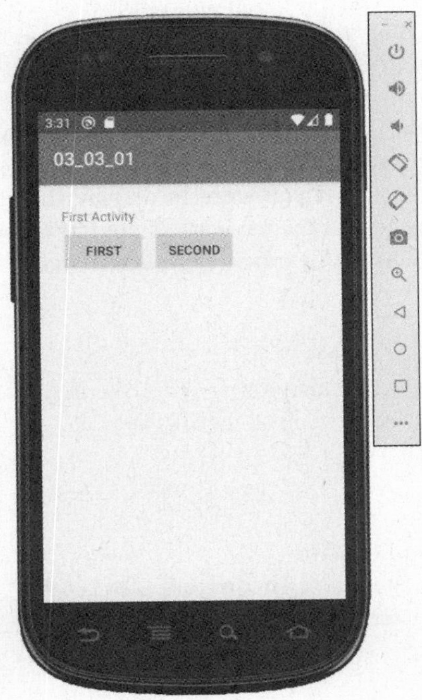

FIGURE 3-5: Create user interfaces for the three activities.

Each of the activities requires the same bit of code in the onCreate() method:

```
this.Caller.setText(intent.getStringExtra("Caller"))
```

You can also add code to the onCreate() method to change the button captions as needed. The MainActivity can call both the FirstActivity and the SecondActivity implicitly, as shown here:

```
fun onFirstLocClick(view: View){
    val goto = Intent("android.intent.action.FIRST")
    goto.putExtra("Caller", "Main Activity")
    startActivity(goto)
}

fun onSecondLocClick(view: View){
    val goto = Intent("android.intent.action.SECOND")
    goto.putExtra("Caller", "Main Activity")
    startActivity(goto)
}
```

In both cases, you use the content from the <action> element of the <intent-filter> found in the AndroidManifest.xml file. After creating the Intent, goto, you can add the name of a caller to it and then call startActivity(). This process is similar to the one used for the explicit intent seen in example 01_06_03.

REMEMBER

However, you can't use the implicit approach when dealing with the MainActivity. That's because a lot of other apps have the same <action> value of "android.intent.action.MAIN". If you were to display the entire list of apps, the user could become confused and the navigation wouldn't work as intended. To get around this problem, you use an explicit approach instead, as shown here for the FirstActivity code:

```
fun onFirstLocClick(view: View){
    val goto = Intent(this, MainActivity::class.java)
    goto.putExtra("Caller", "First Activity")
    startActivity(goto)
}

fun onSecondLocClick(view: View){
    val goto = Intent("android.intent.action.SECOND")
    goto.putExtra("Caller", "First Activity")
    startActivity(goto)
}
```

When you run the app, you find that each of the activities will display the name of the activity that called it. As you use the Back button, you can see that the series of activities appears in reverse as Android pops them off the backstack.

Adding UI fragments to the activities

As previously mentioned, a fragment provides added content for your activity in a form that you can share in as many places as needed. You can attach and detach fragments as needed so that the layout of your activity need not change, even when the content does. Use these steps to create a UI fragment for the example:

1. **Right-click** `app\java\com.allmycode.p03_03_01` **and choose New⇨Fragment⇨Fragment (Blank).**

   You see the Configure Component dialog box, shown in Figure 3-6.

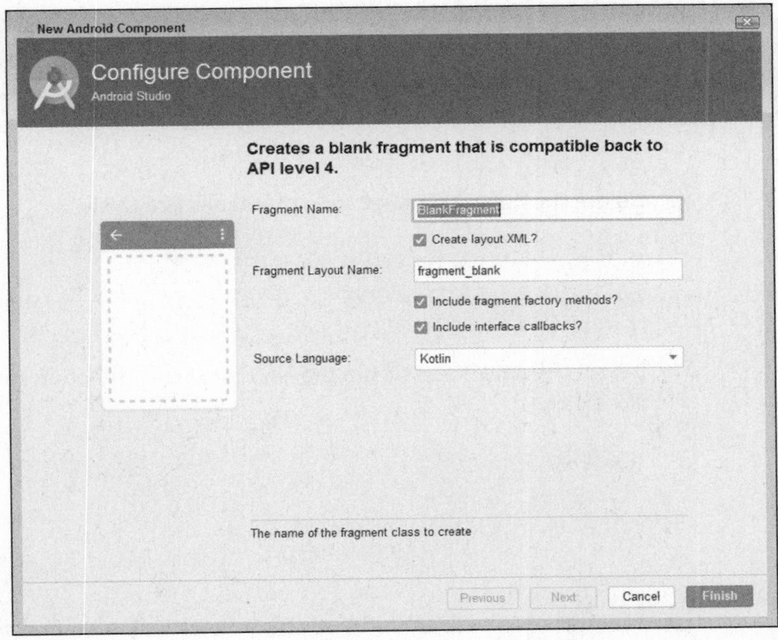

FIGURE 3-6: Configure a new fragment.

2. **Type** SpecialContent **in the Fragment Name field and click Finish.**

   Android Studio creates a new fragment for you. The default fragment contains two parameters, only one of which is actually used by the example.

3. **In the** `SpecialContent` **layout, set the** `TextView id` **value to** aMessage**.**

   The `TextView id` is currently blank, and you may want to update it at some point.

REMEMBER

The template includes some extra code that you don't need for example purposes. The intent of the code is to show you what you might need to fill out the fragment. However, the extra code makes the fragment harder to understand and work with. Most important, the example doesn't use any parameters, so that's the first place to make some cuts.

Creating an Architecture

4. **Delete the code at the top of the `SpecialContent.kt` file that reads:**

```
private const val ARG_PARAM1 = "param1"
private const val ARG_PARAM2 = "param2"
```

5. **Delete the code in the `SpecialContent` class that reads:**

```
private var param1: String? = null
private var param2: String? = null
```

6. **Remove the parameters from `onCreate()` so that the function now looks like this:**

```
private var listener: OnFragmentInteractionListener?
    = null
override fun onCreate(savedInstanceState: Bundle?) {
    super.onCreate(savedInstanceState)
}
```

7. **Delete the button handler code that looks like this:**

```
fun onButtonPressed(uri: Uri) {
    listener?.onFragmentInteraction(uri)
}
```

8. **Delete the parameters from the `newInstance()` function so that it looks like this:**

```
@JvmStatic
fun newInstance() =
    SpecialContent().apply {
    }
```

These changes to the seemingly complete fragment code makes it a lot simpler. Here are the functions you end up with:

- `onCreate()`: Configure the fragment object.
- `onCreateView()`: Create the fragment view.
- `onAttach()`: Perform any required setup during attachment to a specific `context` (your activity).
- `onDetach()`: Perform any required breakdown when the attachment to a `context` is over.
- `newInstance()`: Return a new instance of the fragment object. This function is implemented as a companion object.

Now that you have a new fragment to use, you can try it in the `MainActivity`. The following steps get you started:

1. **Add a `FrameLayout`, `flLayout`, immediately below the `FirstLoc` and `SecondLoc` buttons.**
2. **Add Hide and Show buttons below the `FrameLayout`.**

   Your setup should now look like the one shown in Figure 3-7.

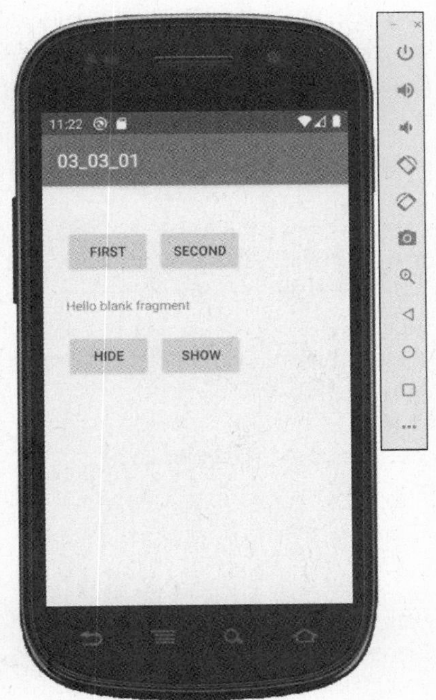

FIGURE 3-7: Configure `MainActivity` to hold the fragment.

3. **Implement the `OnFragmentInteractionListener` interface in `MainActivity` using the following code:**

```
override fun onFragmentInteraction(uri: Uri) {
}
```

   Because this fragment isn't actually doing much interaction by just displaying a message, the associated function doesn't do anything, either.

4. **Add code to instantiate the fragment in the** `onCreate()` **function of** `MainActivity`**, like this:**

```
val transaction =
    supportFragmentManager.beginTransaction()
transaction.replace(R.id.flContent,
                    SpecialContent.newInstance())
transaction.commit()
```

Everything you do with the fragment revolves around a transaction supported by `supportFragmentManager`. In this case, you use a factory method, `SpecialContent.newInstance()`, to replace the content of the `flContent` with the new fragment. Calling `transaction.commit()` actually causes the change to happen.

5. Add the button handler code for the Hide and Show buttons, as shown here:

```
fun onHideClick(view: View){
  if (supportFragmentManager.fragments.size > 0 &&
      supportFragmentManager.fragments[0] != null) {
    val transaction =
      supportFragmentManager.beginTransaction()
    transaction.addToBackStack(null)
    transaction.hide(
      supportFragmentManager.fragments[0])
    transaction.commit()
  }
}

fun onShowClick(view: View){
  if (supportFragmentManager.fragments.size > 0 &&
      supportFragmentManager.fragments[0] != null) {
    val transaction =
      supportFragmentManager.beginTransaction()
    transaction.show(
      supportFragmentManager.fragments[0])
    transaction.commit()
  }
}
```

In both cases, the function begins by verifying that there is a fragment to manage. The `supportFragmentManager.fragments.size` will contain a value that tells you how many fragments are available (only 1 for this example). You access the first fragment in `supportFragmentManager.fragments[0]`.

After you verify that there is a fragment to interact with, the code begins a transaction that either hides or shows the fragment in question. The transaction ends with `transaction.commit()`, as usual.

You can now exercise the fragment by showing and hiding it. If you click Hide and then click Back, the fragment reappears because it's on the backstack. The call to `transaction.addToBackStack(null)` performs this task. If you leave this call out, the action you performed on the fragment won't appear on the backstack (as demonstrated by showing the fragment and clicking Back).

When you create multiple copies of `MainActivity` on the backstack, each of these copies maintains its own fragment state so that clicking Back will show the fragment in those copies where the fragment was active and will hide the fragment otherwise. The app you've created is now set up to help you understand how the backstack works.

ADDING THE FRAGMENT DIRECTLY TO YOUR LAYOUT

After you finish creating the fragment, you have a number of options for including it with an activity. For example, you can add it to the activity layout by choosing the `<fragment>` entry in the Common group of the Palette. When you do this, you see the Fragments dialog box shown here for adding the new fragment. Just select the one you want to use and click OK.

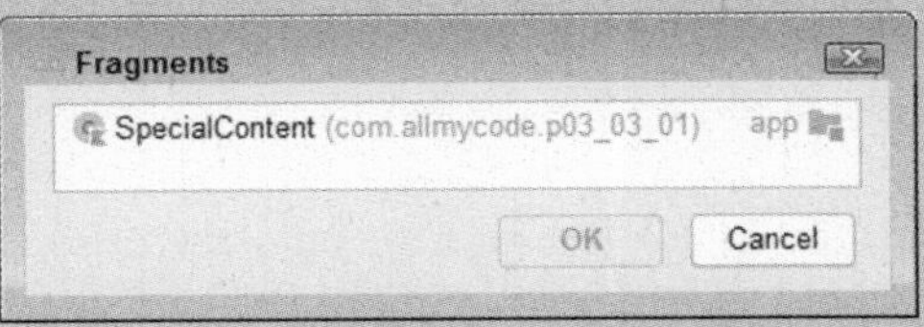

This approach works well if you plan to keep the fragment in place during the entire time you work with the activity. However, it doesn't work well if you want to attach, detach, replace, or remove the fragment from the activity. It's the easy solution when you know that the fragment will remain a constant part of your layout, so you should use it whenever possible. Just be aware that this approach comes with limitations.

WARNING

Many online articles show a considerable amount of code with discussions of how to detach and then attach fragments to your app. The act of detaching the fragment also makes the fragment unavailable. If you look at `supportFragmentManager.fragments.size` immediately after performing a `transaction.commit()`,the fragment seems to still be there. However, when you look at `supportFragmentManager.fragments.size` again in another event handler, you find that the fragment is actually gone and any attempt to attach it fails. This is the why the example shows how to use `transaction.show()` and `transaction.hide()` instead. If you actually want to remove the fragment, using `transaction.remove()` is a better option.

Adding dialog box fragments to the activities

You have a few options available to you to display a dialog onscreen. In many cases, you could opt for the alert dialog created by the code here:

```
AlertDialog.Builder(this)
    .setCancelable(false)
    .setTitle("Alert Dialog")
    .setMessage("This is an alert dialog!")
    .setIcon(android.R.drawable.ic_dialog_alert)
    .setNegativeButton("Close",
        DialogInterface.OnClickListener
    { dialog, which -> dialog.cancel()
    }).setPositiveButton("Ok",
        DialogInterface.OnClickListener
    { dialog, which -> dialog.dismiss()}).create().show()
```

This example creates a basic alert dialog box that displays a simple title and message with two buttons. Click Close and the dialog box calls `dialog.cancel()`; click OK and the dialog box calls `dialog.dismiss()`. To make the alert dialog box appear, you first call `create()` and then `show()`. The example app adds this code to an Alert button that appears below the Hide button onscreen. Figure 3-8 shows how it appears to the user.

REMEMBER

The alert dialog box gets the job done much of the time, but it's inflexible. When you need more flexibility than the alert dialog box can provide, use a dialog box fragment instead. The code for this part of the example is attached to the Dialog button that appears directly below the Show button in the example. Here are the steps needed to create a dialog box fragment:

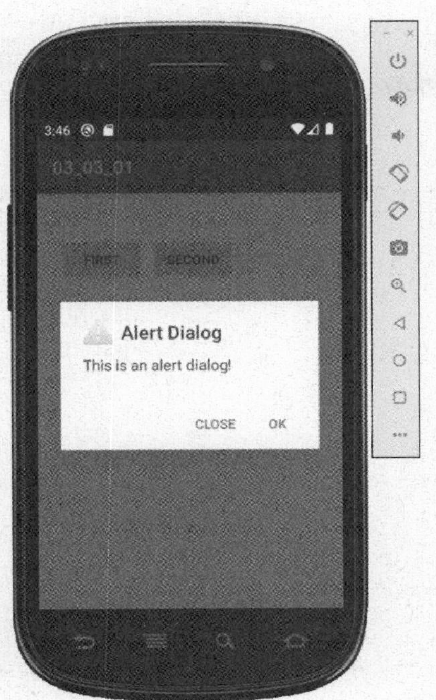

FIGURE 3-8: Display an alert dialog box onscreen.

1. **Right-click** `app\java\com.allmycode.p03_03_01` **and choose New⇨Kotlin File/Class.**

   You see the New Kotlin File/Class dialog box, shown in Figure 3-9.

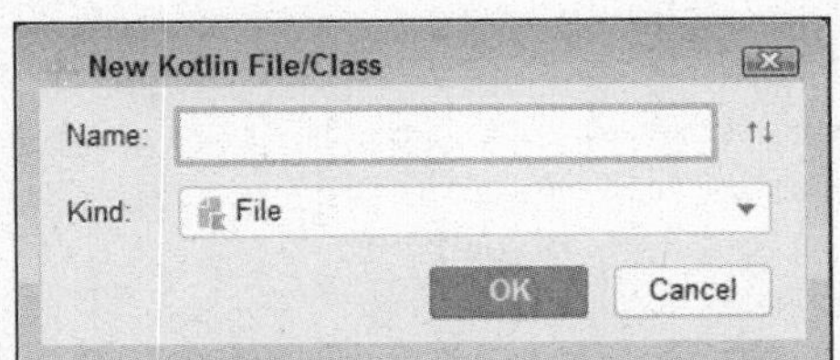

FIGURE 3-9: Create a dialog box fragment class.

2. **Type** FragmentDialog **in the Name field, choose Class in the Kind field, and click Finish.**

   Android Studio creates a new fragment class for you.

   The custom class will also need a layout file so you can design the interface.

3. **Right-click** `app\res\layout` **and choose New⇨Layout Resource File.**

   You see the New Resource File dialog box, shown in Figure 3-10.

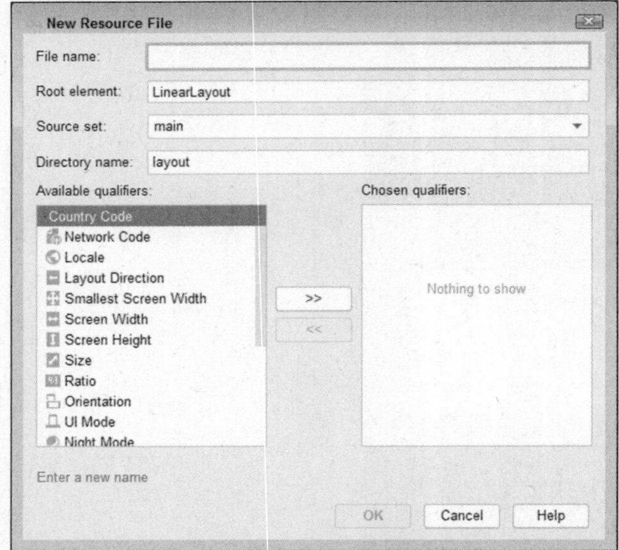

FIGURE 3-10: Design a layout for the dialog box fragment class.

4. **Type** fragment_dialog **in the File Name field and then click OK.**

   You see a new layout file added to the layout folder. Configure the layout so that it provides a basic dialog box design. Listing 3-1 shows the layout for this part of the example.

LISTING 3-1: Dialog Box Fragment Layout Specifics

```
<?xml version="1.0" encoding="utf-8"?>
<LinearLayout
xmlns:android="http://schemas.android.com/apk/res/android"
    android:layout_width="match_parent"
    android:layout_height="match_parent"
    android:gravity="center"
    android:orientation="vertical">

    <TextView
        android:id="@+id/DlgMessage"
        android:layout_width="wrap_content"
        android:layout_height="wrap_content"
        android:gravity="center"
        android:minWidth="250dp"
        android:text="@string/DlgMessageText"
        android:textSize="18sp"/>
```

```
    <Space
        android:layout_width="match_parent"
        android:layout_height="wrap_content"
        android:minHeight="10dp"/>

    <LinearLayout
        android:layout_width="match_parent"
        android:layout_height="match_parent"
        android:orientation="horizontal">
        <Space
            android:layout_width="wrap_content"
            android:layout_height="wrap_content"
            android:layout_weight="1"/>

        <Button
            android:id="@+id/BtnOK"
            android:layout_width="wrap_content"
            android:layout_height="wrap_content"
            android:onClick="@string/BtnOKClick"
            android:text="@string/BtnOKText"/>

        <Space
            android:layout_width="0dp"
            android:layout_height="wrap_content"
            android:layout_weight="1"/>

        <Button
            android:id="@+id/BtnCancel"
            android:layout_width="wrap_content"
            android:layout_height="wrap_content"
            android:onClick="@string/BtnCancelClick"
            android:text="@string/BtnCancelText"/>

        <Space
            android:layout_width="wrap_content"
            android:layout_height="wrap_content"
            android:layout_weight="1"/>
    </LinearLayout>

</LinearLayout>
```

5. **Add the code needed to create the `FragmentDialog` class in `FragmentDialog.kt`.**

   The design of this class is essentially the same as that of the `SpecialContent` class, with some small differences and some simplification as well. Listing 3-2 shows the code required for this class.

LISTING 3-2: Creating the `FragmentDialog` Class

```
package com.allmycode.p03_03_01

import android.content.Context
import android.os.Bundle
import android.view.LayoutInflater
import android.view.View
import android.view.ViewGroup
import androidx.fragment.app.DialogFragment
import com.allmycode.p03_03_01.R.layout.fragment_dialog
import kotlinx.android.synthetic.main.fragment_dialog.*

class FragmentDialog: DialogFragment() {
    override fun onCreate(savedInstanceState: Bundle?) {
        super.onCreate(savedInstanceState)

        val style = DialogFragment.STYLE_NORMAL
        val theme = R.style.ThemeOverlay_AppCompat_Dialog
        setStyle(style, theme)
    }

    override fun onAttach(context: Context?) {
        super.onAttach(context)
    }

    override fun onDetach() {
        super.onDetach()
    }

    override fun onCreateView(
        inflater: LayoutInflater,
        container: ViewGroup?,
        savedInstanceState: Bundle?
    ): View? {
```

```
        return inflater.inflate(fragment_dialog,
            container, false)
    }

    fun onBtnOKClick(view: View){
        DlgMessage.setText("Message Updated!")
    }

    fun onBtnCancelClick(view: View) {
        dismiss()
    }
    companion object{
        @JvmStatic
        fun newInstance() =
            FragmentDialog().apply {
            }
    }
}
```

Most of the code works as before. This shows a minimal class that supports two buttons: OK and Cancel. When the user clicks OK, the message shown on the dialog box changes to "Message Updated!" Clicking Cancel dismisses the dialog box.

REMEMBER

You can't directly access the buttons in the dialog box. You must add some special connectivity to `MainActivity`. If you don't add the connecting code, the app continuously stops and the error messages tell you that Android couldn't locate the required button click handler.

6. **Add the code required to create the dialog box and connect to the button handlers in the `FragmentDialog` class to `MainActivity.kt`.**

   You need to add the three functions shown in Listing 3-3.

LISTING 3-3: Adding Dialog Box Creation and Connectivity Code

```
fun onDlgFragmentClick(view: View) {
    val transaction =
        supportFragmentManager.beginTransaction()
    val MyDialog = FragmentDialog.newInstance()
    MyDialog.show(transaction, "FragmentDialog")
}
```

(continued)

Creating an Architecture

LISTING 3-3: *(continued)*

```
fun onBtnOKClick(view: View) {
    val MyDialog: FragmentDialog =
        supportFragmentManager.findFragmentByTag(
            "FragmentDialog") as FragmentDialog
    MyDialog.onBtnOKClick(view)
}

fun onBtnCancelClick(view: View) {
    val MyDialog: FragmentDialog =
        supportFragmentManager.findFragmentByTag(
            "FragmentDialog") as FragmentDialog
    MyDialog.onBtnCancelClick(view)
}
```

Notice how similar starting a dialog box fragment is to working with a standard fragment. However, make sure you assign a meaningful tag to the `MyDialog.show(transaction, "FragmentDialog")` call or you'll find interacting with the dialog box later to be difficult. Make certain to choose a unique tag.

REMEMBER

The button handlers both work the same, except for the fact that they're accessing different buttons. You have to specify the `FragmentDialog` type when creating the `MyDialog` object. You do this to make calling the button handlers possible after you gain access to the required fragment. The `findFragmentByTag()` function relies on the tag you specified earlier to locate the fragment of interest. After you have the desired fragment, you can simply call the required function within it.

At this point, you can run the app and try out the dialog box. Figure 3-11 shows a typical example of what you see. Now that you have the basics, you can create extremely flexible dialog boxes of any complexity. Try the OK and Cancel buttons. Also, try the Back button. The dialog box goes away. When you click the Back button with an Alert dialog box, nothing happens. This custom dialog box is placed on the backstack so that the user can interact with it in a manner that's closer to other app activities.

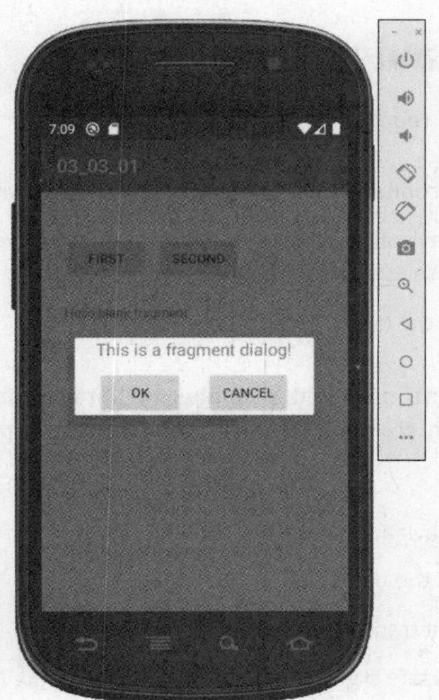

FIGURE 3-11: Displaying a custom dialog box fragment with interesting functionality.

Providing for Navigational Needs

Navigation is critical in an app if you want your user to get from point A to point B without becoming frustrated. You have to start by viewing navigation as another way to structure your app — this time with a workflow in mind.

Creating a single workflow isn't difficult; you just create a line of activities from a starting point to an ending point when the job is finished. It's when you have to start thinking about multiple workflows that things can get difficult. When you add multiple entry and ending points to the workflows, they can become horribly complex.

Using the navigational tools provided with Android Studio can make the task of creating navigation with multiple workflows in a complex app easier. You still have to use the tools to think about how the user will interact with your app, but at least the tools provide an aid to direct your thinking and see graphically how things will likely work. The following sections tell you in detail about navigation and the tools you need to ensure good navigation.

Creating the navigational graph

Navigation implies certain requirements in your app:

- The user can't get lost, confused, or frustrated when working with your app.
- Features like bottom navigation have to work well, and you have to ensure that the right button is selected as a default.
- The app must navigate the backstack in a uniform manner.

The `Navigation` component gives you a number of libraries and a plug-in that reduce the work needed to create good navigation in your app. These elements include:

- Support for common navigation patterns
- Automated handling of the backstack
- Automation of fragment transactions
- Implementation of typesafe argument passing
- Built-in transition animations
- Simplification of the deep-linking process
- Centralized storage of the navigational data

When working with the Navigation component, you automatically get support for activities and fragments. However, you can also add support for custom destinations. To create a complete navigational setup, you interact with the

- Navigation graph
- `NavHostFragment`
- `NavController`

This section begins by looking at the navigation graph. The navigation graph is contained in an XML file, but you can use a designer to interact with it. The "Navigating between activities and fragments" section of Chapter 1 of this minibook provides a brief overview of the navigation graph, but it's time to look at it in more detail, which means creating a test app named 03_03_02 using the same techniques as those in Book 1, Chapter 3. To keep things simple, continue to use the Empty Activity template as your starting point. After you create the project, you can start by defining the navigation graph using the following steps:

1. Open the `build.gradle (Module: app)` **file found in the** `Gradle Scripts` **folder and add the two implementations to the** `dependencies` **element, as shown in the following code.**

```
def nav_version = "1.0.0"
implementation "android.arch.
  navigation:navigation-fragment:$nav_version"
implementation "android.arch.
  navigation:navigation-ui:$nav_version"
```

WARNING

There are two `build.gradle` files. Make sure you open the correct one. Placing the entries in the wrong file will make your application fail.

Even though the `implementation` entries appear on multiple lines in the book, you place them on a single line in the file. The use of multiple lines in the book is to accommodate the book's page size.

The code uses a `def nav_version = "1.0.0"` entry to make updating the navigation version easier. You need both navigation fragment and navigation UI entries, as shown. The Kotlin version of these files is different from the Java version, so make sure you use the right version, depending on the language you use to code your app.

After adding the implementation entries, you see a message at the top of the editor telling you that the Gradle files have changed and you need to sync them with the IDE in order for the IDE to work properly, as shown in Figure 3-12.

FIGURE 3-12: Sync the IDE to your Gradle files before creating the app features.

activity_main.xml ×	MainActivity.kt ×	app ×
Gradle files have changed since last project sync. A project sync may be necessary for the IDE to work properly.		Sync Now

2. Click Sync Now at the top-right side of the editor window.

You see two build processes occur. The first rebuilds Gradle as part of the syncing process. The second rebuilds your app. These processes should take just a few minutes, but be sure to wait until they complete before you proceed with the next step.

3. Right-click the `app\res` **folder of the project and choose New⇨Android Resource File.**

You see the New Resource File dialog box, shown in Figure 3-13.

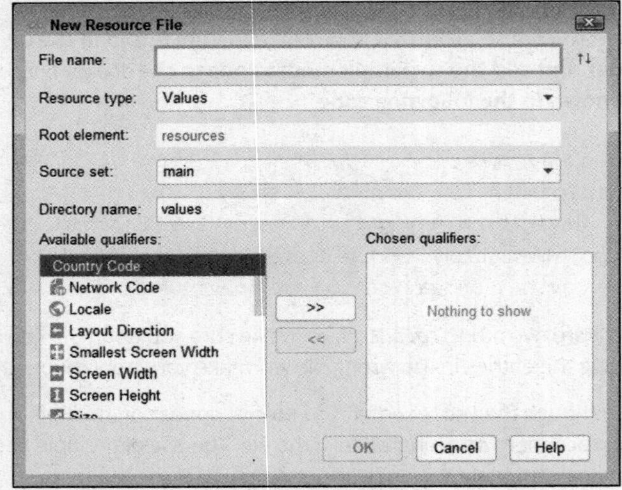

FIGURE 3-13: Create the navigation graph resource.

4. **Type** nav_graph **in the File Name field, choose Navigation in the Resource Type field, and click OK.**

   Note that the filename of your navigation graph must appear in lowercase and can contain the numbers 0 through 9 or the underscore.

   Android Studio creates an empty navigation graph for you. As with the layout files, the underlying file is an XML file, but you see the designer view shown in Figure 3-14, which makes working with the navigational elements easier.

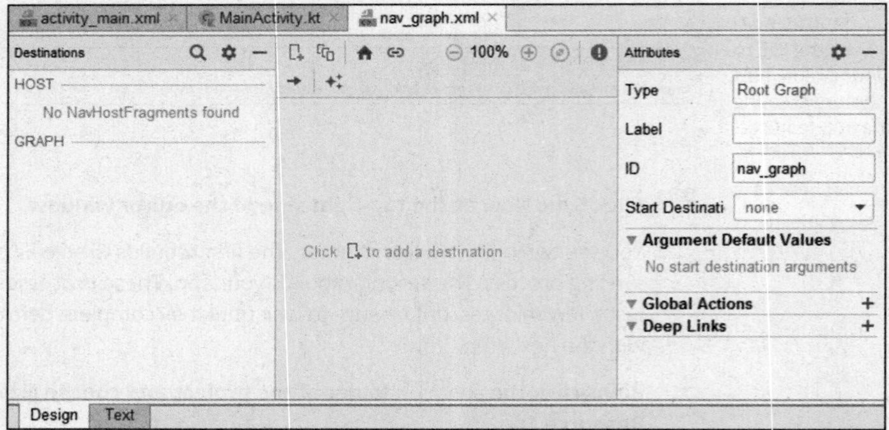

FIGURE 3-14: An empty navigation graph.

No destinations are currently listed in the Destinations pane on the left. That's because the `MainActivity` doesn't have a `NavHostFragment` in it. To make navigation work, you must add and configure this fragment. The next section shows you how.

Adding a NavHostFragment to your activity

A *navigation host* derives from the `NavHost` class, providing a container used to hold destinations. As the user moves around in the app, items are added to and removed from the navigation host. The most common implementation of `NavHost` is `NavHostFragment`.

REMEMBER

The `NavHostFragment` is designed for apps with a single main activity and multiple fragment destinations. When an app has multiple activities, each activity has its own navigation graph and associated `NavHostFragment`. To begin this part of the example, delete the `TextView` that comes with the template. Drag a `NavHostFragment` component from the `Containers` folder of the Palette to a place under the `ContraintLayout` in the Component Tree. You see a Navigation Graphs dialog box like the one shown in Figure 3-15, where you associate `nav_graph` with `MainActivity`. If you had multiple navigational graphs, you'd have to choose which one to use, but in this case, all you do is click OK.

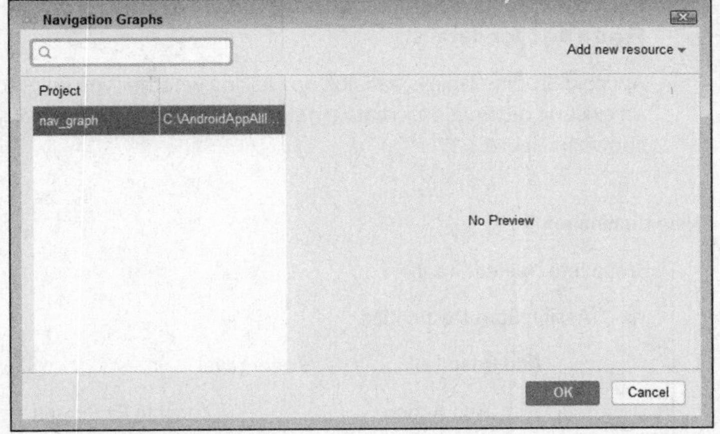

FIGURE 3-15: Associating an activity with a navigation graph.

WARNING

At this point, you see a new fragment added to `MainActivity`. A yellow indicator (some call it a *bang*) may appear next to the entry telling you that something is wrong. The code won't compile until you fix this error, so you need to click the yellow indicator. If you see another pane open that tells you about using a `FragmentContainerView` instead, a problem exists with the version of the navigation components you're using. The message thread at `https://stackoverflow.com/questions/58320487/using-fragmentcontainerview-with-navigation-component` offers a potential fix to the problem, but the easiest approach in most cases is to use an earlier, more stable, version of the navigation components.

Change the `id` value of the `NavHostFragment` to `nav_host` to make it easier to identify. After you successfully add the `NavHostFragment` to the `MainActivity`, you see `activity_main (nav_host)` added to the Host area of the Destinations portion of your `nav_graph`. Now it's time to add destinations to the navigation graph.

Adding destinations

You need to plot how you want your app to work. The graphic interface provided by the navigational graph helps you accomplish your goal. The best way to begin is to create destinations for each entry point in your app. You might have just one main entry point, but someone might also be able to enter your app from other locations to access specific features. In this example, the app has only one entry point that you can call `MainEntry`. The following steps tell how to add this destination.

1. **Click New Destination at the top of the navigation graph editor (see Figure 3-16 for details).**

   Android Studio displays a dialog box asking whether you want to search for an existing destination, create a new destination, or define a placeholder, as shown in Figure 3-17.

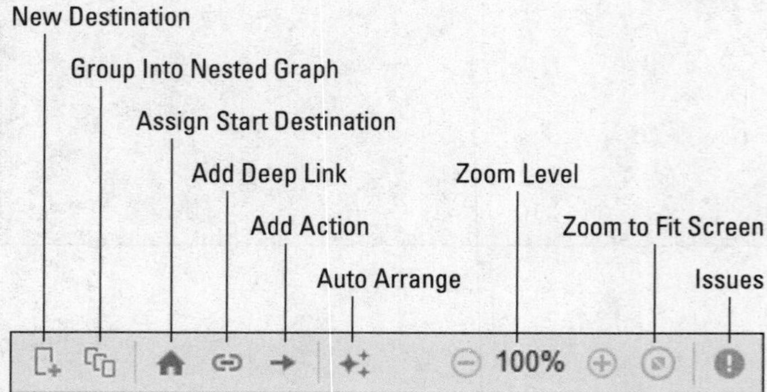

FIGURE 3-16: Navigation graph controls.

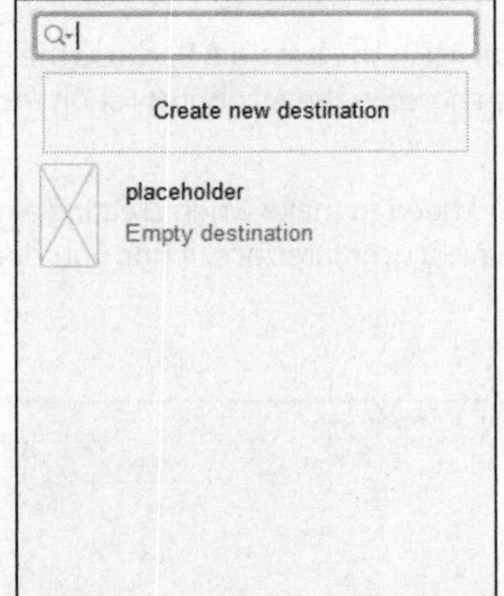

FIGURE 3-17: Choose a destination type for the navigation graph.

2. **Click Create New Destination.**

   You see the Configure Component dialog box, shown in Figure 3-18.

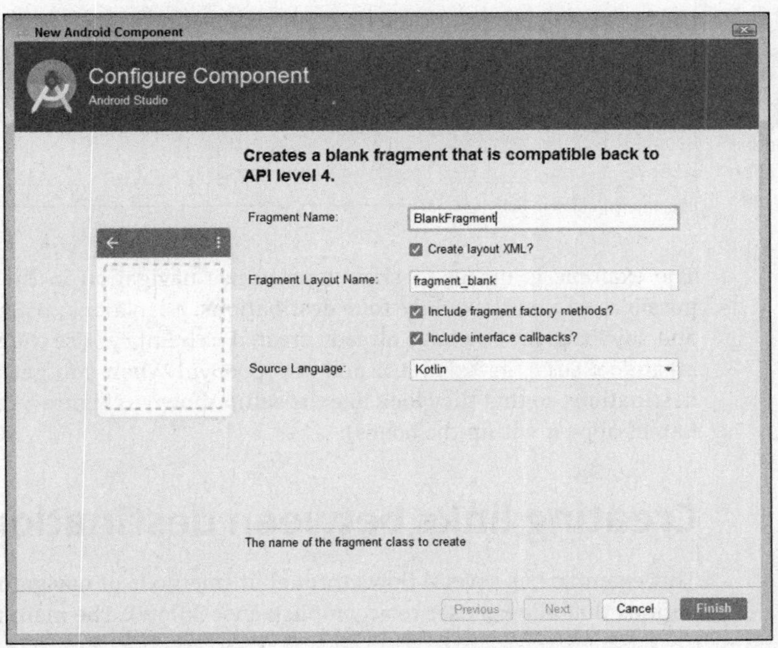

FIGURE 3-18: Define the new destination fragment.

3. **Type** mainEntry **in the Fragment Name field and click Finish.**

   Android Studio adds the new destination to the navigation graph for you, as shown in Figure 3-19. Notice that it automatically assigns it as the start destination (the home icon in the upper-left corner). You also see the destination added to the Graph list in the left side. Because the destination is selected, you see its attributes shown in the Attributes list on the right side of the display.

TIP

Generally, the only decision you need to make when creating a new fragment is whether the fragment will have a user interface. If not, you clear the Create Layout XML option.

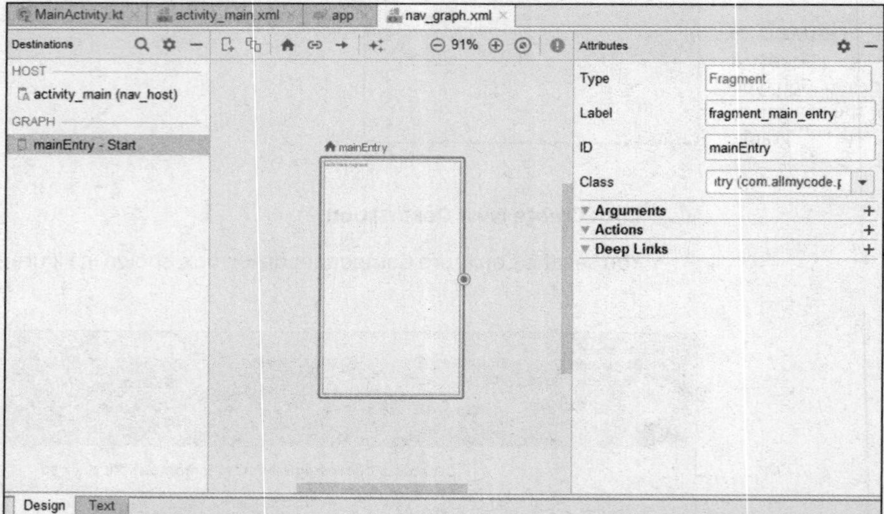

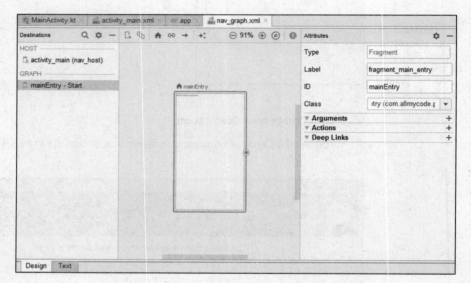

FIGURE 3-19: Seeing the fragment added to the navigation graph.

The example is meant to show how to use navigation in the simplest manner possible, so you have only four destinations: `mainEntry`, `doStuff`, `seeResults`, and `sayGoodbye`. You have already created `mainEntry`. Use the same technique to create `doStuff`, `seeResults`, and `sayGoodbye`. When you get done, arrange the destinations so that they look like the setup shown in Figure 3-20 (the destination names appear within the boxes).

Creating links between destinations

This example has several flows through it (methods of navigating between destinations that allow a user to accomplish a workflow). The main flow is

```
mainEntry->doStuff->seeResults->sayGoodbye
```

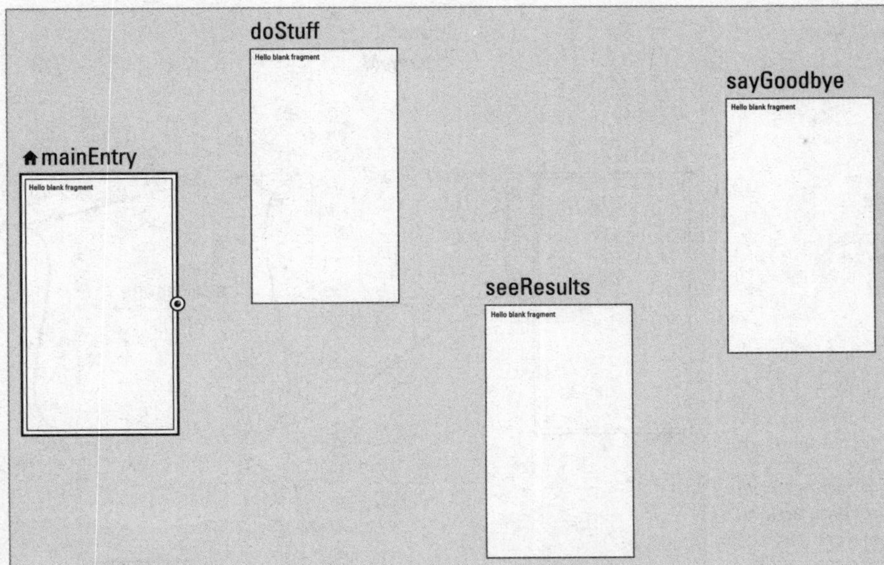

FIGURE 3-20: Arrange the destinations in a way that makes using them easy.

However, a user might not actually want to do something. The user's only need might be to see the current project progress, so a second flow is

```
mainEntry->seeResults->sayGoodbye
```

A third flow might take place when the user hasn't completed a project and plans to continue the next day. In this case, the flow is

```
mainEntry->doStuff->sayGoodbye
```

To add an initial action, you simply draw a line from one activity to another by clicking the starting activity and dragging to the destination activity. You can try it with `mainEntry` to `doStuff`. When you draw the line, you see an arrow points from `mainEntry` to `doStuff`. You can do the same thing with the other destinations in the main flow.

Adding the second and third flows works the same. You begin by selecting the initial destination and drawing a line from it to the second destination. When you get finished, you end up with a series of destinations connected with actions that look like the graph in Figure 3-21.

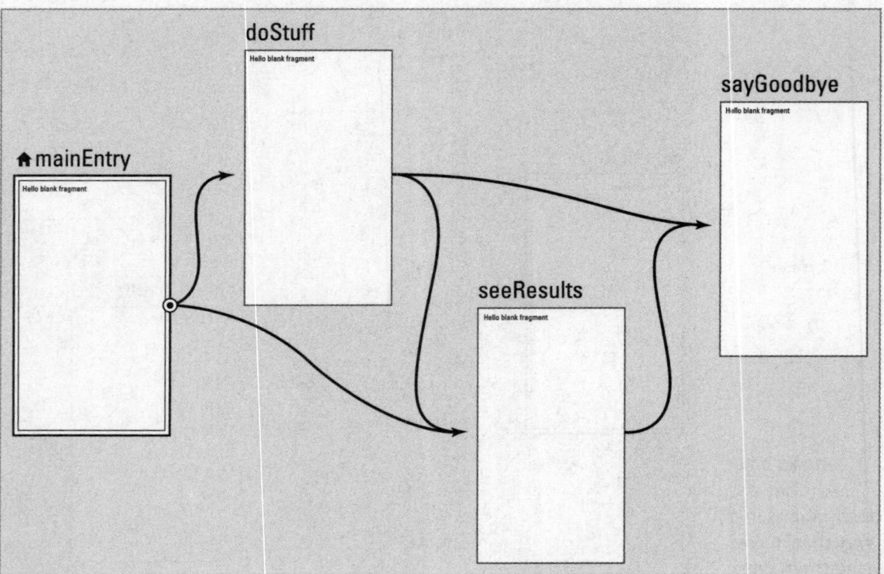

FIGURE 3-21: Create actions between each of the destinations.

Creating the required linkages

You might think that your app is ready to run at this point, but it isn't. A little previous knowledge and reading the automatically generated source code files can prove incredibly helpful if you don't want to spend an entire day trying to determine why your app won't run. To begin, you must modify the MainActivity class heading to look like this:

```
class MainActivity : AppCompatActivity(),
    MainEntry.OnFragmentInteractionListener,
    DoStuff.OnFragmentInteractionListener,
    SeeResults.OnFragmentInteractionListener,
    SayGoodbye.OnFragmentInteractionListener {
```

Then you have to implement the onFragmentInteraction() function, like this:

```
override fun onFragmentInteraction(uri: Uri) {
}
```

At this point, you could build and run your app to see the MainEntry fragment. Of course, you can't navigate anywhere, but at least your app will run. To navigate somewhere, you need some sort of an event, which is what buttons do best. However, now you have design decisions to make.

This example uses the same interface as the example created earlier in the chapter (see Figure 3-5), with the addition of a third button named Previous. However, you don't place the first buttons in a single location because the buttons change depending on the fragment you call. Consequently, these two buttons appear on each of the fragments in their correct location, while the third button, Previous, and the TextView, Caller, appear in activity_main.xml along with the NavHostFragment, like this:

```
<TextView
    android:id="@+id/Caller"
    android:layout_width="wrap_content"
    android:layout_height="wrap_content"
    android:layout_marginStart="24dp"
    android:layout_marginLeft="24dp"
    android:layout_marginTop="24dp"
    app:layout_constraintStart_toStartOf="parent"
    app:layout_constraintTop_toTopOf="parent"/>

<Button
    android:id="@+id/Previous"
    android:layout_width="wrap_content"
    android:layout_height="wrap_content"
    android:layout_marginStart="240dp"
    android:layout_marginLeft="240dp"
    android:layout_marginTop="48dp"
    android:onClick="@string/PreviousClick"
    android:text="@string/PreviousText"
    app:layout_constraintStart_toStartOf="parent"
    app:layout_constraintTop_toTopOf="parent"/>

<fragment
    android:id="@+id/nav_host"
    android:name=
      "androidx.navigation.fragment.NavHostFragment"
    android:layout_width="match_parent"
    android:layout_height="match_parent"
    app:defaultNavHost="true"
    app:navGraph="@navigation/nav_graph"/>
```

Each of the fragments will have entries similar to this one (except SayGoodbye, which has no entries):

```
<Button
    android:id="@+id/FirstLoc"
    android:layout_width="wrap_content"
    android:layout_height="wrap_content"
```

```
        android:layout_marginStart="24dp"
        android:layout_marginLeft="24dp"
        android:layout_marginTop="48dp"
        android:onClick="@string/FirstLocClick"
        android:text="@string/FirstLocText"/>
    <Button
        android:id="@+id/SecondLoc"
        android:layout_width="wrap_content"
        android:layout_height="wrap_content"
        android:layout_marginStart="120dp"
        android:layout_marginLeft="120dp"
        android:layout_marginTop="48dp"
        android:onClick="@string/SecondLocClick"
        android:text="@string/SecondLocText"/>
```

Remember the paths that the user can take. Because `SeeResults` always goes to `SayGoodbye`, it has only one button. You can provide a message that says goodbye in `SayGoodbye` so that it isn't empty.

Of course, now you need to wonder where the event-handling code goes. It all appears in `MainActivity.kt` because the `MainActivity` is actually hosting the fragments. In addition, you have fewer event handlers than you might initially think because the fragments don't require individual event handlers. Only the buttons need individual event handlers, so you can take care of the entire app's requirements using just four functions, as shown in Listing 3-4.

LISTING 3-4: Event Handlers Used to Control Movement between Fragments

```
fun onGoDoStuffClick(view: View){
    Caller.setText("Caller: MainEntry")
    val navController = Navigation.findNavController(
        this, R.id.nav_host)
    navController.navigate(
        R.id.action_mainEntry_to_doStuff)
}

fun onGoResultsClick(view: View){
    val navController = Navigation.findNavController(
        this, R.id.nav_host)
    val Fragments :NavHostFragment =
        supportFragmentManager.findFragmentById(
            R.id.nav_host) as NavHostFragment
    if(Fragments.childFragmentManager.fragments[0]
                is MainEntry) {
        Caller.setText("Caller: MainEntry")
```

```
                navController.navigate(
                    R.id.action_mainEntry_to_seeResults)
            } else {
                Caller.setText("Caller: DoStuff")
                navController.navigate(
                    R.id.action_doStuff_to_seeResults)
            }
        }

    fun onGoSayGoodbyeClick(view: View){
        val navController = Navigation.findNavController(
            this, R.id.nav_host)
        val Fragments :NavHostFragment =
            supportFragmentManager.findFragmentById(
                R.id.nav_host) as NavHostFragment
        if(Fragments.childFragmentManager.fragments[0]
                is SeeResults) {
            Caller.setText("Caller: SeeResults")
            navController.navigate(
                R.id.action_seeResults_to_sayGoodbye)
        } else {
            Caller.setText("Caller: DoStuff")
            navController.navigate(
                R.id.action_doStuff_to_sayGoodbye)
        }
    }

    fun onPreviousClick(view: View) {
        val navController = Navigation.findNavController(
            this, R.id.nav_host)
        val Fragments :NavHostFragment =
            supportFragmentManager.findFragmentById(
                R.id.nav_host) as NavHostFragment
        when (Fragments.childFragmentManager.fragments[0]) {
            is MainEntry -> Caller.setText("Caller: MainEntry")
            is DoStuff -> Caller.setText("Caller: DoStuff")
            is SeeResults -> Caller.setText("Caller: SeeResults")
            is SayGoodbye -> Caller.setText("Caller: SayGoodbye")
        }
        navController.navigateUp()
    }
```

Function `onGoDoStuffClick()` sets the tone for the other functions you see in Listing 3-4. It follows this basic routine:

WARNING

- Set the caller text so that the user can see the previous fragment name.
- Obtain access to the `NavController`, which actually manages the navigation between fragments.
- Use the `NavController` to navigate to the next fragment using the specific action required. Be aware that you must focus on actions, not destinations. Trying to use the wrong action to access the correct destination will still result in an app crash.

You have two ways to get to `SeeResults: MainEntry` and `DoStuff`. The `onGoResultsClick()` and `onGoSayGoodbyeClick()` functions obtain access to `NavHostFragment`, which is the container used to hold the fragments. Notice that you must type cast the call to `findFragmentById()` because you don't want just any fragment — you want the `NavHostFragment`. The `NavHostFragment` contains a list of all the `fragments` in the app, but the topmost fragment in the list is always the fragment that has focus, so you can verify the caller and take an action based on which caller is active.

A call to `onPreviousClick()` can happen in a number of ways, so it relies on a `when` (the Kotlin equivalent of a switch in other languages) to determine what text to display in `Caller`. However, the navigation is simpler in this case. Calling `navigateUp()` always takes you to the previous location.

This example creates a somewhat more complex version of the first example in this chapter using just one activity and four fragments. In many respects, the process of navigation is significantly easier, plus it's more flexible than the app in the first example. However, getting started is more time consuming, so this technique is best suited to projects that require relatively complex navigation.

Performing Background Tasks Using WorkManager

The `WorkManager` lets your app perform tasks in the background in a noncritical manner. You use it when you need to make sure that a task is performed but you aren't necessarily in a hurry to do it. The example in this section, 03_03_03, uses the same techniques as those in Book 1, Chapter 3. You use an Empty Activity as a starting point.

This example does a simple task: writing data to a text file in the background. To begin the process, you need to add permissions to your AndroidManifest.xml file, as shown here in bold:

```
<?xml version="1.0" encoding="utf-8"?>
<manifest
xmlns:android="http://schemas.android.com/apk/res/android"
    package="com.allmycode.p03_03_03">

    <application
        ...
    </application>
    <uses-permission
  android:name="android.permission.WRITE_EXTERNAL_STORAGE" />
    <uses-permission
  android:name="android.permission.READ_EXTERNAL_STORAGE" />
```

The user interface for this example consists of a single button named button that says "Write File." Success and failure messages appear as a Toast at the bottom of the emulator screen. The button handler code looks like this:

```
fun buttonOnClick(view: View) {
    viewModelStore.apply { applyCycle() }
    if (WorkManager.getInstance(this).getWorkInfosByTag(
        "Worker").isDone())
        Toast.makeText(this, "Completed Successfully!",
                       Toast.LENGTH_LONG)
    else
        Toast.makeText(this, "Failed!", Toast.LENGTH_LONG)
}
```

Calling viewModelStore.apply with the name of a function used to create and call the worker thread, applyCycle(), starts the whole process. The last part of the code checks to see whether the work is finished on return from the call; it might not be. Remember that the task is performed within the constraints you set for it, which may mean waiting until conditions are right.

The applyCycle() function has a number of tasks to perform. It creates an environment for the worker thread, creates the worker thread in a specific way, and then queues the worker thread to perform work. However, Android decides when the worker thread actually starts. Here's the code you need for this function, which appears in the `MainActivity` class:

```
internal fun applyCycle(){
    val requestCode = 1
    ActivityCompat.requestPermissions(this,
      arrayOf(
       android.Manifest.permission.WRITE_EXTERNAL_STORAGE,
       android.Manifest.permission.READ_EXTERNAL_STORAGE),
      requestCode)

    val oneTimeRequest =
      OneTimeWorkRequest.Builder(WriteFile::class.java)
        .addTag("Worker")
        .build()
    WorkManager.getInstance(this).enqueue(oneTimeRequest)
}
```

REMEMBER

You must call `requestPermissions()` in the activity, not in the worker class. The call will fail if you try to do it in the worker class. The mysterious `requestCode` is simply a number that the `requestPermissions()` function returns when it successfully obtains the required permissions. The example takes some shortcuts for the sake of clarity, but normally you want to check every permission and every return value.

The `OneTimeWorkRequest.Builder()` function performs a task just one time. Android supplies other builder functions that you can use to perform tasks on a scheduled or other basis. The required argument for this function is the class you want to use for the worker thread. You can also add things like tags and constraints to the request. When you have everything you want in the class, you call `build()` to complete the process. A call to `WorkManager.getInstance(this).enqueue()` places the request on the queue, which eventually calls the worker thread.

The majority of the essential code for this example appears in a `Worker` class that has a single function, doWork(). Here's what this class looks like:

```
class WriteFile(ctx: Context, params: WorkerParameters) :
  Worker (ctx, params) {
  override fun doWork(): Result {
    val permCheck = ContextCompat.checkSelfPermission(
       applicationContext,
       android.Manifest.permission.WRITE_EXTERNAL_STORAGE)
    if (permCheck == PackageManager.PERMISSION_DENIED)
       return Result.failure()
```

```
        val path = applicationContext.getDir("Data",
            Context.MODE_PRIVATE)
        val outFile = File(path, "Test.txt")
        if (!outFile.exists())
            outFile.createNewFile()
        outFile.writeText("This is a test!")
        outFile.outputStream().flush()
        outFile.outputStream().close()
        return Result.success()
    }
}
```

The code performs a minimal permissions check and returns `Result.failure()` if the permissions process somehow failed. Assuming that you do set up permissions correctly, you see a dialog box like the one shown in Figure 3-22 the first time you run the app.

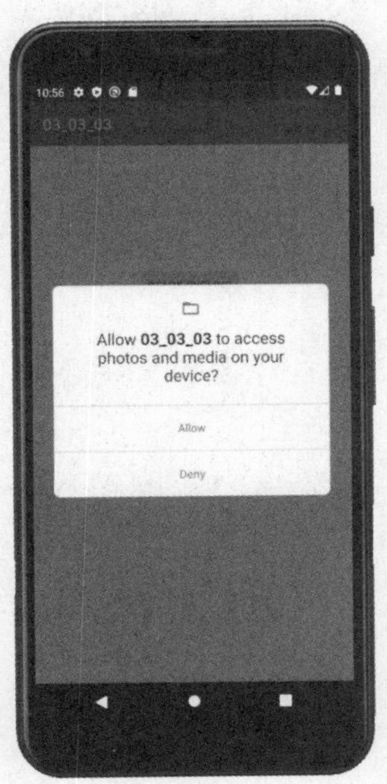

FIGURE 3-22: Writing a file requires user permissions.

Creating an Architecture

TIP

Even when working on the emulator, you must obtain a path to a location where you can write the application data. Otherwise, you get a read-only file system error message, even if you should otherwise be able to write the file. The way to ensure that you don't encounter the read-only file system message is to obtain the path using `applicationContext.getDir()`. You can then create a file object using the `File()` function. When the file doesn't exist, you must create it by calling `createNewFile()`.

The process of writing the file follows the same approach used in other environments. You write some text, flush the cache of data, and then close the file. If all this happens without problems, the code returns a result of `Result.success()`.

» **Ensuring that data remains safe and user accessible**

» **Working with various kinds of data**

» **Accessing special device features**

Chapter 4
Defining an App's Behavior

The best app in the world would be unnoticeable except for the service it provides. When you can focus completely on the task at hand and not even notice the app that is helping you perform that task, you have a really great app. The problem is that most apps don't come close to this ideal because they're actually quite intrusive. They shout, "Here I am. Aren't I truly amazing?" Even a well-behaved app does need to provide notifications at times, but those notifications should come only when they're welcome and expected. This chapter shows you effective ways to work with notifications, permissions, and preferences — three of the cornerstones of great app behavior.

Apps can perform a lot of work for you or help you perform the work yourself, but most of that work somehow involves data. Many users don't actually consider how much data they interact with daily, but the amount of data that people plow through is truly amazing. An app that can manage data seamlessly, in a manner that lets the user see a task rather than data, is providing an essential service. This chapter doesn't tell you everything there is to know about data, but you get an overview of some data management techniques specifically for Android.

Along with useful behaviors and data management, users also expect apps to provide access to the latest gadgetry installed on the host device. When you look through the specifications for modern smartphones, imagining how you might even use some of the gadgets is hard. It's sort of like having one of those knives with 20 different blades and attachments, including a wine cork puller. Having apps that not only access these gadgets without problem, but also suggest uses for them, is really something. This chapter delves into the common camera and the functionality that allows two users to share data, but you get enough of a feel for gadget access to add some gadget support to your new app as well.

Working with Notifications

Notifications are messages that appear outside the app's UI to tell you something potentially useful. However, many notifications are annoying rather than helpful. For example, you're in the middle of a meeting and your phone buzzes to tell you the weather has changed. It's absolutely lovely out there; don't you wish you were outside? After gritting your teeth, you turn off that message forever only to have another immediately pop up. Your grocery is running a special on plastic bags — you'd better get to the store now and buy scads of them! Once again, you turn off that notification . . . and another arrives. The notifications are annoying, and now you've missed something important that your boss said. (Something about people being let go? Was that it?)

The following sections talk about notifications of all sorts, hopefully useful ones rather than the other kind. You also learn about Do Not Disturb mode, which should actually mean no disturbances.

Understanding what notifications do

Notifications are supposed to communicate. They might tell you of an emergency or about the number of messages that an app is currently holding for you. A notification can tell you that a loved one urgently needs to talk with you or that you're going to be late paying a bill if you don't get going. So the type of communication, why you're receiving the communication, and the content of the communication can vary widely. However, you generally see notifications presented in one or these ways:

- An icon in the status bar
- A more detailed entry in the notification drawer
- A badge on the app's icon
- Automatically as a pop-up
- On the device's sign-in screen
- As a dialog box when you start the app

How a notification presents itself can often tell you something about the notification when the app uses notifications correctly. For example, you can see an icon on the status bar at all times, making it a good option for high-priority communication. The only higher-priority notification type might be the pop-up, which should be used rarely (or not at all) because it's incredibly annoying and intrusive. You'd use a pop-up only for the most essential information, like telling someone that her hair is on fire.

REMEMBER

A badge on the app's icon is the most appropriate form of notification for most purposes. The user will generally have to focus attention on the app to see it, so the notification tells the user that there's something important to know about without being intrusive. However, if your app provides a general service for the device as a whole, such as essential gadget support, placing the notification in the notification drawer is also an option.

Perhaps the most annoying notifications of all (except those that are telling you about a bona fide emergency, such as a meteor is about to fall on your head) are the ones that buzz the phone or flash the device's LED. In addition to running rampant on your screen, they're now distressing you in other ways that are almost certainly going to be noticed by other people, who will politely laugh behind your back. To avoid these and other well-intentioned but annoying, notifications check out the guide at `https://material.io/design/platform-guidance/android-notifications.html#usage`. The guidelines tell you about things you must avoid, such as cross-promotion of another product within the notification, or sending notifications from apps that the user has never opened, because they're strictly prohibited by the Google Play Store.

REMEMBER

Some notifications are required. For example, in Chapter 3 of this minibook, you see how to work with `WorkManager`. Because the background processes it creates can use both battery and data, you must provide a notification that the background process is running and its percentage of completion. The notification must also provide the means of stopping the background process should the need arise. This requirement also affects things like `DownloadManager`. The way you manage alarms with `AlarmManager` is somewhat different because there is an alarm, not a process, but you still need to provide some sort of notification — an icon in the status bar or a badge on the app so that the user knows the alarm is active and can stop it if necessary. You don't require a notification for background tasks, such as updating a progress bar (see the "Creating a test app" section of Chapter 2 of this minibook), because they remain active only while the app runs.

SPECIAL LOCK-SCREEN CONSIDERATIONS

Notifications generally appear on the lock screen, which means that anyone can see them even when the user isn't logged into the system. Making the notifications visible can save the user time when the notification is about the weather or a sale at a local store. However, other notifications should remain private, which is why you need to set the visibility level of sensitive notifications.

Android actually supports three visibility levels: public, private, and secret. Most notifications fall into the public category, letting the user see everything on the lock screen. Notifications that are a little more sensitive are private. The user sees basic information, such as the name of the app that created the notification and the app's icon. You can also include a hint as to what the notification is about, but not reveal the actual nature of the notification. Secret notifications never appear on the lock screen. The user must log into the system to see them and isn't aware of them until doing so.

Anatomy of a notification

A notification is a kind of highly formatted dialog box when displayed. There are differences, but if you start by viewing them as special dialog boxes as a developer, you can better understand some of the concepts behind them. The formatting consists of these items:

- **Heading:** The heading is a small strip at the top of the notification that acts as an identifier of notification intent and purpose. It contains these elements:
  - **App icon:** People readily identify apps that they commonly use by the app icon. For example, most people can identify Twitter and Facebook solely by the icons their apps use.
  - **App name:** Some organizations create more than one app but use similar icons for each app. The app name identifies a particular app.
  - **Header text (optional):** Header text is a short piece of information to identify the sender when multiple people, organizations, devices, or other sources use the same app for notifications. For example, the header might contain the email address of the sender.
  - **Time stamp:** Even though this element doesn't appear by default and Google claims that it's optional, it really isn't optional. The most annoying kind of notification is one that's two weeks old and no longer important. Keep your users happy; include a time stamp.

TIP

Fortunately, you don't have to rely on a time stamp alone. You have the ability to programmatically dismiss an outdated notification before the user sees it. This is especially important when dealing with notifications in the notification drawer.

- **Expand indicator:** This is a little down-pointing arrow that tells the recipient that there is more information. Clicking the arrow expands the content to display the additional content (at which point the down-pointing arrow becomes an up-pointing arrow so that the user can close the notification).

» **Primary content:** The primary content area contains the message you want to convey. It normally contains these elements:

- **Content header:** The content header should appear in slightly larger and usually bold text than the rest of the notification. It should provide an extremely brief bit of text that you use to convince the viewer to read more.

  The header can also indicate multiple notifications from a single app. For example, when working with an email app, the content header can indicate the number of pending emails in the user's Inbox.

- **Content text:** This is the actual message. You should be brief enough to give the viewer an idea of why the notification is important without having to expand it. Of course, you can always provide an expand indicator if you need additional for detailed content.

» **Origin indicator:** This is a relatively large icon that tells you about the message origin. Although you often see someone's picture here, some notifications provide organization logos or other indicators of the notification source. The idea is that if you see the face of a friend staring at you from a notification, you're more likely to read it.

» **Actions:** You always need an action to get rid of the notification. Nothing is more annoying than to have a notification that hangs around like gum on your shoes. Other actions you might include are the ability to reply to the notification; open the app that generated the notification; call the person who sent the notification; or go to a website to obtain additional information. The point is not to add a confusing array of actions that have nothing to do with the notification.

One important action is the hierarchy indicator. When an app sends out multiple notifications, but these notifications represent a hierarchy, such as a message thread, the hierarchy indicator tells how many child notifications there are for the current notification so that the user can decide whether to drill down into the hierarchy to learn more.

You can also make one of the actions be a short response from the user. The user can type text into the notification to provide a short answer to a question, such as yes or no to an invitation to dinner.

REMEMBER

You need to be a good citizen when it comes to notifications. The user should have the ability to tell your app that it doesn't need to send additional notifications. Precisely how the user configures an app to stop notifications depends on the version of Android used, but it's essential to heed any user settings.

Assigning a channel to your notification

When viewing a television, you select a channel to determine what will appear on the screen. The channel is important for this reason. Likewise, when you create Android notifications, you also assign a channel to each unique notification. For example, if your email app includes notifications for new mail and for upcoming appointments, you need two channels: one for each notification. The use of separate channels means that users can block just one notification type and keep the rest.

When deciding on how to create channels, consider these issues:

- When developing notifications, consider whether some notifications belong to a single, well-defined group, such as download completion. After all, it doesn't matter what you're downloading; the important issue is that the download has completed.
- Also a good idea is to use the same importance level for all notifications you have grouped together. If a particular download requires a higher importance, you should provide a separate channel for it.
- Always create channel groupings when the number of channels your app supports exceeds ten. You don't want to bury your user in unique notifications that end up not being all that unique.
- Use the same channels for all users when your app supports multiple users.
- Link your channels to specific app settings so that the user can control channels individually.

Android actually supports two scopes of channel. You always configure an app-specific channel for your notification. In addition to the app-specific channel, you can create a system-wide notification channel by assigning your notification to one of the predefined categories using `NotificationCompat.Builder.setCategory()`:

- `CATEGORY_CALL`: An incoming call or other life communication request (as potentially differentiated from an email)
- `CATEGORY_MESSAGE`: Any incoming direct message such as SMS or an instant message

- CATEGORY_EMAIL: Any incoming asynchronous message, usually in bulk form, such as an email
- CATEGORY_EVENT: Any sort of an event, such as one found on a calendar
- CATEGORY_PROMO: A promotion or advertisement
- CATEGORY_ALARM: An indicator from an alarm or timer (including one from an outside source, such as your home alarm)
- CATEGORY_PROGRESS: An indicator that a long-running background process has achieved a particular milestone or goal
- CATEGORY_SOCIAL: Any type of social network, resource sharing, or information update communication
- CATEGORY_ERROR: A notice that something bad has happened to an app, background operation, authentication, device, or something else equally regrettable in its effects
- CATEGORY_TRANSPORT: Any type of notification (not necessarily bad) related to the media transport control for playback

WARNING

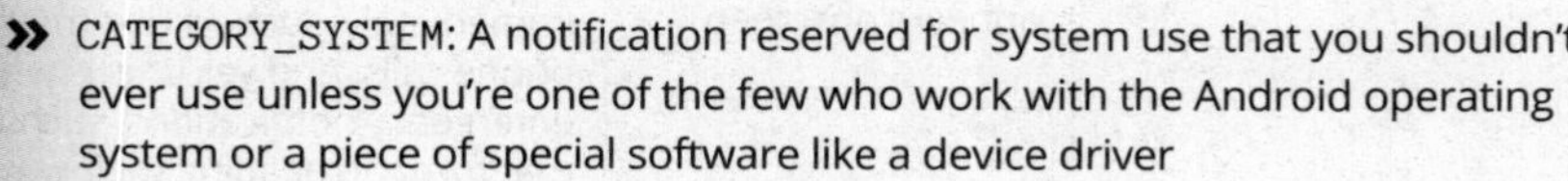

- CATEGORY_SYSTEM: A notification reserved for system use that you shouldn't ever use unless you're one of the few who work with the Android operating system or a piece of special software like a device driver

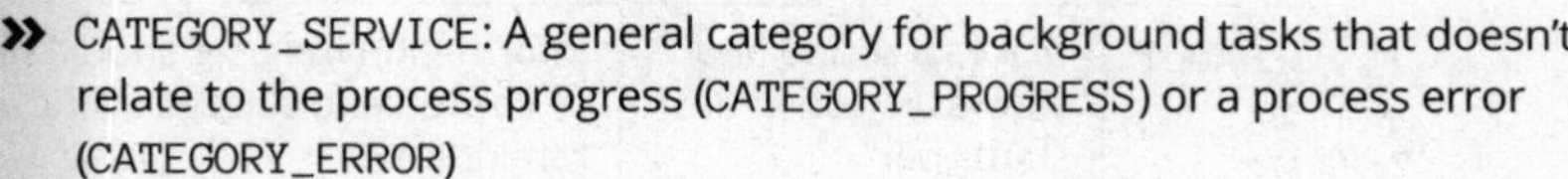

- CATEGORY_SERVICE: A general category for background tasks that doesn't relate to the process progress (CATEGORY_PROGRESS) or a process error (CATEGORY_ERROR)
- CATEGORY_RECOMMENDATION: A recommendation of any sort, including information like news stories that a person might want to read or sources of additional information for working with an app (not to be confused with a promotion, which is covered by CATEGORY_PROMO)
- CATEGORY_STATUS: An update about the status of an app, device, or other items of interest (such as a notice telling you that device support for a new SD card is installed)

Setting the notification importance

Some notifications are more important than others, and notifications come with these importance-level restrictions:

- **Default:** When creating your notification, you can assign an importance level to each channel based on how important you feel the notification is to the user. This is the default importance level.

» **User-assigned:** The problem with assigning a default importance level comes in when you feel that a notification is at one level and the user has a different opinion. Obviously, the user should win, which means that the user should be allowed to change the importance level in Settings.

» **Programmatically assigned:** The default level remains in effect until the user changes it. After the user has changed the default level through Settings, you may lower the importance level but you may not increase it through your app. This restriction keeps the app from deciding that the user really does need to see the notification as important after all.

Android reacts differently to your notification based on the notification level you assign to it, so choosing the correct notification level is important. Choosing the wrong notification level can prove extremely annoying to the user, not to mention interrupt something that's actually more important. Here are the importance levels:

Level	What Happens	Uses
`HIGH`	Makes a sound and appears onscreen	Information that the user must act upon immediately, such as text messages, alarms, and phone calls. And yes, this is where you put those emergency notifications, such as alerting users to that tornado heading their way.
`DEFAULT`	Makes a sound and shows an icon in the status bar	Information the user should review as soon as convenient, such as traffic alerts and task reminders.
`LOW`	Nothing except an icon in the status bar	Content the user may or may not want to review from apps the user has subscribed to as well as noncritical invitations from friends (such as an impromptu party).
`MIN`	A badge on the app, or the notification simply appears when the user opens the app	Content that the user is less likely to act upon immediately, even when opening the app, such as pointing out interesting app features, describing points of interest in a town, weather updates, and promotional content.

Considering the notification types

There are two kinds of notifications. Both of them should be optional and allow the user to opt in, opt out, or pause the notifications as needed. However, most developers view the transactional notifications as somewhat required depending on what sort of information they convey. Here's an overview of notification types:

- **Transactional:** Transactional notifications require instant action on the part of the recipient. You can group them according to these needs:
  - **Immediate interaction:** Normally this is viewed as human-to-human contact, such as a telephone call or the need to perform a particular task with another person, but you could just as easily be interacting with a computer. For that matter, the interaction might be completely automated, such as a message sent to a first responder. The point is that the need is immediate.
  - **Functional requirements:** These notifications might tell you about a pending appointment, the status of your flight, or other issues that help you function better as a person. The notification could also come from your home's alarm system or tell you that a camera near your home has detected movement. The point again is that the need to view the data is immediate: You can't put off detecting a burglar or reacting to a fire.
  - **Device interaction, management, and control:** These sorts of notifications help you deal with apps like your music player, or they help you decide what to do when you've taken a picture with your camera. You also rely on these notifications to tell you about the state of apps running in the background.
- **Nontransactional:** Nontransactional notifications are informative, but you don't necessarily have to see them right away. Your app should make these notifications optional in all cases, and there are other rules you must follow, such as not providing a notification at all until the user has opened the app the first time. You can group such notifications according to these needs:
  - **App maintenance and upgrade:** You can inform the user about new versions of your app or updates that are available for your app. Also, you can provide noncritical notifications of app behavior issues and so on.
  - **Usage tips:** Some apps offer usage tips so that users can have a better experience when working with them.
  - **Surveys and other input:** App developers work hard to give you a great app experience and may ask you to rate their app or fill out a survey.
  - **Hardware updates:** After installing a new piece of hardware, you may see a notification that tells you about how the hardware will make your device better or that the operating system has installed support for it.

Relying on notification updates

Your user doesn't want to be bombarded by notifications, especially when one notification is simply an update of another notification that you sent earlier.

Fortunately, you can update a notification so that a single notification serves the purpose. Update strategies for some notification types are obvious: A progress notification can simply update the progress bar it contains. However, when working with other notification types, you can adopt one of these strategies for updates:

- Reissue the existing notification with modified content.
- Use the `Inbox` style of notification for things like conversations or traffic updates (see `https://developer.android.com/reference/android/app/Notification.InboxStyle` for a discussion of `Notification.InboxStyle`).
- Rely on a notification group with an associated summary. (The system uses this option even if you don't specify a group after the app sends four or more of the same kind of notification.)

Do Not Disturb mode

Users rely on Do Not Disturb mode to keep them from looking at their device at inconvenient times, such as when the boss is talking about a promotion or they're proposing marriage. Of course, if your app generates notifications during this time and it isn't important, the user is likely to be incredibly unhappy. A user has a number of options for setting a Do Not Disturb mode configuration, but the article at `https://www.digitaltrends.com/mobile/do-not-disturb-mode-in-android/` gives you a good idea of what they are.

REMEMBER

As a developer, you can choose to ignore the Do Not Disturb mode settings with certain restrictions. When assigning your notification to the `CATEGORY_ALARM`, `CATEGORY_REMINDER`, `CATEGORY_EVENT`, or `CATEGORY_CALL` system-wide channel categories, Android determines whether to disturb a user, even when in Do Not Disturb mode, based on the user's settings. The user still has final say over whether your app can disrupt Do Not Disturb mode, so you shouldn't count on a notification being received at any particular time.

Creating a notification

You create a notification to tell the user about something special. Android uses a four-step process to accomplish this task:

1. Create a notification channel using the guidelines in the "Assigning a channel to your notification" section of the chapter.
2. Register the notification channel with Android.

3. Create a notification using the guidelines outlined in the "Anatomy of a notification" section, earlier in this chapter.

4. Send a notification using `NotificationManager`.

To get started in creating a notification, create a new app project named 03_04_01 using the same techniques as those in Book 1, Chapter 3. Use an Empty Activity as a starting point. However, because of the way notifications work in newer versions of Android, you must set a minimum API level of 26. This example requires just one button, named `SendNotification`.

Making an icon

One of the problems that seem to plague Android developers is getting their icon to display properly, if at all. You must provide an icon with your notification or the app won't run, so putting off the icon issue until later won't work.

A common issue is that the icon is the wrong size. The website at `https://www.creativefreedom.co.uk/icon-designers-blog/android-4-1-icon-size-guide-made-simple/` has a full list of icon sizes. The best way to go for testing purposes is to create a 24-x-24-pixel icon. You can always create other sizes to support other devices later, but the 24-x-24-pixel icon will work with everything.

TIP

A more difficult issue to deal with than icon size is that the icon background must be transparent. Depending on your graphics application, you may need to set a special transparent configuration option when creating a new file. The image itself will usually show some sort of pattern to let you know that the background is transparent, as shown in Figure 4-1. If your graphics application supports both raster and vector graphics, you must configure the icon for a raster setting. You also need to know that any color you use in creating the icon won't show up when you see it in Android, as you see later in the chapter.

FIGURE 4-1: An icon with a transparent background.

Creating the notification channel

Placing the code for creating a notification channel in a separate function is a good idea because you'll use this function repeatedly while your app runs if you issue notifications regularly. The following code shows a basic createNotificationChannel() function that offers a little flexibility, such as whether to show a badge, but presets other features, such as the notification source:

```
fun createNotificationChannel(
    context: Context, importance: Int, showBadge: Boolean,
    name: String, description: String) {

    if (Build.VERSION.SDK_INT < Build.VERSION_CODES.O) {
        Toast.makeText( this, "API Too Old",
            Toast.LENGTH_LONG)
        return
    }

    val channelId = "${context.packageName}-$name"
    val channel = NotificationChannel(channelId, name,
        importance)
    channel.description = description
    channel.setShowBadge(showBadge)

    val notificationManager = context.getSystemService(
        NotificationManager::class.java)
    notificationManager.createNotificationChannel(channel)
}
```

This createNotificationChannel() function is designed for using with Android API versions 26 and up — the Android-O notification (see https://medium.com/exploring-android/exploring-android-o-notification-channels-94cd274f604c for details). You should use this notification type unless you absolutely have to support older devices. The first part of the createNotificationChannel() function checks whether the caller has an Android-O capability. If not, the example displays a Toast and exits. At some point, you need a better strategy for a production app, but this strategy works for now.

The next steps begin to configure the notification channel. You need a channelId, which is usually the package name and the name of the channel (not the notification). This setting is the in-app channel, not the system-wide channel setting.

The code calls on the NotificationChannel() constructor to create the channel, which includes the NotificationManagerCompat importance level, such as NotificationManagerCompat.IMPORTANCE_DEFAULT. To finish the channel setup, the code defines whether to show a badge and provides a description. The call to `notificationManager.createNotificationChannel()` completes the process of creating a channel based on the characteristics given. To use this function, you add the following code that appears in bold to the app's `onCreate()` function.

```
override fun onCreate(savedInstanceState: Bundle?) {
    super.onCreate(savedInstanceState)
    setContentView(R.layout.activity_main)

    createNotificationChannel(this,
        NotificationManagerCompat.IMPORTANCE_DEFAULT,
        false, getString(R.string.app_name),
        "App Notification Channel")
}
```

Defining and sending a notification

Using the notification channel to actually send a notification comes next. The `onSendNotificationClick()` function handles a user click from the button, as shown here.

```
fun onSendNotificationClick(view: View) {
    val name = getString(R.string.app_name)
    val channelId = "${this.packageName}-$name"

    val notificationBuilder = NotificationCompat.Builder(
        this, channelId).apply {
        setSmallIcon(R.drawable.pizza)
        setContentTitle("Your Pizza is Ready")
        setContentText("Get ready to eat a pizza!")
        setStyle(NotificationCompat.BigTextStyle()
            .bigText("Get ready to eat a pizza!"))
        priority = NotificationCompat.PRIORITY_DEFAULT
        setAutoCancel(true)

        val intent = Intent(applicationContext,
            MainActivity::class.java)
        intent.flags = Intent.FLAG_ACTIVITY_NEW_TASK or
                Intent.FLAG_ACTIVITY_CLEAR_TASK
        val pendingIntent = PendingIntent.getActivity(
            applicationContext, 0, intent, 0)
        setContentIntent(pendingIntent)
    }
```

```
    val notificationManager = this.getSystemService(
        NotificationManager::class.java)
    notificationManager.notify(5,
        notificationBuilder.build())
  }
```

REMEMBER

Even though some elements of this process look similar to those used to create a channel, what you're really building is a notification, so you still begin by performing tasks like getting the app name and the package name to create a `channelId`.

The `notificationBuilder` object doesn't actually send the notification; instead, it builds the notification so that you can send it. To start the building process, you call `NotificationCompat.Builder()` and supply it with the current context and the `channelId`. The call to `apply` begins defining the notification message. All the elements shown in the code are essential to this notification template. If you leave out the call to `setSmallIcon()`, for example, the code will fail with an exception. This is a default priority notification, so you use the `NotificationCompat.PRIORITY_DEFAULT` setting. The notification also automatically cancels after a time.

The `Intent` is essential as well. This is a basic notification, so this intent merely opens the app's `MainActivity` when the user clicks the notification in the notification drawer. Even if the app is already running, the `MainActivity` will receive focus. Clicking the notification also clears it.

All this code goes toward creating a notification that you haven't sent yet. To send the notification, the code begins by creating a `NotificationManager` object. It then calls `notificationManager.notify()` with the number of the notification and the actual notification object. The notification number is for the app's use in updating the notification later; Android doesn't care what number you assign. Notice that you must call `notificationBuilder.build()` to actually create the notification. When this process is complete, you see a notification on the status bar like the one shown in Figure 4-2.

REMEMBER

The first thing you should notice about the P (for pizza) icon on the status bar is that it's white. It has no color as it does in Figure 4-1. If the background of your icon is colored, even a different color from the foreground, what you see is a white square, not an icon. This is why you must make the background of your icon transparent.

When the user pulls out the notification drawer, the notification content can be seen, as shown in Figure 4-3. The content is rudimentary, but when you click the notification, you see the `MainActivity` as expected, and the notification goes away.

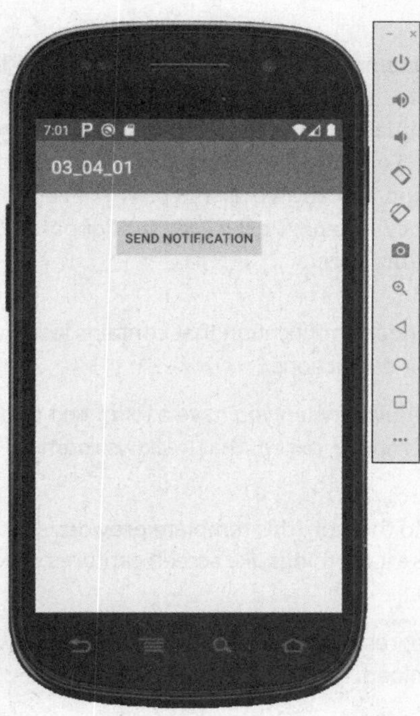

FIGURE 4-2: Seeing the notification on the status bar.

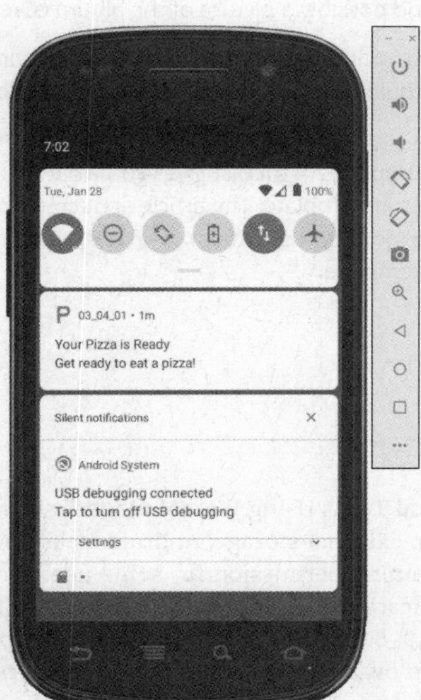

FIGURE 4-3: The notification as it appears in the notification drawer.

Figure 4-3 shows a basic example of just one template, the big text template, as defined by the call to `NotificationCompat.BigTextStyle()`. Android provides more than one template to use for notifications, and you should choose the most appropriate type. To use other styles, you simply choose a different `NotificationCompat` function (as shown at `https://developer.android.com/reference/android/support/v4/app/NotificationCompat`). Here's an overview of the various notification templates:

- **Standard:** This is the standard notification that contains just a short amount of information and one or two actions.
- **Big text:** You use this template when you have a lot of text to display. It looks similar to the standard template, except that it allows room for a lot more information.
- **Big picture:** In addition to the icon, this template provides space for a picture of some type. You can use it for things like screen captures or to see a picture that someone sent you.
- **Progress:** Contains a progress bar that you can update to show the progress of something like a download.
- **Media:** Used to control media playing in the background. You see the standard VCR controls and possibly a picture of the album cover.
- **Messaging:** This template includes a picture of the person sending the message. The message could be a text, but it has potential for other uses as well.
- **Custom:** If none of the templates in this list gives you what you need, you can always try to create a custom template. The article at `https://developer.android.com/training/notify-user/custom-notification` describes how to create a custom template.

Getting Permission

The "Performing Background Tasks Using WorkManager" section of Chapter 3 of this minibook writes data to external storage. Android locks down the system, so you often find yourself obtaining permission for some need. For example, if you have a time-sensitive notification that you want to display in full-screen mode, you must have the `USE_FULL_SCREEN_INTENT` permission to do it. The following sections provide you with an overview of how to work with permissions. Many of the book examples require permissions so that you can see them in use.

Considering permission use

No matter what you want permission to do, you follow the same set of steps to obtain and verify the permission:

1. Add a permission entry to `AndroidManifest.xml`. The problem is that you often need more than one permission. In the `WorkManager` example in Chapter 3, you need permission to both read and write external storage because part of the process verifies that the file doesn't currently exist, which requires reading.

2. Use `ActivityCompat.requestPermissions()` to request the permission in your app code. When working with multiple permissions, you can make a single request using an array of permissions.

3. Verify that the permission is granted using `ContextCompat.checkSelfPermission()`. You may think you have permission when you really don't. Error messages during the app run sometimes hide permissions issues in some other form, such as by saying a file system is read-only when the real problem is not having write permission.

Getting the permission is generally not hard unless you request something at the system level or something that is particularly dangerous. However, whether you should ask for the permission in the first place can be difficult to decide. Here are some best practices to consider:

- Obtain only the permissions you absolutely must have. If possible, try to find other ways to perform the task that don't require the permission.
- Use libraries that require as few permissions as possible. When you use a library, you also inherit the library's permissions requirements.
- Consider precisely how you use the permission so that you can make a case for doing so with the user. Android will ask the user about granting certain permissions. A user who doesn't have enough information can't make an informed decision.
- Make any access to anything outside the app apparent. For example, when you download or save a file, display a message saying that you're performing these tasks.

Anything you can do to keep the user, the app, the device, and the data safe will make it easier for you to maintain a good reputation and obtain better reviews. More important, users can revoke permissions at any time, so it pays to be a good citizen. If the user revokes a needed permission, your app will suffer a loss of functionality, which is why you should always verify that a permission is available before using it and then act accordingly.

TIP

It pays to test your app in an environment where the user hasn't granted one or more permissions or revoked them after granting them. Otherwise, you can't be sure that your app won't crash due to a lack of permissions you thought you had.

Configuring permissions in Android Manifest.xml

The act of gaining permission to do something starts with the `AndriodManifest.xml` file. You include a `<uses-permission>` element in the `<manifest>` element rather than the `<application>` child element. A typical entry appears as an attribute of the `<uses-permission>` element, like this:

```
android:name="android.permission.WRITE_EXTERNAL_STORAGE"
```

Including the entry in `AndroidManifest.xml` isn't enough, however. You must also include a call to `ActivityCompat.requestPermissions()` with an array of permissions, like this one:

```
android.Manifest.permission.WRITE_EXTERNAL_STORAGE
```

The form of both permission entries is similar. You obtain the names of the permissions you need from `https://developer.android.com/reference/android/Manifest.permission`. When you look at the details of a permission, you find notes about usage. For example, you don't need the WRITE_EXTERNAL_STORAGE permission to write files in the application-specific directories returned by a call to `Context.getExternalFilesDir()` or `Context.getExternalCacheDir()` when working with API level 19 or above.

REMEMBER

One of the most important entries in the permission documentation is the entry entitled Protection Level. This entry tells you how Android views a particular permission and what is likely to happen with regard to user interaction when you request it. Android supports four protection levels, three of which you see used in third-party apps:

- **Normal:** Covers areas where you need to access resources outside the app's sandbox, but the resource is unlikely to affect user privacy or the workings of other apps. For example, when you request access to time or time zone information, you have little chance of a security breach. The system grants this level of permission when it installs the app and the user isn't alerted to the need for the resource access.
- **Signed:** To use a signed permission, your app must have a certificate that is signed by the same app that defines the permission. In other words, the other

app must trust your app to grant this permission, and there is a chance that your app could interfere in some way with the other app.

REMEMBER

Some signed permissions aren't meant for use by third-party apps. Of course, documentation being what it is at times, you might find that you don't quite realize that you're not supposed to use the resource in question. This is a good place to look for additional information when you can't solve a permissions problem in other ways.

- **Dangerous:** Any permission that could cause a loss of user permission, damage data stored on the local media, interfere in some minor way with the underlying operating system, or interfere with other apps is dangerous. To use a dangerous permission, you must obtain user approval. The user sees a dialog box that tells about the permission and asks whether the user wants to grant or deny the permission. The example in the "Performing Background Tasks Using WorkManager" section of Chapter 3 of this minibook uses a dangerous permission. You can also read more about dangerous permission prompts at `https://developer.android.com/guide/topics/permissions/overview#dangerous-permission-prompt`.
- **Special:** Some permissions, such as `SYSTEM_ALERT_WINDOW` and `WRITE_SETTINGS`, are so sensitive that your app should avoid using them. These settings can affect the underlying operating system and cause other problems for the user. If your app needs one of these permissions, the system displays a detailed management screen to the user instead of the usual permissions dialog box. The user must grant permission. In some cases, the system will simply deny a special permission because the permission isn't available to third-party apps under any condition.

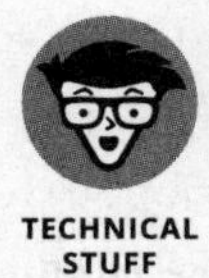

TECHNICAL STUFF

In addition to the special screen and enhanced system monitoring, a special permission generally requires special permission check and usage calls. For example, if you want to use the `WRITE_SETTINGS` permission, you must check whether the user has granted permission by calling `Settings.System.canWrite()`. Be sure you understand any special requirements for using a special permission before attempting to request one.

Complying with User Preferences

Your app has to interact with the user of the app to ensure that it works as anticipated. In some cases, such as notifications, the system performs this task for you, as shown in Figure 4-4. Using these system-supplied settings, the user can choose not to receive notifications from your app.

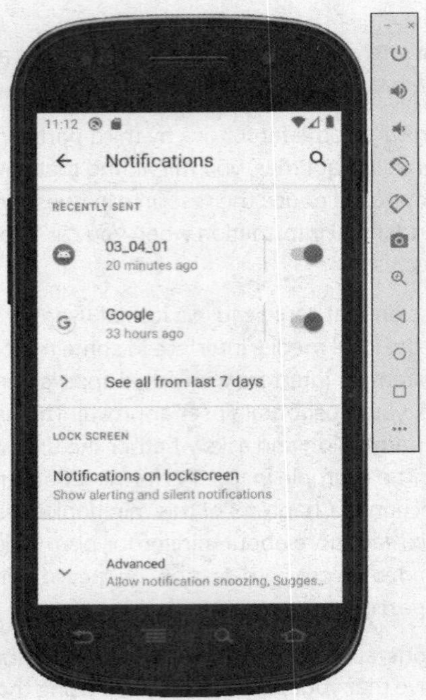

FIGURE 4-4: Notification reception preferences are automatic.

The user can also choose whether to grant permissions. Your app can request a permission and the user can grant it at the outset, but by using the Permission manager in Figure 4-5, the user can choose to revoke the permission later. However, in other situations, you must provide the settings for the user by relying on built-in Android functionality as described in the sections that follow.

Deciding on a preference set

Preferences indicate a user's choice in how to perform a task or configure an interface. Giving the user choices helps the user feel in control of the app and makes the app usage experience nicer. Attitude can make a huge difference in how the user views your app, so providing choices can also boost user acceptance. In some cases, you must offer preferences just to make your app work. For example, a user can't buy anything unless you know where to send the item, which means creating a preference that allows access to one or more shipping addresses.

With all these benefits of providing preferences in mind, you might initially think that a huge preference set that allows the user to address every aspect of the app is what you need, but that's not a useful strategy because it leads to user confusion. Here are some considerations for building a preference set for your app:

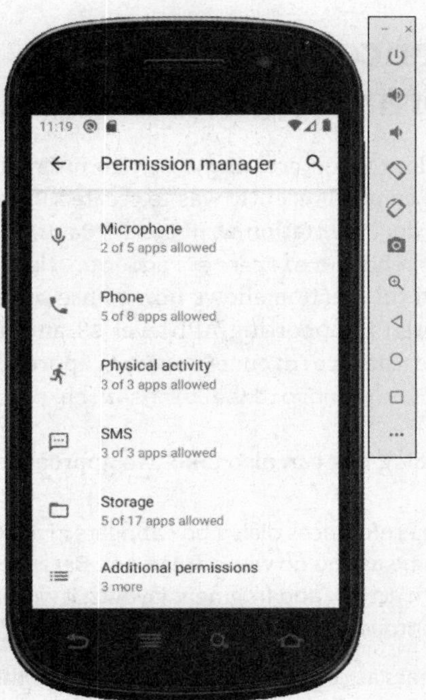

FIGURE 4-5: A user can revoke permissions after the fact.

- Provide options for communicating with your organization in various ways.
- Avoid adding settings for configuration items that the user can set up in other ways, such as notifications and security.
- Create a reasonable list of user interface options, such as color, text size, and so on, but don't include settings that will reorganize the user interface in ways that will make it hard to support.
- Allow the user to choose where, how, and when to store personal data.
- Make it easy to remove historical data that isn't necessary for app functioning.
- Define a method for sharing preferences with others when appropriate.
- Use online preference storage when appropriate for apps that might be used by a single user on multiple devices.
- Keep personal data to a minimum and use best practices to keep personal data safe.

TIP

When working with settings, the Settings option should appear as part of the navigation or on the app menu. Placing the Settings option anywhere else is likely to confuse the user.

Setting preferences using the Preference Library

You have a number of choices when creating a way to interact with the user for preferences. The method used until recently was to create a `PreferenceFragment`; however, according to the documentation at `https://developer.android.com/reference/android/preference/PreferenceFragment`, this method is now deprecated. The example in this section shows how to use the Preference Library approach instead. If you aren't supporting API level 28 and above in your app, however, you can still use the `PreferenceFragment` approach as described at `https://guides.codepath.com/android/settings-with-preferencefragment`.

Designing a Preferences dialog box can also take two approaches:

- **XML:** The layout for the Preferences dialog box appears in an XML file that you inflate much the same as you do with a fragment. Because this is the method you use for both activity and fragment layouts, it will probably feel like the most natural approach.
- **Coded:** The layout appears as code within the app. If you go this route, make sure you create a separate function to hold the layout code to make it easier to change later. Some developers simply prefer code, and this is a perfectly acceptable method.

The example in this chapter takes the XML approach because it's easier to change and understand in most situations. The coded approach can become hard to decipher and you may not get the results you want.

Create a new app project named 03_04_02 using the same techniques you did in Book 1, Chapter 3. Use a Basic Activity as a starting point, instead of the Empty Activity template used in previous examples. The Basic Activity template includes a Settings option right on the menu, so you save yourself a lot of work. Change the default `TextView` component to have an `Id` of `UserName` and a `text` value of `Your Name`. The following sections show how to create this example.

Performing the required setup

As with many of the features you add to an Android app, you must provide a Gradle entry to create preferences. Open the `build.gradle (Module: app)` file and add the following entry to the dependencies section:

```
implementation 'androidx.preference:preference:1.1.0'
```

Creating a layout

The layout appears in an XML file. However, this layout isn't one of the standard layouts supported by Android Studio. Use the following steps to create the layout instead:

1. **Right-click the** `res` **folder and choose New⇨Directory.**

   You see a New Directory dialog box containing a single field in which you can enter a directory name.

2. **Type** xml **and click OK.**

   Android Studio creates the new directory for you.

3. **Right-click the** `xml` **folder and choose New⇨XML Resource.**

   You see the New Resource File dialog box, shown in Figure 4-6.

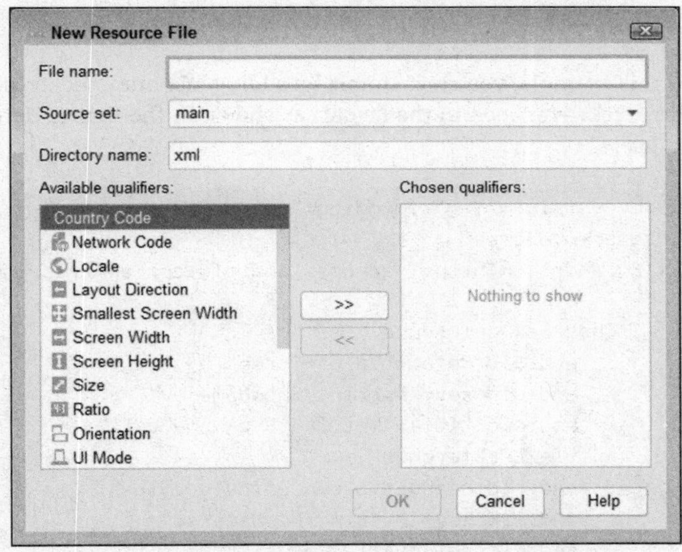

FIGURE 4-6: Create a new preference resource file.

4. **Type** preference_main **in the File Name field and click OK.**

   Android Studio creates and opens the file for you. Notice that the root node automatically uses the name `<PreferenceScreen>`, which is precisely what you need for this example.

At this point, you can begin creating a layout. The easiest way to do this is to use the designer, just as you have for other layouts. The Palette will contain a list of acceptable preference types, as shown in Figure 4-7.

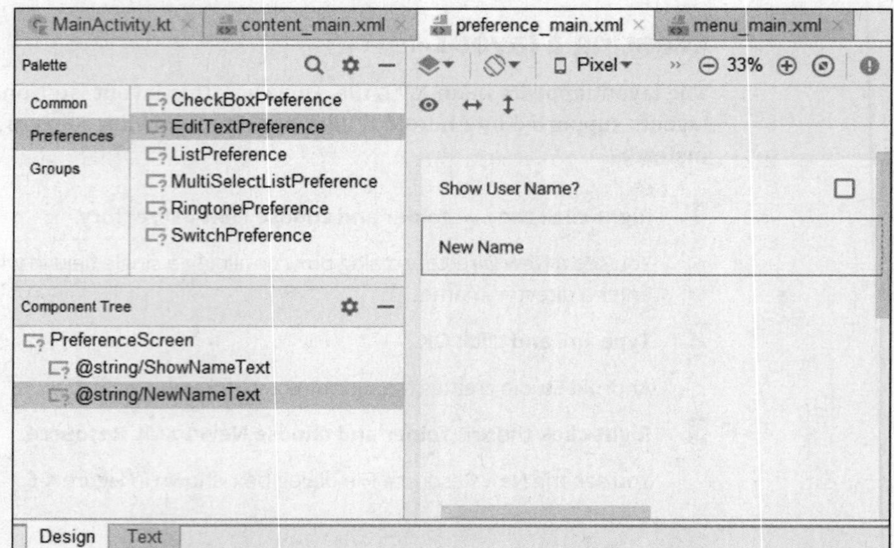

FIGURE 4-7: Each preference appears in a <Preference> element.

For this example, you start simple by adding just one `CheckBoxPreference` and a `EditTextPreference` to the layout, as shown in the figure. Here are the settings you use:

```
<?xml version="1.0" encoding="utf-8"?>
<PreferenceScreen
xmlns:android="http://schemas.android.com/apk/res/android">

    <CheckBoxPreference
        android:defaultValue="true"
        android:key="@string/ShowNameKey"
        android:title="@string/ShowNameText"/>
    <EditTextPreference
        android:defaultValue="Default value"
        android:key="@string/NewNameKey"
        android:selectAllOnFocus="true"
        android:title="@string/NewNameText"/>
</PreferenceScreen>
```

TIP

You can add all sorts of elements to your preferences. If you look down the list of items in Attributes, you see that you can add a summary, create dependencies between preferences, use icons, and create a variety of visual elements, such as dividers between preferences.

Defining the preferences fragment class

You need a class derived from PreferenceFragmentCompat to support a preference fragment. This approach is different from the fragments shown in Chapter 3 of this minibook. The following code shows a basic implementation for a Preferences dialog box of the kind used for this app, which is relatively basic because it has only two components:

```
class NamePreferences: PreferenceFragmentCompat() {
    override fun onCreatePreferences(
        savedInstanceState: Bundle?, rootKey: String?) {

        setPreferencesFromResource(
            R.xml.preference_main, rootKey)

        val showName: CheckBoxPreference? =
            findPreference("ShowName")
        val nameValue: EditTextPreference? =
            findPreference("NewName")

        val PrefChanges: Preference
          .OnPreferenceChangeListener =
          object : Preference.OnPreferenceChangeListener {
                override fun onPreferenceChange(
                    preference: Preference?,
                        newValue: Any?): Boolean {
                    // Add Your Validation Code Here!
                    return true
                }
            }

        showName?.onPreferenceChangeListener =
            PrefChanges
        nameValue?.onPreferenceChangeListener =
            PrefChanges
    }
}
```

You begin by overriding onCreatePreferences(). In fact, this is the only method within the NamePreferences class. The first task is to define the appearance of the Preferences dialog box using setPreferencesFromResource(). Notice that you must tell Android where to start looking for the layout, with the default being rootKey.

The next step is to gain access to the individual components within the Preferences dialog box. Notice that you must specify the component type: `CheckBoxPreference` or `EditTextPreference` in this case. When you have these objects, you can create a listener using `Preference.OnPreferenceChangeListener`. Overriding `onPreferenceChange()` allows you to intercept any preference changes and perform validation on them or work with them in other ways.

REMEMBER

The listener is now listening, but it isn't doing anything with either of the components. To connect the listener to the components, you must assign it to the component's `onPreferenceChangeListener`. Creating the listener alerts you to changes while the Preferences dialog box is open; it doesn't provide a means to access the components on `MainActivity`, which comes in the "Adding menu support" section, later in this chapter.

Saving and restoring the data

Android automatically calls `onSaveInstanceState()` when the app loses focus or is about to shut down. To make things easier, the code defines two constants for accessing the saved data:

```
private const val USER_NAME = "UserName"
private const val SHOW_USER = "ShowUser"
```

The following code implements the `onSaveInstanceState()` function to save the two settings on the Preferences dialog box:

```
override fun onSaveInstanceState(
    outState: Bundle,
    outPersistentState: PersistableBundle) {

    super.onSaveInstanceState(outState,
        outPersistentState)

    outState.putCharSequence(USER_NAME, UserName.text)
    outState.putInt(SHOW_USER, UserName.visibility)
}
```

Notice how the code calls the correct `outState` object function for saving the data. The first value is always a string containing the name of the key used to hold the data. Because it's so incredibly easy to mistype this information (and the compiler won't catch it), using the constants is a better idea.

When you restart the app, you want to access this saved data to ensure that the interface appears as the user expects it to appear. You add this code to onCreate(), as shown in bold here:

```
override fun onCreate(savedInstanceState: Bundle?) {
    ... Default Code ...

    if (savedInstanceState != null) {
        UserName.setText(
            savedInstanceState.getCharSequence(USER_NAME))
        UserName.visibility = savedInstanceState.getInt(
            SHOW_USER)
    }
}
```

When data is available (savedInstanceState will be null on the first execution of the app because you haven't saved any data), the code obtains the saved data and uses it to restore the user interface. In this case, it shows the username unless the user has decided not to display the username.

Adding menu support

You get an options menu with a Settings entry by default when you create the project. That entry doesn't do anything — it just sits there looking pretty, as shown in Figure 4-8.

To display the Preferences dialog box, you must override the onOptionsItemSelected() function, as shown here:

```
override fun onOptionsItemSelected(item: MenuItem):
    if (item.itemId == R.id.action_settings) {
        supportFragmentManager
            .beginTransaction()
            .replace(R.id.preferences, NamePreferences())
            .addToBackStack(null)
            .commit()

        supportActionBar?.setDisplayHomeAsUpEnabled(true)
    }

    return when (item.itemId) {
        R.id.action_settings -> true
        else -> super.onOptionsItemSelected(item)
    }
}
```

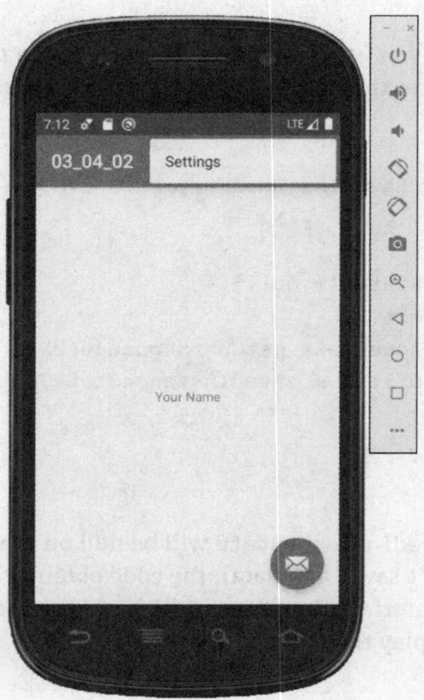

FIGURE 4-8: The Settings option that appears after clicking the ellipses.

The last part of this code is added for you automatically by the IDE. The code in bold provides the functionality for displaying the Preferences dialog box. There are two steps:

1. Display the Preferences dialog box fragment using a `supportFragmentManager` transaction, much the same as you do in Chapter 3 of this minibook. Note that the Preferences dialog box must appear on the backstack for the app to work correctly.
2. Show the left pointing arrow, the Home As Up indicator, by calling `supportActionBar?.setDisplayHomeAsUpEnabled(true)`, as shown in Figure 4-9.

The check box works as you might expect. To change the name, you click New Name to display the dialog box shown in Figure 4-10. The user changes the name and clicks OK to make it permanent or Cancel when there is a change of mind. The behavior shown here is provided as part of the `EditTextPreference` component; you don't have to provide it.

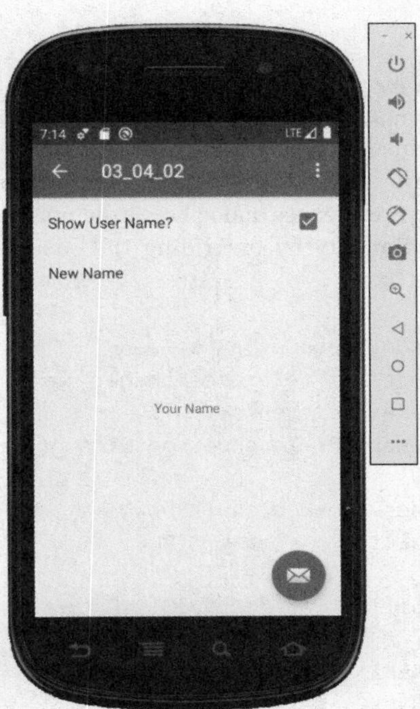

FIGURE 4-9: Display the preference menu onscreen.

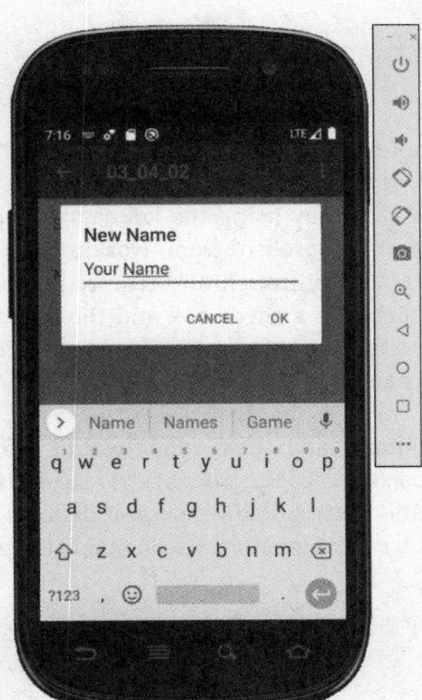

FIGURE 4-10: Changing the user name.

Updating the UI

You can try changing the name and performing other changes, but you'll notice that the changes don't appear immediately on the `MainActivity` display. That's because they don't get saved until the user clicks the left-pointing arrow in Figure 4-9 or the Back button. After the Preferences dialog box is dismissed, any changes take place. You obtain this functionality by overriding the `onSupportNavigateUp()` function, as shown here:

```
override fun onSupportNavigateUp(): Boolean {
    val sharedPreferences = PreferenceManager
        .getDefaultSharedPreferences(this)
    UserName.setText(sharedPreferences.getString(
        "NewName", ""))
    if (sharedPreferences.getBoolean("ShowName", true))
        UserName.visibility = View.VISIBLE
    else
        UserName.visibility = View.INVISIBLE

    if (supportFragmentManager.popBackStackImmediate()) {
        supportActionBar?.setDisplayHomeAsUpEnabled(false)
        return true
    }
    return super.onSupportNavigateUp()
}
```

To gain access to the components on the preferences dialog box, you begin by calling `PreferenceManager.getDefaultSharedPreferences()` to obtain access. You then access each of the values by using the key you set as part of creating the layout. This is a different approach from working with the fragments in Chapter 3, so you need to think through any required data access carefully. Because the `ShowName` component is a check box and the `UserName.visibility` property actually has three settings (`VISIBLE`, `INVISIBLE`, and `GONE`), you need an `if` statement to handle the change.

Notice that you must obtain any data you want before the call to `supportFragmentManager.popBackStackImmediate()`. After this call is made, the fragment no longer exists. This is also where you dismiss the left-pointing arrow by calling `supportActionBar?.setDisplayHomeAsUpEnabled(false)`.

Working with MediaPlayer

You have a number of options when dealing with a media player in Android, but most of them will be overkill except for those situations for which the goal of the app is to create a flexible media player. If your goal is to play some background music for a game or to offer sound effects, you have an easier option than creating a full-fledged streaming solution.

Create a new app project named 03_04_03 using the same techniques as in Book 1, Chapter 3. Use an Empty Activity as a starting point, just as you have in the past. This example requires three buttons configured in a `LinearLayout` (`Horizontal`), like this:

```
<LinearLayout
    android:layout_width="match_parent"
    android:layout_height="match_parent"
    android:layout_marginTop="24dp"
    android:orientation="horizontal"
    app:layout_constraintTop_toTopOf="parent">

    <Button
        android:id="@+id/Play"
        android:layout_width="wrap_content"
        android:layout_height="wrap_content"
        android:layout_weight="1"
        android:onClick="@string/PlayClick"
        android:text="@string/PlayText"/>

    <Button
        android:id="@+id/Pause"
        android:layout_width="wrap_content"
        android:layout_height="wrap_content"
        android:layout_weight="1"
        android:clickable="false"
        android:onClick="@string/PauseClick"
        android:text="@string/PauseText"/>

    <Button
        android:id="@+id/Stop"
        android:layout_width="wrap_content"
        android:layout_height="wrap_content"
```

```
            android:layout_weight="1"
            android:clickable="false"
            android:onClick="@string/StopClick"
            android:text="@string/StopText"/>
    </LinearLayout>
```

The designer will likely complain about some stylistic concerns, but you can safely ignore them. Now you need a resource to use. This example assumes that you're using a local resource, which means creating a new `raw` resource directory by right-clicking `app\res` and choosing New➪Android Resource Directory. You see the dialog box shown in Figure 4-11, where you type **raw** (lowercase) in the Directory Name field and choose raw from the Resource Type drop-down list box.

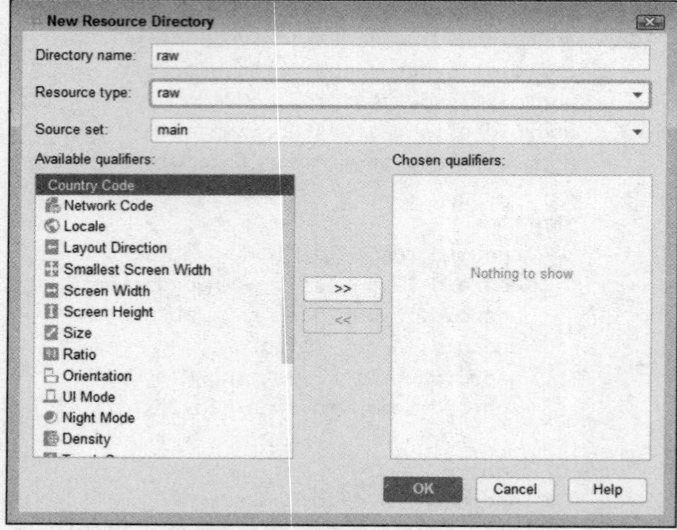

FIGURE 4-11: Creating a directory to hold the music source.

Next, copy a music or other sound file. Right-click the `raw` directory and choose Paste from the context menu. You see a Copy dialog box, in which you choose what to call the file when you move it into the `raw` folder. The filename you choose must not contain any spaces and must be lowercase. Otherwise, you're free to use any name you like (without changing the file extension). The file will appear in the `raw` directory. If you later find that you can't access this file as a resource, recheck the filename; simple names work best. The example uses `citysunshine.mp3` as the example file. You can find public domain sound files at `https://freepd.com/` (and many other sources).

For once, you don't need to jump through any insane hoops to get the smallest feature of Android working. The code is almost too easy when compared to a few of the other book examples. Here's all you need to implement all three buttons:

```
private var mediaPlayer: MediaPlayer ?= null

fun onPlayClick (view: View) {
    mediaPlayer = MediaPlayer.create(
            this, R.raw.citysunshine)
    mediaPlayer?.start()
    Play.isClickable = false
    Pause.isClickable = true
    Stop.isClickable = true
}

fun onPauseClick (view: View) {
    mediaPlayer?.pause()
    Play.isClickable = true
    Pause.isClickable = false
    Stop.isClickable = true
}

fun onStopClick (view: View) {
    mediaPlayer?.stop()
    Play.isClickable = true
    Pause.isClickable = false
    Stop.isClickable = false
}
```

You begin by creating `mediaPlayer`. It's important to declare the object outside `onPlayClick()` because you need to access the same object from all three button handlers. The call to `MediaPlayer.create()` requires just the app context and the name of the resource you want to play. Because you can't be certain that the file exists (or might be corrupted in some way) and `mediaPlayer` might be `null`, you must use `mediaPlayer?.start()` to start playing the file. To pause and stop the media stream, you call `pause()` and `stop()`, as you might expect.

The remainder of the code focuses on ensuring that the user can click only acceptable buttons. You can add visual cues, too. The point is to disable buttons that aren't acceptable for use at a particular time.

Adding Camera Support Using CameraX

Working with any device can be difficult because the device has its own Supervisory Control and Data Acquisition (SCADA) interface. The interface varies by vendor, and you can't ever be sure that the vendor won't decide to change things when you least expect it. You may see the camera (and other devices) as built-in and a cohesive part of the underlying computer, but really, it's not. So, your app has to do things like send commands to start the camera, control its inner circuitry, stop it, activate the flash, and a wealth of other considerations too numerous to list. This complexity is why operating systems rely on *device drivers* (low-level libraries that provide a somewhat common interface to your app) to make interacting with these devices easier because only someone with low-level knowledge can actually control them effectively, which is where CameraX comes into play. Even with a device driver to ease the pain of dealing with all those arcane commands, development is still difficult. CameraX (`https://developer.android.com/reference/kotlin/androidx/camera/core/CameraX`) makes things easier still by providing just a single interface for you to deal with and a lot of automation to perform some tasks for you.

From previous examples in this minibook, you know that API features control just how effective Android is at communicating with the underlying hardware for you. Android actually supports two camera APIs: Camera 1 and Camera 2. Even though the Camera 1 API is deprecated, many developers still use it because it's simpler and easier to use than Camera 2. You can read a comparison of Camera 1 and Camera 2 at `https://infinum.com/the-capsized-eight/conquering-android-camera-api`. This section focuses on Camera 2 because that's what CameraX automates for you. The theory is that using CameraX removes some of the concerns developers have had about working with Camera 2 directly.

However, CameraX does a lot more than alleviate some Camera 2 issues. For example, when working with either of the camera APIs, you soon discover that your math skills had better be nearly perfect and that you need to know about topics like matrix manipulation; otherwise, getting a good picture is a lost cause. In fact, even when you get the API to work, it often provides inconsistent results depending on which camera your device contains. So it's good to know what sorts of things CameraX will do for you that the APIs don't, as follows:

- Provides compatibility with about 90 percent of the devices on the market when using Android Lollipop (API 21) or above.
- Fixes some of the consistency issues that developers face when working with the camera APIs, such as uncertainty over how a list of camera resolutions is sorted after making an API call.

» Reduces the complexity of using advanced camera features such as Portrait, Highly Dynamic Range (HDR), Night Mode, and so on.

» Introduces the concept of USECASES to encapsulate specific tasks in automation. You can now focus on specific tasks, such as Preview, Image Analysis, and Image Capture.

» Builds a lifecycle orientation into camera use so that you gain access to event-handling features such as onResume() and onPause() (see the "Considering the activity lifecycle" and "Considering the fragment lifecycle" sections of Chapter 3 of this minibook for an overview of how lifecycle management works).

» Fixes some known camera API issues, including:
  - Front/back camera switch crashes
  - Optimizes camera closures
  - Orientation issues
  - Flash not firing correctly or at all

As with other examples in this chapter, you follow a basic process when creating a CameraX application, starting with the Gradle dependencies section additions (note that the Implementation code must appear on a single line even though it appears on two lines in the book):

```
def camerax_version = "1.0.0-alpha09"
implementation
   "androidx.camera:camera-core:$camerax_version"
implementation
   "androidx.camera:camera-camera2:$camerax_version"
```

WARNING

In case you're wondering about the version number for CameraX, be aware that there isn't a beta release, much less a full release, as of this writing. Working with alpha-level code means that you should expect inconsistencies, instability, bad documentation, and the like. That's why many articles about using CameraX begin with complaints about these very issues.

Because you're using an external device, you need permission, which means adding an entry to AndroidManifest.xml like this (along with the required code when you actually use the camera in your code):

```
<uses-permission android:name="android.permission.CAMERA"/>
```

Android considers this a dangerous level of permission (see the "Configuring permissions in AndroidManifest.xml" section, earlier in this chapter), so it will ask the user for permission before you do anything with the camera. Of course, this means adding code to ensure that your app *fails gracefully* (it doesn't simply freeze up and possibly lose data) if the user doesn't grant permission.

The next step is to create a layout for your app, which works much like the fragment-based apps used in this chapter and Chapter 3 of this minibook as well. The difference is that you need to use a `TextureView` (`https://developer.android.com/reference/android/view/TextureView`) to make the camera interface work properly. You find the component in the `Widgets` folder of the Palette. You use a `TextureView` because you need to be able to post to it in `onCreate()` so that the camera is active when the app starts, like this:

```
texture.post { startCamera() }
```

The `startCamera()` function performs these basic steps:

1. Get the camera metrics because they're all different:

   ```
   var lensFacing = CameraX.LensFacing.BACK
   val metrics = DisplayMetrics().also {
     texture.display.getRealMetrics(it) }
   val screenSize = Size(metrics.widthPixels,
                         metrics.heightPixels)
   val screenAspectRatio = Rational(metrics.widthPixels,
                                    metrics.heightPixels)
   ```

2. Configure a preview using `PreviewConfig.Builder().apply` that relies on the camera metrics and user requirements.

3. Define the preview characteristics using `Preview(previewConfig)`, which means creating a transform to adjust the camera input to the user's screen, like this:

   ```
   fun updateTransform() {
       val matrix = Matrix()
       val centerX = texture.width / 2f
       val centerY = texture.height / 2f

       val rotationDegrees = when
         (texture.display.rotation) {
           Surface.ROTATION_0 -> 0
           Surface.ROTATION_90 -> 90
           Surface.ROTATION_180 -> 180
   ```

```
            Surface.ROTATION_270 -> 270
            else -> return
        }
        matrix.postRotate(-rotationDegrees.toFloat(),
            centerX, centerY)
        texture.setTransform(matrix)
    }
```

4. Set up a preview listener using `setOnPreviewOutputUpdateListener`.
5. Configure an image capture use case with `ImageCaptureConfig.Builder().apply`.
6. Build the image capture use case using `ImageCapture(imageCaptureConfig)` and implementing a `setOnClickListener` for the button that the user will click to take the image.

These steps get you started. You could take a basic picture using them, but most users will want more. This means implementing various features and various modes, such as the Bokeh mode provided by the iPhone camera.

Sharing with Others

The various fragment examples so far should lead you to the conclusion that an Android app can be extremely flexible. If you come from a desktop-application background, you may be used to the idea that the application is self-contained. Web applications are more like Android applications in that you can embed content from other locations into a web application to create a smorgasbord of data for the user. However, Android kicks the whole concept of sharing up a few notches by making sharing more about getting what you need wherever the data may appear and less about using specific data sources as you would with a web application.

Performing simple share actions with other apps

Android users want to interact with any and every sort of data available, but your app may not offer the functionality to deal with that data, and you may not want to invest time reinventing code that someone else has already created. The idea of using another app's functionality to address your user's need can allow your app to do a lot more than it ordinarily could with less coding on your part. The following sections tell you about the two elements of this process: sending data to other apps and receiving data from other apps.

Sending data to other apps

You see in Chapter 3 of this minibook how to get activities and fragments to interact and exchange data using intents. When you work with a process that involves having the user engaged in a well-defined task, using the intent approach works best. For example, if part of performing a task is to view a document, but your app doesn't support that document type, you can determine whether another app has the required functionality.

However, when the focus is on freeform activities, such as dealing with texts or other kinds of instantaneous communication, no process may be in place to work with the data. In such a case, you need to use an Android Sharesheet instead. A Sharesheet not only works on the local device but also can interact with apps on other devices, such as sending a URL to a friend.

A Sharesheet is a centrally managed repository of apps that can handle specific kinds of data interaction. You don't manage the Sharesheet. You simply provide the means for a user to select a target for the data based on the target's app and user activity that is maintained by the system.

To start the process, you create an intent and set its action to `Intent.ACTION_SEND`. The example in the "Starting Another Activity" section of Book 1, Chapter 6 shows how to perform this task and describes how an intent works. After you create the intent, you call `Intent.createChooser()` and pass it your `Intent` object. The result is an Android Sharesheet that the user can use to choose a target for some data. The article at `https://developer.android.com/training/sharing/send` offers additional insights as to how this process works.

Receiving data from other apps

To receive data from another app, you can use an intent-filter tag in the app manifest, as described in the "Of tags and elements" section of Book 2, Chapter 7. However, you also have the option to create a `ChooserTarget` object that will show up in an Android Sharesheet. If you use Android 10 (API level 29) exclusively, you also have the option to use Sharing Shortcuts. Unlike a `ChooserTarget` object, a Sharing Shortcut can target a specific person, rather than an app as a whole.

Using Slices

A *slice* is a kind of user interface fragment that results from a data search of some type. Most slices rely on content from the Google Search app or from Google Assistant. A user makes a request for information, and you simply find it and display it in your app. As far as the user is concerned, the data environment is seamless, so it's not like embedding in a web app, which lets you sometimes tell that the information comes from another source. However, the downside of using Slices templates is that you must have a minimum of Android 4.4 (API level 19) to use it.

With slices, you can mix content you get from any source you search with standard Android controls like toggles and sliders. The example apps that Android provides shows how to set up things like an itinerary, with live content from the various locations you plan to visit. Another example shows a work itinerary that updates driving time and other essential information based on your current location.

Slices is a work in progress, according to the documentation at `https://developer.android.com/guide/slices`. However, you can get started using Slices templates by using the techniques found at `https://developer.android.com/guide/slices/getting-started`. Make sure to address the installation requirements and the Gradle `dependencies` additions to make Slices active in Android Studio.

» Using color in a layout

» Adding action to the user interface

» Switching elements in and out

Chapter 5
Interacting with the Users

Ultimately, apps perform two tasks: manage data and make it accessible to the user. Even with all the odd sound effects, visual eye candy, and interesting features, the bottom line is that the user is depending on the app to manage and present some sort of data. Just think about all the ways in which an app stores data and then presents it to the user. A personal contact can appear as part of an email, text, phone call, data destination, data sender, meeting participant, photo annotation, and much more. The same can be said of almost every other sort of data you can imagine. Even playing games involves the manipulation of data and presenting it in ways that the user will understand.

This chapter helps you consider the user end of the data pipeline. You discover various techniques of creating engaging user interfaces that will make the user's app experience a lot more pleasant.

Creating a Great Layout

The layout of your app determines how the user interacts with the data — the order in which data elements receive attention. A layout can also create focal points so that more important data receives more attention than less important data. The goal is to create a workflow that the user finds useful in performing tasks quickly. If a user has to stop doing work in order to find a setting or to understand the data, the layout isn't performing well and the user will be less efficient. The most successful layout is the one that the user doesn't notice at all — it simply works.

This section relies on an app named 03_05_01 to provide glimpses into working with layouts in Android. You see how the various elements combine to create an interesting composite user interface to the user. So, begin with the Empty Activity without any controls or components added. Set the minimum API level to 19. In the following sections, you read about layout elements to use with Android.

Defining the View and ViewGroup elements

A *view* is a rectangular area of a layout that contains a single widget. Examples of widgets are

- `TextView`
- `Button`
- `CheckBox`

Every widget you use in your apps is a member of the `View` class. The members you see in the Designer Palette are those that come with Android. Adding libraries in the module `build.gradle` file often adds new controls to the Palette, and each of these new controls is a member of the `View` class as well. You can also create custom controls by creating a class that inherits from the `View` class, or you can save time by inheriting from one of the existing control classes, such as `Button`. Just keep in mind that a view is always a single element of your layout.

A *view group* is usually a collection of one or more views and possibly other view groups. The `ViewGroup` class provides the basis for the containers and layouts found in the Designer Palette. The view group generally acts as a kind of layout and container for the app interface, whether it appears as part of an activity or a fragment.

REMEMBER

A special kind of view group extends the `AdapterView` class rather than the `ViewGroup` class. This kind of view group will accept only controls that derive from the `Adapter` class as children. Examples of `Adapter` class controls are

- ListView
- GridView
- Spinner
- Gallery

TIP

You can create a <merge> element to contain a layout that you won't use in a stand-alone configuration. The reusable layout examples in Book 1, Chapter 6 (01_06_03 through 01_06_06) could benefit from this approach. The <merge> element acts as a different kind of layout root than one of the layout elements, such as the ConstraintLayout. When using a <merge> layout, you must combine it with an <include> element in another file to see the components in the <merge> layout. In addition, you position an <include> that uses a <merge> onscreen using any of the various layouts instead of trying to position the widgets within the <merge> itself.

The <include> element enables you to combine multiple layouts into a cohesive whole. You use this element in Book 1, Chapter 6 to combine two independent layouts (reusable_layout.xml becomes part of activity_main.xml layout).

All the various views and view groups so far create a user interface that appears the moment you inflate it onscreen using setContentView(). Android also supports a lazy view through <ViewStub>. A <ViewStub> remains hidden until you specifically inflate it by calling code like this:

```
ViewStub.inflate()
```

You can't use a <ViewStub> with a <merge>. Instead, you must use it with a ViewGroup or an AdapterView.

Creating a layout using XML

Most of the time, you use the Designer to create layouts because moving components and controls from the Palette to the design area or the Component Tree is a lot easier and faster than performing a lot of typing. However, as you see in the "Using the AndroidX approach" section, at the end of this chapter, some design elements don't just appear in the Palette — you must access them by typing the XML directly into the Text tab.

Some containers are also inaccessible from the Palette. For example, the <merge> falls into the category. However, you don't actually type the <merge> element into the Text tab. Rather, you enter it into the Root Element field of the New Resource File dialog box that you access by right-clicking the layout folder and choosing New⇨Layout Resource File. As shown in Figure 5-1, merge shows as one of the items you can type into the field.

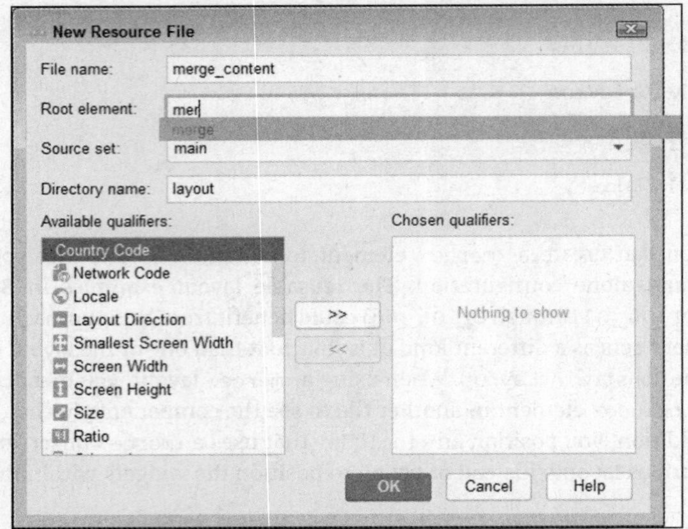

FIGURE 5-1: Defining a <merge> element as the root element.

The resulting <merge> layout has the required namespaces defined, so you simply start adding controls to it. Here is the single control used for an example in this case:

```
<?xml version="1.0" encoding="utf-8"?>
<merge
xmlns:android="http://schemas.android.com/apk/res/android">

    <androidx.appcompat.widget.AppCompatTextView
        android:id="@+id/MergeText"
        android:layout_width="wrap_content"
        android:layout_height="wrap_content"
        android:text="@string/MergeTextText"/>
</merge>
```

To use the merge in your main layout, you add an `<include>`, not something like a `<ViewStub>`. However, to ensure that you can position the items in the `<merge>`, you want to place the `<include>` within a layout, such as a `LinearLayout(horizontal)`. When you move the `<include>` from the Containers folder of the Palette to the design area or the Component Tree, you see the Resources dialog box shown in Figure 5-2, where you select the `<merge>` you want to use.

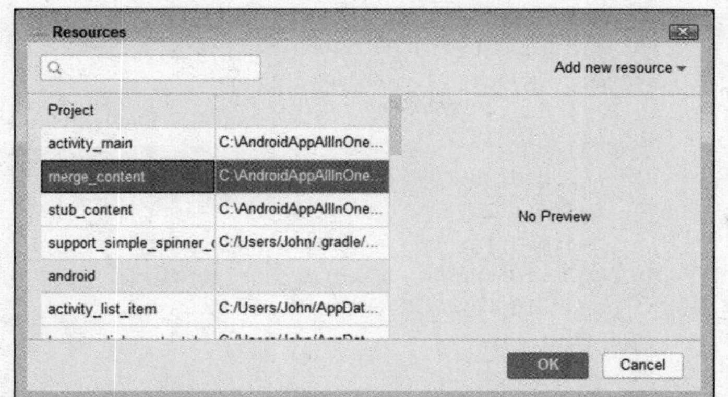

FIGURE 5-2: Selecting the `<merge>` to provide in the `<include>`.

After you have a layout and an `<include>` in place, you can configure the `<merge>` as you would any other control. In reality, however, you're configuring an entire group of controls — the entire `<merge>`. Here's what a `<merge>` might look like in `activity_main.xml` when accessed through an `<include>`:

```
<LinearLayout
    android:layout_width="match_parent"
    android:layout_height="match_parent"
    android:layout_marginTop="8dp"
    android:gravity="center_horizontal"
    android:orientation="horizontal"
    app:layout_constraintEnd_toEndOf="parent"
    app:layout_constraintStart_toStartOf="parent"
    app:layout_constraintTop_toTopOf="parent">

    <include
        android:id="@+id/Merge"
        layout="@layout/merge_content"
        android:layout_width="wrap_content"
        android:layout_height="wrap_content"
        android:layout_marginTop="24dp"/>
</LinearLayout>
```

You must use a full layout with a `<ViewStub>` element. The layout doesn't appear at runtime; you have to inflate it later. Here's what a simple layout used with a `<ViewStub>` might look like:

```
<?xml version="1.0" encoding="utf-8"?>
<LinearLayout
xmlns:android="http://schemas.android.com/apk/res/android"
    android:orientation="vertical"
```

```
    android:layout_width="match_parent"
    android:layout_height="match_parent">

    <TextView
        android:id="@+id/StubText"
        android:layout_width="match_parent"
        android:layout_height="wrap_content"
        android:gravity="center_horizontal"
        android:text="@string/StubTextText"/>
```

CONSIDERING USABILITY AND ACCESSIBILITY ISSUES

The layout, controls, colors, textures, and other visual elements you employ in a user interface can affect the usability and accessibility of the interface. For example, a drop-down list saves space and allows you to place more elements on a single screen. However, a drop-down list also forces the user to work harder because now the user must take a special action to see the list of items the drop-down list contains. Using a drop-down list also reduces the focus of the data element. These issues can make your app less accessible for those with special needs. For example, an elderly person might shake, making it nearly impossible for them to use a drop-down list. If the data element in the drop-down list is essential and the list relatively short, using a list is usually better despite the amount of screen real-estate that a list uses.

Placing common controls in the same place on every screen is also important. Everyone benefits to some degree from a consistent layout, but those who have cognitive or other issues will find that the consistent layout is essential to make your app worth using. You should combine a consistent layout with smart use of defaults so that taking the default action will produce a correct result most of the time. In addition, look to other apps for component and control placement. For example, most users look for a search bar in the upper center or upper right of an app. Placing the search bar on the bottom of the app will make it harder for the user to find.

Color and texture are also essential in making your app usable and accessible. For example, using various shades of red in your app (or any color for that matter) and expecting someone with color perception issues to make sense of them isn't realistic. Online sites such as Vischeck (`http://www.vischeck.com/vischeck/vischeckImage.php`) can help you see your app as someone with a color issue would see it. You just upload a screenshot (or download the app and test locally). Using texture can also reduce the effects of various visual deficiencies. You can use texture to emphasize default actions and to make visual elements clearer.

All positioning is done within the layout rather than the host in most cases. What you're really doing is merging two layouts in this case. The `<ViewStub>` code in `activity_main.xml` looks something like this:

```
<ViewStub
    android:id="@+id/ViewStub"
    android:layout_width="wrap_content"
    android:layout_height="wrap_content"
    android:layout_marginTop="32dp"
    android:layout="@layout/stub_content"
    app:layout_constraintEnd_toEndOf="parent"
    app:layout_constraintStart_toStartOf="parent"
    app:layout_constraintTop_toTopOf="parent"/>
```


Modifying a layout at runtime

You can use a variety of methods to modify the layout at runtime. However, in most cases, the methods employ these techniques:

- Inflate an element
- Deflate an element
- Hide an element
- Show an element
- Rearrange elements
- Change element characteristics (such as title)
- Use a different layout

TIP

In general, you don't want to modify the layout without good reason. Perhaps a particular option becomes unavailable (such as you're out of cheese pizza and you don't want the option to appear on your menu) or you need the user to supply one piece of information before asking for another (depending on country of origin, you provide different address forms). You might also provide different layouts that depend on user preference or move elements around to accommodate special needs (such as larger fonts for those who have viewing difficulties). When the need does arrive, you want to plan ahead for it and use the most appropriate technique. For example, you use a `<ViewStub>` for additional information after the user has provided a necessary input, or you hide the menu item that isn't available. Here's some code that inflates the <ViewStub> and then hides the two buttons on the current layout:

```
fun onShowViewStubClick(view: View) {
    if (ViewStub != null) {
        ViewStub.inflate()
        ShowViewStub.visibility = View.GONE
        Layout2.visibility = View.GONE
    }
}
```

When you decide to have multiple layouts for your app, you can switch between them simply as long as each layout has a different `id` value. The example app has a `Main_Layout` that uses one order of controls (the buttons appear at the bottom) and an `Aux_Layout` that uses a different order of controls (the buttons appear at the top). The controls are the same in each layout. Using different layouts doesn't mean that the layouts must have entirely different controls. Clicking the Other Layout button in one layout calls the same click handler as clicking the Other Layout button in the other layout. Here's the click handler for the `Layout2` button:

```
private var CurrentView = "Main"
fun  onLayout2Click(view: View) {
    if (CurrentView == "Main") {

        setContentView(R.layout.activity_main2)
        CurrentView = "Aux"
    } else {
        setContentView((R.layout.activity_main))
        CurrentView = "Main"
    }
}
```

You can discover the current layout through various means, but sometimes clever programming is error prone, and simple is better. This is one of those cases. Simply create a variable such as `CurrentView` to track the current view and set it appropriately. You can move back and forth between views as needed without problem using this approach.

Considering the common layouts

Android provides you with a number of common layouts that will work with non-adapter widgets. The layouts are

» `ContraintLayout`: Places the controls relative to the parent and sometimes each other based on the limits of the current device. The controls appear in the same order and in about the same place within the limits of a constraint on each device that displays the user interface.

» `LinearLayout`: Creates a horizontal or vertical arrangement of controls with one control in each horizontal or vertical slot. The size of the largest control determines the size of the slot. This layout relies on scroll bars when the layout doesn't fit on the user's screen.

» `FrameLayout`: Defines an area onscreen to place a control, usually graphical, such as a picture.

» `TableLayout`: Relies on a tabular format similar to the tables used for web pages. Control size can vary to accommodate various device sizes. The overall layout remains the same.

» `RelativeLayout` **(legacy):** Makes it possible to position the controls relative to each other, which means that devices of different sizes will have the controls in the same order, but not necessarily in the same place.

Working with adapters

Adapters enable you to create views that contain a number of items. You might have a group of pictures, list of employees, or any other sort of collection, fixed or dynamic. The purpose of an adapter is to hold items. Different adapters hold different items better than. For example, when creating a list of pictures, an `ImageView` works best. This example, however, uses a `ScrollView`, which allows you to display any number of simple or complex items. You use a `LinearLayout(vertical)` to provide structure for the items, and the items appear within a `TextView`. Here is the initial design for this part of the example:

```
<ScrollView
    android:id="@+id/scrollView"
    android:layout_width="match_parent"
    android:layout_height="match_parent"
    android:layout_marginTop="160dp"
    android:layout_marginBottom="20dp"
    android:scrollbarSize="10dp"
    android:scrollbarStyle="insideInset"
    android:scrollbars="vertical"
    app:layout_constraintBottom_toBottomOf="parent"
    app:layout_constraintEnd_toEndOf="parent"
    app:layout_constraintStart_toStartOf="parent"
    app:layout_constraintTop_toTopOf="parent">
```

```
    <LinearLayout
        android:id="@+id/ScrollItems"
        android:layout_width="match_parent"
        android:layout_height="wrap_content"
        android:orientation="vertical"></LinearLayout>
</ScrollView>
```

The designer will complain that the `LinearLayout` is useless, but you can safely ignore that complaint. You fill the `LinearLayout` with `TextView` items in `onCreate()`, as shown here in bold:

```
override fun onCreate(savedInstanceState: Bundle?) {
    super.onCreate(savedInstanceState)
    setContentView(R.layout.activity_main)

    for (value in 0..30) {
        var valueTV: TextView = TextView(this)
        valueTV.setText(value.toString())
        valueTV.gravity = Gravity.CENTER_HORIZONTAL
        ScrollItems.addView(valueTV)
    }
}
```

All the code does is to create a `TextView` with a number in the range from 0 through 30. The number is centered in the `TextView` by adding `Gravity.CENTER_HORIZONTAL`. You then add it to the `LinearLayout`, `ScrollItems`, using `addView()`. The result is the scrollable list shown in Figure 5-3.

Debugging your layout

The previous sections point only to what is possible, because Android provides a lot of flexibility in creating a layout. Unfortunately, the flexibility you have also complicates the task of determining where problems exist in the layout, which is where the Layout Inspector comes into play. These steps get you started with the Layout Inspector:

1. **Start your app.**

   It doesn't matter whether you place it in run or debug mode, but the Layout Inspector will work faster if you're not also debugging the app.

2. **Choose Tools⇨Layout Inspector in Android Studio.**

   You see the Choose Process dialog box, shown in Figure 5-4.

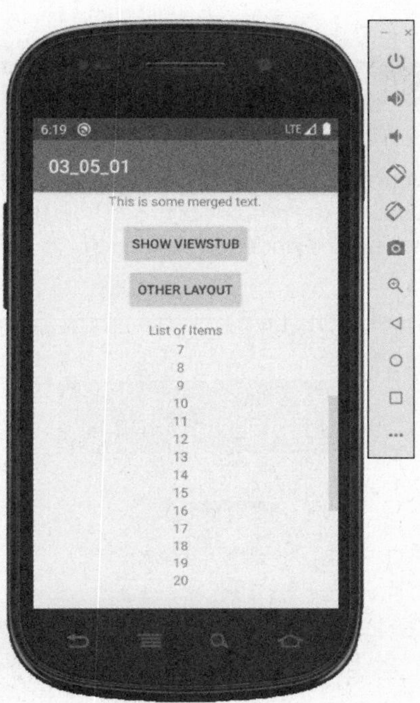

FIGURE 5-3: Viewing the scrollable list.

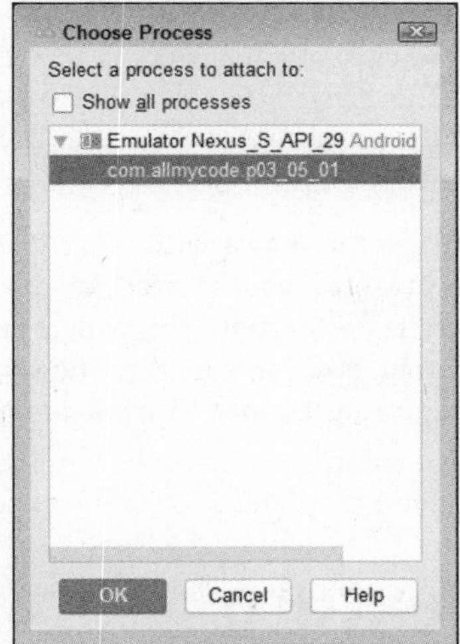

FIGURE 5-4: Select the process you want to inspect.

3. **Highlight the process you want to inspect and click OK.**

   You see the window shown in Figure 5-5, which has the following panes:

   - **View Tree:** Displays every element of the layout so that you can drill down and choose specific items.

- **Load Overlay:** Shows a graphical representation of the layout with the individual controls highlighted. The selected item from View Tree has a border of a different color so that you can pick it out easily.
- **Properties Table:** Contains the properties for the item selected in View Tree. You can drill down into the properties to see how they are set to determine why the display isn't working as expected.

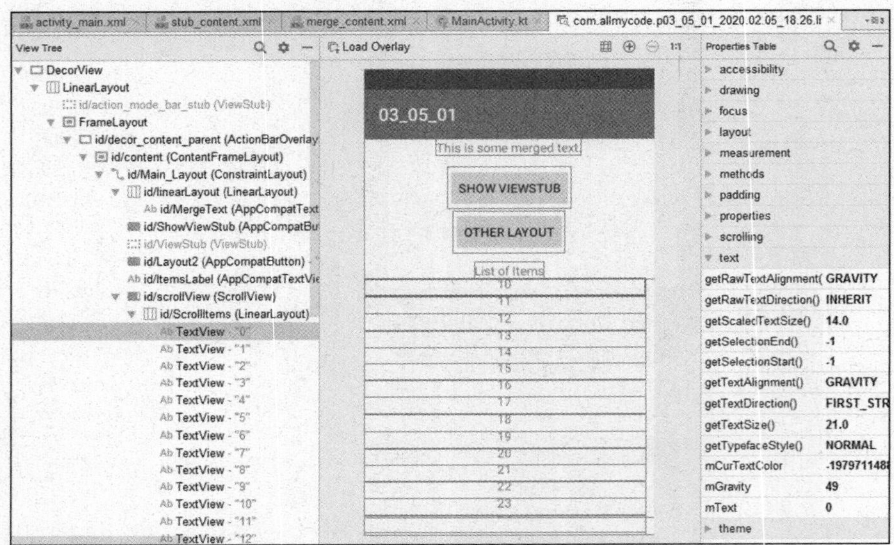

FIGURE 5-5: The Layout Inspector gives you significant detail about your layout.

By comparing what the Layout Inspector shows with what you expected to see, you can locate potential problems in your layout or associated code. More important, drilling down into the properties often tells you which properties to set to obtain a desired result. Unfortunately, you can't modify the settings to try them out while the app is running, but getting an idea of what to try still gives you a significant advantage.

Employing Color and Texture

Some user interfaces focus on shades of gray, or perhaps gray, white, and black. Such user interfaces are boring. Unless your goal is to put your user to sleep, you really do need more than gray, and the addition of white and black won't fulfill the need. Of course, you also don't want to resort to garish displays of colliding colors that will bedazzle the use to the point of unconsciousness. A nice middle ground of color works best. Fortunately, Android Studio offers help in this area, especially if you tend toward the two extremes.

Texture gives your app a feel. The hard outlines of the default controls work best when every control is important. However, if a control becomes less important or simply unavailable because of the task the user is performing, a somewhat fuzzy outline can be helpful because it provides a visual cue. That's what texture is all about — making your app interesting while also providing cues about what to do next with it.

This section relies on an app named 03_05_02 to show how to work with both color and texture using a variety of methods, including styles. The app doesn't do anything special except show off what's available to you as the developer. Begin with the Empty Activity without any controls or components added. Set the minimum API level to 14. (If you want to work with advanced features, such as Palette, you must set the minimum API level to 28.)

REMEMBER

The following sections aren't meant to turn you into a color and texture guru; they're designed to help you make great use of the functionality that Android Studio offers. Going this route won't provide your users with a unique experience, but most users are really only interested in something motivating.

Working with styles and themes

A *style* is simply a kind of template for defining how a particular view looks. You might want to display buttons with particular characteristics, for example. In fact, the Designer often makes style suggestions to you. When you place a series of buttons in a `LinearLayout`, the Designer suggests using one of several styles that make the buttons borderless so that they provide a smooth appearance across the screen. You use a style when the overall appearance of the app works well, but an individual view needs a little extra work.

A *theme* is a style that you apply across an entire app, activity, or view hierarchy. Using a theme saves time because you can apply the styles to the app as a whole, giving every element of the app a consistent appearance. Often, a theme establishes most of the style for an app, and you may tweak that appearance for individual elements using a style.

TIP

In the following sections, you see how to work with styles and themes, but these sections don't necessarily dictate good design choices. You'd do well to combine your development skills with those of someone with design knowledge so that you can create a presentation that looks great.

Working with themes

Your app already has one built-in theme attached to it. Look in the `app\res\values` folder to find `styles.xml`. When you open this file, you see the base application theme shown here:

```
<resources>

    <!-- Base application theme. -->
    <style name="AppTheme"
     parent="Theme.AppCompat.Light.DarkActionBar">
        <!-- Customize your theme here. -->
        <item name="colorPrimary">
          @color/colorPrimary
        </item>
        <item name="colorPrimaryDark">
          @color/colorPrimaryDark
        </item>
        <item name="colorAccent">
          @color/colorAccent
        </item>
    </style>

</resources>
```

A theme consists of the `<style>` element and one or more `<item>` elements. The theme must have a `name` attribute so that you can access it in your code. The `parent` attribute determines what the theme affects, which is the dark action bar used for light activities in this case. Each of the `<item>` entries defines a particular aspect of the theme appearance; in this case, only colors are affected. However, when you add a new `<item>` entry and type **name**, you see a selection of stylistic choices that you can modify, as shown in Figure 5-6. Each `<item>` can modify only one style.

TIP

You can find a code listing of the themes online by using the Google search term `Android "Theme.AppCompat.Light.DarkActionBar" site:android.googlesource.com`. The `themes.xml` file contains a number of versions, so make sure you use the newest possible version to access the latest theme definitions.

```
    <item name=""
</style>          actionBarDivider
                  actionBarItemBackground
                  actionBarPopupTheme
                  actionBarSize
                  actionBarSplitStyle
                  actionBarStyle
                  actionBarTabBarStyle
                  actionBarTabStyle
                  actionBarTabTextStyle
                  actionBarTheme
                  actionBarWidgetTheme
                  Not all variants are shown, please type more letters to see the rest
```

FIGURE 5-6: A list of styles that an `<item>` can modify.

The colors in the `styles.xml` file determine the appearance of your app when you run it. However, the color definitions don't actually appear in this file; they instead appear in `colors.xml`, shown here:

```
<?xml version="1.0" encoding="utf-8"?>
<resources>
    <color name="colorPrimary">#008577</color>
    <color name="colorPrimaryDark">#00574B</color>
    <color name="colorAccent">#D81B60</color>
</resources>
```

REMEMBER

Unlike the `<item>` entries, the `<color>` entries don't have specific names, but you should choose something descriptive, as shown in the example. The default theme for your app appears in the `AndroidManifest.xml` file as the `android:theme="@style/AppTheme"` attribute.

You can create as many themes for your app as you like. All you need is a separate theme entry for each theme. The theme must have a unique name, like this:

```
<style name="AppTheme2"
 parent="Theme.AppCompat.Light.DarkActionBar">
   <item name="colorPrimary">
      @color/colorPrimary2</item>
   <item name="colorPrimaryDark">
      @color/colorPrimaryDark2</item>
   <item name="colorAccent">
      @color/colorAccent2</item>
   <item name="colorButtonNormal">
      @color/colorButtonNormal</item>
    </style>
```

You must then define any new colors in the `colors.xml` file. Where you apply themes is important. In working with app-wide themes, you must place the code for changing the theme before the app draws the app window. For the initial screen, this means placing the code in onCreate(), like this:

```
override fun onCreate(savedInstanceState: Bundle?) {
    if (savedInstanceState != null) {
        var selectedTheme = savedInstanceState
            .getInt("SavedTheme", -1)
        when (selectedTheme) {
            R.style.AppTheme -> setTheme(R.style.AppTheme)
            R.style.AppTheme2 -> setTheme(R.style.AppTheme2)
            else -> setTheme(R.style.AppTheme)
        }
    }
    super.onCreate(savedInstanceState)
    setContentView(R.layout.activity_main)
}
```

For this solution to work, you must provide user preference code to save the desired style. The "Setting preferences using the Preference Library" section of Chapter 4 of this minibook tells you that you have to create and use a user preference setup. Notice that the call to setTheme() must appear before super.onCreate() or the call won't work. There are theoretically low-level techniques for bypassing this issue, but they're definitely for an experienced Android developer and outside the scope of this book. We'll just say that such techniques are extremely error prone.

You can also set a theme for each new activity or fragment that you create by setting the theme before you create the element. Setting a theme at this level is significantly easier than working with MainActivity.

Using the built-in styles

Styles are more easily changed than themes because styles generally apply to individual views or view groups and affect specific aspects of the element in question. During design time, you sometimes see a drop-down list containing choices for a particular view, such as a button. Figure 5-7 shows the selections for setting the style of a button:

When working with other styles, you see other sorts of dialog boxes to assist you in changing the view's style. For example, when working with colors, you see a color chooser of the sort shown in Figure 5-8. You click the color block on the left side of the attribute entry value.

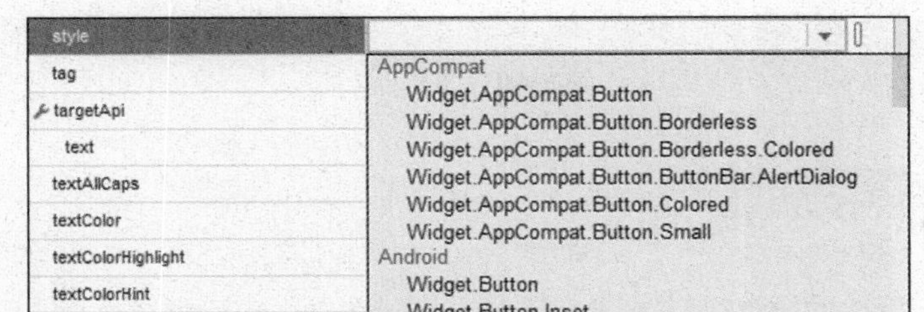

FIGURE 5-7: Choosing a button style during design time.

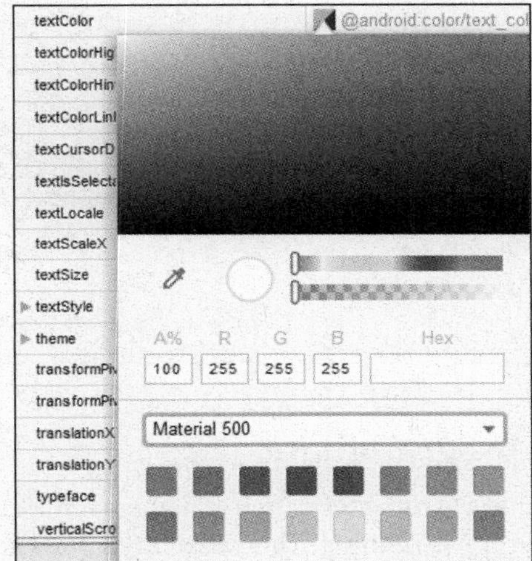

FIGURE 5-8: Use a color chooser to change a color style directly.

As with many other parts of Android design, you can also use a predefined resource by clicking the square on the right side of the attribute value to display the Pick a Resource dialog box, shown in Figure 5-9. You can select from Project, Android, and Theme Attribute colors, or you can create an entirely new resource if you want.

Creating your own styles

As with app-wide themes, you can also create styles that affect individual elements within the `colors.xml` or `styles.xml` files. The important thing is to create the style in the correct file and make it of the correct type. For example, if you want to create a custom color style, it must appear in the `colors.xml` file and be within a `<color>` element. The process, however, is the same as working with a theme; it's just less complex.

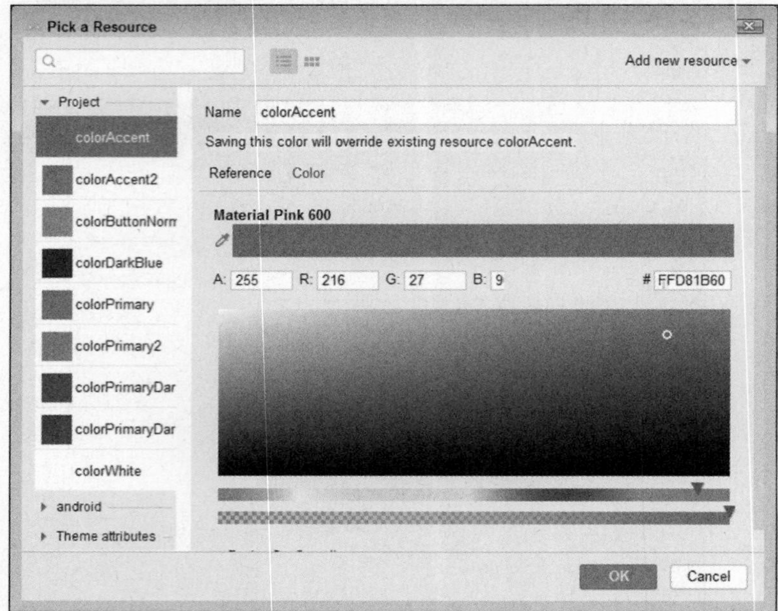

FIGURE 5-9: Rely on standard or custom color selections for your project.

Changing styles programmatically

When you use standard or custom styles, you can change the style of a view any time you want while the app is running. This flexibility differs from working with themes that are applied before you draw the window and are hard to change later. To change the style of a view, you must first obtain the style information and then apply it to the correct object attribute, as shown here:

```
fun onChangeStyleClick(view: View){
    var textColor = ContextCompat.getColor(
        this, R.color.colorWhite)
    var backColor = ContextCompat.getColor(
        this, R.color.colorDarkBlue)
    ChangeStyle.setTextColor(textColor)
    ChangeStyle.setBackgroundColor(backColor)
}
```

In this case, you retrieve the color you need using `ContextCompat.getColor()` from colors.xml. You then apply it to the correct color style using either `setTextColor()` or `setBackgroundColor()`. Note that you can also manually create one-off color changes by using the `rgb()` or `argb()` functions, like this:

```
ChangeStyle.setBackgroundColor(
    argb(0xFF, 0x00, 0x00, 0xA0))
```

TECHNICAL STUFF

Most changeable styles for a view work use the same two-step process. However, some styles aren't changeable through programming, such as the `style` attribute for a `Button`. In this case, you must choose a drawing style during design time and stick with it, or resort to programming tricks like creating two buttons, showing one, and hiding the other as needed.

Creating a palette

The Palette API enables developers to create color schemes based on the graphics used by your application. Making your app color coordinate with the graphics helps create a pleasing view for the user. For example, graphics used for a school will likely contain the school colors. A palette based on the graphics will also use the school colors natively, along with any other elements in the graphics to create a pleasing app for school needs. To begin using the Palette API, add the following implementation entry to the dependencies section of the `build.gradle(Module: app)` file:

```
implementation 'androidx.palette:palette-ktx:1.0.0'
```

To create a palette, you begin with a bitmap. However, most apps save bitmaps as a drawable resource, which means performing a conversion. The following code shows how to obtain a palette from the `pep_extracheese.png` file used in Book 1, Chapter 6.

```
val myPalette = Palette.from(
    BitmapFactory.decodeResource(
        resources,
        R.drawable.pep_extracheese)).generate()
```

That's all there is to it! You now have access to a palette that you can use within your app to create a pleasing appearance. To assign a color to one of the controls, you use code like this:

```
SomeText.setTextColor(
    myPalette.getDarkVibrantColor(1))
SomeText.setBackgroundColor(
    myPalette.getLightVibrantColor(1))
```

The IDE guides you through which functions to use. The value you provide is simply a selection of one of the colors. You can try different numbers to see which colors appeal to you. You can view the palette colors as being of these types based on the bitmap you provide:

- `LightVibrant`
- `Vibrant`

- DarkVibrant
- LightMuted
- Muted
- DarkMuted

Using swatches to create color schemes

The Palette object you created in the previous section also has *swatches*, which are essentially color profiles based on the bitmap you provide. Like the individual color selections, these profiles come in various groups, such as DarkMuted. Consequently, you access a swatch like this:

```
val mySwatch = myPalette.darkMutedSwatch
```

The essential use for swatches is to create themes. You also gain access to new methods that let you choose a color based on how the algorithm sees it being used, such as getBodyTextColor() and getTitleTextColor(). Finally, swatches help you perform analysis on your Palette in preparation for tweaks you may want to make.

Using Animations and Transitions

Playing games can be time consuming — a real waste of resources that most businesses try to avoid. However, games are actually quite good at teaching developers about the use of animations and transitions. For example, a card game can use an animation to suggest a next move when the user hasn't made a move in a while. An action game might use a transition to provide different moves as the user navigates a maze. Business software could take a page from games and use animation to demonstrate what to do next when the user seems stuck. Transitions can give the user a feeling of accomplishment when data is accepted.

Fortunately, the controls and components you use to create Android apps sometimes have the animations and transitions built right into them so that you don't even have to do anything special. For example, a progress bar might have an animation feature to make the movement from one level to the next smoother and more likely to be seen by the user.

This section relies on an app named 03_05_03 to get you started with animations and transitions. Begin with the Empty Activity without any controls or components added. Set the minimum API level to 21. The following sections offer a few ideas on how to use animations and transitions to your advantage in developing apps.

Understanding the need for animations

When most people think about animation, they think about cartoons or games, but those aren't the only place where animation is commonly used, and the other ways can be quite interesting. For example, in pointing where to go, a sign can employ animation to attract attention and make the direction clearer. Animations can also smooth out visual activities so that the activity is easier to follow and easier on the eyes. An animation can help make a process clearer, and you sometimes see them used for step-by-step procedures, such as for putting something together. So, it shouldn't come as a surprise that you can use animations in your app as well and for the same reasons you see them used everywhere else.

Some of the Android controls use animation by default, such as the `ProgressBar`. As shown in the "Creating a test app" section in Chapter 2 of this minibook, you can use coding techniques to make the `ProgressBar` movement smoother. You can also set the `animationResolution` attribute to make the movement smoother. The point is that with a proper setup, a `ProgressBar` comes ready to provide some level of animation for the user. The `SeekBar` provides this same functionality so that when you use it for a music app, the *thumb* (the selector you use to modify the time index) moves smoothly as the music plays.

Android also supplies you with some widgets that handle animation natively, such as the `VideoView` and the `ImageView`. Both controls offer a variety of animation techniques through careful programming. Animating these controls lets you put on an unattended video presentation, such as at a kiosk. Animation relieves the user from having to click from picture to picture, ensuring that the user will tend to view more of the presentation.

Animating graphics

You have various means to animate graphics. This example looks at what amounts to a simple slide show.

Creating the animation list

To begin, you must create an animation list resource using the following steps:

1. **Right-click the `res` folder and choose New⇨Android Resource File.**

   You see a New Resource File dialog box, similar to the one shown previously in Figure 5-1.

   Be sure to right-click the `res` folder and not the `drawable` folder or you'll create an unusable file.

2. **Type** star_animation **in the File Name field.**

   Use a lowercase name or Android Studio will reject it.

3. **Choose** Drawable **in the Resource Type field.**
4. **Type** animation-list **in the Root Element field and click OK.**

   This entry replaces `selector` or some other entry as the root. The dialog box automatically shows a list of options based on what you type. Android Studio creates the required resource file for you.

This example uses some built-in graphics so that no one has to draw anything. These built-in graphics come in handy for testing purposes when you aren't an artist and stick figures hold little interest. With this in mind, here's the code for the resource file:

```
<?xml version="1.0" encoding="utf-8"?>
<animation-list
xmlns:android="http://schemas.android.com/apk/res/android"
    android:oneshot="false">

   <item
     android:drawable="@android:drawable/btn_star"
     android:duration="300"/>
   <item
     android:drawable="@android:drawable/btn_star_big_off"
     android:duration="300"/>
   <item
     android:drawable="@android:drawable/btn_star_big_on"
     android:duration="300"/>
</animation-list>
```

The `<animation-list>` element includes one essential attribute, `android:oneshot`. Setting this attribute to `true` means that you see the animation only once. Because the example will keep the animation going until told to stop, you set this attribute to `false`.

TIP

Each item in the <animation-list> is a separate bitmap found in the @android:drawable resource. You can find a lot of useful bitmaps this way, and this resource helps when your artistic skills are lacking. In addition to the android:drawable attribute, which points to the bitmap, you must also provide an android:duration attribute that tells how long to display each bitmap.

Defining a user interface

This example has a simple user interface consisting of an ImageView and a Button. The ImageView displays the animation and the Button provides the means for starting and stopping the animation. Here's the setup you need for the example:

```
<?xml version="1.0" encoding="utf-8"?>
<androidx.constraintlayout.widget.ConstraintLayout
    xmlns:android="http://schemas.android.com/apk/res/android"
    xmlns:app="http://schemas.android.com/apk/res-auto"
    xmlns:tools="http://schemas.android.com/tools"
    android:layout_width="match_parent"
    android:layout_height="match_parent"
    tools:context=".MainActivity">

    <ImageView
        android:id="@+id/imageView"
        android:layout_width="350dp"
        android:layout_height="350dp"
        android:layout_marginStart="8dp"
        android:layout_marginTop="8dp"
        android:layout_marginEnd="8dp"
        app:layout_constraintEnd_toEndOf="parent"
        app:layout_constraintStart_toStartOf="parent"
        app:layout_constraintTop_toTopOf="parent"/>

    <Button
        android:id="@+id/StartStop"
        android:layout_width="wrap_content"
        android:layout_height="wrap_content"
        android:layout_marginTop="400dp"
        android:layout_marginEnd="8dp"
        android:onClick="@string/StartStopClick"
        android:text="@string/StartStopText"
        app:layout_constraintEnd_toEndOf="parent"
        app:layout_constraintStart_toStartOf="parent"
        app:layout_constraintTop_toTopOf="parent"/>

</androidx.constraintlayout.widget.ConstraintLayout>
```

Note that the `ImageView` is sized to 350 x 350 pixels. This size is for demonstration purposes only. Normally, you'd configure the app to work with the target device.

Starting the animation

You can create an animation using very little code. All you really need is to tell the `ImageView` what resource to use, create an `AnimationDrawable`, and tell the resulting object to `start()` or `stop()` the animation, as shown in the following code:

```
fun onStartStopClick(view: View) {
    imageView.setBackgroundResource(
        R.drawable.star_animation)
    val frameAnimation: AnimationDrawable =
        imageView.background as AnimationDrawable

    if (StartStop.text == "Start") {
        frameAnimation.start()
        StartStop.text = "Stop"
    } else {
        frameAnimation.stop()
        StartStop.text = "Start"
    }

}
```

Communicating with Emoji

Emoji communicate complex emotions, events, ideas, and even words using simple symbols. Because humans have a vast range of emotions, a large number of emoji exist. Of course, you're most interested in the emoji that Android apps support, and you can find them at `https://emojipedia.org/google/` (3,066 at the time of this writing). This list is updated regularly, so if you don't see the emoji you want now, you'll likely see it later.

This section relies on an app named 03_05_04 to provide glimpses into working with emoji in Android. The app doesn't do anything special except show off what's available to you as the developer. So, begin with the Empty Activity without any controls or components added. Set the minimum API level to 26. The following sections tell you about various forms of emoji support in Android.

Keyboard emoji support

Many Android components and controls support emoji natively. You access them using the keyboard, as shown in Figure 5-10 using the 03_04_02 app from Chapter 4 of this minibook. This app doesn't do anything special to provide emoji support; it comes as part of the package. The user just clicks the smiley face at the bottom of the keyboard.

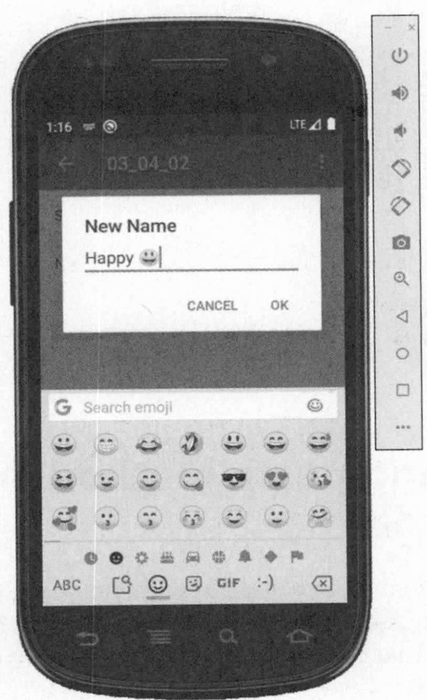

FIGURE 5-10: Accessing emoji using the keyboard in an Android app.

The emoji automatically appear in any control where you can type them, as shown in Figure 5-11. As you can see in the figure, the emoji automatically resize themselves as needed to provide a good presentation onscreen. The emoji tend to be a little larger than the text, so you need to give controls that use them a little more space onscreen.

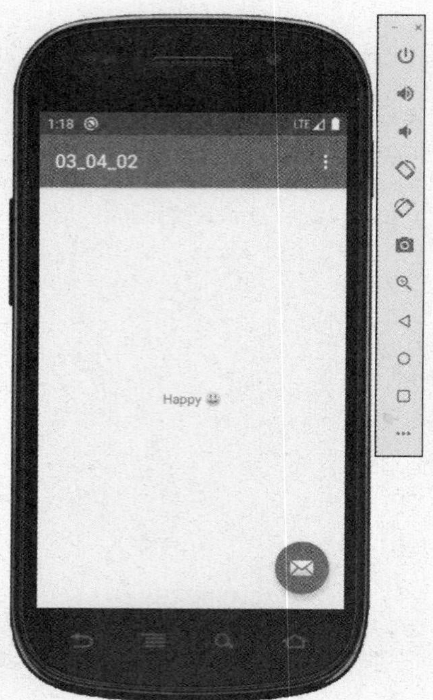

FIGURE 5-11: Displaying emoji in a TextView.

Using the cut-and-paste method on standard controls

If you want to use standard emoji in a static way in your app, you can copy and paste emoji into your app using a standard control, such as a button, using the `strings.xml` file. One site that makes this practice incredibly easy is `https://www.emojicopy.com/`. You simply select the emoji you want to use, click Copy, and then paste the emoji into your `strings.xml` file, as shown in Figure 5-12.

TIP

The appearance of the emoji in the `strings.xml` file isn't all that impressive, but Figure 5-13 shows the results onscreen. This is a standard button — nothing fancy added. The `textAppearance` property is set to `Display2` in this case. So, you get a large button that has all the standard functionality with a friendly grinning cat simply by cutting and pasting. Simple solutions are often the best.

FIGURE 5-12: Copying and pasting emoji into your `strings.xml` file.

```
<resources>
    <string name="app_name">03_05_01</string>
    <string name="EmojiButtonText">😸Grin😸</string>
</resources>
```

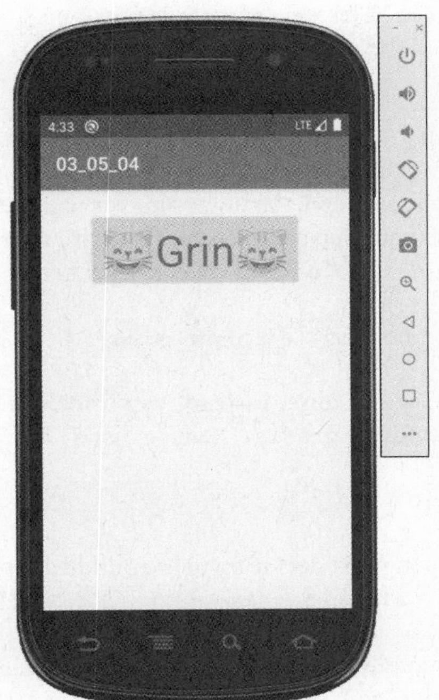

FIGURE 5-13: Viewing the result of cutting and pasting in a standard button.

Using the AndroidX approach

Android supports several levels of programmatic emoji using Unicode characters. The two basic choices are

- **Bundled support:** All the emoji are part of your app.
- **Downloaded support:** The app downloads the fonts from a font provider such as Google Play Services (`https://developers.google.com/fonts/docs/android`).

REMEMBER

The problem with using the bundled fonts is that you may not have access to the latest set of emoji. Here are problems with using the downloaded support:

- You must have an Internet connection to use this approach.
- Downloading the fonts can delay app appearance onscreen.
- It's more complicated.

Because using bundled fonts is straightforward and will meet your needs most of the time, the example in this section relies on bundled fonts. However, the techniques shown also provide a good starting point for using downloaded fonts. Adding full emoji support to your app begins with an addition to the dependencies section of the `build.gradle (Module: app)` file, shown here:

```
implementation 'androidx.emoji:emoji-bundled:1.0.0'
```

If you wanted to use downloaded fonts instead, you'd include this entry in the dependencies section of the `build.gradle (Module: app)` file:

```
implementation 'androidx.emoji:emoji:1.0.0'
```

WARNING

You can't use both entries; you must decide on using bundled fonts or downloaded fonts for the application as a whole.

After you sync your app with the new addition, you have access to a number of emoji-specific features, including a series of controls. You must type the controls in the XML because they don't appear in the Palette. Figure 5-14 shows the controls in question.

<androidx.emo
emoji.widget.EmojiButton (androidx.emoji.widget)
emoji.widget.EmojiEditText (androidx.emoji.widget)
emoji.widget.EmojiExtractTextLayout (androidx.emoji.wi...
emoji.widget.EmojiTextView (androidx.emoji.widget)
Press Ctrl+Space to view tags from other namespaces

FIGURE 5-14: Accessing the special emoji controls.

The example uses an `EmojiButton` widget so that you can compare the cut-and-paste method to the Unicode approach. Here are the configuration options for the `EmojiButton`:

```
<androidx.emoji.widget.EmojiButton
    android:id="@+id/GrinButton"
    android:layout_width="wrap_content"
```

```
    android:layout_height="wrap_content"
    android:layout_marginTop="120dp"
    android:text="@string/GrinButtonText"
    android:textAllCaps="false"
    android:textSize="44sp"
    app:layout_constraintEnd_toEndOf="parent"
    app:layout_constraintStart_toStartOf="parent"
    app:layout_constraintTop_toTopOf="parent"/>
```

The `GrinButtonText` entry in `strings.xml` looks like this:

```
<string name="GrinButtonText" >
   &#x1F638; Grin &#x1F638;
</string>
```

Notice how the Unicode character appears. If you don't include the `#`, you get an unresolved entity reference error. If you don't include the `x`, you see an unescaped `&` character or nonterminated character error.

TIP

You can obtain a full list of emoji, along with their hexadecimal Unicode values, at `https://unicode.org/emoji/charts/full-emoji-list.html`.

Before you can use the fonts, you must load them, even if they're included with your app. This means adding the following code in bold to the `onCreate()` for your app:

```
override fun onCreate(savedInstanceState: Bundle?) {
    super.onCreate(savedInstanceState)

    val config: EmojiCompat.Config =
        BundledEmojiCompatConfig(this)
            .setReplaceAll(true)
            .setEmojiSpanIndicatorEnabled(true)
            .setEmojiSpanIndicatorColor(Color.BLUE)
    EmojiCompat.init(config)

    setContentView(R.layout.activity_main)
}
```

REMEMBER

Notice that you must load and configure the fonts before you call `setContentView()`. Otherwise, the app won't load at all and you continuously see `EmojiCompat.init()` error, with little explanation of why it occurs. Now that you have all the code in place, you can run your app and compare the two versions of the emoji button, as shown in Figure 5-15.

FIGURE 5-15: Comparing pasted emoji to Unicode emoji.

4

Programming Cool Phone Features

Contents at a Glance

» Using Android animation

» Creating random play

Chapter 1

Hungry Burds: A Simple Android Game

What started as a simple pun involving an author's last name has turned into this minibook's Chapter 1 — the most self-indulgent writing in the history of technical publishing. This chapter describes a very simple Android game. The goal of the game is to feed cheeseburgers to Barry Burd. You feed Barry by tapping on the screen.

In case you're wondering, the name Burd has no etymological connection with animals that fly. According to one theory, the name Burd comes from the Russian word *boroda,* which means *beard.* Another conjecture ties it to longer Russian surnames such as Burdinsky and Burdstakovich. U.S. census data reveals that roughly 2 people in 100,000 have the last name Burd. Compare that with 11 in 100,000 who spell their names Bird, and a whopping 32 in 100,000 for Byrd.

Introducing the Hungry Burds Game

When the game begins, the screen is mostly blank. Then, for a random amount of time (ranging from a quarter of a second to a whole second), a Burd image fades in and out of view, as shown in Figure 1-1.

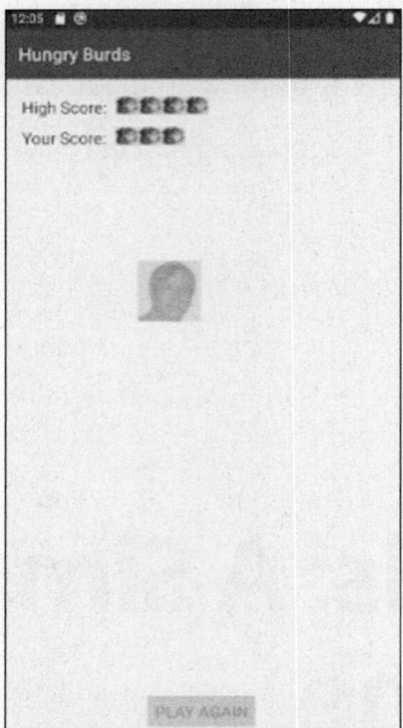

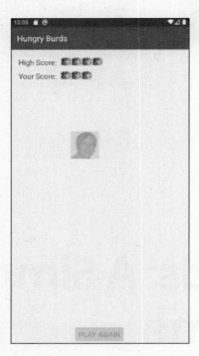

FIGURE 1-1 Playing Hungry Burds.

If the user touches the Burd before it fades away, the app feeds Barry by displaying a tiny cheeseburger. The new cheeseburger shows up at the top of the screen next to the words *Your Score*. In the meantime, a row labeled *High Score* shows the largest number of cheeseburgers eaten during any round of play. (Refer to Figure 1-1.)

A PLAY AGAIN button sits quietly at the bottom of the screen. When the game ends, the PLAY AGAIN button comes alive, and the user can enjoy another fun-filled round of Hungry Burds.

WARNING

For many apps, timing isn't vitally important: For them, a consistently slow response is annoying but not disabling. But for a game like Hungry Burds, timing makes a big difference. Running Hungry Burds on a slow emulator feels more like a waiting game than an action game. If your emulator is slow, run the app on a real-life device.

The Hungry Burds Kotlin code is about 200 lines long. As game programs go, that's miniscule. But this chapter's example can't be dozens of pages long. That's why many features that you see in a realistically engineered game are missing. Here are a few of them:

- **The Hungry Burds game doesn't access data over a network.** The game's High Score leaderboard doesn't tell you how well you did compared with your friends or with other players around the world. The leaderboard applies to only one device — the one you're using to play the game.

  Google Play Game Services is a collection of network-enabled tools to help you add leaderboards, achievements, and multiplayer features to your game app. Game Services belongs to a category of things called *back-end services*. When you publish an app, you can sign up for one or more of these back-end services. For information about publishing your app, visit Book 6.

- **The game runs only in portrait mode.** In the app's `AndroidManifest.xml` file, the `activity` element has an `android:screenOrientation="portrait"` attribute. This keeps the app in portrait mode and saves everyone from having to worry about orientation changes. Android Studio marks this attribute as an error because professional developers frown on such restrictions. But the code runs, and limiting play to portrait mode keeps this chapter's example reasonable in size.

TIP

  If your app's `AndroidManifest.xml` file has an `android:screenOrientation="portrait"` attribute, the file should also contain a `<uses-feature android:name="android.hardware.screen.portrait"/>` element. For details about the uses-feature element, see Book 5, Chapter 2.

- **The screen measurements that control the game are crude.** Creating a visual app that involves drawing, custom images, or motion of any kind involves some math. You need math to make measurements, estimate distances, detect collisions, and complete other tasks. To do the math, you produce numbers by making Android API calls, and you use the results of your calculations in Android API library calls.

  Hungry Burds does only a minimal amount of math, and makes no API calls that aren't absolutely necessary. As a result, some items on the screen don't always look their best.

- **The game has no settings.** The number of Burds displayed, the duration of each Burd's display, and the size of each Burd's display are all hard-coded in the game's Kotlin file. The constants' names are `numberOfBurds`, `maximumShowTime`, `minimumShowTime`, `maximumImageEdge`, and `minimumImageEdge`. As a developer, you can change the values in the code and reinstall the game. But the ordinary player can't change these numbers.

- **The game may not be challenging with the default constants.** Is this good news? After playing Hungry Burds a few times, you can play it over and over again and always win. Of course, real games don't work that way. A real game presents some sort of a challenge. Otherwise, the winner gets no sense of achievement.

If you want Hungry Burds to be challenging, dig into the code and change the values of constants such as maximumShowTime and minimumImageEdge. Experiment to find values that make the game interesting. And, if there are no such values, don't be disappointed. Hungry Burds is a learning tool, not a replacement for Grand Theft Auto.

The Hungry Burds Project's Files

The project's build.grade file is nothing special. The only thing you have to watch for is minSdkVersion. The minSdkVersion has to be 21 or higher. That's because the Kotlin code calls the SoundPool.Builder class's constructor and the View class's generateViewId method. Those features aren't available in Android API levels below 21.

The project's activity_main.xml file is in Listing 1-1. The file's only noteworthy items are two of the PLAY AGAIN button's attributes. The button starts off being disabled and unclickable. That way, when the game starts, the user can't press PLAY AGAIN. Later, when a round of play ends, the app's Kotlin code enables the PLAY AGAIN button.

LISTING 1-1: The Main Activity's Layout File

```
<androidx.constraintlayout.widget.ConstraintLayout
    xmlns:android="http://schemas.android.com/apk/res/android"
    xmlns:app="http://schemas.android.com/apk/res-auto"
    xmlns:tools="http://schemas.android.com/tools"
    android:id="@+id/screenLayout"
    android:layout_width="match_parent"
    android:layout_height="match_parent"
    tools:context=".MainActivity">

    <LinearLayout
        android:id="@+id/highScoreRow"
        android:layout_width="match_parent"
        android:layout_height="wrap_content"
        android:layout_marginStart="20dp"
        android:layout_marginTop="20dp"
        android:layout_marginEnd="20dp"
        android:orientation="horizontal"
        app:layout_constraintEnd_toEndOf="parent"
        app:layout_constraintStart_toStartOf="parent"
        app:layout_constraintTop_toTopOf="parent">
```

```
    <TextView
        android:id="@+id/highScoreTextView"
        style="@android:style/TextAppearance.Medium"
        android:layout_width="wrap_content"
        android:layout_height="wrap_content"
        android:layout_gravity="center_vertical"
        android:text="@string/high_score"/>

    <LinearLayout
        android:id="@+id/highScoreBurgersLayout"
        android:layout_width="match_parent"
        android:layout_height="match_parent"
        android:layout_gravity="center_vertical"
        android:layout_marginStart="10dp"
        android:layout_marginLeft="10dp"
        android:orientation="horizontal"/>
</LinearLayout>

<LinearLayout
    android:id="@+id/yourScoreRow"
    android:layout_width="match_parent"
    android:layout_height="wrap_content"
    android:layout_marginStart="20dp"
    android:layout_marginTop="10dp"
    android:layout_marginEnd="20dp"
    android:orientation="horizontal"
    app:layout_constraintEnd_toEndOf="parent"
    app:layout_constraintStart_toStartOf="parent"
    app:layout_constraintTop_toBottomOf="@id/highScoreRow">

    <TextView
        android:id="@+id/yourScoreTextView"
        style="@android:style/TextAppearance.Medium"
        android:layout_width="wrap_content"
        android:layout_height="wrap_content"
        android:layout_gravity="center_vertical"
        android:text="@string/your_score"/>

    <LinearLayout
        android:id="@+id/yourScoreBurgersLayout"
        android:layout_width="match_parent"
        android:layout_height="match_parent"
        android:layout_gravity="center_vertical"
        android:layout_marginStart="10dp"
        android:layout_marginLeft="10dp"
        android:orientation="horizontal"/>
</LinearLayout>
```

(continued)

LISTING 1-1: *(continued)*

```
    <Button
        android:id="@+id/playAgainButton"
        style="@android:style/TextAppearance.Medium"
        android:layout_width="wrap_content"
        android:layout_height="wrap_content"
        android:clickable="false"
        android:enabled="false"
        android:onClick="playAgain"
        android:text="@string/play_again"
        app:layout_constraintBottom_toBottomOf="parent"
        app:layout_constraintEnd_toEndOf="parent"
        app:layout_constraintStart_toStartOf="parent"/>

</androidx.constraintlayout.widget.ConstraintLayout>
```

The `res/drawable` directory of the Hungry Burds project has two files: `burd.png` and `burger.png`. The `burd.png` file is a picture of Barry. The `burger.png` file is a tiny picture of a cheeseburger. When the game runs, the Kotlin code adds `ImageView` objects containing these `.png` files to various layouts within `activity_main.xml`.

The Main Activity

The Hungry Burds game has only one activity: the app's main activity. So you can digest the game's Kotlin code in its entirety in one big gulp. To make this gulp palatable, Listing 1-2 has an outline of the main activity's code. (If outlines don't work for you and you want to examine the code in its entirety, see Listing 1-3.)

LISTING 1-2: An Outline of the App's Kotlin Code

```
package com.allmycode.hungryburds

// Import classes.

class MainActivity : AppCompatActivity(), View.OnTouchListener {

    // Declare variables.

    public override fun onCreate(savedInstanceState: Bundle?) {
      // Get the size of the device's screen.
      // Get the high score from the last run.
```

```
        // Display the high score (a number of cheeseburgers).
        // Prepare a sound to make when the user touches a Burd.
    }

    override fun onStart() {
        showABurd()
    }

    private fun showABurd() {
        // Add a Burd image of random size at some random
        //   place on the screen. (At first, the Burd is
        //   invisible because it's transparent.)
        // Make this activity be the Burd image's onTouch listener.
        // Create an animation to make the Burd fade in and then fade out.
        // Start the animation.
    }

    override fun onTouch(view: View?, event: MotionEvent?): Boolean {
        // Remove the Burd image's touch listener
        //   so that a second touch has no effect.
        // Display a new cheeseburger image in the Your Score row.
        // Play a sound.
    }

    private fun getListenerFor(view : ImageView) : AnimatorListener {
        override fun onAnimationEnd(animation: Animator?) {
            // If the count of Burd images shown is less than 10,
                showABurd() // Again!
            // Otherwise,
            //   save the high score and enable the PLAY AGAIN button.
        }
    }
}
```

The heart of the Hungry Burds code is the code's game loop, as shown in Figure 1-2.

When Android executes the `onStart` method, the code calls the `showABurd` method. The `showABurd` method does what its name suggests by animating an image from alpha level 0 to alpha level 1 and then back to alpha level 0. (Alpha level 0 is fully transparent; alpha level 1 is fully opaque.)

When the animation ends, the `onAnimationEnd` method checks the number of Burds that have already been displayed. If the number is less than ten, the `onAnimationEnd` method calls `showABurd` again, and the game loop continues. Otherwise, the game ends with a newly enabled PLAY AGAIN button.

```
public override fun onStart() {
    // ...
    showABurd()
}

private fun showABurd() {
    // ...
    addToScreen(burd)
    // ...
    animatorSet.also {
        it.addListener(getListenerFor(burd))
        // ...
        it.setTarget(burd)
        it.start()
    }
}

private fun getListenerFor(view : ImageView) : AnimatorListener {
    return object : AnimatorListener {
        // ...
        override fun onAnimationEnd(animation: Animator?) {
            // ...
            if (++countShown < numberOfBurds) {
                showABurd() // Again!
            } else {
                saveHighScore()
                playAgainButton.isEnabled = true
                playAgainButton.isClickable = true
            }
        }
    }
}
```

FIGURE 1-2: Showing one Burd after another.

The main activity implements `OnTouchListener`. When the user touches a Burd, the activity's `onTouch` method adds a cheeseburger to the Your Score display, as shown in the following snippet:

```
override fun onTouch(view: View?, event: MotionEvent?):
   Boolean {
     view?.setOnTouchListener(null)
     addBurgerTo(yourScoreBurgersLayout)
     soundPool.play(soundId, 1f, 1f, 0, 0, 1f)
     countTouched++
     return true
 }
```

The Code, All the Code, and Nothing But the Code

Following the basic outline of the game's code in the previous section, Listing 1-3 contains the entire text of the game's `MainActivity.kt` file.

LISTING 1-3: The App's Kotlin Code

```
package com.allmycode.hungryburds

import android.animation.Animator
import android.animation.Animator.AnimatorListener
import android.animation.AnimatorInflater
import android.animation.AnimatorSet
import android.annotation.SuppressLint
import android.content.Context
import android.content.SharedPreferences
import android.media.AudioAttributes
import android.media.SoundPool
import android.os.Bundle
import android.util.Size
import android.view.MotionEvent
import android.view.View
import android.widget.ImageView
import android.widget.LinearLayout
import androidx.appcompat.app.AppCompatActivity
import androidx.constraintlayout.widget.ConstraintLayout
import androidx.constraintlayout.widget.ConstraintSet
import kotlinx.android.synthetic.main.activity_main.*
import java.util.Random


class MainActivity : AppCompatActivity(), View.OnTouchListener {
    private val numberOfBurds = 10
    private val maximumShowTime = 1000L
    private val minimumShowTime = 250L
    private val maximumImageEdge = 200
    private val minimumImageEdge = 50

    private var countShown = 0
    private var countTouched = 0
    private var highScore = 0
    private var random = Random()

    private lateinit var displaySize: Size

    private lateinit var prefs: SharedPreferences

    private lateinit var soundPool: SoundPool
    private var soundId = 0

    private var isStarted = false
```

(continued)

LISTING 1-3: *(continued)*

```
public override fun onCreate(savedInstanceState: Bundle?) {
    super.onCreate(savedInstanceState)
    setContentView(R.layout.activity_main)

    val metrics = resources.displayMetrics
    displaySize = Size(metrics.widthPixels, metrics.heightPixels)

    prefs = getPreferences(Context.MODE_PRIVATE)
    highScore = prefs.getInt("highScore", 0)
    displayHighScore()

    prepareSound()
}

override fun onStart() {
    super.onStart()
    isStarted = true
    showABurd()
}

private fun displayHighScore() {
    for (i in 1..highScore) {
        addBurgerTo(highScoreBurgersLayout)
    }
}

private fun addBurgerTo(layout: LinearLayout) {
    layout.addView(ImageView(this).apply {
        setImageResource(R.drawable.burger)
    })
}

private fun prepareSound() {
    soundPool = SoundPool.Builder()
        .setAudioAttributes(
            AudioAttributes.Builder()
                .setContentType(
                    AudioAttributes.CONTENT_TYPE_SONIFICATION
                )
                .setUsage(AudioAttributes.USAGE_GAME)
                .build()
        ).build()
    soundId = soundPool.load(this, R.raw.beep, 1)
}
```

```
private fun showABurd() {
    val duration = (random.nextInt((maximumShowTime
            - minimumShowTime).toInt()) + minimumShowTime)
    val imageEdgeSize = (random.nextInt(maximumImageEdge
            - minimumImageEdge) + minimumImageEdge)
    val burd = ImageView(this).also {
        it.setImageResource(R.drawable.burd)
        it.setOnTouchListener(this)
        it.layoutParams = ConstraintLayout.LayoutParams(
            imageEdgeSize, imageEdgeSize
        )
    }
    addToScreen(burd)
    val animatorSet = AnimatorInflater.loadAnimator(
        this,
        R.animator.fade_in_out
    ) as AnimatorSet
    animatorSet.also {
        it.addListener(getListenerFor(burd))
        it.duration = duration
        it.setTarget(burd)
        it.start()
    }
}

private fun addToScreen(view: View) {
    view.id = View.generateViewId()
    screenLayout.addView(view, 0)
    ConstraintSet().apply {
        clone(screenLayout)
        connect(
            view.id,
            ConstraintSet.LEFT,
            screenLayout.id,
            ConstraintSet.LEFT,
            random.nextInt(displaySize.width) * 7 / 8
        )
        connect(
            view.id,
            ConstraintSet.TOP,
            screenLayout.id,
            ConstraintSet.TOP,
            random.nextInt(displaySize.height) * 4 / 5
        )
        applyTo(screenLayout)
    }
}
```

(continued)

LISTING 1-3: *(continued)*

```
@SuppressLint("ClickableViewAccessibility")
override fun onTouch(view: View?, event: MotionEvent?): Boolean {
    view?.setOnTouchListener(null)
    addBurgerTo(yourScoreBurgersLayout)
    soundPool.play(soundId, 1f, 1f, 0, 0, 1f)
    countTouched++
    return true
}

private fun getListenerFor(view: ImageView): AnimatorListener {
    return object : AnimatorListener {
        override fun onAnimationStart(animation: Animator?) {
        }

        override fun onAnimationRepeat(animation: Animator?) {
        }

        override fun onAnimationCancel(animation: Animator?) {
        }

        override fun onAnimationEnd(animation: Animator?) {
            screenLayout.removeView(view)
            if (isStarted) {
                if (++countShown < numberOfBurds) {
                    showABurd()
                } else {
                    saveHighScore()
                    playAgainButton.isEnabled = true
                    playAgainButton.isClickable = true
                }
            }
        }
    }
}

private fun saveHighScore() {
    if (countTouched > highScore) {
        highScore = countTouched
        val editor = prefs.edit()
        editor.putInt("highScore", highScore)
        editor.apply()
    }
}
```

```
    fun playAgain(view: View) {
        playAgainButton.isEnabled = false
        playAgainButton.isClickable = false
        countShown = 0
        countTouched = 0
        highScoreBurgersLayout.removeAllViews()
        displayHighScore()
        yourScoreBurgersLayout.removeAllViews()
        showABurd()
    }

    override fun onStop() {
        super.onStop()
        isStarted = false
    }
}
```

Setting Up the Game

The game's one and only activity begins the way most Android activities begin. First, you have some property declarations, and then you have an onCreate method. This section explores that introductory code.

Declaring properties

The activity's properties are used throughout the game's run. As usual, you use val rather than var to declare any property whose value doesn't change.

In Listing 1-3, notice the use of the word lateinit. You can probably guess what that's about. It's about late (rather than early) initialization. Here's the story:

Kotlin is fussy about initializing properties. Other languages may let you get away with something, like this:

```
// Bad code:
var total : Int

// and later...

total += nextValue
```

GETTING THE SCREEN SIZE

To display images at random places on a device's screen, the Hungry Burds code needs to know the size of the device's display. How complicated can that be? You can measure the screen size with a ruler, and you can determine a device's resolution by reading the specs in the user manual.

Of course, Android programs don't have opposable thumbs, so they can't use plastic rulers, and they can't browse user manuals. On top of that, a layout's characteristics can change depending on several runtime factors, including the device's orientation (portrait or landscape) and the amount of screen space reserved for Android's notification bar and buttons.

To help with all this, Android has `DisplayMetrics`. A `DisplayMetrics` instance has information about the display's width, height, and pixel density. The only hitch is that you can't get a `DisplayMetrics` instance before you execute `onCreate`. Consider the following code:

```
// Very bad code!
class MainActivity : AppCompatActivity(), View.OnTouchListener {

    var metrics = DisplayMetrics()

    // More code goes here.

    public override fun onCreate(savedInstanceState: Bundle?) {
        super.onCreate(savedInstanceState)
        setContentView(R.layout.activity_main)

        displaySize = Size(metrics.widthPixels, metrics.
    heightPixels)

        // And so on.
```

This code doesn't generate a compile time error, the call to construct a `DisplayMetrics` instance doesn't fail, and the assignment to `displaySize` moves happily along. Everything goes fine until you try to use the `displaySize` variable's `width` and `height` values. With this sidebar's faulty code, both `displaySize.width` and `displaySize.height` are 0. That's not good.

To avoid this kind of trouble, Listing 1-3 assigns values to `metrics` and `displaySize` in the body of `onCreate`, and the use of `lateinit` makes `displaySize` available to other methods in the main activity.

But Kotlin will have none of it. If you haven't given `total` an initial value, you shouldn't be adding something to `total`.

Sometimes, Kotlin's insistence on initializing properties makes things difficult. A property declaration goes outside any method declarations, so Android evaluates these declarations before calling `onCreate`. The problem is, some values aren't available before Android calls `onCreate`. Take, for example, the `prefs` property in Listing 1-3, shown previously. This property has type `SharedPreferences`, but you can't call `getSharedPreferences` until you've started running `onCreate`. What's a programmer to do?

In Listing 1-3, Kotlin's `lateinit` keyword puts the initialization of `prefs` on the back burner. The `lateinit` keyword tells the compiler to be patient and wait for the `prefs` property to get a value. "I know what I'm doing," says the `lateinit` programmer, "and I promise to assign a value to `prefs` before I call the `prefs` object's `getInt` method." And Kotlin responds by saying, "Okay. I trust you."

Similar issues apply to the game's `displaySize` and `soundPool` properties. So, in Listing 1-3, the declarations of these properties use `lateinit`.

You can read more about `SharedPreferences` in Book 3, Chapter 4.

TECHNICAL STUFF

In the app's `prepareSound` method, the value of `soundId` depends on `soundPool`, so you'd expect the `soundId` declaration to use `lateinit`. But Kotlin doesn't permit the use of `lateinit` on primitive types such as `Int`. Some blog posts suggest exotic workarounds, but initializing `soundId` to `0` works nicely.

The onCreate Method

To begin a run of Hungry Burds, Listing 1-3 gets the device's screen size. The code also gets the highest score from the device's previous Hungry Burds runs. To get the highest score, Listing 1-3 uses Android's `SharedPreferences` class.

In Book 3, Chapter 4, you can read about Android's `MediaPlayer` class. The `MediaPlayer` works well for playing songs and videos, but it's not good for brief sound bursts — things like beeps, thunderclaps, happy "you win" rings, or discouraging "bah-waahhh" horns. For such momentary sounds, you use the `SoundPool` class. The sidebar explains why.

Starting with API level 21, you create a `SoundPool` by making a `SoundPool.Builder` and chaining methods one after another until you reach the `build` method. On your way to the `build` method, the `setAudioAttributes` method uses its own `AudioAttributes.Builder` class. By the time you're done with all the `build` calls, you have a real, live `SoundPool` instance.

DIFFERENT WAYS TO PRODUCE SOUNDS

To prepare a file for `MediaPlayer`, Android compresses the file and packages the compressed version with an app's APK. Android can't interpret the bits in a compressed file. So, before the user's device plays the audio or video file, Android takes time to uncompress the file. As a result, the user experiences a brief delay. For a song or a video clip, the delay is tolerable, but with a sound that congratulates you for tapping a Burd image, the delay would be deadening.

Some audio clips are very short. They don't take up much space, so they can be packaged without compression in an app's APK file. Android's `SoundPool` class loads these files quickly and plays them almost immediately.

But wait! There's another step. When you populate the `SoundPool` instance with an actual sound file resource, you get an `Int` value that identifies the sound. Listing 1-3 puts this value in its `soundId` variable. When the user taps a Burd, the app calls the `SoundPool` instance's `play` method and passes that `soundId` as a parameter. Sure enough, the sound file bursts from the device's speakers.

Displaying a Burd

In Listing 1-3, the last statement in the `onStart` method is a call to the `showABurd` method. The next few sections describe how the app goes about showing a Burd.

Creating random values

A typical game involves random choices. (You don't want Burds to appear in the same places every time you play the game.) Truly random values are difficult to generate. But an instance of the `java.util.Random` class creates what appear to be random values (*pseudorandom* values) in ways that the programmer can help determine.

For example, a `Random` object's `nextDouble` method returns a `double` value between 0.0 and 1.0 (with 0.0 being possible but 1.0 being impossible). The Hungry Burds code uses a `Random` object's `nextInt` method. A call to `nextInt(10)` returns an `int` value from `0` to `9`.

If `displaySize.width` is 720 (which stands for 720 pixels), the call to `random.nextInt(displaySize.width)` in Listing 1-3 returns a value from `0` to `719`. And because maximumShowTime differs from minimumShowTime by the Long value 750L, the expression

```
random.nextInt((maximumShowTime - minimumShowTime).toInt())
```

stands for a value from 0 to 749. (The toInt call fulfills the promise that the nextInt method's parameter is an Int, not a Long value.) By adding back minimumShowTime (in Listing 1-3), you make duration a number between 250 and 999. The same kind of calculation sets imageEdgeSize to a number between 50 and 200. The imageEdgeSize is the height and width of the next Burd image being displayed.

Creating a Burd

Android's ImageView class represents objects that contain images. You put an image file (a .png file, a .jpg file, or a .gif file) in your project's res/drawable directory. In the Kotlin code, a call to the ImageView object's setImageResource method associates the ImageView object with the .png, .jpg, or .gif file. Consider the following lines in Listing 1-3:

```
val burd = ImageView(this).also {
    it.setImageResource(R.drawable.burd)
    it.setOnTouchListener(this)
    it.layoutParams = ConstraintLayout.LayoutParams(
        imageEdgeSize, imageEdgeSize
    )
}
```

This code uses Kotlin's also function along with the special it identifier. In Kotlin, also, apply, and let are scope functions. A *scope function* allows you to apply several methods to an object without repeating the object's name before each method application. Inside an also block, the word it refers to the block's target object (the object that comes immediately before .also in the code). If you don't like the way Listing 1-3 creates a new ImageView instance, you can replace the also code with the following four statements:

```
val burd = ImageView(this)
burd.setImageResource(R.drawable.burd)
burd.setOnTouchListener(this)
burd.layoutParams =
    ConstraintLayout.LayoutParams(imageEdgeSize, imageEdgeSize)
```

The also version is nice because also puts the creation of the new ImageView into a tidy code bundle. One glance at the also block makes it clear that the code sets a particular object's properties. Here's what happens inside the `ImageView` instance's `also` block:

- **The call to `setImageResource` associates the `app/res/drawable/burd.png` file with this `ImageView` instance.**
- **The call to `setOnTouchListener` tells Android that `this` main activity handles the image view's touch events.** You can read more about that in the "Handling a Touch Event" section, later in this chapter.
- **The assignment to the image view's `layoutParams` property tells Android how large the view should be.** You've already used `Random` to set the value of `imageEdgeSize`. You want to apply that `imageEdgeSize` to your brand new Burd image. You don't simply say "Make each image's edges be `imageEdgeSize` pixels long." Instead, you say "*In a ConstraintLayout*, make each image's edges be `imageEdgeSize` pixels long." Each of Android's `LayoutParams` classes are the inner classes of one layout or another. There's `ConstraintLayout.LayoutParams`, `LinearLayout.LayoutParams`, `ViewGroup.LayoutParams`, and a bunch of others.

Placing a Burd on the constraint layout

In Listing 1-3, the `addToScreen` method does what its name suggests: It puts a new view on the device's screen. Adding a view to a particular place in a constraint layout involves several steps:

1. **Give the view an `id`.**

   In a layout's XML file, you can write

   ```
   android:id="@+id/newBurd"
   ```

   But you can't do that in the middle of a Kotlin file. Instead, you call the `View` class's `generateViewId` method.

2. **Add the view to the constraint layout.**

   By default, the new view goes in one of the layout's two upper corners. Which corner gets the view depends on a device's language setting. For most languages, it's the upper-left corner. But for right-to-left languages, it's the upper-right corner.

3. **Get a constraint set.**

   To reposition your new view in the activity's constraint layout, you make an instance of Android's `ConstraintSet` class. In Listing 1-3, you start with a `clone` of a `ConstraintSet` from the activity's own constraint layout. You position the new view by making changes to this clone.

4. Connect new constraints to the constraint set.

The code in Listing 1-3 connects two constraints to the constraint set. The first constraint sets the distance between the new view's left edge and the screen's left edge. The second constraint sets the distance between the top of the view and the top of the screen. Figure 1-3 shows you the meanings of the `connect` method's parameters.

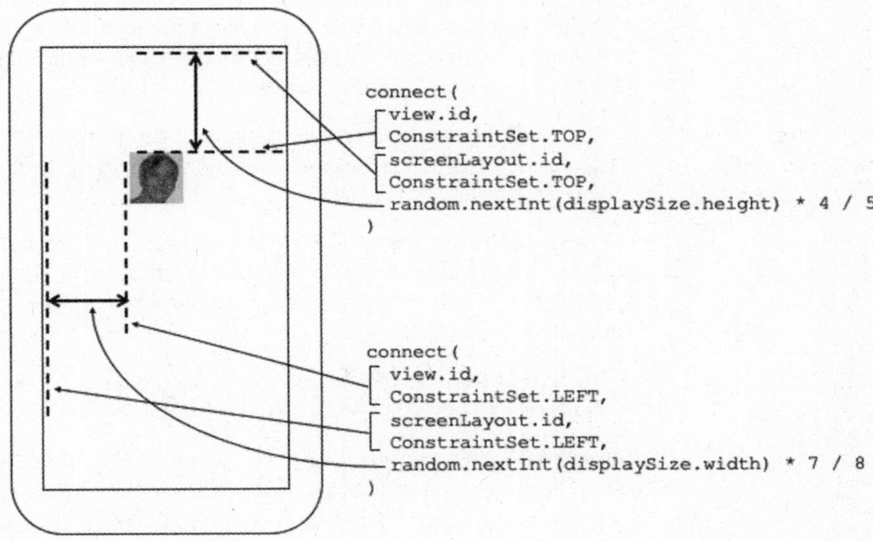
connect(
view.id,
ConstraintSet.TOP,
screenLayout.id,
ConstraintSet.TOP,
random.nextInt(displaySize.height) * 4 / 5
)
connect(
view.id,
ConstraintSet.LEFT,
screenLayout.id,
ConstraintSet.LEFT,
random.nextInt(displaySize.width) * 7 / 8
)

FIGURE 1-3: Positioning a view in a constraint set.

Listing 1-3 generates values randomly to determine the position of a new Burd. A Burd's left edge is no farther than ⅞ of the way across the screen, and the Burd's top edge is no lower than ⅘ of the way down the screen. If you don't multiply the screen's width by ⅞ (or some such fraction), an entire Burd can be positioned beyond the right edge of the screen. The user sees nothing while the Burd comes and goes. The same kind of thing can happen if you don't multiply the screen's height by ⅘.

TECHNICAL STUFF

The fractions ⅞ and ⅘, which help determine each new Burd's position, are crude guesstimates of a portrait screen's requirements. A more refined app would carefully measure the available turf and calculate the optimally sized region for positioning new Burds.

5. Apply the constraint set to the app's screen.

In Listing 1-3, the constraint set's `applyTo` method takes care of that step.

Animating a Burd

Android has two types of animation:

- **View animation:** An older system in which you animate with either tweening or frame-by-frame animation, as described in this list:
  - **Tweening:** You tell Android how an object should look initially and how the object should look eventually. You also tell Android how to change from the initial appearance to the eventual appearance. (Is the change gradual or sudden? If the object moves, does it move in a straight line or in a curve of some sort? Will it bounce a bit when it reaches the end of its path?)

    With tweening, Android considers all your requirements and figures out exactly how the object looks *between* the start and the finish of the object's animation.
  - **Frame-by-frame animation:** You provide several snapshots of the object along its path. Android displays these snapshots in rapid succession, one after another, giving the appearance of movement or of another change in the object's appearance.

    The `animation-list` example in Book 3, Chapter 5 is an example of frame animation.

  View animation has two significant shortcomings. First, view animation doesn't apply to things that aren't views. With view animation, you can change the position of a bouncing ball, but you can't change the price of bananas or the value of one dollar in euros. Those things don't extend the `android.view.View` class.

  In addition, view animation doesn't make lasting changes to a view's values. You can make a view *appear* to move, but the view doesn't really move. Imagine view animating a button from a corner of the screen to the center. The button seems to be in the center but, when the user taps the center of the screen, nothing happens. On the other hand, if the user taps the original corner, the button responds. That's pretty strange!

  So, what's better than view animation?
- **Property animation:** A newer system (introduced in Android 3.0, API Level 11) in which you can modify any property of an object over a period of time.

  With property animation, you can change anything about any kind of object, whether the object appears on the device's screen or not. For example, you can increase an `earth` object's average temperature from 15° Celsius to 18° Celsius over a period of ten minutes. Rather than display the `earth` object, you can watch the way average temperature affects water levels and plant life.

Unlike view animation, the use of property animation changes the value stored in an object's field. For example, you can use property animation to change a widget from being invisible to being visible. When the property animation finishes, the widget remains visible.

To make Burd images fade in and out, the Hungry Burds app uses property animation. A file named `fade_in_out.xml` sits quietly in the project's `app/res/animator` folder. Listing 1-4 has the code.

LISTING 1-4: An Animator Resource File

```
<?xml version="1.0" encoding="utf-8"?>
<set xmlns:android="http://schemas.android.com/apk/res/android"
    android:ordering="sequentially">
    <objectAnimator
        android:propertyName="alpha"
        android:valueFrom="0.0"
        android:valueTo="1.0"
        android:valueType="floatType"/>
    <objectAnimator
        android:propertyName="alpha"
        android:valueFrom="1.0"
        android:valueTo="0.0"
        android:valueType="floatType"/>
</set>
```

The file in Listing 1-4 describes an *animator set.* The set contains two `objectAnimator` elements — one for fading in and the other for fading out. The fade-in animator brings an object from alpha level 0.0 (complete transparency) to alpha level 1.0 (complete opacity). The fade-out animator does the opposite.

WARNING

If you create an animator set and you don't specify an `android:ordering="sequentially"` attribute, the set defaults to `android:ordering="together"`. In Listing 1-4, removing that attribute would make Android play the fade-in and fade-out animators simultaneously. If you were a *For Dummies* author and you were testing your code, you'd see each image pop quickly into view and then disappear slowly. You'd wonder why this was happening, and you'd waste a lot of time trying to figure it out. When you finally found the strange behavior's cause, you'd feel pretty foolish, but you'd remind yourself that everyone makes mistakes. That's exactly what would happen.

In Android, inflation has nothing to do with the price of oil or the air in a balloon. Inflation is the way you pull information into your Kotlin code from an XML file.

In Listing 1-3, the showABurd method inflates the fade_in_out.xml file. The next few lines apply a listener for the animation, set the animation's duration to a randomly generated value, and link the animation to a new Burd image. Last, but not least, the code calls start.

Handling a Touch Event

Listing 1-3, earlier in the chapter, contains the following code:

```
val burd = ImageView(this).also {
    it.setImageResource(R.drawable.burd)
    it.setOnTouchListener(this)
// ... Etc.
```

The main activity listens for the user to touch the Burd image. What's a touch, and how does it differ from a click?

When you click a button, you generate more than one event. Pressing down on the button is a touch event. Lifting your finger up and off the button is another touch event. If you slide your finger along the surface of the button, those are even more touch events. A click isn't a simple thing. A click is a combination of touch events. In game development, the time it takes to respond to a click might as well be an eon. If you program Listing 1-3 to listen for click events, half the user's taps go unnoticed. That's why the main activity isn't an OnClickListener. Instead, the header of the MainActivity class's declaration makes that class implement the OnTouchListener interface.

When the user touches a Burd, Android calls the onTouch method in Listing 1-3. The onTouch method does a number of interesting things:

- **The onTouch method tells Android to stop listening for touch events on that Burd.** You don't want the user to get six points for sliding a finger along a Burd image. After one touch to a particular image, that Burd is cooked!
- **The onTouch method updates the user's score.** Calling addBurgerTo puts a tiny picture of a burger next to the app's Your Score text view.
- **The onTouch method plays a victory sound.** Having prepared the sound-Pool object in onCreate, the code calls that object's play method. The play method's parameters are as follows:

  ```
  play(which_sound, leftVolume, rightVolume, priority, loop, rate)
  ```

- The first parameter is the `soundId` — a value that the `prepareSound` method in Listing 1-3 creates.
- The next two `Float` values (both `1f`) play the sound at 100 percent of the device's current volume level.

  If both values were `0f`, you'd hear nothing at all.
- Higher-priority sounds take precedence over lower-priority sounds but, in Listing 1-3, you have only one sound. So, the lowest possible priority (namely, `0`) is okay.
- The loop parameter tells Android how many times to replay the sound, with 0 meaning "don't replay." The special loop value –1 would mean "repeat indefinitely." (Hitting the Android device with a hammer would certainly override that directive.)
- For the `play` method's last parameter, the value `1f` represents normal speed. You can set this value as low as 0.5 (for half speed) or as high as 2.0 (for double speed).

» **The `onTouch` method increments the count of successful Burd image touches.** (There's nothing particularly interesting about this, so just march on and read the next bullet.)

» **The `onTouch` method returns `true`.** The value `true` tells Android that this touch event has been handled. A return value of `false` would tell Android to pass the buck to some other code that can handle the image's touch event.

In Listing 1-3, a `SuppressLint` line comes right before the `onTouch` method's declaration. When you override `onTouch`, you run the risk of squelching some of Android's accessibility features. A program named Lint runs in the background to warn you about such things. Normally, Lint would recommend that you fire your own click event inside your `onTouch` method's body, but the listing's `@SuppressLint("ClickableViewAccessibility")` annotation tells Lint to ignore the `ClickableViewAccessibility` issue.

TIP

A better version of the Hungry Burds game would heed Lint's warning. For more details, visit `https://developer.android.com/guide/topics/ui/accessibility/custom-views.html#custom-touch-events`.

Finishing Up

In Listing 1-3, the `getListenerFor` method creates an object — one that responds to the animating of a Burd image. This `AnimatorListener` object contains bodies for the methods `onAnimationStart`, `onAnimationRepeat`, `onAnimationCancel`, and `onAnimationEnd`. Nothing happens in three of the four methods, and that's okay.

The `onAnimationEnd` method checks the count of Burds that have already been shown. If that count is less than `numberOfBurds`, the `onAnimationEnd` method calls `showABurd` again, and the game loop continues. If not, the method calls `saveHighScore` to update the app's shared preferences. The method also enables the PLAY AGAIN button, whose listener can start another round of play.

What happens if something interrupts a round of play? What if a phone call comes in? What if the user taps Android's Home button or swipes up from the bottom of the screen? If you're not careful, the game keeps running without anyone playing it. In the worst case, you have two copies of the game playing simultaneously, both displaying Burd images on the same white background.

To keep these weird things from happening, Listing 1-3 overrides the `onStart` and `onStop` methods. Android calls `onStop` when an activity ceases to be visible, but calling `onStop` doesn't automatically end the app's game loop. (In fact, calling `onDestroy` wouldn't automatically end the game loop! How about that?)

To block the relentless appearance of Burd images, the `onStop` method in Listing 1-3 sets `isStarted` to `false`. At that point, an `if` statement in the `onAnimationEnd` method refuses to call `showABurd`, and the repeated display of a *For Dummies* author's face comes to a screeching halt.

But wait! The user can end the phone call and return to the Hungry Burds game. If that happens, the `onStart` method in Listing 1-3 sets `isStarted` to true and calls `showABurd`. In that case, Hungry Burds takes up right where it left off. Play on, fair user!

- **Using the Facebook SDK for Android**
- **Surfing the web from inside an activity**
- **Posting on Facebook with Android code**

Chapter 2
An Android Social Media App

A reader from Vancouver (in British Columbia, Canada) writes:

"Hello. I just thought I would ask that you include the area that seems to get attention from app developers: programs connecting with social sites. I look forward to reading the new book! Best regards, David."

Well, David, you're inspiring readers to create a Facebook app. This chapter's example does two things: It visits a web page, and it creates a post about that page. An app can perform many more tasks — for example, query data, manage ads, upload photos, and do lots of other things that Facebook users want done. For simplicity, though, this chapter's app performs only two tasks: surf and post.

The essence of this chapter's Facebook code is two short statements. To visit a website, the app executes

```
webView.loadUrl(url)
```

And, to create a post, the app executes

```
shareDialog.show(linkContent)
```

Of course, these two statements serve only as a summary, and a summary is never the same as the material it summarizes. Imagine standing on the street in Times Square and shouting the statement, "Share dialog dot show link content." Nothing good happens because you're issuing the correct command in the wrong context. In the same way, the context surrounding a call to `shareDialog.show(linkContent)` in an app matters an awful lot.

The next several sections cover all the context surrounding your calls to `webView.loadUrl(url)` and `shareDialog.show(linkContent)`.

Setting Things Up on Facebook's Developer Site

This chapter's examples talk directly to Facebook's server. The exchange between the app and Facebook doesn't involve Facebook's regular website, so Facebook's server has reason to be cautious. If the server could talk, it would say, "What is this app that's trying to send commands to me directly? Is the app malicious? Why should I trust it?"

Before Facebook's server will listen to your app, you have to register the app on Facebook's developer site. You can do this before you've written a single line of code!

Here's what you do (in a general way because the exact steps change):

1. **Log on to Facebook.**
2. **Visit `developers.facebook.com`.**

   This page knows who you are. After all, you logged on in Step 1.

   An announcement welcoming you to Facebook for Developers appears. It's time for you to add developer credentials to your Facebook account.

3. **Click buttons and answer questions until the page tells you that you've become a developer.**

   Chances are, you'll see another welcome message along with an option to Create First App. If you don't, return to the `developers.facebook.com` page and look for an option to create a new app.

   At this point, the developer site prompts you for your app's display name.

4. **Type a display name.**

   If you're undecided, try My First App or I Love This Android Book. Tempting as it may be, you can't use the word Facebook anywhere in the display name. That's understandable.

   As of the spring of 2020, the site asks for a contact email address, and the bottom-right corner has a Create App ID button. One way or another, you should find a button to indicate that you're finished telling Facebook about the app's existence.

5. **Press Create App ID (or select whatever option takes you to the next step).**

   Facebook's server now knows about your app. You see a dashboard page with all kinds of options. Each option offers dozens of ways to add functionality to your app. Fortunately, this chapter's first example involves none of these options. What a relief!

6. **Look for your app's newly generated App ID.**

   The App ID is a 15-digit number. If the stars are aligned, you can find the App ID by selecting the Settings⇨Basic tab on the left side of the page.

7. **Copy the App ID.**

   In an old movie, someone would tell you to memorize the ID and swallow the paper you wrote it on. Don't do that.

When you register a real app — one meant for use by the general public — you linger a lot longer between Steps 5 and 6. You select options on the app's dashboard and configure each option to fit your needs. When you've finished running this chapter's examples, try exploring some these options. When you do, you'll discover many additional services that your Facebook app can offer.

A Minimal Facebook App

You can import this chapter's code from either of this book's websites (`http://allmycode.com/Android` or the book's page at `www.Dummies.com`) by following the instructions in Book 1, Chapter 3. As is true for any Android app, this chapter's project contains about 130 files and about 45 different folders, and that doesn't count all the stuff that you generate with each run. This chapter centers around the project's Kotlin files. But two other files require some attention.

The build.gradle file

Android has no built-in support for communicating with Facebook. Yes, the raw materials are contained in Android's libraries, but to deal with all of Facebook's requirements, someone has to paste together those raw materials in a useful way. Fortunately, Facebook's developers have done all the pasting and made their library — the Facebook SDK for Android — available for general use. To add the library to your project, put the following line in the `dependencies` section of the project's `build.gradle (Module: app)` file.

```
implementation 'com.facebook.android:facebook-android-sdk:[7,8)'
```

On that line, the range `[7,8)` tells Gradle to use any version of the SDK from version 7.0.0 up to (but not including) version 8.0.0. Changes in version 8.0.0 probably won't break any of this project's code, but you never know.

The manifest file

This project's `AndroidManifest.xml` file has two elements that don't appear in Android Studio's automatically generated file. Here's the scoop:

- **This app uses the Internet to communicate with Facebook's server.** To make communication possible, add the following XML element to the manifest file:

  ```
  <uses-permission android:name="android.permission.
    INTERNET"/>
  ```

  Add this line immediately before the start of the `application` element.

- **The app identifies itself with Facebook's server.** Add these lines immediately after the `activity` element's end tag:

  ```
  <meta-data
      android:name="com.facebook.sdk.ApplicationId"
      android:value="your_app_id_number"/>
  ```

  In place of *`your_app_id_number`*, paste the number that you copied in Step 7 of the section entitled "Setting Things Up on Facebook's Developer Site," earlier in this chapter. You do this to assure Facebook that your app is the genuine article. Of course, if you're being conscientious, you'll put something like `@string/app_id` in the `AndroidManifest.xml` file and add an `app_id` element in the project's `strings.xml` file.

REMEMBER

The file's `meta-data` element belongs inside the `application` element but outside any `activity` elements.

At last it's time for this show's main event!

A Bare-Bones Main Activity

Listing 2-1 contains the essential parts of the Facebook app's Kotlin code.

LISTING 2-1: Posting to Facebook

```
package com.allmycode.p04_02_01

import android.net.Uri
import android.os.Bundle
import androidx.appcompat.app.AppCompatActivity
import com.facebook.share.model.ShareLinkContent
import com.facebook.share.widget.ShareDialog
import kotlinx.android.synthetic.main.activity_main.*

class MainActivity : AppCompatActivity() {
    override fun onCreate(savedInstanceState: Bundle?) {
        super.onCreate(savedInstanceState)
        setContentView(R.layout.activity_main)

        postButton.setOnClickListener {
            val shareDialog = ShareDialog(this)

            if (ShareDialog.canShow(ShareLinkContent::class.java)) {
                val linkContent = ShareLinkContent.Builder()
                    .setContentUrl(Uri.parse(urlField.text.toString()))
                    .build()
                shareDialog.show(linkContent)
            }
        }
    }
}
```

Believe it or not, the 26 lines in Listing 2-1 are enough to post to a news feed or a user story. Figure 2-1 shows the app's first screen.

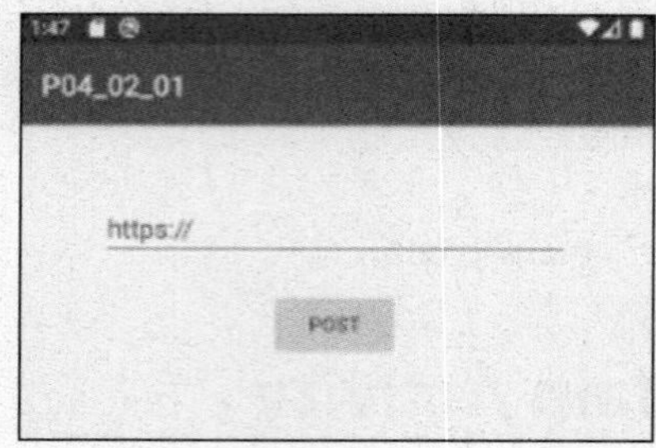

FIGURE 2-1: The simple Facebook app starts running.

The screen has two elements: a text field and a button. You type a URL in the text field and then press the POST button.

If you're not already logged into Facebook on this device, the app displays a Facebook login page. (See Figure 2-2.)

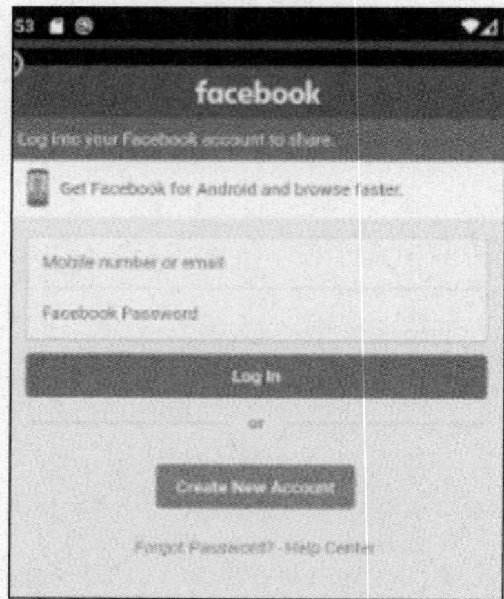

FIGURE 2-2: Logging in to Facebook.

At this point, you enter your email address and password.

REMEMBER

Your app hasn't been deployed in production yet. Only you, the developer who registered the app on the Facebook for Developers page, can create a post. If you want other people to test your app, you have to skip ahead to this chapter's "Who tests your Facebook app?" section.

When you press Log In, the app's response differs depending on whether you've installed the official Facebook app. If you have, your device revs up the Facebook app. If not, your device displays a Share dialog. (See Figure 2-3.)

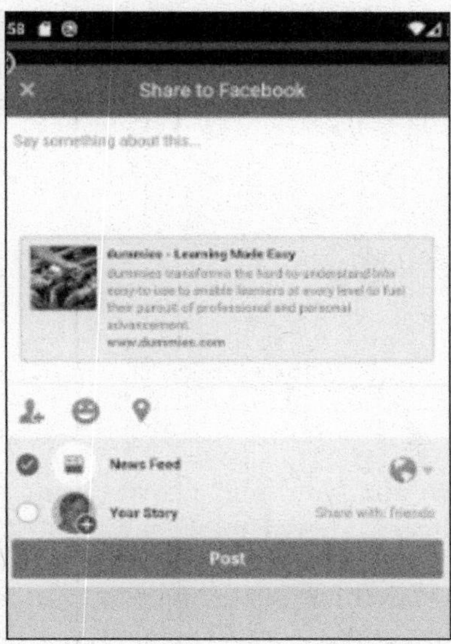

FIGURE 2-3: The Share dialog.

The Share dialog is part of the Facebook SDK for Android. With this Share dialog, you can post to Facebook without having the official Facebook app. Near the top of the Share dialog, a big text field invites you to "Say something about this." In that hint, the word "this" refers to the site whose URL you typed on the main activity page.

The dialog also displays some information about that site. For example, in Figure 2-3 the share dialog displays "dummies — Learning Made Easy" and some other things. This information comes from `meta` tags on the site's web page. The web page's tags look something like this:

```
<meta property="og:title" content="dummies - Learning Made Easy"/>
<meta property="og:description" content="dummies transforms the ..." />
<meta property="og:url" content="https://www.dummies.com/"/>
<meta property="og:image" content="http:// ... .jpg">
```

In this HTML code, the letters `og` stand for *Open Graph* — a standard that's been adopted by the folks at Facebook. Near the bottom of the Share dialog, you can select News Feed, Your Story, or both. When you click Post, the app sends your Share dialog's content to Facebook. (See Figure 2-4.)

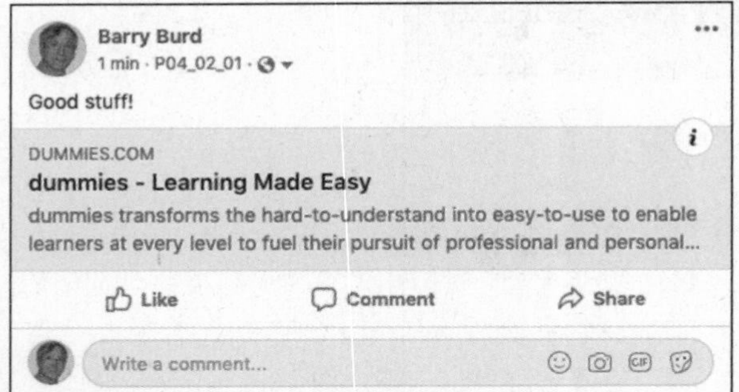

FIGURE 2-4: A new Facebook post.

TIP

As you experiment with this app, you might create some dummy posts. In this context, a dummy post isn't a post *For Dummies*. Instead, it's a post that you create for testing purposes only. The post's text is something like "Testing 1 2 3," and you have no intention of leaving that post on your Facebook page. To delete an unwanted Facebook post (dummy or otherwise), use your web browser to visit Facebook. In the menu bar at the top of the page, click your Facebook picture. Doing so takes you to an administrative page for your account. As part of the unwanted post, you'll find an ellipsis icon with a handy Delete option.

The code in Listing 2-1 is mostly self-documenting. The condition

```
ShareDialog.canShow(ShareLinkContent::class.java)
```

checks to make sure that the app can create a post. For example, following only this section's instructions, the app is still in development and you haven't registered any test users on the Facebook for Developers site. In that case, only you, the person who registered the app on the Facebook for Developers website, can use this app to create a post. If others log on with their own Facebook account, the `canShow` condition is `false`.

If the `canShow` condition is `true`, the code builds a `ShareLinkContent` instance (another class in the Facebook SDK for Android) and feeds that instance to the Share dialog's `show` method. The call to `show` jump-starts either the Share dialog in Figure 2-3 or the honest-to-goodness Facebook app. Good stuff indeed!

Enriching the Minimal App

To understand what this section's example does, imagine the following scenario: You want to encourage people to create Facebook posts about some of your website's pages. To this end, one of your Android app's activities includes a group of radio buttons. (See Figure 2-5.)

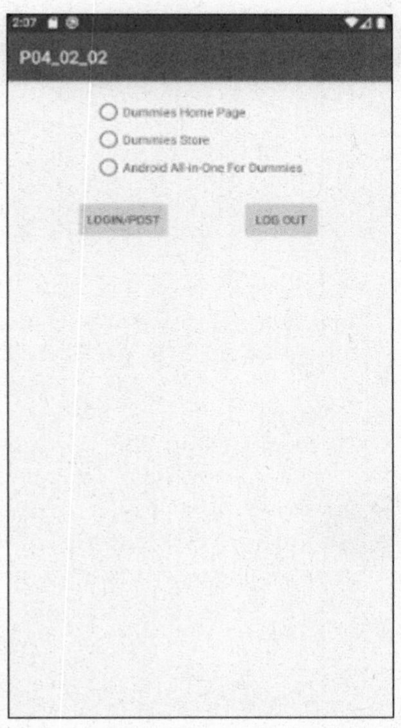

FIGURE 2-5: Nudging users to mention your pages.

Each radio button refers to one of your pages. When a user selects a radio button, the app displays a preview of the button's page. (See Figure 2-6.)

When the user presses the LOGIN/POST button, the app displays the Share dialog in which the user can create a post. (Refer to Figure 2-3.)

When the user creates a post, the Share dialog goes away, and your app's main activity reappears. To help guide the user's choices, you disable the radio button that the user previously selected. (See Figure 2-7.)

Listing 2-2 contains this enhanced app's main activity.

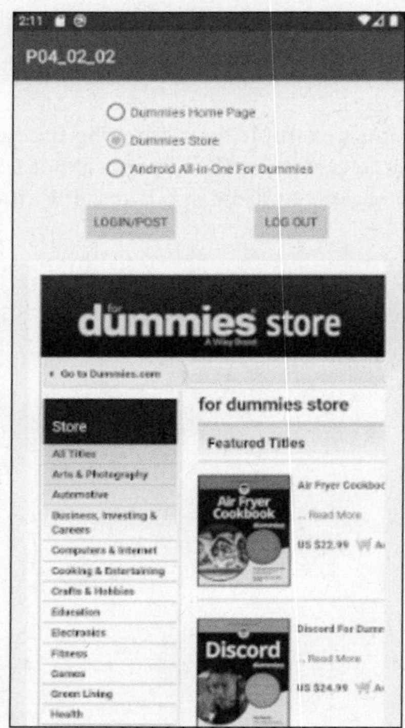

FIGURE 2-6: Previewing a web page.

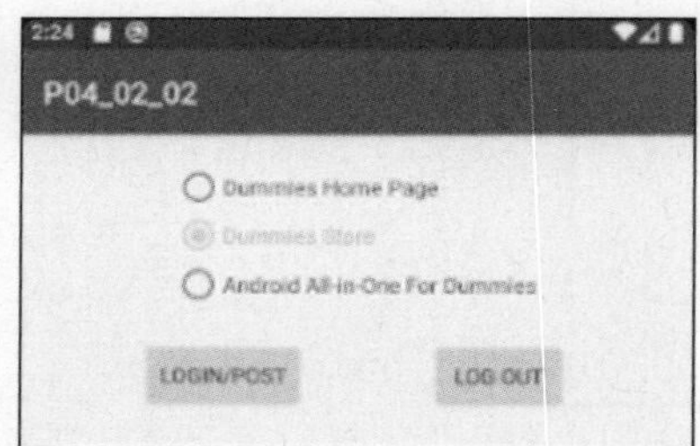

FIGURE 2-7: No reason to mention the Dummies Store a second time.

LISTING 2-2: Building a Better Facebook App

```
package com.allmycode.p04_02_02

import android.content.Intent
import android.graphics.Bitmap
import android.net.Uri
import android.os.Bundle
import android.view.View
import android.webkit.WebSettings
import android.webkit.WebView
```

```
import android.webkit.WebViewClient
import android.widget.RadioButton
import androidx.appcompat.app.AppCompatActivity
import com.facebook.CallbackManager
import com.facebook.FacebookCallback
import com.facebook.FacebookException
import com.facebook.login.LoginManager
import com.facebook.share.Sharer
import com.facebook.share.model.ShareLinkContent
import com.facebook.share.widget.ShareDialog
import kotlinx.android.synthetic.main.activity_main.*

class MainActivity : AppCompatActivity() {
    var callbackManager: CallbackManager? = null

    override fun onCreate(savedInstanceState: Bundle?) {
        super.onCreate(savedInstanceState)
        setContentView(R.layout.activity_main)

        val mySettings: WebSettings = webView.settings
        mySettings.setAppCacheEnabled(true)
        mySettings.cacheMode = WebSettings.LOAD_CACHE_ELSE_NETWORK
        mySettings.javaScriptEnabled = true
        mySettings.loadWithOverviewMode = true

        webView.webViewClient = object : WebViewClient() {
            override fun onPageStarted(
                view: WebView?,
                url: String?,
                favicon: Bitmap?
            ) {
                super.onPageStarted(view, url, favicon)
                progressBar.visibility = View.VISIBLE
            }

            override fun onPageFinished(view: WebView?, url: String?) {
                super.onPageFinished(view, url)
                progressBar.visibility = View.GONE
            }
        }

        urlRadioGroup.setOnCheckedChangeListener { _, checkedId ->
            webView.loadUrl(getUrlString(checkedId))
        }

        postButton.setOnClickListener {
            val shareDialog = ShareDialog(this)
```

(continued)

An Android Social Media App

LISTING 2-2: *(continued)*

```
            callbackManager = CallbackManager.Factory.create()
            shareDialog.registerCallback(
                callbackManager,
                object : FacebookCallback<Sharer.Result?> {
                    override fun onSuccess(result: Sharer.Result?) {
                        findViewById<RadioButton>(urlRadioGroup
                            .checkedRadioButtonId).isEnabled = false
                    }

                    override fun onCancel() {
                    }

                    override fun onError(error: FacebookException) {
                    }
                })

            if (ShareDialog.canShow(ShareLinkContent::class.java)) {
                val linkContent = ShareLinkContent.Builder()
                    .setContentUrl(Uri.parse(getUrlString
                        (urlRadioGroup.checkedRadioButtonId))
                    ).build()
                shareDialog.show(linkContent)
            }
        }

        logoutButton.setOnClickListener {
            LoginManager.getInstance().logOut()
            resetActivityScreen()
        }
    }

    private fun getUrlString(checkedId: Int): String? {
        return when (checkedId) {
            R.id.dummies_home -> getString(R.string.dummies_home_url)
            R.id.dummies_store -> getString(R.string.dummies_store_url)
            R.id.dummies_android ->
                getString(R.string.dummies_android_url)
            else -> ""
        }
    }

    override fun onActivityResult(
        requestCode: Int,
        resultCode: Int,
        data: Intent?
```

```
    ) {
        super.onActivityResult(requestCode, resultCode, data)
        callbackManager!!.onActivityResult(
            requestCode,
            resultCode,
            data
        )
    }

    private fun resetActivityScreen() {
        urlRadioGroup.clearCheck()
        dummies_home.isEnabled = true
        dummies_store.isEnabled = true
        dummies_android.isEnabled = true
        webView.loadUrl("about:blank")
    }
}
```

The next several sections dissect the code in Listing 2-2.

Working with a radio group

You want your app to offer alternatives to the user. For a medium-to-large collection of alternatives, you may create a spinner — a component more commonly known as a drop-down list. (See Figure 2-8.)

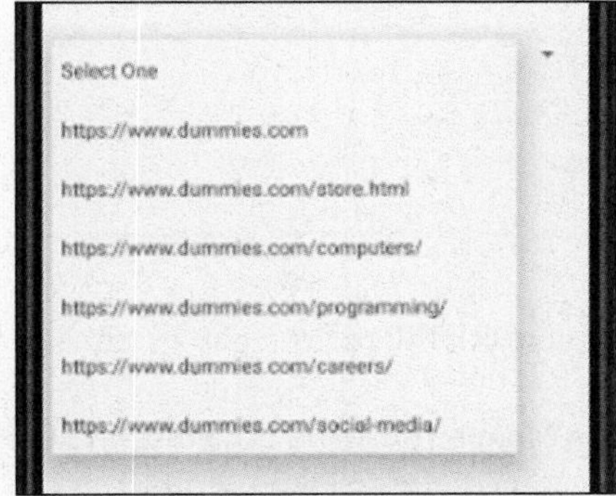

FIGURE 2-8: An Android spinner.

When you have a small number of alternatives, you create a radio group. For example, the radio group in Figure 2-5 contains three radio buttons with the following labels: Dummies Home Page, Dummies Store, and Android All-in-One For Dummies.

Listing 2-3 shows you the XML layout code for the radio group in Figure 2-5. The code's `RadioGroup` element contains three `RadioButton` elements, each with its own `android:text` attribute. Each `android:text` attribute refers to one of the radio buttons' labels.

LISTING 2-3: Declaring a Radio Group

```
<RadioGroup
    android:id="@+id/urlRadioGroup"
    android:layout_width="wrap_content"
    android:layout_height="wrap_content"
    android:layout_marginTop="20dp"
    app:layout_constraintEnd_toEndOf="parent"
    app:layout_constraintStart_toStartOf="parent"
    app:layout_constraintTop_toTopOf="parent">

    <RadioButton
        android:id="@+id/dummies_home"
        android:layout_width="wrap_content"
        android:layout_height="wrap_content"
        android:text="@string/dummies_home_label"/>

    <RadioButton
        android:id="@+id/dummies_store"
        android:layout_width="wrap_content"
        android:layout_height="wrap_content"
        android:text="@string/dummies_store_label"/>

    <RadioButton
        android:id="@+id/dummies_android"
        android:layout_width="wrap_content"
        android:layout_height="wrap_content"
        android:text="@string/dummies_android_label"/>
</RadioGroup>
```

The app's Kotlin code interacts with the radio group in three ways:

- **When the user selects a radio button, the code displays the web page associated with that button. (Refer to Figure 2-5.)** To accomplish this, Listing 2-2 creates an `onCheckedChangeListener`:

```
urlRadioGroup.setOnCheckedChangeListener { _, checkedId ->
    webView.loadUrl(getUrlString(checkedId))
}
```

The listener's method takes two parameters: a RadioGroup (which goes unused in Listing 2-2) and the id of the checked radio button (checkedId in Listing 2-2). The code finds a web page's URL by calling its own getUrlString method on checkedId.

» **When the user presses LOGIN/POST, the code displays a Share dialog with a reference to that button's page. (Refer to Figure 2-3.)** In Listing 2-2, the shareDialog.canShow code isn't very different from the corresponding code in Listing 2-1. The only change is Listing 2-2's use of the checkedRadio ButtonId property.

```
val linkContent = ShareLinkContent.Builder()
    .setContentUrl(Uri.parse(getUrlString
            (urlRadioGroup.checkedRadioButtonId))
    ).build()
```

This property tells the code which of the group's buttons is currently checked. With that piece of information, Listing 2-2 calls its getUrlString method to find the appropriate URL.

» **After the user has created a post, the code disables the radio button associated with that post. (Refer to Figure 2-7.)** When a Share dialog finishes its work, the dialog sends a result back to the app's main activity. The result contains lots of information, but one important piece of information is the status of the attempted post: Did the post succeed, did the user cancel the post, or did the attempted post result in an error? When a main activity (or any other activity) receives a result, Android calls the activity's onActivity Result method.

The code in Listing 2-2 refers to two different onActivityResult methods. One method belongs to the main activity; the other belongs to a CallbackManager — a class from Facebook's SDK for Android.

- In Listing 2-2, the main activity's onActivityResult method doesn't do much on its own. In fact, the main activity's onActivityResult method simply passes the buck to the CallbackManager instance's onActivity-Result method.

```
override fun onActivityResult( ...
{
    callbackManager!!.onActivityResult(...)
}
```

- In turn, the CallbackManager instance's onActivityResult method invokes one of three methods: onSuccess, onCancel, or onError. These three methods belong to a FacebookCallback instance — one that's registered to respond to the Share dialog's results.

In Listing 2-2, the callback's onCancel and onError methods don't do anything. But onSuccess method does what it's supposed to do. The method finds whatever radio button the user selected to create the post and then disables that radio button.

```
override fun onSuccess(result: Sharer.Result?) {
    findViewById<RadioButton>(urlRadioGroup
        .checkedRadioButtonId).isEnabled = false
}
```

The result is shown in Figure 2-7, shown previously.

TECHNICAL STUFF

In recent versions of Android, you don't explicitly override an activity's onActivityResult method. Instead, you use AndroidX features to define a registerForActivityResult method and an ActivityResultContract subclass. Neither Facebook's documentation nor the Facebook developers' blog posts seem to have caught up with these newer Android techniques, so this chapter's example relies on the older features. One way or another, the code works.

Controlling the web view

When you're finished typing a URL in a web browser's address field, your eyes naturally go toward the center of the browser window. This happens because you expect the browser to display a web page. But when you select a radio button, as you do in this section's example, your brain doesn't immediately tell you to look for a web page. That's why the code in Listing 2-2 displays a circular progress bar. (See Figure 2-9.)

When the app's main activity first appears, the progress bar is out of sight.

```
<ProgressBar
    android:visibility="gone"
    ...                         />
```

To make the progress bar show up, you assign a WebViewClient to the activity's webView component in the Kotlin code.

```
webView.webViewClient = object : WebViewClient() {
```

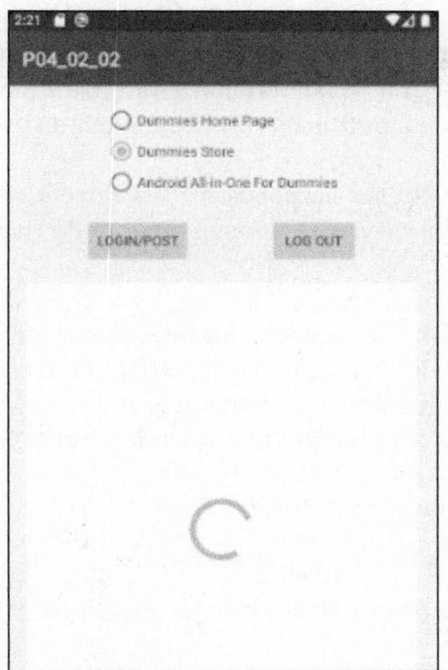

FIGURE 2-9: Waiting for a web page.

A `WebViewClient` manages the behavior of its `webView` instance. In Listing 2-2, the client tells the `webView` to show the progress bar when the page starts loading and get rid of the progress bar when the loading finishes.

```
override fun onPageStarted( ...
{
    ...
    progressBar.visibility = View.VISIBLE
}

override fun onPageFinished( ... {
    ...
    progressBar.visibility = View.GONE
}
```

Other `WebViewClient` methods include handy things like `doUpdateVisitedHistory`, `onFormResubmission`, `onReceivedError`, `onReceivedLoginRequest`, `onScaleChanged`, and many more.

Who tests your Facebook app?

First, you register your app with Facebook. You do this by following the steps in the section entitled "Setting Things Up on Facebook's Developer Site." Then, you run your app and login with your own Facebook user ID. Everything goes smoothly.

Next, you load the app on a friend's device and have your friend try the app. That's when things take a turn for the worse. Your friend sees a message saying that she's not authorized to create a post using this app. What do you do next?

Here's what you do: You revisit the Facebook for Developers site and tell the site to let your friend run the app. If you're not sure how to do that, follow this section's steps.

WARNING

By the time you read this book, the Facebook for Developers site may have changed a bit. If this section's steps don't match exactly what you find on the site, don't worry. Poke around a bit until you find words like Roles and Test Users. If you spend a few minutes looking for the right menus and buttons, you should be okay.

1. **Log on to** `developers.facebook.com`**.**
2. **In the page's upper-right corner, select My Apps.**

   A drop-down list appears. The list shows your Facebook apps' names.
3. **Select one of your apps.**

   Any of your registered Facebook apps will do. But the wording of these instructions favors the app in Listing 2-2.

   After making your selection, the developer site displays your app's dashboard. Look for a navigation bar along the left side of the dashboard. In the navigation bar, select Roles⇨Test Users.

   When you make this selection, the developer site shows you a list of your app's test users. At this juncture, the list is probably empty.
4. **Look for an Add button. When you find that button, click it.**

   A dialog with the title Create Test Users appears.
5. **Look for a way of indicating that you intend to authorize test users for this app.**

   Maybe it's a Yes or No switch. Maybe it's something else. One way or another, say "yes" to having test users.
6. **Look for a Create Test Users button. Go ahead and click that button.**

   To your surprise, Facebook has created some test users for you. They have silly names and fake email addresses, but they're available for you to use. Of course, you want your real-life friend to be a tester for your app.
7. **Click Add to set up a new test user.**

   That makes sense. Right?

   The resulting page gives you the option of adding administrators, developers, testers, and analytics users.

8. **Click Add Testers.**

   An Add Testers dialog appears.

9. **In the Add Testers dialog, type your friend's Facebook ID or username, and then click Submit.**

   The site returns you to the page that lists your app's administrators, testers, and others. Your friend's name appears in the Testers category but, beside your friend's name, you see the word *Pending.* What does that mean? It means that your friend hasn't yet accepted the offer to test your app.

10. **Have your friend buy a copy of this book so that she can follow the next several steps.**

   Remember, technical book authors aren't rich. We can use the spare change.

Greetings to you, app tester! Please follow these steps:

1. **Add developer credentials to your Facebook account.**

   To do, so, follow Steps 1 through 3 in the section entitled "Setting Things Up on Facebook's Developer Site," early in this chapter.

2. **On the developer site, look for something indicating that you should read a notification.**

   Check your user image at the top of the page. If that image has its own little red circle (commonly known as a *notification dot* or *notification badge*), click the image.

3. **In the resulting drop-down list, select Requests.**

   When you do, the developer site shows you a message inviting you to test a particular app.

4. **Click Confirm.**

   That's it! You're an official tester! You can copy the app to your own device or use the original app developer's device. The next few steps cover the case in which you use the app developer's device.

TIP

   For help testing the app on your own Android phone, refer to Book 1, Chapter 3.

   The app has already been installed and tested on the developer's device. The developer is still logged into Facebook.

5. **Launch the app.**

   The main activity appears. (Refer to Figure 2-5.)

6. **Click LOG OUT.**

   In Listing 2-2, the logout button's listener calls

   ```
   LoginManager.getInstance().logOut()
   ```

   so that the app's developer is no longer logged in. The listener also reenables the radio buttons and resets the web view.

   When you follow the next two steps, the app prompts you for your email and password.

7. **Select one of the radio buttons.**
8. **Press LOGIN/POST.**

   From there, you can use the app's features to log onto Facebook and mention the developer's site in your news feed.

   Happy posting!

» Creating an Android app with native code

Chapter 3
Going Native

Sometimes, you have to get your hands dirty. You have to pop the hood and figure out why smoke comes out of your car. You have to bake a cake for that special friend who's allergic to the ingredients in store-bought cakes. Or, in order to build the perfect mobile app, you must bypass Android's comfortable Kotlin coating and dig deep to find your true inner geek. You must create part of an app in the primitive, nuts-and-bolts, down-and-dirty language called C (or, if you want to use object-oriented programming techniques, C++).

Developers have depended on low-level programming languages like C/C++ for years to give them an advantage and that's what this chapter is about. Instead of driving the minivan of apps, you can drive a souped-up Ferrari. Of course, just as a Ferrari requires in-depth maintenance, your souped-up app will require special skills to maintain as well. Besides discovering how to work with native code using the Native Development Kit (NDK), you also discover the pros and cons of using this approach.

The Native Development Kit

The creators of Android realized that developers would want to use non-Kotlin code. So Android has a framework that mediates between Kotlin and other languages. As you might have guessed from this section's title, that framework is *NDK* — Android's *Native Development Kit.* With Android's NDK, you can write code that executes directly on a mobile device's processor without relying on a virtual machine to carry out the instructions.

Understanding why you need the NDK

Book 2, Chapter 3 explains how Kotlin puts a virtual machine between your processor's hardware and a running application. Kotlin programs don't turn directly into sets of instructions that your processor can then run. Instead, your processor runs another set of instructions; namely, a virtual machine. (The block diagram in Book 2, Chapter 3, Figure 3-3 shows the process your code goes through to run on an Android device.) The virtual machine interprets a Kotlin program's instructions and carries out these instructions on your processor's behalf.

This added layer of software (between the Kotlin instructions and your processor's circuits) has both benefits and drawbacks. Isolation from the hardware enhances portability and security. But the added software layer might slow down a program's execution. The layer also prevents Kotlin from micromanaging the processor.

Another potent reason for using non-Kotlin code is to avoid rewriting code that you already have — code written in another programming language. Imagine having a thousand-line C/C++ program that reliably computes a decent daily investment strategy. The program does lots of fancy calculations, but the program has no user-friendly interface. The code has no windows, no buttons, and nothing nice for the user to click. You want to package this program inside an Android application. The app presents choices to the user, computes today's investment strategy with its complicated formulas, and then displays details of the strategy (in a friendly, colorful way) on the user's screen.

You can try rewriting the C/C++ program in Kotlin. But translating between two semi-related languages (such as C/C++ and Kotlin) is a virtual rat's nest. The translation is often messy and unreliable. A better plan is to write the user interface as an Android Kotlin app and let your Kotlin app defer to your existing C/C++ program only for the intricate investing strategy calculations. All you need is a way to exchange information between a Kotlin program and a C/C++ program. (The example in this chapter relies on C, but the techniques will also work with C++.) In short, here are the reasons you really want to use the NDK in some situations:

- **Execution:** C/C++ code is compiled into the same machine language that the processor uses, so there is no interpretation required and the code executes significantly faster.
- **Processor access:** Using C/C++ means that you have access to processor features that Kotlin keeps hidden from view.

» **Debugging:** Low-level access means you can see how the processor is interacting with your code in a way that Kotlin makes impossible, so you no longer have to battle the bugs that often appear in code libraries.
» **Platform library access:** The platform libraries make it possible to work with the processor and peripheral devices at a level that makes seeing the actual bits easier and helps you understand why your code works as it does. You gain access to libraries such as `ffmpeg` (used to process audio and video) and `jnigraphics` (used to process bitmaps) that have no equivalents in Kotlin.
» **Unsupported device access:** Often a new device will ship with support for C/C++, but not any other language. If you need this device for your work, then the only way to interact with it (until someone puts the required support together in a Kotlin library) is to rely on C/C++ code.

There is never a free lunch when it comes to development. You might wonder why everyone doesn't engage in mix-code app development. Here are some reasons that using the NDK may not be the silver bullet solution that you think it is:

» Mixed code development takes more time because C/C++ development is slower and requires more lines of code than Kotlin does.
» You now need people with expertise in two languages instead of one.
» Sometimes bugs hide in programming language interfaces.
» The app won't be as safe or as reliable as it would be using Kotlin code alone.
» Debugging two languages makes finding errors an order of magnitude harder.

Knowing what you get

The NDK package isn't a single entity. It's actually a combination of three entities:

» LLDB debugger
» CMake (a utility for compiling C/C++ code)
» Java Native Interface (JNI) through NDK

The JNI part of the package requires a little explanation. When you work with the NDK, the underlying C/C++ code interacts with the Java bytecode created after you compile a Kotlin or Java app. The NDK doesn't care whether you use Kotlin or Java; it cares only about the compiled result, which is accessed through the JNI.

Getting the NDK

Fortunately, the SDK manager makes getting the NDK and its associated components easy. The following steps get you started:

1. **Choose Configure⇨SDK Manager from the Android Studio main menu or Tools⇨SDK Manager from within the IDE.**

   You see the Settings for New Projects dialog box, with Android SDK highlighted.

TIP

   It doesn't seem like it should matter, but the installation will normally go faster and better if you perform it without a project loaded from the Android Studio main menu.

2. **Select the SDK Tools tab.**

   A list of tools appears, including LLDB, NDK (Side by Side), and CMake, as shown in Figure 3-1.

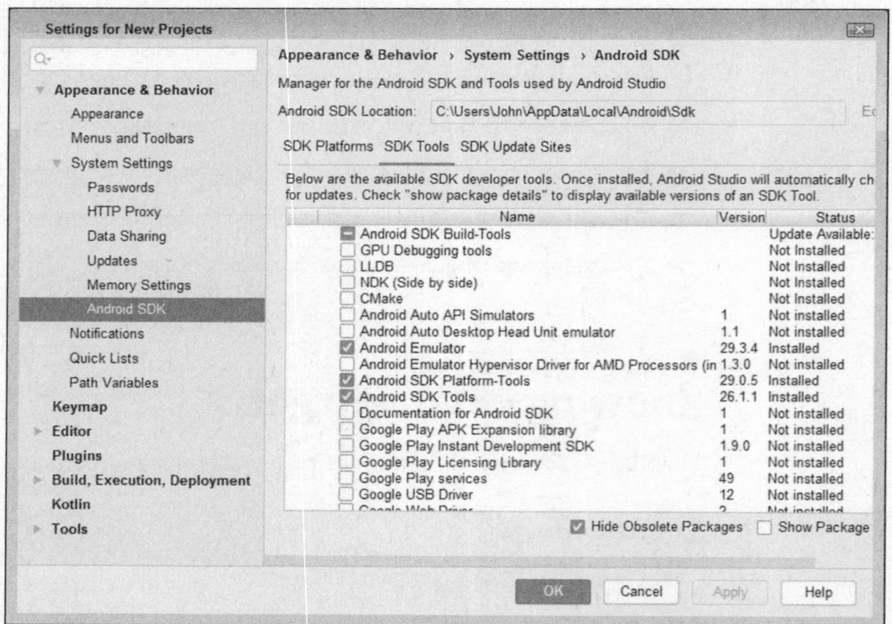

FIGURE 3-1: Locate the three tools needed to implement native code support in your app.

3. **Select the LLDB, NDK (Side by Side), and CMake options.**

   Notice that down arrows appear next to each option, as shown in Figure 3-2. A down arrow shows that Android Studio will download and install the latest version of the tool for you. However, you may not always want the latest version — your project might call for some other version.

	Name	Version	Status
	Android SDK Build-Tools		Update Available
	GPU Debugging tools		Not Installed
⤓	LLDB		Not Installed
⤓	NDK (Side by side)		Not Installed
⤓	CMake		Not Installed
	Android Auto API Simulators	1	Not installed
	Android Auto Desktop Head Unit emulator	1.1	Not installed
	Android Emulator	29.3.4	Installed
	Android Emulator Hypervisor Driver for AMD Processors	1.3.0	Not installed
	Android SDK Platform-Tools	29.0.5	Installed
	Android SDK Tools	26.1.1	Installed
	Documentation for Android SDK	1	Not installed
	Google Play APK Expansion library	1	Not installed
	Google Play Instant Development SDK	1.9.0	Not installed
	Google Play Licensing Library	1	Not installed
	Google Play services	49	Not installed
	Google USB Driver	12	Not installed
	Google Web Driver	2	Not installed

Hide Obsolete Packages   Show Package

FIGURE 3-2: When necessary, you can choose specific tool versions.

4. (Optional) Select Show Package Details.

You can view the various versions of each tool, as shown in Figure 3-3. Instead of choosing the current version, you may check one of the older versions instead. The example uses the versions of the packages shown as selected in the figure.

	Name	Version	Status
	LLDB		
	2.0	2.0.2558144	Not installed
	2.1	2.1.2852477	Not installed
	2.2	2.2.3271982	Not installed
	2.3	2.3.3614996	Not installed
	3.0	3.0.4213617	Not installed
⤓	3.1	3.1.4508709	Not installed
	NDK (Side by side)		
	16.1.4479499	16.1.4479499	Not installed
	17.2.4988734	17.2.4988734	Not installed
	18.1.5063045	18.1.5063045	Not installed
	19.2.5345600	19.2.5345600	Not installed
	20.0.5594570	20.0.5594570	Not installed
	20.1.5948944	20.1.5948944	Not installed
⤓	21.0.6113669	21.0.6113669	Not installed
	CMake		
⤓	3.10.2.4988404	3.10.2	Not installed
	3.6.4111459	3.6.4111459	Not installed

FIGURE 3-3: Choose an older version of the package when needed.

5. Click OK.

You see a Confirm Change dialog box like the one shown in Figure 3-4. Notice that the dialog box includes specific version number information. If you choose to install multiple versions of a tool, you see one entry for each version in the list. The dialog box also tells you about the package download size and the amount of space it uses on disk.

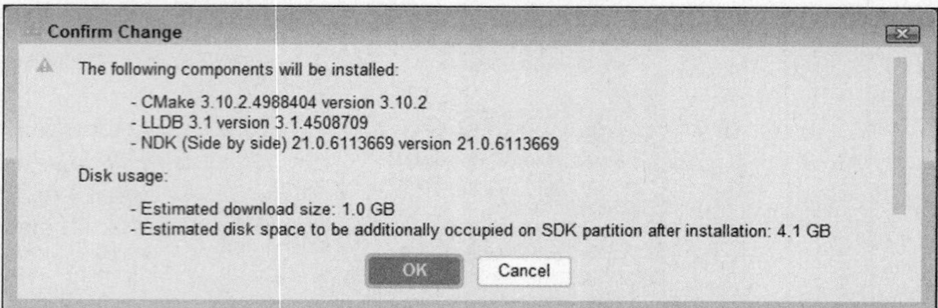

FIGURE 3-4: Verify that you are installing the packages you need.

6. **Click OK.**

   The SDK Quickfix Installation dialog box appears, as shown in Figure 3-5. This dialog box tells you about the status of the download and provides any error messages. It's time for a coffee break because the process takes a while to complete.

   Eventually, after your coffee is cold and the doughnut gone, the SDK Quickfix Installation dialog proclaims the installation complete (or at least subtly mentions it).

7. **Click Finish.**

   You're ready to start a new adventure!

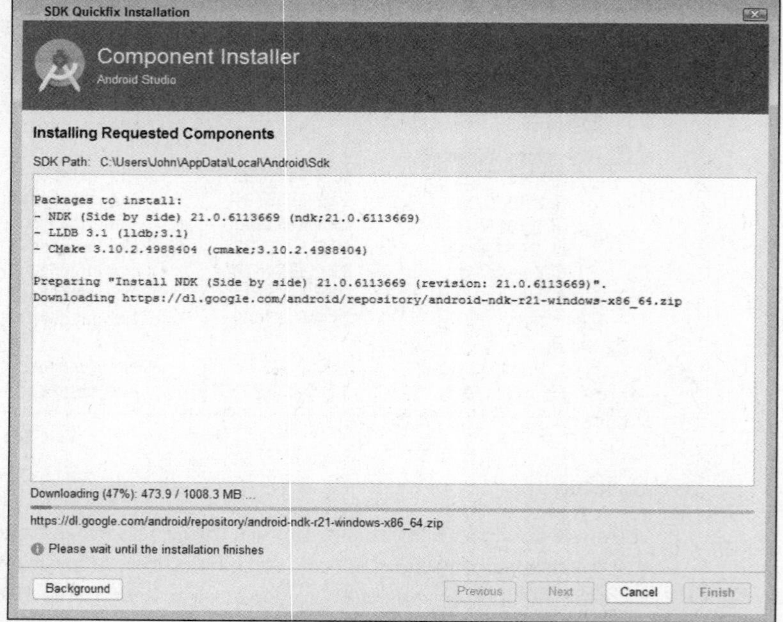

FIGURE 3-5: The SDK Quickfix Installation tells you about installation progress and problems.

Creating an Application

Older versions of Android Studio forced you to jump through all sorts of very odd hoops to create even the smallest project enabled with C/C++ support. Well, worry no more! After you install the latest tools, the process is simpler than ever before. The following sections take you through the application creation process for a simple app.

Starting with the template

To create a simple NDK-enabled application, do the following:

1. **Start a new Android Studio project.**

   You see the Choose Your Project dialog box, as usual. However, if you scroll down, you see a new project type, Native C++, as shown in Figure 3-6.

2. **Select Native C++ and click Next.**

   You see the normal Configure Your Project dialog box, where you select the project options.

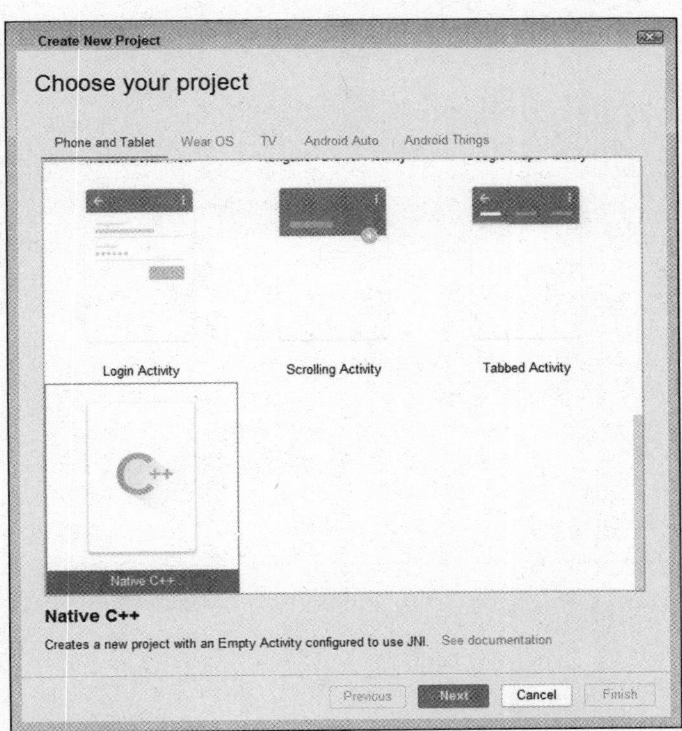

FIGURE 3-6: Installing NDK provides you with a new project type as well.

3. **Type** 04_03_01 **in the Name field and** com.allmycode.p04_03_01 **in the Package Name field.**

   Later in the chapter, you discover that the minimum API level supported by the NDK for native code modules is 16, based on the `platforms.cmake` file content. Don't worry about the `platforms.cmake` file for now; just know that you must set the API level correctly or you could experience problems.

4. **Choose API 16: Android 4.1 (Jelly Bean) in the Minimum API Level field and click Next.**

   You see the Customize C++ Support dialog box, shown in Figure 3-7. This dialog box lets you choose a specific version of C++ to support in your app. Selecting Toolchain Default, as shown in the figure, is the option least likely to cause you problems unless you really do need a specific version of C/C++ for your project.

5. **Click Finish.**

   Android Studio creates an Empty Activity–like project for you with C/C++ support included.

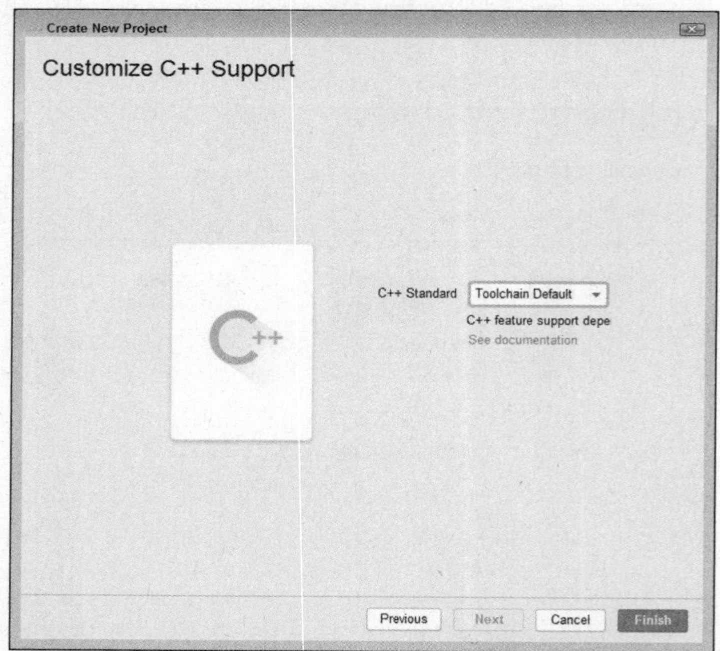

FIGURE 3-7: Choose a version of C++ to use.

Seeing the essential project differences

From an Android perspective, the project you created in the previous section is like an Empty Activity project, but there are important differences that you see almost immediately, and these differences help you create a C/C++ project with a lot less effort. You begin with the Android Project window, shown in Figure 3-8.

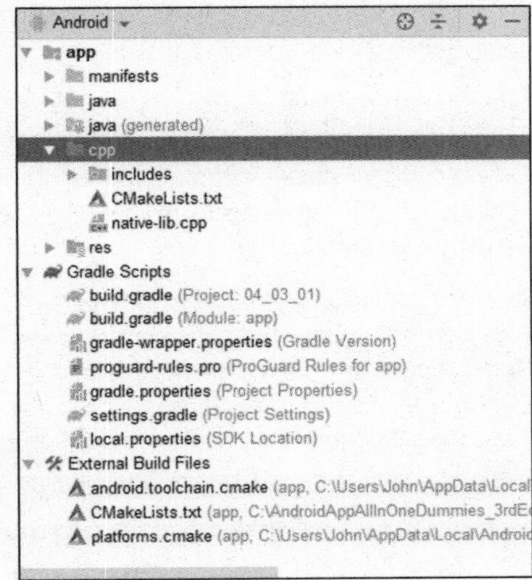

FIGURE 3-8: The Android Project window contains some additions.

The first project difference to note is the `cpp` folder (highlighted in the figure), which contains the essential file types normally used in a basic C/C++ app. Here's what you find:

- `includes`: Provides access to the header files normally used with an Android-type C/C++ app, as well as the header files needed to work with NDK.
- `CMakeLists.txt`: Contains instructions that CMake will use to compile the C/C++ portion of the app.
- `native-lib.cpp`: Contains example code that you use and study for this example.

You also find an External Build Files folder that contains the build files for CMake. In most cases, you won't ever touch these files because the instructions they contain work well with the Android environment. The only time you need to touch them is when you want to do something special, such as optimize the output for a particular processor. Here is how each of these files is used:

- `android.toolchain.cmake`: This file contains all the arguments needed to create a *toolchain,* which is a group of tools used to turn C/C++ source into a binary executable that will work on the current or target device. Developers call the process of turning human-readable code into a binary form *making* the executable, and the instructions to perform the task appear within a *make* file. When working with the NDK, the toolchain consists of a
  - **Compiler:** Turns the human-readable source into a binary form, an *object file,* that the target processor can execute natively. A standard compiler works with the current devices, and a *cross-compiler* transforms the binary into a form that matches a different device. The IDE will use either a compiler or a cross-compiler, but not both.
  - **Linker:** Translates memory addresses in the binary file so that they work with any library files needed to make the code work. You can't have two pieces of executable code occupy the same memory address at the same time, and the linker helps ensure that the addresses you use will work. After the translation, the linker combines all the object files into a single executable file.
  - **Librarian:** Manages the library files containing packaged routines used in your code.
  - **Other tools:** Depending on your configuration, this file may include information for other tools, such as a debugger or IDE. Even though this information no longer appears in `.mk` files, the information at `https://developer.android.com/ndk/guides/android_mk.html` and `https://developer.android.com/ndk/guides/application_mk.html` tells you about variables you can use within the `android.toolchain.cmake` file to alter the manner in which the make process occurs.
- `CMakeLists.txt`: This file contains the instructions to build the binary file. It tells which source files to use, the libraries to include, and the target of the linking process, among other things. This file normally contains the following instructions as a minimum:
  - `cmake_minimum_required()`: Determines the minimum release level of CMake to use to perform the make process.
  - `add_library()`: Provides the name of your source file and output library filename. If you modify the file located in your project for simple tasks, you won't need to touch this entry.
  - `find_library()`: Specifies the name of the external NDK library to use. The default setting usually works fine.

* `target_link_libraries()`: Contains a list of libraries to link to the native code library you're building. Unless you have a complex project that uses both the NDK library and multiple third-party libraries (or other custom libraries you've built), you won't need to change this entry.

- `platforms.cmake`: This file contains a list of platforms that the native code library can target. If the project you create doesn't target a specific platform, such as SDK level 22, the build process will target the minimum SDK level, which is 16.

Considering the build.gradle (Module: app) differences

Including special files in your app and using them to define how to build the native code library for your app doesn't complete the process. As with every other part of your app, you must tell Gradle to build the native code library, which means including entries in the `build.gradle (Module: app)` file.

In this case, there are actually two entries: the build configuration and the build command. Here is the build configuration shown in bold in the `defaultConfig` entry:

```
defaultConfig {
    applicationId "com.allmycode.p04_03_01"
    minSdkVersion 16
    targetSdkVersion 29

    ... Other Entries ...

    externalNativeBuild {
        cmake {
            cppFlags ""
        }
    }
}
```

The default setup doesn't use any special entries, except to say that it has no `cppFlags`. Here are the common entries you find in this entry:

- `arguments`: The `arguments` entry defines the operation of the CMake utility itself. For example, `arguments "-DANDROID_ARM_NEON=TRUE"` would specify that you want to enable or disable NEON for the armeabi-v7a Application Binary Interface (ABI). The "What is an ABI?" sidebar tells you more about what an ABI is all about. You can find more Android-specific CMake arguments described at `https://developer.android.com/ndk/guides/cmake`.

You can also interact with CMake directly on your system. Of course, first you have to find it. On a Windows system, the executable you need will likely appear in the `\Documents and Settings\`*<User Name>*`\AppData\Local\Android\Sdk\cmake\`*<Version>*`\bin` folder. A Mac or Linux system will have an `/Android/Sdk/cmake/`*<Version>*`/bin` folder, too, that has the `CMake.exe` file in it. To interact directly with CMake, you open a command or terminal window, change directories to the one that contains `CMake.exe`, and then type **CMake /?** or **CMake --help**. You see the internal help system, which describes the various arguments you can use with CMake, tells you that the `-D` command-line switch requires a name and value pair as input, and creates a CMake cache entry.

- `cFlags`: Use the `cFlags` entry to define the operation of the C/C++ compiler using macro constants. The macros supported by a C/C++ compiler depend on the vendor. However, many of these macros are standardized. For example, including `cFlags "-D__STDC_FORMAT_MACROS"` enables format macro constants that allow you to do things like print an `int64_t` type when working with an older compiler. If you're using a newer compiler and have no concerns about printing certain data types, you probably won't need this entry.

Android development has relied on libc++ since Lollipop (API level 21). If you don't specify a preference, your app will rely on libc++. The site at `https://libcxx.llvm.org/docs/UsingLibcxx.html` describes many of the libc++ extras. When working in Windows, you can find the compiler in the `\Documents and Settings\`*<User Name>*`\AppData\Local\Android\Sdk\build-tools\`*<Version>* folder as `llvm-rs-cc.exe`. Mac and Linus users will have a similar `/Android/Sdk/build-tools/`*<Version>* directory. To discover more about the command-line switches that this compiler has to offer, open a command line or terminal window, type **llvm-rs-cc –help**, and press Enter.

- `cppFlags`: Use the `cppFlags` option to define flags that specify optional behaviors from your C/C++ compiler. For example, if you specify `cppFlags "-fexceptions"`, the compiler outputs exception information. You can learn more about the essential `cppFlags` entries at `https://developer.android.com/ndk/guides/cpp-support`.

WHAT IS AN ABI?

The acronym *ABI* stands for *Application Binary Interface.* An ABI is like an API, except that an ABI describes the way one piece of software communicates with another on a binary level. For example, in an API, you'd say, "To create a string that represents an object, call the object's `toString()` method." In an ABI, you might say, `"A signed double word consists of 8 bytes and has byte-alignment 8."`

The acronym *ARM* comes originally from the term *Advanced RISC Machines*, which in turn comes from *Advanced Reduced Instruction Set Computing Machines*. The company named ARM, Ltd., designs and licenses its ARM processors for use in mobile devices around the world. (ARM, Ltd., doesn't build processors. Instead, the company does all the thinking and sells ideas to processor manufacturers.)

The ARM EABI is ARM's *Embedded Application Binary Interface. Embedded* refers to the tendency of ARM processors to appear in specialized devices — devices other than general-purpose computers. For example, the main processor inside your laptop isn't an embedded processor. Your laptop's main processor does general-purpose computing — word processing one minute and playing music the next. In contrast, an embedded processor sits quietly inside a device and processes bits according to the device's specialized needs. Your car is loaded with embedded processors.

You may argue that the processor inside your mobile device isn't a special-purpose processor. Thus, the *E* in *ARM EABI* doesn't apply to mobile development. Well, argue all you want. This terminology's usage can wobble in many directions, and regardless of what you think is inside your phone, many phones use ARM processors. The underlying NDK functionality creates code according to ARM EABI specifications. You can find a list of supported ABIs at `https://developer.android.com/ndk/guides/abis`.

The build command entry in the `build.gradle (Module: app)` file consists of an `externalNativeBuild` entry that looks like this:

```
externalNativeBuild {
    cmake {
        path "src/main/cpp/CMakeLists.txt"
        version "3.10.2"
    }
}
```

It may look relatively complex, but it isn't if you take it apart. First, you tell Gradle that you want to perform an external build using CMake. The path to the file containing the items to make appears in `"src/main/cpp/CMakeLists.txt"`. You want to use `version "3.10.2"` of CMake to perform the task. The hardest part of the process is discovering where the `CMakeLists.txt` file actually appears on your hard drive. Fortunately, the IDE makes this easy by presenting the location of whatever folder you highlight at the top of the IDE, as shown in Figure 3-9.

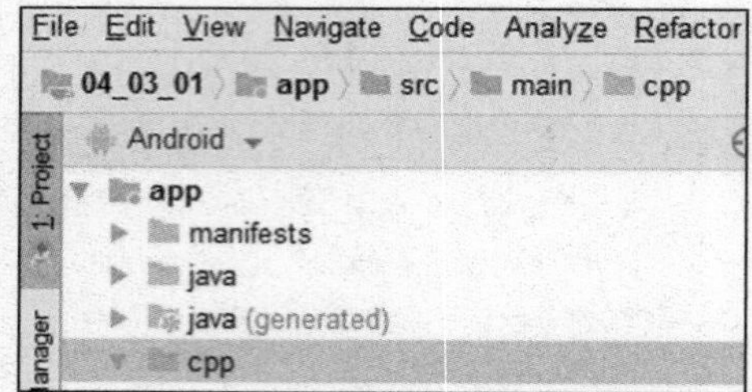

FIGURE 3-9: The IDE provides the location of the folder you point at.

You don't need the project or the App part — just the part that remains. Even if you aren't used to working with your hard drive directly, this approach makes things easy. Another way to locate the same information is to switch to Project view, as shown in Figure 3-10. Just follow the hierarchy down as shown.

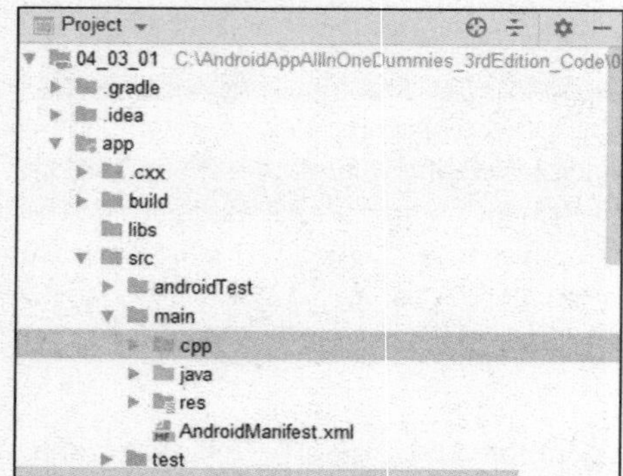

FIGURE 3-10: Using Project view to locate a folder.

Understanding the default template differences

The Android templates always include a `"Hello World!"` entry, and this one is no different. When you start the project, you see a `TextView` with `"Hello World!"`, but you also see a difference. This version has an `id` of `sample_text` for a reason. You need access to the `TextView` to complete the default template functionality. Otherwise, the layout isn't any different than normal.

The code in MainActivity.kt has some additions. As always, you have an onCreate() function that contains the startup code for the app. This version sets the sample_text.text value by calling an external function named stringFromJNI() found in the C++ file included with the template. When you start this app, you don't see "Hello World!" but instead see the mystery string from the C++ file. Here is onCreate() with the additional code in bold:

```
override fun onCreate(savedInstanceState: Bundle?) {
    super.onCreate(savedInstanceState)
    setContentView(R.layout.activity_main)

    // Example of a call to a native method
    sample_text.text = stringFromJNI()
}
```

To access the external C++ file, you need some additional code within MainActivity.kt that creates the connection. Here's the code in question:

```
/**
 * A native method that is implemented by the 'native-lib' native
 * library, which is packaged with this application.
 */
external fun stringFromJNI(): String

companion object {

 // Used to load the 'native-lib' library on application startup.
    init {
        System.loadLibrary("native-lib")
    }
}
```

The external fun stringFromJNI(): String declaration simply tells the compiler that this function is defined somewhere else and not to look for it during the compilation process. Otherwise, you'd receive an error message from the compiler, telling you that stringFromJNI() isn't defined.

The companion object loads the external library specified by System.loadLibrary("native-lib"). The question is where you get the name for this external library. The name appears (in bold) in the CMakeLists.txt file as part of the target_link_libraries entry shown here:

```
target_link_libraries( # Specifies the target library.
                       native-lib
```

```
# Links the target library to the log library
# included in the NDK.
${log-lib} )
```

Whatever you call your library in this entry is what you need to call it in your Android code. There really isn't a good reason to change the library name, however, so generally you use the name supplied.

Getting an overview of the C++ file

This section isn't designed to turn you into a C or C++ developer. In fact, the best it can do is give you a quick overview of the inner workings of a C++ file designed to access the JNI. If you really want to know more about C++, check out *C++ All-in-One For Dummies*, 4th Edition, by John Paul Mueller and Jeff Cogswell (Wiley), to get the answers you need.

TIP

Unless you have an old C file that you really must use with Android, you normally work with C++ files and receive a number of benefits as a result. Working with straight C means writing a lot of extra code to obtain no benefit at all from the resulting binary.

The example template comes with a C++ file called `native-lib.cpp`. Inside this file, you find the following short C++ example:

```
#include <jni.h>
#include <string>

extern "C" JNIEXPORT jstring JNICALL
Java_com_allmycode_p04_103_101_MainActivity_stringFromJNI(
        JNIEnv* env,
        jobject /* this */) {
    std::string hello = "Hello from C++";
    return env->NewStringUTF(hello.c_str());
}
```

The `#include` statements access external header files. A header file contains definitions that a C++ app needs to perform various tasks. Because the definitions are common, developers place them in a single, standard file to make access easy. In this case, the example uses the `<jni.h>` header, which contains definitions used to access the JNI, and the `<string>` header, which contains definitions used to work with strings.

The `extern "C" JNIEXPORT jstring JNICALL` entry tells the C++ compiler that the following function should be exported as an external function with a `jstring` output. The uppercase entries are macros that provide a level of automation for you when writing JNI code. The `JNIEXPORT` macro tells the compiler to put the function that follows into the output binary's dynamic table. Otherwise, when you call `external fun stringFromJNI(): String` in your Android, the call will fail because the Android compiler won't be able to see the function. The `JNICALL` macro tells the C++ compiler to format the function calling convention so that it makes sense to the Android compiler. Otherwise, even if the Android compiler can see the function, it won't be able to make sense of how to call it.

The function name of `Java_com_allmycode_p04_103_101_MainActivity_stringFromJNI()` comes next. Most of this name is stripped off before you see it in your Android code, but when you create the C++ code, you must include it all. However, notice that the part that is stripped off is essentially just a path to the `MainActivity`, with the addition of a `1` in front `03` and `01`. The function takes two arguments:

- » `JNIEnv*`: Points to a structure storing all JNI function pointers. Using the associated `env` variable provides access to the full list of JNI functions so that you can use them in your C++ code. You can find a list of these functions at `https://docs.oracle.com/en/java/javase/13/docs/specs/jni/functions.html#interface-function-table`.
- » `jobject`: Points to a JSON object containing key/value pairs with input arguments to your function from the Android app. Most developers rename the input argument (which is commented out by default) to `thiz` or `instance` to avoid problems with the C++ `this` pointer.

The next step of the code uses standard C++ methods to create a string named `hello` with a value of `"Hello from C++"`. To return this value, you must convert it to a form that Android understands by calling `env->NewStringUTF(hello.c_str())`. The first part of this conversion is C++ specific; it's the `c_str()` function, described at `http://www.cplusplus.com/reference/string/string/c_str/`. The second part of this conversion is Java specific: the `NewStringUTF()`, described at `https://docs.oracle.com/en/java/javase/13/docs/specs/jni/functions.html#newstringutf`.

Seeing the result

This may seem like a lot of work to create a string, and it is, but the result shows that you can access C++ from your app with a little effort. Building this project takes longer than you might expect because of the extra steps involved. However, when you get done, you see the output shown in Figure 3-11. Note that the `sample_text textSize` attribute is set to 36sp in the figure to make the text easier to see.

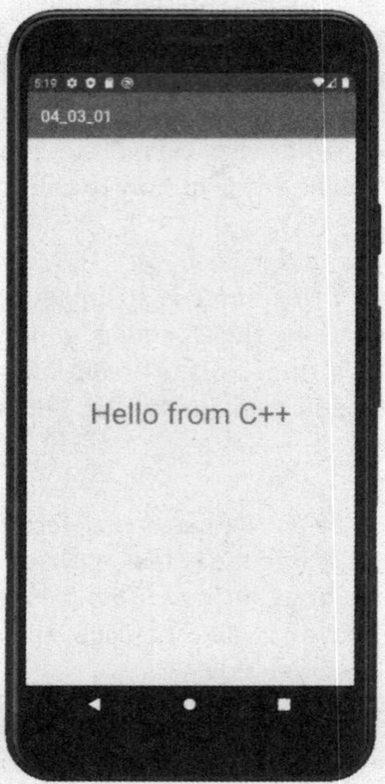

FIGURE 3-11: Seeing the C++ string output.

WARNING

This example won't run with all the emulators that Android Studio provides because of various low-level problems. The Pixel 3a emulator is one of the emulators that works well with the example and is the optimal choice in this instance.

5 Apps for Tablets, Watches, TV Sets, and Cars

Contents at a Glance

- Managing multipanel activities
- Writing apps that run on both phones and tablets

Chapter 1
Apps for Tablets

Don't think about an elephant.

Okay, now that you're thinking about an elephant, think about an elephant's legs. The diameter of an elephant's leg is typically about 40 centimeters (more than four-tenths of a yard).

And think about spiders of the *Pholcidae* family (the "daddy longlegs") with their hair-like legs. And think about Gulliver with his Brobdingnagian friends. Each Brobdingnagian was about 72 feet tall, but a Brobdingnagian adult had the same physical proportions as Gulliver.

Gulliver's Travels is a work of fiction. An animal whose height is 12 times a human's height can't have bone sizes in human proportions. In other words, if you increase an object's size, you have to widen the object's supports. If you don't, the object will collapse.

This unintuitive truth about heights and widths comes from some geometric facts. An object's bulk increases as the cube of the object's height. But the ability to support that bulk increases only as the square of the object's height. That's because weight support depends on the cross-sectional area of the supporting legs, and a cross-sectional area is a square measurement, not a cubic measurement.

Anyway, the sizes of things make important qualitative differences. Take an activity designed for a touchscreen phone. Zoom that activity to a larger size without making any other changes. Then display the enlarged version on a ten-inch tablet screen. What you get on the tablet looks really bad. A tiny, crisp-looking icon turns into a big, blurry blob. An e-book page adapts in order to display longer line lengths. But, with lines that are 40 words long, the human eye suffers from terrible fatigue.

The same issue arises with Android activities. An activity contains enough information to fill a small phone screen. When the user needs more information, your app displays a different activity. The new activity replaces the old activity, resulting in a complete refresh of the screen.

If you slap this activity behavior onto a larger tablet screen, the user feels cheated. You've replaced everything on the screen even though there's room for both the old and new information. The transition from one activity to the next is jarring, and both the old and new activities look barren.

No doubt about it, tablet devices require a design that's different from phone designs. And to implement this design, Android has fragments. You first start discovering fragments in Book 3, Chapters 3 and 4, and this chapter adds to that knowledge by emphasizing the differences between smartphone and tablet presentation. This chapter specifically uses the navigational graph technique explored in Example 03_03_02 of Book 3, Chapter 3.

Gaining Perspective

The examples in previous minibooks rely on the perspective of either a Nexus S or a Pixel 3a smartphone used in the portrait orientation (unless you chose some other smartphone setup during the initial configuration). Of course, you could just assume that no one will ever have any other sort of smartphone and will never use it in landscape orientation. You could go further and just assume that tablet users will be happy with the space-wasting view of a smartphone app, but the users of those devices will soon provide you with a rude awakening. Different devices have different perspectives of your app. The following sections help you understand how to configure Android Studio to support testing with multiple device perspectives so that you can create better layouts for your apps. These sections do rely on Example 03_03_02 from Book 3, Chapter 3, but you can easily understand the material without having to create the example if desired.

BALANCING FLEXIBILITY WITH EFFECTIVENESS

A number of the apps you find on your tablet don't really size, nor do they rotate when the user rotates the device. In some cases, they don't play well on smartphones, or they might work on the smartphone but look a bit odd on a tablet because they use space inefficiently. Some game apps are this way, as are quite a few utility-type and procedural apps. Did the app designers make a mistake? Should every app completely contort itself to precisely match the host device, regardless of whether the contortion makes sense? You must ask these questions as you design your app. Only you and the user really know what you need or want from the app.

In many of the utility app cases, it's actually a good thing that the app doesn't rotate it because the user could miss important information if it did. The design may be inflexible, but it shows precisely what it needs to show in a manner designed to ensure that the user gets the right information. However, you have to look for opportunities to make your app as flexible as is possible without reducing its effectiveness in getting the job done. For example, you could break a procedural app into smaller steps or present the text separately from the pictures on a smartphone, all while keeping them combined on a tablet. You have alternatives to explore.

If your app manages a heating or security system and the picture really isn't optional, but neither is a full view of the controls, you need to ensure that the app installs properly and that the user understands the restrictions. Part of ensuring that an app works right is to create the right level of flexibility. The examples in this chapter assume maximum flexibility so that you see them doing things like properly resizing, rotating, and presenting information effectively.

Creating the right devices

Creating great apps means choosing a set of test devices that match what you expect users will have (or at least provide a broad enough spectrum that the app should work on all current devices, even those you haven't tested). As the chapter progresses, you build a flexible app designed around the ideas presented in Book 3, Chapters 3 and 4. In this section, you look again at one of those apps, Example 03_03_02.

You can use a number of techniques to see problems with Example 03_03_02, which is designed to work on a smartphone in portrait mode. One of those techniques is to work with the emulator controls, shown in Figure 1-1. Notice that two of the controls let you turn the emulated device — which you can do either to the left or to the right. Turning the device shows that the example doesn't rotate when the screen rotates, making it quite impossible to use the app in landscape mode, as shown in Figure 1-2.

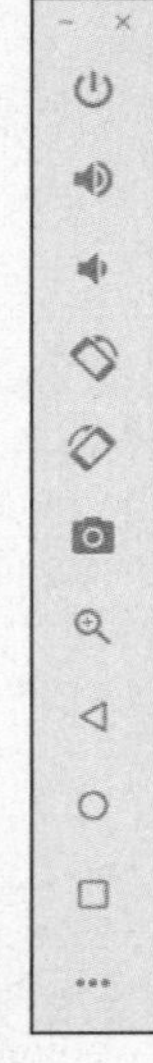

FIGURE 1-1: Emulator controls let you reconfigure the device.

FIGURE 1-2: The example doesn't rotate when turned.

The "Creating an Android virtual device" section of Book 1, Chapter 2 gives you the basics of creating a virtual device. When creating a virtual device, remember that you can choose a startup orientation, as shown in Figure 1-3, and it often helps to have one of each running as you test (see the next section of this chapter for more details).

As shown in Figure 1-4, the maximum resolution of a tablet is nearly twice that of the maximum of a smartphone. The emulator offerings supplied with Android Studio represent the most popular resolutions. However, some devices do provide slightly higher resolutions, and you may need to test against them using a physical device and the USB technique described in the "Testing Apps on a Real Device" section of Book 1, Chapter 3.

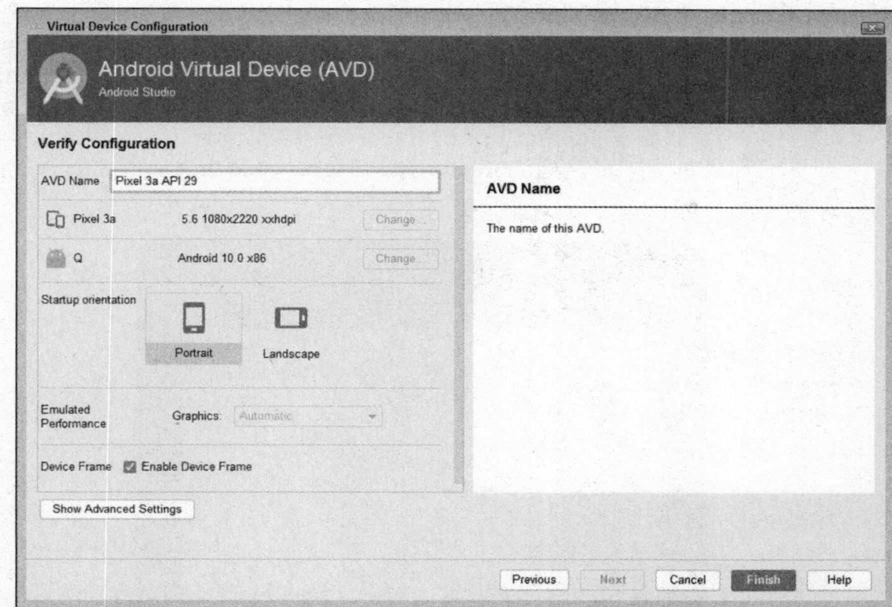

FIGURE 1-3: Test simultaneously in portrait and landscape mode by having one of each.

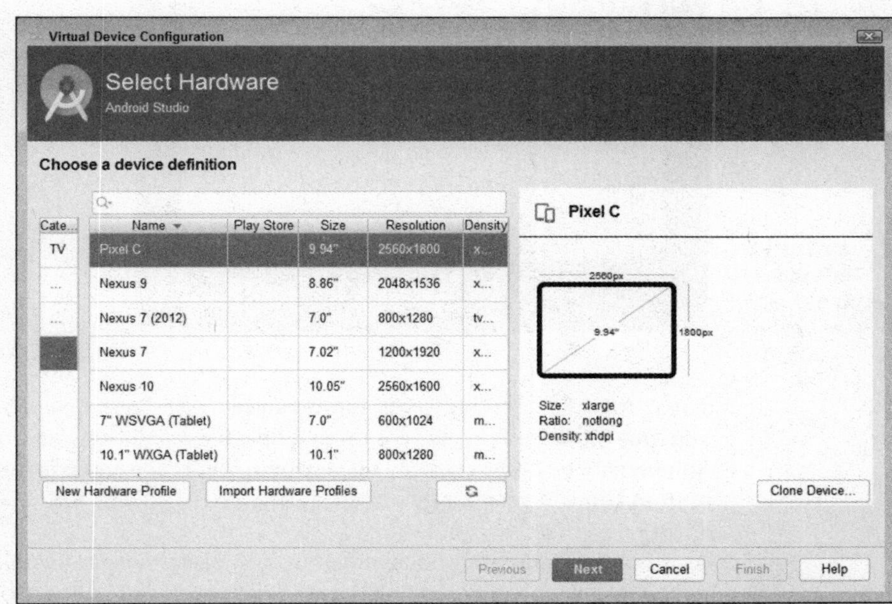

FIGURE 1-4: Tablets can have four times the screen real estate of smartphones.

Running Example 03_03_02 on a high-resolution tablet demonstrates that it doesn't scale very well, as shown in Figure 1-5. The text is so tiny that your user will easily go blind, and the controls are all jammed into the upper-left corner. Between the inability to rotate the display and a lack of scaling, the Example 03_03_02 is a failure, despite looking good in Book 3, Chapter 3.

FIGURE 1-5: The example app doesn't scale well, either.

When creating a testing setup for apps used with both smartphones and tablets, you want to be sure to have a range of device resolutions and form factors. Also helpful is to be able to quickly display both landscape and portrait versions of your app, as shown in Figure 1-6.

REMEMBER

As a final consideration for emulation, you can choose to install any API version you want on an emulator, but a real device may not support the latest Android version. An inability to update to the latest version may make special layout features unavailable, so if your app uses them to create the best possible display, you may also find that some people can't use your app.

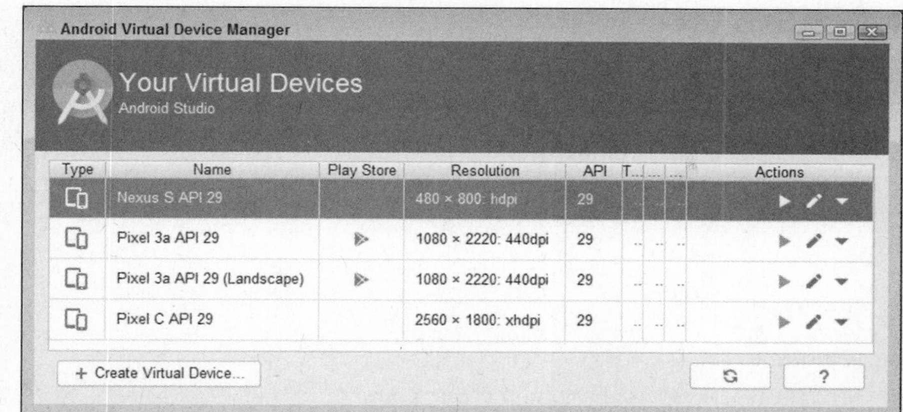

FIGURE 1-6: Define a range of device sizes and orientations to ensure that your app appears correctly onscreen.

Running code on multiple devices

You may have noticed that even with great machine resources, starting an emulation to test your app can take a while, depending on what you expect the app to do. Sometimes, the more efficient approach is to start the testing process on multiple emulators when your goal is to see how the layout works. To use multiple devices to run the app, follow these steps:

1. **Choose Run⇨Select Device.**

   You see the context menu, shown in Figure 1-7.

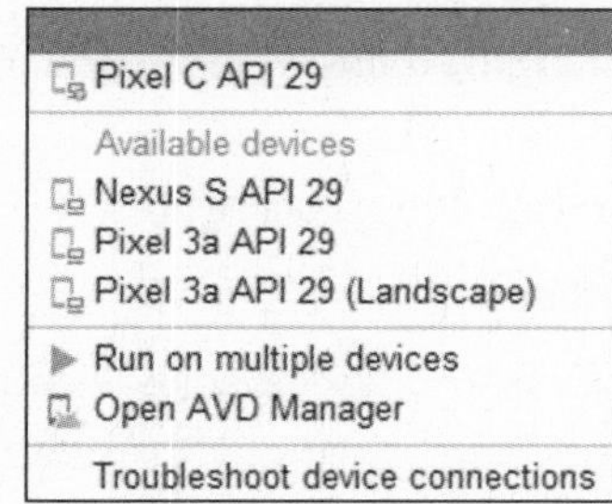

FIGURE 1-7: Accessing the multiple-device capability.

2. **Click Run on Multiple Devices.**

   You see the Select Deployment Targets dialog box, shown in Figure 1-8.

3. **Select the devices you want to use and click Run.**

   Android Studio compiles the app, starts the selected emulators or attached devices, and installs the app on the devices. This process requires longer than the usual time. However, you can then work with each device independently to see various app changes.

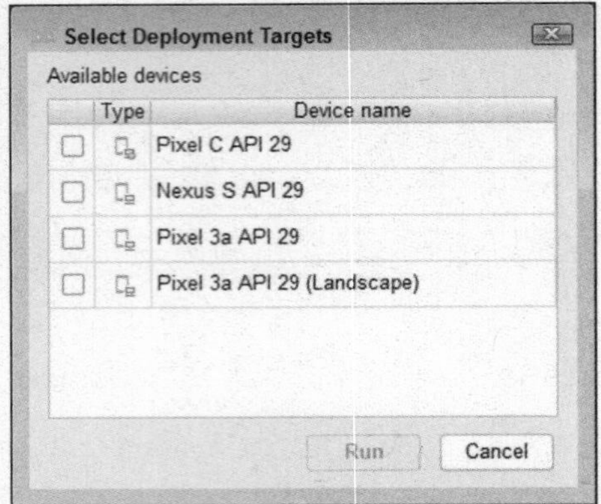

FIGURE 1-8: Choose which devices to use for the emulation.

Copying the project

Clearly, the example app has some design deficiencies, but it makes a good starting point for this chapter, which means making a copy so that you get to keep the original. Use these steps to create a copy of Example 03_03_02.

1. **Create a new folder named 05_01_01 in your source code folder.**

   You see the new empty folder.

2. **Copy all the folders and files in the 03_03_02 folder.**
3. **Paste all the folders and files into the 05_01_01 folder on your system.**

   You see a copy of the files and folders in the new folder.

4. **Choose the Open an Existing Android Studio Project option from the main Android Studio window.**

   Android Studio displays an Open File or Project dialog box.

5. **Select the 05_01_01 folder and click OK.**

   The app won't run correctly at this point, so don't even try. In fact, it may not compile, either.

6. **Open AndroidManifest.xml and change** `package="com.allmycode.p03_03_02"` **to read** `package="com.allmycode.p05_01_01"`**.**
7. **Right-click the** `java\com.allmycode.p03_03_02` **folder and choose Refactor⇨Rename from the context menu.**

   You see the Warning dialog box shown in Figure 1-9, telling you that Android Studio will rename the package instances for you.

8. **Click Rename Package.**

   You see a Rename dialog box like the one shown in Figure 1-10.

FIGURE 1-9: Rename the package instances in your app.

Rename
Rename package 'com.allmycode.p03_03_02' and its usages to:
p03_03_02
Search in comments and strings
Search for text occurrences
Refactor
Preview
Cancel
Help

FIGURE 1-10: Define how you want the rename process to proceed.

9. **Type** p05_01_01 **in the field supplied, check both options, and click Refactor.**

   Android Studio generates a Refactoring Preview like the one shown in Figure 1-11.

10. **Click Do Refactor.**

   After a few moments, the Refactoring Preview dialog box goes away and you can see that the directory names and other elements have been renamed.

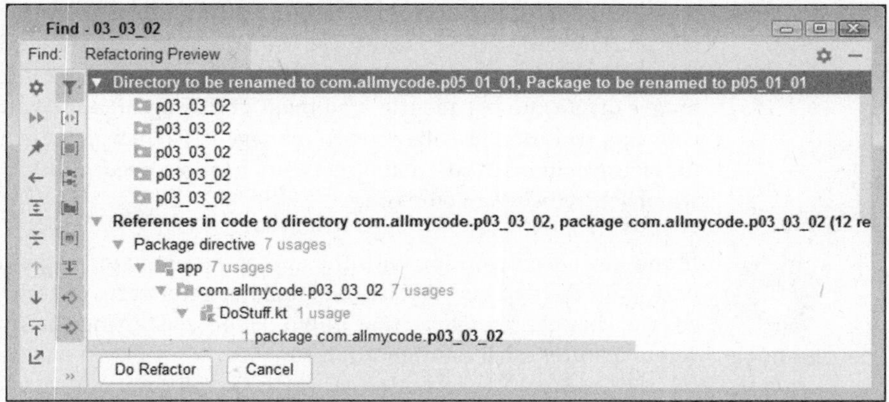

FIGURE 1-11: Verify the refactoring process.

11. **Open** `settings.gradle`**, change the** `rootProject.name` **entry to** `05_01_01`**, and then click Sync Now.**

    Android Studio syncs the change with the rest of the app.

12. **Click Build⇨Make Project.**

    The copied project should compile without error.

Because you're changing things, open `res\values\strings.xml` and change the `<string name="app_name">03_03_02</string>` entry to read `<string name="app_name">Layout Validation</string>` so that the example has a better name than the example number. This technique comes in handy any time you want to retain an existing project but also use it as a starting point for a new project.

Seeing presentation differences

The new example you've created, 05_01_01, has two problems that you've already noted. The first is that it doesn't change orientation when the user changes the device from portrait to landscape presentation. The second is that the text isn't the right size for each device; what looks nice on a smartphone causes the user to squint when working with a tablet. The following sections address both of these issues.

Correcting the orientation problem

It seems as if your app should be able to automatically reorient itself without additional code, but some apps truly are directional, and you see them all the time when you try various apps in Google Play Store (meaning that they have been vetted by Google). For example, a utility to control a furnace might actually work when placed in landscape mode, except, you couldn't conveniently see things like the temperature schedule because adding this information requires a longer display. Consequently, you must decide on an appropriate orientation for your app and then provide code to manage it. The example in this section allows for changes in orientation and reorients itself as needed (a little trick is involved when you're using an emulator).

REMEMBER

If you have been working with the app on an emulator without orientation support, stop the app and restart the emulator afterward. Otherwise, you might not see the change, strange as that might sound. Restarting the emulator apparently resets features such as orientation support.

To begin, you must tell Android that you're interested in knowing about certain changes in configuration, like orientation. Open the `AndroidManifest.xml` file and add the following code, in bold, to the activity.

```
<activity android:name=".MainActivity"
  android:configChanges="orientation|screenSize">
  <intent-filter>
    <action android:name="android.intent.action.MAIN"/>

    <category android:name="android.intent.category.LAUNCHER"/>
  </intent-filter>
</activity>
```

You can add other configuration changes to the `android:configChanges` attribute. However, for now, all you need is to know about orientation and screen size.

The next change appears in `activity_main.xml` file, where you need to add a new `TextView` to display the orientation information received by the code you add in a moment. Name the new control `LastChange` and give it a default `text` value of `N/A`.

The last change is in `MainActivity.kt`. You need to add an `override` for `onConfigurationChanged()`, which is where all the change information appears (so it can get rather complex). Here's the code you use for this part of the example:

```
override fun onConfigurationChanged(newConfig: Configuration) {
    if (newConfig.orientation ==
        Configuration.ORIENTATION_LANDSCAPE) {

        LastChange.setText("Landscape")
    } else if (newConfig.orientation ==
        Configuration.ORIENTATION_PORTRAIT) {

        LastChange.setText("Portrait")
    } else {
        LastChange.setText("Unrecognized")
    }
    super.onConfigurationChanged(newConfig)
}
```

REMEMBER

Notice that the code that interacts with the change must come before the call to `super.onConfigurationChanged(newConfig)`. Otherwise, nothing will happen.

When running the app on an emulator, you see a new little symbol on the bottom of the display with the rest of the controls, as shown in Figure 1-12. This little symbol looks like a box with an arrow in each corner. You must click that symbol to change the orientation of the app.

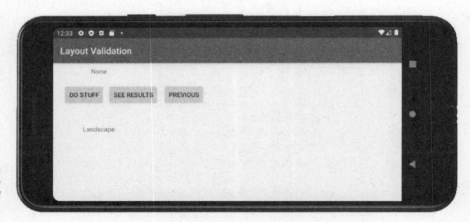

FIGURE 1-12: Look for the little orientation symbol on you emulator.

After you click the orientation symbol, you see the app reorient itself as shown in Figure 1-13. Of course, the text size isn't right, and now the various controls appear shoved over to the left instead of being centered.

FIGURE 1-13: The app now reorients itself correctly.

REMEMBER

As you play with the app, you notice that it maintains state properly and doesn't suddenly display a different page without clicking the appropriate button. Your app must work as expected at all times, which includes changes of configuration such as a changed orientation.

Organizing the layout to match the device

You could slowly drive yourself nuts trying to obtain the right Android layout using programmatic means. A much easier method involves using layouts effectively. For this example, you need to modify how you approach the layout so that it can work well in different orientations and on different-sized devices. To start, consider that activity_main.xml currently uses a ConstraintLayout, which works well when you know you need to work with a specific-sized device at a specific orientation. Using a several LinearLayout setups works better in this case, so activity_main.xml now uses a setup that looks like the one in Figure 1-14.

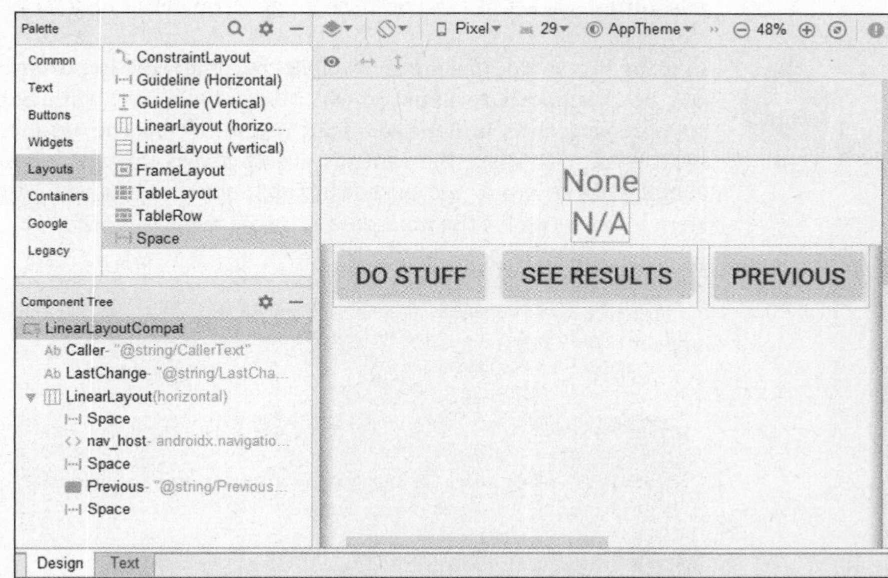

FIGURE 1-14: Using a different layout makes the design more flexible.

REMEMBER

When changing a design, you don't have to start from scratch. You can simply start by using the Text tab to type new names for the elements you want to change, such as by changing the ConstraintLayout to a LinearLayout, as shown in the figure. This design also rearranges a few things and sets some properties differently — all of which you can perform on the Design tab. The new design is actually simpler, and you don't specify any screen positions. For example, here's the new code for the Caller TextView control:

```
<TextView
    android:id="@+id/Caller"
    android:layout_width="wrap_content"
    android:layout_height="wrap_content"
    android:gravity="center_horizontal"
    android:text="@string/CallerText"
    android:textSize="24sp"/>
```

Notice that the control now specifies a textSize attribute value of 24sp, for scalable pixels (sp). Use sp whenever possible to account for differences in device dots-per-inch (dpi) values. Android supports a range of size qualifiers, and it's important to know which one to use. The article at https://blog.mindorks.com/understanding-density-independent-pixel-sp-dp-dip-in-android describes the differences between dp, sp, dip, and so on. Trying to keep them straight could make you crazy! The reason the example now uses 24sp for the text is that it provides a good presentation across smartphone and tablet devices. The text in the pushbuttons is set to 18sp because it shows up better onscreen.

TIP

In using this setup, spacing and weights become more important. For example, the nav_host supports two Button controls and a Space, while activity_main.xml supports spaces around the nav_host and a Button. The weights for each element must equal 1 to space the controls evenly across the device screen, so nav_host actually has a layout_weight setting of 3, not 1, as is used for the other elements. Here is the setup for the horizontal LinearLayout for activity_main.xml:

```
<Space
    android:layout_width="0dp"
    android:layout_height="wrap_content"
    android:layout_weight="1"/>

<fragment
    android:id="@+id/nav_host"
    android:name="androidx.navigation.fragment.NavHostFragment"
    android:layout_width="wrap_content"
    android:layout_height="wrap_content"
    android:layout_weight="3"
    app:defaultNavHost="true"
    app:navGraph="@navigation/nav_graph"/>

<Space
    android:layout_width="0dp"
    android:layout_height="wrap_content"
    android:layout_weight="1"/>

<Button
    android:id="@+id/Previous"
    android:layout_width="wrap_content"
    android:layout_height="wrap_content"
    android:layout_weight="1"
    android:onClick="@string/PreviousClick"
    android:text="@string/PreviousText"
    android:textSize="18sp"/>

<Space
    android:layout_width="0dp"
    android:layout_height="wrap_content"
    android:layout_weight="1"/>
```

None of the controls uses any sort of positioning any longer because the combination of the `LinearLayout` controls makes it unnecessary. Of course, you give up the ability to precisely position controls in the process. A `ConstraintLayout` comes in handy when positioning is critical or you want special effects.

The last odd sort of change is that all the fragments must now have two Button controls and a Space, even `fragment_see_results.xml`. The solution is to include a blank button. Here's the code used to create this new setup:

```
<?xml version="1.0" encoding="utf-8"?>
<LinearLayout
    xmlns:android="http://schemas.android.com/apk/res/android"
    xmlns:tools="http://schemas.android.com/tools"
    android:layout_width="match_parent"
    android:layout_height="match_parent"
    android:orientation="horizontal"
    tools:context=".SeeResults">

    <Button
        android:id="@+id/GoSayGoodbye"
        android:layout_width="wrap_content"
        android:layout_height="wrap_content"
        android:layout_weight="2"
        android:onClick="@string/GoSayGoodbyeClick"
        android:textSize="18sp"
        android:text="@string/GoSayGoodbyeText"/>

    <Space
        android:layout_width="0dp"
        android:layout_height="wrap_content"
        android:layout_weight="1"/>

    <Button
        android:id="@+id/InvisibleButton"
        android:layout_width="wrap_content"
        android:layout_height="wrap_content"
        android:layout_weight="2"
        android:clickable="false"
        android:textSize="18sp"
        android:visibility="invisible"/>

</LinearLayout>
```

Because the `visibility` attribute is set to `"invisible"`, you don't even see the Button onscreen, but the effect of the button is felt through the layout, with Goodbye appearing on one side of the display and Previous on the other. Of course, the main concern is whether these changes have actually fixed the problems noted earlier. Figure 1-15 shows the smartphone landscape view, and Figure 1-16 shows the tablet landscape view. The new design works for simple apps. However, as you see in later sections of the chapter, apps with complex layouts require a bit more planning.

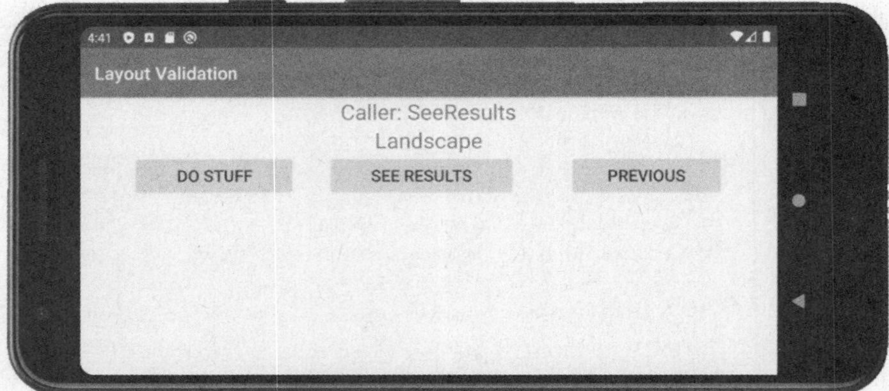

FIGURE 1-15: The new layout works great on a smartphone no matter the orientation.

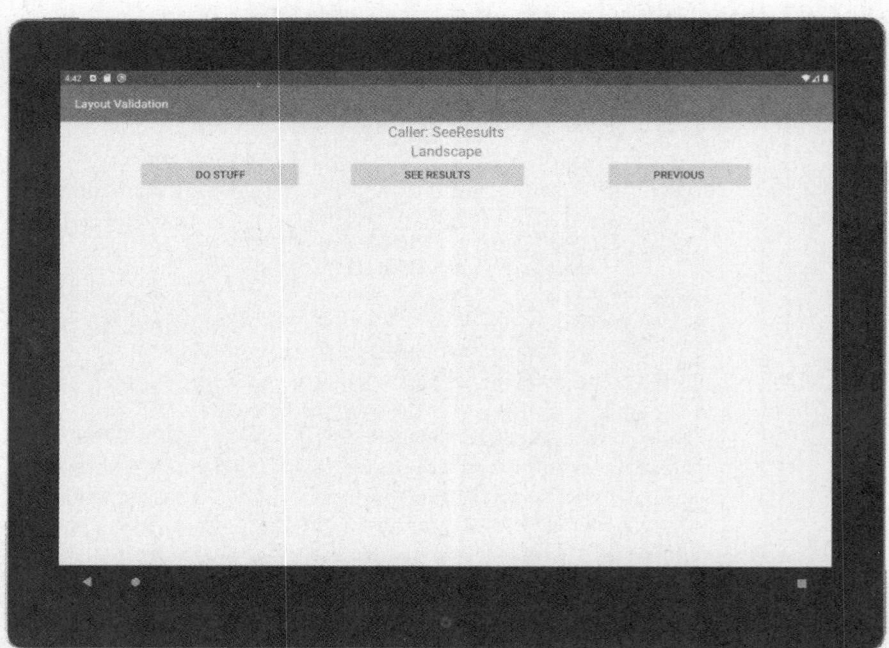

FIGURE 1-16: Tablets can now use the layout as well and the viewer won't squint.

Developing a Nested Navigational Graph

The navigational graph is a lot more flexible than previous examples would have you believe. You can create complex navigation that makes high-end apps possible with a lot less work than you needed to perform in the past. This section conveys the first part of that process, creating a nested navigational graph that groups fragments in such a manner as to make supporting multiple device types considerably easier. When using a nested navigational graph, what you create is a setup in which you use a fragment alone on a smartphone or placed side by side with another fragment on a smartphone in landscape mode (with the requisite reduction in font size). When working with a tablet, you might see four fragments in a group placed in various ways depending on whether the tablet is in portrait or landscape mode. The purpose of all these configurations is to use screen real estate more effectively when working with complex apps.

The example in this section begins by copying the example in the previous section using the technique discussed in the "Copying the project" section, earlier in this chapter. Call this example 05_01_02. As you follow the steps, substitute `05_01_02` for `05_01_01` as needed. You don't need to do anything other than copy the project to start the sections that follow.

Understanding the uses for nested navigational graphs

The essential idea behind a navigational graph (as described in Book 3, Chapter 3) is to outline a process consisting of a series of workflows. In that chapter, you see three workflows:

```
mainEntry->doStuff->seeResults->sayGoodbye
mainEntry->seeResults->sayGoodbye
mainEntry->doStuff->sayGoodbye
```

The problem with this setup is that `doStuff` might actually require a number of steps that won't fit on a single smartphone screen. To make the fragments work, you have to fit them on a single screen of the smallest device you want to support. However, in order to use screen real estate efficiently, a larger screen might show multiple fragments. You have a problem here that you can solve using a nested navigational graph by maintaining the individual fragments but grouping them together into a single nested graph within the main graph.

Consider a series of forms used to make a sale from an online shopping cart. The app you create makes the shopping process easier because a user can safely store personal information locally. So, you might break this process into four parts, as shown here:

1. Verify the content of the shopping cart and total price based on that content and details like shipping method.
2. Obtain the buyer's personal information and shipping address if different from the buyer's address.
3. Obtain credit card or other means of purchase.
4. Finalize the sale by requiring buyer verification of details.

The process must follow all four of these steps, so grouping them makes sense. However, a buyer need not necessarily want to make another purchase. The `seeResults` part of the overall process might simply display current orders. So, a buyer might want to make a new purchase and see it added to the list of pending orders, see just the pending orders, or just make a purchase. The three original workflows still work, but `doStuff` is now more complex. Examples of other kinds of nested graph include:

- Login or other verifications
- Setup or other wizards
- Gaming or other activity flows
- Demos that allow limited interaction
- Any complex multiscreen workflow or process

Developing an app design

A complex app doesn't just sprout out of your mind like a patch of petunias. You don't get up in the morning, proclaim you'll be brilliant, and create the design from scratch without reworking it a little. Most people start with an overview, which is what you can consider the original design from Book 3, Chapter 3 to be. You augmented that design in this chapter as example 05_01_01, and you see this augmented design in Figure 1-17.

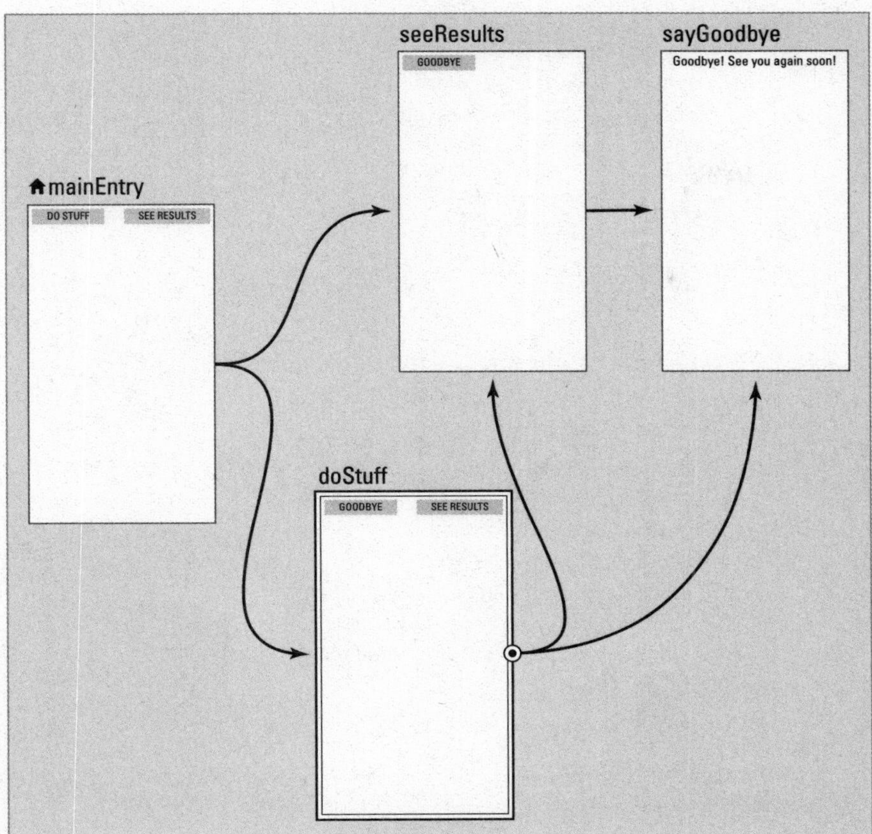

FIGURE 1-17: An augmentation of the original Book 3, Chapter 3 design.

Apps for Tablets

Follow these steps to implement the design changes considered in the previous section of the chapter:

1. **Add three new fragments below** `doStuff` **and name them:**
   - `personalInfo`
   - `creditCard`
   - `finalize`

   You use the same process as you do in the "Adding destinations" section of Book 3, Chapter 3.

2. **Delete the existing links among** `doStuff`, `seeResults`, **and** `sayGoodbye` **by clicking each link and pressing Delete.**

3. **Create new links as shown in Figure 1-18 to create the new workflow.**

   You use the same process as you do in the "Creating links between destinations" section of Book 3, Chapter 3.

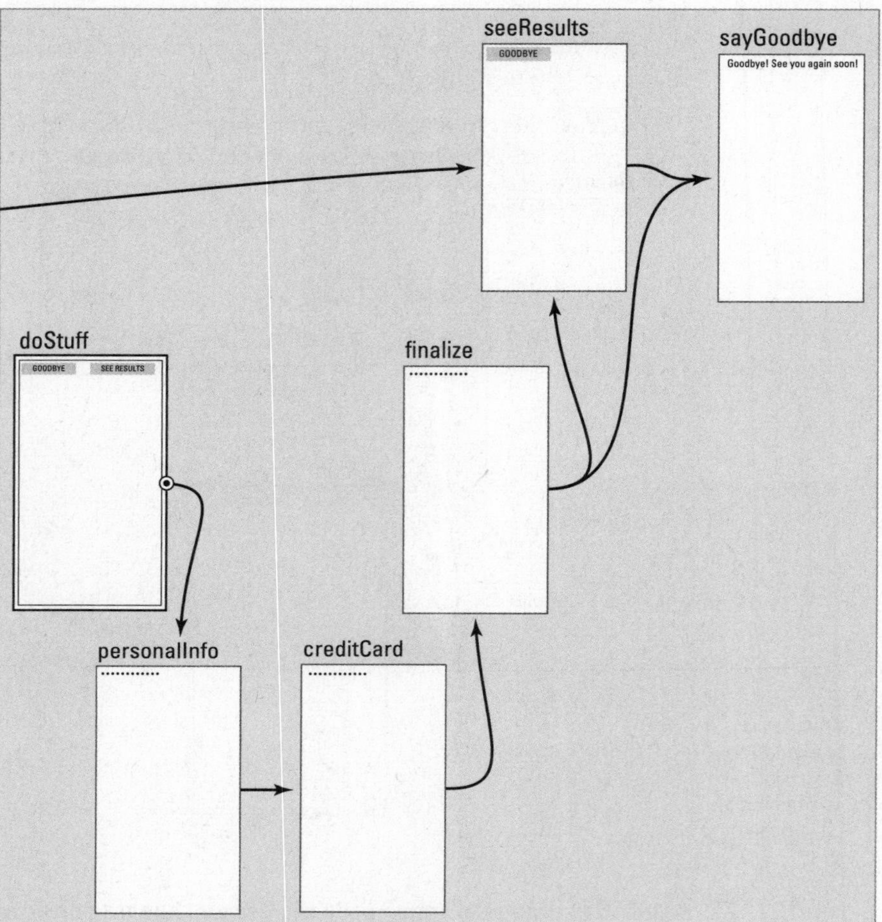

FIGURE 1-18: Define the new links for the updated design.

4. **Rename** `doStuff` **to** `verifySale` **by highlighting the** `doStuff` **block in the design and typing** verifySale **in the ID field of the Attributes pane.**

   You see a dialog box asking whether to perform the update locally or globally.

5. **Click Yes to perform the update globally.**

   The navigational graph designer applies the change globally.

6. **Perform Steps 4 and 5 to rename** `seeResults` **to** `seeOrders`**, with a Label of** `fragment_see_orders`**.**

7. **Shift-click** `verifySale`**,** `personalInfo`**,** `creditCard`**, and** `finalize`**.**

   You see all four blocks highlighted.

8. **Click Group Into Nested Graph on the toolbar (the icon that looks like three blocks grouped).**

   You now see the grouped items as a single block with an ID value of `navigation`, which clearly isn't helpful. If you wanted to maintain the original design, you could always use `doStuff` for an ID because this single grouped block encapsulates what you used to call `doStuff`, but a better name might be `purchaseGoods`.

9. **Highlight the grouped block and type** purchaseGoods **in the ID field of the Attributes pane.**

   The final graph looks like the one in Figure 1-19.

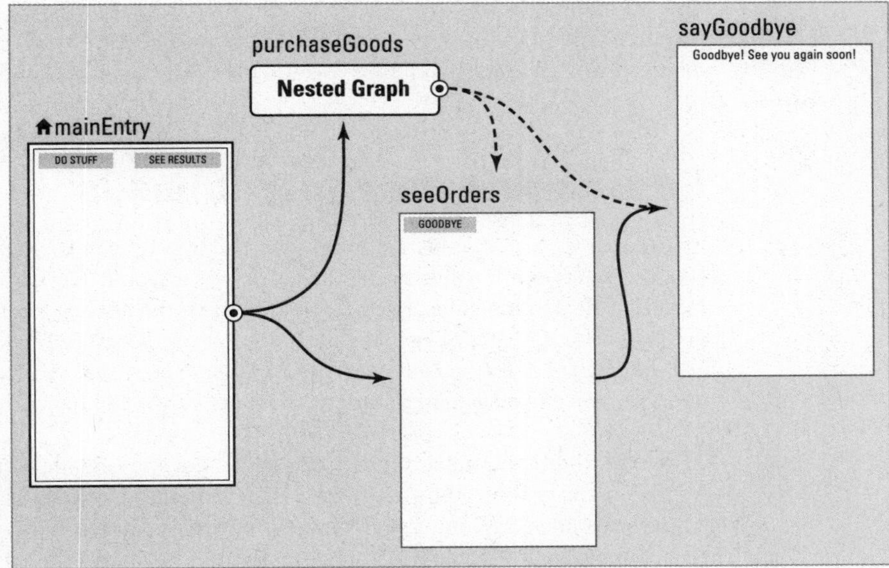

FIGURE 1-19: An updated graph that considers a more complex process.

You should note a few things aspects of this new design. For one thing, all the nested graph links are dashed so that you can easily see that clicking one of them won't show the actual actions. To see the actions contained within a nested graph, you must double-click the block, which reveals the content.

The second thing to note is that the Destinations pane takes on a new meaning, as shown in Figure 1-20. Notice that when you go into a nested graph to see its individual elements, you can't see any of the elements outside the nested graph. You click Root (with the left-pointing arrow) to leave the nested graph and return to the overview.

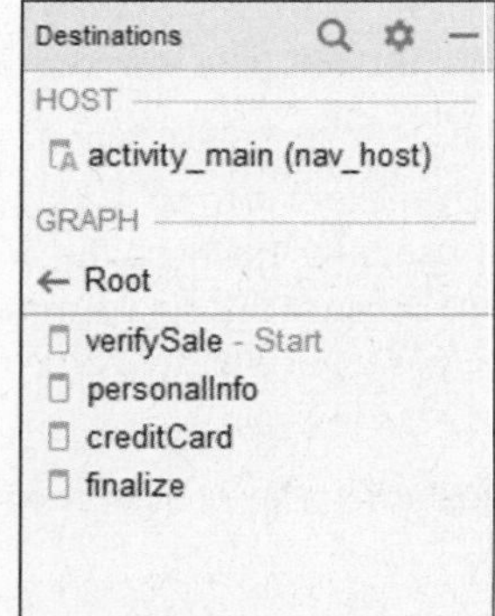

FIGURE 1-20: Seeing Destinations from within the nested graph.

REMEMBER

The fragment file for verifySale is still titled fragment_do_stuff.xml, and the fragment file for seeOrders is still titled fragment_see_results.xml. You could change these filenames and likely would for a large project, but for now, just leave them as is.

Considering the content needs

At this point, you should try to compile the app by choosing Build⇨Make Project. You see two unresolved reference errors as a result. The errors come from the fact that the actions have changed. Double-click the entries to modify the actions: action_doStuff_to_seeResults becomes action_finalize_to_seeResults, and action_doStuff_to_sayGoodbye becomes action_finalize_to_sayGoodbye. If you like, you can also change the Caller.setText() call to "Caller: Finalize".

Of course, these actions don't completely fix the app linkages, but they're a start. The problem is that you now have a different flow, and using the Button controls as the app has done makes the app brittle and not very adaptive to the content. What you really need is a quick method of navigating the graph that isn't so brittle. In addition, you want the fragments to contain only content. So, begin by removing the buttons from all the fragments and adding two buttons to activity_main.xml so that it looks like Figure 1-21.

To keep things easy, change the fragments so that they all have a simple TextView that describes the current page, like this:

```
<?xml version="1.0" encoding="utf-8"?>
<LinearLayout
    xmlns:android="http://schemas.android.com/apk/res/android"
    xmlns:tools="http://schemas.android.com/tools"
    android:layout_width="match_parent"
    android:layout_height="match_parent"
```

```
    android:orientation="horizontal"
    tools:context=".DoStuff">

    <!-- TODO: Update blank fragment layout -->

    <TextView
        android:id="@+id/textView"
        android:layout_width="wrap_content"
        android:layout_height="wrap_content"
        android:layout_weight="1"
        android:gravity="center_horizontal"
        android:text="This is the Main Entry page."
        android:textSize="24sp"/>
</LinearLayout>
```


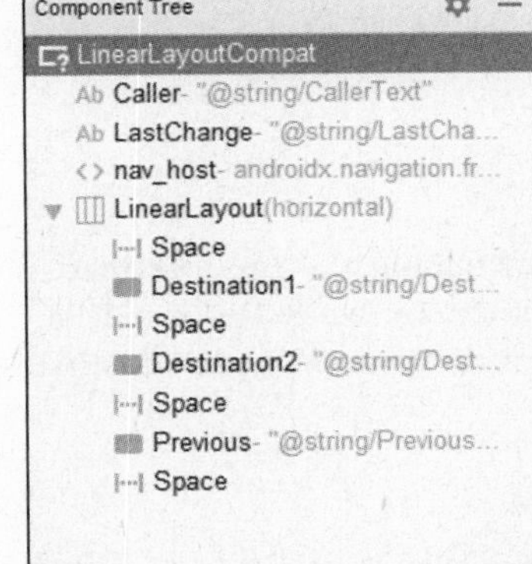

FIGURE 1-21: Reorganize the layout to place all controls on `activity_main.xml`.

The `nav_graph.xml` file requires changes as well. Set the `Label` attribute for each of the destinations to match the `ID` attribute. You also need to add information about the buttons for each of the destinations by adding arguments on the Attribute pane. Click the + icon to see a dialog box like the one shown in Figure 1-22.

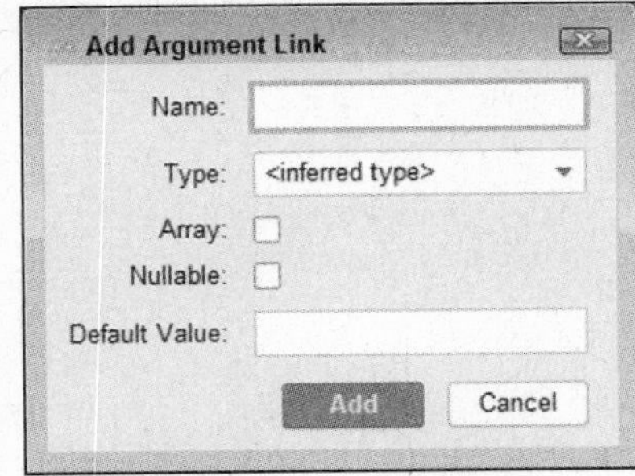

FIGURE 1-22: Add button information to each destination.

For this example, type **Button1** or **Button2** (when the destination has two buttons) in the Name field, select String as the Type, and type the text that should appear on the button in Default Value, such as **Buy Goods** for `Button1` of `mainEntry`. Figure 1-23 shows an example of how your entries should look for `mainEntry`.

FIGURE 1-23: Add arguments to handle the button text.

Making these changes allows you handle the two destination buttons using a single function for each. Both functions work the same, but `onDestination1Click()` is a little longer because it contains more destinations. Here is the `onDestination1Click()` code:

```
fun onDestination1Click(view: View){
    val navController = Navigation.findNavController(
        this, R.id.nav_host)
    val Fragments: NavHostFragment =
        supportFragmentManager.findFragmentById(
            R.id.nav_host) as NavHostFragment
    val ChildFragment =
        Fragments.childFragmentManager.fragments[0]

    val thisCaller = navController.currentDestination
    Caller.setText("Caller: " + thisCaller!!.label)

    when (ChildFragment) {
        is MainEntry -> navController.navigate(
            R.id.action_mainEntry_to_doStuff)
```

```
        is DoStuff ->  navController.navigate(
            R.id.action_doStuff_to_personalInfo)
        is personalInfo -> navController.navigate(
            R.id.action_personalInfo_to_creditCard)
        is creditCard -> navController.navigate(
            R.id.action_creditCard_to_finalize)
        is finalize -> navController.navigate(
            R.id.action_finalize_to_seeResults)
        is SeeResults -> navController.navigate(
            R.id.action_seeResults_to_sayGoodbye)
    }

    ChangeButtons(navController)
}
```

This function works similarly to those you have worked with in the past, but in reality it provides a simplification because you no longer micromanage everything. The `navController` provides access to the various locations that you want to manage, while `ChildFragment` tells you about the current destination. For example, you use `ChildFragment` to determine the name of the caller based on its `label` property. `ChildFragment` also lets you know about the destination type so that you know where the app should go next.

Part of the magic in this version of the app is that `navController` changes to match the current destination. So, after you call `navController.navigate()`, `navController` no longer points to the previous destination; it points to the new destination instead. The call to `ChangeButtons(navController)` configures the buttons to match the new destination using the following code:

```
fun ChangeButtons(navController: NavController) {
    val newCaller =
        navController.currentDestination!!.arguments
    if (newCaller!!["Button1"] != null) {
        Destination1.visibility = View.VISIBLE
        Destination1.setText(
            newCaller!!["Button1"]!!.defaultValue.toString()
        )
    } else
        Destination1.visibility = View.INVISIBLE

    if (newCaller!!["Button2"] != null) {
        Destination2.visibility = View.VISIBLE
```

```
        Destination2.setText(
            newCaller!!["Button2"]!!.defaultValue.toString()
        )
    } else
        Destination2.visibility = View.INVISIBLE
}
```

This is where the default argument values you configured in Figure 1-23 come into play. Each of the destinations has between zero and two buttons. When there is button text to display, the code uses the argument text to update the button. Otherwise, the button is invisible. Figure 1-24 shows the result of making the app useful with a nested navigational graph.

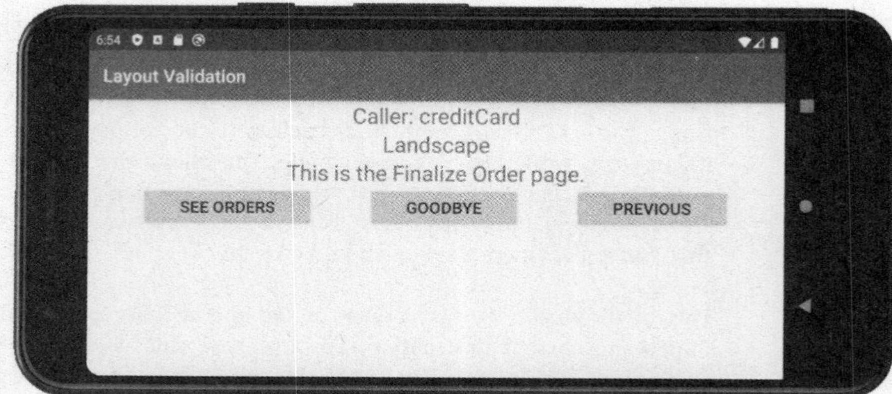

FIGURE 1-24: The fragments now have only content, so you can easily rearrange them.

Creating a Responsive App

You can do more than you've seen in this chapter to create an app that works equally well on a smartphone or a tablet (or any other device, for that matter). Here are some other methods of adding flexibility and responsiveness to consider:

- **Choose when to use a navigation bar or a navigation drawer.** When working with a larger device, rely on a navigation bar, displayed at the bottom of the app, to provide a better view of app features in an easily accessed manner. However, when working with a smaller device, use a navigation drawer (hidden on the app bar) instead to conserve space.

- **Make full use of Toolbar functionality.** You see part of this feature in action in the "Complying with User Preferences" section of Book 3, Chapter 4.
- **Restrict your app to specific device sizes when necessary.** You have a number of options in this regard, which are explained at `https://developer.android.com/guide/practices/screens-distribution.html`.
- **Create different layouts based on smallest screen width.** After designing a layout using fragments that contain only content, you can rearrange the fragments in any pattern that a particular device will accommodate and then place that layout in a special folder for devices of that size, as explained at `https://developer.android.com/training/multiscreen/screensizes`.
- **Define different layouts based on device orientation.** This technique relies on the same approach you use for screen widths. You can use the resulting special folders by orientation, smallest screen width, or both.

» **Creating a basic wearable app**

» **Creating a watch face app**

Chapter 2 Developing for Android Wear

Android wearables commonly come in a single form: the watch. However, that's the end of the commonality. The first section of this chapter gives you a brief overview of just a few ways in which wearables are used today. The diversity will amaze you!

Many of this book's concepts work on all kinds of devices. But when a person describes a particular feature, it's easy to think "smartphone or tablet." In this chapter, you veer briefly from that path and deal exclusively with wristwatches (known formally as *Android Wear devices*, or *wearables* for short). The apps won't make you the next talk of the town with regard to wearables, but you'll gain insights into the commonality of and differences among wearable app development.

Seeing Where Wearables Are Used

It's usually helpful to have an idea of just where your apps might end up. Seeing what other people have dreamed up can give you ideas for your own amazing app. You may find yourself asking why a wearable can't seem to do something, and then wind up creating an app to do it. The following list offers just some basic ideas of what wearables do today:

- **Withings ScanWatch (`https://www.withings.com/us/en/scanwatch`):** Has a host of health-related features, including the ability to detect your sleep apnea and display an EKG. It'll also help you get ready for your next fitness event by tracking your running, walking, and swimming.
- **Skagen Falster 3 (`https://www.skagen.com/en-us/falster3-learn-more`):** Looks gorgeous, and you can use it to make calls Dick Tracy–style. It also comes with 8GB of RAM to hold part of your music collection, and the 1GB of RAM ensures that you can run some hefty wearable apps. Just in case you get lost, this watch can help you find where you are by displaying a micro-map containing GPS information.
- **Huami Amazfit T-Rex (`https://en.amazfit.com/t-rex.html`):** Provides the Swiss army knife of watches with durability that even the military likes (with 12 military-grade certifications to prove it). What is amazing about this watch is that it actually does look like one of those ultra-sophisticated mechanical watches that people used to wear not long ago, but now you can change the watch face to match your personality of the day. As you might expect for such a watch, it comes with 14 sports modes that you can use to track your performance in a manner particular to your favorite sport.
- **Coolpad Dyno 2 (`https://coolpad.us/dyno/`):** Defines the wearable that children want. As you might expect, it's a little light on features but high on durability. It also provides special kid features like an SOS button that a child can press to get in contact with Mom and Dad instantly. The parent also decides who can communicate with the child, and the watch has many other features that make the 4LTE communication safer.
- **TicWatch Pro 4G/LTE (`https://www.mobvoi.com/us/pages/ticwatchpro4g`):** Enables the rest of us to find a watch that doesn't cater to fitness needs. This watch provides about the same level of connectivity as a standard smartphone, supports Google Pay (so that you don't have to carry a wallet around) and an SOS mode for those creepy areas of town, and provides access to Google Assistant so that you can discover a new restaurant in your area on a whim. Of course, it does provide heart monitoring (which seems to be a somewhat standard feature), but the focus is on what most people need just to live their lives.
- **Motiv Ring Fitness (`https://mymotiv.com/`):** Works with your Android device. However, you have to write the code needed to access it, which makes this device a wearable kind of add-on. It can actually perform many of the tasks that a watch can, such as track your health and help you buy things at the store, but in a smaller format.

» **Jacquard Jacket** (`https://atap.google.com/jacquard/collaborations/levi-trucker/`): Interacts with your smartphone, the one in your pocket, through various gestures on the left sleeve. Google has created this jacket in collaboration with Levi's. This jacket has many features that you might expect, like the ability to obtain schedule updates and (it's not easy to envision this) take a selfie. It will also tell you when you leave your jacket behind at a restaurant and help you track down your smartphone.

TIP

The point of the last two entries in this list is that you shouldn't focus on equating wearables to watches. Android Studio is currently set up to work with watches unless you find a handy third-party template. Third parties are stepping up with a host of different Input Method Editor (IME) add-ons, as described at `https://developer.android.com/training/wearables/ui/wear-ime`, so the basic interactions in this chapter will likely get superseded by new innovations at some point. Eventually, you can count on the Wear OS taking off in new directions because people don't want to be hampered by having to constantly monitor their smartphone or tablet.

Setting Up Your Testing Environment

From a coding perspective, working with a wearable project doesn't have to be significantly different than any other Android project. However, the user interface is different because you work with a significantly smaller device. You also have to consider the emulator you use to test the app and so on. With all this in mind, the following sections tell you about a basic wearable app project using the usual Hello World example.

TIP

You may have a perfectly wonderful mobile app that you want to move to a wearable device. Android also enables you to add a wear module to your existing mobile project. The instructions at `https://developer.android.com/training/wearables/apps/creating.html#add-wear-os-module` tell how to perform this task.

Creating the project

Most of the classes and methods that you use to write phone apps work on Android Wear apps as well. For evidence (but not proof) of this fact, follow these steps:

1. **In Android Studio, start a new project and select the Wear OS option.**

   You see a list of templates like the one shown in Figure 2-1.

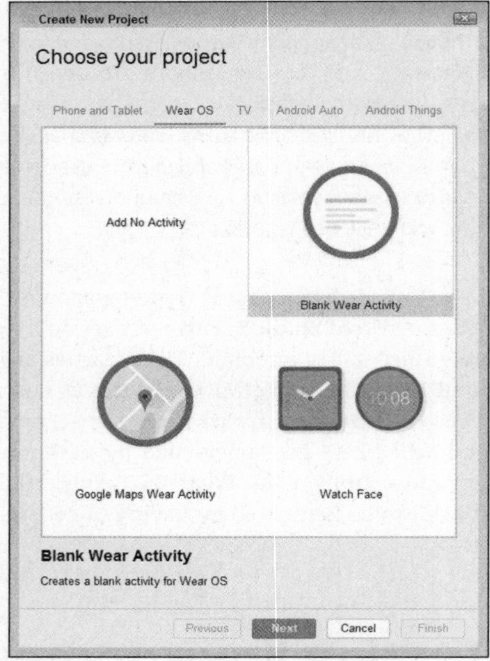

FIGURE 2-1: The Wear OS templates focus on watches.

2. **Choose the Blank Wear Activity template and click Next.**

   You see the Configure Your Project dialog box, shown in Figure 2-2. Most of the features don't look any different from a standard app. However, notice that the minimum API level defaults to API 28: Android 9.0 (Pie). In looking at online offerings, you find that this is actually a good level to choose, despite the fact that it limits the smartphones you can pair with your app if you wanted to do so.

REMEMBER

   The Pair with Empty Phone App option on this page lets you pair your wearable app with a phone. However, Android recommends against this and states outright at `https://developer.android.com/training/wearables/apps/creating` that a wear app should run independently of a phone app. The suggestion is to test your app on an actual watch by uploading the app using Wi-Fi or Bluetooth. This chapter uses the emulator just to make things easy and ensure that you can follow along, even if you don't currently own a smartwatch (or other wearable device).

   If you check the Pair with Empty Phone App option, what you see is a dual project containing both a `mobile` and a `wear` folder.

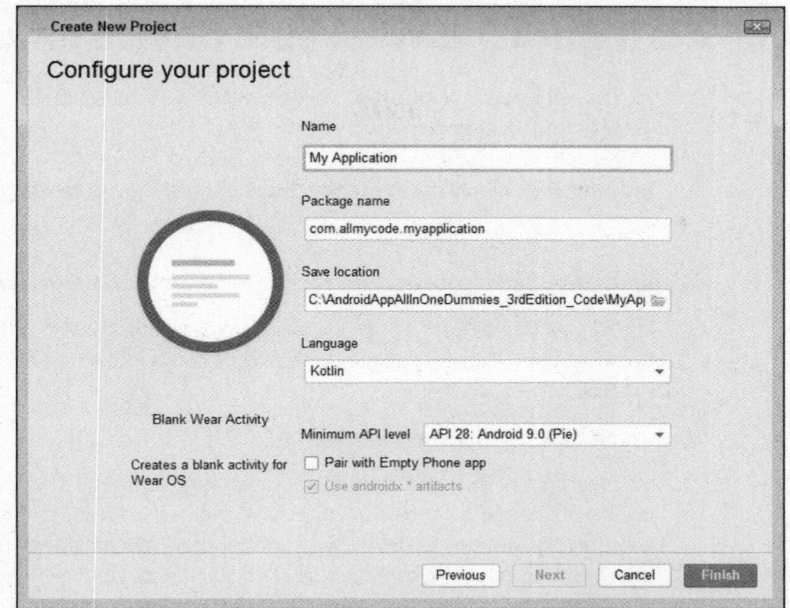

FIGURE 2-2: Define the basic parameters of the app you want to create.

3. **Type** 05_02_01 **in the Name field, type** com.allmycode.p05_02_01 **in the Package Name field, and click Finish.**

   Android Studio begins creating your project for you.

TECHNICAL STUFF

If you like to poke around in a new project before doing anything else, you may notice that the Component Tree shows an error for the `FrameLayout`, as shown in Figure 2-3, before you've touched anything. This error is tied to the `app:boxedEdges="all"` entry, which supposedly is missing a namespace entry, except that the namespace entry is there as part of the `<androidx.wear.widget.BoxInsetLayout>` element. When you see this error, you click the offending line to display a red light bulb on the left side of the editor. Click the light bulb and choose Suppress: Add tools.ignore="Missing Prefix" Attribute from the context menu.

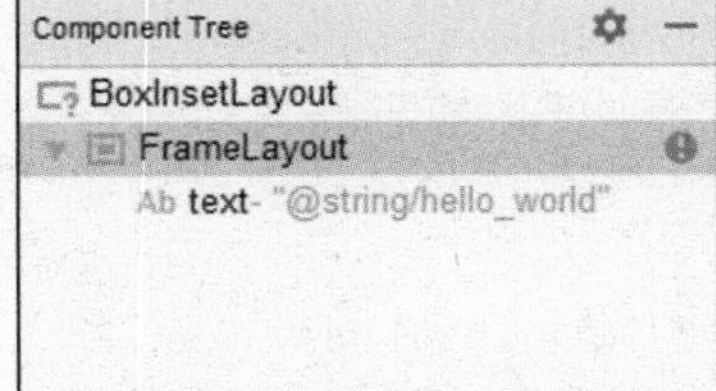

FIGURE 2-3: Already an error and you haven't even touched anything!

Configuring a wearable device emulator

To run this chapter's example, the only thing you need is an Android Wear AVD. Here's how you get one:

1. **In Android Studio's main menu, choose Tools ➪ AVD Manager.**

   The AVD Manager opens.

2. **In the AVD Manager window, click the Create Virtual Device button.**

   The Virtual Device Configuration dialog box appears. The left side of the dialog box contains a Category list, and the middle contains a list of hardware profiles.

3. **In the Category list, select Wear OS.**

   You see a list of devices for the Wear OS that replaces the Phone device listing you normally see, as shown in Figure 2-4. Unlike the Phone category, the Wear OS category focuses on device types rather than specific device models. All these devices have the same density and slightly varying resolutions. Otherwise, the only real difference is the shape. You have a choice of these basic shapes:

   - **Square:** A form commonly found for larger wearables that provides the most usable screen space.
   - **Round:** A circular form commonly found with moderately sized wearable displays, often oriented toward fashion.
   - **Round chin:** A circular form that is mostly round with a squared-off portion at the bottom. It provides a luxury look but has the least usable screen space to offer.

4. **Select Android Wear Square and click Next.**

   This chapter relies on a specific AVD so that it's easier for you to compare the output from your app with the screenshots in the book. However, any of the choices would likely work fine, and if you're really determined to see a round or a round chin display instead, feel free to select it.

TIP

It's true. To run this chapter's example, any Android wear choice will do. But to run the emulator on your development computer, some choices might be better than others. Some AVDs consume too much memory. The Android Wear Square selection tends to work best.

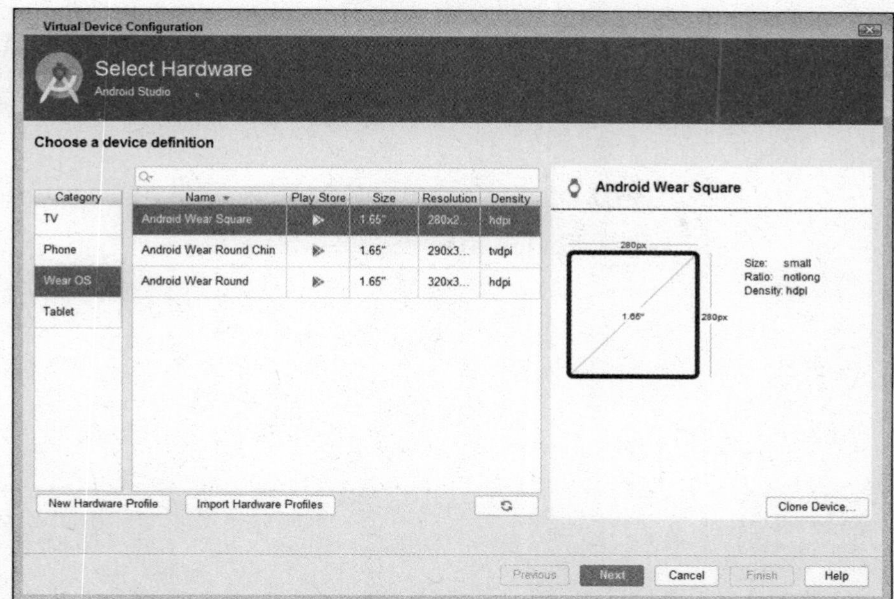

FIGURE 2-4: The Wear OS category contains only a few basic types.

5. **Click Next.**

   You see the Select a System Image dialog box, shown in Figure 2-5. Notice the tabs at the top of the table with Recommended selected by default. The recommended options will work best on most development computers, so you should select one of them unless you have a particular need. For example, if you select the Other Images tab, you see that you can choose an armeabi-v7a processor rather than an x86 processor.

REMEMBER

   Notice that the highest available API level is 28. Because you select API level 28 in Step 2 in the "Creating the project" section, earlier in the chapter, you must choose an API level 28 device now.

   The Target column is also important for a system image in this situation. The option that will cause fewest problems when creating your app is the Android 9.0 (Wear OS) target.

   Also remember that the previous examples in this book use API level 29, so you must download the API level 28 release.

6. **Click the Download link for the Android 9.0 (Wear OS) target, shown highlighted in Figure 2-5.**

   You see a Component Installer dialog box appear. The progress bar shows the download process, which can take a while. It might be a good idea to read a good book or have some coffee. At some point, the download and installation process will complete.

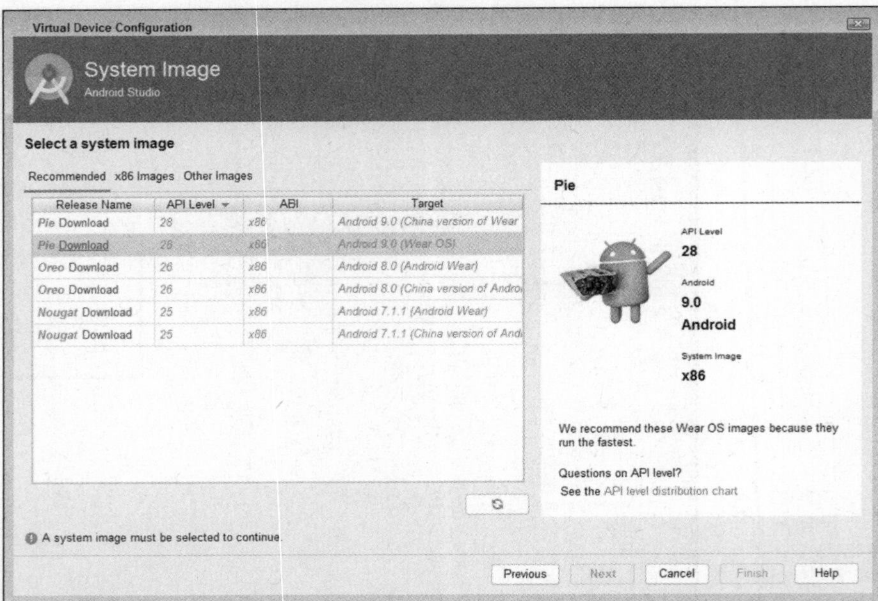

FIGURE 2-5: Select one of the recommended options for best performance.

7. **Click Finish.**

   The Component Installer dialog box goes away. You return to the Select a System Image dialog box.

8. **Click Next.**

   You see the Verify Configuration dialog box, shown in Figure 2-6.

9. **Click Finish.**

   You see the new device appear in the Android Virtual Device Manager dialog. Notice that the Type column shows a watch icon, rather than a smartphone and tablet icon.

10. **Close the Android Virtual Device Manager dialog.**

11. **Choose Run⇨Select device.**

    A context menu appears.

12. **Click the Android Wear Square API 28 entry.**

    The IDE is now configured to use an appropriate device for testing.

To ensure that your configuration works, choose Run⇨Run 'app'. You see the default project output shown in Figure 2-7.

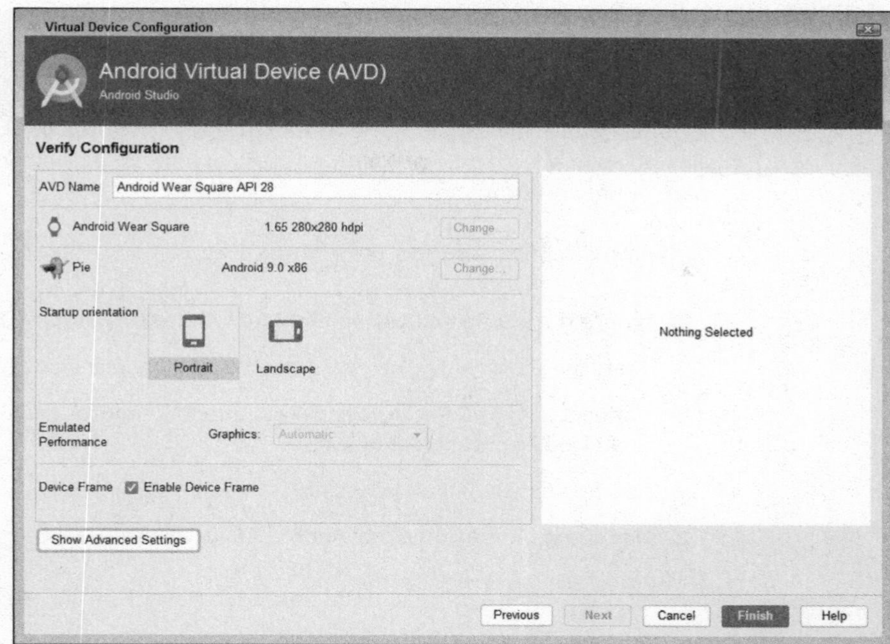

FIGURE 2-6: The configuration used for the examples in this chapter.

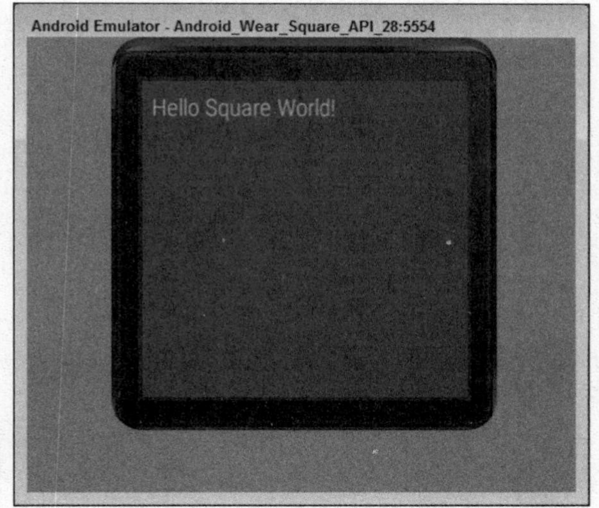

FIGURE 2-7: A quick test of your environment.

Developing for Android Wear

Other testing configurations

For the full Android Wear experience, you may want two devices — a wearable and a phone (modern wearables are far more capable than the offerings of the past). The obvious question is, are both of them emulated, or just one? Are they both real, or only one of them?

To help answer this question, the Android documentation provides a few scenarios:

- **Ignore the phone and use an emulated Android Wear device.**

  That's the scenario that we recommend for this chapter's example.

- **Connect a real phone to your development computer and use an emulated Android Wear device.**

  See the brief list of tips in this section.

- **Use a real phone and a real Android Wear device.**

  Again, see the brief list of tips.

The Android developer training pages have detailed instructions on setting up phones for testing with Android Wear, so this section of the chapter doesn't dwell on the details. Instead, you get some of the highlights. These highlights might help you see the forest for the trees while you march step-by-step through the instructions on the Android developer site's pages.

The Android developer site's pages on testing with real devices are `http://developer.android.com/training/wearables/apps/creating.html` and `http://developer.android.com/training/wearables/apps/bt-debugging.html`. When you set up a phone for testing with Android Wear, you perform some or all of the following steps:

- Install the Android Wear app from the Google Play Store on your phone.
- Use the Developer options in the phone's Settings screen to enable USB debugging on the phone.
- (With an Android Wear emulator) Type the following command in your development computer's command prompt window or Terminal app:

  ```
  adb -d forward tcp:5601 tcp:5601
  ```

  This command forwards your emulator's communications to the connected phone.

- (On a real wearable device) Use the Developer options in the device's Settings screen to enable ADB debugging on the Wear device.

- In the Android Wear app on the phone, pair the phone with the emulator (or with the real wearable device).

For connecting a real wearable device, you have two options:

- **Connect the device to your development computer using a USB cable.** Alas! Some Android wearables don't have USB ports.
- **Create a Bluetooth connection between the phone and the wearable.** For this option, you have to enable the Debugging over Bluetooth option on the wearable. You also have to set up Debugging over Bluetooth in the Android Wear app on the phone and type the commands

```
adb forward tcp:4444 localabstract:/adb-hub
adb connect localhost:4444
```

  on your development computer.

Wearable Apps: What's the Big Deal?

The previous sections spend considerable effort to convince you that Wearable apps are very much like phone apps. But if things are so similar, why have a separate Android Wear chapter? Why not just write "Follow the steps you followed in all the other chapters" and be done with it?

The answer is, some aspects of wearable app development are different from their phone and tablet counterparts. The most obvious difference is screen size. You can't display very much on a one-inch screen, so you have to design your app accordingly. To make doing so viable, you also have access to special wearable classes:

- `BoxInsetLayout`: Defines a layout that works well with round screens by creating a box, within which you place the display elements. The previous example in this chapter uses this layout.
- `SwipeDismissFrameLayout`: Enables a user to dismiss any view by swiping the screen from left to right. You need this ability when an app, such as a map view, needs some method for dismissing the activity as a whole. The article at `https://developer.android.com/training/wearables/ui/exit` tells more about this layout and its use.

» `WearableRecyclerView`: Provides a curved layout, such as the layout used for the main Wear application launcher. This view maximizes the use of screen real estate so that you don't have to create a scrolling list of options but can instead place the options around the outside circumference of the display. Obviously, short options should appear at the top and bottom of the list because the top and bottom have the least space to offer. You can see more about this interesting layout at `https://developer.android.com/training/wearables/ui/lists`.

» `AmbientModeSupport`: Provides ambient mode support when used with the `AmbientModeSupport.AmbientCallbackProvider` interface. *Ambient mode* means that your app remains displayed at all times, such as in a particular kind of watch face. You aren't actually expecting the user to do much other than look. *Interactive mode* is what most developers think about because the user is doing something with the app. You can read more about this app at `https://developer.android.com/training/wearables/apps/always-on`.

REMEMBER

Another difference for wearables is the specific classes in the API. Like any other Android development project, the wearable API is in a constant state of flux, and you might find that your favorite class is deprecated before you get to enjoy it fully. Of course, these changes happen for a reason. Each update supposedly makes the API better and easier to use. Given that the API will probably change sooner than later, make sure you check up on your favorite classes (and their upgrades) at `https://developer.android.com/training/wearables/ui/wear-ui-library#deprecations`.

Case Study: A Watch Face

In any language, the meanings of words change over time. Eventually, the original meanings fade into obscurity. Only linguists and lexicographers know how words' meanings have evolved.

Take, for example, the word *telephone*. In the late 1800s, this word came from *tele* (meaning *across*) and *phone* (meaning *sound*). In the 1900s, when these devices became widely available, people shortened the word from *telephone* to *phone*.

In the 2000s, phones expanded their functionality to include texting, web surfing, game playing, and other activities not directly related to sound or to sending sound across regions of space. Way back when our grandparents were young (as early as the year 2015), phones were replacing credit cards as a primary method of making point-of-sale payments. Now, in the year 2065, we use phones to wash our clothes, mow our lawns, build our cities, and raise our children. Who among us remembers even remotely that the word *phone* came from a root word related to *sound?*

The same kind of thing is true about "watches" and "wearables." Nowadays, people wear watches to look good and to make positive impressions on other people. But in the old days, watches were about telling time. The word *watch* originates from workers on watch duty carrying devices to help them mark time. Even in the early 2000s, some fashion-challenged people wore watches to keep track of the current time. In fact, using the instructions in the sections that follow, you find out how to create your own watch face that will help you keep track of the time.

Defining the watch face project

As do most Android projects, this project begins at the main screen, where you define the project parameters. Because this project is a little different, use these steps to create your project:

1. **In Android Studio, start a new project and select the Wear OS option.**

   You see a list of templates like the one shown previously in Figure 2-1.

2. **Highlight the Watch Face template.**

   The title of this dialog box is misleading. A Watch Face isn't an activity. But the creators of Android Studio can't worry about every little detail.

   REMEMBER

   When you select Watch Face in this step, you're telling Android Studio to write a lot of code for you. In later sections, you explore some of this code. For now, just keep clicking.

3. **Click Next.**

   You see the Configure Your Project dialog box, shown previously in Figure 2-2. Notice that the template actually shows a watch face icon in place of the round face icon shown in Figure 2-2. Like the previous project, you should use a minimum API level of API 28: Android 9.0 (Pie).

4. **Type** 05_02_02 **in the Name field, type** com.allmycode.p05_02_02 **in the Package Name field, and click Finish.**

   Android Studio begins creating your project for you.

Testing the watch face app

The first thing you want to do after creating this project is to see it run. The following steps help you test the new app. However, you'll find that this app runs differently from those you may have worked with in the past.

1. **Choose Run⇨Edit Configurations.**

   You see the Run/Debug Configurations dialog box, shown in Figure 2-8.

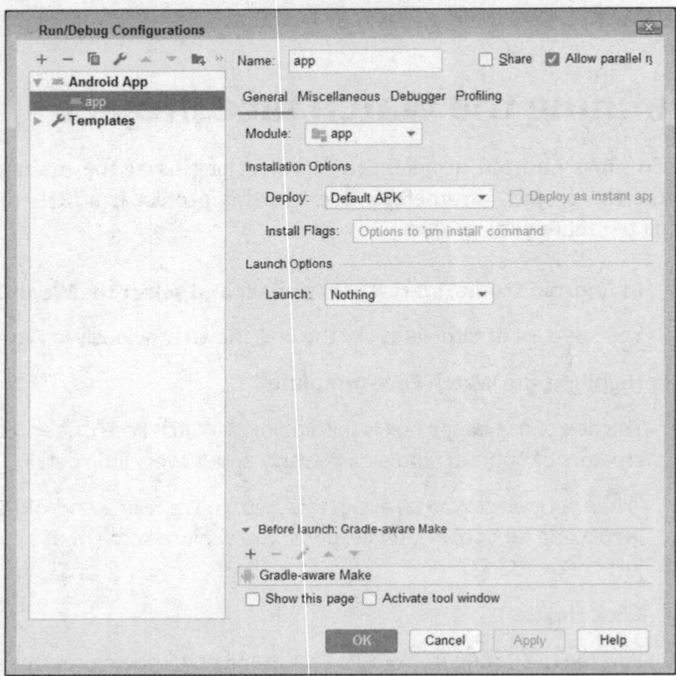

FIGURE 2-8: You must reconfigure the run conditions.

2. **Choose Nothing in the Launch field, as shown in Figure 2-8, and click OK.**

   You're launching a service, not an activity. This project is affecting the emulator wallpaper.

3. **Choose Run⇨Select Device and choose Android Wear Square API 28 from the context menu that appears.**

   For help with AVDs, refer to the "Setting Up Your Testing Environment" section, earlier in this chapter.

4. **Choose Run ⇨ Run 'app'.**

   When you do, the wheels start churning. When the emulator appears, you see the normal watch face, but no app. However, you're not running an app; you're changing the watch face.

5. **Click the lightning-bolt icon on the emulator and drag down.**

   You see a list of configuration items.

6. **Click the sprocket.**

   The Settings menu appears, as shown in Figure 2-9.

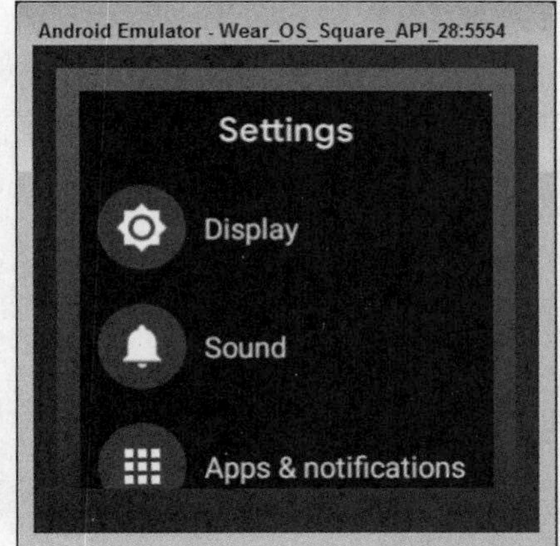

FIGURE 2-9: Access the emulator's Settings menu.

7. **Click Display.**

   You see the Display settings. Notice that the top item is Change Watch Face.

8. **Click Change Watch Face.**

   The display shows two items. The first is the current watch file and the second is an option to see more watch faces, as shown in Figure 2-10.

9. **Click Change Watch Faces.**

   One of the options in the list is My Analog. It normally appears at the bottom of the list, as shown in Figure 2-11.

10. **Click My Analog.**

    The new watch face appears onscreen, as shown in Figure 2-12.

FIGURE 2-10: Choose to see more watch faces.

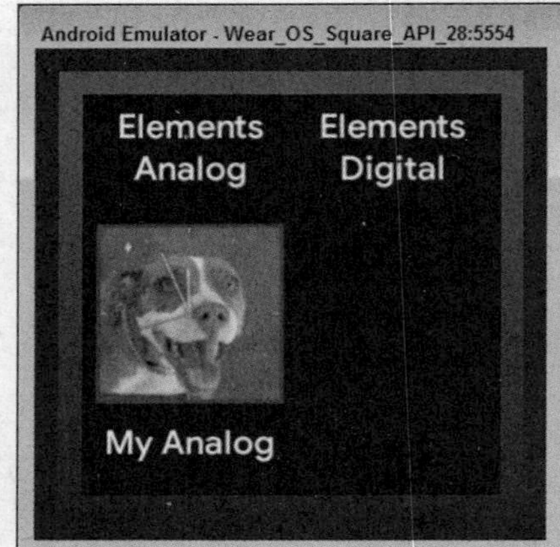

FIGURE 2-11: Locate the newly created watch face.

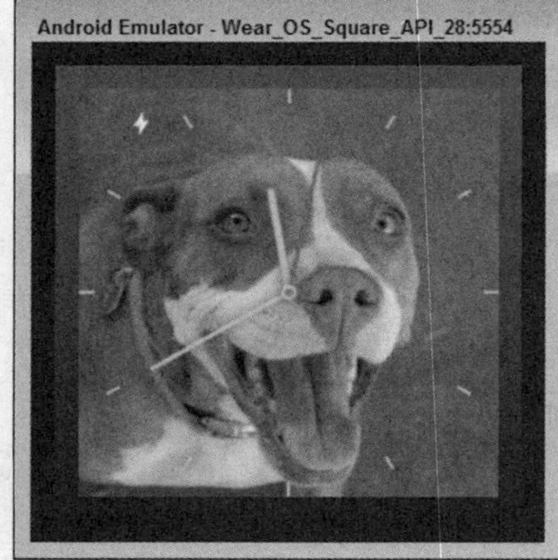

FIGURE 2-12: The emulator is using the new watch face.

Dissecting the skeletal watch face project

Many interesting things lurk inside a typical watch face project's code. This section describes a few of them. As you read this section, you can follow along by examining the code that Android Studio creates in the previous set of steps.

The manifest file

When Android Studio creates a skeletal app, you get an `AndroidManifest.xml` file. The `AndroidManifest.xml` file for the skeletal watch face app contains elements that don't appear in skeletal phone apps.

- **The `<uses-feature>` element:** The following code:

  ```
  <uses-feature android:name="android.hardware.type.watch"/>
  ```

  tells the Google Play Store that your app is for wearable devices. The Google Play Store won't offer to load your app on phones, tablets, or other nonwearable gizmos.

  The Google Play Store consults a manifest file's `<uses-feature>` element, but an Android device does *not* consult that element. In other words, having a `uses-feature ... type.watch` element in your app's manifest file does *not* prevent an ordinary phone from installing your app. Using Android Studio's Run ⇨ Run 'app' command, you can bypass the Google Play Store and run a wearable app on a phone, a tablet, or an Android-enabled toaster oven. If you don't have an entire project (but have only a project's `.apk` file), you can use Android's `adb` command to side load the `.apk` file onto a nonwearable device. We don't promise that your wearable app will run smoothly (or run at all) on a nonwearable device, but the `<uses-feature>` element won't prevent you from trying.

- **The references to preview images:** Android Studio's skeletal watch face app has an `app/res/drawable` folder. And within that folder, you find a few preview images, such as `bg.png` and `preview_analog.png`. Unlike most of the items in the Project tool window's `drawable` branch, you don't display these images within the app itself. Instead, Android displays these images when the user scans the list of installed watch faces.

To tell Android about these images, you put references to the images in the manifest file's `<meta-data>` elements:

```
<meta-data
    android:name="android.service.wallpaper"
    android:resource="@xml/watch_face"/>
<meta-data
    android:name="com.google.android.wearable.watchface.preview"
    android:resource="@drawable/preview_analog"/>
<meta-data
    android:name=
        "com.google.android.wearable.watchface.preview_circular"
    android:resource="@drawable/preview_analog"/>
```

» **The references to wallpaper:** When you create this chapter's watch face app, you don't create an activity. That's fine, but if your watch face isn't an activity, what is it? The answer: Your watch face is a service. More specifically, your watch face is a *live wallpaper* service.

The live wallpaper feature appeared in Android version 2.1 to provide animated, interactive backgrounds for users. To establish your watch face as a live wallpaper, you put several elements in the `AndroidManifest.xml` file. These include the following:

- A `<meta-data>` element pointing to your app's `res/xml` folder
- The `android.service.wallpaper.WallpaperService` action in an intent filter
- A `<uses-permission>` element with the name `android.permission.BIND_WALLPAPER`

All these elements turn your watch face into a kind of background for the display on a wearable device.

The Kotlin code

Your app's main Kotlin file extends `CanvasWatchFaceService` (a class in the `android.support.wearable.watchface` package). A full tour of the file is much more than you need for this first watch face app, but it's important to point out a few highlights.

The heart of the code is the `onDraw()` method. That's not surprising because the name `onDraw()` means "Here's what you do when you want to draw my watch face." In Android Studio's skeletal app, the `onDraw()` method contains the code in Listing 2-1.

LISTING 2-1: The `onDraw()` Method

```
override fun onDraw(canvas: Canvas, bounds: Rect) {
    val now = System.currentTimeMillis()
    mCalendar.timeInMillis = now

    drawBackground(canvas)
    drawWatchFace(canvas)
}
```

A *canvas* is where the things that you draw will eventually appear. You draw on a canvas with methods such as `canvas.drawLine()`, `canvas.drawArc()`, `canvas.drawBitmap()`, `canvas.drawRect()`, and `canvas.drawText()`. One form of the `canvas.drawText()` function takes four parameters:

- **The first parameter (`text`) is the string of characters to be drawn on the screen.** You can supply any text desired here as long as it somehow relates to the watch face. Remember that you're not creating an app; you're working with a service that displays a watch onscreen.
- **The second and third parameters (`x` and `y`) are float values.** These values store measurements. One value (x) is the number of pixels from the left of the device's screen to the leftmost edge of the text. The other value (y) is the number of pixels from the top of the screen to the top of the text.
- **The fourth parameter (`paint`) is a value of type `Paint`.** When creating a `paint` object, what you're doing is defining a kind of brush. It has a color and a width, along with many other features. Here's how you define a basic `paint` object:

  ```
  var myColor = Paint()
  myColor.setColor(Color.parseColor("#FFFFFF"))
  myColor.strokeWidth = 30f
  ```

In the Android world, what's already been drawn is either valid or invalid, with "invalid" meaning "The drawing is obsolete." Android calls the `onDraw()` function whenever the current drawing becomes invalid. And to make the drawing obsolete, your app's code calls the `invalidate()` function.

When the device is in ambient mode, your code's `onTimeTick()` function calls `invalidate()`:

```
override fun onTimeTick() {
    super.onTimeTick()
    invalidate()
}
```

When the device is in interactive mode, your code sends itself a `MSG_UPDATE_TIME` message at regular intervals, and the receipt of that message triggers an `invalidate()` call:

```
fun handleUpdateTimeMessage() {
    invalidate()
    if (shouldTimerBeRunning()) {
        val timeMs = System.currentTimeMillis()
        val delayMs = INTERACTIVE_UPDATE_RATE_MS -
                timeMs % INTERACTIVE_UPDATE_RATE_MS
        mUpdateTimeHandler.sendEmptyMessageDelayed(
            MSG_UPDATE_TIME, delayMs)
    }
}
```

Enhancing the skeletal watch face project

Android Studio creates the skeletal app that's described in the previous section. You get the skeletal app for free simply by clicking buttons when you create a new project. Of course, freebies have disadvantages. For one thing, they seldom do exactly what you want your app to do. For another, looking at canned code isn't as satisfying as writing your own code. Here's how to add the date to the watch face (and you can use this approach for your own additions):

1. **Add the following two new `import` statements to the beginning of `MyWatchFace.kt`.**

   ```
   import java.time.LocalDateTime
   import java.time.format.DateTimeFormatter
   ```

2. **Create a new function for drawing the time, like this one:**

   ```
   private fun drawDate(canvas: Canvas) {
       val paint = Paint()
       paint.setColor(Color.WHITE)
   ```

```
    paint.style = Paint.Style.FILL
    canvas.drawRect(90f, 160f, 190f, 190f, paint)

    paint.setColor(Color.BLACK)
    paint.textSize = 20f
    val localDate = LocalDateTime.now()
    canvas.drawText(
        localDate.format(
            DateTimeFormatter.ofPattern("M/d/y")),
        95f, 180f, paint)
}
```

This function performs two tasks. First, it draws a white square on the background. Second, it adds the current time in black.

You obtain the current time using `LocalDateTime.now()`. However, this time is unformatted. To format the time, you use `localDate.format()`, with a formatter, which is `DateTimeFormatter.ofPattern("M/d/y"))` in this case. The article at `https://developer.android.com/reference/java/time/format/DateTimeFormatter` tells you more about using patterns to format both time and date.

3. **Add `drawDate()` to `onDraw()` using the following code in bold:**

```
override fun onDraw(canvas: Canvas, bounds: Rect) {
    val now = System.currentTimeMillis()
    mCalendar.timeInMillis = now

    drawBackground(canvas)
    drawDate(canvas)
    drawWatchFace(canvas)
}
```

The order in which you draw the watch face elements is important. If you were to draw the date after the watch face, the hour and minute hands would disappear behind the data, which would look quite odd indeed!

That's it! You're done! When you run the app, you see a display like the one in Figure 2-13.

Developing for Android Wear

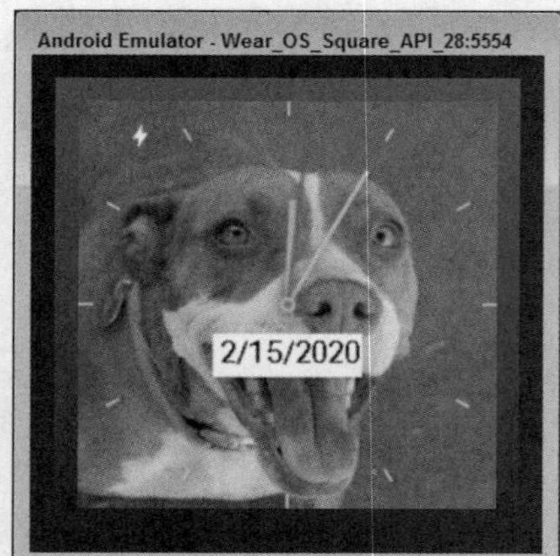

FIGURE 2-13: The skeletal watch face app with the date display added.

» Running Android Studio's TV app

» Creating an Android TV app

Chapter 3 Developing for Android TV

Do you remember the first time you heard about "the cloud"? Most people understand that "the cloud" doesn't refer to condensed water vapor; it refers to that collection of hardware and software that feeds us our contacts, our calendars, and our bookmarks wherever we go. Some buzzwords like the word "cloud" enter our psyches without fuss or fanfare. Other buzzwords knock us on the head and say "Pay attention to me. I will become important."

You may have had an interesting response when you first heard about the *ten-foot experience,* and may have wondered why anyone needed a ten-foot TV screen. Most of us have seen 70-inch TV screens in stores and may have wanted to know how a ten-foot device would fit into the average consumer's living room.

In the phrase *ten-foot experience,* "ten feet" doesn't refer to the screen size. It refers to the user's distance from the device. The basic idea is, when a user isn't right up against a screen (the way we are with computer monitors and cellphone screens), the user interface must be designed accordingly. You can't have lots of detail on a television screen because the user can't see very much detail. In addition, many TVs don't have the kinds of input facilities that computers (or even smartphones) have. Most TVs now ship with a USB port where you can plug in a keyboard or other input device and it works fine, but you buy such a device separately. Even so, most people are limited to a remote control or a game controller, which are crude instruments compared with a keyboard or mouse. The onscreen keyboards found with most TVs today would work fine if a TV had a touchscreen, but moving around the keyboard with a remote control can be time consuming and frustrating.

The ten-foot experience plays an important role in the creation of good Android TV apps. For many apps, the user doesn't do any continuous (smooth) scrolling. Instead, scrolling jumps from one item to the next. Of course, when the user searches for a favorite program, you need text or speech input. For text input, a keyboard appears on the screen, and the user scrolls from key to key (a slow and tedious process) using the remote unless the user has a keyboard plugged into the TV. For speech input, the user says a phrase out loud. When the device's voice recognizer gets the phrase all wrong, the user says the phrase a second time (much louder this time). Yelling titles into a remote control device can be embarrassing if you're living in a house with other people.

Anyway, this chapter provides a brief introduction to Android's TV app development environment.

Getting Started

To get started with Android TV development, follow the same steps that you follow for creating a Phone and Tablet project, but make the following changes:

- When you see the Choose Your Project dialog box, select TV and then Android TV Activity. Note that, unlike other template types, you have a choice only between adding no activity at all or using the Android TV Activity template.
- Type **05_03_01** in the Name field of the Configure Your Project dialog box and type **com.allmycode.p05_03_01** in the Package Name field.

After you create your project, plug an Android TV device into your development computer. If you don't have such a device (or don't want to move the device from your living room to your office), create an Android TV AVD on your development computer. To do so, follow the steps that you follow in the "Configuring a wearable device emulator" section of Chapter 2 of this minibook for creating an Android Wear AVD. (The only change is to select TV instead of Wear when you pick a device category.)

REMEMBER

Android Studio currently provides two TV emulators based on their resolution: 720p and 1080p. There are no 4K or other emulators, so you need a device to test apps for these environments. The emulator screenshots in this chapter rely on the 720p version. The 720p emulator will probably work best for a wide range of app types, but you may want to target 1080p for high-end apps.

TIPS FOR GETTING THE EMULATORS TO RUN

The TV emulators use far more processing power than any other emulator you run for Android development. In fact, not only will you find them sluggish, but the app may not install because of a lack of resources. Testing the emulators on several systems shows that your older Intel i7 processor may not do the trick, even though it does have eight cores and you've souped it up to 4.90 GHz (see the 9700K specs at `https://www.intel.com/content/www/us/en/products/processors/core/i7-processors/i7-9700k.html`). Your system should have a bare minimum of 16GB RAM (more is always better), an SSD, and a gaming graphics card. Yes, that sounds like a whole lot of hardware, and you might not have it. Here are some techniques to get the setup to run if you make changes to the emulator setup. (These changes occur on the Verify Configuration page of the Virtual Device Configuration dialog box with the advanced settings showing.)

- Use the 720p emulator whenever possible.
- Set the Graphics field to Software – GLES 2.0 if you don't have a high-end graphics card.
- Set the Boot Option to Cold Boot to ensure that you get a clean start with each run (the startup time will increase).
- Reduce the Multi-Core CPU setting to 3 or 2 (startup time will increase substantially).
- Reduce the Internal Storage to 256 MB (unless you plan to store more data than that during app execution).
- Reduce the size of the SD Card to Studio-managed 128 MB.
- Clear the Enable Device Frame option (which will affect the appearance, but not functionality, of your app).

The article at `https://developer.android.com/studio/run/emulator-troubleshooting` offers additional information that you might find helpful in getting the emulator to run reliably and a little faster.

When you see the Select a System Image dialog box, you must download one of the Android TV images, even if you have downloaded other system images for other uses in the book. This chapter uses the Q system image. As part of obtaining the Android TV image, you must read and accept a special licensing agreement. The installation process will proceed much like the one outlined in the "Configuring a wearable device emulator" section of Chapter 2 of this minibook. Unlike phones and watches, you generally use a TV in the landscape position and don't need to worry that someone will change the orientation on you. However, if you insist, Android Studio will let you create a portrait orientation emulator.

TIP

This is one time when you might want to select Hardware – GLES 2.0 in the Graphics field of the Verify Configuration dialog box if possible. The TV emulator runs so slowly without this feature that you might end up old and gray before the emulator even comes online. However, to use this feature, you need a high-end graphics card in your system. A graphics card with good gaming features works best. You might consider an NVidia Titan V (`https://www.nvidia.com/en-us/titan/titan-v/`) to be overkill, but you really do need serious processing power to move quickly.

You probably would have tried various settings and updating your hardware without reading about them in this chapter. One way or another, you get a skeletal app with an enormous amount of meat on its bones. (The word "skeletal" doesn't do justice to this newly created app — you're really seeing the most basic form of app you can create, yet it requires an enormous amount of code.) The Project tool window's tree is shown in Figure 3-1.

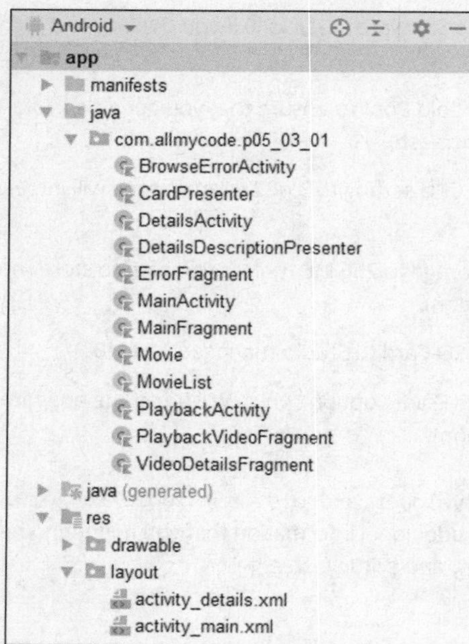

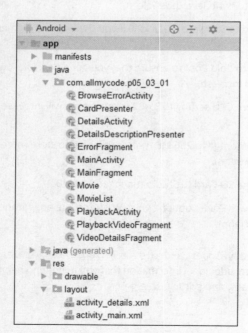

FIGURE 3-1: Android Studio's skeletal TV app.

Running the Skeletal App

Most television sets don't have touchscreens. Some, however — like the Music Computing MCLCDTTV65104k — provide a touchscreen by default. In addition, you can obtain a touchscreen overlay for your television that you mount to the front of the set and plug into the USB port on your set. This chapter focuses on most TVs and limits the gizmos to those that come with the emulator. When creating your app, remember that your user won't have access to a mouse or any of the other usual amenities of computers. All this said, when you start the emulator, you see the same set of controls that you had when working with a phone, tablet, or wearable device. The controls onscreen also react to a click, so except for the form factor, working with this app is much like working with the other apps in this book.

To run the app, be sure to select a usable emulator or have your physical device plugged into your computer's USB port. Choose Run⇨Run 'app' as normal. When the emulator starts, which usually takes a while, you see a Finish Setting Up Your TV screen, like the one shown in Figure 3-2. You don't actually have to do anything on this screen, but it's the first sign that something useful is happening with your app. However, if you want, you can play around with this fully functional screen when your app isn't running.

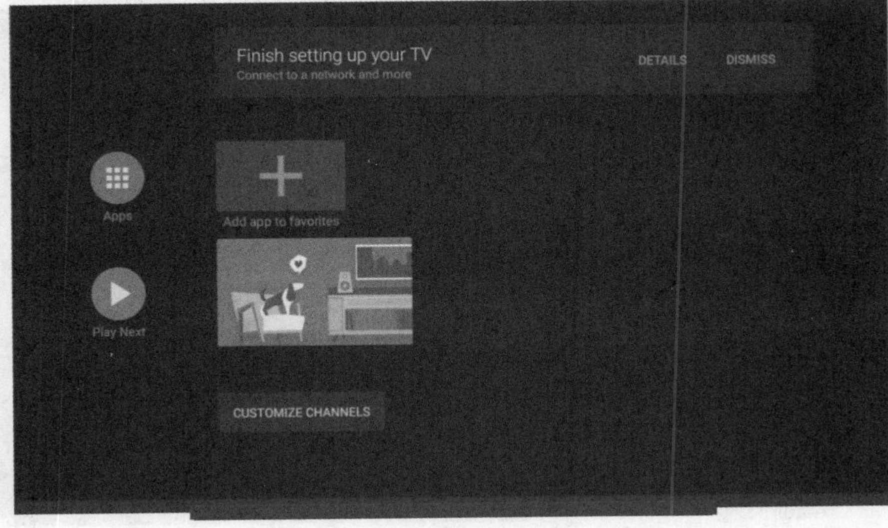

FIGURE 3-2: You see this emulator screen when your app isn't running.

You may see a screen that asks about what sort of storage you want to use. This screen goes away after a few seconds, so you can ignore it. Normally the Videos by Your Company display appears next, as shown in Figure 3-3.

FIGURE 3-3: The skeletal app's main activity.

However, in some cases, you may need to click Apps on the Finish Setting Up Your TV screen to display the list of apps shown in Figure 3-4. The Videos by Your Company app appears on the right end (the one with a ticket stub with a right-pointing arrow on it).

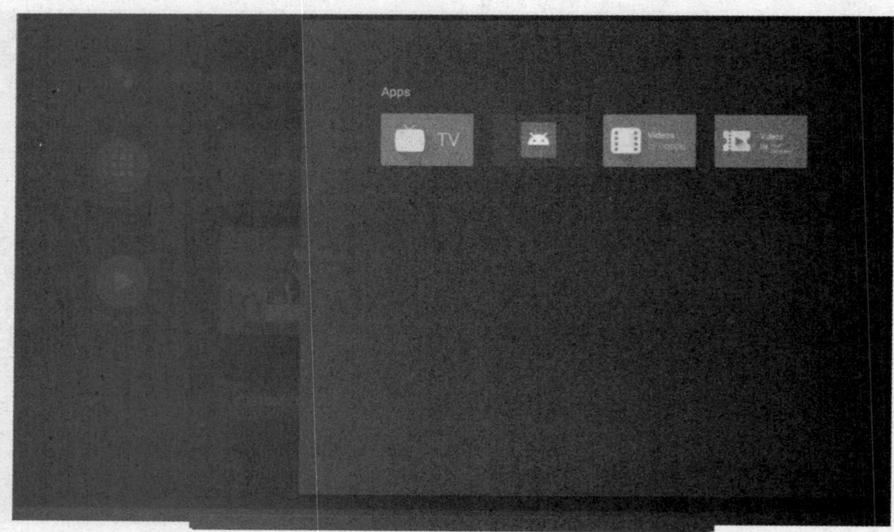

FIGURE 3-4: Start your app manually when required.

The app's layout has several rows. In Figure 3-3, the top row has the heading Category Zero and has several Movie ABC entries. The next several rows don't look like real rows. In fact, only one of the headings (Category Zero) appears immediately to the left of its corresponding items. The Category Two row heading appears roughly midway between the top and bottom of the screen, but the movie items in the Category Two row appear near the bottom of the screen. This happens because the items are taller than the headings, and the layout tries to keep as many headings on the screen as possible. When the user scrolls from one heading to another (say, from Category Zero to Category Two), the rows of items scroll proportionately so that the Category Two heading is immediately to the left of its Category Two items.

In Figure 3-4, Category Zero is highlighted. If you scroll rightward from Category Zero, you see a highlighted version of a video (the leftmost video in the Category Zero row). See Figure 3-5.

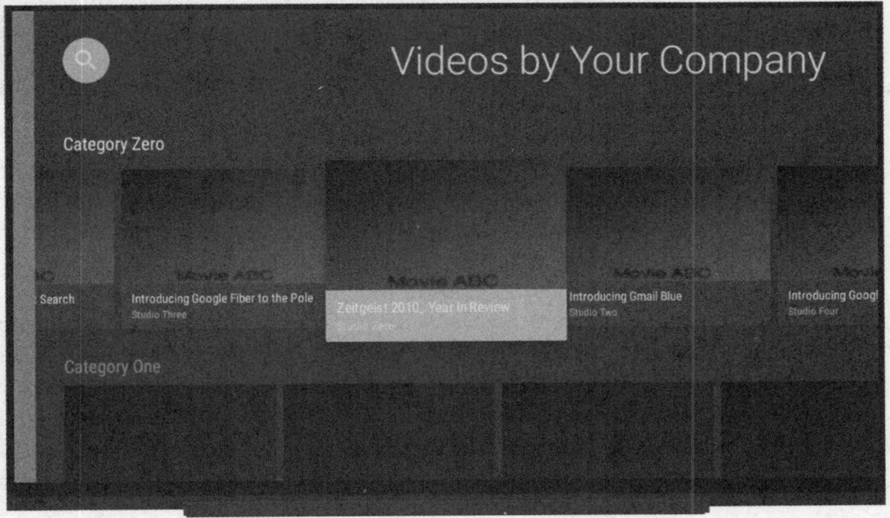

FIGURE 3-5: You've scrolled to one of the videos.

If you press Enter with a video selected, you see what should be a detail screen for that particular video. However, the screen is essentially blank.

The emulator's Back button returns you to the grid full of videos. If you scroll downward, you eventually reach a list of preferences. (See Figure 3-6.)

The richness of Android Studio's skeletal TV app might seem strange. But there's method to this madness. It's all about the ten-foot experience, also known as the *lean-back experience*.

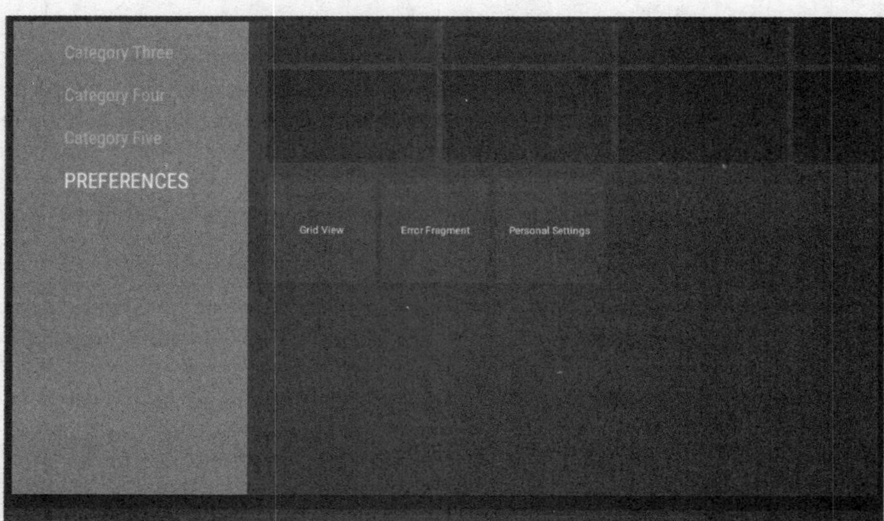

FIGURE 3-6: Some preferences.

When you use a computer, you're in work mode. You lean forward and try to accomplish something. (It might be something frivolous, but it's an accomplishment nevertheless.) When you watch television, you're not in work mode. You want to minimize any accomplishment phase. Your primary purpose is to lean back and enjoy the show. You want to relax. So, with Android TV, it's especially important that the user interface is unobtrusive. You want every interface to look like every other interface. That way, you can use simple reflexes to navigate from category to category, from movie to movie, and from a highlighted movie to details about the movie. If the skeletal app has so much prebuilt scaffolding, it's to make that scaffolding be the same for every app's interface. With such a familiar interface, users can ignore the app's interface and relax with their favorite movies.

Dissecting the TV App

The TV app comes with a lot of code, and it's helpful to wander about and explore it in detail. The app helps you create a consistent appearance in your own offerings. The following sections help you take the app apart so that you can better see how it works.

Adding to the standard AndroidManifest.xml

Many of the apps in this book have an `AndroidManifest.xml` file that borders on simple, but that's not the case with this app. In addition to the usual

MainActivity, you also have a DetailsActivity, PlaybackActivity, and BrowseErrorActivity. Each of these activities has its own .kt file, as shown previously in Figure 3-1. They also appear as activities in the <application> element.

However, these activities aren't the main event. What you really find interesting are the <uses-feature> entries shown here:

```
<uses-feature
    android:name="android.hardware.touchscreen"
    android:required="false"/>
<uses-feature
    android:name="android.software.leanback"
    android:required="true"/>
```

The first entry, android.hardware.touchscreen, lets you click the screen and have something happen. If you load this app on a regular TV, it may not have a touchscreen, so working with the app will be harder. Some TVs also ship with what is called a multitouch display that uses multiple touch gestures. In other words, the display can detect more than one touch at a time. To get this functionality, you change android.hardware.touchscreen to something like android.hardware.touchscreen.multitouch.distinct.

The second entry merely tells the compiler that this software runs on an Android TV and not another device. It replaces the android.hardware.type.television entry that you may find in older examples. Along with the addition of the android.software.leanback feature, you also find that the <intent-filter> element and <category> entry also reflect the TV nature of the app by using <category android:name="android.intent.category.LEANBACK_LAUNCHER" />.

Looking into build.gradle (Module: app)

Even build.gradle reflects the change in app venue. Most of the entries are similar to those that you use to build other app types, but note the leanback addition shown in bold in the following code:

```
dependencies {
    implementation fileTree(dir: 'libs', include: ['*.jar'])
    implementation
        "org.jetbrains.kotlin:kotlin-stdlib-jdk7:$kotlin_version"
    implementation 'androidx.leanback:leanback:1.0.0'
    implementation 'androidx.appcompat:appcompat:1.0.2'
    implementation 'com.github.bumptech.glide:glide:3.8.0'
}
```

Developing for Android TV

Defining a layout

What will underwhelm you the most about this app is the lack of layout. You find some interesting generic graphics in the `drawable` folder and two activity layouts in the `layout` folder. However, both layouts are incredibly simple because you perform most of the display work within the code. For example, here's the `activity_main.xml` file, which is a far cry from most of the examples in the book:

```
<?xml version="1.0" encoding="utf-8"?>
<fragment xmlns:android="http://schemas.android.com/apk/res/android"
    xmlns:tools="http://schemas.android.com/tools"
    android:id="@+id/main_browse_fragment"
    android:name="com.allmycode.p05_03_01.MainFragment"
    android:layout_width="match_parent"
    android:layout_height="match_parent"
    tools:context=".MainActivity"
    tools:deviceIds="tv"
    tools:ignore="MergeRootFrame"/>
```

Oddly enough, `MainActivity.kt` is similarly devoid of content. All you really have in that file is the `override` for `onCreate()`. The overview of the work to do to present a list of movies appears in `MainFragment.kt`, where you find a list of tasks to perform in `onActivityCreated()`:

```
override fun onActivityCreated(savedInstanceState: Bundle?) {
    Log.i(TAG, "onCreate")
    super.onActivityCreated(savedInstanceState)

    prepareBackgroundManager()

    setupUIElements()

    loadRows()

    setupEventListeners()
}
```

The first two items on the list, `prepareBackgroundManager()` and `setupUIElements()`, are what you expect for creating a display. The last step, `setupEventListeners()`, makes the app interactive so that something happens as the result of a click. However, when you get to `loadRows()`, things get interesting because now you're dealing with data. The `loadRows()` function creates an `adapter` — a data source — as shown in Listing 3-1. The sections that follow discuss this part of the app in more detail.

LISTING 3-1: Providing a Data Source

```
private fun loadRows() {
    val list = MovieList.list

    val rowsAdapter = ArrayObjectAdapter(ListRowPresenter())
    val cardPresenter = CardPresenter()

    for (i in 0 until NUM_ROWS) {
        if (i != 0) {
            Collections.shuffle(list)
        }
        val listRowAdapter = ArrayObjectAdapter(cardPresenter)
        for (j in 0 until NUM_COLS) {
            listRowAdapter.add(list[j % 5])
        }
        val header = HeaderItem(i.toLong(),
            MovieList.MOVIE_CATEGORY[i])
        rowsAdapter.add(ListRow(header, listRowAdapter))
    }

    val gridHeader = HeaderItem(NUM_ROWS.toLong(), "PREFERENCES")

    val mGridPresenter = GridItemPresenter()
    val gridRowAdapter =
        ArrayObjectAdapter(mGridPresenter)
    gridRowAdapter.add(resources.getString(R.string.grid_view))
    gridRowAdapter.add(getString(R.string.error_fragment))
    gridRowAdapter.add(
        resources.getString(R.string.personal_settings))
    rowsAdapter.add(ListRow(gridHeader, gridRowAdapter))

    adapter = rowsAdapter
}
```

The adapter and the presenter

Central to the mission of the code in Listing 3-1 are the notions of an adapter (`MovieList.list`), found in `MovieList.kt`, and a presenter (`CardPresenter`), found in `CardPresenter.kt`. An *adapter* stores data, and a *presenter* displays the data that an adapter stores. That's the way Android's TV classes separate data from presentation. The `loadRows()` function provides the functionality needed to move the data from `MovieList.list` to `cardPresenter` using the `ArrayObjectAdapter`.

Developing for Android TV

It's a classic principle of app development:

> *Data and presentation don't belong in the same parts of your code.*

If you interleave your data code with your presentation code, modifying the presentation is difficult to do without messing up the data. Data is data, whether it's displayed on a 70-inch TV or a 1-inch watch screen.

Imagine dealing with data about a movie, as described earlier. In a more realistic app, the data might include the title, the release date, a synopsis, the actors' names, a link to a trailer, and other information. A user might view the data on an Android TV. But in another setting, the same user might view the same data on a computer, a smartphone, or whatever other device is available. With the presentation code separated from the data code, you can provide several alternatives for displaying the same data. With one class to store the data, you can plug in a big TV display one time, a smartphone display another time, and a ten-inch laptop display the next time. You can offer the user a choice of interfaces — one for daytime browsing and another for nighttime perusal. You're ready for any kind of display because the code to control the data doesn't care what display logic is behind it.

Imagine changing the way you store each movie's release date. Instead of storing an ordinary Gregorian calendar date, you decide to store each movie's *Star Trek* star date. (According to one online calculator, the first *Matrix* movie was released in the United States on star date −323754.8.) With the data decoupled from the display, you don't have to inform your display code about this data storage change. The data code already has a function named `getReleaseDate()`, and the presentation code calls this method during the app's run. While you're setting up the data code to handle star dates, you modify the `getReleaseDate()` method to convert between star dates and Gregorian dates. The display code doesn't know about this change, and what the display code doesn't know won't hurt it.

Using the Adapter class

Figure 3-7 illustrates the relationships among classes used in Listing 3-1.

For an adapter, TV apps normally use the `ArrayObjectAdapter` class (a member of the `'androidx.leanback:leanback:1.0.0'` package). When you construct a new `ArrayObjectAdapter`, you supply a `Presenter` in the constructor call, such as the following:

- `val rowsAdapter = ArrayObjectAdapter(ListRowPresenter())`: Applies a dimming effect to each of the rows, as described at `https://developer.android.com/reference/android/support/v17/leanback/widget/ListRowPresenter`

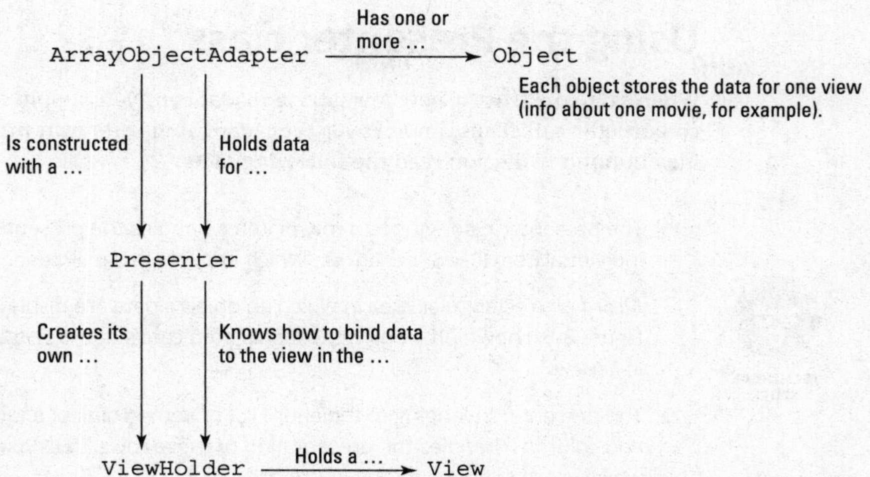

FIGURE 3-7: Adapters, presenters, and other good stuff.

- `val listRowAdapter = ArrayObjectAdapter(cardPresenter)`: Determines how to display the individual movies you want to display
- `val gridRowAdapter = ArrayObjectAdapter(mGridPresenter)`: Creates a grid in which to place each of the movies contained within cardPresenter

Thus, each `ArrayObjectAdapter` has its own presenter.

Each presenter constructs its own `ViewHolder`. (The `ViewHolder` class is an inner class of the `Presenter` class. Each presenter actually constructs its own `Presenter.ViewHolder`.) The next section tells you how this process works within the presenter.

A `ViewHolder` holds a view. (Don't look so surprised!) An instance of the `ViewHolder` class has no methods of its own and has only one public field. The public field is the `view` field. A `ViewHolder` instance's `view` field refers to whatever view the `ViewHolder` is holding. A presenter displays views, and a presenter gets its views from the `ViewHolder`. You can think of the `ViewHolder` as a cache for views.

In Listing 3-1, a call to an adapter's `add()` function adds an object to the adapter. This adding process happens in a number of ways:

- Adding a list of movies to a row (`listRowAdapter`)
- Adding rows of movies to a movie collection (`rowsAdapter`)
- Adding the rows of movies and other display details to a grid (`gridRowAdapter`)

Using the Presenter class

When you construct a new `ArrayObjectAdapter`, you supply a presenter in the constructor call. Thus, an `ArrayObjectAdapter` has its own presenter. Keep that idea in mind while you read the following facts:

- The presenter belonging to a row of items handles the presenting of an individual item (`CardPresenter`, which appears in `CardPresenter.kt`).

  A *card* is a rectangular area in which an object's data are displayed. In Figure 3-5, shown previously, the highlighted card's title is *Zeitgeist 2010_ Year in Review*.

- The presenter belonging to the entire list of items (think of a table with rows and columns) handles the presentation of those rows (`ListRowPresenter`, which is provided for you by Android).

- The presenter belonging to an entire grid handles the presenting of grid elements (`GridItemPresenter`, which appears in the `MainFragment.kt` file as an `inner class`).

The `CardPresenter` class offers a good example of how a presenter is constructed. Listing 3-2 shows the essential code given with the example app. (It has other elements as well, but these are the functions you should focus on.)

LISTING 3-2: The Presenter

```
override fun onCreateViewHolder(parent: ViewGroup):
        Presenter.ViewHolder {

        Log.d(TAG, "onCreateViewHolder")

        sDefaultBackgroundColor = ContextCompat.getColor(parent.context,
            R.color.default_background)
        sSelectedBackgroundColor =
            ContextCompat.getColor(parent.context,
                R.color.selected_background)
        mDefaultCardImage = ContextCompat.getDrawable(parent.context,
            R.drawable.movie)

        val cardView = object : ImageCardView(parent.context) {
            override fun setSelected(selected: Boolean) {
```

```
            updateCardBackgroundColor(this, selected)
            super.setSelected(selected)
        }
    }

    cardView.isFocusable = true
    cardView.isFocusableInTouchMode = true
    updateCardBackgroundColor(cardView, false)
    return Presenter.ViewHolder(cardView)
}

override fun onBindViewHolder(viewHolder: Presenter.ViewHolder,
    item: Any) {
    val movie = item as Movie
    val cardView = viewHolder.view as ImageCardView

    Log.d(TAG, "onBindViewHolder")
    if (movie.cardImageUrl != null) {
        cardView.titleText = movie.title
        cardView.contentText = movie.studio
        cardView.setMainImageDimensions(CARD_WIDTH, CARD_HEIGHT)
        Glide.with(viewHolder.view.context)
            .load(movie.cardImageUrl)
            .centerCrop()
            .error(mDefaultCardImage)
            .into(cardView.mainImageView)
    }
}

override fun onUnbindViewHolder(viewHolder: Presenter.ViewHolder) {
    Log.d(TAG, "onUnbindViewHolder")
    val cardView = viewHolder.view as ImageCardView
    // Remove references to images so that the garbage collector can
    // free up memory
    cardView.badgeImage = null
    cardView.mainImage = null
}
```

Developing for Android TV

The presenter in Listing 3-2 has three required methods:

» **The** onCreateViewHolder **method does what its name suggests. It creates a** ViewHolder **instance.**

The ViewHolder instance has a view. How nice!

- **The** `onBindViewHolder` **method binds data to a** `ViewHolder` **instance.**

  In Listing 3-2, the view in the `ViewHolder` gets the properties needed to interact with the movie data. In particular, the card's title, `cardView.title–Text`, becomes the content of `movie.title`.

- **The** `onUnbindViewHolder` **method can do some cleanup when the data in a view becomes obsolete.**

  In Listing 3-2, the `onUnbindViewHolder` method removes the references to the images so that the garbage collector can free the memory they use.

IN THIS CHAPTER

» Using Google Play in auto apps

» Performing the development prerequisites

» Creating a basic app

Chapter 4
Developing for Android Auto

Some of the things you can do in your car today are absolutely amazing! The limitations of a radio and CD player have vanished from newer cars. These days, cars offer a slew of ways to entertain you while you drive. You have music options from an inordinate number of sources, and the car can tell you about the weather, movies, or latest sports scores. It can even read to you from a book. Voice control makes the driving experience fuller and yet reduces the risks from inattentive driving.

Cars talk and can receive your requests for information or changes in configuration. They give you instructions for getting from point A to point B and tell you about road and weather conditions. Your car can even check on your house status before you get home. (One app enables you to turn the lights on and change the house temperature if you have the right setup in your home.)

In case talking to your car isn't enough, you can also talk with Google Assistant or Alexa (for example, Ford makes Alexa available through an app). There are also safety apps, such as the one that will dial 911 automatically for you if the car gets into an accident. The possibilities for programming your car to perform exciting new tasks are nearly limitless. The point of this chapter is to help you grasp the possibilities.

To program your 64 Mustang to perform incredible tasks never before seen in such a car, however, your car must have Android capability available. Even the newest cars may not have this capability, so verify that before you begin development. You must also consider the potential trade-offs involved. Some upgrades really aren't upgrades at all as far as the user is concerned, and you need to develop your app with that in mind.

WARNING

Your app must also consider the environment from a safety perspective. If your app distracts a driver at the wrong time, it could cause an accident. For example, some features in Ford cars are disabled during driving, such as getting movie times and locations. You can obtain this information when stopped and even set the GPS based on which movie theater you select, but once you start driving again, the feature becomes unavailable. Some places in the world also place significant limits on what an auto app can do, so you need to check local regulations.

After you consider the parameters of your app, you follow a process similar to all of the other apps in this book. First, you select an emulator; then you create the app itself in basic steps. This chapter won't make you an Android Auto app programming guru, but it'll get you started with a very basic app.

Checking Auto Compatibility

What sort of an app you build, when the user can interact with it, and how the app is presented are just a few of the questions you must ask yourself when working with Android on a car. The environment can actually vary depending on how a user configures accessory devices. For example, a Ford with Sync 3 (`https://www.ford.com/technology/sync/`) comes with these features:

- » Certain built-in apps that let you ask about weather, sports, and movie times at local theaters
- » Voice-activated apps (some are, some aren't)
- » Apps that are available at all times and others that are available only when the car is stopped
- » Functionality that's available from tablets when plugged into the USB port, such as searchable music (you can tell the car what you want and the car will find it on the tablet)

» Sync3-compatible apps (such as Ford+Alexa, `https://media.ford.com/content/fordmedia/fna/us/en/news/2017/01/04/alexa-car-ford-amazon-shop-search-home.html`) after pairing a smartphone to the car

» Extended Android Auto support after connecting a smartphone to the car through the USB port

You can't make any assumptions about your app environment because this is just Ford using Sync 3. Every other vendor out there has its own idea of just how to make Android work with its cars. The Android Auto connection is becoming more popular, however, with vendors such as BMW joining in (see `https://www.digitaltrends.com/android/bmw-making-wireless-android-auto-free-in-most-cars-in-2020/`). If you follow car technology, you may be knowingly nodding your head at this point because Apple tried the same thing with CarPlay (`https://www.apple.com/ios/carplay/`), which still hasn't standardized any car vendor's offerings. Even so, the article at `https://thedroidguy.com/android-auto-top-5-functionalities-1065927` offers five reasons that Android Auto is better than CarPlay. Make sure you pay attention to the Current Limitations section at the end of the article, which helps you understand precisely how much planning you need to do for your app. The smart developer will understand the app market and choose accordingly.

TIP

Even if everything else is just right, however, the car user may choose not to use Android Auto because Android Auto can actually interfere with built-in features. For one thing, Android Auto may not work quite as planned unless you configure the car and the smartphone precisely (see the article at `https://www.techradar.com/news/pros-and-cons-to-using-android-auto-on-a-2019-honda-passport` for one example). The voice control is still available, but only for features on your smartphone rather than those built in to the car. It seems to be one or the other, but not both with some cars. For example, when creating an Android Auto setup on a Sync 3–equipped car, you gain all sorts of smartphone-typical voice-assisted information and entertainment sources, but you lose the ability to search your music database or set the car's temperature using voice command. Even the GPS support becomes manual, which is a real pain when you're on the road and suddenly have to switch destinations. So whether Android Auto is a perk or not depends on just how gadget-fixated the driver is. Some will choose the comfort of the built-in features.

However, your app may not necessarily depend specifically on Android Auto to work. The Ford+Alexa and other apps demonstrate that you can work with the car's native ability, which means that you can let the user keep familiar functionality while still providing value-added services. It all depends on how you set up and configure your app.

CONSIDERING DEVELOPMENT ALTERNATIVES

You can use Android, yet focus on creating apps for specific vehicles using that vehicle's built-in functionality. For example, you can build Sync 3 apps for Ford using the AppLink API described at `https://developer.ford.com/pages/applink/`. The AppLink API provides Android support, so you still create an Android app using Android Studio, but you employ the AppLink API to do it, realizing that the resulting app will work only on Ford and Lincoln cars equipped with Sync 3. The trade-off is that the resulting app will interact directly with the vehicle in the same manner as the apps the user is used to working with; the app won't disable existing features.

Tesla is one of the more interesting offerings when it comes to creating apps that work with the underlying car software directly. You can read about this offering at `https://teslaapi.dev/`. The API supports multiple languages, including: cURL, Python, Node.js, and Java. You also have access to Android, iOS, and JavaScript development, which means you can create something specific to Tesla using most of the powerful platforms available today. Oddly enough, Tesla is one of those vehicles that currently has no plans to support Android Auto.

REMEMBER

Support for Android apps (no matter what form they take) is a relatively new car feature. You can find a list of cars that currently offer some level of Android support at `https://www.android.com/auto/compatibility/`. This list simply shows the models of cars that potentially have Android support. A Ford Taurus may fall within the range of years that support Android, but if it doesn't have Sync 3 installed, you don't get the required support. The smartphone must also meet specific standards and some features. For example, FordPass Connect requires a certain model year and a smartphone that uses a compatible AT&T network (see `https://owner.ford.com/fordpass/fordpass-sync-connect.html`).

Choosing the Google Play Services

Android Auto (described at `https://play.google.com/store/apps/details/Android_Auto_Maps_Media_Messaging_Voice?id=com.google.android.projection.gearhead`) isn't the end of the line when it comes to accessing specialized apps and online functionality. The Android Auto app does provide considerable functionality in the form of all those Google apps you've come to love, plus a few specifically designed for people who drive. Of course, it provides full Google Assistant functionality so that you interact with your smartphone and its capabilities in hands-free mode. If you have a voice activation button on your car's steering wheel, you can click it to gain instant access to Google Assistant without moving your hands from the steering wheel to the screen.

In addition to native Android Auto functionality, you can also download apps from Google Play Services. Here are a few of the apps to choose from today:

- **Amazon Music (`https://www.amazon.com/b/?node=13337243011`):** Allows access to all your Amazon Music offerings and all the usual Amazon Music features, such as Prime offerings. This particular app can work with your vehicle in a number of ways, including the use of built-in or add-on Alexa support for cars that have it. Essentially, you can ask for music, including music you have purchased through Amazon music, in a variety of ways depending on your mood.
- **NPR One (`https://one.npr.org/`):** Tracks current local, regional, and national news and other items of interest and presents them in a commercial-free setting that only National Public Radio (NPR) can provide. The app lets you skip stories that don't interest you.
- **OverDrive (`https://app.overdrive.com/`):** Accesses the contents of more than 20,000 libraries. Although you shouldn't read books or stream video when driving, streaming audiobooks can be a great way to travel. You can also interact vocally with your local participating library to place a book on hold or perform other library-related tasks.
- **Pandora (`https://www.pandora.com/`):** Streams high-quality and personalized radio-type broadcasts. The app theoretically evolves to present streamed music based on your input. This is the app for people who don't have time or energy to select individual songs from a playlist or audio library. The streaming capability now includes podcasts as well.
- **Scanner Radio (`https://scannerradio.app/index.html`):** Scans the police and fire bands and presents you with live conversations about fires and other incidents. This type of app comes in handy when you need to be aware of potential hazards while driving as soon as they happen.
- **Spotify (`https://www.spotify.com/us/`):** Makes both free and subscribed access to Spotify, the largest music streaming service in the world, available while you drive. Free access does come with ads.
- **Tidal (`https://tidal.com/`):** Provides a high-quality listening experience from an audio library of 60+ million tracks (enough so that you'd never have to listen to the same track twice). According to the developer, this app currently works on more than 400 car types that support Android Auto.
- **Waze (`https://www.waze.com/`):** Delivers real-time road information by relying on input from fellow drivers. You can also use this as a GPS to find the best route given current road conditions, rather than the usual methods of shortest distance or most efficient gas mileage. If you want to join a carpool, Waze can help here as well.

REMEMBER

Now that you have an idea of what's available today, you have to consider what you might want to develop (remembering the caveats in the previous section). The instructions at `https://developer.android.com/distribute/best-practices/launch/distribute-cars` tell you about the submission requirements for your Android Auto app. Book 6, Chapter 1 tells you more about publishing an app in general, which you'll find helpful in jumping through the required hoops. One thing to remember is that even though Google Play Store supports all sorts of host devices, cars generally support only smartphones today, so you need to target your app's platform accordingly.

Considering Notification Limits

When you're working with your smartphone or tablet, you can receive notifications at any time. Of course, you can set preferences not to receive notifications from certain apps, but generally, most people receive most notifications all the time. Distracted driving is a serious problem, and you won't find a lack of laws regarding it, so any Android app you create for a car needs to observe certain restrictions when making notifications. A notification must be

- **Important enough to interrupt the driver:** Some examples are the imminent failure of a car's safety feature or the presence of a pedestrian standing in the way of the car. A friend request from Facebook isn't important enough to interrupt the driver, and you should avoid notifying the driver.
- **Appropriate when driving:** You can think about this restriction in two ways:
  - You can let the notification, such as an important text message, wait until the car is stopped. Most APIs make it possible to detect when the car has stopped at a stop light or for other reasons.
  - The driver doesn't need to know about the notification until the driver exits the vehicle. Advertisements about car insurance fall into this category.
- **Sufficient priority:** When presenting a notification, the car's software may decide that your notification simply isn't high enough priority to display when other notifications have a higher priority. The fact that the right front tire is losing pressure rapidly is definitely higher priority than the telephone call from Mom.
- **Not illegal to present:** State laws are just now starting to catch up with technology. Such laws are very likely to become enforceable through car software at some point. Your notification might not appear because presenting it may become illegal based on the history of presenting such notifications

causing distractions. A recent article by Rural Mutual Insurance at `https://www.ruralmutual.com/resource/auto/hands-free-not-risk-free/` points out the risks of hands-free apps not being risk free. In short, any nonessential interaction you have with the driver may eventually become illegal.

AVOIDING INTERACTION LIMITS

Interaction limits keep drivers safe. For example, browsing a list of artists and songs while driving isn't safe because the driver will focus on the panel and the selections rather than on the road ahead, so the car prevents the user from browsing using the car's features when the car is in motion. Older setups relied on checking the accelerator and brake to determine movement, which people overcame by hard-wiring the circuitry to make the car always appear to be stopped. Newer setups have an accelerometer to detect motion, which is a lot harder to overcome unless you want to take your dashboard apart and delve into the intricacies of car circuitry.

People seem to have this strong need to drive as well as do something else, usually with the focus on the something else. The articles at `https://www.nhtsa.gov/risky-driving/distracted-driving` and `https://www.thezebra.com/distracted-driving-statistics/` provide some interesting statistics and observations about distracted driving and highlight the need for interaction limits. As a developer, you can write your apps in a way that keeps the driver safe from distracting notifications from the outset, without the need for interaction limits in the first place:

- If a notification can wait until the driver has left the vehicle, it's always better to wait.
- Making distracting sounds is always a bad idea, and most cars won't allow your apps to make sounds anyway, except for playing music or reading an audiobook. Android Auto now has a switch to turn off all notification sounds (see the article at `https://www.androidpolice.com/2020/01/30/you-can-finally-silence-notifications-in-android-auto/`).
- Using voice, rather than text, so that the driver can hear the notification or other information is always better than forcing the driver to read the panel.
- Keeping designs simple so that the driver doesn't have to figure anything out is important.
- Reduce everything to a single task at a time so that the driver isn't trying to multitask while driving.
- Allow voice interactions at all times instead of requiring the driver to interact through the panel.

Notifications also have limits in their manner of presentation. The notification that makes a sound or vibrates the device and then presents some sort of visual presentation on a smartphone or tablet may appear differently on a car. For example, some cars have a bar across the top of the display to present certain notifications. The textual notification display is the only presentation you receive. Here are some other notification types:

- **Image:** This is a picture of a person or entity that is contacting the driver by text or call.
- **Icon:** This is an indicator of the app that's making the notification, and it's sometimes paired with the image of the person calling, texting, or posting. For example, a notification of someone posting from Facebook may show both the image of the person making the post and the Facebook icon.
- **Text-to-Speech (TTS):** Instead of presenting pure text, the text appears on the panel, and the car reads the text for the driver. Using this approach keeps the driver's focus on the road rather than the panel. Because TTS relies on a computer reading the text, the text you choose should be understandable when read by a computer voice. Short, common words with few syllables work best.
- **Close icon:** Notifications always come with some means of being dismissed without being read. If the driver is busy, the notification should automatically dismiss itself after a short time to keep from distracting the driver.
- **Sound:** The notification sound is not a ringtone but a sound that is provided by the system (rather than by your smartphone or other paired device). The sound is short-lived and simply alerts the driver to the presence of an essential notification. You use sound only when the notification is high priority — something that affects the driver's safety or alerts to driver to either car or environmental concerns.
- **Voice commands:** Most newer cars provide voice commands to interact with notifications. Using voice commands allows the driver to deal with the notification without looking at the panel and while keeping both hands on the wheel. Any notification you create must react properly to voice commands.

Creating an Emulator

Before you can do much development, you need a car with Android Auto installed, or an emulator. This chapter focuses on using the emulator, but the following sections offer a quick guide to using your car as a development platform.

Configuring your car for development

You can't move your car to your office, so you need a smartphone with enough functionality to perform the development and then plug it into the car's USB port. You don't enable developer mode in the car; instead, you enable it on your smartphone by using these steps:

1. **Open the Android Auto app on your smartphone.**

   If you don't have Android Auto installed, your smartphone won't connect to the car, even if the car is Android Auto enabled. Normally, your smartphone will automatically detect the need to install Android Auto when you plug it into the car's USB port.

2. **Choose About.**
3. **Tap the gear icon in the upper-right corner.**

   You see Android Auto details.

4. **Scroll to the bottom of the page.**

   One of the entries shows the Android Auto version.

5. **Tap the version entry ten times.**

   Your smartphone tells you that developer mode is enabled.

RELYING ON REAL HARDWARE WITHOUT USING YOUR CAR

Not many people are willing to experiment with their new car in building Android Auto apps. Ideally, one of the car or experimental device vendors will put a kit together, similar to those kits you find all over the place on the Internet for building Internet of Things (IoT) projects. However, a long search turned up nothing of a kit nature from anyone. If you see such a kit, make sure you contact either John (`John@JohnMuellerBooks.com` or Barry (`android@allmycode.com`) with your insights.

The lack of a kit hasn't stopped some people. One of the better approaches is to use an existing development board, such as the TI Development Board, as described at `http://www.ti.com/cn/lit/an/spraco0/spraco0.pdf`. Many people are using the Android Auto retrofit kits found on places such as Amazon (`https://www.amazon.com/exec/obidos/ASIN/B07KRPSRKH/datacservip0f-20/`) as a starting point. Some people are grabbing the hardware from cars that have made their way to the scrap heap because of an accident. One enterprising person even created a kit from scratch (see `https://www.mathieupassenaud.fr/build-your-own-android-auto-head-display/` for details). The point is that you need hardware found in the car, not an actual car, to perform your testing.

TIP

If you encounter problems with this procedure, make sure that your car actually does support Android Auto, that you have the latest updates installed, and that the car "sees" the smartphone attached to the USB port (which is normally confirmed by a notification, with the smartphone serving as an audio source). Make sure that you have the latest version of Android Auto installed on the smartphone as well. When all else fails, contact the car vendor to determine whether some special handshake is required to make the setup work.

Defining an emulator

Most developers rely on an emulator to perform most of the development work for their Android Auto app. To get started, you need to configure the emulator using the sections that follow.

Install the SDK support

Before you can do anything else, you need to install the required SDK support, as described in the following steps.

1. **Choose Configure⇨SDK Manager or Tools⇨SDK Manager.**

   You see the Settings for the New Projects dialog box.

2. **Select SDK Tools.**

   The list of SDK Tools includes Android Auto API Simulators and Android Auto Desktop Head Unit Emulator, as shown in Figure 4-1.

3. **Select the Android Auto API Simulators and Android Auto Desktop Head Unit Emulator options (along with any other required updates) and then click OK.**

   You see the Confirm Change dialog box, shown in Figure 4-2. Make sure both entries are there. The figure shows the versions of the emulators used in the book. If you use different emulator versions, you may see differences in outputs.

4. **Click OK.**

   The Component Installer appears, and you see the various steps needed to install the software. The process usually goes quickly.

5. **Click Finish.**

   The Component Installer closes, and you see either the Android Studio main display or the IDE.

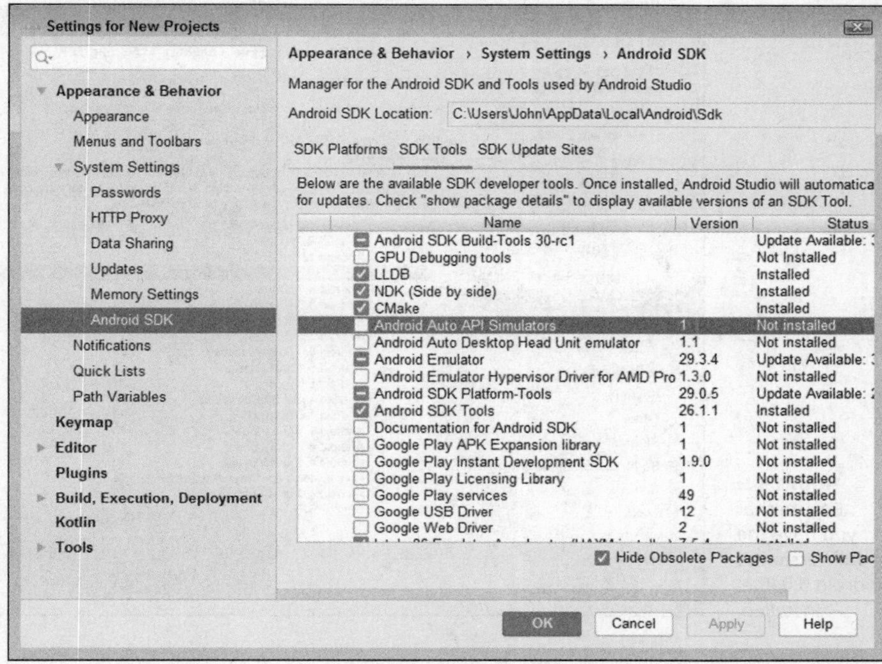

FIGURE 4-1: Android Emulator tools you need to work with Android Auto.

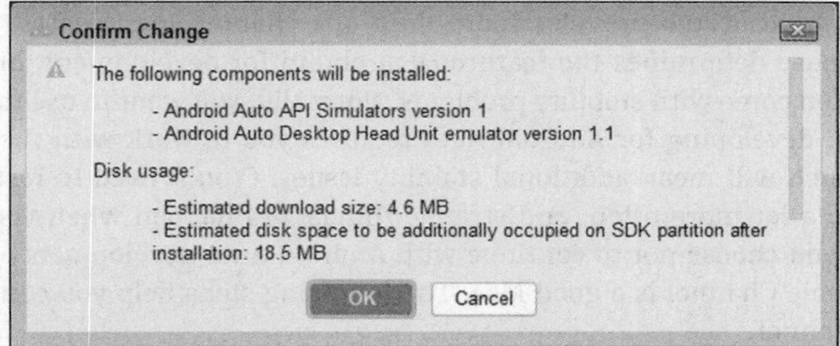

FIGURE 4-2: Verify that you're installing the right features.

6. **Perform Steps 1 through 5, choosing SDK Platform instead of SDK Tools, to fully install Android 9.0 (Pie) on your system.**

   If the entry reads Partially Installed, as the highlighted one shown in Figure 4-3 does, the emulator won't set up correctly.

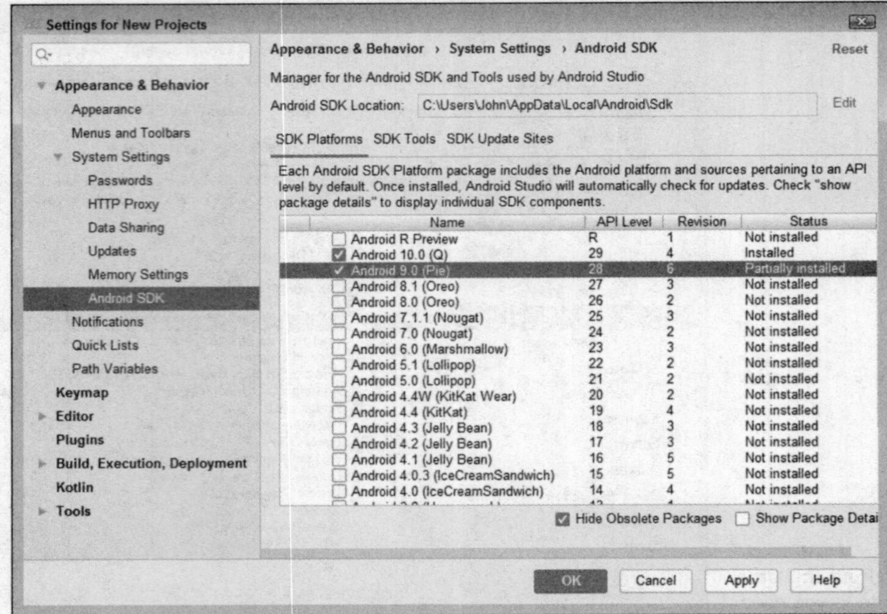

FIGURE 4-3: Ensure that you have the full version of Android 9.0 (Pie) installed.

Using the Canary Channel for updates

Android Studio provides more than one channel for updates. The channel you choose determines the features you obtain for development, but newer features often come with stability problems. Normally, you want to use the Stable Channel, but developing for Android Auto requires you to work with the Canary Channel, which will mean additional stability issues. (You'll need to restart Android Studio a lot more often, and strange things will happen when you run your code.) If you choose not to continue with Android Auto development, going back to the Stable Channel is a good idea. The following steps help you configure the Canary Channel.

1. **Choose Configure⇨SDK Manager or Tools⇨SDK Manager.**
2. **Select Appearance & Behavior/System Settings/Updates.**

   You see the settings shown in Figure 4-4.

3. **Choose Canary Channel from the Automatically Check Updates for drop-down list.**

   You see a warning message.

4. **Click Check Now.**

   You see an update dialog box like the one shown in Figure 4-5, outlining the various updates available to you.

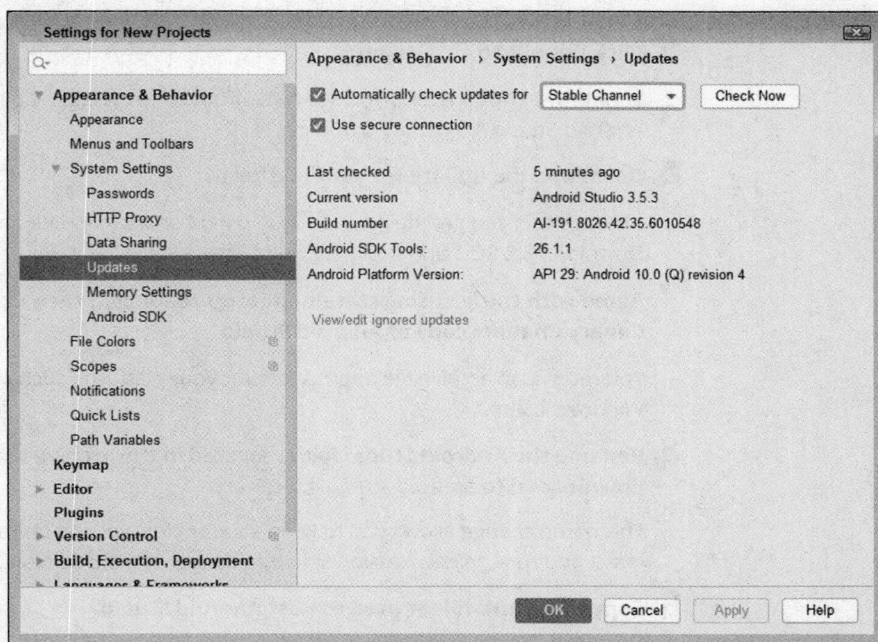

FIGURE 4-4: Change the channel used for updates.

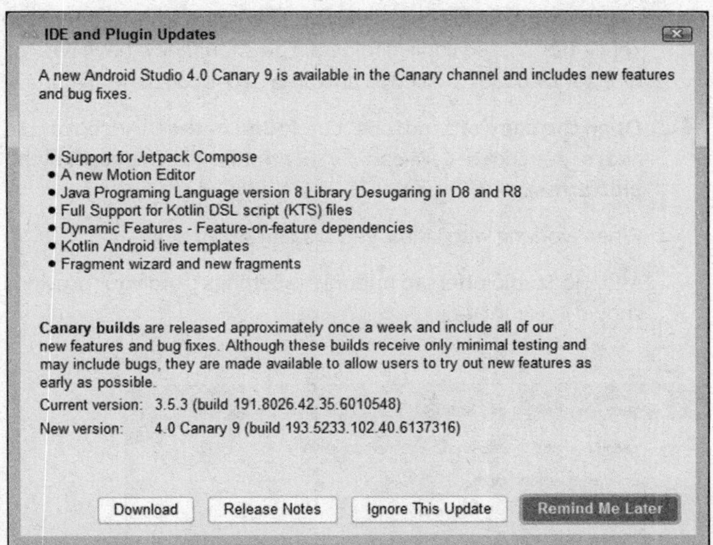

FIGURE 4-5: Obtain the updates needed for this project.

5. **Click Download.**

   Your browser opens, and you see a site from which you can download the Android Studio 4.0 Canary 9 update.

6. **Download the update for your platform.**

   Make certain you get the Android Studio 4.0 Canary 9 update and not the Download 3.6 RC 3 update.

7. **Agree with the licensing statement after reading it; then download the Canary Channel copy of Android Studio.**

   You receive an archive file appropriate for your platform, such as a `.zip` file for Windows users.

8. **Rename the Android Studio folder located in the archive that you downloaded to** android-studio-4.0-canary.

   This name change allows you to keep your original version of Android Studio intact and run the new version side by side with the old version.

9. **Copy the entire folder used to host Android Studio.**

   For example, on a Windows system, you'd copy the file to `C:\Program Files\Android`. Mac users should drag the files to their `Applications` folder, and Linux users should copy the files to the `/usr/local/` (for personal copies) or `/opt/` (for shared copies) folders. You should now have two folders in that directory: `Android Studio` and `android-studio-4.0-canary`.

10. **Open the copy of** `studio64.exe` **found in the** `C:\Program Files\Android\android-studio-4.0-canary\bin` **folder (or the equivalent for other platforms).**

    When working with Linux, you look for `studio.sh`.

    Android Studio offers to import the settings from your previous installation, as shown in Figure 4-6.

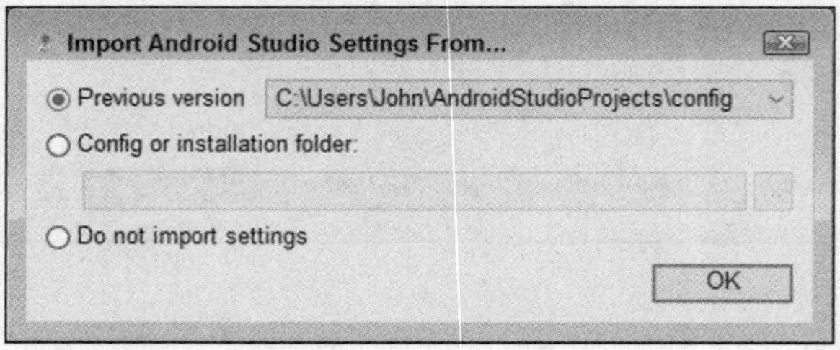

FIGURE 4-6: Obtain the updates needed for this project.

11. Choose the correct location for the settings and then click OK.

You see the Android Setup Wizard dialog box, shown in Figure 4-7. This wizard doesn't perform a full install; it instead performs an update install.

12. Follow the prompts to complete the installation process.

Android Studio starts.

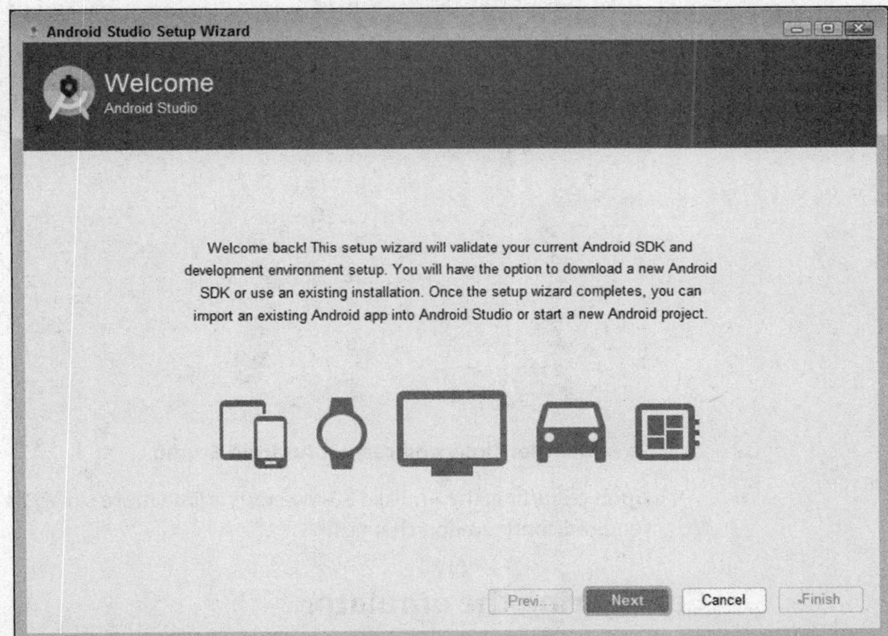

FIGURE 4-7: Complete the Canary Channel version setup process.

TIP

Your platform provides a method for making the Canary Channel version of Android Studio available in the same manner as you access your normal version. Both copies appear as Android Studio, but the Stable Channel version uses a green icon, while the Canary Channel version uses a yellow icon.

Make the Android Studio configuration change

The Android Automotive emulator won't appear in the list of available emulators until you make a required configuration change, as described in the following steps.

1. **Locate the `studioFlags.xml` file on your system.**
   - **Windows:** `C:\Users\<User Name>\.AndroidStudio3.5\config\options`
   - **Linux:** `~/.AndroidStudio3.5/config/options`
   - **Mac:** `~/Library/Preferences/AndroidStudioPreview3.5/options`

2. **Open the file in a pure text editor, preferably one that's designed to work with XML files, and make the addition shown in bold in the following code.**

   You can open the file in Android Studio if desired.

```
<application>
  <component name="StudioFlags">
    <option name="data">
      <map>
        <entry key="npw.templates.automotive"
               value="true" />
        <entry aid:table="cell" aid:crows="1" aid:ccols="1"
  key="gradle.ide.new.sync"
               value="false"/>
        <entry aid:table="cell" aid:crows="1" aid:ccols="1"
  key="gradle.ide.single.variant.sync"
               value="false"/>
      </map>
    </option>
  </component>
</application>
```

3. **Save the file. Close and restart Android Studio.**

   Upon restarting, the Android Studio starts a little more slowly as it makes required configuration changes.

Configuring the emulator

After you have the required SDK and Android Studio changes in place, you can finally create an emulator. The following steps show you how:

1. **Choose Configure⇨AVD Manager or Tools⇨AVD Manager.**

   You see the Android Virtual Device Manager dialog box.

2. **Click + Create Virtual Device and choose the new Automotive category.**

   The dialog box lists a minimum of two entries, as shown in Figure 4-8. The Automotive emulator format appears in more vehicles than the Polestar 2 emulator does. However, you need to choose the emulator that best fits the target for your app. The example in this chapter relies on the Automotive emulator.

3. **Highlight Automotive (1024p landscape) and click Next.**

   You see the Select a System Image dialog box, shown in Figure 4-9.

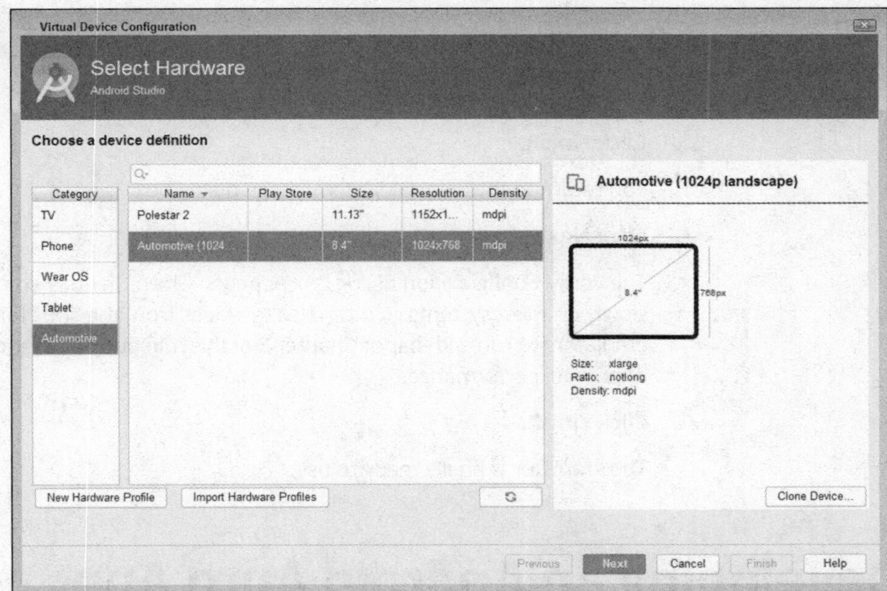

FIGURE 4-8: Choose the emulator you want.

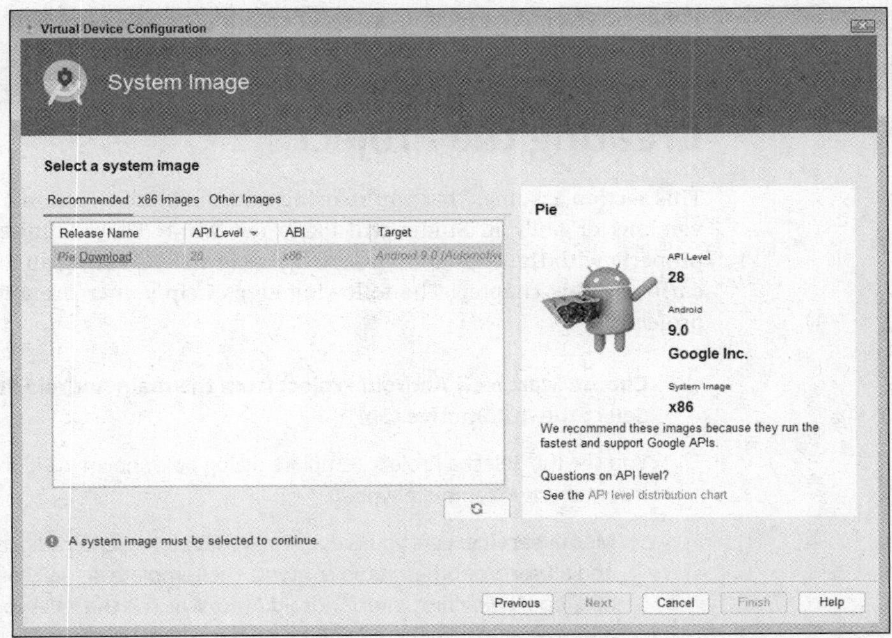

FIGURE 4-9: As with any emulator, you need a system image.

4. **Click Download to download the automotive part of the SDK.**

   You see the Component Installer dialog box.

5. **Click Finish.**

   You return to the Select a System Image dialog box.

6. **Click Next.**

   The Verify Configuration dialog box appears. Given that this emulator runs slowly on most systems, you can use the ideas from the "Tips for getting the emulators to run" sidebar of Chapter 3 of this minibook as a resource for improving performance.

7. **Click Finish.**

   The emulator is finally ready to use.

Developing an Android Auto App

If you survived the grueling ordeal of creating an emulator, you're finally ready to create a basic app. The following sections get you started.

Creating the Project

This section assumes that you're using Android Studio Version 4.0 Canary 9. Older versions of Android Studio will likely not work. They definitely won't interact properly with the emulator you configure in the "Creating an Emulator" section, earlier in this chapter. The following steps help you create a new Android Auto project:

1. **Choose Start New Android Project from the main Android Studio menu. Select the Automotive tab.**

   You see the Select a Project Template dialog box, shown in Figure 4-10. It contains two template types:

   * **Media service:** Lets you create apps that play music, radio, audiobooks, and all sorts of other audio content. The template actually offers two levels of support. The first is for Android Auto, which is the level you should select if you want to offer an app in the near future. The second is for Android Automotive OS, which is still in development.
   * **Messaging service:** Provides the means for users to receive incoming notifications, read messages aloud using text to speech, and send replies via voice input in the car. This template supports only Android Auto.

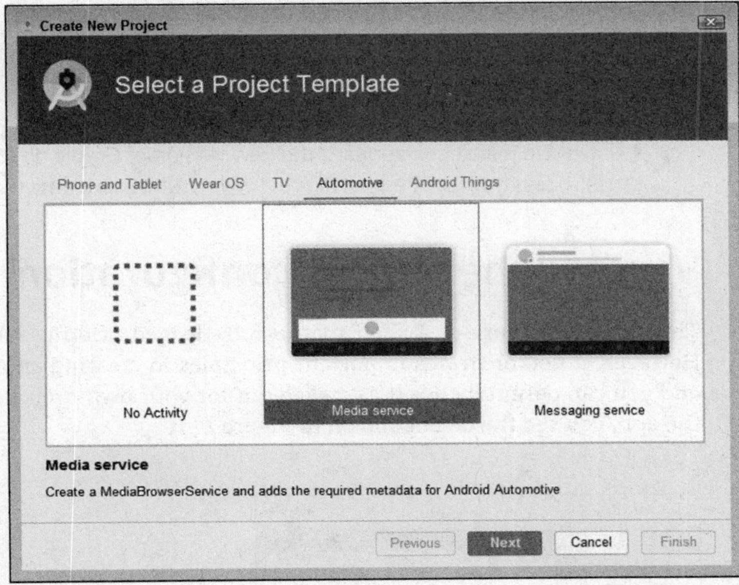

FIGURE 4-10: Select an automotive project template.

2. **Highlight the Media Service template and click Next.**

   You see the Configure Your Project dialog box.

TECHNICAL STUFF

   Unlike most dialog boxes used for project configuration, this one includes a Use Legacy Android Support Libraries check box. Selecting this option could cause your app to fail because of the restrictions that using old libraries causes. However, using the legacy libraries will also make your resulting app more stable than using the Canary Channel libraries, so you have to consider this trade-off when putting your project together.

   This dialog box also specifies a minimum API level of API 28: Android 9.0 (Pie). Given the experimental nature of Android Auto, you should likely stick with this level.

3. **Type** 05_04_01 **in the Name field, type** com.allmycode.p05_04_01 **in the Package Name field, and then click Finish.**

   Android Studio creates the project for you.

REMEMBER

   During this process, you might see a notification from your firewall that it needs permission to unblock some features of the OpenJDK Platform binary. You must allow access or you won't have the required functionality in the project.

   The old version of Gradle won't work with this project, so the next step is to update it.

4. **Open the** `gradle-wrapper.properties` **file and change the** `gradle-4.8-bin.zip` **entry to read** `gradle-6.1-rc-1-all.zip`**. Then click Sync Now.**

   A download dialog box appears, the new version of Gradle downloads, and the sync process begins. The sync process will require more time than usual.

Viewing the project configuration

This project is more of a shell than a full-fledged offering when you create it. However, it demonstrates important principles in creating an Android Auto app, and you can definitely use it as a skeleton for your own projects. When you open the app, you see the layout shown in Figure 4-11.

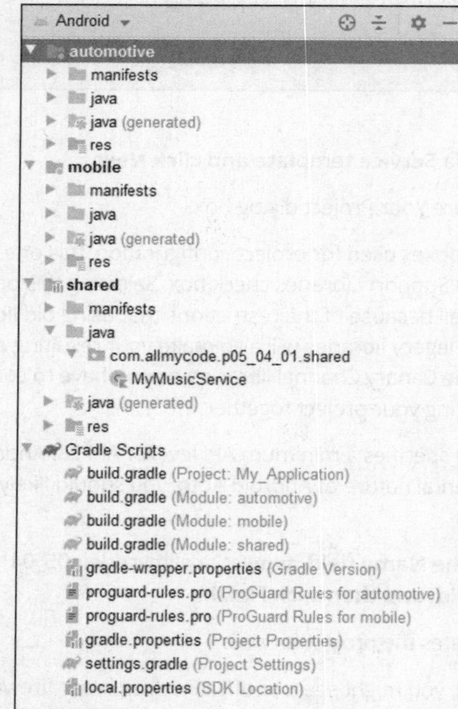

FIGURE 4-11: Parts of an Android Auto app.

The project consists of three modules:

- **automotive:** Contains the automotive-specific portions of the app. Except for a unique manifest and some resources, this part of the project doesn't contain any written code files (just those used for testing and those that are automatically generated). It also contains resources specific to this part of the project, but it contains no layout files because the OS, not the app, draws the UI. The most important part of this module is the `AndroidManifest.xml` file, which contains the following `<uses-feature>` element required for automotive apps:

```
<uses-feature
    android:name="android.hardware.type.automotive"
    android:required="true"/>
```

REMEMBER

Automotive apps also start without an `<activity>` element. You can add an `<activity>` element with `<intent-filter>` entries, but the `<intent-filter>` must never have the `"android.intent.action.MAIN"` or `"android.intent.category.LAUNCHER"` attributes.

- **mobile:** Provides an interface for a smartphone, which is currently the Hello World example that you see as a starting point for other smartphone apps in this book. There are no surprises here; the manifest, code files, layouts, and resources all look like those of a standard smartphone app. Your physical mobile device (not emulated) must have Android Auto installed and have access to a music source before the app will run on it.
- **shared:** Implements the majority of the project's functional code, including `MyMusicService`, shown in Figure 4-11. This is where you look for insights into how the app created for the smartphone pairs with the service created for the car. Only the automotive portion of the project is fully functional at this point, so you run this service on the Automotive emulator that you create in the "Defining an emulator" section, earlier in this chapter.

REMEMBER

The automotive and mobile modules link to the shared module through a `build.gradle` entry in each module's `dependencies` section: `implementation project(path: ':shared')`. This entry tells Gradle to add the shared module into the other two modules, so what you see in the shared module appears in both outputs. Note that Figure 4-11 shows a project-level `build.gradle` file, along with one `build.gradle` for each of the modules.

In looking at `AndroidManifest.xml` for the shared module, you see a service entry similar to the one used for the Android Wear example in Chapter 2 of this minibook. You also see this interesting `<meta-data>` element:

```
<meta-data
    android:name=
        "com.google.android.gms.car.application"
    android:resource="@xml/automotive_app_desc"/>
```

This entry references the following XML file:

```
<?xml version="1.0" encoding="utf-8"?>
<automotiveApp>
    <uses name="media"/>
</automotiveApp>
```

The combination of the two entries tells Android Auto that this is a media app and that it should appear in the media portion of the UI.

REMEMBER

The purpose of all these modules is to create an *app bundle*, which contains multiple APKs so that each device downloads the code required to make it work properly through Dynamic Delivery of modules (see `https://developer.android.com/guide/app-bundle/dynamic-delivery` for details).

Performing required configuration tasks

As with the Android Wear example in Chapter 2 of this minibook, the automotive portion of this example requires some reconfiguration on your part because it runs as a service rather than as an app. The following steps help you perform these required configuration tasks.

1. **Choose Run⇨Edit Configurations.**

   There are three Android App configurations, as shown in Figure 4-12, and you must choose the correct one or the app won't run.

2. **Highlight the automotive entry.**

   You see the run and debug options for the automotive module.

3. **Choose Nothing in the Launch field of the Launch Options group.**
4. **Click OK.**

   Android Studio makes the appropriate changes in the project configuration.

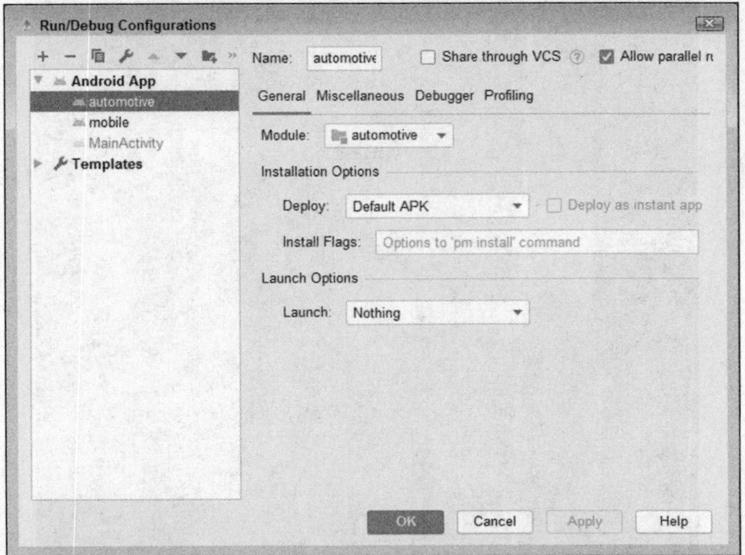

FIGURE 4-12: Reconfiguring the correct app.

Touring the Media Service app

Because this example works with a service, you need to perform a few steps before starting it:

1. **Choose Run⇨Select Device.**

   You see a list of devices to choose from.

2. **Click Automotive (1024p landscape) API 28.**

   Android Studio sets the device to use for running the app.

3. **Choose Run⇨Run.**

   You see a list of modules to run.

4. **Click Automotive.**

   Gradle builds the app, the emulator starts, and you see the app loaded into the emulator. This process can require some amount of time to complete, so it's important to be patient.

Once the app starts to run, you see the home page of the Media Service as shown in Figure 4-13. The only functional part is a drop-down list box where you can choose the music source, which defaults to Bluetooth Audio.

FIGURE 4-13: The app's home page, where you can choose an audio source.

The project template doesn't supply much functionality, so when you choose My Application as a source, you won't see much. However, if you choose the Local Media source and click the Browse icon (which looks like a musical note), you see what your app output would look like if you added some functionality, as shown in Figure 4-14.

This part of the app is fully functional now despite the skeletal nature of this example project. Click Ringtones and then Calypso Steel, and you hear the associated ringtone over your computer speakers. When the ringtone plays, you see the usual controls associated with media, Skip Back, Play/Pause, and Skip Forward. When working with the ringtones, skipping forward selects the next ringtone and clicking back selects the previous ringtone. It's interesting to play with this part of the app to see how your app should behave.

Click the Apps button (the grid icon) to see a list of apps installed in the emulator, as shown in Figure 4-15. You see that My Application is listed as one of the apps. However, if you click it, you find that it tells you no media is available. Likewise, clicking Bluetooth Audio tells you that the Bluetooth functionality is disconnected. However, clicking Settings does display a rudimentary Settings feature.

The Notifications button (the bell icon) does display a notifications screen, but the default screen simply tells you that there are no notifications. Clicking the little bar at the bottom of this screen takes you back to the previous screen in the emulator. As mentioned earlier, what you get from the template is an app skeleton, nothing more.

FIGURE 4-14: Seeing how the browse feature will likely work in a completed app.

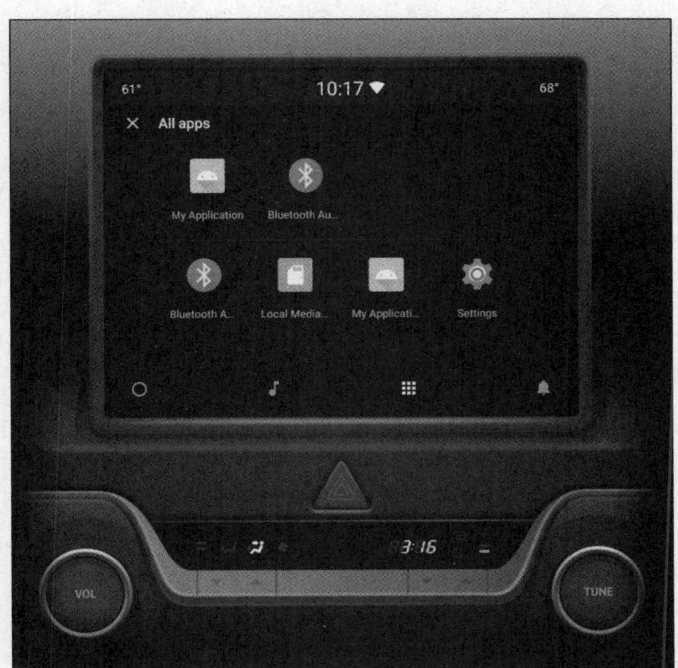

FIGURE 4-15: Choosing one of the installed apps.

6

The Job Isn't Done Until . . .

Contents at a Glance

IN THIS CHAPTER

» Creating a developer account

» Prepping your code

» Uploading your app

Chapter 1 Publishing Your App to the Google Play Store

First-time app publishing is both exciting and scary. It's exciting because, after months of development work, you're finally doing something "real" with your app. It's scary because you're exposing your app to the public. You're afraid of pressing the wrong button on the Google Play developer page and accidentally telling the world that your app kills kittens.

Well, you can relax about killing kittens. The Google Play developer page helps you get things right. And if you get something wrong, you can correct it pretty quickly. As for the excitement of publishing, there's nothing quite like it.

In this chapter, you take those courageous steps. You create a developer account and publish your first app.

Creating a Google Play Developer Account

Choosing Android for your app platform has some distinct advantages. To develop for the iPhone, you pay an annual $99 fee. Over a ten-year period, that's about a thousand bucks. As an Android developer, working over the same ten-year period, you pay $25. That's all.

To create a Google Play developer account, visit https://play.google.com/apps/publish/signup. On this page, you do the following:

- **Agree to the Google Play developer distribution rules.**
- **Pay the $25 fee.**
- **Provide your account details.** These details include your name, email, phone, and (optionally) your website URL.

  If you're working with a team, you can provide your coworkers' email addresses and set up each coworker's permissions on your account.

  If you plan to collect money through your app, you can set up a merchant account. When you do so, you provide your business name, contact name, address, phone, website URL, customer service email, and credit card statement name. There's also a What Do You Sell drop-down list. Do you sell Automotive and Marine supplies? Nutrients and Supplements? Timeshares? And what about Other? Do you sell Other?

  The information that you provide when you first sign up isn't cast in stone. You can change this information later using the Google Play's Settings page.

Preparing Your Code

At this point, you're probably tired of looking at your own app. You've written the basic app, tested the app, fixed the bugs, tested again, added features, done more testing, stayed up late at night, and done even more testing. But if you plan to publish your app, please follow this advice: After you've finished testing, test some more.

Ask yourself what sequences of buttons you avoided clicking when you did your "thorough" testing. Then muster the courage to click the buttons and use the widgets in those strange sequences. And while you're at it, tilt the device sideways, turn the device upside down, hold the device above your head, and try using the app. If your device is a phone, interrupt the app with an incoming call.

Are you finished testing? Not yet. Have your friends test the app on their devices. Whatever you do, don't give them any instructions other than the instructions you intend to publish. Better yet, don't even give them the instructions that you intend to publish. (Some users won't read those instructions anyway.) Ask your friends about their experiences running your app. If you sense that your friends are being too polite, press them for more details.

TIP

You can "publish" your app on Google Play so that only your designated friends can install the app. For more information, skip ahead to the section entitled "The App Releases page."

REMEMBER

When you test your app, be your app's worst enemy. Try as hard as you can to break your app. Be overly critical. Be relentless. If your app has a bug and you don't find it, your users will.

Un-testing the app

When you test an app, you find features that don't quite work. You check the logs, and you probably add code to help you diagnose problems. As you prepare to publish your app, remove any unnecessary diagnostic code, remove extra logging statements, and remove any other code whose purpose is to benefit the developer rather than the user.

In developing your app, you might have created some test data. (Is there a duck named "Donald" in your app's contact list?) If you've created test data, delete the data from your app.

Check your project's `AndroidManifest.xml` file. If the `<application>` element has an `android:debuggable="true"` attribute, remove that attribute. (The attribute's default value is `false`.)

Choosing Android versions

An app's `build.gradle` file specifies three SDK versions: `compileSdkVersion`, `minSdkVersion`, and `targetSdkVersion`. (In case you're wondering, Book 1, Chapter 4 tells you all about these SDK versions.) When you create a new project, Android Studio sets the compile and target SDK versions to the newest full release. You shouldn't change these values. Google released API Level 28 in August of 2018, and by November 2019, all new apps and updates to existing apps were required to target Level 28 or higher. This requirement will update each year with new versions of the Android SDK.

TIP

To read about the yearly version requirements, visit `https://developer.android.com/distribute/best-practices/develop/target-sdk` and `https://android-developers.googleblog.com/2019/02/expanding-target-api-level-requirements.html`.

Your app's `minSdkVersion` is a completely different story. When you create a new project, Android Studio asks you for a Minimum SDK version. This `minSdkVersion` number is important because it shouldn't be too low or too high.

- **If the minSdkVersion number is too low, your app isn't using features from newer Android versions.** If your app is very simple, this is okay. But if your app does anything that looks different in newer Android versions, your app's vintage look might turn users off.
- **If the `minSdkVersion` number is too high, Google's Play Store won't offer your app to users with older devices.** In fact, if your app's `minSdkVersion` is API 26, a user who visits the Play Store on an Android Nougat device doesn't even see your app. (You might have already encountered the `INSTALL_FAILED_OLDER_SDK` error message. Android Studio can't install an app on the emulator that you selected because the emulator's SDK version is lower than the app's `minSdkVersion`.)

  You don't want to eliminate users simply because they don't have the latest and greatest Android devices. So to reach more users, keep the `minSdkVersion` from being too high. If your app doesn't use any features that were introduced after API Level 23, set your `minSdkVersion` to 23.

Try running your app on emulators with many API levels. When you run into trouble (say, on an emulator with API Level 21) set your project's `minSdkVersion` to something higher than that troublesome level. You can change this number by editing the `build.gradle` file.

When you create a new project, the Minimum SDK drop-down list comes with its own Help Me Choose link. When you click this link, you see a chart showing the percentage of devices running Android 8, 9, 10, and other versions. This clickable chart describes the features in each Android version and (most important) shows the percentage of devices that are running each version. With information from this chart, you can choose the best compromise between the latest features and the widest user audience.

The AndroidX libraries allow devices with older Android versions to take advantage of newer Android features. For info, refer to Book 3, Chapter 1 and visit `https://developer.android.com/jetpack/androidx`.

Setting your app's own version code and version name

When you create a new project, Android Studio puts some default attributes in your `build.gradle` file. These attributes include the `versionCode` and `versionName` fields:

```
defaultConfig {
  ...
  versionCode 1
  versionName "1.0"
}
```

The version code must be an integer, and your app's code numbers must increase over time. For example, if your first published version has version code 42, your second published version must have a version code higher than 42.

Users never see the version code. Instead, users see your app's version name. You can use any string for your app's version name. Many developers use the `major-release.minor-release.point` system. For example, a typical version name might be `"1.2.2"`. But there are no restrictions.

Choosing a package name

Your app's package name should identify you or your company. If you have a domain name, start the package name with the domain name's parts reversed. Your domain name can't be `example.com`. But if it could be `example.com`, your first app's package name might be `com.example.earnmeamillion`. Every app must have its own package name, so your second app's package name would have to be different. Maybe it would be `com.example.secondtimeisacharm`.

TECHNICAL STUFF

The Internet Engineering Task Force reserves `example.com` as a placeholder name. Android Studio suggests `com.example` as part of a temporary package name for a new project. You also see `example.com` in Internet-related documentation.

REMEMBER

The Play Store has a few of its own restrictions on things you can use as package names. You can read all about this by visiting `https://developer.android.com/studio/build/application-id`.

Preparing Graphic Assets for the Play Store

When you publish an app to the Play Store, you interact with the Google Play Console. The essential step in this interaction is the step in which you upload your app's installation file. It's the essential step but by no means the only step. You also answer dozens of questions about your app, and you upload many graphic assets. This section describes those graphic assets.

Creating an icon

When you create a new project, Android Studio puts some default attributes in your `AndroidManifest.xml` file. One of them is the `android:icon` attribute:

```
<application android:icon="@mipmap/ic-launcher"
 ... >
```

In that attribute, the name `"@mipmap/ic-launcher"` refers to a bunch of `ic-launcher` files in various parts of your project's `res/mipmap` folder. Before publishing your app, you should replace this default icon name with your own icon's name.

The Play Store also requires you to submit a high-resolution icon — a high-quality version of your app's signature icon. The high-res icon appears here and there on the Play Store's pages.

Android Studio comes with a super-duper icon-building tool named Asset Studio. Here's a quick experiment to get you started using it:

1. **In the Project tool window, right-click the `res` branch.**

   As a result, a context menu appears.

2. **In the context menu, select New➪ Image Asset.**

   The Asset Studio window appears. The window's Name field contains the default name `ic_launcher`. (See Figure 1-1.)

3. **Type something different in the window's Name field . . . or don't!**

   If you don't, your new icon will replace Android's default `ic_launcher` icon. That way, you'll have no trouble finding the icon when you run the app. (Of course, the name `ic-launcher` might confuse other Android developers!)

4. **In the Asset Type radio group, select Image.**

   The alternatives are Clip Art and Text.

5. **To fill in the Path field, navigate to the location of an image on your development computer.**

   At this point, you've specified your icon's foreground layer.

6. **Repeat Step 5 with the dialog box's Background Layer tab selected.**

   For the Background Layer, the Asset Type radio group has only two choices: Color and Image.

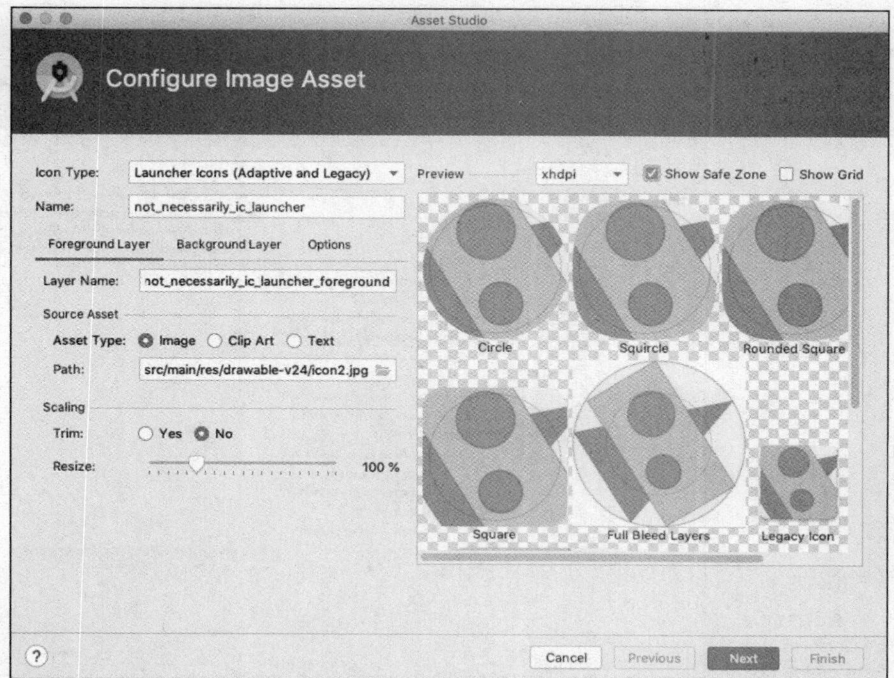

FIGURE 1-1: The Configure Image Asset dialog box.

7. **Press Next.**

   Asset Studio shows you a list of files and the directories to be created. When you select a file in the list, you see a preview of the file's contents. (See Figure 1-2.) If you like what you see, move on to the next step.

8. **Press Finish.**

   Presto! You're back to Android Studio's main window.

9. **Run your app and look for your brand-new icon.**

   Nice icon! Isn't it?

To create images for Asset Studio, you can use almost any drawing software. You can also create icons by visiting `https://romannurik.github.io/AndroidAssetStudio/`. In addition, you can download prepackaged icon packs from Google's Play Store.

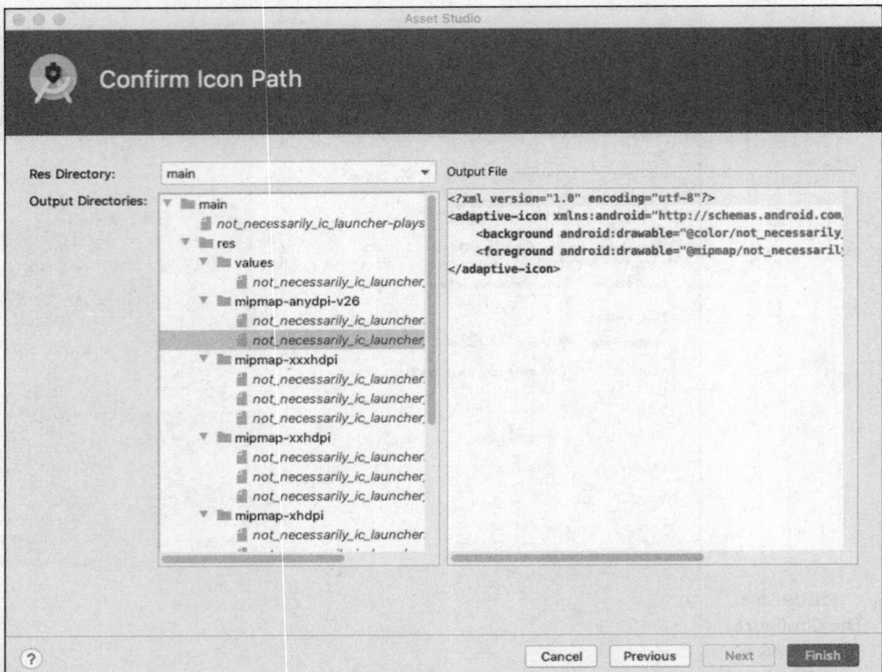

FIGURE 1-2: The Confirm Icon Path dialog box.

There's no shortage of documentation to help you create stunning Android icons:

- To read about the Play Store's design specs, visit `https://developer.android.com/google-play/resources/icon-design-specifications`.
- Android's adaptive icons look different depending on the device that's running your app. To find out about adaptive icons, visit `https://developer.android.com/guide/practices/ui_guidelines/icon_design_adaptive`.
- For guidelines on submitting graphic assets of any type, visit `https://support.google.com/googleplay/android-developer/answer/1078870`.

Creating screenshots

Along with every app that you submit to the Play Store, you must submit at least two screenshots. The Google Play Console has slots for phone screenshots, tablet screenshots, TV screenshots, and wearable screenshots. Each screenshot must be JPEG or 24-bit PNG with no alpha transparency. The minimum length for any side is 320 pixels, and the maximum length for any side is 3,840 pixels.

You have many ways to take screenshots of your running app. When you run the emulator, you get a camera icon on the emulator window's side menu bar. Another way to get a screenshot is to use Android Studio's built-in Screen Capture facility. Here's how you do it:

1. **Use Android Studio to run your app on an emulator or real device.**
2. **Look for a camera icon along the left side of the Logcat tool window.**

   If you don't see the camera icon, look instead for a tiny "more stuff" icon. That icon looks like two angle brackets (>>). When you select that icon, you see the camera icon. (See Figure 1-3.)

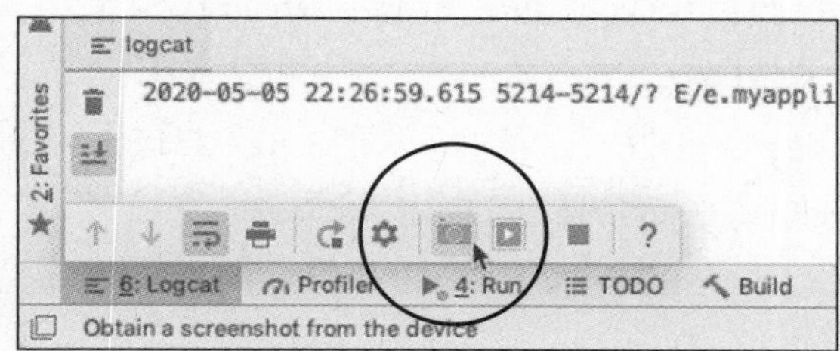

FIGURE 1-3: Getting a screenshot.

3. **Click the camera icon.**

   A new window appears. The window shows a screen capture of your device or emulator. You can click the Save button immediately. But you can also click Recapture or Rotate, or make other adjustments.

If Android Studio's Screen Capture facility isn't your thing, you have several alternatives. For example, you can use your operating system's screen capture facility to take a screenshot of a running emulator.

In Windows

1. **Launch your app in the emulator.**
2. **Click the emulator window (so that the emulator window is the active window).**
3. **While you hold down the Alt key, press the Print Screen key in the upper-right corner of the keyboard.**

TIP

   Depending on your keyboard's make and model, the key might be labeled PrintScr, PrtSc, or some other variant of Print Screen.

4. **Open an image-editing program.**

   If you don't already have a favorite image-editing program, try IrfanView (`www.irfanview.com`). It's full-featured and completely free.

5. **Press Ctrl-V to paste your new screenshot into the image-editing program.**

On a Mac

1. **Launch your app in the emulator.**
2. **Press Cmd+Shift+4.**

   This tells the Mac that you intend to take a screenshot.

3. **Press the spacebar.**

   This tells the Mac that the screenshot will capture a single window.

4. **Click anywhere inside the emulator window.**

   Your computer creates the screenshot and places it on the desktop.

TIP

You can use your development computer's screen capture facility to take a screenshot from a physical device. Start by searching for a program that mirrors an Android device's screen on your computer. After installing the program, follow this section's instructions for taking a screenshot in Windows or on a Mac.

In theory, you can press the Volume Down and Power buttons simultaneously to take a screenshot. The trouble is, the exact sequence of presses and button holds varies from one make and model to another. Check your device's documentation (and other sources) for more info.

Your options for creating screenshots are endless. If all else fails (and, in fact, all else seldom fails), you can get screenshots from running emulators and devices using your computer's command line. Search the web for `adb shell/system/bin/screencap`.

Providing other visual assets

If your app is featured on the Play Store (or rather, *when* your app is featured), a *feature graphic* appears on your store listing page. Your feature graphic must be a JPEG or 24-bit PNG file with no alpha transparency. Its dimensions must be 1,024 by 500 pixels.

The blog page at `http://android-developers.blogspot.com/2011/10/android-market-featured-image.html` has time-tested advice on creating feature graphics. The key is to create an eye-catching image that promotes your app without replicating your app's screen. You should also make sure that the image looks good no matter what size screen displays it.

Why stop after you've uploaded screenshots and a feature graphic? You can also upload a 180-by-120-pixel promo graphic and a 1,280-by-720-pixel TV banner. If that's not enough, you can throw in a promotional video and a 4,096-by-4,096-pixel Daydream stereo image.

Who knows? Maybe next year you'll be able to upload a hologram!

Creating a Publishable File

When you create an app that runs on an emulator or a device, Android Studio packages your app in one of two ways: as an Android Package (APK) file or an Android App Bundle (AAB) file. You can upload either kind of file to Google's Play Store.

- **If you upload an APK file, the Play Store copies that file to users' devices.** The APK filename extension is `.apk`.
- **If you upload an AAB file, the Play Store creates custom APK files for the users' devices.** When a user wants to install your app, the Play Store picks and chooses the parts of the AAB that are required for that particular user's device. As a result, the Play Store sends a leaner APK file to the device. The custom APK file has only the components needed by that user's device.

  In addition, the Play Store can send a reduced-feature app — one that downloads and starts running very quickly. While the user explores the app's most basic features, the Play Store readies more components for download to the device. Without any special actions on the user's part, the app's feature set grows as needed. This is called *Dynamic Feature Module Delivery,* or *Dynamic Delivery* for short. (See `https://developer.android.com/guide/app-bundle/dynamic-delivery` for more details about Dynamic Delivery.)

  For any large, multifaceted app, AAB files are the way to go. But you can't deploy an AAB file directly to a device. For a simpler app, an APK file is good enough.

  The AAB file name extension is `.aab`. (Big surprise, right?)

Differences among builds

You may not be used to using *build* as a noun. In geek language, the noun *build* refers to a file or set of files that, in some way or another, are ready to run. When you ask Android Studio to run your app, your computer creates a build of the app and then *deploys* the build onto an AVD or a physical device.

As you develop an application, you create several different builds, each with its own characteristics and each for its own purposes. Android's official terminology classifies builds in two ways: by build variant and by flavor.

- **The differences among *build variants* are visible to the app developer.** By default, a new Android Studio project describes two different build variants — *debug* build and *release* build. When you create, test, and modify your app, you run debug builds. But to publish an app to the Google Play Store, you must create a release build.

  The next section lists some important characteristics of a release build.
- **The differences among *flavors* are visible to the user.** Android Studio doesn't assign flavors to a new project. The creation of flavors is up to each app's developer. Many apps come in two flavors: free and paid. Another breakdown by flavors is by country: one flavor for most countries, another for countries with special content restrictions.

To manage your app's build variants and flavors, go to Android Studio's main menu bar and choose Build⇨Edit Build Types or Build⇨Edit Flavors.

What is a release build? Funny that you should ask! Here are some facts about release builds:

- **A release build contains your digital signature.** A *digital signature* is a sequence of bits that only you (and no one else) can provide. If your APK or AAB file contains your digital signature, no one can pretend to be you. (No one can write a malicious version of your app and publish it on the Play Store site.)

  When you follow this section's instructions, you use Android Studio to create your own digital signature. This signature lives in a directory on your computer's hard drive. You can't examine this signature with an ordinary text editor (Notepad or TextEdit, for example), but you should treat that directory the way you treat any other confidential information. Do whatever you normally do with data to prevent the loss of the data and to keep others from using it.

  TIP

  You can read more about digital signatures in this chapter's "Understanding digital signatures" sidebar.

UNDERSTANDING DIGITAL SIGNATURES

When you digitally sign a file, you add a sequence of bits that only you can add. You use sophisticated software to create the sequence and to embed the sequence in your file. The software to create this sequence uses techniques from number theory. (Sometime between 1777 and 1855, Carl Friedrich Gauss called number theory "the queen of mathematics," and he wasn't kidding!)

Digital signing actually involves two sequences of bits:

- **A private key:** A sequence that you don't share with others.
- **A public key:** A sequence that you do share with others.

The private key never leaves your office, but you can display the public key on a neon sign in Times Square. If you tell someone your private key, you'd have to . . . (well, you know). But you can hire a pilot to write your public key with white smoke in the sky over the Golden Gate Bridge.

To sign an app, you run software that adds a certificate to your app. A *certificate* is a bunch of information that includes your private key, your public key, some information to identify you, and some other information. Like your signature on a contract, a certificate's private key is difficult to fake. But with the certificate's public key, a program on the user's device verifies that your app is authentic.

A user gets keys from your app's certificate. But as a developer, you store keys apart from any certificate. You keep public and private keys in a place where your software can retrieve them — a *key store* file. When you digitally sign an app, software grabs keys from a key store file, uses the keys to create a certificate, and melds the certificate into your build file. If you visit your user home directory, and drill down to an `.android` subdirectory (starting with a dot), you probably find the `debug.keystore` file. When you test an app on an emulator or on your own device, Android Studio quietly signs your app with a simple key from this `debug.keystore` file. (For help finding your user home directory, see Book 1, Chapter 2.)

A key store file contains sensitive information, so every key store file is password-protected. Android's `debug.keystore` file is password-protected. But unlike most key store files, the `debug.keystore` file's password is freely available. The password is `android`. Anyone can sign any app using keys from the `debug.keystore` file. That's okay because the `debug.keystore` file's keys don't work for apps that you publish on the Play Store (or anywhere else, for that matter). So before publishing your app, Android Studio adds your own keys to the app.

(continued)

(continued)

After downloading your app, a user's software applies a public key to verify that your app is signed properly. And what does that prove? Well, if a hacker tampers with your app somewhere between publication and the user's downloading, the test for proper signing detects the tampering. "Sorry," says Android, "I refuse to install this app."

But what about a malicious hacker who creates a damaging app and uses Android's freely available tools to sign it? To the world in general, the app looks fine. Signing doesn't verify that an app's developer has good intentions.

The weak link in the chain is the fact that Android apps are *self-signed.* When you add a digital signature to your app, no one else signs with you.

For scenarios that require more security (scenarios not normally associated with mobile devices), a developer can get help from a certificate authority. A certificate authority is an organization that issues special digital signatures — signatures that the world recognizes as very trustworthy. To get such a signature, you convince a certificate authority that you're a good person, and you pay some money to the certificate authority. Some certificate authorities issue signatures for free. These free signatures are okay, but they aren't as trusted as the paid signatures, and they don't have the same clout as the paid signatures.

For more information about Android app signing, visit `http://developer.android.com/tools/publishing/app-signing.html`.

- **A release build's code is obfuscated.** Obfuscated code is confusing code. And, when it comes to foiling malicious hackers, confusing code is good code. If other people can make sense of your Kotlin code, they can steal it. They can make money off your ideas, or they can add snippets to your code to rob users' credit card accounts.

  You want developers on your team to read and understand your code with ease, but you don't want some outsider (like our friend Joe S. Uptonogood) to understand your code. That's why, when you follow this chapter's instructions, Android Studio creates files with obfuscated code.

  TIP

  You can read more about obfuscated code in this chapter's "Don't wait! Obfuscate!" sidebar.

DON'T WAIT! OBFUSCATE!

Nestled quietly inside your project's directory is a `proguard-rules.pro` file. When you ready your project for upload to the Play Store, Android Studio creates two additional files named `proguard-android.txt` and `proguard-android-optimize.txt`. These three files contain configuration information for the compiler. The compiler minifies, preverifies, and obfuscates your code.

To *minify* code is to make the code smaller by removing unnecessary classes, fields, and methods. This includes classes belonging to the Kotlin and Android libraries.

Preverifying code means performing a certain kind of safety check on the code. This safety check looks for places where the code can escape from its virtual machine and start running wild on the rest of the device's operating system. Code that doesn't pass this check gets a failing grade from the compiler.

When you *obfuscate* something, you make it difficult to read. You scramble stuff and generally do the opposite of what you're supposed to do when you write clear, maintainable code.

Why do this? An obfuscated program can be executed without modification by an appropriate device. The device doesn't need a password and doesn't have to decrypt anything in order to run the code. In fact, an obfuscated program contains nothing unusual as far as the Android runtime (ART) is concerned. But for a person trying to reverse-engineer your code, the obfuscation is a nightmare. That's because the human mind doesn't process code mechanically. Instead, humans get the big picture; humans have to understand things in order to work with them; humans feel stress when they work with things that are terse, circuitous, and highly compressed.

So with obfuscated code, evil people can't easily figure out how your code works. They have trouble stealing your tricks, and (more important) they can't easily add viruses to your published code.

Before publishing on the Play Store, you must obfuscate your app's code. Fortunately, the steps in this chapter's "Creating the release build" section do the obfuscation for you. Android's compiler turns your code into a dizzying mess for anyone trying to tinker with it.

(In case you're wondering, the word `proguard` in the configuration filenames has nothing to do with the open source ProGuard project. In days gone by, Android used ProGuard to obfuscate code. Android moved away from ProGuard but didn't bother to change the filenames.)

» **A release build's code is zipaligned.** Zipaligned code is easier to execute than code that's not zipaligned. Fortunately, when you follow this chapter's steps, Android Studio zipaligns your code (and does so behind your back, without any intervention on your part).

BYTE OFF MORE THAN YOU CAN VIEW

The Android operating system (along with all other UNIX-like systems) has a `mmap` program. The letters `mm` in `mmap` stand for *memory-mapped* input and output. The `mmap` program grabs data from a file and makes the data available to applications. The `mmap` program is a real workhorse, providing quick and efficient data access for many apps at once.

The nimbleness of `mmap` doesn't come entirely for free. For `mmap` to do its work, certain values must be stored so they start at four-byte boundaries. To understand four-byte boundaries, think about a chunk of data in your application's APK file. A *byte* is eight bits of data (each bit being a 0 or a 1). So four bytes is 32 bits. Now imagine two values (Value A and Value B) stored one after the other in your APK file. (See the figure in this sidebar.) Value A consumes three bytes, and Value B consumes four bytes.

Without four-byte alignment, the computer might store the first byte of Value B immediately after the last byte of Value A. If so, Value B starts on the last byte of a four-byte group. But `mmap` works only when each value starts at the beginning of a four-byte group. So Android's `zipalign` program moves data, as shown in the lower half of the figure below. Instead of using every available byte, `zipalign` wastes a byte in order to make Value B easy to locate.

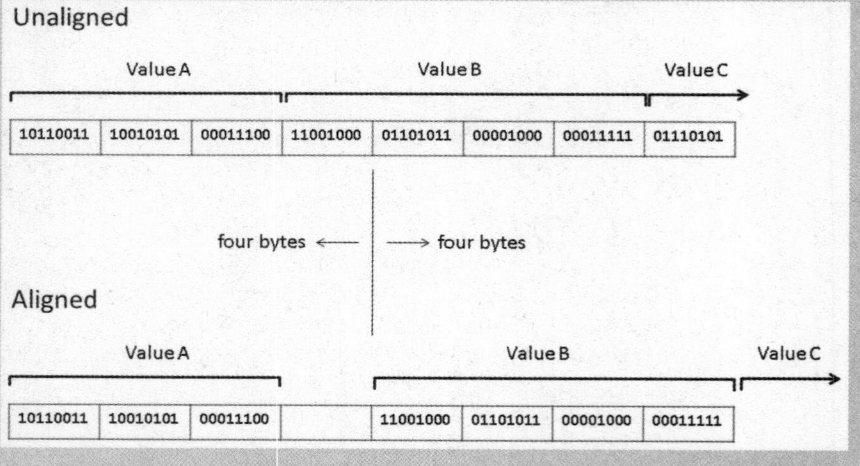

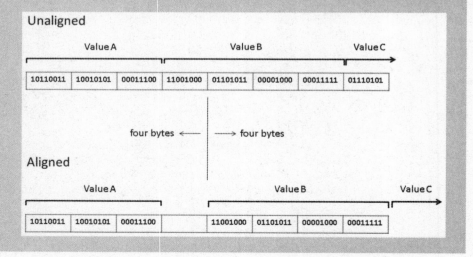

TIP

You can read more about zipalignment in this chapter's "Byte off more than you can view" sidebar.

» **Android's build tools may reduce your release build's file size.** Maybe your code is somewhat bloated, or your `res` folders have more bytes than they need. Android Studio's build process can take care of all that. In Android Studio's Project tool window, double-click the `build.gradle` file (the one labeled *Module*). In that file, add two lines in `buildTypes/release` section, like so:

```
buildTypes {
    release {
        minifyEnabled true
        shrinkResources true
        proguardFiles getDefaultProguardFile(
                'proguard-android-optimize.txt'),
                'proguard-rules.pro'
    }
}
```

With `minifyEnabled` set to `true`, the compiler puts your project's code on a diet. And with `shrinkResources` set to `true`, the compiler slims down your `res` folders' files.

WARNING

If you use something called JNI, setting `minifyEnabled` to `true` can break your code. For details and workarounds, visit `https://developer.android.com/studio/build/shrink-code`.

Creating the release build

Several paragraphs leading up to this section give lengthy descriptions of the ways release builds differ from debug builds. With all that chatter about release builds, you'll be surprised to find out that creating a release build isn't very complicated. Just follow these instructions:

1. **Make the changes described in this chapter's "Preparing Your Code" section.**
2. **In Android Studio's main menu, choose Build ➪ Generate Signed Bundle / APK.**

   The first page of a dialog box appears. The box's title is Generate Signed Bundle or APK. (See Figure 1-4.)

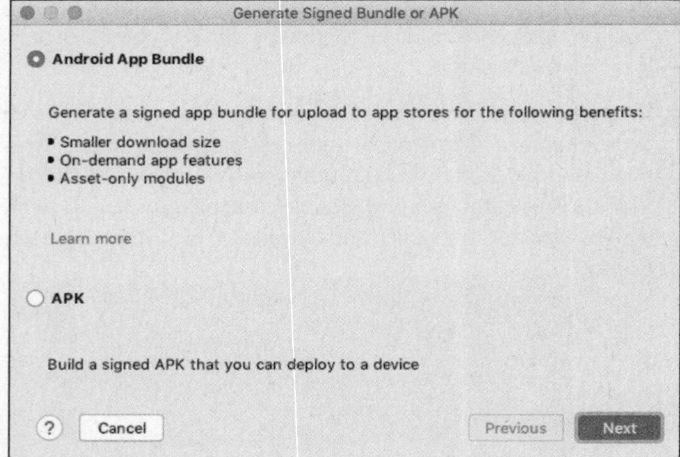

FIGURE 1-4: Bundle or APK?

3. **Select either Android App Bundle or APK.**

   If you need help choosing, refer to the start of the "Creating a Publishable File" section, earlier in this chapter.

4. **Click Next.**

   The top of the dialog box's next page has a drop-down list in which you select one of your project's modules. If your project has only one module (named app, for example) Android Studio grays out the drop-down list. (See Figure 1-5.)

   Your next task is to put something in the dialog box's Key Store Path field.

   TIP

   For some good bedtime reading about key stores, see the "Understanding digital signatures" sidebar.

   At this point, it helps to understand the difference between a key store file and a single key. A *key* is what you use to digitally sign your Android app. A *key store file* is a place to store one or more keys. In this section's instructions, you create two passwords — one for the new key store file and another for the key that you'll be putting in the key store file. For details, see the sidebar entitled "Understanding digital signatures."

   The Key Store Path field offers you three options: (a) Click a button to start creating a new key store file; (b) Click a button to choose an existing key store file (one that's already on your computer's hard drive); or (c) Type the full pathname of an existing key store file in the Key Store Path field. In what follows, you pursue the first option.

5. **Click the Create New button.**

   A New Key Store dialog box opens. (See Figure 1-6.)

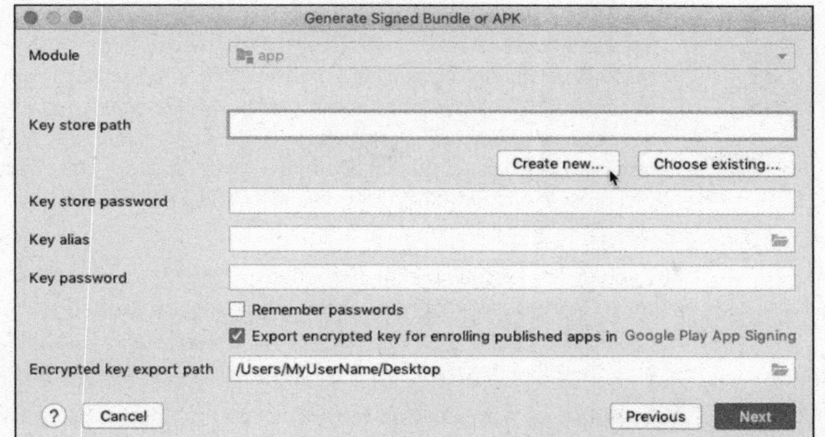

FIGURE 1-5: A bunch of questions about keys and key stores.

FIGURE 1-6: The New Key Store dialog box.

6. Click the folder icon at the rightmost end of the Key Store Path field. (Refer to Figure 1-6.)

In the resulting dialog box, you navigate to a folder on your computer's hard drive. In addition, you make up a name for your new key store file.

Where do you want to put your new key store file and what do you want to name the file? The choice is yours. One way or another, name the key store file `whatever_you_want.jks`. The extension `.jks` stands for *Java key store.*

TIP

Signing all your Android projects with the same key is generally a good idea. Android treats the key as a kind of fingerprint, and two apps with the same fingerprint can be trusted to communicate with one another. When two apps have the same key, you can easily get these apps to help one another out. But reusing a key has a potential downside. It's the same problem you have when you reuse a password. If your one and only key is compromised, all your apps are compromised.

If you decide on maintaining only one key, resist the temptation to put the key store file in your app's project directory. When you do that, you're hinting that the key store belongs exclusively to your current Android project. But when you publish more apps, you'll want to use this key store to sign other projects' files.

7. **Do whatever you must do to confirm your choice of a key store file's location and name.**

   Click OK, or something like that.

   Returning to the New Key Store dialog box, you see that the box has two Password fields and two Confirm fields. (Refer to Figure 1-6)

8. **Enter passwords in the Password and Confirm fields.**

   Do yourself and favor and make 'em strong passwords.

REMEMBER

(In the lingo of *For Dummies* books, this is a Remember icon.) Please remember to remember the passwords that you create when you fill in the Password and Confirm fields. You'll need to enter these passwords when you use this key to sign another app.

A key store file may contain several keys, and each key has a name (an *alias,* that is).

9. **Type a name in the Alias field.**

   The alias can be any string of characters, but don't be too creative when you make up an alias. Avoid blank spaces and punctuation. If you ever create a second key with a second alias, make sure that the second alias's spelling (and not only its capitalization) is different from the first alias's spelling.

10. **Accept the default validity period (25 years).**

    If you create a key on New Year's Day in 2021, the key will expire on New Year's Day in 2046. Happy New Year, everybody! According to the Play Store's rules, your key must not expire until sometime after October 22, 2033, so 25 years from 2021 is okay. (A recent Google search to find out how the creators of Android decided on the date October 22, 2033 came up empty. What kind of party will you throw when this day finally rolls around?)

11. **In the Certificate section, fill in the six fields. (Refer to Figure 1-6.)**

The items *First and Last Name, Organizational Unit,* and so on are part of the *X.500 Distinguished Name* standard. The probability of two people having the same name and working in the same unit of the same organization in the same locality is close to zero.

When you finish, your dialog box resembles Figure 1-6.

12. Click OK.

The Generate Signed Bundle or APK dialog box from Figure 1-5 reappears. This time, many of the box's fields are filled in for you. (See Figure 1-7.)

You may see a check box labeled Export Encrypted Key for Enrolling Published Apps in Google Play App Signing. If you do, make sure that the check box is selected. (If you opted to create an APK file rather than an Android App Bundle in Step 3, you don't see that check box.)

When you export an encrypted key, key's file extension is `.pepk`. To learn what `.pepk` files are all about, see the section entitled "The App Signing page," later in this chapter.

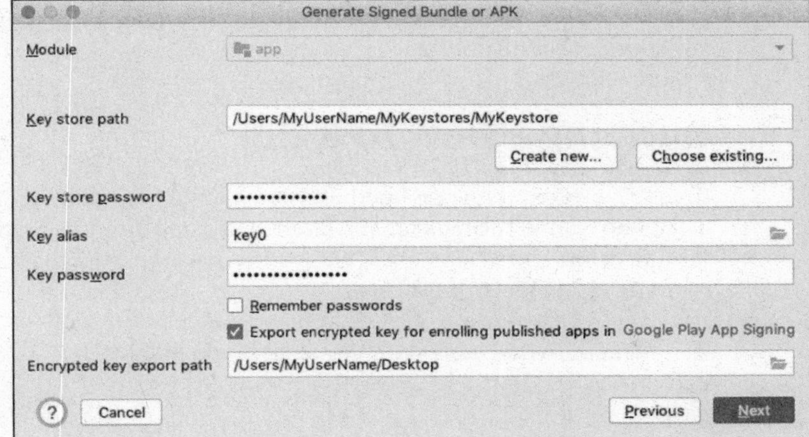

FIGURE 1-7: Filling in the fields of Figure 1-5.

13. Click Next.

One last Generate Signed Bundle or APK page appears. (See Figure 1-8.)

On this final Generate Signed Bundle or APK page, take note of the Destination Folder. Also, be sure to select Release in the Build Variants list. If you have a choice between V1 and V2 signature versions, select both. (To find out what the names V1 and V2 mean, visit `https://developer.android.com/about/versions/nougat/android-7.0.html#apk_signature_v2`.)

And finally . . .

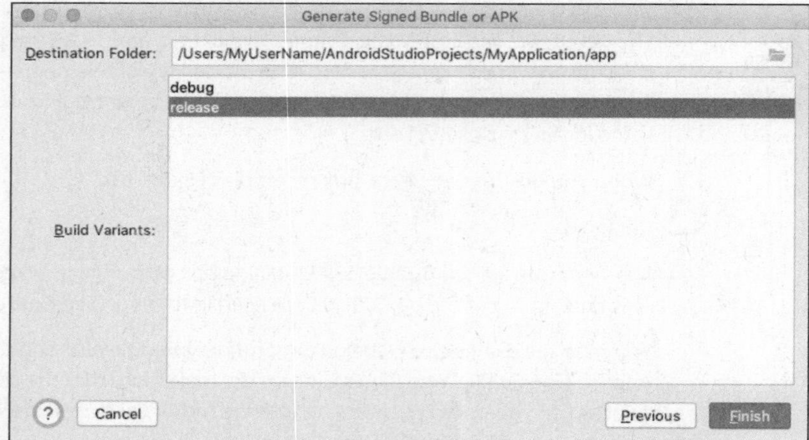

FIGURE 1-8: The penultimate step.

14. Click Finish.

Android Studio offers to open the folder containing your shiny, new AAB or APK file. That's great! Open the folder and stare proudly at your work.

Congratulations! You've created a distributable version of your app and a reusable key store for future updates.

Running a new APK file

If you've created a release build and you want to try running it, don't click the usual Run icon in the toolbar, and don't select Run⇨Run 'app'. Without first performing some extra steps, those things won't work. If the file that you've created is an APK file, follow these steps:

1. **Make sure that you're running at least one AVD.**

   If you're not, select Tools⇨AVD Manager and get an AVD going.

2. **At the top of Android Studio's Project tool window, the word *Android* is one of several drop-down list items. Change the selection from Android to Project. (See Figure 1-9.)**

   For help finding the Project view, refer to Book 1, Chapter 4.

3. **Expand the Project view tree to find your project's app/release branch.**

   Chances are, the `app/release` folder has a file named app-release.apk. If it doesn't, look elsewhere for the `app-release.apk` file.

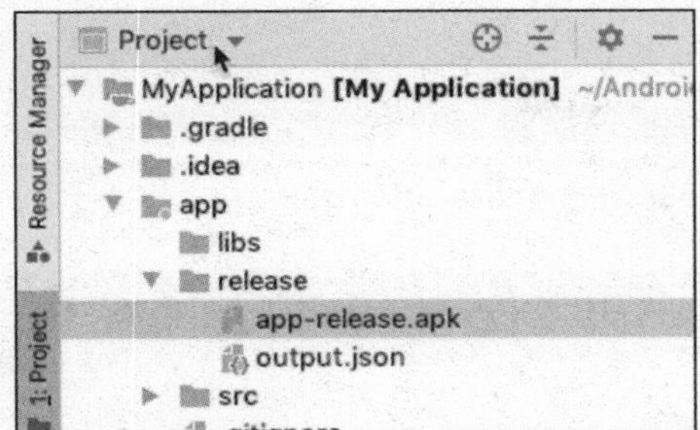

FIGURE 1-9: Finding the APK file.

4. Drag the `app-release.apk` file from the Project view to the AVD screen.

   When you do, Android installs your signed app on the AVD.

5. **Click the app's icon to launch the app on the AVD.**

   Watch your app run!

TIP

If you're comfortable using your operating system's command line, there's a quick way to make sure that your APK file has a digital signature. Look in a subdirectory of `Android/Sdk/build-tools` for a file named `apksigner.jar`. Then run the following command (all on one line that may wrap on its own):

```
java -jar path_to_apksigner.jar verify --print-certs path_to_build.apk
```

The output may be overzealous with its warnings, but you should see information about the signature that you created.

Running the app in a new AAB file

You can't deploy an AAB file to an Android device. Instead, you need a tool that sifts an APK file out of the AAB file and then deploys the APK file to the device. As of May 2020, the appropriate tool runs only from your development computer's command line — the Windows Command Prompt or the macOS Terminal application. The instructions that follow are intentionally sketchy because the details are likely to change over time. Anyway, if you're determined, these instructions can get you started:

1. **Visit** `https://github.com/google/bundletool/releases` **and download the latest bundletool jar file.**

2. **Collect all the information you need.**

   Table 6-1 lists the things you need to know to use `bundletool`.

The Information You Need	This Chapter's Nickname for the Information
On your computer's file system, the location of:	
The `java` program (`java.exe` or simply `java`)	*JAVA_COMMAND*
The `bundletool` jar file	*BUNDLETOOL_JAR*
Your AAB file	*AAB_FILE*
Your key store file	*KEYSTORE_JKS_FILE*
Your key store's password	*KEYSTORE_PASSWORD*
Your key's alias	*KEY_ALIAS*
Your key's password	*KEY_PASSWORD*
A new name (ending in `.apks`) for the collection of APK files that will be generated when you issue the `bundletool` command	*APKS_FILE*

3. **Launch your computer's command-line application — the `cmd` app in Windows or the Terminal app on a Mac.**

4. **In the command-line window, type the following command (all on one line that wraps a few times on its own):**

```
JAVA_COMMAND -jar BUNDLETOOL_JAR build-apks
  --bundle=AAB_FILE
  --output=APKS_FILE
  --ks=KEYSTORE_JKS_FILE
  --ks-pass=pass:KEYSTORE_PASSWORD
  --ks-key-alias=KEY_ALIAS
  --key-pass=pass:KEY_PASSWORD
```

   If all goes well, the result is a shiny, new `.apks` file. That file encodes some APK files that have been extracted from your AAB file.

   The only remaining task is to deploy an APK file on your Android emulator.

5. **Make sure that one (and only one) AVD is running, and that no physical devices are connected to your computer.**

   Doing so keeps the next command from being a bit more complicated.

6. **In the command-line window, type the following command (all on one line that may wrap on its own):**

```
JAVA_COMMAND -jar BUNDLETOOL_JAR install-apks --apks=APKS_FILE
```

This command analyzes your emulated device, decides which APK (or combination of APKs) to install on that device, and then proceeds to install your app.

7. **On the emulated device, find your app's launch icon and run the app.**

Good work!

TIP

If you get stuck trying to use `bundletool`, visit the online reference page: `https://developer.android.com/studio/command-line/bundletool`.

Another way to build and run an AAB file

If you want to test an AAB file and `bundletool` isn't your cup of tea, you can follow this section's steps. With these steps, you can also fine-tune a build to target specific release versions and specific flavors of your app. You can use one key to sign your app's free version and another key to sign the app's paid version.

Here's what you do:

1. **Create a signing key by following Steps 1 through 12 in the section entitled "Creating the release build."**

   Hey! That's most of the section's steps, isn't it?

2. **In the Generate Signed Bundle or APK dialog box, click Cancel.**

   Lo and behold! You're back to Android Studio's main window.

3. **Click the Build Variants tool button.**

   You can find that button along the left edge of the Android Studio window. (See Figure 1-10.)

   Clicking that button brings the Build Variants tool window out of hiding. This tool window has an Active Build Variant drop-down list.

4. **In the Active Build Variable drop-down list, select Release. (Refer to Figure 1-10.)**

   Now, when you select Run➪Run 'app', Android Studio will try to build and run your project's release version. The only problem is, Android Studio won't try to run a signed version. Before that can happen, you have a few more steps to follow.

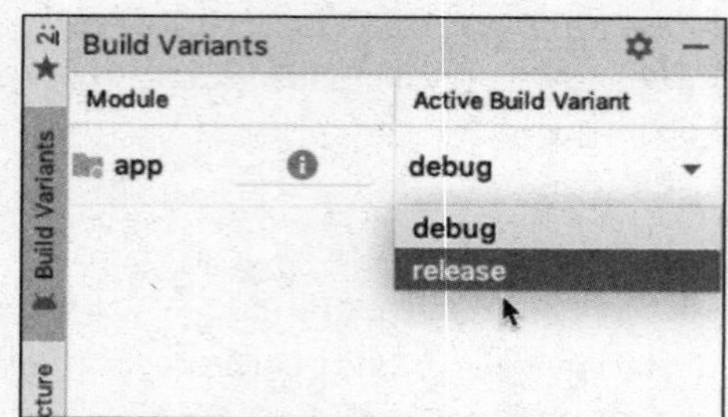

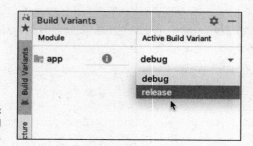

FIGURE 1-10: Selecting a build variant.

5. **In Android Studio's main menu bar, choose File⇨Project Structure.**

   The Project Structure dialog box appears. (What else would you expect?)

   You're about to create something called a *signing configuration.* The signing configuration says, "One way to sign a build is to use the key that was created in Step 1."

6. **In the Project Structure dialog box, choose Modules⇨Signing Configs.**

   The dialog box now contains two plus sign icons — one below the word Modules and another in the Signing Configs tab. (See Figure 1-11.)

FIGURE 1-11: Creating a signing configuration.

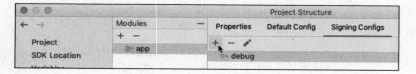

7. **Click the Signing Configs tab's plus sign icon.**

   A new message box requests that you enter a signing config name.

8. **In the message box, type** release **and then click OK.**

WARNING

   Using the name `release` doesn't automatically connect this signing configuration with your project's release build variant. Making that connection comes later in these steps.

9. **In the list near the top of the Signing Configs tab, check to make sure that the release item is selected.**

   If not, select it.

10. **In the body of the Signing Configs tab, fill in the information about the signing key that you created in Step 1.**

    Android Studio wants the path to the key store file, the file's password, a particular key's alias, and that key's password. (See Figure 1-12.)

Project Structure
Properties Default Config Signing Configs
debug
release
Store File
/Users/MyUserName/MyKeystores/MyKeystore
Store Password
a81XNNqPQLy0tl
Key Alias
key0
Key Password
plY80ir2DFZp9mHKj
Cancel Apply OK

FIGURE 1-12: Don't even think about it! This screenshot's passwords are fake.

11. Click Apply.

At this point, you've created a signing configuration. As a final step, you have to associate that configuration with your project's release build.

12. In the Project Structure dialog box, select Build Variants⇨Build Types. (See Figure 1-13.)

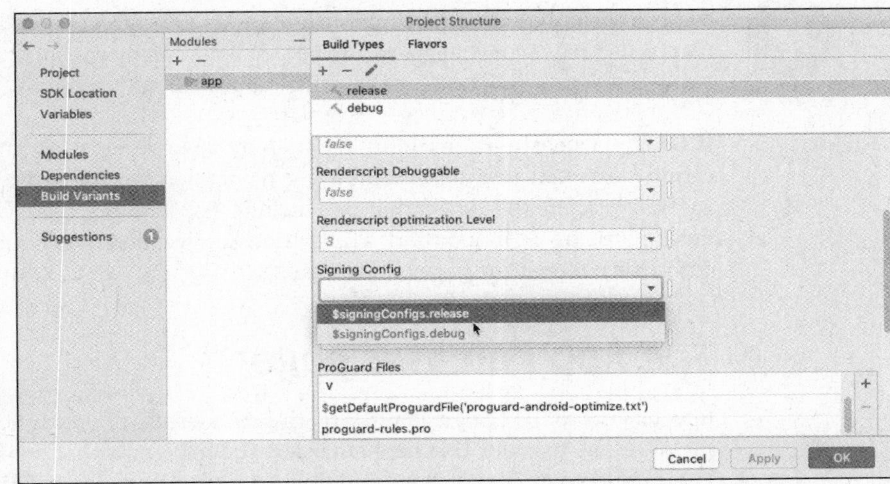

FIGURE 1-13: Connecting a signing configuration to a build.

13. **In the list near the top of the Build Types tab, check to make sure that the release item is selected.**

14. **Look for the Signing Config drop-down list in the Build Types tab. In that list, select SigningConfigs.release. (Refer to Figure 1-13.)**

15. **Click OK.**

    Well, whaddya know? You've returned to Android Studio's main window.

16. **Check the Build Variants tool window to make sure that it's still in release mode.**

17. **In Android Studio's toolbar, click the Run icon.**

    And that's it! Your app runs in the AVD window.

Publishing Your App

To start this section's adventure, visit `https://play.google.com/apps/publish`. Look for a button or link with words like Create Application. Click that button or link and get ready to roll.

REMEMBER

Nothing permanent happens until you click the Rollout button. If the Rollout button makes you nervous, there's also a friendly Save Draft button. So you can pause your work, think about things for a while, and log on again later. For more extreme situations (severe cases of Developer's Remorse), there's an Unpublish link.

TIP

Neither the Rollout nor the Unpublish requests take effect immediately. In particular, a Rollout request triggers a review of your app by the folks at the Play Store. You must wait a few days for their final approval.

If Google's website is anything like its May 2020 version, clicking Create Application takes you to a place with a big navigation bar along the left side. Pages accessible from the navigation bar include App Signing, Store Listing, Content Rating, Pricing & Distribution, Translation Service, and many others. This section describes a few of the pages in detail.

The App Releases page

In your visit to the Google Play Store, the grandest of all events is the uploading of the APK file. To make this happen, select the navigation bar's App Releases item. That's where you find buttons and links for uploading APK or AAB files. In particular, the page offers you a few different upload tracks.

» **Tracks intended for app testing:**

- **Internal track,** with up to 100 testers. You supply the testers' email addresses. Each email address must be associated with a Google account.
- **Closed (alpha) track,** with up to 2,000 testers. You supply the testers' email addresses or the names of Google Groups.
- **Open (beta) track,** with an unlimited number of testers. Anyone with a compatible device can be a tester.

» **Track intended for general release: Production track,** with users instead of testers. Your app is listed on the Google Play Store.

TIP

For more information about each of the tracks, visit `https://support.google.com/googleplay/android-developer/answer/3131213`.

Publishing Your App to the Google Play Store

WHAT? MORE TESTING?

When testing your app with friends and relatives, you don't always get reliable results. Sure, your friends are polite, but they might also know something about your app — something that other users won't already know. So your casual acquaintances living on other continents should test your app, too. In fact, you should test so much that you'd have trouble mailing your APK file to all your testers.

That's why the Play Store allows you to publish an app with invitation-only access. After uploading an app to the internal or closed track, you provide a list of testers — a relatively small number of people who can download the app from the Play Store. When these people use your app, the Play Store keeps track of crashes, application not responding (ANR) occurrences, and other unwanted events. The Google Play Console can filter its reporting of these events by Android version and device type.

If you want more testing, you can use Android's built-in testing tools. Book 3, Chapter 2 has the details. Other popular testing frameworks include Robotium, UI Animator, Selendroid, Testdroid, and Dynatrace.

And, if you want even more testing, you can enroll your app with a *testing farm* — a service that automates the testing and tests your app on many different devices simultaneously. Amazon Web Services (AWS) has its own full-featured testing farm.

For each of these tracks, you supply an APK or AAB upload, a name for this release, and an explanation of what's new in this release. When you follow the steps in the "Creating a Publishable File" section, earlier in this chapter, Android Studio creates a file named `app-release.apk` or `app-release.aab` and puts the file in your project's `app/release` subdirectory. So, when the big upload moment comes, drag that `app-release` file to the Drop Your File Here box, or click the Browse button and use your File Explorer or Finder to navigate to this `app-release` file.

The Store Listing page

On the Google Play Console's Store Listing page, you describe your app to potential users. You answer many questions and upload several files. This section lists several of the items on the page.

TIP

As you scroll down among these items, a Save Draft button stays at the bottom of your web browser's screen. Click the Save Draft button frequently to keep from losing any work that you've done.

- **Title of your app:** A great title can jump-start an app's popularity, so make your title something snappy.
- **Short description:** You may enter up to 80 characters.
- **Full description:** You may enter up to 4,000 characters.
- **Graphic assets:** Refer to the section entitled "Preparing Graphic Assets for the Play Store,"earlier in this chapter.
- **Your app's category:** Is it a game? If so, what type of game? (Choose from Action, Adventure, Card, Puzzle, Racing, Role Playing, and many other types.) If it's not a game, what type of app is it? (Choose from Business, Communication, Education, Finance, Health, and a bunch of other types.)
- **Tags to associate with your app:** For some suggestions, click the Save Draft button and then click the page's Manage Tags button.
- **Content rating:** Complete a questionnaire to determine your app's content rating under several standards (international and otherwise). Does your app involve violence, sexuality, potentially offensive language, or references to illegal drugs? Does your app involve the exchange of any personal information?
- **Your contact details:** You must supply an email address, and users have access to this address. Optionally, you can supply a website and a phone number.

- **Language translations:** You specify the default language for your listing on the Play Store. You can provide translations in other languages, or have Google Translate furnish its own guesses. (This can accidentally lead to some fairly amusing results.) You can also purchase translations straight from the Google Play Console. For a very simple app, translation costs as little as $5 per target language.

The App Signing page

The "Creating a Publishable File" section, earlier in this chapter, draws a sharp distinction between APK files and AAB files. An APK file represents an installable app, and an AAB file represents several APK files. You can upload either kind of file to the Google Play Store. If you upload an APK file, the Play Store downloads that file to users' devices. If you upload an AAB file, the Play Store manages the creation of your app's actual APK files and downloads those files to users' devices.

Whatever you send, the file must be digitally signed. So says the same "Creating a Publishable File" section. But if you upload an AAB file and the Play Store creates all the APK files, who signs those APK files?

The App Signing page presents you with the option of letting the Play Store add your signature to each of the APK files. To make this happen, you can upload the `.pepk` file that you create in Step 12 of the section entitled "Creating the release build," earlier in this chapter. Yes, you're handing your very own digital signature over to Google. It's a bit like telling someone your banking PIN or your mother's maiden name. But in return, you're reducing the complexity of delivering a sleek, customized app to each of your users. If you want the benefits of Dynamic Delivery, you have to let Google manage your app signing key.

Other pages

The Google Play Console has other pages, too, and here are some of them:

- **Device catalog:** On the Device catalog page, you specify which devices are explicitly supported for running your app, and any devices that are explicitly excluded. In May 2020, the Device catalog lists over 16,000 devices.
- **App content:** On the App content page, you describe your app's privacy policy. You specify the app's target age group. You tell Google if your app contains ads.

» **Pricing & distribution:** In which countries can your app be distributed? You can pick and choose from more than 150 countries.

  Will you charge for your app, or will it be free? For many developers, this question requires some serious thinking so the next chapter delves deeply into the alternatives. For now, the only thing you have to know is that changing your mind is a one-way street. You can change an app from being paid to free, but you can't change an app from being free to being paid. Of course, you can publish a new app that's very much like the original free app, except that the new app is a paid app.

» **In-app products:** Will you sell products or offer subscriptions through your app? For a discussion about this possibility, see the next chapter.

» **Services & APIs:** A *back-end service* is computing done on the cloud. And why would your app need to deal with the cloud? Maybe your game has a leaderboard, and you want to compare the scores of users around the world. To make this comparison, you need information that's stored outside the user's own device. This function, and many other functions that apps perform, require access to a server.

  Maybe you want to send data to your users using Google Cloud Messaging. Maybe you want Google's search engine to look for content within your app. Maybe you want Google to handle your in-app billing. All these things involve back-end services.

  Licensing is another very commonly used back-end service. Licensing protects your app from illegal use. For more info, see the "About app licensing" sidebar.

ABOUT APP LICENSING

If you license your app, no device can run your app unless the device checks in with a server. The server ensures that the device has permission to run your app. Here are some scenarios for an app (free or paid), with and without licensing:

- **Best case scenario with licensing:** A user buys your app and copies the .apk file to another user's device. The other user hasn't paid for your app. The other user tries to run the app but can't run it because of the licensing restrictions.
- **Worst case scenario without licensing:** A user buys your app and copies the .apk file to a file-sharing website. People download and install your .apk file and run the code for free. (Ooo! That's bad!)

- **Worst case scenario with licensing:** A user buys your app, cracks the licensing, and copies the `.apk` file to a file-sharing website. People download and install the cracked version of your `.apk` file and run the code for free. (That's bad, too.)
- **Best case scenario without licensing:** No one ever tries to steal your app. Or, if someone steals your app, the additional distribution of your app works to your advantage.

All things considered, it's best to do licensing with any paid app. Licensing is also a good precaution with a free app (to help you maintain ownership of the app's concept).

To enable licensing in your app, you must install the *Google Play Licensing Library* (also known as *LVL* — the *Licensing Verification Library*) using the Android SDK Manager. You must add that library to your app's project. You must obtain the app's licensing key (a sequence of about 400 gibberish characters) from the Google Play Console and add the key to your main activity. You must add additional code in your app to check a device's license and to respond (based on the result of the check). The additional code implements one of three possible policies:

- **Strict policy:** Whenever the user tries to launch your app, the device asks the Google Play server for approval to run the app. If the user tries to launch your app when the device has no connectivity, the user is out of luck. Life's tough.
- **Server-managed policy:** The user's device stores a copy of the user's license. The device uses the copy when network connectivity is unavailable. The license is obfuscated (so it's tamper-resistant), and the license keeps track of trial periods, expiration dates, and other stuff. This is the default policy, and it's the policy that Google highly recommends.
- **Custom policy:** Create your own policy or modify either of the preceding policies by adding Kotlin code to your app.

This chapter's "What? More testing?" sidebar describes how you can use the Google Play Console to register testers for your soon-to-be-published app. You can also name some special testers for your app's licensing scheme. Your testers attempt to run the app when (as they know darn well) they shouldn't get permission. The Google Play Console keeps track of successes and failures so that you can find out whether your licensing scheme works correctly.

For all the details about the licensing of apps, visit `http://developer.android.com/google/play/licensing/`.

Publishing Your App to the Google Play Store

Leave No Stone Unturned

Do lots of homework before you publish on Google's Play Store by checking out these resources:

- Visit `https://developer.android.com/studio/publish/preparing` for a comprehensive list of required steps.
- Visit `https://developer.android.com/docs/quality-guidelines/core-app-quality` for an exhaustive list of criteria that your app must satisfy.
- Visit `https://developer.android.com/distribute/play-policies` for a glimpse at the Play Store's upcoming changes.

  And finally . . .

- Visit `https://developer.android.com/distribute/best-practices/launch/launch-checklist` to make sure that you're ready for your app's big rollout.

Publishing Elsewhere

Google's Play Store isn't the only game in town. (It's a very important game, but it's not the only game.) You can also publish on the Amazon Appstore, on several independent websites, or on your own website.

The Amazon Appstore

This section has a few notes about publishing on Amazon Appstore. The steps for publishing with Amazon resemble the steps for publishing with Google. Publishing on Amazon's Appstore is less expensive than publishing on Google's Play Store (if you call not paying a one-time $25 developer fee "less expensive"). The Amazon Developer Portal pages look a bit different from the Google Play Console pages, but the basic ideas are almost all the same. Amazon's focus is primarily on tablets and Fire TV, but the store lists apps for phones as well.

Digital rights management

When you publish an app, you have the option of applying Amazon's *digital rights management (DRM)* to your app. This is the Amazon equivalent of Google's Licensing Verification Library. Like the DRM for Amazon Kindle books, the Appstore's DRM electronically grants permission to run each app on a device-by-device basis. And like any other scheme for managing users' privileges, the Appstore's DRM inspires vast waves of controversy in blogs and online forums.

Amazon doesn't publish gobs of information about the workings of its DRM scheme. But one thing is clear: Without digital rights management, any user can run your application. With DRM, a user can replace his or her device and, by logging on to the new device as the same Amazon user, have access to his or her rightfully purchased apps. Users can run paid apps without having an Internet connection because when a user buys an app, the user receives an offline token for that app. There's no doubt about it: When you publish a paid app, DRM is the way to go.

Amazon answers some questions about DRM in a blog post with the following unwieldy URL: `https://developer.amazon.com/public/community/post/Tx16GPJPAW8IKLC/Amazon-Appstore-Digital-Rights-Management-simplifies-life-for-developers-and-cus`. For reference, you can also check `https://developer.amazon.com/docs/app-submission/understanding-submission.html#about_drm`.

A few other differences

Amazon's graphic assets requirements are different from Google's. The image sizes are different, and the number of images that you must submit are different. Fortunately, when you're submitting your app and you encounter these differences, you can save your Developer Portal work, set the Developer Portal aside, and create more images. You can find Amazon's image requirements at `https://developer.amazon.com/docs/app-submission/asset-guidelines.html`.

Amazon's app-signing procedure is a bit different from Google's. By default, Amazon applies its own certificate to each app published on the Amazon Appstore. The certificate is unique to your account. But otherwise, it's a boilerplate certificate.

Then there's the optional SKU. When you submit an app, Amazon's Developer Portal lets you supply a SKU. The acronym *SKU* stands for *Stock Keeping Unit*. It's a way that you, the seller, keep track of each kind of thing that you sell. For example, imagine that you sell only two kinds of shirts: green ones and blue ones. When the customer buys a shirt, the only thing the customer decides is whether to buy a green shirt or a blue shirt. Then you might assign SKU number 000001 to your green shirts and 000002 to your blue shirts. It's up to you. Instead of 000001 and 000002, you might assign 23987823 to your green shirts and 9272 to your blue shirts. Anyway, when you submit an app, you can create your own SKU number for that app.

TIP

For a nice summary of the Amazon Appstore's guidelines and recommendations, visit `https://developer.amazon.com/docs/app-submission/faq-submission.html`.

Other venues

Some of the lesser known Android app websites offer apps that consumers can't get through Google Play or Amazon Appstore. In addition, many sites offer reviews, ratings, and links to the Google and Amazon stores. You can search for these sites yourself, or you can find lists of such sites. To get started, visit Android Authority (`https://www.androidauthority.com/best-app-stores-936652/`) and Joy of Android (`http://joyofandroid.com/android-app-store-alternatives`).

Sites differ from one another in several ways. Does the site specialize in any particular kind of app? Is the site linked to a particular brand of phone? Are the site's reviews more informative than those of other sites? Does the site vet its apps? Is the site's interface easy to use? And here's a big one: How does a user install one of the site's apps?

Before there were app stores, there were websites with files that you could download and install. Installing meant clicking an icon, issuing some commands, or doing other things. That model is still alive in the desktop/laptop world. But for mobile devices, for which installation procedures can be cumbersome, the one-stop app store model dominates.

Some Android app sites still use the download-and-install-it-yourself model. For a patient (or a truly determined) consumer, the install-it-yourself model is okay. But most mobile-device owners are accustomed to the one-step app store installation process. Besides, some mobile service providers put up roadblocks to keep users from installing unrecognized apps. On many phones, the user has to dig into the Settings screen to enable installation of apps from unknown sources. On some phones, that Settings option is either hidden or unavailable.

For users who know and trust your work, there's always one oft-forgotten alternative. Post a link to your app's APK file on your own website. Invite users to visit the page with their mobile phones' browsers and download the APK file. After downloading the file, the user can click the download notification to have Android install your app.

Here's one thing to consider. To preload the Google Play Store on a device, the device manufacturer must obtain Google's approval. The approval comes in the form of a certification, which asserts that the device and its software meet certain compatibility standards. Because of the expense in meeting the standards or in obtaining certification, some device manufacturers don't bother to apply. Their devices don't have the Play Store preloaded. Many of these devices have alternative app stores preloaded on their home screens but the Play Store app is conspicuously absent. Some users find workarounds and manage to install the Play Store app, but many users rely on apps from other sources. To reach these users, you have to find alternative publishing routes. (The percentage of users who live in this uncertified world could be very small, or it could be quite large. The stats aren't readily available. One way or another, these people deserve to have access to your app.)

» Not charging for your app (if that's your thing)

» Increasing your app's downloads

Chapter 2

Monetizing and Marketing Your App

The *Honeymooners* television series aired from 1955 to 1956 on the CBS television network in the United States. Comedian Jackie Gleason played Ralph Kramden, a bus driver living in a small Brooklyn, New York, apartment with his wife, Alice. (In earlier sketches, actress Pert Kelton had played the role of Alice. But Kelton was blacklisted by McCarthy's House Committee on Un-American Activities, so actress Audrey Meadows assumed the role of Alice.)

One of Ralph Kramden's fatal flaws was his affinity for get-rich-quick schemes. In a hilarious *Honeymooners* episode, Ralph and his buddy Ed Norton (played by Art Carney) did a live television infomercial for their Handy Housewife Helper gadgets. Ralph's sudden stage fright made him stumble and shake instead of effectively showing off his product.

While we're on the subject of getting rich quickly, we can segue seamlessly to the subject of making money from your Android app. This chapter tells you how to set a price for your app and when to offer it for free, how to handle advertising and earn revenue from it, and much more.

Choosing a Revenue Model

In the old days (whenever they were), making money was simple. You provided either a product or a service. You charged a certain amount per unit for the product (more than it cost you to acquire that unit), or you charged a certain amount per hour for the service. If you charged $10 for one widget, you charged $20 for two widgets. You didn't overthink the process because information didn't spread very quickly or very far. If you had an interesting twist on the sales of your goods or services, very few people would know about it.

Along came the phenomenon known as advertising. The more effectively you advertised, the more products or services you sold. (We know it's difficult to believe, but some advertisements made false claims about the things they were selling!) There were also sales promotions. An article entitled "Sales Promotion Has an Interesting History as Well" (`https://www.zabanga.us/marketing-communications/sales-promotion-has-an-interesting-history-as-well.html`) identifies the first such promotion as a penny-off coupon. The C. W. Post Company issued the coupon for Grape Nuts cereal in 1895. No longer was the amount of money you earned strictly proportional to the number of units people wanted to buy. The amount depended on psychological factors (which you, the seller, could influence) and on variations in pricing (which you could determine).

The information age has companies whose revenue streams resemble labyrinths. One company spends millions to create software, and then gives away the software so that other companies will buy its consulting services. Another company gives away all its services but collects data on the use of those services and sells the data to other companies. Company A makes money by advertising Company B which, in turn, makes money by advertising Company A.

When you first think about profiting from your app, you might think, "Either I sell the app and make money or I give the app away for free and make no money at all." That's not the way it works. Not at all.

This section describes the many ways that you can profit from the distribution of your Android app. Unfortunately, the section doesn't contain any here's-exactly-what's-right-for-you advice. There's no single, one-size-fits-all revenue model. Many models are better for some kinds of apps and worse for other kinds of apps. Some models are best for the country you live in, but not for other countries. We can try to classify apps into certain categories based on their ideal revenue models, but the boundaries between categories are thin, and the criteria for placing apps' categories are subtle. You have to think about your own app and decide which model (or which combination of models) is best for you.

Charging for your app

You can set a price for your app. If you publish on Google's Play Store, you pay a 30 percent commission. That's not bad considering that Google has paid $80 billion to app developers to date (see `https://www.androidpolice.com/2020/02/03/google-play-has-paid-out-developers-over-80-billion-to-date/`). If you decide to charge for your app, what price should you set? The following sections offer you some advice.

TRIPLING DOWN

Many developers today create dual versions of their apps for both Android and iOS. You may end up being one of them. As the article entitled "iOS App Store vs. Google Play Store" at `https://www.lifewire.com/ios-app-store-vs-google-play-store-for-app-developers-2373130` explains, the two venues are quite different, so you need to think about how to make one app work in both if you go this route.

Because the iOS App Store approval process is slow, cumbersome, and possibly gruesome, the Google Play Store route makes more sense for that experimental app. However, as expressed by the article "Top Apple's App Store developers are earning 64% more than Google Play's" (`https://macdailynews.com/2019/06/18/top-apples-app-store-developers-are-earning-64-more-than-google-plays/`), your chances of earning a good living from your app are better with the iOS App Store. The question becomes one of whether you truly have the makings of a top developer, or is your app nice, but not that nice?

The strategies for making money constantly evolve, so you should keep looking for new ways of doing things. Consider this article: "Tinder is now bypassing the Play Store on Android to avoid Google's 30 percent cut" (`https://www.theverge.com/2019/7/19/20701256/tinder-google-play-store-android-bypass-30-percent-cut-avoid-self-install`). Epic took the same route for its *Fortnite* game (`https://www.theverge.com/2018/8/3/17645982/epic-games-fortnite-android-version-bypass-google-play-store`). It's not hard to imagine that Google is already considering methods of making this problem go away so that it can continue to grab 30 percent of the revenues.

Whether you use one of these approaches alone or decide to go all out and triple down is entirely up to you. The point is to have a strategy that ultimately results in sales that will keep you afloat as you create new, amazing apps.

Consider the competition, including the free competition

Check other apps with functionality that's similar to your app. Look at the prices for those apps. Ask yourself where your app fits in. Does your app have more features? Does your app present a smoother user experience? If so, you can charge a bit more. If not, you had better lower your asking price. If you find free apps that do what your app does, ask yourself why a user would choose your paid alternative.

Use psychological pricing

Studies have shown that, as far as consumers are concerned, whole numbers aren't equidistant from one another. In a consumer's mind, the price $0.99 is much less than the price $1.00. In the United States, we can't remember ever seeing a gasoline price that didn't end in nine-tenths of a cent per gallon. This phenomenon, which sets prices at a bit less than a round number, is known as *odd pricing.*

Odd pricing is just one form of *psychological pricing.* Another psychological pricing principle is that users don't like spending amounts that seem to be strange or arbitrary. What do you think if you're asked to pay $1.04 for something? Why are you being asked to pay four extra cents?

Vary your price

On Google Play Store, you can't turn a free app into a paid app. Some vendors offer a free version and a separate, paid version. Usually, the free version has ads and the paid version doesn't. The paid version is definitely separate, though. With a paid app, you can increase or decrease the price as needed to meet market demand.

There are two competing strategies for evolving your pricing, and you might want to use a combination of these strategies:

- **Start high; eventually go lower.** If your app has little or no competition, you can start high. Attract users who think of themselves as high rollers, and get the highest price from these users that you can get.

  As a variation on this strategy, consider premium pricing. With *premium pricing,* you intentionally set a high price in order to convince users that you have a high-quality app. (Of course, if you try this trick, you had better not disappoint your users. You must maintain the perception of high quality. If your app is truly a high-quality app, you have a leg up.)

  If you start with a high price, your sales eventually slow down. This decrease can happen because you've found all the people who are willing to pay the higher price, or because other developers have started undercutting your price. One way or another, you can lower your price.

And then, there's the competing strategy . . .

» **Start low; eventually go higher.** Start by undercutting the competition. Then, when you've developed a good reputation, raise the price of your app.

If your app is popular (so popular that people might notice a change in price), you should consider the timing of your change. Decrease the price when the change will be noticed. (For example, if your app has a seasonal aspect, lower the price very conspicuously as that season's purchases rev up.) Increase the price in small increments when users are least likely to notice. Alternatively, you can coordinate price changes with other changes. You can increase the price when you release a new version with new features. Or, when you increase the price of one of your apps, you can announce loudly that you're decreasing the price of another app.

REMEMBER

Some people will never buy your app; instead, they'll do everything in their power to steal it from you. For one thing, there are all sorts of alternatives to buying from the Google App Store (see `https://www.digitbin.com/alternatives-play-store-paid-apps-free/` and `https://whatsupandroid.com/google-play-store-alternatives/`). People also find articles such as "How can I download paid apps for free on the Google Play Store?" at `https://www.quora.com/How-can-I-download-paid-apps-for-free-on-the-Google-Play-Store` that describe how to circumvent the system. If you price your app too high, more people will likely want to steal it rather than pay for it. Often, pricing comes down to figuring out what people think is fair, which can be really tough to determine because most people aren't talking. Just in case you're wondering, people even have licit ways to get your app for free (despite its being a paid app), as described in "How to Get Paid Apps for Free from Google Play Store Legitimately" at `https://www.guidingtech.com/get-paid-apps-free-google-play-store-legitimately/`.

Look for statistics and other hard data

A chart posted at `www.appbrain.com/stats/free-and-paid-android-applications` indicates that, on Google Play Store, about half of all free apps have fewer than 500 downloads. Compare this with the paid apps: Between 80 percent and 90 percent of all paid apps have fewer than 500 downloads. Interestingly, for paid apps, these percentages don't vary directly in proportion to price.

» For apps priced less than one dollar *and* for apps priced more than ten dollars, about 90 percent have fewer than 500 downloads.

» For apps in the middle (apps priced between $2.50 and $5.00), the percentage of apps with fewer than 500 downloads drops to a more comfortable 80 percent.

WARNING

PROMOTIONAL PRICING

Promotional pricing means temporarily lowering your price in order to attract more users. You'd like users to pay the higher price. But if they don't buy at the higher price, they might buy at the lower price. What's more, a temporary drop in price might be enough to attract lots of new users, even if it's a drop from an unreasonably high price to a slightly less unreasonable price. The Google Play Store offers a promotional price setup based on a promo code the user enters when buying the app in the store. You can read about this strategy at `https://developer.android.com/google/play/billing/billing_promo`.

The trick with promotional pricing is to do it at the right time and with the right price. If you lower your price too frequently or for a long period of time, users start thinking of the promotional price as the "real" price. They lose all interest in the regularly posted price. If the discounted price is too close to the regular price, users don't see much of an advantage in rushing to buy. (Think of the penny-off coupon in the 1895 Grape Nuts cereal promotion mentioned at the start of this chapter. Would you get in your time machine to take advantage of that one?)

If the discounted price is too low, you might earn less during the promotion than you spend to maintain your app. On a temporary basis, earning less might be okay. But if the promotion doesn't help to attract buyers at the regular price, it's not okay.

When you offer a promotion, avoid any taunting of users who purchased the app at the regular price. If you can avoid advertising the promotion to those users, do so. Consider offering something extra to your existing paid users (especially the ones who purchased your app very recently).

Some countries have laws governing the use of promotional pricing. Your app will probably be offered for sale in these countries, so check the laws before you go crazy with promotional pricing. Fortunately, if your promotion is through the Google Play Store, Google will help ensure that you meet the requirements of other countries.

Some aspect of psychological pricing operates favorably in the \$2.50 to \$5.00 range. You might not understand why this happens (and in fact, we don't know why it happens). Even so, the fact of a sweet spot that occurs between \$2.50 and \$5.00 is worth noting.

One way or another, it never hurts to search for statistics. Trends change, so look for pages that are updated frequently. Be skeptical of facts and figures from years gone by.

When you look for hard data, lots of good things happen. At best, you learn that your preconceived notions about app pricing are wrong and that you should modify your pricing strategy. At the very least, you become aware that what you intend to do isn't backed up by the facts. So you keep doing what you intend to do, but you do it with your eyes wide open.

TIP

Search the web for information about *pricing strategies*. You'll find a lot of good reading there. If you want a one-stop shopping-stats page, pay a visit to `https://quoracreative.com/article/mobile-marketing-statistics`.

Offering an extended free trial

Google Play buyers can return an app within two hours for a full refund. If you want the trial period to last longer, you have to outfit your app. One way to do it is to have the app record the time when it was first launched and compare this to the current system time. Of course, saving this information in `SharedPreferences` isn't foolproof. A user with some programming skill can hack the scheme and can share this hack with others. (After your app has been hacked, there's no going back. You can't track down all sources of illicit information and stop them in their tracks. Bad information spreads very quickly. No matter what you do, a tip about hacking your app will be available online forever.)

Instead of storing times and dates on the user's device, you can send this information to a server along with the device's identification number. Have the app check that server regularly. Like the `SharedPreferences` scheme, this server-based scheme isn't foolproof. But storing times and dates on a server is harder to crack than storing information on the user's device.

TECHNICAL STUFF

On a phone, you get the device's identification number by calling the `TelephonyManager` class's `getDeviceId` method. For a device that's not a phone, you can ask for the `Settings.Secure.ANDROID_ID` field.

Another way to implement a multiple-day trial period is to create two apps with two different licensing arrangements. The free trial app's license expires in 30 days. But as the trial app breathes its dying breath, it reminds the user to visit the Play Store and purchase the paid app.

If you don't like maintaining two separate apps, you can cut the cake in a different place. Create one app that implements both the trial version and the full version. Distribute this app freely. But as part of this dual-version app's logic, have the app check the user's device for the presence of a second, paid app. The second app does nothing except either exist or not exist on a user's device. If the second app exists, the dual-version app behaves like the full version. But if the second app doesn't exist, the dual-version app behaves like the trial version.

One way or another, the Play Store's app licensing tools are more reliable than most home-grown date-checking techniques. Using licensing to police the trial period is a good idea. For a few words on the Play Store's app licensing tricks, see Chapter 1 in this minibook.

Freemium apps

A mobile app with a paid-only revenue model is rare indeed. By one count, there were ten times as many free apps as paid apps in 2017. Statista can tell you all about downloaded apps at `www.statista.com/statistics/241587/number-of-free-mobile-app-downloads-worldwide` and `www.statista.com/statistics/241589/number-of-paid-mobile-app-downloads-worldwide`. (Statista is a paid service that you can view for free by going through a sign-in process. Simply click the View for Free link.) You may also find the statistics on the Business of Apps site at `https://www.businessofapps.com/data/app-statistics/` helpful.

In the "freemium" revenue model (no, this isn't a made up word; check out `https://www.investopedia.com/terms/f/freemium.asp`), one useful version of your app serves as advertising for an even more useful version. This form of advertising has several advantages over more traditional advertising modes:

- **The advertising is well-targeted.** People who install your free version are potential buyers for your paid version.
- **It directly demonstrates your app's benefits.** Instead of reading or hearing about your app, users experience your app.
- **It's repetitive without being annoying.** A potential customer probably uses the free version on a regular basis.
- **It can be inexpensive.** You incur an expense when you create the app, and you have to create the app anyway. But after you've published the app, the marginal cost of each free download is almost nothing. (This assertion assumes that you don't offer services for each active user. Yes, the free users might find bugs, and fixing the bugs takes your time and effort. But the effort you spend fixing these bugs doesn't count as an advertising expense. You'd be fixing these bugs no matter who found them.)
- **It enhances your reputation.** This one is a "biggie." With conventional advertising, you can come off as a snake oil salesman. But with a free version of your app, you're a benevolent developer (a benevolent developer who might occasionally ask for well-deserved remuneration). Think back to the last few times you upgraded from free to premium. For many people, it wasn't because they needed the enhanced features. Instead it was because, through repeated use of the app, they had formed a certain respect for the originator.

As with several other revenue models, the main question is, "How much?" In the freemium model, which parts of your app do you give away for free? Which parts do you keep for the paid version? As usual, there's no prepackaged answer. But here are some general strategies:

- **Divide your users into two categories — the high rollers and the not-so-high rollers.** The high rollers might be the corporate users; the others are individuals. The high rollers need premium features and have the resources to pay for those features. The others don't. Which features of your app appeal primarily to the high rollers? Put those features in the premium version.
- **If you don't incur a cost each time someone uses a particular feature, give that feature away for free. If you incur an ongoing cost, charge for that feature.** An app on a phone or tablet can do only so much work. Maybe, to implement certain features, your app ships work out to a server. Access to the server costs money, and the amount of money depends on the workload. The more people use these costly features, the more revenue you must have. (Otherwise, you'll go broke.) So tie the price of the app to the use of these features. The app's premium version includes these costly features; the app's free version doesn't.
- **If volume usage is relevant for your app, create a soft paywall.** A *hard paywall* is an all-or-nothing restriction on the use of a resource. But with a *soft paywall,* users get 500 whachamacallits for free each month. Users who need more than 500 whachamacallits each month buy a recurring subscription or additional groups of items. You can change the number when you see the need. But when you do, be aware of the impression you make on your existing users (both the free users and the paid users). For some good reading about recurring subscriptions, see the "Subscription pricing" section, later in this chapter.
- **Advertise or nag in the free version.** If the previous approaches are like carrots, this approach is like a stick. With this approach, you entice users to pay for your app by putting something undesirable in the free version. Unfortunately, Android has no `emitUnpleasantOdor` method. So, for the undesirable feature, most developers advertise or nag.

  Nagging involves displaying a pop-up alert box reminding the user to buy the retail version. You decide how often you want the pop-up to appear, and what the user must do to dismiss it.

  The advertising option has a few advantages over the nagging option. For one thing, advertising can be unobtrusive. (Who ever heard of unobtrusive nagging?) When advertising is unobtrusive, users tend not to associate it with the app or with the developer. So, with advertising, your image remains largely untarnished. And don't forget that advertising can bring you some revenue while you wait for users to purchase your app's full version.

TIP

When using the advertising option, rotate the ads; also, make them unobjectionable. If you want the user to click the ad, make sure it's something that the app user will want. Having a variety of advertisements might actually interest the user. Some people might keep the free version of the app just to get the ads!

- **(Not recommended) In the free app, include only enough functionality to demonstrate the paid app's usefulness.** Apps that involve saving data tend to use this strategy. With the free version, you put the app through its paces. You examine the results to see how effectively the app does its job, but you can't save the results. The user is disappointed because, in the final analysis, the free app is nothing but a tease. (A less reprehensible alternative is to provide enough storage capacity for one analysis or one file — enough to save something, but not enough for someone to conduct business.)

  With this approach, you undermine some of the freemium model's advantages. For one thing, you lose the repetition advantage. A potential user tries your app once to find out whether it's worth buying. Months later, when the need for your app arises in a more serious context, the user has forgotten about your app and finds another app in its place.

  More important, this approach ignores the benefits of customer loyalty. Instead of impressing users with your generosity, you annoy users with your stinginess. You lead a user to the brink of success. But then, at the last minute, you confront the user with a mean-spirited roadblock. Whether you think of your app this way or not isn't relevant. What's relevant is that users feel this way.

  If you have a killer app, and all you need to do is assure users that your app can perform its supposedly herculean tasks, this approach is for you. Otherwise, you should avoid using it.

For most apps, the percentage of free-version users who become paid-version users is in the single digits. But that's okay, because free users aren't "deadbeat" users. Free users form an important part of your marketing ecosystem. They help spread the word about your app. If your app has any social aspects, the more users you have (free or paid), the better. And if anyone checks your app's usage statistics, free users count. So, by all means, give the free users access to your app's essential features.

Selling things with your app

You may want to add the ability to sell things with your app. To set up in-app billing, you make additions to your app's code. You create a service, a broadcast receiver, an AIDL file, and some other stuff. You add a permission in the app's `AndroidManifest.xml` file:

```
<uses-permission
android:name="com.android.vending.BILLING"/>
```

On Google's Developer Console, you visit the in-app billing pages. You select the kind of billing you want for your app.

TIP

For help with getting to the Play Store's Developer Console, refer to Chapter 1 in this minibook.

- **Managed product:** The Play Store manages this one-time sale.
- **Unmanaged product:** You manage this sale.
- **Subscription:** The Play Store manages this recurring sale. (See the next section.)

In the Developer Console, you give the product a name (a *title*). You enter a description and specify the price. You can accept the default conversions into other countries' prices, or you can name your own local prices.

The Play Store can manage the billing for your product, but the Play Store doesn't deliver content. Delivery of the purchased content is up to you. For some of the gory details about in-app billing, visit `https://developer.android.com/google/play/billing/billing_library_overview`.

GO GLOBAL

While you're developing an app, you're worried about the user interface, the layout, and the code logic. Translating the app into other languages might not be foremost in your thoughts. But research shows that attention to international markets pays off. For example, the article at `https://sensortower.com/blog/app-revenue-and-downloads-1h-2019` tells you about the 15 percent increase in worldwide app sales year over year. The article at `https://sensortower.com/blog/sensor-tower-app-market-forecast-2023` shows the growth in sales by region, and it doesn't take long to notice that U.S. sales are being eclipsed by those in other regions. The Google Play Store sales will increase 136 percent in the U.S. by 2023. In the same time frame, sales will increase 196 percent in Europe and a whopping 408 percent in South America.

When you *localize* an app, you translate the app's text into the user's native language. Localization is important, but in today's market, users expect more. An app's characters should look and dress like regional characters. Characters should act in a way that

(continued)

(continued)

matches local customs. The game's actions should even be tailored to regional styles of play. For example, while users in the United States tend to play for long periods of time, users in Asia play in short bursts, taking time out to do other things between intervals of play. These and other subtle considerations go beyond localization and involve the broader issue of *culturalization.*

When you publish an app, you provide the app's title, a short description of the app, and a long description. You can purchase translations for these entries, you can add your own translations, or you can ignore the translations problem. Research shows that the third alternative — ignoring the issue — is a bad idea. The sales for apps with localized Play Store listings are six times those of apps without localized listings.

When you reach the pricing page, you name your price. Imagine entering USD 0.99 (almost one U.S. dollar). You do this because you remember our advice about odd pricing. (Refer to the "Use psychological pricing" section, earlier in this chapter.) You also click the Play Store's Auto-Convert Prices Now button. The Play Store converts your price in local currencies for the 130+ countries where your app will be sold. The price in Japan is set to JPY 118. For Columbia, the price is COP 2,428. These numbers violate the rule about avoiding prices that seem strange or arbitrary.

In the United States, users don't stop to think about spending $0.99 for an app. In the consumer's mind, $0.99 is an easy "throwaway" amount. Every country has its own throwaway price, but that price might not be the result of mechanically converting $0.99 in the country's local currency. The folks at Google tested the throwaway theory when they varied apps' prices by only a few yen in the Japanese market. They found that, at a certain threshold amount, lowering the price by one or two yen caused a doubling in sales. The moral of this story is, pay careful attention to local pricing. In the Play Store's Developer Console, you can click Auto-Convert Prices Now and be done with it. But you can set the price manually for at least 65 countries, and doing so might pay off nicely.

Customization for the global market doesn't end with app pricing. You might even modify your business model from country to country. In-app purchases and subscriptions work better in some countries than in others. And the use of certain payment methods varies from one country to another. For example, in the United States, the credit card is king. But in India there are only three credit cards for every 100 people (`https://www.thehindubusinessline.com/money-and-banking/indias-credit-card-boom-faces-threat-from-payment-apps/article30128957.ece`). India represents a huge growth-potential country. Japan's users like direct carrier billing, and Germany is big on using PayPal. In some countries, gift cards are the best way to go.

When you market your app, think carefully about the international market. Think about it at every step in the development, publishing, and marketing process.

Subscription pricing

Some apps require care and feeding when they run. They consume data that needs to be updated periodically, or they consume services that you must provide. For apps of this kind, subscriptions might be appropriate.

A subscription charges the user repeatedly. As an app's developer, you get to choose what "repeatedly" means. The options are monthly, yearly, and seasonal. (The seasonal option is like the yearly option, except that renewal occurs only during a certain part of the year — a part that you specify with start and end dates.)

If your app's content requires regular refreshing, the subscription model is worth your consideration. You can build up a steady income flow, and that's worth a lot.

REMEMBER

Subscription pricing works only if your content requires it. Some apps have artificially imposed subscription policies (having the app self-destruct after a certain period of time). Apps of this kind work well for big business clients, but they have little appeal for individual users. For more information on subscription billing through the Play Store, visit `https://developer.android.com/google/play/billing/billing_subscriptions.html`.

Earning revenue from advertising

There was probably a time when you had to jump through hoops before you could display ads inside your app. You'd find people who wanted to advertise their goods or services, write code to display their ads, strike up an agreement on the price for your advertising, and so on. Nowadays, displaying ads isn't difficult at all. The process is like a smooth-running assembly line.

This section outlines the steps you need to take to display ads in your app. We can't provide much detail because the details change frequently. Instead, this section's outline describes what you can expect to do when you dive into the advertising game. Google's AdMob (`https://admob.google.com/home/`) facility handles all the nitty-gritty details, and the AdMob web pages guide you through every step of the process.

Here are the basics of the steps you take:

1. **Visit** `https://apps.admob.com/signup/`.
2. **Sign in with a Google account.**

   You can use the same account that you use when you sign in to the Play Store's Developer Console.

3. **Enter the required information about yourself.**

   Don't worry. It's not too much information.

4. **Click a Monetize New App button, or something like that.**

   You see a page where you enter the name of your app. AdMob finds your app on the Play Store.

5. **Enter some information about the ads that you want to display.**

   How do you want the ads to appear? The choices are banner or interstitial:

   - **A *banner* ad appears as a small band somewhere on the app's screen.** A banner ad can appear or disappear any time during the run of your app.
   - **An *interstitial* ad takes up a large part of the device's screen.** An interstitial ad shows up only when the user won't be terribly annoyed by the ad's appearance. For example, if your app is a game, you might code your app so that an interstitial ad appears only between rounds.

   If you're familiar with time/space trade-offs, you'll recognize where the two types of ads fit in. A banner ad consumes very little space but can appear almost anytime. An interstitial ad consumes less time in order to gain some space.

   In this step, you also specify the refresh rate for ads, and some other things.

TIP

   The *refresh rate* is the amount of time that each ad remains on the user's screen (before being replaced by another ad). Research shows that a rate of 60 seconds or longer works best.

   At some point, the web page displays an *ad unit ID*. This ad unit ID number goes into your app's code. When a user runs your app, the app sends this ID number to the AdMob servers. The more the AdMob servers receive your ID, the more money you earn.

6. **Make a note of your ad unit ID.**

   Meanwhile, back on your development computer . . .

7. **Use the Android SDK Manager to install the Google Repository.**

   You'll find the Google Repository entry in the Android SDK Manager's Extras category.

8. **Add stuff to your project's files.**

   Here are a few of the things you do:

   - **Put your ad unit ID in the `strings.xml` file.** Doing so identifies your app so that you can earn money for displaying ads.

- **Put a** `com.google.android.gms.ads.AdView` **element in your activity's layout.** This element can display ads.
- **Add code to your app's activity.** The code loads ads into your layout's `AdView` widget. For a banner ad with AdMob, the code is pretty simple:

```
AdView adView = (AdView) findViewById(R.id.adView);
AdRequest = new AdRequest.Builder().build();
adView.loadAd(adRequest);
```

Visit `https://developers.google.com/mobile-ads-sdk/docs/admob/android/quick-start` for all the details.

When your app goes live, the amount that you earn varies from one advertiser to the next. In most cases, the amount hangs on a "cost per something or other" measure. Here are a few possibilities:

- **Cost per click (CPC):** Your payment depends on the number of users who click the ad in your app.
- **Cost per thousand impressions (CPM):** An *impression* is the appearance of an ad on a user's screen. A single impression isn't very impressive, but for every thousand ads that appear, you get paid.
- **Cost per action (CPA):** You earn money whenever a user performs a certain action. What constitutes an action depends on the advertiser. Examples of actions are clicks, sales, and registrations.

One way or another, advertising is a relatively low-maintenance way to earn some money for publishing your app.

Variations on in-app advertising

Your app is a place where others can advertise. Given that fact, you have dozens of ways to tweak the advertising model. If your app complements an existing company's business, get the company to sponsor your app. You can meld references to the company's products and services into your app's interface. If you do it tastefully, users don't feel that they're being pressured. (This isn't a new idea. In the earliest days of U.S. television, shows integrated ads into their regular scripts. George and Gracie would move seamlessly from a kitchen comedy routine to a minute-long discussion of Carnation Evaporated Milk.)

Incentivized advertising is another option. With this option, advertisers reward users who perform certain actions within your app. For example, your app stores and displays recipes. For every ten recipes that the user completes, the app rewards the user with a coupon for cooking utensils. The advertiser gets the business, the user gets the goods, you get the revenue, and your app gets used. Everyone wins.

Both sponsorship and incentivized advertising are very well targeted. You're not promoting automobiles for 10-year-olds or weight-lifting equipment for people with weak backs. Instead, you're riding a wave. It's a synergetic wave between your app's theme and a company's wares.

Donationware

If you're not trying to earn a fortune but you'd like some spare change from your most loyal users, try this strategy. Use in-app billing, as described in the "Selling things with your app" section, earlier in this chapter. But instead of delivering a product, deliver a "thank you."

The rate of return will be very small. But many of us have done some donating for our favorite apps. So for all the apps that have ever been published, the return rate isn't zero.

Offering your app for free

You might argue against the decision to put this "absolutely free" subsection inside the "Choosing a Revenue Model" section. But for a novice developer, "absolutely free" is a choice worth considering. For one thing, a free app attracts more users than a paid app. With your free app, you can start building your reputation among users. This reputation might be for you as a developer, or for the apps in your ongoing development plans. Besides, when you publish your first app, you learn a lot about the process. That's worth something even if it's not monetary.

Revenue or no revenue, an immeasurable benefit is derived from giving freely to the community. When you think about publishing apps, don't forget about giving.

Getting paid to develop apps for others

Don't forget about this option. Find a local business or a big company. Write code or design user interfaces. Create the artwork for apps. Do what you do best and leave the rest to the business moguls.

Marketing Your Application

Imagine trying to find your friend at a gathering that has one million attendees. It wouldn't be easy. Take the scenario one step further. You don't know the person. You're looking for anyone with gray hair and blue eyes who weighs less than 150 pounds. What are your chances of finding this particular person?

Now imagine that you're not at a social gathering. You're surfing on Google's Play Store, and the Play Store has more than a million apps. You narrow your search to find a trivia quiz game. At first, the Play Store displays the top dozen trivia quiz games, so newly posted games aren't included. You widen the search by clicking the page's See More button. After the Play Store displays its first 300 trivia quiz apps, you stop clicking the See More button. What are the chances that you'll land on Super Novice's new app?

These stories aren't meant to discourage you. They're meant to remind you that your app doesn't market itself. Here are some ways for you to market your app:

- **Create a website.** Use search engine optimization (SEO) techniques to get your site noticed.
- **Contact the press.** This suggestion includes traditional journalists as well as reviewers and bloggers. The worst they can say is "I'm not interested in writing about this." If they offer to write about your app for a fee, you can always say no.
- **Use social media.** You know the sites: Facebook, Twitter, Pinterest, Instagram. Post regularly to build a following.
- **Add social features to your app.** Nothing says "Try this app" like a post made directly from the app. You can also build loyalty by having users post to one another within the app.
- **Create your own blog or podcast.** This requires work, but it can pay off big time.
- **Pay for advertising.** Through AdMob, you can have other apps display ads for your app. If you don't mind spending some money, you can set up a regular paid ad campaign. But you can advertise for free in a house ad campaign. When you allocate advertising space to promote your own wares, you're creating a *house ad*. AdMob doesn't charge for this kind of advertising. You create a house ad to promote one of your apps within another of your apps. Alternatively, by agreement with another developer, you can advertise your app in the other developer's app (and vice versa).

- **Update your app regularly (as a marketing strategy).** An update can call attention to your app. A study by BI Intelligence (`www.businessinsider.com/app-update-strategy-and-statistics-2015-1`) found a positive correlation between the frequency of updates and user's ratings. That's good news.
- **Get help from Google's Play Store.** The Play Store has a page with the title "Optimization Tips." This page analyzes your app and lists things that you've done (and haven't done) to enhance your app's visibility. For example, with one of your apps, the page may remind you to design for tablets. It tells you to add custom drawables for tablet screen densities, and upload at least one screenshot for 7-inch and 10-inch tablets. Google's research shows that apps customized for tablets monetize ten times as much as apps designed with only phones in mind. (In addition to the Google Play Store, you should seek out articles such as the one at `https://www.apptamin.com/blog/optimize-play-store-app/`.)

Brick Breaker Master: An App Marketing Case Study

The epistolary novel has a long and noble history. In Rousseau's *Julie*, or *The New Heloise*, two lovers pass letters back and forth. Goethe's *The Sorrows of Young Werther* is a collection of letters from Werther to his friend William. Shelly's *Frankenstein* includes a sea captain's letters. More recently, such notables as Stephen King, Gary Shteyngart, and Daniel Handler (writing as Lemony Snicket) have featured diaries, news articles, and letters written by their novels' characters.

As far as we know, this section is the first use of the epistolary style in a *For Dummies* book.

We can't claim full credit for this accomplishment. The interchange that's documented here, which first appeared in a previous edition of the book, is mostly real. It's a bunch of excerpts from an email conversation between Barry and a reader. In these email messages, the reader (Daniel Levesque) does most of the heavy lifting. All Barry does is ask the right questions. Barry trimmed some paragraphs to keep it relevant, and this book's copy editor made some useful changes. Otherwise, the words that you see here are true and unadorned.

From: Daniel Levesque

To: Barry Burd

February 25, 2013

Good morning, Barry.

I'm about to finish the book *Beginning Programming with Java For Dummies.* Then I will start later this week *Java For Dummies* . . ..

From: Barry Burd

To: Daniel Levesque

February 25, 2013

Daniel,

I'm glad that you're enjoying my books. Have you noticed the last name of the project editor [Paul Levesque, from a previous edition]? (When your email arrived, I thought he was contacting me.) . . .

From: Daniel Levesque

To: Barry Burd

February 25, 2013

Yes, I saw his name when I bought the book . . ..

Many emails later . . .

From: Daniel Levesque

To: Barry Burd

August 14, 2013

Hi Barry,

A while ago, you helped me with a couple of questions when I was reading your Java and Android *For Dummies* books. After all this "study," I finally published my first game!

Many emails later . . .

From: Daniel Levesque

To: Barry Burd

June 12, 2014

Hello Barry,

I just published my second Android game of 2014: "Space Garbage!" The goal of the game is very simple: survive in space while avoiding the floating objects! . . ..

Many emails later . . .

From: Daniel Levesque

To: Barry Burd

February 1, 2015

Hi Barry,

I thought I would let you know that I just released my first game of 2015. It is my very first game using a game engine, and I am quite happy with the result. The game, Brick Breaker Master, is currently number 20 in the Google Play "Top New Paid" category!!!

Best regards,

Daniel Levesque

From: Barry Burd

To: Daniel Levesque

February 3, 2015

Daniel,

I'd love for you to send me some tips on your getting to the number 20 spot. I'm revising my *Android All-in-One* book, and I'd like to quote you in the chapter on publishing apps. Do you have any advice for up-and-coming developers?

Barry

From: Daniel Levesque

To: Barry Burd

February 4, 2015

Hi Barry,

It's very difficult to do any marketing when you have a very small team or if you work on your own. Here's what I did with Brick Breaker Master to promote installs:

- I figured out that Google uses some kind of algorithm to rank "new paid apps" and "new free apps," so I tried to generate several installs EVERY day for the first month.
- I sent a message to my 200+ LinkedIn contacts, asking them to install the game and give me a good rating (not sure how many actually did it).
- I built a new App page on Facebook and asked all my family members and friends to "share" the page with their contacts. (I figure that I probably got 50 shares through this, although the potential was more like 500.)
- I sent messages to my followers on Twitter every three days with a screenshot of one of the game levels. (I didn't tweet too often — didn't want my followers to get upset and then unfollow me.)
- I updated my website as soon as I published the game on Google Play and the Amazon Marketplace.
- I submitted a summary of the game to the top ten Android review sites with the hope that they would publish a free review. (Most of them have an automated reply saying that they receive too many requests to guarantee a review but that for $100 they will . . . you get the picture). I didn't want to spend $1,000 for ten reviews without knowing in advance what rating they would give my game! Unless you know for sure that you have a knock-out app, this approach is very risky.

I hope this will help with your chapter in the book.

Best regards,

Daniel

» Creating a custom distribution system

» Personalizing your approach

» Getting others to recognize you

Chapter 3
Creating Public Support for Your App

Chapter 2 of this minibook delves into the traditional methods of selling an app or selling services based on an app. The traditional approach doesn't always work, though. You can upload your app to Google Play Store, perform intense marketing, and still come up completely dry because no one can see you for the trees. It can make you want to walk down the center of Main Street in a clown suit sporting a sign saying, "I created an app! Buy it!" Unfortunately, given the prevalence of cute cat videos on YouTube, everyone will likely ignore you just the same. So, this chapter is about what you do when the traditional approach fails and you find yourself with an app that no one seems to want to buy.

Some of the suggestions in this chapter require a person with a special kind of outlook and interesting gifts to pull off. Not everyone is just naturally cute and talented enough to pull of something like Patreon, a service described in this chapter, or to generate the next viral upload to YouTube. However, you won't know until you try, which actually is the point of this chapter: to try something, anything, to get noticed and attract supporters. Use this chapter to gain some ideas of what you can try when seeking attention for your app.

REMEMBER

This chapter can't possibly consider every technique for getting noticed and garnering support for an app. If you find that you've been exceptionally successful with a particular approach that doesn't appear somewhere in this book and want to share it with someone, be sure to contact either John (John@JohnMuellerBooks.com) or Barry (android@allmycode.com) with your insights. Of course, we're interested in hearing about safe methods of promotion, not crazy stuff involving the Grand Canyon and tricycles.

Obtaining Support through Patreon

People often connect the idea of patronage to the arts, especially artists who are part of a group. Patrons of the arts abound — just watch the Public Broadcasting System (PBS) sometime to see how much patrons support the efforts of the public television stations. The following sections build a case for developing an app based on patronage, rather than as a packaged product (think shrink-wrapped software of the sort that you used to need for desktop systems).

Discovering that patronage isn't new

Patrons exist for all sorts of people who find it hard to earn a living doing something that is of benefit to everyone. For example, Galileo depended on the Marchese del Monte and the Grand Duke of Tuscany, Cosimo II de Medici, for support during his life as a mathematician, scientist, and inventor. The paper at `https://escholarship.org/content/qt94q0q1gq/qt94q0q1gq.pdf` describes Galileo's system of patronage in detail. This paper by Mario Biagioli is enlightening because it explores the full effect of obtaining patronage, which goes well beyond physical means in the form of monetary support. For Galileo, patronage affected his social status, focuses of learning, and a great many other aspects of life. His patrons, in turn, received social status and knowledge from having supported Galileo.

The concept of patronage need not apply simply to one person performing what will be their life's work. It could apply to a one-time event or a one-time application. For example, Farm Aid (`https://www.farmaid.org/`) provides an annual event to help farmers experiencing hard times (see `https://www.washingtonpost.com/entertainment/music/farm-aid-weaves-blues-country-rock-tapestry-at-jiffy-lube/2016/09/18/b12cd414-7db5-11e6-ad0e-ab0d12c779b1_story.html` as an example). Your app designed to help people locate assistance in the aftermath of a hurricane can certainly be patron supported, even though the app is a one-off project. You won't get people to buy such an app; you need patrons to support it.

The most interesting aspect of patronage is the work it requires of the person seeking the patronage — not the same amount of work required to earn a living and pursue interests such as art and science at the same time, but an entirely different kind of work. Galileo must have been charismatic in a manner that attracted the attention of his patrons, and such charisma is necessary today as well. When viewing modern artists who rely on a system of patronage, it becomes obvious that they have a certain something. You might have a certain something, too.

Considering crowdfunding

Modern patronage can occur in the same way as it always has: You connect with individuals who are especially well endowed financially and willing to share it for a good cause. The more common route nowadays, however, is to use *crowdfunding*, with large groups of people taking the place of a single patron and contributing through websites such as Patreon (`https://www.patreon.com/`). When you visit the Patreon site, you see a listing of the main categories of individuals who use it to help support their work. The list doesn't include Android app developers specifically, but you do find niches that can apply to apps:

- **Gaming:** `https://www.patreon.com/c/gaming`
- **Education:** `https://www.patreon.com/c/tutorials-and-education`
- **Other:** `https://www.patreon.com/explore`

Defining why you should use crowdfunding

The app store has made using the shrink-wrap model of single software sales less viable because there are so many offerings to choose from, and developers often see users go to other products rather than invest in pricey upgrades. Using the crowdfunding approach has these significant advantages:

- **Subscriptions cost less:** When a user sees a small price for an annual subscription, it's more likely that the user will continue to support the app.
- **Establishment of a relationship:** Rather than do a poor job of trying to please everyone, a developer can focus on doing a great job of pleasing a group that is actually interested in the app.
- **Cash flow:** The issue that plagues developers most is inconsistent cash flow. A crowdfunding solution provides incremental, but consistent, payments that the developer can rely upon to keep the lights on.

» **Alignment:** Because the developer focuses on fewer people who provide incremental payments, it's possible to deliver the kinds of updates patrons want at a rate that's acceptable to the patrons.

» **Stable development environment:** Creating a stable development environment enables the developer to explore functionality that would normally prove difficult or impossible to fund. For example, if enough patrons want a particular analysis feature, the developer can add it even if the feature would normally not appeal to the market as a whole.

REMEMBER

Keeping things in perspective is essential. You should use crowdfunding if it works for your app, but you must also consider these potential pitfalls:

» **Subscription fatigue:** Even if you have the most devoted and joyous group of supporters in the world, you need to continually create something interesting or the users will wonder what they're getting for their subscription. As users grow tired of their subscription, your revenue stream falls.

» **Implementation details:** Rather than a single release, you now have a Continuous Integration/Continuous Delivery (CI/CD) model that can prove difficult to implement. You can read a good overview of the process at `https://www.infoworld.com/article/3271126/what-is-cicd-continuous-integration-and-continuous-delivery-explained.html`.

Understanding the development angle

Patreon is bristling with apps of every kind. The starting point is the Patreon app (`https://play.google.com/store/apps/details?id=com.patreon.android`) that many people who rely on Patreon use to communicate with their supporters. Then there are the pages of support information that talk about interacting with various Patreon app features, such as `https://support.patreon.com/hc/en-us/articles/115005429546-Will-my-podcast-benefits-work-with-my-favorite-podcast-app-` and `https://support.patreon.com/hc/en-us/articles/115005666886-How-do-I-post-in-the-mobile-app-as-a-creator-`.

TIP

You can find a page specifically designed for Fledgling Developers at `https://www.patreon.com/fledglingdevelopers`. The goal is to create free apps without ads but *with* Patreon supporters. As you look down the page, however, you see that a great deal more is involved than simply creating apps. For example, one of the current goals at the time of this writing is to buy a new laptop for one of the members, and you can see a progress bar toward obtaining it. When you become a member, you gain access to private blog posts that aren't available to the general public, among other incentives. Here are some other groups that you might want to check out:

- **Imagination Overflow:** https://www.patreon.com/imaginationoverflow
- **Sketchware Team:** https://www.patreon.com/sketchware

DO ICONS REALLY HELP?

In reading some of the advice online about getting an app into the hands of users, you find that one of piece of advice crops up consistently but also seems counterintuitive. Apparently, a great icon makes a significant difference. At first, an icon might not seem that it should matter much. Yes, you want something professional, but investing heavily in something that doesn't add to the functionality of the app seems silly . . . until you start taking a good look around. Icons, like logos, provide a quick method of identification. A person can see the Facebook, Twitter, and other icons and immediately know what they represent. No one quite agrees on the recipe for the perfect icon (or else everyone would be doing it), but here are some guidelines to consider:

- **Detail:** Make the icon detailed enough so that it becomes easily recognizable, but not so detailed that everyone has a hard time making out the specifics.
- **Aesthetic unity:** When creating an icon or series of icons, make sure they work with the underlying app and with each other. If you use little hearts for image elements in one part of the design, you should use them in every other image element as well.
- **Recognizable:** The icon should be easy to recognize at a glance. Often this means using a transparent background. (In the "Making an icon" section of Book 3, Chapter 4, you discover the necessity of a transparent background when working with Android icons). The article "The World's 21 Most Recognized Brand Logos of All Time" (https://www.impactbnd.com/blog/most-recognized-brand-logos-identities) points out that most of these icons have a white or transparent background so that the outline of the icon shows through.

Most people don't have the skills to create a great icon, so getting someone else to do it, although expensive, is the best idea because you live with an icon long after you design it. If you truly feel inclined to create an icon, make sure to follow the advice of articles like the one at https://www.smashingmagazine.com/2016/05/easy-steps-to-better-logo-design/.

Just in case you're wondering, strong support also exists for creating apps that help other Patreon creators work with their patrons. You can find them at `https://www.patreon.com/apps`. So, you don't necessarily have to be creating the next super app; you can do something a bit more mundane.

Determining the trade-offs

How much of the crowdfunding money makes it to the developers? Currently, Patreon takes 5 percent for itself and another 5 percent for transaction fees. The remaining 90 percent actually makes it to the developers. The developers don't have to sign a contract with Patreon, so developers keep 100 percent ownership of their work and full control of their brand.

TIP

There are alternatives to Patreon, with Gumroad (`https://gumroad.com/`) being one of the top options among them. When choosing a crowdfunding provider, you need to consider precisely what the provider wants in return. Most providers need a certain percentage of what you obtain from your patrons as a starting point. Some also require contracts that require you to give up a percentage of your ownership and perhaps some control over your brand as well, so it pays to be careful in making a selection.

Developing Your Own Distribution Stream

You have an app on Google Play Store, have already set up a Patreon account, and now you're looking to do more to promote your app because it still isn't moving. The fact of the matter is that you're competing with thousands of other developers, so your chances of standing out from the crowd are slim unless you're willing to be all over the place, making it hard for anyone to ignore you for very long. The difficulty is in coming up with a strategy that works with your skill set, comes relatively naturally, and doesn't consume more time than it's worth to maintain. Plus, your efforts have to feel natural or you won't keep doing them. With all these points in mind, consider the material in the following sections to be a starting point for brainstorming your own approach.

Creating podcasts

A *podcast* is a type of presentation that many compare to radio talk shows, with a presenter discussing one focused topic in a specific time frame. A single presenter can provide podcasts in a range of topics in an episodic format. The length of a podcast varies, but articles like the one at `https://blog.pacific-content.com/`

how-long-is-the-average-podcast-episode-81cd5f8dff47 seem to indicate that podcasts are statistically about 43 minutes in length, which, oddly enough, is about the same amount of time as someone spends watching a television show. Obviously, this television show, podcast, radio talk show, or whatever you want to call it is about your app.

When you try to look for advice on creating a podcast specifically for Android users, you normally find are lists of apps that provide podcasts or techniques for building a podcast app, neither of which is helpful. Podcasts follow a variety of formats, with the most successful presented by charismatic people with a great online appearance. The least successful are those unscripted types with a mumbling, fumbling presenter whose five minutes of presentation seem more like an hour.

Allowing the viewer to see you isn't essential, but podcasts that reveal someone with a smiling face at some point during the presentation seem a lot more approachable. You should also ensure that people can actually see your app as you work with it, and you want to go through your demonstration slowly enough to allow people to follow along. Practicing the podcast before you film it is a good idea, but everyone has their own way of getting the job done.

REMEMBER

A disoriented, nonfocused set of app musings doesn't do anyone any good. Having a strict focus in your presentation is essential to being successful. Of course, trying to figure out what people want can be difficult, but you can usually find plenty to present in these topics:

- **How-to:** Step-by-step procedures to perform a specific task or perform a configuration. A how-to can help sell your app by showing the user what it can do to solve problems the user is having.
- **Common issues:** As people write in about your app, you notice certain patterns in overcoming issues that you can talk about, saving you support time and the user frustration.
- **Tips:** A set of usage tips specifically designed for a tightly focused group of users can help sell your app and give users ideas. It's often surprising how a set of good tips will get users thinking about your app in new ways, and you may suddenly find users working with your app in ways you never imagined. The point is to make the tips specific to a group as well as tightly focused.
- **App updates:** Updating your app doesn't mean that users will automatically notice the new features. In fact, the law of inertia generally dictates that the user will do everything possible not to notice the new features. Getting users to see the advantage in employing new features helps sell new copies or subscriptions, or simply grow your user base by making your app more attractive to a patron.

MONITORING INTERACTION EFFECT

Nothing will provide instant success. In fact, you may spend a lot of time and effort trying to get anyone to notice anything you're doing. However, if you show up enough times in enough places, people will begin to notice. The problem can become whether the kind of notice you attract is the notice you actually want. Unfortunately, there aren't any absolute measures to employ, but here are some ways to gauge the overall reactions that people are having to your app:

- Track likes and dislikes for the app package as a whole.
- Request feedback when interacting directly with the user.
- Consider the number of app downloads.
- Monitor server load (when an app uses server resources.)
- Look for online comments.
- Determine whether others talk about the app.

» **Community focus:** If you find that your users are especially adept at interacting with and talking about your app, you may want to use that buzz to your advantage. You can create a tightly focused podcast created from user interviews, list group/chat submissions (those messages people upload to a server and other people answer online, such as Medium.com, `https://medium.com/`, and Stack Overflow, `https://stackoverflow.com/`), or other sources to show how other users are working with your app. This sort of podcast gives your app a real-world feel.

WARNING

Creating a podcast about anything other than your app is a bad idea. The worst sort of podcasts make comparisons to the competition, saying, "We're better because . . ." You want to maintain a positive spirit and keep your focus solely on what your app can do for the user. The user community needs to make its own decision on how your app compares to others. This focus on the positive doesn't mean that you can't encourage users to provide reviews or other positive feedback about your app.

Developing YouTube videos

Finding YouTube statistics online isn't hard. Not all these statistics agree, and the statistics that look reasonably accurate are bound to change quickly. One thing, however, is certain: YouTube is incredibly popular, and ignoring this venue for promoting your app is ill advised. With this idea in mind, here are more YouTube statistics to consider (based on the amalgamation of statistics from several recent sites):

- It's the second largest search engine after Google.
- It has more than a billion users each month.
- Twenty-five percent of all content on YouTube is viewed on mobile devices.
- One billion views come from mobile devices each month.
- It appears in 56 countries.
- Seventeen percent of all Internet traffic flows through YouTube.
- Users watch six billion hours of video each month.
- YouTube content is accessed by hundreds of millions of devices.
- One hundred hours of new video is uploaded every minute.

Regardless of whether you believe all these statistics, the fact remains that you need YouTube to help promote your app because someone, somewhere, is likely to see it and like your video enough to tell others about it. If you're lucky, a good video will go viral and you won't have to worry much about promoting your app in the near future. Of course, luck goes only so far, so pursuing other venues is still a good idea.

REMEMBER

At this point, you're wondering why everyone isn't investing heavily in YouTube content. It's because, as always, there is no free lunch. (You'll likely hear this phrase more often than you'll ever want to, but it's important.) To obtain the benefits of YouTube, you must make a significant investment, as outlined here:

- The cost of producing a video, unless you do it on your own, is significantly higher than other forms of interaction, like a blog post.
- The learning curve for producing videos is quite steep, and not many people can produce a great video.
- Your video is apt to get lost on YouTube unless the right person sees it and helps make it viral.
- Making changes to a video is not nearly as easy as making edits to a blog post.
- Building a following of supporters on YouTube is about as difficult as building supporters for an app.

Even though the costs of creating a video are high and you'll need to put a great deal of effort into producing one, the benefits are definitely appealing. However, even if you produce a great video, it's relatively easy to miss the target anyway. Consider the following when putting a video together for an app:

- Keep the video short and targeted to a particular aspect of your app, such as performing a task that isn't easily demonstrated through other means. Most people use videos to present these types of content:
  - Tutorials on how to use the app
  - App interaction strategies with the larger world
  - Education on a specific topic that the app addresses
  - Demonstrations
  - Product reviews
- Make sure to tell people about your app at the end of the video and provide links to learn more about it.
- Presentation is everything in a video, so hiring actors who can provide that bright, cheery smile is a plus.
- Create a fun, memorable video because otherwise no one will watch it.
- After adding the fun, don't forget to keep the professionalism in place as well.
- Ensure that the video is actually targeted to the audience you want to reach. Generic videos seldom succeed.
- Present visual cues such as the organization logo, app icon, and other memorable visual elements as often as possible.

REMEMBER

Avoid confusing a YouTube video with a podcast. You use podcasts for more informational and detailed needs. A YouTube video is for lighter content meant to promote your app. According to Statista (`https://www.statista.com/statistics/1026923/youtube-video-category-average-length/`), the average length of a YouTube video is only 11.7 minutes, compared to around 43 minutes for a podcast. Consequently, you have far less time to make your case in a YouTube video and have to hope that your audience actually stays through the whole thing.

Employing social media

Most people recognize the value of word of mouth when it comes to making anything popular, and social media is today's word-of-mouth avenue for many people. Social media can provide an effective way to promote your app when managed correctly. In fact, 33 percent of the people who download your app will do so because someone else recommended it.

Statistics show that around 52 percent of people discover apps through their family, friends, and colleagues, and most of those conversations happen on social media today. The paper entitled "Mobile App Marketing Insights: How Consumers Really Find and Use Your Apps," at `https://think.storage.googleapis.com/docs/mobile-app-marketing-insights.pdf`, offers all sorts of interesting statistics on just how people interact with apps and how they promote them to each other, but you quickly find that social media is king in many respects with respect to promotion. Interestingly, 68 percent of the apps used daily have something to do with social needs and communication.

WARNING

Before you go off and make your first post on Facebook about your new app, however, you want to make sure that you have a separate Facebook account for your app. No one wants to hear about last year's fishing trip while trying to discover something about your app, and forcing them to do so says that you're not a professional. Your app social media account should also have a formal appearance compared to your personal account. In addition to providing a presence on the social media apps of your choice, you can also contemplate these approaches to making social media work for you:

- **Consider using paid ads.** Some social media apps, such as Facebook, make it relatively simple to provide ads.
- **Rely on influencer marketing when possible.** This marketing orientation includes choosing the right venue. For example, 80 percent of all micro-influencers rely on Instagram to post original content. Contrast this with Snapchat, which accounts for only a little less than 40 percent (most influencers use multiple content channels).
- **Create a channel for User-Generated Content (UGC).** According to the Nielsen article at `https://www.nielsen.com/us/en/press-releases/2012/nielsen-global-consumers-trust-in-earned-advertising-grows/`, 90 percent of customers will listen to peer recommendations, but only 33 percent will listen to an ad.
- **Promote your best reviews, no matter where they appear.** About 60 percent of people think that ratings and reviews are essential when deciding to download an app.
- **Use the right platform for the correct effect.** For example, Facebook encourages community building, so this is the social media venue you use to build communities of users. Instagram, on the other hand, helps users gravitate toward a well-rounded aesthetic. Twitter is great for creating the buzz that generates new users.

Answering questions

Getting on community support sites and answering questions might seem like the least likely way to generate sales along with a great way to waste a lot of time, but answering questions really does help. When you begin providing answers to user questions, the users begin to see you as a trusted source of helpful information. Also, users start to know you as a person (at least, to a noncreepy extent), which builds a personal rapport. This rapport makes users trust your app offerings as well.

REMEMBER

However, if you take this route of answering user questions, be sure to follow these guidelines:

- Answer questions only when you can be sure of providing a correct answer.
- Never offer opinions.
- Maintain strict professionalism and don't take the bait to argue with a heckler.
- Keep advertising out of your answers.
- Provide links to other resources, including your apps, when specifically asked.
- Take off-topic conversations to email.
- Include all needed resources with your answers, including graphics and code when the site supports them.
- Keep answers as short as possible without leaving out important details.

Taking the Personal Approach

Making your users feel special is important because happy users buy more products and recommend those products to friends. Most developers don't take a very personal approach because it requires a lot of time and effort. Plus, you end up hearing about all sorts of things that have nothing to do with your product in many cases. The problem has become so significant that many people now claim that reaching a human at many product-support lines is impossible. The developer would rather not deal with users at all and instead assign a robot to perform the task.

However, you aren't a successful developer with millions of users just yet (or you probably wouldn't be reading this book). One way to differentiate your app from every other app out there is to provide great support. Great support generates buzz, which is precisely what you need to build a group of loyal users who are rabid supporters of your app. The problem is that you still have constraints on your time. The following sections offer a few ideas on how you can personalize your user contact, yet continue to use your time efficiently.

Creating a blog

Blogs can work well because they feel more personal than the Frequently Asked Questions (FAQ) pages used by many organizations today. A FAQ feels cold and impersonal because it's meant to provide information without any sort of feeling. On a blog, you often see some opinion mixed with the author's personal style that looks more like an article than a FAQ.

A blog can put you in contact with people who might be interested in your app long before you actually build it. By providing updates on app progress and then reading any comments on the updates you've given, you can make small tweaks to your app before issues become major causes of user distress. The updates also build excitement for your app and can help you gain some level of investment money through prerelease purchases.

After you release your app, the blog can serve as a means for pointing to app-specific resources, such as YouTube videos. Many blog platforms natively support podcasts, so you can make the podcasts available in a venue that allows some level of monitoring on your part for potential customers. Each blog post should contain pointers to any social media you support, along with an app-specific website for additional information and downloads. In short, blog posts can act as a means to advertise all the avenues you use to support your app.

TIP

In addition to promotion, a blog can provide a written record of updates you have made and propose for the future. You can use it to help provide support for your app for those people who would prefer written support to something like a podcast. In fact, you can make some blog posts by simply cleaning up the script you use to make your podcasts or YouTube videos, so you get dual usage from a single effort.

Blogs also offer the possibility of guest posts. If you can convince someone with industry name recognition to provide a quick post, it will definitely attract attention. Of course, you can do the same thing with podcasts and YouTube videos, but a blog offers the potential of allowing the substance of the interview to sink in through the written word. The point is to stop yelling about your app yourself and get someone else to do it for a while (after all, you've become quite hoarse in your efforts).

EMPLOYING SEARCH ENGINE OPTIMIZATION (SEO)

People often rely on searches to find what they need, including a search for apps. Sometimes digging through the offerings in the Google App Store or other app store is just too cumbersome, so a potential user will conduct a search. This is where *SEO,* which is the art of making your site look better through key-word usage, comes into play. (You may also see a specialized form of SEO for apps listed as App Search Optimization, or ASO.) By making links to your product appear first, or at least high, in the search results, you improve the chances that someone will find your app. If you want to try the SEO process yourself, try the suggestions in the article at `https://thetool.io/2017/seo-for-mobile-apps`. However, SEO can be difficult, and most of us need help, which is why you might want to try one of these SEO professionals to ease your burden:

- **GummiCube:** `https://www.businessofapps.com/marketplace/gummicube/`
- **MobleDevHQ:** `https://mobiledevmemo.com/mobiledevhq/`
- **PreApps:** `https://www.businessofapps.com/marketplace/preapps/`
- **SearchMan:** `https://searchman.com/`

You may have also noticed that most sites today have an https, rather than an http, protocol. The https indicates that the site has an SSL certificate that helps guarantee a secure connection. An SSL certificate costs money, though, and some developers don't want to invest in one. Unfortunately, any idea you have of appearing near the top of any search list depends on having that https address because sites such as Google don't even consider sites with an http address, for the most part.

People also like stories, and the story of your app can prove interesting to users. When people understand the motivations and goals behind an app, they're more likely to support it. This is actually one area in which a blog has a significant advantage over other media because you can carefully hone your written version of the story to present a specific aspect of you without the usual downsides that a video presentation would incur (including voice intonations that tend to be distracting rather than helpful).

Answering your email

How you handle email can be tricky. If you choose to support email, the email should actually address the user's questions and not simply provide a form response that will tend to frustrate and infuriate your users. Nothing is worse than sending out a form email that tells the writer to visit your website where your FAQ sheet answers all questions, even though it doesn't. Making the response a no-response sender makes things worse because the user can't even write back. Here are a few tricks that you can use to make the process of answering your email faster and yet keep it personal:

- **Use form paragraphs.** If you find that users ask some questions often, you can create a form paragraph to answer that particular element of the email.
- **Rely on blog posts.** One reason to write blog posts is to provide a personal and friendly response to common user questions. If a question will consume more space to answer completely than an email can comfortably accommodate, provide a friendly reference to the blog post.
- **Create scripted fill-in-the-blank responses.** Some questions follow a pattern that readily adapts itself to a fill-in-the-blank response. The basic answer is the same in every case but the details differ, and customizing those details also customizes the email.
- **Develop a list of question-answering volunteers.** Community support works because well-informed users help users with fewer skills and less experience. To maintain this group of well-informed users, you need some sort of incentive, such as free subscriptions or access to special app features.

REMEMBER

It's essential to use humans to review the incoming emails and choose the correct response. Robots can go only so far in providing support functions. At some point, you likely need to provide a time-consuming, custom response. Keeping individual users when you first start out is essential to your success, so shortchanging this aspect of product support will mean that your app is less likely to succeed.

While you're answering the user email, make sure to take full advantage of your email response. Here are a few things to consider including with it:

- Promote your latest product and provide a link to it.
- Encourage the user to review your product online.
- Provide a link to the various resources that your organization supports.
- Detail a good reason to buy a subscription or app update.
- Make a memory (help the person remember your app by associating it with something) with a quote from a happy user or simply something of interest.

Considering App Store Alternatives

You have alternatives to selling your app in the Google Play Store. Whether these alternatives make sense depends on the app, what it can do, what you expect as an audience, and what personal abilities you can call on to promote it. For example, Amazon used to have its own play store, but now you can sell on Amazon through its regular sales channel in the Apps & Games department (`https://www.amazon.com/s?k=android&i=mobile-apps`). (What used to be termed as an app store now supports Amazon game controllers and Fire TV Voice Remote, so you couldn't get it for your tablet or smartphone.)

Often, a particular vendor will support an app store that focuses on the devices that the vendor creates. Here are some examples:

- **Huawei App Store:** `https://appstore.huawei.com/` (This particular store focuses on the Chinese market.)
- **LG SmartWorld:** `https://www.lg.com/global/lg-thinq`
- **Samsung Galaxy Store:** `https://www.samsung.com/global/galaxy/apps/galaxy-store/`

Independent app store vendors exist as well. These stores don't have the attraction of supporting Android as a whole or even a particular kind of device. However, they normally have some sort of hook that makes them highly appreciated by the community, such as being easier to search or allowing less *shovelware* (the kind of app that was poorly designed in the first place and is now mainly unsupported because no one is using it). The following table discusses various independent app store vendor offerings.

Store Name	URL	Hook
AppBrain	`https://www.appbrain.com/`	Combines an app store with a promotion site that helps you get your app into other stores as well. This site seems to focus mainly on consumer apps.
Appland	`https://www.applandinc.com/`	Combines app launches and app downloads for Android, Windows, and iOS offerings. This site seems to focus more on corporate than consumer apps.

Store Name	URL	Hook
Appolicious	`https://appolicious.com/`	Enforces extremely strict guidelines for app submission that makes it hard to get your app listed. After the app is listed, however, users have far fewer apps to wade through to find yours. Users also have higher confidence that they'll have a good experience.
Aptoide	`https://en.aptoide.com/`	Is easier to search and navigate, making apps stick out in their particular category.
F-Droid	`https://f-droid.org/en/`	Offers strong support for open source apps and flags any app commercial aspects.
Itch.io	`https://itch.io/`	Provides specific support for game apps, so locating a game based on genre is easier. The interface also supports both developers and gamers better than some other offerings.
GetJar	`https://www.getjar.com/`	Presents a simple, clutter-free interface that works well for less experienced users.
Kongregate	`https://www.kongregate.com/`	Focuses mostly on games and entertainment, but you can find a few other categories of apps here. The impressive feature of this site is that you can find mobile, cartridge, PC, and web-based offerings in a single location, which makes it perfect for developers who want to target more than one platform.
neXva	`http://www.nexva.com/`	Was designed for vertical markets in which the developer needs more control over how the app is distributed. This orientation makes it easier to find apps that meet somewhat esoteric needs and that would normally get buried in the Google App Store.

Store Name	URL	Hook
SlideME	`https://www.getjar.com/`	Offers a less crowded alternative to the Google App Store with a different, but largely similar, interface and offerings.
uptodown	`https://en.uptodown.com/`	Supports Windows, Mac, and Android apps, which makes it convenient if you plan to develop apps for more than one of these platforms. This site supports only free apps. It also has a worldwide market, which makes it easily accessible in places like China that have a hard time accessing the Google App Store.

Getting your app into other countries may prove nearly impossible in some cases. For example, many app stores that cater to people in the United States don't provide support to the Chinese market. You need to do your homework before entering other markets to ensure success. For example, here is a list of common app stores in China:

2345	360	Anzhi Market
AppChina	Baidu	Coolmart
Flyme	HiAPK	HiMarket
MaoPao	Oppo	PP Assistant
Tencent Myapp	VIVO	Wandoujia

Getting Awards

Awards help attract attention for your app. When you can get others to talk about your app, that's one thing. When you can get people to say that your app is the best available, that's quite another. For Android app developers, the big award of the year is the annual Google Play Award Winners (see `https://play.google.com/store/apps/editorial_collection/promotion_topic_googleplayawards2019` for the 2019 winners). Even if your app doesn't appear here, you may still want to give the awards a look to see how you might improve your app. The following sections provide some advice about awards.

Looking for awards in all the right places

The truth is, getting Google to recognize your app if it isn't already receiving a lot of exposure in other ways is a long shot at best. Fortunately, you can submit your app for possible recognition to a number of sites. If you can submit your app, you're at least in the running. Most of these sites have requirements that you must meet, such as a submission fee or a time to submit it by and only new apps need apply. Here are some sites to consider for submitting your app for recognition:

- **Apple Design Awards:** `http://developer.apple.com/design`
- **Best Mobile Apps Award:** `http://www.bestmobileappawards.com/`
- **DICE Awards:** `https://www.interactive.org/`
- **Global Mobile Awards:** `http://www.globalmobileawards.com/`
- **Independent Games Festival:** `http://www.igf.com/`
- **International Mobile Gaming Awards:** `http://www.imgawards.com/`
- **Media Excellence Awards:** `http://mobilexawards.com/`
- **Mobile Premier Awards:** `http://mobilepremierawards.com/`
- **Webby Awards:** `http://www.webbyawards.com/`

The list doesn't include the Appsters Award or AppCircus because there are no current links for them. If you have links for either of these sites, or have additional sites you feel are essential to add to the list, contact John (`John@JohnMueller-Books.com`) or Barry (`f`) with the required information.

TIP

The list in this section may not provide enough opportunities for you or may not have categories that match your app. Oddly enough, there is actually a site devoted to helping you find the right place to submit your app for a potential award: Awards Finder (`https://awardsfinder.com/`). If your app has the right criteria, this site will help you find one or more places to make a submission. You obtain very basic information about the award and a link for finding out more. The links aren't always recent or relevant, but you can usually find an updated link by searching for it.

Strutting your stuff

After you have an award, or two, or three in hand, you want to be sure to proudly display it everywhere. Doing so may seem obvious, but you can easily find examples of an award that appears on the app's support site but nowhere else, which means that hardly anyone sees it, and those who do are looking for support, not an award. Here are some other places you should put notifications of your award:

- The app's *splash screen* (the screen that you see flashed before the main app screen appears)
- The app's About screen
- The app's main site
- At the end of any video or podcast
- In your correspondence
- Every public venue where your app appears
- On promotional items

Index

Symbols

A

B

C

D

E

F

G

H

I

M

N

O

P

Q

R

T

U

About the Authors

Barry Burd received an M.S. degree in Computer Science at Rutgers University and a Ph.D. in Mathematics at the University of Illinois. As a teaching assistant in Champaign-Urbana, Illinois, he was elected five times to the university-wide List of Teachers Ranked as Excellent by their Students.

Since 1980, Dr. Burd has been a professor in the Department of Mathematics and Computer Science at Drew University in Madison, New Jersey. He has lectured at conferences in the United States, Europe, Australia, and Asia. He is the author of several articles and books, including *Java For Dummies, Beginning Programming with Java For Dummies*, and *Java Programming for Android Developers For Dummies*, all from John Wiley & Sons, Inc.

Barry lives in Madison, New Jersey with his wife of 40 years. In his spare time, Barry enjoys eating chocolate and avoiding exercise. You can reach Barry at android@allmycode.com.

John Mueller is a freelance author and technical editor. He has writing in his blood, having produced 115 books and more than 600 articles to date. The topics range from networking to artificial intelligence and from database management to heads-down programming. Some of his current books include discussions of data science, machine learning, and algorithms. His technical editing skills have helped more than 70 authors refine the content of their manuscripts. John has provided technical editing services to various magazines, performed various kinds of consulting, and writes certification exams. Be sure to read John's blog at http://blog.johnmuellerbooks.com/. You can reach John on the Internet at John@JohnMuellerBooks.com. John also has a website at http://www.johnmuellerbooks.com/. Be sure to follow John on Amazon at https://www.amazon.com/John-Mueller/.

Barry's Dedication

For Harriet, Sam, and Jennie; Sam and Ruth; Abram and Katie; Benjamin and Jennie. And also for Basheva.

John's Dedication

This book is dedicated to my long-time friend and technical editor Russ Mullen. The two of us have worked on so many projects together that it boggles the mind. I'll miss him greatly and wish him well on his continued journey.

Barry's Acknowledgments

I heartily and sincerely thank Katie Mohr for her hard work and support in so many ways. Thanks to Guy Hart-Davis and Susan Christophersen for their efforts in editing this book. Thanks to the staff at John Wiley & Sons, Inc. for helping to bring this book to bookshelves. Thanks to Jeanne Boyarsky, Frank Greco, Chandra Guntur, and Michael Redlich for their advice on technical matters. And a special thanks to Richard Bonacci, Peter Lubbers, and Cameron McKenzie for their long-term help and support.

John's Acknowledgments

Thanks to my wife, Rebecca. Even though she is gone now, her spirit is in every book I write, in every word that appears on the page. She believed in me when no one else would.

Guy Hart-Davis deserves my thanks for his technical edit. I'm looking forward to continued work with him.

Matt Wagner, my agent, deserves credit for helping me get the contract in the first place and taking care of all the details that most authors don't really consider. I always appreciate his assistance. It's good to know that someone wants to help.

A number of people read all or part of this book to help me refine the approach, test application code, verify the extensive text, and generally provide input that all readers wish they could have. These unpaid volunteers helped in ways too numerous to mention here. I especially appreciate the efforts of Eva Beattie, who provided general input, read the entire book, and selflessly devoted herself to this project.

Finally, I would like to thank Katie Mohr, Susan Christophersen, and the rest of the editorial and production staff.

Publisher's Acknowledgments

Acquisitions Editor: Katie Mohr

Project and Copy Editor: Susan Christophersen

Technical Editor: Guy Hart-Davis

Proofreader: Debbye Butler

Production Editor: Umar Saleem

Cover Image: © kirill_makarov/Shutterstock